STUDIES IN MODERN HISTORY

General Editor : L. B. NAMIER, Professor of Modern
History, University of Manchester

THE BEGINNING OF
THE THIRD REPUBLIC IN FRANCE

A HISTORY OF THE NATIONAL ASSEMBLY
FEBRUARY–SEPTEMBER 1871

THE BEGINNING OF THE THIRD REPUBLIC IN FRANCE

A HISTORY OF THE NATIONAL ASSEMBLY
(February–September 1871)

BY

Rev. FRANK HERBERT BRABANT, M.A.
CANON OF WINCHESTER

MACMILLAN AND CO., LIMITED
ST. MARTIN'S STREET, LONDON
1940

COPYRIGHT

PRINTED IN GREAT BRITAIN
BY R. & R. CLARK, LIMITED, EDINBURGH

AMICO
DILECTISSIMO

DAVID CECIL

Introduction

PREFACE

THIS book is a study of a parliamentary Assembly, and not a history of France. This accounts for the rather tenuous treatment of such subjects as the Peace and the Commune. The Commune, especially, is described as seen from Versailles.

The material, that lies before the student, is of two kinds — on the one hand, the evidence of the journalist, all the daily potpourri of rumours and reports, that surrounds and besets the life of a great Assembly, the gossip of the lobbies, the " sketches " of the Press Gallery, " The Week in Parliament ", the " Toby M.P." of the time, the anecdotes of leading personalities, the cream skimmed off reports of debates and interviews : [1] on the other hand, we have the memoirs of deputies themselves,[2] some of them comments written down in the heat of the moment, some expressing the calmer judgment of men, who try to look back on their experiences as already belonging to History. With the help of these (to which, of course, must be added the later books on the history and biography of the period),[3] I have tried to avoid what is ephemeral in contemporary gossip, and also what is pedantic in remoter verdicts, to form a picture of the National Assembly, as it lived and moved. Special attention is paid to the formation and growth of groups and parties.

Part I takes the story to the end of the Commune : on

[1] Such books as *L'Assemblée nationale*, by Bosq (journalist) ; *Mes petits papiers*, by Hector Pessard (journalist) ; *Souvenirs parlementaires*, by Claveau (official reporter).

[2] Such as Lacombe's *Journal*, de Meaux's *Souvenirs*, de Marcère's *Assemblée nationale*.

[3] See Bibliography (classified) on p. 523.

vii

the whole, during these four months the centre of interest lies outside the Assembly. It is not till June that it begins to occupy the foreground. Part II, then, studies the inner life of the Assembly more closely, and gives more definite pictures of parties and personalities.

A foreigner must always feel a doubt as to whether he can sufficiently understand another country to describe the habits and motives of its public life. It is usual to console oneself with the reflection, " What an Englishman loses in vividness of impression, he gains in impartiality of judgment ", but it may well be doubted whether this is always true. Where impartiality means the stern suppression of personal prejudices, it may be impressive enough. Froude's tribute to the Middle Ages is generous in a flaming Protestant, and Macaulay's recognition of Louis XIV's exquisite courtesy, when he received James II as an exile, comes grandly from a Whig. But self-control is striking only, when there are passions to be controlled, and in this history (if it is not too presumptuous to mention our own subject on the same page as Froude and Macaulay) — in this study of French politics, few Englishmen find it hard to keep their heads. Accustomed to a parliamentary monarchy, our sympathies swing easily backwards and forwards from the Royalist's respect for order to the Republican's love of liberty : accustomed to our Anglican Via Media, we can appreciate both the fervour of the Catholic and the independence of the anti-clerical : the sharp division of French opinions strikes strangely on our cushioned compromises.[1]

Impartiality is therefore neither an important nor a difficult virtue for such a study, and I should care very

---

[1] It is interesting to notice that in a discussion during the year 1873, on a Bill forbidding attacks on the National Assembly, both sides appealed to English political practice. Gambetta reminded them of the English love for " fair play " (he used the English word) between the parties. The right retorted that the English would not tolerate attacks on the Crown, to which they argued that the supreme authority of the Assembly corresponded at that moment.

little, if a reader caught fervent Royalism or red-hot Republicanism from these pages. In writing of a period, now fifty years removed, in a country other than our own (and politically almost unrecognisable after the War of 1914–18), to speak of calm judgment is mere pretentiousness. One's utmost ambition would be to stir some spark of interest in the period and actors which would call for the slightest exercise of impartial judgment.

But though we can consider it without passion, French history always has qualities, with which the annals of no other country can vie. Drama in the clash of ideas, clearness and logic in their exposition, charm of personality and speech — all that indescribable " style ", which stamps what is French beyond mistake, — is present in the life of one of the most distinguished and most "French" of French Parliaments.

I have to express my gratitude to the President of the French Chamber of Deputies for allowing me to consult (in the Archives of the Chamber) the unpublished minutes of the Commission on Decentralisation, of which I have made use in my Appendix.

F. H. B.

Winchester, 1939

CONTENTS

CONTENTS

INTRODUCTORY CHAPTER

SKETCH OF THIERS' LIFE

INTRODUCTORY CHAPTER

SKETCH OF THIERS' LIFE

" As regards M. Thiers . . . I entertain a deep feeling of
gratitude and respect for his memory, and as critic and historian
I can but admire his flexibility of mind, his general ability, his
eloquence, his grasp of practical matters, his lucidity, activity
and courage. Few men, I think, have loved France as well as
he did " (TAINE, *Life and Letters*, Pt. III. p. 197).

THERE are historical characters, which dazzle the eye by the
complexity of their elements ; the jewelled points of red
and gold tremble against the background of darkness ;
they toss up jets of fire, that seem to aspire to the stars ;
the night is startled by the sudden flares of contrasted
colours, which burn their way into silence ; to write of
them is the joy of the romantic historian, such as Mr.
Lytton Strachey breathlessly looking down into the crater
of Gladstone's political mind, or lending an ear to the hissing
of that beautiful hooded snake, Francis Bacon.

Others attract by the steady brilliance of one single
quality, like a searchlight slowly cleaving the dark till it
reach its object. Such was Thiers — a luminous intelligence
ever directed to a desired end.

Again and again, the turbulent nineteenth century in
France sought to escape from that dry light. The romantic
advocates of France as the liberator of oppressed nationalities chafed at the little man in spectacles, who gave them
facts and figures, when they wanted causes and catchwords.
The Social Revolution of 1848 pushed aside the pedestrian
eloquence, that discoursed of Political Economy, when the

3

air was full of Fraternity, Justice, and the Right to Work.
He was silenced by the drums and trumpets of the Second
Empire; his dull repetition of facts seemed flat and
monotonous, when set against the subtle schemes of
Napoleon III with their strange amalgam of hesitation and
precipitancy — half Jingoist, half Utopian; the majority
of the Corps Législatif in July 1870 clamouring for a march
on Berlin had no time to listen to that flute-like voice demanding papers.   But the Empire rose and fell; revolutions
raged and died away; wars were won and lost, and still the
little man in spectacles was left on the stage; in 1871 the
boasting Marshals were silent; the great national resistance
of Gambetta was over; the generals, who had sworn to
return to Paris dead or victorious, had come back, alive
and defeated; the orator, who had cried " Not an inch of
our soil nor a stone of our fortresses ", had signed the
capitulation; the time for heroes — and heroics — was
over, and in her agony France turned to the man, who had
understood.

Was there ever such a revenge?   The man, whom Louis-
Philippe had dismissed, now become the arbiter of the
return of the Orleans Princes to France!   The man, whom
the Second Empire had failed to employ, entrusted with
the task of concluding a war begun by them!   The great
aristocratic families, accustomed to take their orders from
the King, now crowding round the little bourgeois and
fixing all their hopes of a restoration on him!

To the end, his amazing prescience held; thrown over
by the impatience of the Royalists, he died, rejected but
right.   He told them they could never restore the Monarchy;
they replied with shouts of indignation, but the Monarchy
was not restored.   He told them they would have to found
a Republic; they turned him out of office, but two years
later they founded the Republic, almost in the manner he
had predicted.   It was enough to exasperate a saint — the
more, as there was no calm modesty about Thiers; he did

not take much pains to conceal his views upon his own infallibility and the fallibility of others. Far more ardent and generous souls rushed into the fray ; far more exhilarating and exciting policies took up the challenge of events, and, as soon as the dust had cleared, Thiers was discovered erect, shouting, gesticulating, intriguing, " the very essence of bourgeois mediocrity " (so Flaubert described his policy), yet, when France was sinking into anarchy, the only man, who knew what must be done and could get men to do it — the only speaker, who, if passion still left a corner into which persuasion could penetrate, was sure to convince his hearers.

He was born at Marseilles on April 15th, 1797, and at first sight his parentage seems uninteresting ; his mother had an intrigue with a married man, and only the fortunate death of his legitimate wife allowed a marriage and averted a scandal. His father deserted the family, and was not seen again, till the fame of his son lured him to Paris. But, traced further back, the genealogical table grows more suggestive. On the paternal side, one ancestor had been a rich merchant, and another architect at Marseilles in charge of public expenditure and municipal building. On the maternal side, he had as great-grandmother a Greek from Cyprus, and the same line gave him a rather distant connection with the one poet of the First Republic—André Chénier.

It would perhaps be unjust to deny any obligation from the son to the scapegrace of a father. Pierre Louis Marie seems to have been an amusing rogue ; he had been at different times a merchant, an army contractor, the manager of an acting company and the lessee of a gambling-house ; he had an inexhaustible flow of completely fascinating and utterly untrustworthy conversation ; if at the conclusion of his more improbable stories he saw signs of incredulity, he hastened to add " But I was there ". His speciality consisted in giving long and highly technical descriptions of shipbuilding to experts on the subject, and

relating how he had sailed round the world with Captain
Marchand to sailors, who did not believe a word he said.
One can see where Adolphe got his conversational powers
and his (better justified) claim to omniscience.

At school, Adolphe was at once the pet and the terror
of his masters, atoning for a thousand mischievous tricks
by his precocious intelligence and his remarkable memory;
in an age when children were apt to be remarkable for their
romanticism, he already gave signs of his realist attitude
to life. When the news of Napoleon's victories arrived,
and hearts swelled with pride and excitement, he calmly
expounded the strategy of the campaign. One can
already trace the historian of Bonaparte, who was never a
Bonapartist.

In 1816 he left Marseilles for the University town of
Aix to study law, turning his back on the noise and confusion of a great seaport to enter the cultured circles and
elegant salons of a quiet academic city. But he never quite
lost what he had learned, when as a boy he used to wander
round the busy harbour and watch the shipping come in
from all over the world. In his speech on Property (September 14th, 1848) there is a direct allusion to these early
days. "In our youth we have all seen cotton arriving
from India, marvellously perfect, as if the threads had been
drawn by the hands of fairies; I have seen them myself."
In 1829 he had everything settled for a voyage round the
world with Captain Laplace, but the sudden political crisis
kept him at home; to the end of his life he kept a taste
for high adventure — and low adventurers.

In 1832, when he was arranging for the arrest of the
Duchesse de Berri, he met Deutz in the Champs Élysées on
a winter evening with a pistol in each pocket; in the later
years of his life Jules Simon said in jest, " Thiers would
like me better, if I were a little less respectable ".

Like so many boys, who had been at school under
Napoleon, he hated the Bourbons; he used to address a

circle of student friends at one of the Aix forges and thunder against the Jesuits and the Ultras, while the blacksmith stood entranced, his hammer suspended in the air ; his views shocked the Royalist salons, but who could resist his conversation, the animated gestures, the malicious epigrams, the naïve self-confidence, the inexhaustible information ? Old-fashioned Conservatives shrugged their shoulders indulgently. " He writes well," they said, " but he thinks badly."

In 1820 the local Academy of Letters and Arts offered a prize for the best essay on Vauvenarges ; none of the competitors signed their names, but the judges had not much difficulty in concluding, which was the work of the audacious young liberal from the fervent speeches in its favour of one of Thiers' personal friends. They quieted their consciences by giving it a *proxime accessit* and awarded the prize to a theme with a Paris postal address. Unfortunately for the learned body Thiers had written that one also.

His life at Aix produced a friendship and an affair of the heart, but the friendship had more to do with the heart than the affair. It was here that he formed with his fellow student Mignet an intimacy, that survived even the fact that they were both historians and both wrote about the same period — a severe test of affection.

His love-affair was less successful ; he had won the heart of Mlle Bonnafoux, who was charming but poor ; the " but " was to his honour ; however, amid the excitements of Parisian life he did not remain faithful to the engagement. The father demanded satisfaction and they fought a duel at Montmartre ; no blood was shed, as the father fired and missed, while Thiers threw away his pistol.

He had arrived at Paris in 1821, very much of a Dick Whittington, with no political connections and heralded by nothing more substantial than his reputation as a young liberal from the provinces. From 1821 to 1828, without

B

making any great sensation in the political world, he steadily secured his position in the ranks of the Opposition ; he took three steps which qualified him as member of the party, which opposed the King without attacking the monarchy. In the first place he became a journalist ; he had brought an introduction to Manuel, the leading orator of the Opposition, by whose influence he became a contributor to the *Constitutionnel*. In the second place, he became a friend and protégé of Talleyrand, who showered upon him the protection of his all-powerful mots : " Il est petit, mais il grandira ", " Il n'est pas parvenu, il est arrivé ". Lastly he produced his *History of the French Revolution*, which charmed the public by the lucidity of its explanations and delighted his own party by its defence of Liberalism.

In 1827, when he was dining with Sainte-Beuve, a guest exclaimed, " My dear friend, you know you will be a Minister", and Thiers showed no sign of surprise.

The 1830 Revolution began in defence of the freedom of the Press and Thiers was soon in the forefront of the battle ; he had founded the famous *National* newspaper, in which he wrote the historic phrase, " The King reigns but does not govern " ; about this time he met Lamartine ; the poet and the historian were always poles apart ; the one was an idealist and the other a realist, but Lamartine was impressed by him. " He had enough gunpowder in him to blow up ten governments . . . what convinced me of his superiority was his contempt for his own party."

When Charles X published the " Ordonnances ", it was Thiers, who drew up the protest of the journalists — " Obedience ceases to be a duty . . . for our part we resist " ; as he signed it, he said, " It is heads we need at the bottom of this paper". It was Thiers, who drew up the proclamation, which contained the words, " The Duke of Orleans has declared that he accepts the Charter " ; when it was pointed out to him that the Duke had done nothing of the kind, he altered the phrase, to " He has not decided ; he is waiting for our good pleasure ", and hurried off to Neuilly ; there he interviewed the Duchess and Louis-Philippe's clever sister Madame Adelaide. He was eloquent, convincing, as much at his ease as if he had dined with royalty every day of his life. " We must not let the destiny of France float in the air," he said in the course of convincing Madame, and, when he had succeeded, " Today you are placing the crown in your family ".

When Louis-Philippe first met the little journalist, who had done so much to give him the throne, he said, " M. Thiers, are you ambitious ? " The question hardly needed an answer, but Thiers was still young and there were other and older friends of the Orleans family, whose claims had to be considered ; so he only obtained the humble post of Secretary General of Finance, with a seat on the Council of State.

In October 1830 he was elected deputy and became Under Secretary of Finance in the Laffitte Ministry ; his first speech at the tribune, where he was to win so many triumphs, was a failure ; his diminutive stature and his Southern accent excited ridicule. " He can hardly be seen " (such was the malicious gossip of the lobbies), " but, to make up for it, he can be heard only too well." The Ministry was blamed for its weakness in repressing disorder, and it was said that during the sacking of the Archbishop's Palace Thiers refused to let the troops interfere, saying, " How great the people is in its anger ! " When the vigorous Ministry of Casimir-Périer was formed,[1] he was not included.

Thiers realised that he must learn to adapt himself. First he set himself to improve his public speaking. In this he soon succeeded ; in 1831 he delivered an excellent

[1] It was Casimir-Périer who made to his supporters the immortal remark, " The Government does not need your votes, when it is right ; it is when the Government is wrong, that it depends on your loyalty ".

speech on Foreign Affairs ; the next year he amazed the Chamber by preparing a Budget report in a day and a night. Even Legitimists said with a smile, " He knows everything and especially those subjects, of which he is completely ignorant ".)

Secondly, he saw that established governments are not too grateful to those who remind them of their revolutionary origins and he set himself to curb his liberal ardour. In 1832, after the sudden death of Casimir-Périer, the King sent for him with the appeal " Be my Pitt ",[1] and towards the end of 1832 he entered the Soult Ministry. As Minister of the Interior he showed his loyalty to the dynasty by securing the capture of the Duchesse de Berri, and in 1835 he proved his conservative principles by being present at what the Republicans called " the massacre of the rue Transnonain " (when the troops, irritated by a shot from a window that killed their general, fired indiscriminately on the crowd), and by supporting the severe " September Laws ". (During the year 1833 — between his first and second terms of office at the Interior — he was Minister of Commerce and Public Works.) He took great interest in the schemes of building at Paris and was always riding about to inspect their progress. People got used to seeing him on his horse, " Vendôme " ; on the occasion of the restoration of Napoleon's statue, he galloped in front of the royal cortège, shouting " I take the King's orders ", and waving his hand with a gesture said to have been copied from a picture of Austerlitz. The drums sounded, the veil fell from the statue, and Thiers was carried by his

---

[1] This comparison is not without interest. Both were conservative statesmen after a liberal start ; both were reformers in the sense that they hated disorder and confusion ; both swayed assemblies by silver-tongued persuasion. But Thiers never felt any of Pitt's sentiment towards the King and Constitution ; his mind was wider and more flexible, and his free-and-easy style was in complete contrast with Pitt's rather conscious integrity and the measured magnificence of his oratory. His temperament was more like that of Fox, though he had a sounder judgment and a closer grasp of the *métier* of statesmanship.

charger into the very middle of the band.

But there were occasions, when the amusement of the crowd was tempered by respect. During the street riots Thiers rode the same horse imperturbably, while officials of the Department who accompanied him were killed at his side; the soldiers said, half mocking, half impressed, " He has had an ' auditeur ' killed under him ".

In 1834 he married Mlle Dosne, an event, which caused rather an unnecessary outburst of gossip. The Dosnes were a family of the most bourgeois respectability; the father had made his money in building speculation, and in his frequent absences Thiers became great friends with Mme Dosne, an intelligent woman, passionately interested in politics. This was enough foundation for the scandalous rumour that the attachment extended further than a common interest in public affairs and that the marriage with the daughter was meant to cover an attachment to the mother.[1]

Thiers had learned to identify himself fully with the King's Conservative policy; they became for a time great friends and Louis-Philippe called him " mon cher petit Président ". The King now wished to efface the title " King of the Revolution " by seeking marriage alliances with Legitimist thrones, and Thiers vainly tried to secure at Vienna or St. Petersburg a wife for the Duke of Orleans. But, while he sympathised with the royal policy of the *juste milieu*, he sought to balance a tame home policy by a spirited programme abroad. This was partly due to a fervent patriotism, which never left him during all the

[1] The Duc de Broglie relates how, after the attempt of Fieschi to kill Louis-Philippe by an infernal machine, the wives of the Ministers and courtiers were eagerly awaiting the news; when it arrived, Mme Thiers did not open her mouth or ask about her husband but Mme Dosne had a terrible expression of pain and anxiety; she felt that a word from her would underline the indifference of her daughter; the Duchesse de Broglie kind-heartedly told her that Thiers was safe, but (adds her son) " I am not sure that Mme Dosne was very grateful for having been so quickly understood " (*Revue des Deux Mondes*, 1/1/25, pp. 69, 70).

vicissitudes of his public career, but it was also connected
with a great interest in military affairs and an admiration
caused by long study of Bonaparte's campaigns ; he spent
a whole day on the battlefield of Austerlitz. No one had
more contempt for romantic Bonapartism ; he laughed
at the legend of Napoleon as the liberator of oppressed
nationalities, and he had too much philosophy and common
sense to be carried away by the glamour of war. But
his administrative genius was fascinated by the technical
problem of handling and controlling vast masses of men,
and he was never happier than in the middle of a camp ;
it was a hard fate which decided that the only war waged
under his direction should be a civil war.

All this brought him up against the most obstinate side
of the King's character — his passion for peace. Twice the
King and his Minister measured swords, and twice the
Minister was beaten. In 1833 he demanded intervention
in Spain and the King resisted with all his arts of cajolery
and indignation. One scene at the Council was so stormy
that, when the King had withdrawn, Thiers said to his
colleagues, " I do not know, gentlemen, how far His
Majesty's attitude suits you ; for my part I cannot tolerate
it " ; in 1837 he resigned. He now joined Guizot in the
famous Coalition and after a violent election, in which
references to secret influence thinly veiled an attack on
the King himself, he returned to power in 1840. During
this year the great Eastern crisis began ; France warmly
took the side of Egypt and Mehemet Ali ; when the other
Powers took action against Egypt without consulting
France, Thiers demanded war ; in face of immense public
excitement, the King remained as firm as a rock ; " Ah,
if you would only be my Peace Minister ! " he said, as he
parted again from his Foreign Secretary and called on
Guizot to succeed him.

During the eight remaining years of the July Monarchy,
Thiers lived in his famous study, Place St-Georges ; he

seldom had direct relations with Louis-Philippe, but
the adversaries respected each other, like duellists who
have felt one another's skill ; there were angry moments,
when tempers rose and Thiers vented his anger in such
epigrams as " The King prays every morning ' Give us this
day our daily platitude ' ", but the more normal attitude
of the fallen Minister was represented by the title, half
affectionate, half familiar, by which the King was known in
the household, " Papa Doliban " ; [1] Thiers did not show
the same forbearance towards his successor in office and
it is difficult to acquit him of factiousness, when, having
denounced Guizot for subserviency to England, he afterwards attacked him for hostility to England in the affair
of the Spanish Marriages, by means of documents supplied
by his old enemy, Palmerston.

During these years he gave himself up to his " dear
studies ", as he loved to call them. The first three volumes
of the *Consulate and Empire* appeared in 1845. In the
evenings he held receptions, which became a feature of
Paris life and recalled the salons of the eighteenth century ;
though a prince of talkers, he knew how to listen. In the
holidays he loved to travel, especially in Italy, and he was
a passionate collector ; at the Ministry of the Interior he
kept two gazelles, and, as the officials watched him stroking
them and whispering into their ears, they recalled his arts
of political seduction, so that for a long time his protégés

[1] Louis-Philippe said, " When once Thiers has got an idea inside his head,
the devil himself could not get it out " (de Marcère, *Histoire de la République*,
ii. 80). One day Thiers threw his portfolio on the table exclaiming : " Ah,
Sire, if after having struggled against the majority in the Chamber of Deputies
and the Chamber of Peers, I am still resisted by the Queen and the princes,
I cannot carry on " (de Marcère, *Ass. nat.* i. 314). In his Memoirs he asserts
that " our princes have not fully carried out, as in England, the constitutional
form of monarchy " (p. 117) — in private conversation he sometimes described
the Orleans régime as " la monarchie fourbe " (" not playing fair ") (Lacombe,
i. 105). But in 1850 Thiers hurried to see the dying king in exile — " I served
the King," he said, " and I loved him, although he opposed me ; I should
never have forgiven myself, if I had let him die without seeing him " (Reclus,
M. Thiers, p. 236).

were called " Thiers' gazelles ". At home he filled his rooms with tropical plants ; he returned from his travels laden with statues and pictures ; they were not always authentic, and his taste was not sure enough to make much difference between a copy and an original ; Mme Thiers specialised in Chinese and Japanese pottery.

He refused to take part in the banquets, which led to the fall of the July Monarchy ; in the critical days of 1848 he tried without success to form a ministry, which might save the throne.

The revolution, which created the Second Republic, marks an important turning point in his life ; hitherto he had been regarded as a brilliant politician with no particular principles, sceptical about institutions, and taking up causes or laying them down as suited his own hand. The anarchy and disorder of 1848 first revealed him as a Conservative leader.

His first impression was one of doubt ; he did not share the republican optimism of the moment, but he suspended judgment. " The time for kings is past " ; " Universal suffrage is an impenetrable mystery." But the confusion, that ended in the street-fighting of the June days, and the wild social Utopias, that turned the heads of the Paris workmen, filled him with disgust. He published a book, in which he expounded and defended the doctrine of Property, and on September 14th he attacked, in the Constituent Assembly, the proposal to inscribe the right to work in the Constitution ; he said, " I shall always ask you Socialists this question : Where are the means of realising what you promise ? " [1] " I am not slavishly attached to facts ; I want generalisations, but *after* the facts " ; he used characteristic formulae of crystal clearness. " By means of personal property, the stimulus to work is

[1] " Vos moyens ? " compare the same reiterated objection, twenty-three years later, when " Guerre à l'outrance " was defended in the National Assembly (see p. 124).

made strong; by the principle of inheritance, it is made infinite." "Socialism applies to private industry the principles, that ought to be reserved for government.")

This Conservatism drove him to what he always regarded as one of the great mistakes of his life — his support of Louis Napoleon for the Presidency; as he said later in a frank moment, "We voted for him, because we were frightened"; he looked upon the Prince as witless and incompetent, "cultivated but chimerical"; he said to his intimates that he intended to give him mistresses and then to govern in his name; he referred to him as "the flag *we* have chosen to represent Order". He had a rude shock, when he found that Napoleon was not disposed to be anyone's flag. The Prince wrote his own electoral manifesto and refused to accept Thiers' corrections; he turned the Élysée into a military establishment against Thiers' advice;[1] true, he offered Thiers a place in his Ministry, but the latter preferred to wait and see.

In the Legislative Assembly Thiers was the heart and soul of the Right. He infuriated the Left by such pronouncements as "A Republic can only exist on condition that it is not governed by republicans", "The Constitution of 1848 is a dirty piece of paper". In supporting the law of May 31st, which mutilated Universal Suffrage, he intentionally caused a tempestuous scene by referring to the "vile multitude". Reaction carried him even into the clerical camp; in the Commission, that drew up the Educational Law of 1850, Thiers stood shoulder to shoulder with the Catholics, Falloux and Dupanloup; under the July Monarchy, he had seemed rather a Voltairian in the matter of religion; now he said, "I, who have never flattered anyone, even kings, I say as loudly as I can, that

---

[1] Napoleon used to relate maliciously the words of Thiers on the subject: "The nation will be delighted to see its civic chief magistrate adopt civilian dress. . . . Besides, if you were to adopt a military costume, your successor might be awkwardly situated if he could not do the same" (Vandam, *My Paris Notebook*, p. 301).

I love the heroes of religion ; I feel a sense of deep admiration for the soldiers of Turenne hearing Mass ".[1] In 1845 he had urged the Government to take steps against the Jesuits ; now he said, " I am not afraid of Ultramontanism ; I am ready to give it my hand ".[2] In a public letter he went so far as to say, " Education by the clergy, which I used not to like, seems to me better than what is being prepared for us ; the new University claims to teach our children a little mathematics, physics and natural science and a great deal of demagogy ".[3] " What terrifies me is the introduction into our schools of thirty-seven thousand Socialists and Communists, veritable anti-curés in the communes. . . . What has our primary education produced ? Half-educated people and jobbers." [4]

It was in September 1851 that Carlyle met Thiers at Paris and described him as " a little brisk man towards sixty, with a round white head, close-cropt and of solid business form and size ; round fat body tapering like a ninepin into small fat feet and ditto hands ; the eyes hazel and quick, comfortable, kindly aspect, small Roman nose ; placidly sharp fat face, puckered eyeward (as if all gravitating towards the eyes) ; voice of thin treble, peculiarly musical. . . . I have not heard such a mild, broad river of discourse, rising anywhere, tending anywhither. . . . But he is willing to stop too, if you address him and can give you a clear and dainty response about anything you ask " [5] ; " a fine healthy creature and without any ' conscience ' good or bad ".[6] Mme Thiers was " a brunette of forty, pretty enough of her kind, an insignificant kind ".[7]

It did not require much prescience to see that the dispute between the President and the Assembly would end in a *coup d'état*, but Thiers had at least the merit of

---

[1] *Procès verbaux de la commission de 1849*, p. 194.
[2] *Ibid.* p. 239.   [3] *Ibid.* p. 23.
[4] *Ibid.* pp. 35 and 92 (speeches during the Commission debates).
[5] *Last Words of Thomas Carlyle*, p. 169.
[6] *Ibid.* p. 187.   [7] *Ibid.* p. 181.

framing the " mot de la situation ", when he said " L'Empire est fait ". Nevertheless, he was not expecting the visit of the officer, by whom he was turned out of bed on the night of December 2nd and carried off to prison at Mazas, appealing to his character as a deputy and muttering, " I have a strong desire to shoot you ". He was exiled from the country, but after eight months Louis Napoleon let him return, tearing out a page (so the story goes) from his *Consulat et empire*, in which Thiers had defended the 18 Brumaire (the elder Napoleon's *coup d'état*) and saying, " Here is his passport ".[1]

Thiers returned once more to his studies ; he wrote the last eleven volumes of his *History*, and his mania for omniscience led him into a new passion for astronomy and biology ; at the Observatory he met Leverrier, and Pasteur at the laboratory ; they both began by admiring him and ended by being bored at his questions. Under all this intellectual activity his heart was sore ; in a will, which he drew up at the time, he speaks of his " inconstant and ungrateful country ".

He was not much shocked at the Draconian methods of the Imperial Government ; he always liked the strong hand. But two things he could not abide ; one was the person of the Emperor. He could not forget that bitterest of all wounds to self-respect — the being outwitted by someone we despise, and most of the Emperor's political ideas seemed to his calm and sober mind a sentimental and incoherent system of mystification. " I like the kitchen," he said of the Second Empire, " but I cannot stand the cook." Louis Napoleon, who had a telling if rather heavy gift of repartee,[2] replied, " That is because I

---

[1] Grenville-Murray, *Round about France*, p. 61.

[2] When Victor Hugo published *Napoleon the Little*, the Emperor retorted, " written by Hugo the great " ; he was perhaps at his best, when dealing with his troublesome, democratic nephew Jerome : " You have nothing of the great Napoleon about you ", said the latter ; " Well, at any rate I have his relations ", was the reply.

would not employ him to taste the dishes for me ". He repaid Thiers' dislike with interest and referred to him as a " meddlesome, arbitrary and irrepressible personage " ; he is even said to have added (perhaps with a smile, for the Emperor loved to be enigmatic), " I have not the faintest doubt that he is my personal enemy to an even greater extent than my political enemy. If he had had the disposal of me, I should have disappeared, for he is a moral as well as a physical coward." [1]

Secondly, Thiers was revolted by the foreign policy of the Second Empire, which seemed to him a perpetual sacrifice of the true interests of France to phrases and abstractions ; he had no good word to say for the " policy of nationalities " which in practice meant the creation of two new powerful neighbours — Germany and Italy, who, so far from being grateful for the services of France, took the earliest opportunity of turning their forces against her. Even this policy (he maintained) was not honestly carried out. While the liberation of Italy was encouraged to please the French democrats, the debt was cancelled by the refusal to let Italy have Rome as her capital, for fear of offending the French Catholics. While (to show her generosity) France let Bismarck establish the predominance of Prussia and deserted her old friend Austria, she played with the idea of annexing Luxembourg as a " compensation " and rattled her sabre at her ancient foe across the Rhine.

Such inconsistencies could only lead to war. Thiers foresaw it, and perhaps at no period of his career was his prestige greater — not even, when he was almost omnipotent sovereign in 1871 — than when he stood forth, free from all responsibilities of office, as representative of the common-sense attitude of so many of his fellow countrymen, liberal and conservative, to critise the tortuous policy of the later Empire. That policy may be regarded as subtle,

---

[1] Vandan, *Undercurrents of the Second Empire*, p. 37.

generous, or brilliant ; it can hardly be regarded as sensible
or coherent. The Emperor's failing health showed itself in
an increasing love of mystification, which made malicious
observers call him " a sphinx without a secret ", and his
gradual concessions to parliamentary government drove
him into an uneasy oscillation between old friends and
new counsellors.

Thiers returned to public life in 1863 as deputy for
Paris ; he had refused to stand as candidate for the
Republican party, but accepted a programme of the constitutional Opposition, comprising all the elements from
Right to Left which were hostile to the Empire. In January
1863 he delivered his famous speech demanding the five
" necessary liberties " — of the person, of the Press, of
elections, of representation, of majority government.

But it was above all in the field of foreign policy that
he made his most significant orations, and here he leaned
towards the Right ; he was a fervent nationalist and a
champion of the Pope's temporal power, on political rather
than religious grounds ; with all his strength he opposed
the aid given by the Empire to the unification of Italy and
Germany — sometimes by sweeping anticipations of the
future, " Italian unity will be the mother of German
unity ", " We have not a fault left to commit " (after
Sadowa) ; sometimes by cries of injured patriotism, " We
are sometimes Italians, sometimes Germans — Frenchmen
never ", " I love Italy, but there is something I love more
and much more — France ".

Nevertheless his Nationalism was never Jingoistic, and
in 1870, amid the wild excitement of the public and the
tumultuous opposition of the majority in the Corps Législatif, he resolutely opposed the declaration of war. " I
cannot take the responsibility of a war founded on such
motives . . . you have obtained the substance and you
are breaking off relations on a question of form. . . . No
one was more grieved than I by the events of 1866 [Sadowa],

no one desires reparation for them more than I do, but I am profoundly convinced . . . that the occasion is wrongly chosen."

After Sedan, all eyes turned towards Thiers ; Mérimée on behalf of the Empress wrote two letters asking for his advice ; he replied, " To ask me for my advice . . . , when we are on the very edge of the abyss I have so often predicted, . . . is to create for us both an impossible position. One can foresee catastrophes, but to foresee is not the same as to prevent." [1]

When the September Revolution swept away the Empire, Thiers refused to accept office ; he said, " I disapprove of the dissolution of the Corps Législatif by force, . . . but I remember that we are in the presence of the enemy ". He was ready to help the Government of National Defence (especially in preparing the Paris fortifications), but he would not make himself responsible for their policy ; he had no love for revolutions and he was sceptical about the *levée en masse* — Gambetta's policy for carrying on the war.[2]

Personally he was often on the verge of despair : " I am terribly sad. . . . If in my lifetime my country loses the position, which it has so far occupied in the world, I shall never be consoled ; I shall hide myself. . . . I shall plunge myself into my studies ; you will never hear me spoken of again." [3]

On September 9th, Jules Favre, the Minister for Foreign

[1] D'Haussonville, *Mon journal pendant la guerre*, pp. 41, 42.

[2] " I said to Thiers that the National Guard seemed to be preparing seriously. ' I much desire it,' he answered, ' and I have a little hope and yet . . . who can feel certain ? Only three times have the masses of the people been deeply moved ; at the Crusades by a religious feeling ; at the Reformation, by a feeling of freedom and moral reform ; and in 1789, when the middle classes after having suffered so long in their interests and their *amour-propre*, felt that up till then they had been nothing and wished to be everything. Apart from these three periods, the majority of the people have been almost inert. Shall we be able to wake them up ? " (*Journal de Comte d'Haussonville*, p. 87).

[3] *Ibid.* p. 147.

Affairs, sent him on a diplomatic tour, and he visited London, Vienna, Florence and St. Petersburg, seeking for intervention in favour of France. He summed up his failure in another famous phrase, " Europe exists no longer ". The meagre result of his journey was an offer on behalf of Russia to ask Bismarck to arrange an interview with Thiers; he accepted, and on November 1st–4th he met for the first time at Versailles the German Chancellor, whom he called " a savage with genius ". The Prussians were ready to grant an Armistice, but would not promise to allow Paris to be provisioned. For terms of peace they demanded Alsace.

Thiers returned to Paris, advising the Government to accept, and after their refusal retired to Tours. Gambetta, who was there as head of the Delegation, consulted him about strategy, but bitterly complained of his pacifism. In December Thiers went to Bordeaux, and it was there he heard the news of the surrender of Paris.

Character. — The first impression, left by half an hour's interview with Thiers, was always that of his brilliant powers of conversation, not, like Lamb's, adorned by flights of fancy, not dignified, like Coleridge's, by the stately labour of intellectual construction, not weighty, like Dr. Johnson's, with long-matured reflections on life and conduct, but shrewd, positive, concerned with action and persuasion to action — for he depended for his political influence almost as much upon his talk as upon his speeches — sometimes hasty and ill-tempered in judgments on individuals, but redeemed from being mere political gossip by a historian's knowledge of the past and by occasional prophetic glimpses of the future. The terms were caustic, familiar often to the point of coarseness, the standpoint that of the ordinary bourgeois, made clear and cutting by a vivid personality.

It is difficult to analyse conversation, but one may note

his skilful use of slightly malicious anecdote ; two examples may serve as illustrations. One evening in the lobbies of the National Assembly he heard a bitter Orleanist holding forth to a group of deputies on the theme that Thiers aspired to be dictator. " My dear friend," he answered, " one day King Louis - Philippe wished me to enter a ministerial combination, that did not suit me ; I refused and he insisted, saying, ' You want to make me believe that you don't care for office '. I was rather annoyed and said, ' Sire, whenever your Majesty has said that you only accepted the burden of a crown with regret, I have always believed you '." [1]

On another occasion, when a Royalist deputy was grumbling at his complacency towards the Radicals, he said, " When I was young — a long time ago — I was a Voltairian ; one day I went with one of my friends to see an old _curé_, who was much attached to my family ; the venerable priest tried to catechise us and invited us to carry out our religious duties. ' What is the use ? ' we answered, ' we have not got faith.' ' Go on doing your duties,' was the reply, ' and faith will come in time.' Well, the Radicals did not believe in the wisdom and power of moderation ; perhaps they still don't, but they are practising it and doubtless they will end by believing." [2]

One can see in his speeches a fairly faithful mirror of his conversation ; he had long ago broken with that pomp of philosophic generalities, that seemed the essence of a great speech under the Restoration ; he was always familiar, easy, lucid, seductive in style ; in the last period of his life he adopted the method of anecdotes — purged, naturally, of the sparkling indiscretion of his private talk. " He proved his points by telling stories and by the way he told them. . . . People are so fond of stories that they grant the good story-teller the conclusion he wishes to

[1] H. Pessard, _Mes petits papiers_, Series 2, p. 147.
[2] _Ibid._ p. 278.

draw, as a kind of extra reward."[1]

Great talkers are always suspected of being conceited; in the case of Thiers we must distinguish political ambition from personal vanity. Of his ambition there can be no doubt; Mme de Lieven said of him, " He has the pride of Satan "; he said to Mme Adelaide, when they were standing before a picture of Turenne, " That is what I ought to have been; don't smile; I am serious ". In 1840 Guizot ended a letter from the London embassy, " On this question I await instructions from the Government ". " Instructions ! " cried Thiers, " I would never have written that."[2]

As he grew older, he began to think himself infallible; opposition irritated him more and more. He judged without mercy all, who presumed to carry on the Government against his advice — Guizot, Louis Napoleon, Gambetta. He often changed his views, but he was always certain that his policy of the moment was the only possible one. It was less a love of domination than a hatred of muddle — always his bugbear; he was the last person to suffer fools gladly, and he constantly under-rated his opponents.

All this may be pardoned and even admired in one, who felt he alone could save his country; there was, however, another side to his egoism, which was less impressive; he had a mania for knowing every subject better than anyone else; " his foible was omniscience ". He was probably influenced by the example of Napoleon's omnicompetent mind. A dictator, whose every word is law and who makes everyone else's business his own, is bound by his position at least to appear to know everything; in a constitutional statesman, often out of office, it has a touch of the ridiculous.

The anecdotes about Thiers' omniscience (or his claim

---

[1] E. Faguet, *Propos littéraires*, Series 2, p. 334.
[2] Reclus, *M. Thiers*, p. 262.

C

to it) are endless. He said to Soult, " During your famous siege of Genoa, it had two lines of defence ". " But I was there," answered the Marshal, " and it only had one." " I assure you, Marshal, that it had two." One day he said to Guizot, " I never make mistakes " ; he gave detailed lectures on Japanese porcelain to the lady, who painted his portrait ; [1] he asked Bertrand (secretary of the Académie des Sciences) for advice on a mathematical point and then contradicted him on that very point.[2] One day he said of McMahon, " He is no more fit to be President than I to be " — there he hesitated and the courtly interviewer made the obvious comment, " Ah, M. Thiers, you find it hard to think of anything you cannot do ". In 1866, when he was crossing the Channel, he explained the principles of steering to the captain with details on the winds and the working of a ship ; Guizot, who was on board, said in his serious voice, " When is he going to climb the mast ? " [3] It is no doubt absurd to pretend to know everything, but it is only fair to remember that he did know a good deal. " Often ", says Hector Pessard,[4] " I have seen generals enter his study with a slight smile of disdain, and leave stupefied by the technical knowledge of this civilian born to command." [4]

One side, then, of Thiers' mind was made up of a certain restlessness and vivaciousness, and his conversation was like a firework display — a splutter of irritation at the incompetence of others, and quick changes of interest in his own versatile mind.

But, when one goes deeper, one finds a luminous serenity of intelligence — the " dry light " of Matthew Arnold — , which contrasts with the mobility of his temperament ; as Berryer said of him, he was " mobile but sincere ". There were two different levels to his character

---

[1] De Meaux, *Souvenirs*, p. 74.   [2] Taine, *Correspondance*, vol. iii. p. 171.
[3] Weiss, *Notes*, p. 154.   [4] *Mes petits papiers*, Series 2, p. 47.

— the one shrewd and crafty, scintillating with all the arts of the accomplished partisan ; the other adorned with the gifts of an intelligent and disinterested statesman ; with one side of his character he loved simplicity, lucidity of ideas, and efficiency in government ; with the other he liked to weave a complicated web for the purpose of disentangling it ; you never knew in which mood you might find him.[1]

This quality is essential to understanding his rôle as President of the Third Republic ; the statesman in him would have liked to be left alone as dictator with Napoleonic powers, but the politician loved the play and puzzle of parliamentary intrigues and enjoyed the opportunities of public speaking, in which he knew that he was far superior to the Emperor ; he therefore preferred a dictatorship through the tribune — a strong government, not silent but talking endlessly — a régime of free speech in which the President did most of the speaking ; his ideal constitution was one in which he was allowed to talk half the day in order to persuade people to let him do what he wanted during the other half.

This luminous intelligence — always giving itself airs of philosophic detachment, which made those smile who knew the eager fighter attached to it [2],— may be defined as common sense.

His methods of administration lacked originality and a sense of the future ; his speeches were distinguished by insight rather than foresight ; he did not believe in the future of railways, which he called toys for children ; [3] he supported the old professional army and only accepted

---

[1] Jules Simon defined him well as having " an ever-changing surface with a depth of persistent seriousness " (*Gouvernement de M. Thiers*, ii. 243).

[2] Thiers always began talking about returning to his " dear studies " at the precise moment he met with a political disappointment.

[3] Clemenceau says (Martet, p. 35) : " I detested Thiers fervently and the sentiment was quite mutual. But we agreed on one thing ; we could not bear railways."

universal service very reluctantly. He was opposed to Free Trade, Public Education and the income tax ; [1] he foresaw neither the religious nor the social conflicts on the horizon. It was perhaps significant that his greatest services were rendered in 1871–3, when France had no future. But he possessed common sense to the point where it verges on brilliance. He may not always have had better arguments, but he always knew how to put them better than other people ; he made figures enthralling and commonplaces vivid ; his advice sounded so persuasive that it seemed folly to disagree with him ; he shared, with the first Napoleon, the faculty of making everyone else seem " idéologues ".[2]

Up to a point, the French are delighted with common sense and, as long as the business man was needed, his position was unassailable. But from 1871 to 1873, as security increased and men had leisure to renew the old disputes, he began to lose grip ; old hatreds and resentments got the upper hand [3] and Thiers, who might have been the Richelieu of the old régime or the Gambetta of the new, was too independent to follow kings or mobs. His view of the future of France was modest and unexciting — only made plausible by his own interesting personality ; the parties rallied to catchwords he detested, " the Christian Monarchy " and " the Athenian democracy " ; his " l'avenir aux plus sages " seemed like " safety first ", and, when in 1877 the country, weary of excitement,

---

[1] Weiss wrote in June 1871 : " Practical men think him too ' routinier ' for the present situation ; he cannot get to work in reorganising the army nor in the great reforms needed in Education, nor in the ' legislation des cultes ' nor in Finance " (*Notes et impressions*, p. 324).

[2] Faguet (*l.c.* 334) says with reference to his speaking : " The great power of all eloquence is to make people believe that the idea, which the orator has just put into their heads, is one which they have held from their cradles ".

[3] In August 1871 he wrote to Girardin : " My policy in the midst of a country eaten up with absurd discussions can only be one of union, and it is not popular ; people love hating one another " (Pessard, *Mes petits papiers*, Series 1, p. 179).

turned to him again, it was too late.[1]

In one sphere at least, he could not be accused of over-moderation ; no one could doubt the ardour of his patriotism. His accent when he spoke of " le pays " was unforgettable ; Jules Favre has left a moving description of how he pleaded with Bismarck at Versailles.[2] He was no enemy of Germany (he judged Bismarck more calmly than most of his contemporaries), but he believed that its unification was a menace to France ; he was no Clerical, but he believed that French prestige was bound up with the occupation of Rome ; in 1871 he knew how to maintain the dignity of France in days of humiliation ; he indulged in no idle blubbering or threats of revenge ; he did not go round Europe on his knees begging for allies ; the honour of France was to be vindicated by keeping her word and paying her debts.

Was he deficient in emotion ? He certainly hated sentimentality ; he was true to his favourite mottos, " Take everything seriously, but nothing tragically " ; he hated Romanticism (he used to say " Le romantisme, c'est la Commune "), and one day Louis-Philippe put him next to the Princess Clementine to cure her of a taste for Hugo ; he had little feeling of loyalty to Kings or causes. But he had a genius for friendship, which even the political differences of 1873 did not quite break, and he could move the Assembly to its depths when he spoke of France as " le noble blessé ".

His attitude to Religion was very characteristic ; he entered politics at a time, when it was almost impossible for a Liberal to be religious ; during the Second Empire, the Marquis de Castellane relates how his mother, trying to convert Thiers, spoke of the Gospels as the " most beautiful books that ever were written ". " I can still hear him

---

[1] Heine wrote of him in 1840 : " He could only succeed indefinitely, if his hearers could be content to hear of material needs indefinitely ; the day when some movement of opinion should turn the attention of France to objects of another order, would he satisfy them ? " (Reclus, p. 167).

[2] See p. 109.

reply in his little, piping voice, " I beg your pardon, Madame ; there is one even more beautiful — the Manual of Epictetus ".[1] But later he described himself as " deeply spiritualist " for reasons delightfully characteristic. " I have proved mathematically and from the study of history the existence of the Supreme Being, and that by irrefutable arguments." [2]   " Are you a Protestant ? " asked de Marcere. " I am very much of a Catholic ", he answered. " But are you a Catholic right through ? " " Ah, I see, perhaps you are right ; I am a passionate spiritualist ; I have proved mathematically and by History and Geology that there is a Supreme Being." [3] He said in his will : " I hope to see my dear ones again, and in this consoling certainty, I move towards the end of my days in perfect submission to the Supreme Ruler of all things ".[4] If he was personally a Deist *à la* Renan,[5] he was historian enough to know the importance of the Catholic Church for the people ; he spoke of Catholicism as a " pure moral ancient creed . . . the work of God as some think, the work of men as others think, but, as all admit, the profound work of a sublime reformer, interpreted during eighteen centuries by Councils, great assemblies of the wisest minds of every age ".[6]   He believed profoundly that the position of France in Europe must be Catholic, and that Protestantism and Materialism were alike pro-German ; his own personal convictions he never put more delightfully than in an answer to the Marquis of Belcastel, who pressed him about his relations to God, — " I am neither of the Court nor of the Opposition ".

[1] *Memoirs of Castellane*, p. 36.

[2] Mme Adam, *Nos amitiés politiques avant l'abandon de la revanche*, p. 396.

[3] De Marcère, *Assemblée nationale*, i. 296.   [4] Reclus, p. 254.

[5] Like Renan, he hated anti-Clericalism and all its propaganda ; he wrote to Fournier, Ambassador at Rome : " The supposed persecution of Galileo is a childish invention ; the trial was absurd, not cruel " (Letter of 16/9/72, Bouniols, *Thiers au pouvoir*, p. 246).

[6] *Consulat et empire*, t. iii. 1. xii. (quoted *procès-verbal* of the Commission of 1849, preface, p. 19).

PART I

THE PEACE AND THE COMMUNE

CHAPTER I

THE PARIS–BORDEAUX CONTROVERSY

AT midnight on Friday, the 27th of January, the Prussian bombardment of Paris came to an end : the city was starved out. On the Saturday, Jules Favre, Minister for Foreign Affairs, went to see Bismarck at Versailles in order to arrange the details of an Armistice : owing to obstacles put in his way by the German military staff, it was not till ten in the evening that he was able to send the following telegram to Gambetta, head of the Delegation at Bordeaux, who was organising the defence in the provinces : "We are signing a treaty with Count Bismarck today : we have agreed upon an Armistice of twenty-one days ; an Assembly is convoked at Bordeaux for the 12th of February ; have the Armistice executed and convoke the electors for Feb. 8th: a member of the Government will start for Bordeaux ".[1]

On Sunday morning, at one o'clock, a full meeting of the Government of National Defence was held at Paris. This Government, which had been struggling for four months against the Prussians without the walls and the growing anarchy within, had been formed on September 4th, the day when, on receiving the news of Sedan, the Paris mob stormed the Corps Législatif, and so brought the Second Empire to an end. The Republican deputies (about thirty in number) intended to induce the Corps Législatif of the Empire to set up a Committee of Public Safety, but most of their supporters believed that this legislative body had fallen with the régime, which had created

[1] Jules Favre, *Gouvernement de la défense nationale*, ii. 409.

it. The Revolutionaries (led by Blanqui, the apostle of a vague and pre-Marxian communism, the arch-conspirator, who had passed thirty-five years in prison) had sent two battalions of the National Guard to break down the defences of the Palais-Bourbon. In spite of Gambetta's appeals, the mob refused to wait, for a Commission to report on a new Constitution, and dragged their deputies off to the Hôtel-de-Ville.

It was a critical moment : all the revolutionary leaders were present at the famous centre of insurrection. Blanqui himself and Félix Pyat were on the spot : Millière was throwing out lists of the new Government from the windows on to the heads of the crowd. Workmen were running up the Red Flag. The deputies were taken unprepared. At this moment someone called out " The deputies for Paris to be the Government ", and the phrase instantly caught the popular imagination. " Had it not been for this fortunate idea ", says Jules Simon, " we should have had the Commune, perhaps that very day, and the Prussians would have been in Paris within a week." [1]

General Trochu was the President and Minister for War : he had served in the Crimean War, and in 1867 had written a book called *The French Army*, in which he eulogised the young soldiers and attacked the Imperialist legend of the Old Guard and the *corps d'élite*. In September 1871 anyone, who had criticised the Army of the Empire, seemed a god-send. His own personal position was not too easy. He had promised to defend Paris, if the Emperor would return to the capital. As his advice had been disregarded, he had intended to resign, but he had sworn to the Empress that he would die for her, " as a Breton, a Catholic [2] and a soldier ". When the Corps Législatif

---

[1] Jules Simon, *Souvenirs du 4 septembre*, p. 414.

[2] He was the only important representative of the Right in the Government : before he took his seat at the head of the council table, he said, " You are all resolute defenders of Religion, Property, and the Family, I hope " (*Souvenirs du 4 septembre*, p. 423).

was invaded by the mob, General Lebreton (one of the officers of the Chamber) appealed to him to rally the soldiers, who were refusing to defend the deputies. After some hesitation he accepted, but on his way met Jules Favre, who was going to the Hôtel-de-Ville and who called out to him, " There is no longer any Government ". His immense popularity with the crowd and the Army and his remarkable gift of eloquence [1] made him indispensable as head of the new Government. But the defence of Paris was a hopeless business : he was too good a soldier not to see it,[2] but he was too good an orator to admit it ; and he must be held partly responsible for the greatest fault of the National Defence Government — an official optimism, which withheld the truth from the people. The bewildered incredulity, with which the surrender was received, did much to produce that state of irritation, which led ulti-mately to the Commune.

Jules Favre was the Minister for Foreign Affairs : he was one of the great Republican orators, both at the Bar and at the tribune. Pleading before the Chamber of Peers in 1834, he began, " I am a republican ". He defended Orsini after his attempt to murder the Emperor. In the Corps Législatif he was the leader of the little Republican band. He was a sincere man and a real patriot, with a grave face, sweet and dignified, but he was too sensitive for the burden now placed upon him. When decision was required, he too often burst into tears or coined un-fortunate phrases, which cannot be lived down, such as the declaration that France would never surrender an inch of her soil or a stone of her fortresses. When after the war he addressed the National Assembly for the first time, " there was a general murmur of respectful

---

[1] It was said of him under the Empire, " He speaks too well : don't trust him " (Bosq, *L'Assemblée nationale*, p. 92).

[2] In his speech at the National Assembly (13/6/71) he called the siege " a heroic folly necessary in order to give time to the Powers to intervene " (*Annales de l'assemblée nationale*, t. 3, p. 370).

surprise, so worn and aged had he grown ".[1]

Jules Ferry was Maire of Paris : he was also a member of the Bar. He had leaped into fame by the title rather than the contents of his first pamphlet : Haussmann was Préfet of the Seine and was carrying out the transformation of Paris into its modern appearance in a manner, which his opponents described as wasteful. Ferry's pamphlet was called *Les Comptes fantastiques de M. Haussmann,* a brilliant parody of the name of Offenbach's famous opera.[2] He was probably the strongest member of the Government. The Prince Napoleon once said : " *Au fond* Gambetta is a good fellow who only wants peace and quiet. He is a good-natured lion. Ferry is quite different : he is as cold as a surgeon."[3] It was he who saved his colleagues on October 31st, when they had been shut up in the Hôtel-de-Ville by the Blanquists. " A subterranean passage was discovered ", says Simon, " leading from a neighbouring barracks to the place of our confinement. Ferry ventured into it first, and appeared like a destroying angel saying to the revolutionaries : ' You can go home : I do not wish blood to be spilled, but do not suppose that you will be free to do what you like, when you have left this place. If you make any further trouble, you are done for.' "[4] His personal appearance was not attractive. His nose was Jewish, and his mutton-chop whiskers were famous. He was not liked by his own party, and his opponents said he could not accuse without condemning, nor attack without hating. He seemed a complete contrast to Jules Simon, the supple and courteous Minister of Education. It was fitting that, ten years later, in the great struggle over Catholic Education, the first should be on the side of intolerance and the second should speak for liberty.

[1] E. King, *French Political Leaders,* p. 237.
[2] *Tales of Hoffmann.* It is said the title was suggested to him by the editor of the *Temps.*
[3] Lano, *Après l'empire,* p. 195.
[4] Simon, *Soir de ma journée,* p. 142.

Jules Simon was so captivating in his speech and so unctuous in his manner that the Bishop of Orleans used to say, " He will be a Cardinal before me ". He was a philosopher, a pupil of Victor Cousin and a lecturer at the Sorbonne. After the *coup d'état* of 1851 he publicly attacked Louis Napoleon and was suspended. His melancholy look and student's stoop hardly prepared one for the subtlety and energy of his speeches (" the steel blade in the velvet sheath "). He was a Deist, hostile, though always polite, to Catholicism. He was what we should call an academic liberal. " Bring me liberty in any form ", he said to a Bonapartist, " and I am ready to serve you." At the National Defence Government he sat aloof and distant, never taking a line of his own and conciliatory to all points of view : his colleagues said, " He has the nature of a priest : he only wants the tonsure ".[1] But a great store of energy lay under his air of indifferent serenity.

The wittiest member of the Government was Ernest Picard, the Minister of Finance, and he was probably the wisest. He said to his colleagues, " You will only have a comic-opera siege ", and he proposed negotiation when Paris was blockaded.[2] He had also been a member of the parliamentary opposition under the Empire. With his open face, his long hair, sticking up like a note of interrogation, and his malicious eye, stout, pleasant-featured and hale, he talked away with sparkling epigrams and exquisite irony. He had little respect for democratic formulae ; he openly believed in strong government and said, " As we cannot suppress Universal Suffrage, and as it is hard to mutilate it, we must ' filch it ' ".[3] In the Corps Législatif he had been leader of the Gauche Ouverte (that is the liberal section of the Left), and in the Government he represented liberal tendencies against the exclusivism of Gambetta,

---

[1] Goncourts, *Journal*, t. 5, p. 54.   [2] Weiss, p. 330.
[3] *Taine Letters*, iii. 226. The verb used is " escamoter ".

who said, " We can only govern with parties ". At the
first meeting of Ministers he claimed the Interior for himself, as signifying the policy of a truly national Government
resolved " to use all the forces of the country ". When
Gambetta was chosen by 5 votes to 4, he rose and handed in
his resignation, but he was persuaded to accept the Ministry
of Finance.[1] He protested against Gambetta's partisan
appointments, and he demanded the election of a Constituent Assembly.

Arago and Garnier-Pagès had both served the Second
Republic of 1848. Emmanuel Arago had been General
Commissary for the Rhine Department. He spoke with
real power in his thunderous voice, but he was jovial, and
fond of *bon mots* ; afterwards, he proved one of the most
popular members of the National Assembly. Garnier-
Pagès had been Minister of Finance in '48. He was good-
tempered and moderate, but somewhat vain. An observer
of the '48 Assembly described him as " tall, thin and somewhat sickly looking, presumptuous and shallow, yet not
morose or unkind ".[2]

Four members of the National Defence Government had
been sent to Tours to organise the defence of the provinces,
while Paris was besieged, and they had now moved to
Bordeaux. Two of them, representing the Left and the
Right, were political nonentities. Glais-Bizoin (one of the
old opponents of the Empire) was a figure of fun with his
bald head and his mean face, his eyes like gimlets and his
small cheek-bones showing through a forest of short hair,
which covered his cheeks and chin.[3] Admiral Fourichon
was in command of the North Sea fleet ; he represented the

[1] Reclus, *Picard*, pp. 209-11.   [2] Corkran, *Constituent Assembly*, p. 40.
[3] Simon, *Soir de ma journée*, p. 335. See Hector Pessard, i. 153-60, for
a delicious story — too long to reproduce here — of how he wrote an " advanced " drama, which had been rejected by the Imperial censor and was
therefore hailed at Geneva as a work of genius : it was performed there before
a great gathering of Republicans and, after it had proved insupportable
rubbish, the personal courtesy and political views of the Swiss had a hard
struggle with their aesthetic judgment.

Right, but was not a person of much force at the council table. Crémieux, the Minister of Justice (he had held the same post in the '48 Government), " was not only a French revolutionary, but a revolution in history. He was the arrival of the Jew. When twenty-four years old he changed his name from Isaac-Moses to Isaac-Adolphe. He founded the " Alliance Israélite universelle ". His appearance was unprepossessing — flat nose, small eyes, pale hair and short legs — but his voice was attractive, his nature generous and his repartees vigorous. Once, when he was speaking in Court, the President said, " The Court sees with regret that you are not keeping to the point ". He answered, " I beg the Court to continue their regrets for five minutes longer ".[1]   As Minister of the National Defence Government, he distinguished himself by two acts — giving the vote to the Jews in Algeria, which caused much discontent among the Arabs,[2] and dismissing fourteen magistrates for having taken part in the " mixed Commissions " (civil and military) under the Empire.

But the life and soul of the Delegated Government in the provinces (whether at Tours or Bordeaux) was Léon Gambetta. He did not belong to the old Republican families ; he was only thirty-two years old, and his father was an Italian grocer from the South of France. He had rushed into fame as the result of his diatribe against the Empire in the Baudin trial,[3] and in the last Corps Législatif he had been one of the most ardent opponents of Ollivier's " Liberal Empire ".

As Minister of the Interior in the National Defence Government he had stood for a severely Republican policy ;

---

[1] Weiss, pp. 13-18, and *Portraits de Kel-kun*, p. 24.

[2] In the debate on this subject before the Assembly (21/5/74), in spite of the feeling excited, Crémieux kept the members in roars of laughter. His theory was that the Jews might not change their nationality, unless " God decreed that the change should be imposed on them ". " Therefore, gentlemen, I imposed it on them." (General laughter. De Bastard: " You consecrated yourself as the Eternal Father ! ")

[3] See below, p. 451

he was not interested in attempts to conciliate old Orleanist allies or repentant Bonapartists. He was interested in trying to hold together the advanced and moderate members in the Republican party — an art in which he showed a skill worthy of a future leader. One of his first acts had been to replace all the Maires of Paris and 29 out of 30 Préfets by tried Republicans. He sent Challemel-Lacour to Lyons, where the Commune had broken out and where he succeeded in restoring order, while winking at the Red Flag on the Hôtel-de-Ville, as the " historic standard of the city ". At Marseilles Esquiros expelled the Jesuits ; Gambetta altered the word " expelled " to " dissolved " and replaced him by Gent. He allowed the Préfets to recognise the newly elected municipal councils or not, as they wished. He opposed the idea of immediate elections for a Constituent Assembly and, when the Delegation attempted to hold them, he was sent to Tours in order to bring them to heel, leaving Paris in a balloon.

Once out of Paris, his policy diverged more and more from that of his more moderate colleagues. He took over all the military direction into his own hands with an energy and patriotism, that nobody denied, though its wisdom has been a matter of controversy. He refused to consent to a General Election, unless there was a preliminary *épuration* (weeding-out) of functionaries, and all persons, who had stood as official candidates under the Empire, were disqualified, and on December 25th he dissolved all the General Councils of the Departments as being too Royalist. Even so correct a Republican as Jules Grévy protested against his action, and three Préfets sent in their resignations.[1]

It was the part of the Government, which remained at Paris, that met on the Sunday after the Armistice : the directors of the railways were sent for in order to make urgent arrangements concerning food supplies, after which

[1] De Roux, *Origines de la 3e République*, pp. 75-82.

the Ministers, though worn out with fatigue and anxiety, drew up a decree regulating the elections for the coming National Assembly, to which was to be referred the momentous question of Peace or War. It was to meet at Bordeaux on February 12th : for the elections the law of the Second Republic (March 15th, 1849) was to be in force. This meant universal suffrage : the voters were to be convoked in their cantons, and included all males of twenty-one years : the candidates had to be at least twenty-five years old, and were to be elected by " scrutin de liste " (*i.e.* one electoral list of candidates for each Department) ; the only electoral disqualification was a judicial sentence of degradation or incapacity. The army were to take part, and public functionaries were eligible, except that a Préfet might not be chosen in his own Department. The total number of deputies was fixed at 768 (including six representatives for Algeria and nine for the colonies) ; thus in a country, large areas of which were occupied by the enemy, a considerable section of its population prisoners in Germany, its administration in chaos, its railways disorganised, its postal and tele-graphic services disordered, it was proposed to elect an Assembly in eleven days ; Bismarck, when he heard the clauses of the Armistice read, exclaimed " It is im-possible ! " [1]

If the only obstacles had been material ones ! But more serious difficulties swam before the eyes of the tired Ministers on that Sunday morning. How would Gambetta take the news at Bordeaux ? He had worked miracles in the South ; he was in the midst of organising a new army to prolong the desperate resistance, which in his view the honour of France imperiously demanded. What reception would he give to a telegram informing him that the Paris Government, on its own initiative, and without consulting the rest of France, had suspended the conflict ? And

[1] Simon, *Gouv. de M. Thiers*, i. 3.

D

how would he feel about the electoral decrees ?   His
colleagues recalled with anxiety how, at Paris, he had
strenuously advocated the view that no one, who had held
office under the Second Empire, ought to be allowed to
stand as a candidate.   He had submitted to the majority
of his colleagues, when it had been a question of holding the elections the previous September, but would he
submit, now that he was surrounded by his republican
admirers at Bordeaux, the Dictator of the South ?   It was
owing to apprehensions of this kind that Favre had
announced in his telegram the mission of a member of the
Paris Government.   At all costs unity of action between
the two Governments must be maintained.

Jules Simon was chosen for this delicate task ; [1] he had
been deputy for the Gironde, and he still had many friends
in that Department.   His personal qualities also marked
him out for the post ; half philosopher and half politician,
he concealed under the most gentle and winning of manners
a resolute will of his own.   He was given two decrees, one
for public use, the other only to be used in the last extremity.   The first authorised him to exercise authority
with his Bordeaux colleagues, in order to carry out the
orders of the Paris Government ; decision was to be by
a majority and there was to be no casting vote ; [2] the
second decree contained the clause " In the improbable
case of resistance being offered by the Delegation to the
decrees of the Paris Government, Jules Simon is invested

[1] At a second meeting on Sunday attempts were made to give him a
colleague. Trochu (President of the Council) proposed Pelletan ; Garnier,
Pages and Arago (Minister of Justice) offered to accompany him. General
Vinoy said he could not keep order in Paris, if the Government were imprudent
enough to leave. It was decided by five votes to four that Simon should go
alone. (*Procès-verbal du gouvernement de la défense nationale—Annales de
l'assemblée nationale*, t. 20, p. 185.)

[2] At the moment the Delegation at Bordeaux consisted of four Ministers —
Gambetta, Fourichon, Crémieux and Glais-Bizoin. Gambetta had the casting
vote ; Simon had protested against this arrangement, and had proposed that
he should only have a veto on certain defined issues (Déposition de Jules
Simon — *Annales*, t. 23, p. 444).

with full powers of the most absolute kind to see that the decrees are executed ".[1]

He left Paris on Tuesday, January 31st, at 7 A.M.[2] in a special train of two carriages, accompanied by Lavertujon, one of the Secretaries of the Government, and his son, Gustave. The latter has left a description of the journey; he calls it " a wearisome and tragic Odyssey "; the train moved very slowly (the line had been damaged), and there was time to observe from the windows the detailed traces of the German invasion. At first Jules Simon exclaimed " It is terrible ! ", as they passed some battered ruin, but after a time he could bear it no longer and turned his back on the window, murmuring broken phrases : " This journey seems like the stations of the Cross. . . . Everywhere we shall meet German troops. . . . How long shall we take to reach Bordeaux ? " " Twenty-six hours ", they told him ; he groaned. " We are going more slowly than an omnibus." [3]

At Juvisy the train suddenly stopped ; the Prussian officers politely regretted that they had received no orders. Simon protested : " Favre told me everything was settled ". There was nothing to be done but to send a wire back to Versailles, and pass the time of waiting miserably in an inn, where the rare treat of eating white bread was more than counterbalanced by the noisy Bavarian troops, who were drinking and smoking there, and the still more distressing behaviour of the French proprietress, who (with a candour, that in less tragic circumstances might have had its humorous side) informed the Minister for National Defence that the Prussians were

[1] The Council agreed that, if Gambetta threatened open resistance, Simon might give way " on secondary points such as the date of the convocation of the Assembly " (*Annales*, t. 20, p. 186).

[2] Crémieux afterwards complained of the delay of three days in leaving Paris; Simon replied (Déposition v.s.) that " Favre had to go to Versailles to get a safe-conduct, Bismarck was away, and there was a delay of twenty-four hours ".

[3] Simon, *Soir de ma journée*, pp. 357-63.

very polite, that business had not been so bad, and that she had nothing to complain of.

They took refuge in the fields and spent an hour wondering if the capricious Chancellor had some new trick in store and whether they ought to return to Paris. At last, after another half-hour, the safe-conduct (which Bismarck had forgotten the day before) actually arrived, and at five in the evening they reached Orleans. After dinner Simon asked the hotel-keeper to get a carriage ready, as they were going off. " Going off ! " he exclaimed ; " leaving Orleans ! but you won't be able to pass. There are no trains and the bridge is mined." They patiently explained that it was precisely for that reason they had ordered a carriage ; as they left the city, the Prussian Royal Guards crossed their bayonets and Simon had to lean out of the window in the pitch dark, while military lanterns were flashed on his papers.

At Vierzon they left the Germans behind, and at half-past twelve the train steamed into Bordeaux. On the platform they met several friends, who shook them by the hand, saying excitedly, " Well, you know what is happening here ". " I know nothing," Simon answered. " I have been shut up in a railway carriage for more than twenty-six hours." " There are placards up on the walls against you ; we hope you are going to act at once." But the Minister of Public Instruction was the last person to be rushed into precipitate decisions ; after all (he reminded them) Gambetta might have been wrongly informed or carried away by unreflecting patriotism.

As they walked through the streets, however, it was hard for him not to feel anxious ; the walls were covered with copies of a proclamation, which began : " Whereas it is just that all the accomplices of the régime, which began with the crime of December the 2nd and ended with the capitulation of Sedan, leaving to France a legacy of ruin and invasion, should, for the present, be punished by the

same political disqualification, which has befallen the
detestable régime, of which they were the culpable instruments ; Whereas it is a necessary punishment for the
responsibility they have incurred by consciously aiding and
abetting the ex-Emperor in the accomplishment of the
various acts of government that have placed the country
in danger ". The decree, that followed, excluded from the
new Assembly all Ministers, senators, councillors of state
and Préfets, who had held office between 1851 and 1870, and
all, who had accepted an official candidature at elections
from the Imperial Government.[1]

This Bordeaux decree was dated Tuesday January 31st ;
Gambetta had received the telegram announcing the
Armistice on Sunday morning and had notified it to the
generals, Préfets and sous-Préfets. He had then waited a
whole day, and, no member from Paris having arrived, lost
patience and sent a wire to Favre asking for more details ;
he received a reply from Bismarck : " The Armistice will
last till February 19th ; hostilities are continuing before
Belfort and in Doubs, Jura and the Côte d'Or, till an
agreement is reached ".[2]

This message " exasperated " [3] Gambetta. Not only
had the Paris Government signed a capitulation on their
own, paralysing the rest of France, but they had not even
taken the trouble to include the armies still fighting in
the East [4], which had thus fallen into the Chancellor's trap.

---

[1] Simon, *Gouv. de M. Thiers*, i. 10, 11.

[2] Favre, *Gouv. de la défense nationale*, iii. 15.

[3] Gambetta's own phrase before the Commission of Enquiry.

[4] See Freycinet (*Souvenirs*, p. 238) : " By an anomaly without precedent
in the history of war, the Paris Government had taken upon themselves to
trace the line of demarcation of our forces, though it knew nothing about
their positions and sometimes not even of their existence (as in the case
of the Army of Garibaldi and the recently formed Army Corps of Pourcet).
They had to refer to the maps of the Prussian staff, that is to say to sign with
their eyes shut ; but, what is more serious, they accepted this exclusion of
the army of the East from the Armistice and never told us. . . . We ordered
our troops to stop fighting, and the Prussian Government never warned us
that their own forces were continuing to march." General Clinchant sent a
message to the German General, Manteuffel, who refused to recognise that

There were not wanting those, who counselled Gambetta to denounce the Armistice, refuse to convoke the Assembly, and declare himself dictator. But he shrank from civil war and contented himself with promulgating the ineligibility decree ; he followed it up on February 1st by a fierce proclamation.

After a noble tribute to the resistance of the besieged capital, he went on : " Something awaited us, more menacing, more heart-breaking than the fall of Paris. An Armistice has been signed without our being warned or consulted. We have only lately learned of the criminal carelessness of its provisions. It delivers to the Prussians Departments occupied by our soldiers, and compels us to remain inactive for three weeks and to convoke a National Assembly, when the country is in such a terrible situation. . . . Delegates of the Paris Government, we are ready to obey . . . in order to prove to the world . . . by our example that Democracy is not only the greatest of all parties but also the most conscientious of Governments. But no one has come from Paris and we must act. . . . Prussia counts on the Armistice to weaken, discourage and dissolve our armies ; Prussia expects that an Assembly, called after a series of defeats and the terrible fall of Paris, will necessarily be in a state of panic and ready to accept a shameful peace. . . . Let us make use of the Armistice as a school of instruction for our young troops . . . in place of the reactionary assembly of cowards, for which the enemy wishes, let us install an Assembly, that is truly national and republican, desiring peace, if honour is assured

---

the Armistice extended beyond the armies of Paris and the North : after some vanguard actions, the French troops were obliged to cross the Swiss frontier ; Garibaldi's Army was placed in the same position at Montrollan, but here the Germans did not attack. J. Favre, questioned before the Commission of Enquiry (*Annales*, t. 23, pp. 320-22), answered (1) that Bismarck conveyed to him the impression that the Armistice was general, and (2) that he was not present, when the demarcation of zones took place. " It was carried out by two staff-officers, M de Valdan and his secretary in the presence of Moltke : I had absolutely nothing to do with it."

. . . but capable of willing war also, ready for anything rather than to lend a hand in the destruction of France." Then followed a fiery appeal to the patriotism of all parties in Gambetta's finest style : " Let us not betray our history ; let us not surrender our country to the hands of barbarians.   Who will sign such a peace ?   Not you, Legitimists, who are fighting so bravely under the flag of the Republic to defend the soil of the old kingdom of France.   Nor you, sons of the bourgeois of 1789, whose great work was to seal the indissoluble pact of union between the old provinces.   Not you, workers of the towns, whose intelligence and generous patriotism have always looked on France in her strength and unity as the leader of modern nations.   Not you, labourers and proprietors of the country districts, who have never spared your blood in defence of the Republic, to which you owe your possession of the soil and your title of citizen." [1]

This proclamation and the decree on ineligibility were sent out to all the Préfets ; they did not meet with universal acceptance.   Achille Delorme, Préfet of Calvados, replied : " Your proclamation is very fine, but I cannot accept that part which refers to the Armistice.   It is a public accusation against the Paris Government, and is inevitably an appeal to civil war."   Gambetta wired back (February 1st, 7 P.M.) : " Hand over your powers to your general secretary, and order him to publish the proclamation.   This is a formal order to you both." [2]   Other Préfets objected to its moderation.   The Préfet of Bouches-du-Rhône, Gent, declared he could not accept the elections, and telegraphed to Gambetta, " On, on, my great friend ; an effort worthy of you . . . only dictatorship can save France ".   It was not till February 3rd that he consented to obey. [3]

[1] Zevort, *Histoire de la 3e République*, pp. 143-4.
[2] Favre, *Gouv. de la défense nationale*, iii. 33-34.
[3] Simon, *Gouv. de M. Thiers*, i. 38 : telegrams of January 27th and 30th (" Enquête sur les actes du Gouvernement de la défense nationale ", *Annales de l'assemblée nationale*, t. 20, pp. 657, 659).

The city of Bordeaux, as Simon left the station, seemed to him " full of alarm and resentment ",[1] bands of street urchins were calling out " No elections ! Guerre à l'outrance ! " His friends assailed him with questions : " What are you going to do ? " " I have only just left the train ", replied the unruffled philosopher. " Let me consider the situation and see Gambetta. Keep calm ; I shall do my duty, but no one, I suppose, will bear me a grudge, if I wish to avoid civil war, which would be a great evil." [2]

M. Zevort, Rector of the Academy, had offered to put up the Minister of Public Instruction ; from his house Jules Simon sent for Fourcand, Maire of Bordeaux, informed him of his mission, and enquired as to the state of the city. Fourcand replied that personally he was opposed to Gambetta's decree, but the majority of the municipal council and the larger part of the National Guard and of the population were enthusiastically on his side. That being so, he could only maintain a position of complete neutrality.[3]

Simon then proceeded to the Prefecture ; he has himself described the scene : " The quiet, cultured, good-natured town had become at once a political capital, a gigantic Stock Exchange, and the Headquarters of an Army Corps ; the Place des Quinquonces was completely hidden by long rows of cannon." At the Prefecture itself, the hall of the Conseil-Général and the Préfet's own cabinet were thronged with journalists and reporters. Gambetta himself, if he needed a little quiet, had to retire behind a screen. " He addressed crowds from his balcony, deputa-

---

[1] Simon, *op. cit.* p. 6.   [2] *Soir de ma journée*, p. 364.
[3] Enquête (t. 23, p. 445. Simon's evidence) : " Fourcand declared that there were at Bordeaux two quarters of the city hostile to the Gouvernement of Paris, that he could not carry out my order. . . . I could only defeat Gambetta by civil war." On the other hand, Fourcand (t. 24, p. 170) represents himself as saying, " You can count on me. I do not accept the mutilation of Universal Suffrage."

tions from the top of the staircase, and private persons
behind the door. The great staircase itself was like that
of a railway station, when the train is just starting.
Ministers and generals forced their way through by free use
of the elbow. The crowd was brightened by the great
variety of uniforms. Even the civil functionaries had let
themselves go, and a director of telegraphs had as many
feathers to his cap as a general and as many stripes on his
arm." [1]

Pushing his way through this motley throng, Simon
reached the private study of Crémieux, where he found
the Delegation waiting for him ; Gambetta had ordered
Freycinet [2] to draw up a report on the military situation,
and it was at once read to the meeting ; it was stated that
150,000 men, ready to enter upon a campaign, had been
annihilated by the action of the Paris Government ;
why had they not consulted Bordeaux before drawing
up the terms ? Simon replied that he had not nego-
tiated the Armistice himself, and that he knew nothing
of the detail of the negotiations. Freycinet asked,
" Why, at least, did you not let us know ? " To this
Simon replied that he had not been informed of the
terms of Favre's original telegram. Here Gambetta
broke in ; he said that he was astonished and indignant that in affairs of such importance the entire
Government at Paris and Bordeaux had not acted
together.

At this point the discussion became violent ; protests
and criticisms were poured upon Simon's devoted head.
He remained perfectly calm and " let himself be insulted " (as Glais-Bizoin described it afterwards) ; [3] he
was not there (he said) to discuss regrettable events of the

---

[1] Simon, *Gouv. de M. Thiers*, i. 48.

[2] Freycinet, *Souvenirs*, p. 245.

[3] In a pamphlet called *Five Months of Dictatorship* ; Jules Simon in replying
accepted the phrase, " Charged as he was with interests of such importance,
he had no right to think of himself " (*Gouv. de M. Thiers*, i. 12).

past ; he was there to remind them of the problems of the future. The electoral question was the question of the moment, and on this the Paris Government would never give way. " After we have so often reproached the Empire with its official candidates, are we going to apply the same system so audaciously and on so wide a scale ? When we have the chance of founding the Republic on the will of the nation, are we going to found it on the decree of four men ? " What was the danger of letting Bonapartists stand at the coming elections ? " A handful of Imperialists reduced to a tiny minority in the Chamber would be far less formidable than a party exiled from public life, which should be able to appeal to our own principles against us." Finally he warned those, who were demanding a continuation of the war : " Do you want to turn France into a Poland or into a wilderness ? " [1] But he made little impression on his colleagues. Some of them (especially Admiral Fourichon) appeared to agree with his points, but they were completely dominated by the personality of Gambetta, and Gambetta refused to give way an inch ; he was in a state of exasperated patriotism and ready for a quarrel with Paris ; he also seems to have dreaded the influence, which the Bonapartists still exercised in the country districts, and he could not get it out of his head that Bismarck, who he knew had tried to get Favre to convene the Corps Législatif of the Empire and whom he suspected of having offered to treat with Napoleon III, was hoping to use the Bonapartist vote to secure a shameful peace. But Freycinet, who knew him well, has left it on record that in his view Gambetta's insistence on the ineligibility decree was " not the result of his own personal opinion " ; his open and large-hearted tolerance of all parties, when it was a question of serving France, contrasted strangely with this mass-proscription. All he would say, when pressed, was that " it was not right that the men, who had ruined France,

---

[1] *Gouv. de M. Thiers,* i. 14-16.

should pronounce on her destinies ".[1]

At half-past four the municipal council were admitted, and a stormy debate ensued. Jules Simon was so constantly interrupted that he exclaimed, " But I am a deputy of Bordeaux ! I am in my own constituency. I cannot understand why you and you " (naming several members of the Council) " interrupt every word I say, when I am explaining to you the intentions of the Government." Gambetta was very violent ; referring to the Bonapartists he said, " We must finish with them, once and for all ". The municipal councillors declared that the elections at Bordeaux would take place in accordance with Gambetta's decree. Simon said, " You are entering upon a conflict with the Government ". They answered, " We know of no Government except the one here ; we should see you enter it with pleasure. We have obeyed it for four months, and we shall continue to obey the decrees it passes by a majority."

The meeting broke up in disorder ; Gambetta, as he descended the great staircase, called out " You are not Republicans ! " while Glais-Bizoin followed trying to calm him.[2]

Simon took the opportunity of a private talk with his colleagues; Glais-Bizoin approved of the ineligibility decree ; Fourichon disapproved of it, but felt himself unable to desert Gambetta ; " You are right, my dear Simon," he said, " a thousand times right ; you know that I am with you from the bottom of my heart ". " Yes, Admiral, I know ; what troubles me is that you will not say so." " I am your friend ; I hope you do not doubt it." " Yes, an old friend." " But, even if I voted with you, we should not have a majority ; for Crémieux and

[1] Freycinet, *Souvenirs*, p. 248. Antoine Claveau says (*Souvenirs*, p. 3) : " Pushed on by Ranc, the most daring of his friends and the most Jacobin of men, Gambetta had sworn to stop the elections, which would put an end to his dictatorship ". His subsequent conduct shows that the charge is unfair, but the reference to Ranc's influence may well be true.

[2] Simon, *Gouv. de M. Thiers*, i. 18 ; Enquête (*Annales*, t. 25, p. 218 : Évidence de Silvy).

Glais-Bizoin will never abandon Gambetta, he has so many supporters here." " Then it is an impasse." " No, patience ; some favourable incident may happen."

On his return to the Rector's house, Simon had to make up his mind what to do. There were not lacking people to advise him ; Thiers was at the Hôtel de France, surrounded by Royalists and Conservatives, who were far from averse to a conflict with Gambetta, and who had persuaded him he was in personal danger so that he had turned his apart-ment into a fortress and was continually guarded by a gigantic attendant called Sablot d'Emborguez. Thiers strongly advised Simon to publish the decree, which con-ferred full powers upon him. " You have no time to waste ; take Gambetta's place as Minister of the Interior. You will have at least one legion of the National Guard on your side ; the rest may be neutral. You must sound General Billot's army ; make any use of me you like ; if my name or presence is necessary, I am ready." He was very violent against Gambetta and very ready to dramatise the situation, reiterating, " He will have you arrested ".

Simon shrugged his shoulders : " It is a trap to force my hand ; a rumour set going by those, who want an open conflict. I know Gambetta ; he is incapable of such an action,[1] and for the same reasons, that stop

---

[1] The account in *Soir de ma journée*, drawn up by Simon's son, who was with him, is a little too anxious to represent his father as wrapped in Olympian calm far above all fear and resentment. Thus " he was far from feeling any personal animosity against Gambetta. Did he not remember the long hours of intimacy under the Empire in the little room of the place de la Madeleine ? " (p. 365). Simon, in his own evidence before the Commission (*Annales*, t. 23, p. 444), is more human ; he says he had voted against Gambetta's appoint-ment as Minister of the Interior ; and that they had had a difference of opinion about the personnel of the University ; he states that " our personal relations have ceased ". They drifted finally towards the Right and Left wings of the Republican parties. Gambetta's friends were slow to forgive ; Edmond Adam (a hot Gambettist) wrote to his wife on February 17th, 1871 : " Jules Simon is detestable ; he pretends (so Duclerc tells me) that on his arrival at Bordeaux, Gambetta concealed himself from fear " (Mme Adam, *Mes angoisses*, p. 26). Gambetta had his revenge, when he turned out Simon's Ministry in May 1877.

me from using the army." [1]

As to Thiers' advice, he regarded it as impracticable. Was it likely that the Delegation would allow him to publish his decree in the streets side by side with theirs, and how could he get into communication with the rest of France ? " I am a kind of prisoner here ; I can't correspond with the Préfets, who obey Gambetta : as for the telegraph, it is in his hands ; I can't communicate with the Paris Government, for Stenackers, the Director of Posts, refuses to let the pigeons go without an order from Gambetta." Even the post could not be trusted ; he had already sent off some letters, and none of them had arrived.

Also, he was determined at all costs to avoid civil war, unless it became inevitable. " People say to me, ' What are you waiting for ? The Army will follow you.' They do not shrink from a battle in the streets. Ah ! it is easy to pass for a strong man by using force, but at what a price ! I will never yield to reactionary pressure, inspired by political motives." [2] What then was to be done ? The best plan would be to send for some of his Paris colleagues. Three members of the Paris Government could be at Bordeaux by nine in the morning of February 6th, and would give him the majority ; he believed that, when matters got to that point, the Delegation would submit. Thiers agreed with this, and Cochery was sent off immediately to the capital.

On Thiers' advice Simon had letters sent off to personal friends in the provinces ; they were addressed in various hands so that the post should not recognise his writing, and sent to private persons (such as bankers and professors) so as not to arouse suspicion. [3]

On February 2nd Simon interviewed the representatives

[1] Simon, *Soir de ma journée*, pp. 367, 370, 371, 372 ; *Gouv. de M. Thiers*, i. 22.   [2] *Soir de ma journée*, pp. 367, 368.
[3] Simon, *Gouv. de M. Thiers*, i. 24.

of the Press, who asked if he had with him a decree invest-
ing him with full powers ; he read it to them and reports
were published in the evening papers. At the Delegation,
Gambetta and Crémieux attacked him violently, and the
offending papers were seized.[1]

Simon also approached the generals and magistrates.
One general, who had promised support, refused at the
last moment, but General Foltz declared himself ready
to render every assistance. Simon said, " I expect Gambetta's resignation at nine o'clock on Monday, February
6th ; if it does not take place, the Prefecture is to be
occupied at once ". Foltz objected that he had only a
limited number of men under his orders and that it needed
an order from the Minister of War to transfer regiments
from one territorial division to another. Simon quieted his
scruples by nominating him Minister of War on the spot.
This decree together with the other was deposited with
Cellerier, the Premier President ; in case of Simon's arrest
before February 6th, he was to publish them and Foltz
was to seize the Prefecture.[2]

Meanwhile the state of the city grew more and more
alarming ; the extremists of the Republican party (led by
a fanatic called Lhuillier) were clamouring for Gambetta
as dictator. On the other side, also, opinion was beginning
to assert itself. Two important persons (afterwards
members of the Assembly) waited on Simon and implored
him to use force. The Royalist Press demanded energetic
action.[3] Taine, who was staying at Pau, drew up a protest
against " Gambetta's unjust and dangerous electoral law ",
and got many signatures. " Whereas ", it ran, " the
delegation at Bordeaux has no powers except what it
holds from the Paris Government . . . and the electoral
decree from Paris is the only one which is liberal and demo-

---

[1] Enquête (Annales, t. 23, p. 445 : evidence of Jules Simon).
[2] Simon, Gouv. de M. Thiers, i. 24-25.
[3] Ibid. p. 26.

cratic . . . we declare that we will vote as our consciences direct, without paying any attention to the ineligibility decree." [1]

On February 2nd an intervention of Bismarck brought matters to a head, and (as the Chancellor probably intended) nearly provoked civil war. He sent a telegram to Gambetta formally protesting against the ineligibility decree as violating the freedom of election laid down in the Armistice; Gambetta at once had a copy posted on the walls with the following comment :

CITIZENS,

Several days ago we said that Prussia, in order to satisfy her ambition, counted upon an Assembly, into which, owing to the shortness of the interval and other material difficulties of every kind, the accomplices and flatterers of the fallen dynasty might enter as the allies of M. de Bismarck. The exclusion decree of January 31st ruined their plans. The insolent claim put forward by the Prussian Minister to intervene in the constitution of a French Assembly is the most striking justification of the measures taken by the Government of the Republic. The lesson will not be lost for those, who have any feeling for the honour of the nation.

The Minister for War and the Interior

LÉON GAMBETTA [2]

Jules Simon considered that this ill-timed and unjustifiable interference of the German Chancellor put him into an impossible position, as though he were acting as agent for Germany ; he very wisely decided to take the offensive. Accordingly on Friday, February 3rd, he went to the Delegation and read over to them once again the Paris decree. When it had been received with the usual threats of disobedience, he declared that he could no longer deliberate with colleagues, who openly resisted the Government ; he would therefore take measures to publish the decree.

[1] Taine, *Vie et correspondance*, iii. 7.
[2] Simon, *Gouv. de M. Thiers*, i. 27.

Crémieux replied that he had no right to do so ; he was only one member of the Delegation and must submit to the majority. In answer, Simon read the second decree conferring full powers upon him, and, without replying to the violent protests it provoked, went straight to the offices of *La Gironde,* a friendly newspaper, where he handed in copies of both decrees for publication preceded by the following statement : " At 8.45 this morning I received a copy of M. Bismarck's telegram. I understand and share the irritation it has caused. But the decree of the Paris Government is dated January 28th, and it was inserted in the *Journal Officiel* and the *Bulletin des Lois* on the 29th ; I am here to carry it out ; I have never hesitated in demanding that it should be obeyed. I demand it today, as I did yesterday, because I regard it as indispensable to the welfare of my country. It matters little to me that political opponents find themselves in agreement on this point with the Republican party, to which I belong. At this moment everything ought to give way before the most imperious of civic duties." Copies of the documents were sent to other papers, to the Mairie and the Prefecture.

On Saturday the Delegation forbade the publication and placarding of the decrees ; no telegraph office was to transmit them, and the Préfet ordered the Commissioner of the Police to seize copies of all papers, which contained " an alleged decree signed Jules Simon ".[1] The representatives of the Press sent a protest calling on Simon, by virtue of the unlimited powers he had received from Paris, " to protect in our persons and property, the liberty of the Press and the authority of the laws ". He was, at the moment, anxiously awaiting the arrival of his Paris colleagues, and he contented himself with a protest to the Delegation. " The decree I published is perfectly regular and I formally maintain it ; the papers, which have published it, have acted in conformity with the law, and their

---

[1] Simon, *Gouv. de M. Thiers,* i. 31.

seizure is illegal." [1] The situation was tense : the Republican extremists called on Gambetta to retire to Lyons and to carry on the National Defence from there ; crowds surrounded the Prefecture calling out " Long live the dictator ! " On Saturday a meeting was held at the Grand Theatre demanding that he should assume the dictatorship. Lhuillier forced his way into the Prefecture, saying he came to speak to Gambetta on behalf of the people. Spuller replied that the Minister was ill, and could not see him. Lhullier said, " I do not know who you are ", but was finally persuaded to go away. [2]

Rumours ran round the town that Simon was to be arrested. Fourichon called to see him in the evening and said, " Gambetta wanted to arrest you ; I opposed it energetically. He gave up the idea but I thought I ought to warn you." When he had gone, Simon said with a smile, " An excellent fellow Fourichon ; he is obviously quite sincere ; he quite believes what he told us ; he wishes to give a proof of his friendship, but his story does not hang together ". [3] Nevertheless he took the precaution of sleeping out that night. Glais-Bizoin said to him afterwards, " It has been decided not to leave you any means of addressing the public, but you will retain your personal liberty ". [4]

More moderate counsels now began to prevail. The

[1] Simon, *Gouv. de M. Thiers*, i. 32-4.

[2] Déposition de Dalloz (*Annales*, t. 25, p. 83).

[3] Gustave Simon's account, suggests that his father treated the whole question of arrest with a philosophic detachment. But Silvy, in his evidence before the Commission, says : " He told me he intended not to sleep at his house that night. . . . I doubt if Glais-Bizoin and Crémieux would have ever consented to his arrest, but two of Gambetta's advisers, Ranc and Alain-Targé, were believed not to shrink from extreme measures. But I am inclined to think that the rumour was an exaggeration " (*Annales*, t. 25, p. 218). J. Simon in his evidence (t. 23, p. 446), says, " I took several precautions ", and only rejects with scorn the idea that Gambetta meant to *shoot* him. Antoine Claveau (*Souv. parl.* p. 2) relates that Simon spent the night with an old school friend of his, Paul Dhormoys, and adds that Thiers also spent the night out. Spuller, Gambetta's intimate friend, said before the Commission (t. 25, p. 51), " There was never any question of touching a hair of anyone's head ".

[4] *Soir de ma journée*, p. 373 ; *Gouv. de M. Thiers*, i. 32.

E

Journal Officiel had refused to insert the Paris decrees, in response to a note from Laurier to Dalloz, the editor. "Don't insert anything without orders. . . . Help me to gain time. . . . Gambetta has given up the plan of going to Lyons. . . . We are going to send Crémieux to discuss the matter with the Paris Government. The situation is very serious . . . the problem is how to gain twenty-four hours." [1]

In several of the former discussions the Bordeaux Delegation had raised doubts as to the authenticity of the decrees from Paris ; Simon had suggested they should send a wire to Paris, but that was rejected on the ground that it would pass through Bismarck's hands ; a pigeon started off but never arrived ; finally, on the Sunday, Crémieux left for Paris. [2]

Meanwhile, at Paris, Bismarck's intervention had caused anger and alarm. On February 3rd the Chancellor had informed Favre of the telegram he had sent to Bordeaux. He added : "From the first I expressed the fear that it would be difficult under the present circumstances to hope for complete freedom of election. Full of this apprehension (which M. Gambetta's action seems to justify), I asked myself whether it would not be wiser to convoke the Corps Législatif, which represents an authority freely chosen by universal suffrage. Your Excellency declined the proposal, and gave me the formal assurance that no pressure would be brought to bear on the elections."

This letter was not only the first intimation the Paris Government had of Bismarck's telegram to Gambetta ; it was the first news they had had of Gambetta's ineligibility decree. Nothing better conveys an impression of the isolation of the two Governments of France. Favre replied on Saturday at midday : "You are right to appeal to my loyalty ; you will never find it lacking. . . . I have not

---

[1] Evidence of Dalloz (*Annales*, t. 25, p. 81).
[2] Simon, *Gouv. de M. Thiers*, i. 34, 35.

opposed the whole system of official candidatures under the Empire in order to return to it myself in favour of the present Government. . . . If the decrees to which you refer, have really been issued by the Bordeaux Delegation, we shall repeal them." [1]

Favre then proceeded to Versailles, and protested strongly against Bismarck's interference, which could only have the effect of increasing Gambetta's prestige. The Chancellor replied : " He will not obey you : we are in no mood for waiting. The military Council are at me all day ; they wish to resume hostilities : our Armistice Convention is broken in pieces." Favre answered that the difficulties would be surmounted, if he would only trust them and leave them freedom of action. [2]

On the same day (Saturday, February 4th) Liouville arrived from Bordeaux with Jules Simon's message and a copy of the ineligibility decree. [3] It was immediately rescinded at an evening meeting of the Council of Ministers, who published a proclamation in which they said : " We do not admit the right to impose arbitrary restrictions on universal suffrage. . . . To recall our past dissensions, when the enemy is on our soil, is to belittle by means of old resentments the great work of saving the country." Trochu proposed to withdraw the powers of the Bordeaux delegation and remove the Government to Bourges in order " to resist Gambetta's revolutionary action ", but Liouville emphasised the strength of Gambetta and the dangers of civil war. It was decided to send three representatives to Bordeaux and, if Gambetta still resisted, the National Assembly was to be called at Poitiers. [4]

---

[1] Favre, *Gouv. de la défense nationale*, iii. 21-4. The *procès-verbal* of the Government records a " long, confused and violent debate ; it was decided to postpone the question of Gambetta's dismissal till the text of the decrees was known (*Annales*, t. 20, p. 191).

[2] Favre, *Gouv. de la défense nationale*, iii. 25.

[3] These pieces had been published at Paris, but were considered as a forgery, perpetrated by Rochefort (*Annales*, t. 20, p. 191).

[4] *Ibid*. p. 192.

On Sunday, however, the debate was renewed with vigour. Trochu now appeared to feel that, if Gambetta were arrested, it would be an act of servility to Bismarck : Favre, however, wished to send an order of arrest that night, and General Clement Thomas offered to take it. But Ferry, Trochu and Le Flô urged that it would make a martyr of Gambetta, and it was decided that Favre should content himself with sending Simon the power to arrest him *au besoin*.[1]

Three members of the Government, Garnier-Pagès, Pelletan and Arago, set off to Bordeaux to support Simon : Crémieux, who had left Bordeaux for Paris on the 5th, met his three colleagues at Vierzon, and they were all at Bordeaux by the fateful hour of nine o'clock on Monday morning — Simon's " Zero-time ".

The moment they arrived, it was evident that the crisis was over : the *Journal Officiel* at once consented to publish Jules Simon's decree, the orders to General Foltz were withdrawn, and a meeting of the Government was held at the Prefecture.

Gambetta was not present ; he sent a letter of resignation and wired to the Préfets : " It is my duty to abandon my position as a member of the Government, with which I am no longer in agreement either in ideas or aspirations ". Freycinet tried to remonstrate with him on a decision which would split the Republican party into two camps. He replied : " This is only an incident which the serious questions soon to be settled will wipe out of men's minds. It is perhaps a good thing that, after having been denounced as a dictator, I should retire from the scene of my own free will." He shook hands with all those, who had worked with him, and said farewell. " Let me thank you for the devoted support you have consistently given me. I have played my part ; there is nothing for me to do but to retire." One of the generals present has recorded his

[1] *Annales*, t. 20, pp. 192-4.

feelings : " I confess I loved that man ".[1]

At the Council of Ministers, after Gambetta's letter of resignation had been read, it was proposed to replace him at the Interior by Jules Simon. Crémieux protested ; he admitted his party had been defeated, but he hoped the majority would not press their victory to extremes : in view of the dispositions of the Préfets, the swing from Gambetta to Simon would be too violent. It would be better to appoint someone less involved in recent controversies ; he proposed Arago, who accepted with some reluctance, saying to Simon : " Well, it will be only for a few days. In any case, you will be Minister in all but name, for I am ignorant of what has been happening in the Departments and unacquainted with the personnel." [2]

The crisis was over ; it has been described at length, because it forms an indispensable prelude to the election of the Assembly, and because it introduces, in characteristic attitudes, some of the actors in the political drama. On none of them need our judgment be very severe. In the tragic circumstances it was natural that violent things should be said. But Gambetta showed, as on so many occasions, that combination of the flaming orator from the Midi and the cunning Genoese shopkeeper, which made him fiery in speech and moderate in action. Those, who describe the duel between him and Simon as " the battle between the lion and the cat ", do not show profound penetration ; Gambetta might roar and toss his mane, but, *au fond*, there was as much fox as lion in him. Doubtless he let his outraged patriotism and his personal position at Bordeaux carry him to the verge of an armed conflict, but, when he realised that the feeling of the country would be against him, above all, when he felt doubtful how far his

[1] Simon, *Gouv. de M. Thiers*, i. 41-4 ; Freycinet, *Souvenirs*, p. 248 ; Deschanel, *Gambetta*, p. 109.

[2] Simon, *Gouv. de M. Thiers*, i. 44 ; *Soir de ma journée*, p. 374.

Préfets would support him, he gave way quietly and with dignity.[1]

(Jules Simon has been blamed for the " excessive sensitiveness, the wealth of precautions, the pedantic trifling which wasted so much precious time ".[2] An impartial judgment would recognise that he showed both cleverness and wisdom in dealing with a most delicate situation ; wisdom because firmness was necessary in view of the fact that Bismarck was only waiting for the least concession to Gambetta in order to resume hostilities ; [3] cleverness, because civil war could only be avoided by saving the face of the Bordeaux Delegation and outvoting them by a majority of colleagues instead of issuing orders to the Army to arrest them.)

[1] A public rupture was just avoided. The Delegation did not openly resist the Paris decree ; they professed to doubt its authenticity. It is referred to in their proclamations as the "so-called decree". Laurier in begging Dalloz not to accept Simon's communication to the *Journal Officiel*, urged that it would give the conflict an official existence for the first time.

[2] Sorel's judgment. See Desjoyeaux, *Fusion monarchique*, p. 162.

[3] The German military staff were so doubtful about a peaceful solution that for a moment von Moltke actually suspended the disarming of the French troops. Favre, *Gouv. de la défense nationale*, iii. 37.

CHAPTER II

THE ELECTIONS

THE policy of the Paris Government had triumphed, but only in the nick of time, and, as Jules Simon took his seat at the Prefecture to help Arago with his ministerial work, he was not without opportunities of enjoying, with his philosophic smile of malicious indulgence, some of the confusions caused by the abrupt transition from one Government to another. Thus, called off to lunch at a rather busy moment, he asked an inspector-general of Public Instruction, who had been a favourite pupil of his, to occupy his post for an hour while he was away ; he had hardly sat down to his meal and unfolded his napkin, when a note was brought to him from his temporary substitute : " My dear master, I am leaving the office and feel it my duty to let you know. I wish to preserve the most complete neutrality between Gambetta and yourself. Therefore it is impossible for me to remain at the post of confidence, where you have placed me."

Again, a Préfet wired to the Ministry of the Interior under the impression he was addressing Gambetta : " All goes well ; the list is accepted everywhere. I have carefully had Jules Simon's name crossed out." Eight days later the same Préfet sent the new Minister of the Interior " the most sincere and cordial congratulations ".[1]

French Préfets are apt to be like that — devoted servants of the Government that is in ; only in the Depart-

---

[1] Simon, *Soir de ma journée*, p. 155 ; Simon, *Gouv. de M. Thiers*, pp. 39, 40

ment of the Nord was it found necessary to replace the Préfet, Paul Bert, who had published an ineligibility list beginning "Brame, ex-Minister of the Empire; Plichon, ex-Minister of the Empire; Des Rotours, official candidate 1868–9", and on receiving news of the Paris electoral decrees, declared that, "even if authentic", they were produced by a Government, "that had been for four months in prison and cut off from the public opinion of the provinces".[1]

On February 2nd Herold (the new Minister of Interior at Paris) issued a circular to the Préfets. In the Departments occupied by the enemy, where there were no Préfets, the Maires of the chief towns were to act for them; the vote was to take place at the chief town of each canton; in the occupied territory it was recommended that electoral meetings should be held indoors. "The Government has no candidates to recommend. . . . All they say is, choose men of good reputation and independent character. . . . Let us hope that the control of our country's destinies may not return to the hands of those, who by their servile complacency have hastened on the disasters which are crushing us."[2]

There was little fear of that; Gambetta's apprehensions of a Bonapartist success were quite unfounded; public sentiment was strongly hostile to the Empire, and, although the country districts were full of officials, who had run elections in the past for the fallen dynasty, they stood aside, frightened and discouraged. A tiny group of about thirty deputies could be vaguely called Imperialist from their past careers, but not even all of these could be suspected of much devotion to the Bonapartes.[3] Corsica (the

---

[1] After the February elections it was the provinces who were "backward and misguided", and Paris which was "the last refuge of enlightenment".

[2] Favre, *Gouv. de la défense nationale*, iii. 506-7. (All future references are to Volume III.)

[3] Thus Jules Brame (Minister of the Empire in 1870) drifted into the Orleanist ranks, and Admiral La Roncière de Noury (deputy for Eure) joined

" rotten borough " of the party) returned Paul Abbatucci, who had been a supporter of the Empire in the Corps Législatif ; Conti, a poet who had been Napoleon's private secretary ; Galloni d'Istria ; and Gavini, a famous Préfet, under the Empire, of the Alpes-Maritimes (he had been called the " King of Nice "), who said in his election address : " I shall demand an appeal to the people so that they can themselves pronounce on the maintenance of the dynasty, which had its home in our island ".[1]

So far Jules Simon felt satisfied (he had been right against Gambetta), but, as telegrams poured in announcing Royalist successes and Republican defeats, his brow darkened. " This is what I feared," he said, " our poor, beloved Republic was born in a day of disaster, when all was lost and we could only save our honour. Honour is much, but people expected more of the Republic ; they expected the impossible." [2]

The elections of February 8th, 1871, are an interesting political study. No elections before or since were held in France under such conditions, nor perhaps had they been paralleled in the history of any great nation. Forty-three Departments were occupied by the Germans, who posted up the electoral decrees themselves. No attempt was made to interfere (Bismarck wished for a rapid decision), but postal communication was forbidden and circulation was very difficult. 420,000 Frenchmen were prisoners in Germany, 240,000 disarmed at Paris, 90,000 interned in Switzerland ; deputies heard of their elections from regiments, hospitals, even prisoners' camps.

For twenty years the electors had looked to the Imperial officials to direct their votes, but the Bonapartists were now silent. The Republican Government, weakened and divided, did not even try to give a lead to the country.

the Right Centre. The Empress Eugénie's bitter comment (rebuked by her husband) was, " In France it is a crime to be unfortunate ".

[1] *Dictionnaire de biographie parlementaire.*
[2] Simon, *Soir de ma journée*, p. 376.

In a few Departments some canvassing and preparation of lists had gone on after the abortive convocation of the electors in October 1870, but mostly there was no party organisation and lists were drawn up in the most haphazard manner. Only in a few places (Paris for instance) were formal addresses drawn up by the candidates.

Under these conditions, free from all pressure and direction, France chose an Assembly, which many consider the most competent and distinguished it has ever possessed — certainly the most aristocratic assembly ever returned by universal suffrage. The great surprise of the elections was the resurrection of the old Legitimist party, 180 strong. The usual Republican explanation (quite classical in this context) was " clerical influence ". " The electorate ", says Zevort, " was under the all-powerful influence of the only body of men not disorganised by the *levée en masse*, the clergy." [1] It is perhaps more plausible to point to the country gentry and notables, who had been exasperated by Gambetta's dissolution of the Conseils Généraux and the municipal councils, but there is a simpler and more probable explanation. M. Halévy puts it very tersely. In 1870 Prévost Paradol had said : " [Under the Empire] to be elected deputy, it is necessary to be one of three things — a Government official, a Red Republican or a landed proprietor ". The war had smashed the Imperial Government ; Gambetta's policy of war *à outrance* had frightened the peasants away from the Republic, so they turned once more to the châteaux ; [2] their inmates had been loyal to the King and hostile to the Empire ; many of them had shut themselves up since 1830, refusing allegiance to Orleans and

[1] *Histoire de la 3e République*, i. 15. So Jules Simon : " The Legitimist success is to be explained by the interference of the clergy " (*Gouv. de M. Thiers*, i. 56) ; de Luz (*Henri V*, p. 329) admits that elections were organised and controlled by the clergy, and quotes from the Baron de Montfleury : " The Reverend Father Rouquaire, Superior of the Jesuit House of Val . . . said to me, ' It is absolutely necessary that you should stand for the Assembly ' ".

[2] *Fin des notables*, p. 12.

Bonaparte alike. They had fought for France and sent their sons to fight for France; the electors cared little about their political views but they still looked on them as natural leaders. In default of the politicians they called back the gentry to public life. " Almost a century after the Revolution . . . the old nobility still kept their prestige and influence." [1] " As by a miracle, the France of olden times started from the soil." [2] The eloquent words of the Legitimist de Meaux deserve quotation : " The Legitimist families had furnished the smallest number of servants to the Empire and the largest number of servants to the national defence. . . . I do not know whether in the military history of the French nobility there is a more honourable page than the part they took in a hopeless cause and under a detested republic. . . . Never since the fall of the Bourbon Monarchy had the old noblesse counted so many representatives in a political assembly." [3]

The lists of these deputies included names of the famous ancient families — the Maillés, the Durforts, the Harcourts, the Gontaut-Birons, the Mortemarts, the Uzés, the Rochefoucaulds. Some of them had been members of former Assemblies : Aubry,[4] Benoist d'Azy,[5] Fresneau,[6] Larcy,[7] de Vogüé,[8] General Changarnier,[9] Audren de Kerdrel.[10] Others were new men destined to play their

---

[1] Dreyfus, *La République de M. Thiers*, p. 72.   [2] Halévy, p. 12.

[3] De Meaux, *Souvenirs politiques*, p. 9.

[4] Member of the Legislative Assembly of '49, sent to the Abbaye after the *coup d'état*.

[5] Deputy under the Orleans Monarchy, '41–8 ; member of the Legislative Assembly of '49 ; presided at the meeting of deputies held to protest against the *coup d'état*.

[6] Member of the Legislative Assembly.

[7] Deputy, '39–46 ; member of the Assembly of '49 ; protested against the *coup d'état*.

[8] Representative, '48–9 (Constituante).

[9] Member of the Constituante, and Legislative Assembly ; commanded the National Guard in '49 ; exiled to Belgium after the *coup d'état*.

[10] Constituante and Legislative ; one of the few Royalists, who sat in the Corps Législatif of '52, but resigned before the proclamation of the Empire.

parts in the new Assembly — Cazenove de Pradines, Dampierre, Lucien Brun.

They had the misfortune to lack a leader ; an aristocratic group needs leadership more than any other, yet is most recalcitrant to it.   There was a man marked out for the post, the man, who with Montalembert and Berryer had reorganised the Catholic party under the July Monarchy, and had carried the law, which gave freedom to the Catholic schools under the Second Republic — the Viscount de Falloux ; but he now refused to enter the National Assembly.   He was pressed to stand ; the Departments of Maine-et-Loire and Île-et-Vilaine offered him a place on their lists, but he pleaded ill-health — he suffered from attacks of neuralgia, which sometimes paralysed him.   The Viscount de Meaux, who knew him intimately, believed that this was no insuperable obstacle and sadly pondered over his *grand rifiuto*.   Certainly it was no lack of interest in political affairs, that held him back, for he will be seen interviewing Ministers, addressing meetings of deputies, bearding Thiers ; he himself in his *Memoirs*[1] (after an obvious excuse that he stood aside to allow his friend Cumont to enter public life) reveals what was perhaps the real reason — the old quarrel about the abstention of Legitimists under the Empire,[2] which had alienated the Count de Chambord's sympathies from him.   " To return in a moment of success, in order to impose myself upon him was not to my taste."   The Duc de Broglie says in his *Memoirs* :[3] " It is the greatest reproach one can bring against the Count de Chambord and his party that they made so little use of such a man ".   In February 1871 they paid the penalty.

Failing a political leader, the Legitimists had at least a spiritual one — the famous Dupanloup, Bishop of Orleans. He was in touch with all the important political personages

---

[1] ii. 443.   [2] See pp. 248-251.
[3] Quoted Desjoyeaux, *Fusion monarchique*, p. 110.

of the day.   Thiers was an old friend, and had stayed at the
Episcopal Palace after his fruitless journey in 1870 to
obtain diplomatic support for France from Europe ; he
had prepared the Prince de Joinville for his first communion ; he had given the Count de Chambord his first
lessons in the Catechism.   Unfortunately his position was
somewhat compromised by the divisions in the Church
during the Vatican Council.   Dupanloup had been one of
the leaders of the Liberal opposition to the infallibility
decree ; the *Univers*, the extreme Catholic organ of Louis
Veuillot, never ceased to attack him ; Mgr. Chigi, the Papal
Nuncio at Paris, mistrusted him ; and Pope Pius IX would
never make him a Cardinal.

This was serious in view of the ultramontane atmosphere,
that surrounded the Count de Chambord.   " The pure
Legitimists ", writes the Duc d'Aumale, ''differ from their
ancestors, who were by nature Voltairians, and who put the
throne above the altar. . . . Nowadays the altar is higher
than the throne . . . there is always a smell of incense
about them." [1]

Beyond the frontiers of the Legitimist party there
stretched a vaguely Conservative Centre (about 220 in
number) devoted to the cause of peace and order.   In
reaction from Gambetta and the advocates of war they
were classed for the moment as Royalists, but the party
contained diverse elements.   There were the Orleanists
proper, some really devoted to the cause of the Princes,
some representatives of that bourgeoisie which had set up
the July Monarchy in its image and cared for constitutional, liberal and parliamentary government, whatever its
title, ready to accept a liberal monarchy or a conservative
republic or even (it was whispered) a republic presided over
by a Stadtholder of royal blood)— what Thiers afterwards
called " une république princière ".

In this party among members of former assemblies were

<hr>

[1] *Écrits politiques*, p. 140.

Gouvion-St-Cyr,[1] Bocher,[2] de Goulard,[3] Le Flô,[4] the Marquis de Maleville,[5] Martel,[6] Mathieu-Bodet,[7] St-Marc Girardin,[8] Daru.[9] General Ducrot represented the Army and Admiral Fourichon the Navy. The old Orleanist nobility were represented by the three Dukes — de Broglie, Decazes and Audiffret-Pasquier. The Duc d'Aumale and the Prince de Joinville (sons of Louis-Phillipe and uncles to the Comte de Paris, the Orleanist heir to the throne) were both elected, one for Oise, the other for the Haute-Marne. An attempt was made in the latter Department to invalidate the election on the ground that the Prince belonged to a family, which had been exiled from France, but it was overruled.[10] The more liberal section of the party were afterwards to form Thiers' supporters — the Left Centre; [11] their leaders were to be men like Bethmont, Casimir-Périer, Victor Lefranc, Léon de Maleville, Feray, Waddington, and above all, Thiers' old colleague under the July Monarchy — Dufaure.

The Republicans numbered about 200, also split into two groups of about 100 each; a moderate section rallied round Jules Simon, Jules Favre and the Paris Government

[1] Entered the Chamber of Peers in 1841.

[2] Member of the Legislative Assembly of '49.

[3] Deputy, '45–8; detained at Mazas after the *coup d'état*.

[4] One of the *questeurs* of the Legislative Assembly; expelled from France after the *coup d'état*.

[5] Deputy and Peer of France, '37–48.

[6] Representative in '39; sat in the Corps Législatif of the Empire, '63–70, where he voted with Thiers' " third party ".

[7] Sat in the Constituante; after the *coup d'état* joined Louis Napoleon's " Commission consultative ", but resigned after the decree confiscating the Orleans property.

[8] Professor of history at the Sorbonne; deputy '34–9 and '42–8.

[9] Peer of France; Constituante and Legislative; imprisoned at Vincennes after the *coup d'état*; joined Thiers' " third party " and was Minister of Foreign Affairs in '70 (under Ollivier — the " Liberal Empire " period).

[10] The Duc d'Aumale said in his election address, " In my opinions, in my past, in the traditions of my family I find nothing that separates me from the Republic ".

[11] It is not possible at this stage to be very exact in the classification of the parties; groups had not yet been formed; many deputies did not arrive till late; owing to multiple elections, many constituencies were vacant; the

of National Defence, while the Extreme Left supported Gambetta and demanded war to the bitter end.) Clément Laurier (who had been Gambetta's Director-General) said in one of his last circulars to the Préfets, " We must have war to the last stage of exhaustion ". They believed that a stand might yet be made on the central plateau of France and in the fortresses of the North, that if they held out long enough, even the gigantic strength of Germany could not defeat a nation in arms, and that in the long run Europe would be bound to intervene rather than see France blotted off the map. This view prevailed in the occupied Departments of the East, where many Gambettists were elected; in the Haut-Rhin, Keller, though a Royalist, was in favour of resistance, almost the only member of the Right who took that view. Paris, as usual, voted for the extremest Republicans it could find. On February 10th Jules Favre wrote bitterly from Paris : " The confusion of votes has been so great that the counting has not yet finished at the time I am writing (11 P.M.). But we know that we are completely beaten. Garibaldi and Gambetta head the list ; then Delescluze, Pyat, Tolain and all the men of October 31st.[1] Not one member of the Government of National Defence, but Rochefort is there to give it distinction." [2]

membership of the Assembly did not exceed 630. The following rough sketch must suffice for the moment :

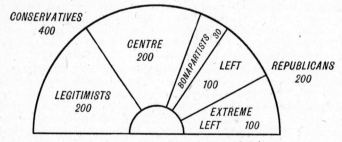

CONSERVATIVES
400

CENTRE
200

BONAPARTISTS 30

LEFT
100

REPUBLICANS
200

LEGITIMISTS
200

EXTREME
LEFT   100

[1] The date of the revolutionary attack on the National Defence Government.   [2] Simon, *Soir de ma journeé*, p. 166.

The Republican deputation for Paris contained many veterans of the Second Republic : Louis Blanc, Victor Hugo, Jules Grévy, Henri Martin the historian, Schoelcher, Edgar Quinet; many of the members had recently distinguished themselves under the September Republic — Edmond Adam, Floquet, Naquet, Rochefort, Peyrat, Clemenceau, then beginning his political career.

The more moderate peace section of the Republicans appeared at the Assembly in about equal numbers — Jules Favre, Jules Ferry, Arago, Ernest Picard represented the National Defence Government ; Jules Simon, after being defeated at Paris,[1] Bordeaux and Montpellier, was preparing to retire into private life when he was elected for the Marne.[2]

But, on the whole, the longing for peace expressed itself by the choice of non-Republican candidates ; in the country districts the Left had no organisation and its doctrines still recalled the fear of Socialism, which in 1851 had driven the peasants into the arms of the Empire. Tired of the war, France sought to be represented by men, who had neither been concerned with declaring it nor with carrying it on. In many places the lists of candidates were simply headed " Peace " and " War ".

Afterwards, a great controversy arose as to whether there had been any other issue than that of the continuance of the war.[3] Gambetta held that, after signing the

[1] Dufaure refused to put Simon's name on the Republican lists on the ground that it would be easier to defend a member of the National Defence Government, if he were not a deputy. On this Simon comments : " I failed to understand the force of this, as J. Favre and Picard were both on his lists ; as it turned out, Paris elected neither Picard nor me — nor Dufaure " (*ibid.* p. 162).

[2] He got very tired of the procession of people condoling with him. " Do you think politics are so very attractive ? " he asked. " I shall arrange my life on other lines." He wrote to his wife : " I am going to see if I can get employment as an *administrateur* of a company, or in a bookshop, or on a newspaper. I could not bear taking pupils, and I don't want a Government post on any terms." Thiers pressed him to accept a vacancy in one of the many colleges, which had elected him, and when Simon refused, saying, " I do not feel ready for a fresh effort ", was visibly annoyed (*ibid.* pp. 158, 377-8).

[3] Even the Comte de Paris wrote on January 31st : " If the Assembly vote

peace, the Assembly had exhausted its mandate and ought to return to its electors ; [1] the Royalist majority maintained that it had received constituent powers and could settle the future government of France.

The truth seems to be (and it is borne out by contemporary testimony) that hardly anyone (even the most professional politician) had any thought for the distant future at all. The present was too full of anguish. Thiers once said, " Universal Suffrage has no sense of vision, only a sense of touch ", and in this case the electors could hardly be blamed, when the immediate problem was whether France should continue to exist as a nation ; in comparison with this it seemed almost a visionary question whether it should be a republic or a monarchy.

Three typical elections will illustrate the movement of the majority in favour of peace and against the extremists. In the Loire, as there were not enough candidates to fill up the Conservative list, places were offered to the Republican leaders at Montbrison, who had administered the Department to the general satisfaction under the September Government ; they refused, expecting that the Conservative successes would only be temporary and not wishing to break away from the rest of their party. So Thiers and Trochu were placed on the list and the Loire deputation presented a varied selection of local notables, unanimously resolved to oppose Gambetta and make peace, but differing in their party loyalties ; Dorian, Minister of Public Works in the National Defence Government, sat on the Left ; Arbel (a distinguished *maître des forges* at Rive-de-Gier) and Cunit (a lawyer of Saint-Étienne) joined the Left Centre, while Bouillié (a capable tradesman, Maire of

the Treaty, ought it to pass on to its constituent functions, or would it not be better for it to seek fresh authority at new elections, which can be held more at leisure ? " (Desjoyeaux, *Fusion monarchique*, p. 165).

[1] Which did not prevent Gambetta from fully recognising the constituent powers of the Assembly, when it was clear they were going to be exercised in favour of the Republic.

F

Rennes) and Montgolfier (a civil engineer) and Callet became members of the Right Centre ; Jullien, de Sugny and de Meaux (all leading members of the Conseil Général) joined the Legitimist Right.[1]

In the Department du Nord each *arrondissement* was asked to choose a candidate and the central Republican committee at Lille promised to put them all on its electoral list. The *arrondissement* of Aresne chose de Marcère, but the Lille committee turned him down as unorthodox ; thereupon the president of the Conservative committee offered to put him on their list. De Marcère went to see him and told him frankly that, if the Assembly were called upon to decide on the form of government, he would vote for the Republic. The Conservative president expressed his indifference on the point ; other and more important interests were at stake, and he thought de Marcère perfectly capable of defending them. The conservative list obtained from 200,000 to 300,000 votes, while the Republicans polled 50,000.[2]

In the Department of Tarn-et-Garonne, Freycinet (Gambetta's friend and military adviser) was on both the Conservative and Republican lists. At the last moment the Republicans, sure of success, asked him as a matter of party loyalty to withdraw his name from the other side ; he reluctantly consented and was soundly beaten. 16,000 votes were cast for the Republicans, and 40,000 for their opponents.[3]

The French *scrutin de liste* allows multiple elections. Gambetta and Trochu were elected in nine Departments, while Thiers was chosen in twenty-six. It was a veritable plebiscite. One night, after dinner in his little room at the Hôtel de France, the old man reflected in silence on the verdict of his country ; his wife and sister-in-law, Mlle

[1] De Meaux, *Souvenirs politiques*, pp. 4-6.
[2] De Marcère, *Assemblée nationale*, i. 31.
[3] Freycinet, *Souvenirs*, p. 258.

Dosne and his faithful giant were with him. He stood there, his left knee bent on the chair, his arm spread over its back and his head bent. Suddenly he looked up: " You are not praying ? " he said ; " but it is necessary to pray. I am not devout but I am praying because, in the disaster of nations, when humanly speaking all seems lost, and it is not possible to see whence help can come, one feels sure that it is God Who rules the world." [1]

[1] Quoted in Loth, *L'Échec de la restauration monarchique*, p. 31 (note).

CHAPTER III

THE NATIONAL ASSEMBLY MEETS AT BORDEAUX

THE new deputies were now beginning to arrive, many of them straight from the war, still in their uniforms, without having had time to see their families. They had the greatest difficulty in finding rooms ; the hotels were overflowing, and the municipality were obliged to requisition apartments. An eyewitness writes : "Mattresses were placed on landings and even on billiard tables. . . . I was told there were deputies, who had to take refuge in hospitals ; others were reduced to sleeping in the harbour at the bottom of fishing-boats." [1]

Most of them felt a sensation of being lost, as they entered the crowded and animated city. Many of the younger of them had come straight from regiments and hospitals ; others had travelled through desolated Departments, past the dark, deserted Gare du Nord at Paris, and they blinked their eyes at the bustle and gaiety of the temporary capital of France. Many of the older deputies were men who had long retired from politics and lived in the country, superintending their estates and their local charities. These old Legitimist noblemen seemed like ghosts of the past, as they shouted "Vive le roi ! " to the astonished and amused passers-by ; and over all shone the joyous southern sun ; the theatres were open ; large placards on the walls announced a play by Félix Pyat (they added as an additional attraction, "Pièce interdite") ; newsboys hawked at the top of their voices a paper un-

---

[1] Claveau, *Souvenirs politiques*, p. 4.

suitably entitled *Victoire*. The streets were filled with ex-employees of Gambetta's Government with their stripes and plumes ; stragglers from the armies ; *francs-tireurs* in their picturesque uniforms ; contractors offering their services ; inventors of marvellous machines guaranteed to wipe out the Germans in ten minutes ; Republicans from Paris haranguing the people among the vegetables in the market-place. Jules Claretie wrote : " Paris is no longer Paris ; all Paris is at Bordeaux . . . this city is at once exotic and Parisian, a Boulevard des Italiens at San Francisco ".[1]

Underneath all this riot of colour, confusion utter and inextricable. " Giddiness and anarchy " are the impressions of an eyewitness. " After forty years it lingers in my memory like a fever." [2] The deputies, most of them new to public life and hardly knowing each other by sight, wandered about in search of Government offices — or even of a quiet corner to discuss things together. Some of them knew little about the result of the elections ; de Meaux was astonished to meet so many Royalist friends on the steps of the Assembly ; [3] de Broglie, arriving a week late, met his nephew the Vicomte d'Haussonville, who spoke to him about the attitude of the Legitimists. " There are plenty of Legitimists here then ? " asked the Duke. " They are here in force ; they claim to be two hundred and talk of restoring the Monarchy at once." The Duke was " thunderstruck ".[4]

On Sunday, February 12th, a preliminary meeting of the Assembly was held ; it was meant as a kind of dress rehearsal and took place at the Grand Théâtre, not long ago the scene of popular meetings demanding Gambetta as dictator, now hastily transformed into a meeting-place for the Assembly. It was a fine eighteenth-century building,

---

[1] Reclus, *L'Avènement de la 3e République*, pp. 16, 17.
[2] Claveau, *op. cit.* p. 2.
[3] De Meaux, *Souv. pol.*, p. 7.
[4] Quoted *Fusion monarchique*, p. 169.

the work of Victor Louis. (The outer hall served as a
conference room. Inside, the level of the seats was raised
to that of the stage ; the tribune of white wood towered up
in the prompter's place ; the orchestra, pit, and balcony
were for the use of deputies ; the public looked on from
the boxes, while the " questure " and the officials of the
Chamber were relegated to the roof ; [1] the hall had no
windows and had to be continually lit by gas.)

The preparatory sitting was held in the *foyer*. The
Count Benoist d'Azy (a Legitimist seventy-five years of
age) took the chair as the oldest member. De Larcy asked
how many members were present, and Arago, the Minister
of the Interior, replied that only a certain number of
telegrams and *procès-verbaux* had arrived ; nothing had
come as yet from the occupied Departments, and the results
of the Paris elections would not be known till tomorrow.
In spite of this, the President proposed to appoint a provisional bureau ; the four youngest members, de Castellane
(27 years old), Duchâtel (33), L'Ebraly (29) and Paul de
Rémusat (40), took their seats as secretaries ; (proceedings
only lasted three-quarters of an hour.[2])

(On Monday, February 13th, the Assembly was opened.[3])
A crowd gathered round the approaches to the theatre,
jeering at the Conservative members and shouting " Vive
la République ! ", as deputies of the Left passed by.
General Garibaldi, conspicuous in his red shirt against the
black coats of his colleagues, " like a wild poppy in a dark

---

[1] Antoine Claveau, who was *secrétaire-redacteur* (official reporter), had to
listen to the debates, hidden behind a dozen deputies in an *Avant-scène* on
the left, and to reach his bureau had to climb along a shaky bridge. He says,
" I looked down on abysses, which made me giddy " (*Souv. pol.*, p. 7). Use
had been made, to staff the Assembly, of the personnel of the old Corps
Législatif.

[2] *Annales de l'assemblée nationale*, t. 1, pp. 1-2.

[3] In spite of the demand of a great number of deputies, the Archbishop of
Bordeaux, from fear of trouble, had refused to allow a Mass of The Holy
Spirit, at the opening of the Assembly (Loménie, *La Restauration manquée*,
p. 99).

cornfield ",[1] excited their enthusiasm, when he walked in to take his seat as deputy for Nice.

The sitting opened with the resignation of the Government for National Defence. Jules Favre had arrived from Paris the day before,[2] and hurried off to visit Thiers, whom he found " alert, resolute and in full possession of power, though as yet without the title ". Favre expressed his intention of retiring from politics ; after having been the author of the famous phrase " Not an inch of our territory nor a stone of our fortresses ", he could not honourably sign a treaty, which would dismember France. Thiers replied : " You are preferring popularity to duty ; you need not worry about your declarations during the war ; our disasters have so cruelly altered our position that you are released from your word. Can you or can you not be of use in the negotiations, which are about to open ? That is the only question ; I regard you as indispensable ; I am about to assume responsibility for them myself ; I have a right to my opinion, and it is my duty to impose the task on you." [3]

They then proceeded to the Assembly, where Favre took his seat with his ministerial colleagues on the front bench on the Left. He laid down office in a voice broken with emotion, that moved all who heard him. " A tear seemed hidden in every wrinkle of his large face." " We accept in advance ", he said, " the judgment, which your equity will pass on our conduct. I ask your permission to return for a few days to my post, where I have delicate duties to perform. My first care will be to take back to

---

[1] Claveau, p. 10.

[2] Before leaving Paris, he had a last interview with Bismarck. The Chancellor was much impressed with the orderly character of the elections, though still a little apprehensive of Gambetta's plans in the South ; he consented to prolong the Armistice till February 21st, adding, " I beg you not to lose an hour " ; he refused to give any hint as to peace terms, alleging an express order to keep silence from the German Emperor (Favre, *Gouv. de la défense nationale*, iii. 49).

[3] Favre, *ibid.* pp. 54-6.

those, with whom we are negotiating, the affirmation that, whatever may happen, France is ready to do her duty bravely." [1]

Subdued applause showed the patriotic apprehensions, with which deputies viewed the coming week; but the sitting was not to end without an explosion of party passion. At the opening, the President had read the following letter from Garibaldi :

CITOYEN-PRÉSIDENT,[2]

As a final duty towards the cause of the French Republic, I have given it my vote, which I now depose into your hands ; I also renounce the mandate of deputy, with which several Departments have honoured me.

The official report has " Mouvement en sens divers " ; [3] if for the Left Garibaldi was a hero, who, when his country had refused to stir a finger, had alone remembered her debt to France, the Catholic Right could not be expected to feel much sympathy for the champion of the Roman Republic. Many of them complained that he had been worse than useless during the war, and had let General Manteuffel march past him without an attempt at resistance.

When the sitting was over and the President had left the chair, the General was seen advancing slowly to the tribune. Whether he had been urged on by members of the Left, who wanted a demonstration, or whether he were simply obeying an instinct for self-advertisement, or whether he really wished to add further explanations to his letter of resignation, no one ever knew, for at his appearance a great clamour arose from the benches of the Right. " The sitting is over ! To the door with him ! A foreigner shall not lay down the law to us ! You cannot speak ;

[1] Claveau, p. 8.
[2] This was the hall-mark of the Reds ; more moderate people said " M. le Président ".
[3] *Annales*, t. 1, p. 4.

you have resigned ! " Deputies, who were filing out into
their bureaux for the verification of powers, hurried back ;
the Left supported the General ; the public galleries joined
in on the same side ; Gaston Crémieux, a visitor from
Paris, called out to the Royalists, " You are a pack of
rustics ; you do not represent France ".[1] The President
returned to his seat and, standing with his hat on, implored
his colleagues to leave the Chamber quietly and ordered
the galleries to be cleared. A long tumult followed within
and without the doors. Garibaldi slowly walked out, acclaimed by a small group of Republican deputies, and left
that night for Caprera.[2]

On Tuesday and Wednesday the Assembly was occupied
with the verification of powers. Never had it been so
speedily done : where further information could not be
procured, a simple statement from the deputies sufficed.
The only trouble arose over the Préfets elected in their own
Departments (contrary to the decrees of the Paris Government) ; five of Gambetta's Préfets were disqualified on
these grounds — Cyprien Chaix, Marc-Dufraisse, Mestreau,
Lamorte and Girot-Pouzol.[3]

On Thursday the 16th the Paris deputies took their
seats. The rowdies in the streets received them with
rapture, yelling to the Conservative deputies " Hats off to
the people ", and pointing out the Republican heroes, of
the capital — Victor Hugo with his National Guard's kepi
on his head ; Colonel Langlois with his arm in a sling ;
Millière, destined in a few weeks to be shot as a rebel on
the steps of the Panthéon ; Delescluze, who was to die at
the barricades, fighting for the Commune ; Rochefort,
who was to be sentenced to deportation ; Félix Pyat, who

---

[1] A month later Crémieux was shot during the disturbances, that accompanied the Commune at Marseilles ; there were those, who said that the
General, who gave the order, had not forgotten the famous insult, which he
hurled at the Royalist majority.

[2] Claveau, p. 11.

[3] Bosq, *Souvenirs de l'assemblée nationale*, p. 10.

had been concerned in all the risings at Paris in 1848 ; Charles Floquet, who addressed to the Tsar, when he visited Paris in 1867, the famous apostrophe " Vive la Pologne, monsieur " ; Cournet, a future member of the Commune ; Ledru Rollin, Razoua, Farcy, Peyrat ; Clemenceau, " remarkable for the strangeness of his face, his dead (almost blue) colour, his deep eyes black and burning, his short hair, his moustache as black as though it had been dyed, his energetic and striking expression ".[1] As they took their seats in the boxes of the pit on the Left, " in attitudes of rather stagy ferocity ", murmurs broke out on the Right ; a deputy called out, " Paris sends us revolutions every twenty-four hours by telegraph " ; Fresneau, a Legitimist deputy, rushed to the tribune and, making an excuse of wishing to speak on the *procès-verbal* of the last sitting, referred to " colleagues notoriously covered with the blood of civil wars ". The Left replied with a furious manifestation, in which the public galleries joined. The old President besought the speaker at the tribune to " leave all that on one side ".[2]

Later in the debate Franclieu from the Right rose to complain of the insults offered to deputies at the door. Floquet replied, " Do you take the cry ' Vive la République ! ' for an insult ? " The authorities, however, felt some alarm, especially as some of the Bordeaux National Guard joined in the manifestations, and half a squadron of cuirassiers were called in to protect the Theatre.[3]

The Assembly was still in a state of excitement, as it turned its attention to the conclusion of the verification of powers : the election of the Orleans Princes was adjourned for further consideration ; a moving demonstration occurred, when the Maire of Strasbourg led in the deputies of Alsace to take their seats.

---

[1] De Marcère, *Assemblée nationale*, i. 37.

[2] Claveau, pp. 13-15 ; *Annales*, t. 1, p. 45.

[3] *Annales*, t. 1, p. 47. Later on, Thiers (perhaps remembering the Gunpowder Plot) had frequent inspections of the vaults under the Theatre.

The Assembly now proceeded to constitute itself. Jules Grévy was elected President by 519 votes to 6. He was a Republican, but of the moderate Left ; the Conservative majority were grateful for his famous amendment, moved at the Constituent Assembly of 1848, which would have made the Empire impossible ; [1] he had also dissociated himself from Gambetta in September 1870.

The four Vice-Presidents, Martel (Centre Gauche), Benoist d'Azy (Droit), Vitet (Centre Droit) and Léon de Maleville (Centre Gauche),[2] were elected by big majorities. There was a party contest for the "questure" (the members responsible for the internal arrangements of the Chamber). Baze (the well-known questeur of the Assembly dissolved by Louis-Napoleon) and General Martin des Pallières (Centre Dr.) got 458 and 430 votes, but the third post was hotly contested ; Princeteau, a Legitimist, got in by 222 votes ; the candidates of the Left (Rolland and Magnin) obtained 145 and 147 votes.

The six secretaries were Bethmont (Centre G.), Paul de Rémusat (Centre G.), de Barante (Centre Dr.), Johnston (Dr.), de Castellane (Dr.) and de Meaux (Dr.). Between two divisions the President read out what he called a "grave resolution", which ran as follows : " M. Thiers is named Chief of the Executive of the French Republic ; he shall exercise his functions under the control of the National Assembly and with the help of Ministers, whom he shall choose, and over whom he shall preside ".[3]

[1] He had proposed that the President of the Republic should be elected by the Assembly and responsible to it — a system realised in fact by Thiers from 1871-3.

[2] The Centre had not yet actually broken into a Left and a Right, but it was soon to do so.

[3] *Annales*, t. 1, pp. 55-8.

CHAPTER IV

THIERS IN POWER

M. WEISS, a Royalist journalist of independent judgment, who afterwards rallied to the Republic, wrote the following severe passage on the Conservative attitude at Bordeaux : [1]

Those, who saw Bordeaux in the opening days of February, can recall the scene, so full of expectation and suspense — those deputies arriving from their Departments in groups of five or six, who had to be restrained from proclaiming the Monarchy in the Tourny Avenue, before the Assembly had found a building to sit in ; those unexpected figures of Legitimists, who seemed to have stepped out of a pre-1830 tapestry, to plunge into the water of universal suffrage and find new life and confidence from it ; Thiers still uncertain as to the number of constituencies, which had elected him, and surrounding himself with Royalists and Fusionists ; Gambetta preparing to retire to San Sebastian, while his followers were busy accusing Jules Favre of having caused the loss of our armies and the fall of the revolutionary government ; everyone trying to find the Prince de Joinville and the Duc d'Aumale in spite of the incomprehensible zeal they displayed in concealing themselves ; last of all, Blanqui [the old Paris revolutionary] coming secretly to Bordeaux to see if there was any way of throwing this Assembly of rustics and landlords into the Garonne as promptly as possible, and saying to his lieutenants in tones of disappointment, " My friends, there is no longer anything we can do ". The great mass of the nation would have refused nothing to the Assembly, which was its creation ; the middle classes had learned from our disasters the lesson, which stood out so clearly for all to read . . . that a nation, which had repudiated its historic and age-long dynasty, . . . had been crushed by a nation, that had been faithful to its old monarchical creed. . . . The Republicans

[1] From a brilliant essay called "The Royalist Illusions" in *Combat constitutionnel*, p. 75.

during the first moments at Bordeaux and before the formation of
the Left Centre were a desperate and divided minority. . . . The
more moderate section . . . asked nothing better than to make
their peace with a Monarchy, provided it was a liberal Monarchy. . . .
Such was the precise state of affairs, when on February 12th the
National Assembly held its first meeting ; yet twenty-four hours
had not elapsed [1] before it had taken its first step towards the
establishment of the Republican régime ; a Royalist majority . . .
had chosen for its President a pure republican, M. Grévy ; five days
later . . . it voted to Thiers the title of " Chief of the Executive of
the French Republic ". Let those responsible accuse themselves of
having been lacking at once in foresight and in courage. We can
understand that in the midst of the torturing obscurities of the
moment, the Royalists did not wish to proclaim the King by
acclamation, but we do not understand why, as monarchists, they
did not refuse to take a step which committed them to a Republic.
. . . Let no one lay the blame on Thiers and his cunning devices ; they
were as clear as the day, and a child could have seen through them.

This vigorous statement raises in a clear form the
question, which a historian of the National Assembly must
try to answer : Ought the Royalists to have restored the
Monarchy on the spot ? or, if that was impracticable, ought
they to have made Thiers chief of a Republic ?

For the pure Legitimist, the Orleanists were and are the
villains of the piece ; Dreux-Brézé says bitterly :

A deputy at Bordeaux said to me : " If the Assembly found itself
faced tomorrow with the abdication of the Comte de Chambord in
favour of the Comte de Paris, or with a formal promise from the
Comte de Chambord that he would renounce the crown after a vote
formally recognising his right, then the proclamation of the Monarchy would only be a matter of hours ".[2]

Lucien Brun, Legitimist deputy for the Rhône, on his
way to Bordeaux met the Marquis de la Guiche, a more
moderate member of the Right ; they fell into conversation about what was to be done, and Brun said : " Well,
we have to save France ; we are going to restore the

---

[1] This is a rhetorical exaggeration ; Grévy was not elected till February
16th.   [2] *Notes et souvenirs*, p. 85.

Monarchy. It is simple enough ; let the Orleans Princes go to fetch the Comte de Chambord and bring him to Bordeaux — and Monarchy is restored." " Wait a minute ", said the Marquis, " it cannot happen as easily as that." From that moment Brun felt " that the cause of Monarchy was lost ".[1]

Loth, who tells the story in his strongly anti-Orleanist book, *L'Échec de la restauration monarchique*, says that the Comte de Chambord was at Geneva waiting for the Orleans Princes. " Their proper place was not with the Army but with their King." [2]

In another chapter [3] we shall trace the history of the relations since 1848 between the older and the younger branches of the Bourbon family ; when they were both in exile, strenuous but ineffectual efforts were made by the wisest leaders on both sides to bring about a fusion of their supporters.

In 1871 the Orleans Princes still believed that their cousin demanded from them an act of penitence for 1830, which they regarded as an insult to the memory of Louis-Philippe. It is not easy suddenly to bring to a successful conclusion negotiations, which have hung fire for twenty years, even when there is a throne in prospect ; but there were willing hands on both sides ready to attempt the task.

Aumale and Joinville landed at St. Malo on February 16th, and sent two members of the Assembly (the Duc de Decazes and the Marquis de Castellane) to inform Thiers of their arrival ; he was lunching with his wife and sister-in-law, and on receiving the news burst into one of his famous fits of passion.[4] When he had cooled down, he sent

---

[1] Loth, *L'Échec de la restauration monarchique*, p. 16.
[2] *Ibid.* p. 20.   [3] See pp. 260–5.
[4] De Castellane (*Men and Things of my Time*, p. 37) says : " He turned pale and then livid ; then taking hold of the first plate that came to his hand, he flung it with all his might across the dining-room and cried, ' Don't let your Princes come to this country or I'll have them shot ' ". Unfortunately, as every reader of Castellane's *Memoirs* knows, the Marquis' imagination is much more vivid than his memory.

Trubert (one of the Princes' confidential friends) to meet them at Angoulême and implore them not to come to Bordeaux. They replied that it was their right and their duty to take their seats in the Assembly. On the 18th, Rémusat and Bocher met them at Libourne and said : " Thiers goes on his knees to you ; your presence would cause grave complications. After all, the law exiling you from France is a law and cannot be evaded ; if you come to Bordeaux, Thiers will resign and leave you responsible for the situation." Rémusat added : " The truth is that you embarrass him, as you always have embarrassed him." Finally, on the understanding that the Government would support their admission to the Assembly, the Princes agreed to the postponement of the question and left for Biarritz on the 23rd.[1]

It is not clear what else they could have done.[2] Weiss, in the passage quoted above, implies that they ought to have gone straight to Bordeaux ; Loth says they ought to have gone to Geneva to join the Comte de Chambord. It is clear that, as a matter of fact, they took the advice of their parliamentary friends, who all said quite frankly that the moment for taking a decisive step had not yet come ; the country had more important things to think about. The Comte de Paris (grandson of Louis-Philippe and Orleanist heir to the throne) in a letter of February 18th, expresses this in a straightforward way : " I do not think that it is my business to prejudice the decision of the Assembly on the future government of France by negotiations which might seem to aim at disposing of France without her

---

[1] Desjoyeaux, *Fusion monarchique*, p. 171.

[2] Whether they ought ever to have been elected to Parliament is another question ; there is much to be said for the view, which Berryer took in 1849, that it is part of the dignity of a Royal Family, which has been deposed, *not* to demand the posts of ordinary citizens. The Princes had very little influence in the Assembly itself ; many Royalists felt that their position as members of a royal House was compromised by the jostle and contact of parliamentary life, while their presence at the centre of political life was always a cause of suspicion to the Comte de Chambord's exiled Court.

consent. . . . As long as our relations with Prussia are the principal affair of the moment, questions about the future ought to be reserved." [1] The Orleans House had always been essentially a parliamentary monarchy, and they naturally waited for Parliament to give the signal.

What of the Comte de Chambord ? Ought he to have left Geneva (where he had gone to be as near France as possible) and to have presented himself at Bordeaux with the words " Here is your King " ? He would have performed such a regal act to perfection, and it is very possible that the Assembly would have voted for monarchy by acclamation : how long a monarchy so acclaimed would have lasted is another question. But the very people, who tell us that he was only waiting for the Orleans Princes, inform us in the same breath that he had the most respectable of reasons for keeping away from Bordeaux. " He felt an invincible repugnance to seem to owe his return to the favour of foreigners . . . when he was still young, he declared to the Vicomte de La Rochefoucauld, ' I am so French that I would rather never enter France than seem to owe my return, I do not say to foreign bayonets but even to foreign influence '." [2]

After this it is rather bewildering to be told as an argument for immediate restoration that " the Germans would have raised no objections ". [3] It is said that in October 1870 Bismarck had offered to restore the Bourbon Monarchy ; [4] and the Count himself once said to his nephew,

---

[1] *Fusion monarchique*, p. 173.   [2] Loth, p. 17.   [3] *Ibid*. p. 23.

[4] On October 1st the Comte de Chambord wrote to the King of Prussia : " [In France] they are beginning to understand that the principle of hereditary Monarchy . . . can, alone, in the hour of crisis, offer a harbour of safety. . . . I am ready if my country calls me, to fulfil the mission which a sacred duty imposes on me, and I am equally resolved to return on the morrow to exile rather than sign her humiliation. . . . If victory has its demands it is for the wisdom of Princes to restrain them within limit of justice. It is to your Majesty's heart that I appeal." Bismarck replied insultingly : " The least pressure from without would only trouble, and not favour the inclination of France towards a Monarchy ", as though the Comte de Chambord had asked for foreign pressure (de Luz, *Henri V*, pp. 315-19).

the Duc de Parme, when out hunting (so the story goes),
" If I had consented to a surrender of territory, I should
today be King of France ".[1]

In any case, Bismarck certainly told the Archbishop of
Rouen that " he would like to see Monarchy restored in
the person of Henry V, but he reproached the Comte de
Chambord with want of energy ". The King of Prussia
also thought the Count incompetent, but he wished to see
the legitimate line restored ; when the German troops
were passing through Varennes, he called his officers
together and said, " You know what crime was committed
here eighty years ago ; when a nation treats its king like
that, the hand of God lies heavy upon it ".[2]

The Comte de Chambord, also, felt unable to take the
step ; it would be too much to say that, like his cousins,
he waited on the Assembly : that was not a habit of the
Bourbons, and least of all of the grandson of Charles X ;
he waited on Heaven. " It is for France to speak ", he
said, " and for God to act." But if the Assembly had
summoned him, he would have probably felt free of his
scruples and have recognised in its vote the call of God.

The responsibility therefore, whether from the Legitimist or the Orleanist angle of vision, must lie with the
leaders of the parliamentary majority. Ought they to
have recalled the King ? De Meaux, a member of the
Moderate Right, says frankly, " At that moment, no one
believed a Restoration possible ". Weiss, in the passage
quoted at the beginning of this chapter, over-simplifies
the situation.[3]

The enthusiasm of the Royalist deputies was the irresponsible enthusiasm of grey-haired schoolboys. It did not

[1] De Luz, p. 324.

[2] Loth, *L'Échec de la restauration monarchique*, p. 24.

[3] To do him justice, Weiss seems to have taken the same view, at the time ;
Claveau met him at Bordeaux in February and he said, " They are making
fools of themselves." " Who are ' they ' ? " " Everybody ; Thiers is to be
President of the Republic." " Oh, a stillborn Republic ! " " No, it will last."
(Claveau, p. 4.)

last when they met together under responsible leaders. At a meeting of the Right under the presidency of de Kerdrel, the Marquis de Belcastel (one of the most honest and outspoken of the Legitimists) had mentioned the chances of a Restoration ; the chairman " stopped him short and in a tone of irritation treated his remarks as imprudent ".[1] Nor is it true that the lessons of the war had converted the nation to monarchy, for a reason which the Royalists always failed to understand — namely that in the eyes of the ordinary voter France *had* been led to disaster by a monarch ; they were not subtle enough to understand the distinction by which the Right treated the Empire as " political Caesarism " and the worst form of democracy.

As for the moderate section of the Left, " so ready to make their peace with a monarchy ", let de Marcère speak. He was a Conservative and a Catholic, afterwards a member of the Left Centre. He writes :

I learn from the books I read that the majority of the Assembly were Royalists. I saw the majority and lived among them attentive to all that was going on around me, impartial and free from party prejudice. My opinion is that it would rather have adopted a Republic than a Monarchy. . . . The truth was that the question was not and could not have been put ; that the personal ambitions of party men and the disinterested preferences of friends of the fallen dynasties would alike have been ashamed to show themselves in face of the issue of life and death for France, which sat so heavy on all hearts." [2]

These well-weighed words of one who proved in the end no great friend to the Third Republic, represent the situation.

As to the anecdote of Blanqui's abandoning the plan

---

[1] Hanotaux, i. 154 (*n*). A Royalist deputy, the Comte de Douhet, drew up a motion asking for the " intervention of the successors of the illustrious Royal Family which gave us Alsace and Lorraine ", to obtain a mitigation of the Prussian peace conditions, but he was prevented by his friends from proposing it at the tribune (de Roux, *Origines de la 3e République*, p. 91).

[2] *L'Assemblée nationale*, t. i. p. 42.

of raising a popular movement against the Assembly, it
does not alter the fact that in all likelihood the proclamation of monarchy would have provoked civil war ; it
would have at once united the divided Republican party,
and kindled the half-suppressed Gambettist sympathies of
the South ; de Meaux says : " We had no military force to
carry out the orders of the Assembly ; the only armed force
remaining was the National Guard in the great cities,
and the great cities were delivered to demagogues ".[1] To
this Loth can only retort that such a rising could not have
been worse than the Commune, which actually broke out a
month later. But what would the Commune have been
like in February, with the Government at Bordeaux,
nothing organised, the Armistice about to expire, no peace
preliminaries settled, and the Paris mob face to face with
monarchy, not merely the fear of monarchy ? The German
troops would have had to interfere and all order in France
would have gone to pieces ; besides, would it have been
confined to Paris ? It is well known that Thiers only
prevented the great cities from joining in March by the
solemn assurance that the Republic was not in danger ; in
February the Commune would have broken out in Lyon,
Marseilles, Toulon, and in twenty cities at once.

De Meaux continues : " How could we restore the
Monarchy with the Royal House divided and a monarch
separated from his heirs ? . . . What would have been the
fatal opening of his reign ? " It was the answer to this
last question perhaps, which made even the most fervent
Legitimist hesitate ; already France foresaw the loss of
Alsace and Lorraine. Even supposing the Count de
Chambord had consented to put his name to such a treaty,
what a humiliating beginning for a monarchy, which rests

---

[1] De Meaux, p. 32. This is Thiers' own judgment (*Notes et souvenirs*,
p. 118) : " The Assembly was so far from being able to restore the Monarchy
(with the greatest cities of the South in revolt and Paris in the hands of 200,000
fanatics) that it could not even have managed to wrest the power from
Gambetta without the energetic intervention of Jules Simon ".

far more on national and personal prestige than does an
anonymous republic, where the acts of the Government are
the acts of all ! Many a Royalist resigned himself to vote
a provisional Republic with the secret consolation that a
disastrous peace would appear forthwith on the debit side
of that detested régime.

It is hard not to feel that the majority of the Assembly
were well-advised. It may be true that after February
12th, 1871, there was no more chance for a Restoration ;
but, if so, it is because there was never any chance at all.[1]

But, granted all that, does it follow that the Conservatives did right in proclaiming Thiers head of the French
Republic ? During the controversy between Simon and
Gambetta, Thiers had appeared surrounded by Monarchists.[2]
The Orleanists did not forget that he had belonged to
their fold. Had he not helped more than any contemporary to found the July Monarchy, and himself brought
the famous message to the Duc d'Orléans offering him the
Lieutenancy of the Kingdom ? Had he not been Minister
to Louis-Philippe and visited him in his exile ?

It is true that the Legitimists did not seem to have many
reasons for trusting him (he had arrested the Duchesse de
Berri, the Comte de Chambord's mother) ; but under the
Second Republic he had rendered yeoman service to the
cause of order and property. He had rallied to the Catholic
cause and helped to carry the Education Law ; he had
delivered the famous speech on " the vile multitude ",
meant to provoke the fury of the Left ; he had supported

[1] Or rather the last chance would have been somewhere between 1850
and 1870 ; if Legitimists and Orleanists had made up their quarrel and there
had been a united royal house, France might well have turned in that direction
(*after* the Peace and the Commune). We may accept the Duc de Broglie's
judgment that " if the fusion had been accomplished during the Empire, the
Comte de Chambord would have been accepted as King, after its fall, by everybody " (*Fusion monarchique*, p. 128).

[2] Even as late as February 19th, when Thiers offered Jules Simon a post
in his Ministry, the latter said to his son, " I should have thought that Thiers
would want to surround himself with Orleanists " (*Soir de ma journée*, p. 379).

the law restricting universal suffrage ; he had strenuously
defended the Papacy and the French occupation of
Rome ; he had been a friend of Berryer and well received
in the Legitimist salons of the Duchesse de Gallieni and the
Duchesse Pozzo di Borgo.

To the Orleanist Princes during the Empire he had
assumed an attitude of detached and rather paternal
affection ; on July 5th, 1870, he wrote to the Duc de
Chartres, the younger brother of the Orleanist heir :

I have demanded liberty for my country. I am demanding it
and I shall go on demanding it obstinately, resolved to accept it
loyally from whoever will grant it . . . and never to rest till we have
it. . . . Your titles for the future rest entirely on the capacity of
your family to give liberty ; to keep in the heart of France the noble
longing and desire for liberty is the only service that a good citizen
can offer to you. . . . I had no responsibility for the faults, which
hurled your family from the throne, and yet I ruined my career for
them . . . because of an attachment based not on personal expecta-
tions, but on ancient memories. . . . I have no ambitions left except
to give useful counsel to my country now and then ; I do not wish
to owe anything to any dynasty present or future. I wish to act
loyally towards them all, but to have no personal tie with any of
them. I ask you, Monseigneur, to forgive this language ; there are
explanations which must be made once in one's life and once for all.[1]

A shrewd Orleanist would not have built much on such a
letter.

On November 3rd, 1870, Bismarck, during an interview, offered to transmit a message to the Princes. Thiers
replied :

I look upon them with respect and affection ; I think they would
be wrong to do anything imprudent at this moment or to behave
as claimants to the throne. . . . But there are certain symptoms
which make one apprehensive lest the Republic of 1870 may follow
the example of the Republic of 1848 ; in that case the return of
the Princes might be useful to France, but today I have no message
for them.[2]

[1] Bouniols, *Thiers au pouvoir*, pp. 4, 5.   [2] *Notes et souvenirs*, p. 86.

Still, much had happened since November. Thiers had
said to Falloux at Tours : " With a Ministry in which I
shall have at my right hand my dear old friends, you and
Larcy, we shall surmount all our difficulties. " My terms ",
replied Falloux, " will be monarchy." " Of course, we are
at one on that point, but time will be wanted ; more time
perhaps than you and I can imagine today." [1]

In December, 1870, it was said [2] that Thiers expressed
himself in terms so favourable to the claim of the Comte de
Chambord that Larcy sent word to the Comte de la Ferté
Mun (the representative of the Prince), and an interview
would have taken place between him and Thiers, had not
each expected the other to make the first move.

On his arrival at Bordeaux, it is also said that Larcy
persuaded him to approve of a motion for the Restoration
brought forward by two deputies (Larcy himself and
Baragnon) ; Daru also had a long interview with him on
the subject. At this juncture he received a letter from
Dufaure, who was at Paris, imploring him not to abandon
the Republic and describing the alarming condition of the
capital. He at once sent for Daru and told him that for
the moment he had given up all thought of a Restoration.[3]

All this is very conjectural, and there is no decisive
evidence that Thiers' first impulse at Bordeaux was
towards Monarchy. What is certain is that he very soon
saw that, in the present condition of the country and in
view of the divisions in the Royalist party, there was
nothing to be done. The pressing question of Peace or
War was far too serious to allow of the additional complica-
tion of constitutional dissensions ; patriotism demanded
a party truce, and demanded it not the less imperiously
because, as long as that truce lasted, he would be the un-
questioned ruler of France. When a Royalist deputy said
to him, " Let us hasten to set up a monarchy ; you shall

---

[1] Falloux, *Souvenirs*, ii. 441-2.   [2] Loth, p. 42.
[3] Loth, pp. 32-4.

be its Richelieu ", the little bourgeois drew himself up and
answered with a haughtiness, that only his amazing abilities
save from being ridiculous, " Not yet ; at this moment
France would not understand anyone else but me taking
the lead ".[1]

On February 15th he sent for some of the more prominent Legitimist leaders — the Duc de La Rochefoucauld,
the Marquis de Juigné, the Comte de Juigné, the Marquis
de Dampierre — and said :

At this moment we can govern only with the help of all respectable parties ; it would be contrary to all the inspirations of patriotism to confuse the work of reconstruction which lies before us by
giving power to one or other of the parties and dividing us, so raising
against that party the hostility of all its disappointed rivals. But it
is evident to me that, if we are wise, the prudence we are going to
display must end in the united Monarchy ; you understand me,
gentlemen, the *united* Monarchy." [2]

" If we are wise ! "   " The united Monarchy ! "   The
Legitimists would have gone away less reassured, if they
could have looked into Thiers' mind and there read what
he thought of the wisdom of the Royalist parties and the
chances of their union.[3]

However, reassured or not, they had no alternative ;
Thiers was inevitable. His prestige in the country was
largely due to his attitude as the steady, clear-sighted
critic of the Empire, the very voice of the liberal conscience of France. In the Corps Législatif he had made his
famous speech on the " necessary liberties " ; he had

[1] Bosq, *Souvenirs de l'assemblée*, p. 6. It is said (this again is in the region
of *on-dits*) that the Bishop of Orleans wrote to Joinville : " Come here as
soon as you can ; Thiers will help us to restore the monarchy " ; and that the
Prince replied, " Do not believe it ; Thiers will only consult his own interests "
(*loc. cit.*).

[2] De Meaux, p. 26 ; Hanotaux, i. 155.

[3] The Marquis de Noailles says : " Thiers was informed secretly by an
important member of the Bonapartist party, the lover of àn Austrian lady,
who frequented the Ctesse de Chambord, that the White Flag would not be
given up and therefore a Restoration was impossible (*Bureau du roi*, p. 164).

denounced the designs of Prussia and warned France of
the danger as early as the Schleswig-Holstein conflict ; he
had criticised the declaration of war in 1870 and had been
shouted down by the Imperialist majority, who called
out, " Go to Coblenz ! " The country remembered those
phrases, sometimes revealing the future, always lighting up
the situation — " The Empire is made " (in 1851) ; " There
are no faults left to commit " (after Sadowa) ; " Europe
no longer exists " (after his fruitless tour of the Continent
in 1870 seeking help for France) ; or that phrase that
stands out so vividly against the muddled cosmopolitan
sentimentality of the Second Empire, " I love Italy but
there is something I love more, and much more, and that
is France."

But, above all, the anarchy and confusion of those
feverish days at Bordeaux called for the energy and
lucidity of his great administrative mind ; his fingers
itched to clear up the muddle (" *gâchis* ", as he called what
he hated most in life). De Meaux says of him very justly :
" What tempted him was not only ambition but also the
love of hard work ".[1]

There was, then, no opposition to the resolution putting
Thiers in power ; the only difficulty occurred as to the
title. " Chief of the Executive ! " grumbled Thiers when
Dufaure showed him the proposed text, " if I am called
' chef ', people will think I am a cook. I want to be
President." " So you will be President of the Council of
Ministers." " Yes, but President of the Republic." [2]

---

[1] De Meaux, p. 27. " I don't want to take up the work of Prime Minister
again ", said Thiers. " Louis-Philippe worried me too much ; neither Charles X
nor Louis-Philippe were real constitutional monarchs. Charles was always
putting forward his conscience, and Louis-Philippe his ' system '." Louis-
Philippe's point of view is expressed in the well-known phrase, " When we go
for a journey, we sleep in the same room ; I let Thiers choose between the
two beds, and I always find him in mine " (de Meaux, p. 28).

[2] Bosq, p. 23. The title was an unfamiliar one. A sentinel, in reply to a
question from Thiers, is said to have answered, " Yes, my Executive " (Bosq,
p. 120).

The Royalist members of the Commission naturally objected to the phrase " the French Republic ". Dahirel and Ventavon went to Thiers and expressed to him the violent opposition, which the words had aroused. He replied :

It is not I who drew up the resolution ; perhaps it would have been better not to have used the words, but, as they have put them in, it is very hard to remove them. A discussion would take a day or two and time is very precious ; the Prussians demand the evacuation of Belfort in order to prolong the Armistice for five days ; a day lost may mean the Prussian entry into Paris ; Heaven knows what misfortunes might result. . . . I have only the right to advise, but I appeal to the wisdom and patriotism of the Right not to raise untimely discussions . . . the word " Republic " means nothing ; the question of the future government of France is entirely reserved.[1]

The Commission finally decided that they would insert in the resolution words reserving the constitutional problem and proposed the following preamble : " Whereas it is of importance, until a definite decision is taken on the institutions of France, to provide immediately for the necessities of government and the conduct of the negotiations."

On Friday, February 17th, the Assembly met to discuss the Commission's report. Thiers naturally did not desire to address the Assembly, till he could speak as a representative of the Government, but an unexpected incident made him break his resolution. Keller, strongly against Thiers' advice, read out a protest on behalf of the deputies for the Departments of Bas-Rhin, Haut-Rhin, Moselle and La Meurthe. It consisted of three propositions : " (1) Alsace and Lorraine do not wish to be cut off from France. . . . (2) France cannot sign or give her consent to the cession of Alsace and Lorraine . . . even an Assembly elected by universal suffrage cannot invoke its sovereignty

---

[1] Chalvet-Nastrac : *Projets de restauration et le général Ducrot*, p. 20.

to sanction or ratify terms that would destroy the integrity of the nation (Approbation from the Left). (3) Europe cannot permit or ratify the abandonment of Alsace and Lorraine. . . . We, the people of Alsace and Lorraine, are prepared on our part to begin the war again today, to-morrow or at any moment." The reading of this protest caused an outburst of patriotic sympathy (" the enthusiasm of despair ", an eyewitness calls it) ; it was referred to the bureaux " avec urgence ".[1]

Thiers rose from his place and said :

> In so serious a matter the Assembly must recognise that we must act with a sense of responsibility . . . we must not let ourselves be carried away by words ; we must know what we are ready to put behind our words. . . . Have the courage of your opinions ; do you want war or peace ? This is a very grave matter ; do not let us behave like children.[2]

A man, who talks like that to an Assembly, is either shouted down or henceforward he can do what he likes with it. For the first time — for the first time of many times — the National Assembly were persuaded by that flute-like voice. After a suspension of one hour, a report was pre-sented and carried " referring the matter to the wisdom and patriotism of the negotiators " ; a few members of the Extreme Left voted against it, and Rochefort called out, " It is a blank cheque ! "

Victor Lefranc then read the report of the Commission in favour of conferring executive powers on Thiers. Louis Blanc protested against the preamble ; the idea of a pro-visional Republic seemed to him an absurdity ; even universal suffrage itself could not legitimately touch the right of the people to govern themselves ; a deputy called out, " You are defending the Republic by divine right ". On a division, about twenty members of the Extreme Left abstained ; on the Extreme Right Belcastel refused to

[1] *Annales*, t. 1, pp. 61-2.   [2] *Ibid.*, p. 63.

vote ; " even for a day ", he said, " I do not want the republican label ".[1]

(The next day was spent by Thiers in forming his Ministry.) He began by including three members of the old National Defence Government.[2] He had already assured Jules Favre that he would retain him as Minister for Foreign Affairs ; his excessive emotionalism made him a very poor antagonist in negotiations to Bismarck, but Thiers probably wished to conciliate Republican opinion by associating as many Republicans as possible with the conclusion of peace. Ernest Picard remained at the Interior, where Thiers appreciated his original wit and his lucid energy. Jules Simon rather reluctantly accepted the Ministry of Public Instruction, after an assurance that he would not be the only Republican in the Ministry.[3] Of all the three appointments this was the most contested. Though Simon was personally popular, his views were abhorrent to the Right ; he was a free-thinker, an advocate of the separation of Church and State and, worst of all, a supporter of compulsory education. Lacombe says in his *Journal* : " It is impossible to make Conservatives tolerate his appointment ".[4] It was suggested that the religious

[1] *Annales*, t. i. p. 64; Bosq, p. 25. Weiss, in the article quoted above, says : " In order to preserve a real neutrality as between Republic and Monarchy, the Assembly should not have allowed the Executive any other title than their own . . . the magistrate charged with the direction of government should have been called ' President of the Executive Council of the National Assembly ' ". This may be wisdom, but is wisdom *post eventum.* The Assembly were in a cleft stick : the Republic existed ; they had allowed the National Defence Government to lay down their powers before them solemnly and regularly ; to upset it would have meant a little revolution, and, as Thiers pointed out, there was literally no time for prolonged debates.

[2] General Ducrot in an interview with Thiers protested against his including the " men of September " in his Ministry. " My dear general," he answered, " the Republican party, which these Ministers represent, is very powerful. I cannot govern without their support. . . . These men are firmer and abler than you suppose ; they have experience and knowledge " (Chalvet-Nostrac, *op. cit.* p. 27, 8).

[3] Thiers said : " If the Republic loses its chances it will be the fault of the Republicans, not mine " (Halévy, *Courier de M. Thiers*, p. 423).

[4] *Journal*, i. 3.

part of the duties of the Minister of Public Instruction should be transferred to the Minister of Justice, but Simon refused his consent ; finally, the Right gave way, consoling themselves with the pledge Thiers had given to Dampierre at a meeting on February 15th, " I will never give way on the question of compulsory education ".[1]

The Ministry of Justice was given to Dufaure. It is said that Thiers did it with a certain hesitation ; he was somewhat afraid of the independence of his rough-tongued old colleague ; in fact the judicial sphere was the only one in which Thiers did not override his Ministers.[2] In return the Garde des Sceaux concerned himself little with the general policy of the cabinet.

General Le Flô, who had served at Paris under the National Defence Government, was Minister for War, and Admiral Pothuau Minister of the Marine ; both these appointments were professional rather than political.

The Right obtained only two posts. The Minister for Agriculture and Commerce, Lambrecht, was a Legitimist. What was more important from Thiers' point of view, he was a Protectionist, and had been a blind supporter of Thiers in the Corps Législatif (in return for which the President of the Council used to refer to him as " the wisest of the wise ") ; he was a poor speaker, a recommendation in the eyes of his chief, who regarded oratory as his speciality.[3]

[1] De Meaux, 79 n. (1).

[2] Jules Simon says : " Dufaure was the only member of the Council with whom Thiers did not feel at his ease ; he treated him with great deference (Soir de ma journée, p. 201). He says : " I still see him " (one day at Versailles, when Thiers, backed by the whole Council, tried to persuade Dufaure to dismiss two subordinates suspected of Bonapartism), " I still see him fastening with jerky movements of his hand the strap, that went round his documents and replying gently to the most earnest entreaties, ' No, M. le Président ' " (ibid. p. 162). As an example of Thiers' interference with his Ministers, see the letter of March 11th which he wrote to Picard : " I wish to make my excuses and those of the Cabinet for two nominations of Préfets, which you will notice perhaps in the Moniteur " (Reclus, Picard, p. 274).

[3] Bosq says of Lambrecht : " He spoke clearly, though one would have liked a little more warmth ; he had a listless voice, which suggested a touch of

The only pure Legitimist in the Ministry was de Larcy, who took the Public Works ; he was an old friend of Thiers and the Right considered that his amiable character made him too conciliatory.[1]

The Ministry of Finance was left vacant for the moment. Thiers asked Buffet, who refused, and on his visit to Paris a few days later secured Pouyer-Quertier, a bluff industrialist from Normandy who had been a supporter of the Empire, but had had his official candidature withdrawn because of his strong Protectionist views.

On receiving his acceptance, Thiers sent a telegram to Bordeaux to ask for the approval of Simon and Dufaure. It arrived at 10 P.M. and the Minister of Public Instruction could not succeed in seeing his colleague ; the old servant who answered the door was " more inflexible than the sentry who threatened Napoleon with his bayonet ". He was obliged to wire back his own consent, and add, " Dufaure is in bed ". Next day the Minister for Justice said, " Another time, don't take the trouble to disturb me ; I approve beforehand all you do ".

Simon sent a letter to Thiers the next day to make his position clear : " Larcy, Dufaure and I wish to enter a caveat on the question of Free Trade ; Dufaure is especially afraid of the effect on English opinion of appointing Protectionist Ministers. It is understood that I myself remain in the Ministry with all my deplorable doctrines — Free Trade, Compulsory Education, etc., etc." [2]

On Sunday, February 19th, Thiers announced the formation of his Ministry to the Assembly ; after explaining that he had attempted to unite representatives of all

disdain for the nonentities all around him " (*Souvenirs de l'assemblée nationale*, p. 42). Claveau says of him : " He had only one fault ; when he spoke he showed that he had not enough teeth ; one saw right down his throat " (p. 24).

[1] " Larcy refused to enter a Government with Simon. Simon arranged to be found reading intently a letter from one of his cousins — who was a nun in the East. Larcy was much impressed " (de Roux, *Origines de la 3e République*, p. 94).

[2] Simon, *Soir de ma journée*, pp. 161-2 ; *Gouv. de M. Thiers*, p. 74.

parties, he passed, by a happy and natural transition, to one of the noblest examples of his grand style :

In a prosperous society, regularly constituted and accepting peacefully and gradually the progress of human thought, each party represents a political system and to unite them into one administration would mean to pit conflicting tendencies one against another, which . . . would lead either to immobility or conflict.

But, alas, is our condition that of a society regularly constituted and peacefully accepting the progress of human thought ? (*Movement.*) Hurled into a war without serious motive and without sufficient preparation, we have seen one half of our land invaded, our army destroyed, our great organisation smashed to pieces, our ancient and powerful unity endangered, our finances upset, the majority of our inhabitants snatched from their work to face death on the battlefield, public order profoundly troubled by the sudden appearance of anarchy, and, after the surrender of Paris, the war suspended for a few days only, ready to break out again, unless a Government that has the esteem of Europe can, by accepting office courageously and taking upon itself the responsibility for painful negotiations, put an end to these terrible disasters.

In presence of such a state of things, is there, can there be, any policy but one ? . . . To rid our country of the enemy who tramples upon it and lays it waste ; to recall from foreign prisons our prisoners — soldiers, officers and generals ; to form once more, with their help, a disciplined and valiant army ; to re-establish order ; to replace at once those administrators, who have resigned or proved themselves unfit ; to re-elect the General Councils, and municipal councils, which have all been dissolved (*Hear, hear*) ; to set up upon its feet again our disorganised administration ; to put a stop to ruinous expenditure, to restore our credit, the only way to face our pressing commitments ; to send back again to the fields and workshops our mobilised soldiers, to re-open our clogged-up roads ; to rebuild our broken bridges ; to revive our industry, everywhere in suspense (that industry which alone can give the means of life to our workmen and peasants) (*Hear, hear*) ; — can anyone say that there is anything more urgent than that ? Is there anyone here, who dares to discuss learnedly articles of a Constitution, while our prisoners die of want in foreign countries, while our population, perishing with hunger, is forced to deliver the last crumb of bread to foreign soldiers ? . . . Ah, doubtless when we shall have rendered to our country that pressing service I have described, when we have lifted up our wounded France [1] from the ground where she lies, closed her wounds, restored her strength, and brought her to herself again, then, once more in health and free again, she shall decide how she wishes to live.

J. Favre then asked the Assembly to appoint a Commission to accompany Thiers and himself to Paris for the Peace negotiations. This proposal was not well received and was only carried after a warm debate; Gambetta expressed the fear that such a Commission might seem to commit the Assembly beforehand.

Feeling that the Assembly might do something foolish in his absence, Thiers persuaded them to adjourn till February 28th. That night he left for Paris.[2]

[1] One cannot translate into English the well-known phrase, "Le noble blessé, qu'on appelle la France".

[2] To occupy their time it was agreed to appoint eight Commissions (of 45 deputies each) to report on the state of the nation. These were: (1) On the army; (2) on the navy; (3) on finance; (4) on railways, roads, etc.; (5) on postal communications; (6) on the occupied Departments; (7) on the internal administration; (8) on commerce. *Annales*, t. 1, pp. 73-85.

CHAPTER V

THE PEACE PRELIMINARIES

AT the Bordeaux station Thiers met and took with him
to Paris the Baron Baude, who was going to attend a
Conference at Brussels, and the Duc de Broglie, who had
just accepted the London Embassy. No one is at his
best on a night journey, and the Chief of the Executive,
waking up at Poitiers from an uneasy slumber, allowed
himself to use language, which deeply wounded the Duc,
and perhaps marked the beginning of that duel to the
death, in which they were eventually to take part. The
conversation turned on the Orleans Princes, and Thiers
said angrily : " Their conduct is unworthy of their name ;
they come to look for a crown in the misfortunes of their
country ". " From that moment ", the Duc used to add,
in telling the story, " I understood that Thiers had given
up working for the Monarchy and henceforward meant to
work for himself." [1]

During the rest of the journey, Favre and Thiers discussed the unknown conditions of Peace, which Bismarck
kept up his sleeve. The Chief of the Executive was in no
optimistic mood ; " If we had treated before the sur-

---

[1] M. Ernest Daudet tells this incident, which he says he heard from the
Duc himself, in *La Chronique de nos jours*, p. 199. As the Duc himself tells
the story, J. Favre and Picard were in the carriage. " After a few trivial
phrases Thiers fell silent, then sank into a deep slumber. . . . We looked at
each other, laughed, and prepared to do the same. . . . We woke up early in
Poitiers. . . . The station was completely empty and they had to search for
food for us in the town." It was in this hungry state that the words were
spoken. (*Revue des Deux Mondes*, 1/2/29, p. 565.)

render of Metz ", he said, " Prussia would have been content with Alsace and three milliards ; now she will demand Lorraine as well and eight milliards — and we are in the dreadful position of having no means of resistance ".

Paris was reached on Monday evening ; as the Armistice was to expire on Tuesday evening, Thiers wired to Versailles to say that he would call on Bismarck the next morning ; it had been thought advisable that he should go alone, as it was hoped that, in a non-official atmosphere, their first contact might be rather a meeting of old friends than a diplomatic duel.[1]

The Chancellor opened the interview in the most courteous tones ; he deplored the fact that the responsibility for making peace should have fallen on Thiers' guiltless shoulders, but he congratulated France on having entrusted her destinies to him.[2] When, after these compliments, he came to business, he did not show himself at all inclined to make the way smooth ; he had been much annoyed because the president of the parliamentary commission, which was to accompany Thiers to Paris, had put forward the idea of getting passports from London : the interference of neutrals (and especially of England) was Bismarck's bugbear at the moment.[3]

He began by refusing to extend the Armistice beyond Thursday. He complained that the French preparations for war were continuing — the 1871 class were being called up ; the Garde Mobile, which Thiers had asked permission to send away from Paris, would go to swell the Army in the provinces.

Thiers protested that a treaty of peace could not be drawn up in forty-eight hours ; the Chancellor replied that the treaty would, no doubt, take five or six weeks, but

---

[1] Favre, *Gouv. de la défense nationale*, p. 90.

[2] Thiers, *Notes et souvenirs*, p. 102.

[3] Jules Favre (who mentions this incident in a letter to Jules Simon) adds : " Public opinion in England is on our side, but the position of the Government is unshaken " (Simon, *Soir de ma journée*, p. 169).

H

that a preliminary statement of the fundamentals of a treaty need not take more than forty-eight hours ; opinion in France and Germany on the questions of territory and indemnities must by now have been definitely formed.

Thiers replied firmly that he would never consent ; he had personally taken trouble to accelerate affairs as much as possible. " If I were thirty years old instead of seventy, I could not have done more. In view of the loyalty of my action, to shut us up within so narrow a ring of time would be an intolerable oppression to which I will not submit, let the consequences be what they may." [1]

Bismarck had of course been bluffing ; he wished to see how far he could bully his opponent. He now played his second card. " I am not the master here ; already they reproach me for being too weak ; I have a formal command from the Emperor not to prolong the Armistice." Thiers replied : " It is surprising that the author of Prussia's greatness should not be master in his own house ". Before the end of the interview, Bismarck got the King's leave to prolong the Armistice till Sunday.

The discussion then turned on the entry of the German troops into Paris. Thiers asked, if to satisfy their pride they were prepared to risk the sacking of Paris, a catastrophe that would dishonour them. The Chancellor replied that the French newspapers were always saying that the German Army, having got to the gates of Paris, dared not enter ; General Trochu had even said that, if the Emperor rode into Paris, he would be in danger of a pistol shot ; the honour both of the Army and its Emperor were being called in question.

Thiers replied that he would speak to the Emperor and make him understand how little his honour was involved in the matter. Bismarck was slightly embarrassed ; the Emperor was useful as an oracle, but he did not like people getting behind his back and consulting the oracle for

[1] Thiers, *Notes et souvenirs*, p. 104.

themselves. " Do not press him too hard ", he said ; " at his age we must be careful of his strength. Besides, he does not like talking business unless his Ministers are present."

" Let us now come to the great question," said Thiers with a sinking heart. Bismarck replied that, as to the general conditions of peace, he would not add much to the terms he had suggested in November. " I have already told you my mind on the matter ; I have already asked for Alsace and a certain part of Lorraine. I will give you back Nancy, but we must have Metz for our security."

Here he glanced at Thiers, but the French representative only answered quietly, " Go on ". " In November ", he continued, " I mentioned four milliards as an indemnity ; today we must have six." " Six milliards ! " replied Thiers scornfully, " it must have been a soldier, not a financier who put such figures into your head. Alsace, Metz, and six milliards ! It is out of the question ; we will discuss this among ourselves, and I will let you know our terms ; if you demand impossibilities, I shall withdraw and leave you to govern France." [1]

Bismarck told Busch [2] that in this interview Thiers spoke of Europe as likely to intervene.

I answered, " If you speak to me of Europe, I shall speak to you of Napoleon ". Thiers would not take this seriously ; " from him France has nothing to fear " ; but I proved to him that he must remember the plebiscite (of 1870 in favour of the Empire), the peasantry and the officers and soldiers. The Guard could only regain their old position under the Emperor ; with a little skill it would not be hard for him to get 100,000 of his soldiers, who were prisoners in Germany. Then all we had to do was to let them go armed across the frontiers, and France would be his again. . . . This must have made an impression on him, for today (Wednesday) when he was going to speak once more about Europe, he pulled himself up and said, " I beg your pardon ".

[1] Thiers, *Notes et souvenirs*, pp. 106-8.
[2] Busch, *Bismarck in the Franco-German War*, ii. 342.

Bismarck's arguments about the Empire were of a kind very popular in the German camp before the February elections, when it was the fashion to suppose that France was sinking into anarchy ; but it can hardly be supposed that Thiers, Chief of the Executive with a freely elected Assembly behind him, attached much importance to them.

On Wednesday the 22nd, Thiers returned and saw the German Emperor at the Prefecture ; he represented to him " respectfully and seriously " the dangers of an unjust peace from the point of view of Europe as a whole. To such generalities the monarch listened courteously but with the air of one who leaves politics to his Ministers ; on the more military question of the entry into Paris, he said that it was "hard to be forbidden to enter a capital which they were proud to have reduced by their arms ". The Crown Prince, who was far more sensitive and large-minded, was touched by Thiers' passionate declaration that he " would never surrender Metz ". We know that the Prince gave the impression in his own circle that he did not think that Germany ought to insist on the surrender of the town, and Bismarck too was hesitating as to the wisdom of the demand.[1]

Unfortunately Thiers does not seem to have been conscious either of the impression he had made on the Prince,[2] nor of the Chancellor's uncertainties. At the

[1] Thiers, *Notes et souvenirs*, pp. 108-9. After the second interview von Keudell sent an urgent message in Bismarck's name to the Grand Duke of Baden that " great care must be taken not to let the French guess that Germany would perhaps have consented to abandon Metz " (Hanotaux, i. p. 123).

[2] Thiers in his *Notes et souvenirs* says : " The Crown Prince touched on the conditions of peace . . . with a delicacy and kindness at least in appearance, that gave me some hope . . . on the entry into Paris he replied in a strain differing very little from the King's " (p. 109). Jules Favre, writing to Simon of impressions gathered at the moment, says : " Thiers found the King and the Prince very polite and abominably greedy ; their demands for money are such that no treaty is possible " (*Soir de ma journée*, p. 170). In the Crown Prince's diary an account is given of the interview. Thiers pointed out the dangers of an entry into Paris (bombs, explosives, etc.). He said : " No Frenchman would ever consent to the cession of Lorraine . . . as for the six milliards, nowhere, not even in England, could so much money be found . . .

second interview with Bismarck, Favre was present and a long discussion took place on the subject of Metz. Thiers reminded the Chancellor that in November he had promised to restore it, whereupon the other closed the debate with an ultimatum. " What was possible in November is no longer possible today, after three months' bloodshed ; if you are resolved not to surrender Metz, it is useless to continue negotiations."

The moment was critical ; Bismarck watched his opponent eagerly to see if he would take him at his word. Thiers answered : " We shall see whether we shall have to break off negotiations ; now let us go on to other points ". The Chancellor breathed again ; Thiers was taking refuge behind his parliamentary commission, and it was not likely that in a matter of peace or war, a committee of deputies would take the responsibility, which their chief had refused to shoulder.

The discussion then passed to the indemnity. The Chancellor referred to the sum of six milliards as very modest ; the war itself had cost four. Thiers answered that in the financial state of France the demand was an impossible one ; it was not an indemnity at all, but a piece of speculation. Bismarck refused to give way ; he was only the mouthpiece of Prussia and must wire to Berlin for instructions.[1]

he had come to appeal to the noble heart of the King of Prussia (who had refused to live in the Palace of Versailles that it might be used for the wounded) and to the Prince who had won so high a reputation in France." Of Thiers himself the Prince says : " He spoke with a little modulation of voice, generally with downcast eyes, preserving all the time a resigned though tactful bearing ; his language was fluent, yet without the least degenerating into the style of the phrase-monger. When I spoke, he looked at me with a bright, sagacious eye, through big, sharply focused spectacles, looking straight into my face. His exterior is more like that of an oldish country gentleman living on his means, than that of a statesman." (*Diaries of the Emperor Frederick,* 257.)

[1] Thiers, *Notes et souvenirs*, pp. 109-10. Dr. Busch (*op. cit.* ii. p. 341) writes that Bismarck related the following scene as having occurred at the interview of the 22nd : " When I demanded *that* of him " (unfortunately Busch could not catch *what*), " Thiers drew himself up to his full height " (a touch

On Thursday, Bismarck sent two German financiers to Paris, who suggested a scheme by which six milliards might be obtained on credit from German banks. Thiers firmly refused ; France would never surrender responsibility for her own affairs.[1] In the evening the parliamentary commission met, and Thiers made his report to them. As Bismarck had anticipated, he stated that there was no hope of getting Metz. His anxieties were now centred round Belfort and the eastern frontier. As to the indemnity, the Commission came to the conclusion " that while we must resist, we must none the less sign the peace ".[2]

On Friday, February 24th, a third interview took place at Versailles ; Thiers rightly describes it as the " most animated and dramatic day " of the negotiations. Before the French representatives set out, they received a visit from M. Kern, the Swiss Minister, who had been to see Bismarck about the need of preserving communications between France and Switzerland. He warned the French

of malice here), " and said, ' Mais c'est une indignité '. . . . After this I spoke to him in German . . . he began in a querulous voice, ' But you are aware that I know no German '. I replied (in French), ' When you spoke just now of " *indignité* ", I found that I did not understand French sufficiently '." M. Matter (*Bismarck et son temps*, iii. 253) treats this as another version of the scene on Saturday (see p. 112). It seems to me quite different in tone and I should place it on the Wednesday ; it is unfortunate that Dr. Busch could not catch what " that " was, but as Bismarck went on to say, that after the passage at arms, Thiers accepted as a concession what he had treated before as an " indignité ", it may refer to the agreement to telegraph to Berlin about the indemnity. Referring to this same discussion, Bismarck told Busch (ii. 342) that Thiers demanded an indemnity of 150,000,000, pleading the great expense of the war to France, especially owing to the rottenness of the war material (" the shoes with pasteboard soles and the arms, especially those from America "). " I replied ' Yes, but just suppose that a man were to attack you and try to flog you, and after having beaten him off you came to demand reparation, what would you answer if he were to try to appease you by saying, " You must take into consideration that the rods, with which I tried to beat you cost me a lot of money and were so badly made " ' ? "

[1] Thiers, *op. cit.*, pp. 110-111.

[2] " The patriotism of Thiers revolted against the proposal of the German banker. He declared that France would honour its signature without anyone's help. Bismarck was furious : " Bring an interpreter ; from now on I shall not speak French " (Dreyfus, M. *Thiers contre l'empire*, etc., p. 266).

that he had found the Chancellor highly irritable. " What
are you coming here for ? " he had cried. " Why are you
meddling ? We have laid down our conditions and, if they
are not accepted, war will begin again." Nevertheless when
they arrived they found Bismarck, though suffering in
health, " calm to outward appearance ". Metz was discussed
first of all and the Chancellor was inflexible. He said he was
far from wishing to drive France to despair ; he recognised
how unstatesmanlike that would be. He had opposed
von Roon's plan for seizing two-thirds of Lorraine ; he
only demanded a small portion of it, but that portion must
include Metz. " In Germany they accuse me already of
losing the battles Count Moltke has won ; do not ask me
for impossibilities."

As to the indemnity, the Chancellor said he had wired
to Berlin and they had insisted on maintaining in the
expenses of the war the pensions for widows and orphans,
the maintenance of prisoners, and the share of the southern
states ; they were prepared to reduce the figure to five
milliards but they would go no further.[1] Hitherto the
interview had been calm ; Thiers now determined to make
one supreme struggle to save Belfort. Bismarck opened by
saying, " Belfort is in Alsace, and all Alsace is to be transferred to Germany ".

For two hours Thiers pleaded. " No," he cried, " I
will never surrender both Metz and Belfort ; you mean to
ruin France in her finances and on her frontiers as well.
Well, take her, administer the country, levy the taxes ; we
shall retire, and you will have to govern France under the
eyes of all Europe — if Europe permits." [2]

Such is Thiers' own summary of what he said during
those famous two hours ; it must be supplemented by
Favre's description of the scene :

I still see him pale, agitated, getting up and sitting down : I

---

[1] Thiers, *Notes et souvenirs*, pp. 111, 112 ; Favre, *Gouv. de la défense nationale*, p. 103.　　　　　[2] Thiers, *Notes et souvenirs*, p. 113.

hear his voice broken with disappointment, his tone at once proud and suppliant; I know nothing grander than the sublime passion of that noble heart, breaking out into protests, threats and prayers; sometimes insinuating, sometimes terrible; gradually kindling into flame when faced with an unjust resistance, at one given moment ready for the last extremities, deaf to the voice of reason so strong and sacred was the feeling that inspired him. . . . He did not really believe that it was possible to resume the war, if Belfort was refused us, but he spoke as though he thought it possible.[1]

If Thiers did not convince the emotional Favre, we may be quite sure that he did not convince the shrewd Bismarck, who was the last person to be shaken by an appeal to sentiment. At first he met the outbursts with an easy and bluff good-nature; he took Thiers by the hand and said: "Believe me, I have done all I could, but as for leaving you part of Alsace it is quite impossible". But after all, he wanted peace concluded, as soon as possible, and when Thiers said, "I sign this very instant, if you give me Belfort; if not, nothing, nothing but the last extremities", the Chancellor replied, "If you wish, I will make an effort with the Emperor, but I do not believe it will succeed". He then sat down and wrote two letters, one to the Emperor, the other to Moltke. "Without him we shall obtain nothing."

Half an hour passed. Thiers says, "Every sound of footsteps in the ante-chamber made our hearts leap". The answer when it came meant more agony of waiting; the Emperor would be out till four; no one could say when the Count would be at home. The French representatives at once declared they would wait till the matter was settled.

Another hour of "inexpressible anxiety"; Bismarck retired to dinner. When he returned, it was to say that the Emperor was back, but would decide nothing without Moltke. When the Count finally arrived, the Chancellor went off to

---

[1] Thiers' own colder and more reserved account does actually agree in essentials with Favre's more dramatic version. He says himself: "I was desperate . . . [I used] now menaces, now entreaties". For another account see Note at the end of this chapter.

discuss the matter with him. " Dumb and motionless ",
says Favre, " we watched the hands of the clock moving
along."   Bismarck entered again, looking satisfied :
" Moltke is on our side ; he will turn the King ".

After another three-quarters of an hour, the Count had
returned from interviewing the King, and the Chancellor
went off to hear his report. The suspense was becoming
intolerable ; at last the door opened and Bismarck, standing on the threshold with his hand on the key, announced
the final offer. " I have an alternative to propose to you ;
according to the King's wish, I demanded the entry of our
troops into Paris ; you explained to me your fears and re-
pugnances, and asked us to give up the clause. We are
ready to do so, if you leave us Belfort. Which will you
have — Belfort or no entry into Paris ? "

Neither of the French negotiators ever forgot the
moment's pause which followed. They did not consult
together ; a look was enough. " Belfort," Thiers exclaimed, " Belfort."

He added a few noble words : " Paris is ready to drink
the cup that is offered her to the dregs to keep for France
a corner of her soil ; the mourning of Paris will be the
ransom of Belfort ". " Reflect well," answered Bismarck ;
" perhaps you will change your mind." But Thiers needed
no reflection : " We should be failing in our duty if we
gave up Belfort ".[1]

It was half-past nine ; the interview had lasted since
midday. The French representatives retired to Paris,
exhausted by the conflict of emotions ; till midnight they
sat with the parliamentary Commission, sharing with them
the anguish of the day. On Saturday they found Bismarck
in a changed mood ; he had received Lord Granville's
dispatch from England suggesting there should be no
indemnities, and he was very excited. Thiers says : " His

[1] Thiers, *Notes et souvenirs*, pp. 114-15 ; Favre, *Gouv. de la défense nationale*,
pp. 104-7.

temper was worthy of a savage ".[1] The Chief of the
French Executive tried to defend the principle that the
surplus of the war contribution should be used to com-
pensate France for a fraction of the debt proportionate to
the taxes imposed on the ceded provinces. The Chancellor
refused to hear a word ; he accused Thiers of going back
on a point which had been already settled. " I see ", he
said, " you only want to begin the war again ; you will get
support and advice from your friends the English." Jules
Favre replied hotly, " It is your own fault if we now find
friends in Europe."

The discussion on the indemnity was still more heated.
Bismarck again produced his financial advisers. Thiers
again refused German aid : France, he said, would build
herself up again by hard work and would pay within the
stipulated time ; nothing more could be asked of her.
Finally he asked leave to send for Alphonse de Rothschild
to take his advice.

Bismarck could not refuse, but he became irritable ;
he said he was ill and that they were wasting time over
provisions already agreed upon ; his conditions were
ultimata, to be taken or left. " Send for an interpreter,"
he exclaimed. " I will not speak French any more " ;
and he burst into a flood of German. Thiers remained
quiet and self-possessed ; at five o'clock the announcement
of dinner caused a diversion. Thiers refused the Chancellor's invitation and would not let Favre bring him anything to eat. At seven-thirty Rothschild was announced
and Bismarck, mellowed by his meal, received him courteously. Thiers accepted his renewed politeness, "like a man
wounded but indulgent ".[2]

On Sunday the last meeting was held to sign the preliminaries. The documents should have been ready at one
o'clock, but the representatives had to wait three hours —

---

[1] Thiers, *Notes et souvenirs*, p. 116.
[2] Favre, *Gouv. de la défense nationale*, pp. 111-14.

an interval filled " with general conversation, which seemed a refinement of torture ". When all was ready, Bismarck called in his colleagues from Bavaria, Wurtemberg and Baden. Thiers demanded that they should each of them append their signature ; the Chancellor replied with a smile, "Do you want to strip the leaves off our German unity already ? " " Ah," replied the Frenchman, " it was we who made it." " Perhaps," said Bismarck, shrugging his shoulders ; then, with a radiant smile, he took up the golden pen (offered him by the ladies of German towns) and signed. Thiers and Favre followed silently and without a sign of emotion ; [1] it was not till they were in their carriage that their feelings got the better of them. Writing next day to Jules Simon, Favre says : [2]

When I had to put the seal to the instrument, I thought I was going to die. . . . It was a spadeful of earth thrown on to the coffin of the beloved being, on whom we smiled yesterday and who is now being lowered into the cold tomb ; Alsace and Lorraine were before me ; it seemed that I was selling them to Prussia. . . . Thiers bore the trial like a hero, but when we had got back into our carriage, he burst into tears ; so we arrived at Paris ; he was crying all the time ; I was suffocated and stupefied. The afternoon was glorious with sunshine ; the road was covered with people welcoming us ; I could have wished to be in my coffin. [3]

Such is the story of the outward events of the negotiations ; what judgment is to be passed on the motives and the ability of the actors and the far-reaching results of what they did ?

M. Hanotaux, in his *Histoire contemporaine*, though he is in the main a great admirer of Thiers, criticises somewhat severely his conduct of the Versailles negotiations. He says : " While Bismarck kept his cards tightly clutched in his two hands " (that is, by refusing to disclose his terms of peace prematurely), " Thiers arrived with his hands wide

---

[1] Favre, *op. cit.* pp. 118-19 ; Hanotaux, i. 126.

[2] I prefer this spontaneous version to the better-known and more elaborate passage in his history.   [3] Simon, *Soir de ma journée*, p. 176.

open before him. France in fact was to be no less unhappy in her diplomatic than in her military operations." [1]

That faults had already been committed on the French side before her representatives arrived at Versailles is true enough. Jules Favre's reckless inclusion of the whole country in the Armistice was a mistake of the gravest order; precious time was wasted in the dispute between the Paris and the Bordeaux Governments, though M. Hanotaux's contention that the absence of Gambetta from the peace negotiations was a great loss to France seems highly questionable. If Gambetta's policy had been followed, Bismarck would probably have refused to recognise the elections as free, and would almost certainly have declined personal negotiations with the Dictator of the South.

M. Hanotaux censures as " very imprudent " the debate in the Assembly on the question of Alsace and Lorraine in which the French were the first to pronounce the terrible formula of cession. He describes as an " incomprehensible error in tactics " the speech of Thiers in which he seemed to make public his intention of surrender: [2] " Have the courage of your convictions; either war or peace ". It should in fairness be remembered that it was not Thiers' fault if Keller's motion was brought forward at all; he occupied as yet no official position, he protested against the whole discussion and would have stopped it if he could. He forced himself to speak, because he feared that the Assembly in a burst of emotion might compromise all possible negotiations beforehand.

However (though not through Thiers' fault) Bismarck was actually aware that the French people wanted peace at almost any price. He had had an interview with Cardinal Bonnechose, the Archbishop of Rouen, and he had drawn from the simple-minded prelate an admission of the pacific sentiments of the French clergy; he had the supreme advantage of observing France from Versailles,

---

[1] Hanotaux, i. 105.   [2] *Ibid.* 113.

while Thiers at Bordeaux knew nothing whatever of German opinion. As far as one can judge, Thiers had only four cards he could possibly have played at Versailles.

First, he might have threatened a continuation of the war; he was hampered here by his firm belief that it was impossible. How long the struggle could have been continued is a problem for military historians; what seems clear to the layman is that psychologically France was beaten. The cessation of hostilities for over a month, and the victory of the Peace party at the elections, meant that the resumption of hostilities would have called for an extraordinary moral effort. Rarely if ever in history has the signing of an Armistice been succeeded by a renewal of fighting; the fact that a nation wants peace is very near to an admission of defeat. It is perhaps fair to remember that Thiers' violent anti-Bonapartism and opposition to the war may perhaps have unconsciously disposed him to despair; it was part of his political creed that war should never have been declared and could not have been worse managed. Bismarck adroitly struck this note at the first interview. " It was not you, upon whom this burden should have fallen."

The second card was an appeal to neutral powers. Since the bombardment of Paris, Europe was becoming alarmed at the increase of German power. On October 30th the Austrian Ambassador, de Wimpfen, sent a dispatch to the Chancellor, in which he said : " The Cabinet of Vienna still believes in the general interest of Europe and in a peace brought about by the impartial arbitration of neutrals." In England (on February 17th, 1871) a debate had taken place in the House of Commons, in which the Conservative Opposition had blamed the non-intervention policy of the Gladstone Government.[1] Bismarck said to Dr. Busch : " I feared that each successive post might bring me some communications from one of the neutral powers like that

[1] Hanotaux, i. 108.

we received from Napoleon in 1866 ".[1]

At the moment a conference had been called at London
to discuss the action of Russia in repudiating the article
of the 1856 Treaty on the neutrality of the Black Sea ; the
fear that France (copying the tactics of Talleyrand at the
Congress of Vienna) might bring the question of the Peace
before assembled Europe, kept Bismarck (he tells us)
" awake at nights ".[2] Was Thiers to blame for not having
used this opportunity ?   It must be remembered again how
isolated he was ; cut off from the usual channels of information (the ambassador for London was only just
crossing the Channel) and absorbed in the endless business
of restoring order, he had little time for sounding neutral
opinion.   It is possible (as M. Hanotaux says)[3] that his
peculiar gifts would have been more in evidence at a
Congress than in private interviews with the acutest
diplomatist in Europe, but it was of course for that very
reason that Bismarck hurried on the negotiations and made
difficulties about extending the Armistice from day to day.

The third card he might have played was to use the
differences of opinion in the German camp itself, more
particularly the conflict between the civilian and military
parties.

Bismarck has been careful to let it be known that after
Sedan he had no clear-cut ideas on the conditions of peace.
He wished to leave himself a free hand ; he had opposed
the march on Paris, but had been overruled by the King's
military advisers.   In February he was in the same position
of uncertainty as to the cession of Metz.   On February 21st
he said to Dr. Busch at dinner :[4] " If the French were to
give us a milliard more, we might perhaps let them have
Metz.   We would then take 800,000,000 francs and build
ourselves a fortress a few miles further back. . . . I do
not like so many Frenchmen being in our house against

---

[1] *Our Chancellor*, ii. 76.   [2] Hanotaux, i. 109.
[3] *Ibid.* p. 114.   [4] *Bismarck in the Franco-German War*, ii. 341.

their will. It is just the same with Belfort ; it is all French there too. The military, however, will not be willing to let Metz slip, and perhaps they are right." The Crown Prince, liberal and humanitarian, leaned in the direction of moderation ; the same day he said to the Chancellor that " Metz might perhaps be sacrificed rather than see fresh thousands fall, on new battlefields ". The Grand Duke of Baden belonged to the same party.

General von Moltke and the military staff took the other side. At a Council held in the Emperor's presence there had been a furious altercation between Moltke and Bismarck ; the subject under discussion was the action to be taken, if, after the Armistice expired, peace was not signed ; the General accused the Chancellor of being too favourable to France.[1] By February 21st military opinion had sobered down ; they were confronted with a regular, and apparently stable, Government at Bordeaux ; public opinion in Germany, impressed with the length and growing expense of the Paris siege, had been profoundly disappointed that the surrender of the capital had not led to immediate peace. Opinion even in the Army was becoming more sceptical as to whether the full military programme could be carried out. We can see from the Crown Prince's diary how pleased and surprised the Moderate party were that the preliminaries were signed with such comparative ease.

All this we can see now, but Thiers had little opportunity of seeing it. Bismarck dropped hints as to disagreements with Moltke, but Thiers naturally took them as mere attempts to evade responsibility. The plain fact seems to emerge that a brilliant and well-informed diplomatist might have saved Metz, and Thiers was neither the one nor the other. He was by nature an orator, and orators

[1] Hanotaux, i. 117. The situation may be compared to the dispute between Clemenceau and Foch as to the annexation of the Rhine, but whereas Bismarck may be rightly called a militarist because he gave way to the demands of the military party, it is unjust to apply the same title to Clemenceau, who successfully resisted that party.

rarely make good diplomatists. Appeals to sentiment were singularly out of place in that little room at Versailles ; he talked too much and too unguardedly. Bismarck said of him : " He is too sentimental for diplomacy ; he is shrewder than Jules Favre, but he too lets himself be bluffed too easily. . . . I like him very much ; he has a fine intellect and good manners and can tell a story very agreeably ; I was often sorry for him." [1] A good negotiator never lets the other side feel sorry for him.

Thiers had only one other card left which he could play — not war but the threat of a rupture : " I shall withdraw and let you govern France ". It was a desperate stake but it could have been risked ; it would have put Germany in a difficult position in the actual state of European opinion. The difficulty was that it was a card which could only be played once ; to use it a second time would have been a pitiful anti-climax. Thiers probably should have used it to save Metz ; he actually employed it for Belfort and he won. It is not, I think, fair to say that he ought to have prevented the entry of the Prussians into Paris at all costs ; it is doubtful how far it actually caused the Commune.[2]

What are we to say of Bismarck ? He was faced with the usual dilemma of a completely successful campaign. If France were left too strong, German opinion would be alarmed ; if France were left too weak, then who would guarantee the payment of the indemnity ? A strong monarchy and anarchy being both undesirable, he chose the course of recognising and treating with a peace-loving, hard-working Republic ; he trusted the bourgeois virtues of Thiers, who hated war and a repudiation of debts as equally unbusiness-like.

On the larger question of the justice of the peace, we

[1] Busch, *Memoirs of Bismarck*, ii. 183; and *Bismarck in the Franco-German War*, ii. 342.

[2] Thiers' view was that the entry of the Prussian troops was a cause of the Commune, though he did not say it would not have happened without that cause.

shall say little ; in the changed Europe of 1939 we need not waste our breath in denouncing the annexation of French territory ; one thing only is eternally relevant. Bismarck was no lover of violence for its own sake, and he did not hate either France or Frenchmen ; his real crime was that he concentrated the whole of his mind on national unity and strength. Alsace and Lorraine were necessary to place the Imperial crown on his master's head and he took them without further question. In doing so, he ignored Europe altogether ; no Conference or Congress closed the 1870 war ; peace was hammered out in a week's private duel between two individuals.

Morley tells us [1] how, on the very edge of war, Napoleon III, on hearing the suggestion of a Congress, " was stirred even to tears at the thought of salvation by his own favourite chimera ". The taunt is just ; the sentimentality of the Second Empire led France to Sedan, but the realism of Germany, breaking rudely away from the tradition of Congresses, led Europe to 1914.

Additional Note

(Extract from Chesnelong, *Les Derniers Jours de l'empire et le gouvernement de M. Thiers,* pp. 82-4)

One day I heard M. Thiers himself describe, with an emotion that communicated itself to me, this last stage of his negotiation with M. de Bismarck. I wrote this account just after hearing it. I know nothing more moving or more touching ; it is all to the honour of M. Thiers, and I reproduce it here because of its deep interest.

" Well, then," said Thiers in opening his supreme attempt to save Belfort for France, " we will bleed ourselves white to pay the enormous indemnity of 5 milliards, which you demand of us. France will submit to the still more terrible necessity of yielding that part of Alsace and Lorraine, from which your armies have driven us. She will accept the loss of Strasburg, in spite of the heroic defence, which has shown how French this city is at heart ; she will give up

---

[1] *Life of Gladstone,* i. 968.

I

Metz, where everything, even the language, is French. It is a cruel mutilation : you impose upon us the law of conquest : we submit with bitter sorrow. But Belfort still resists : you have not conquered it. To give up Belfort, when the fate of war has not snatched it away, would be a dishonour. Though we are conquered, we cannot consent to it."

Bismarck replied : " Belfort can hardly resist for a week. Why should we prolong a murderous contest, when its result is mathematically certain ? We wish for the whole of Alsace ; it has cost us enough blood for us to have the right of taking it back without leaving you anything, for it was ours before it was yours. We only ask to be allowed to re-enter into possession, through a just conquest, of that, which in other days an unjust conquest snatched from us. I understand your sorrow ; I sympathise with it, I should be glad to give way to your demand, but my duty towards Germany does not allow it. Besides, the resolve of my master the Emperor is irrevocable — namely to have peace on the conditions I have offered you without any other modification than the reduction of the indemnity to 5 milliards. If you do not accept it, it means that the war will immediately begin again, and you are in no condition to continue it."

" Well, then," cried Thiers with an emotion born of despair, " we will rather have war than consent to give up Belfort, which is not yet yours. Oh, I know our old Army is imprisoned in Germany : the armies we raised in a hurry and which for four months have held the field against you, are scattered and enfeebled ; France is reeling beneath the weight of her misfortunes : she is drained of men and money : if hostilities begin again, the struggle will be terribly unequal, and all the chances are against us. I know all that. But Belfort is the key of the house : you have not taken it : I cannot deliver it to you. I should be signing the dishonour of France and my own dishonour. I shall ask of France to make a supreme effort, and if it is necessary, she will make it. She is wounded but she is not dead, and, even should she perish, she will at least show to the world what a nation is capable of when reduced to despair. Do not condemn us to this extremity. You have a passion for the greatness and glory of Germany. But the possession of Belfort will add nothing to the greatness of your country, and what glory will she find in a victory, which will be a merciless extermination ? I still hope that you will not allow yourselves to shoulder such a responsibility before God and before history."

Bismarck, moved by this solemn adjuration, then said to Thiers :
" I do not doubt the courage of France, but I see its powerlessness,
and I have no doubt about the result of a renewal of hostilities. All
the same, I am touched by your despair. I cannot, however, take
upon me to make the important concession you ask in the matter of
Belfort. I must refer to the Emperor, who himself will not decide
without having consulted the Marshal de Moltke. I will take your
demand to him, and I promise to support it. In two hours I shall
let you know the Emperor's last word."

It was time for Bismarck's dinner and he invited Thiers to dine
at his table. Thiers declined the invitation and remained alone [1]
in the room, where the conversation had taken place. Worn out with
fatigue and emotion, he lay upon the sofa and, in spite of his
anxieties, fell into a deep and feverish sleep. Great was his astonishment, when he awoke, to find himself covered with Bismarck's war-
cloak. Bismarck had re-entered the room after dinner to take leave
of Thiers before going to the Emperor. He had not woken up his
illustrious visitor, but to preserve him from the cold (it was February
and there was a winter temperature at Versailles) he had covered
him with his own cloak. Thiers related this curious detail very
charmingly, and added with his subtle smile, " This rough man had
some traces of delicacy in the midst of his Pomeranian brutality ".
Two hours passed : Bismarck did not return, and Thiers, whose
impatient ardour had been restored by his short sleep, could not
resist a feeling of restless anxiety. After the delay of more than an
hour, Bismarck arrived. " I have made you wait," he said to Thiers.
" I was pleading your cause, and encountering obstacles. At last,
I bring you the Emperor's last word. Belfort shall remain French,
but in return for it the Emperor will enter Paris at the head of his
victorious army. However, he will not remain there more than
twenty-four hours." " I accept," replied Thiers ; " it will be another
humiliation ; for the last six months we have given up counting our
humiliations. At least honour is saved and we keep the key of the
house."

[1] Favre, however, implies (*Gouv. de la défense nationale*, iii. 105) that he
remained in the room during the hours of waiting. If Chesnelong's version is
correct, Favre must have gone out for a time. Thiers says, " We passed an
hour, Jules Favre and I, in inexpressible anxiety ". Thiers' " naps " were
famous, but it is perhaps natural that he should have omitted it in the official
account of the scene (*Notes et souvenirs*, p. 114).

CHAPTER VI

RATIFICATION OF THE PEACE PRELIMINARIES

When Thiers and Favre returned to Paris on the night of Sunday, February 26th, they found the city in a state of feverish excitement : the news that the Prussians were to enter Paris had provoked grave disorders. At three in the afternoon a great crowd had assembled on the Place de la Bastille to honour the memory of those, who had fallen during the siege, and a gendarme had been drowned with brutal violence.[1]

All night long the tocsin sounded and messages arrived that battalions of the National Guard were gathering to march against the Germans. Thiers left for Bordeaux the next morning, after an anxious and troubled vigil, during which he never closed his eyes.

The populace had carried off the cannons of the National Guard from the parc Wagram to the Parc Monceau ; General Vinoy, who had only 16,000 men under him, received orders from the Government to withdraw from the right bank and concentrate on the left bank of the Seine ; Ferry no longer had any control over the municipal council, of which he was the nominal president ; Cresson had resigned the Préfecture of the Police on February 11th, and no one had been found to take his place.[2]

Favre's only hope was that the entry of the Prussians might be altogether avoided by a speedy ratification of the Peace Preliminaries. Article 3 ran, "*Immediately* after the

---

[1] Favre, *Gouv. de la défense nationale,* iii. 122.
[2] *Ibid.* p. 129.

ratification of the present treaty, the German troops shall evacuate the interior of the city of Paris and the forts on the left bank of the Seine "; Bismarck had prolonged the Armistice till March 12th, counting on long and violent debates in the Assembly before peace should be signed. On Monday afternoon Jules Favre wrote to Simon : " I don't want the discussion in the Assembly stifled, but it seems to me that it might be shortened ; it is a crime to display our weakness and powerlessness under the eyes of Europe. Keep this in mind : Abrégez ! abrégez ! " [1]

Thiers arrived at Bordeaux in the afternoon and went straight to the Assembly. Several deputies had assembled in one of the committee rooms to hear him. He told the story of his struggle with Bismarck, his eyes full of tears and his voice trembling. One who was present says, " No words can describe the painfulness of the scene ".[2]

He then proceeded to the Assembly ; it had been waiting for a long time in silence. He asked his secretary, Barthélemy-Saint-Hilaire, to read the text of the treaty, and the House listened to the Preliminaries in a deep silence broken now and then by the sobbing of the reader or a low murmur of grief from his auditors. A deputy, who had been a soldier, held out his mutilated hand and said to his neighbour, "I suffered less when these three fingers were cut off ".[3]

When he had finished his reading, Tolain from the Left opposed the demand for " urgence " (that is, immediate discussion) ; he asked for a full debate on this " shameful and unacceptable treaty ". Thiers protested : " No one would propose ' shameful ' terms to you ; the shame is for those, who have contributed to the faults that have brought such a situation about. As for me, I swear before my country and before God that I am innocent of these faults."

---

[1] Simon, *Soir de ma journée*, pp. 177-8.
[2] Dampierre (quoted Hanotaux, i. 132).   [3] Hanotaux, i. 132.

After three other members of the Left had urged that before any further discussion, the report on the state of the nation by the eight committees should first be read, " urgence " was voted. Gambetta then proposed that at least the meeting of the bureau to report on the matter should be put off till next day. Thiers replied by hinting at the dangerous state of Paris. " I cannot read to you all the telegrams, which I receive every moment ; respect my silence." [1]

On March 1st the tragic debate took place. Victor Lefranc reported in favour of acceptance of the terms ; he went perhaps slightly too far when he said : " The Government of the Republic in signing this peace will have the right to be proud of the effect of its action in producing stability ". " And shame ", called out a member of the Left. Thiers called out, " Let the member who speaks of shame get up in his place ".

Edgar Quinet opposed the report of the Commission. " As for me ", he said, " I will never sign ; if the present is terrible, let us at least save the future. We can only do that by rejecting conditions, which destroy at once the present and the future." " And the means ? " interrupted Thiers, " the means ? " [2]

Bamberger, a native of Strasburg, implored the Assembly to reject " the greatest iniquity in history ". Hitherto the debate, though tense, had been calm, but the pent-up feelings of the House needed a safety-valve ; the chance interruption of a Bonapartist deputy supplied it. No one can regard the famous scene that followed as

---

[1] *Annales*, t. 1, pp. 88-96. That evening the deputies for Alsace and Lorraine climbed the steps of the Hôtel de France (Thiers' house) for a last appeal. Thiers met them at the door, saying, " I know what you have come to ask. Go away ; it is impossible. Do not speak of it. Go away, I can do nothing : I shall not answer. Go away ! " " But, M. Thiers," they pleaded, " we are sold, we are abandoned. The laws of God and man forbid you to surrender our population as if they were sheep." Thiers could only repeat, " I tell you to go : I cannot listen to you. Go away " (Malo, *Thiers*, p. 493).

[2] *Annales*, t. 1, pp. 98-101.

particularly creditable to the majority. " I persist in thinking ", says an eyewitness, " that the Assembly did not act an admirable part in raging like an animal set loose against one man." [1] But it was perhaps better, if there was to be violence, that it should break out not between advocates and opponents of the Peace, but from their united ranks overwhelming in their fury the common foe.

Bamberger had said, " One man alone ought to sign this treaty — Napoleon III ". Amid the cheers that followed, a voice was heard — " Napoleon III would never have signed a disgraceful treaty ". " Who said that ? " the Assembly called out. " What is his name ? " The interruptor called out from the Bonapartist benches, " My name is Galloni d' Istria ". Amid growing excitement, Haentjens, who was sitting next to him, added, " It would be better to blame the Prussian sovereign than a sovereign, who is the prisoner of our cruel enemies ". Other members of the small Imperialist group intervened, but it was on Conti, the ex-secretary of Napoleon, that the fury of the Assembly vented itself.

" To the tribune ! " they called out, and, as he responded to the general cry, a scene of the wildest excitement began. The Assembly became a raging mob ; Right and Left forgot their differences ; Langlois " rushed on him like a dog " ; Wilson raged like a madman ; the gentle Jules Simon led the tumult. " Speak ! " he cried to Conti, " speak, then ! Dare to defend the author of our disasters ! Say something that honest men can hear ! "

Assisted by Grévy, imperturbable on his presidential chair, Conti faced the tumult, calm and undismayed. But he could hardly complete a sentence ; he reminded them of the oath they had all sworn to the Empire. " And the Emperor ? " they shouted. " Did he not take an oath to the Republic ? " He pleaded that France herself had

[1] Claveau, p. 32.

founded and ratified the Empire by plebiscite. " Come down from the tribune ! " called the Royalist marquis de Franclieu, " butchers have not the right to insult their victims." At last Paul Bethmont from the Centre said, " There is only one way to end this scene ; to vote the deposition of the Emperor Napoleon and his family ".[1]

After a few minutes suspension of the sitting, Target moved the following resolution : " The National Assembly closes the incident, and in the tragic circumstances, through which the country is going, faced by unexpected protests and opposition, confirms the deposition of Napoleon III and his family, already pronounced by universal suffrage, and declares him responsible for the ruin, invasion and dismemberment of France ".

Gavini, a Bonapartist, denied the right of the Assembly to pronounce upon a question, which had not been before the electors, but was shouted down. Conti was again refused a hearing ; Cochery called out to him, " You are outraging the feelings of the Assembly, and at what a moment ! " Thiers said a few words in favour of the resolution. " You have disregarded the truth," he said, addressing the supporters of the Empire ; " today it rises up before you, and it is a punishment from Heaven to see you here obliged to submit to the judgment of the nation, which will also be the judgment of posterity." The vote of deposition was carried with only five dissentients.

After Bamberger had finished his interrupted speech, Victor Hugo mounted the tribune and the Assembly were all ears to listen to the famous Republican poet and exile. He began, " The Empire has committeed two parricides — the murder of the Republic in 1851, and the murder of France in 1871 ". Then followed one literary antithesis after another : " Paris is resigned to her death, but not to our dishonour " ; " We have a double mission — to raise

[1] *Annales*, t. 1, pp. 102-3 ; Claveau, pp. 32-3.

up France and to warn Europe " ; " In this fatal year of Councils and of carnage . . . we have side by side a Gothic Pope, who seeks to live again, and a Gothic Emperor, who also returns upon the scene ". The Right became restless : " To the question ! " they called out. He went on : " We pity Germany, because she has been a people and is now only an Empire " ; " All that France may lose, if we sign this peace, the Revolution will gain ". The peroration was an astonishing anticlimax. " One day France will be terrible again ; she will regain Lorraine and Alsace . . . she will seize Trèves, Mayence, Cologne and Coblentz. . . ." Interruptions broke out ; a member of the Right said, " We protest against this spirit of conquest ". The speaker said, " You don't understand my meaning. . . . After seizing all the left bank of the Rhine " (*interruptions*), " France will cry, ' I give it all back on one condition, that in the future we shall be one people, one republic." To such a blustering fraternity had events driven the pacifist and internationalist of 1849.[1]

Vacherot, Maire of Paris, defended the Treaty : " It is my profound conviction that in no other way can France be saved " ; as a philosopher and idealist, he sadly registered the fact that " it is not only by means of feelings and principles that practical politics are carried on ".

Louis Blanc made the most effective of the attacks on the Treaty ; he appealed to the example of the armies of the Revolution : " At that moment France was regarded as dead by the whole world . . . our fathers conquered, because they believed France to be unconquerable ".

General Changarnier, in a few manly words, warned the Chamber against " the influence of a melodramatic patriotism ", which would lose them the respect and the sympathy of Europe ; Buffet, as deputy for the Vosges, asked leave to abstain from voting ; Thiers, while accepting his claim,

[1] *Annales*, t. 1, pp. 106-9.

appealed to every other deputy to give a vote for or against :
" let us all have the courage to take the responsibility for
what we are doing ".

Brunet (an eccentric Paris deputy, who wished to move
the capital to Bourges or Clermont-Ferrand) spoke next
amid signs of impatience ; Millère and Arago protested
against ratifying so disgraceful a treaty ; Keller (in an
agonised appeal on behalf of his fellow-countrymen, condemned to become Germans) moved the Assembly to its
depths ; Tirard called out, " Let the 750 representatives of
France put themselves at the head of France and we will
save her ".

It was time for the Chief of the Executive to intervene.
His task was difficult, and he wisely spoke only for a short
time ; he had to avoid saying anything that would either
wound the susceptibilities of a French Assembly or rouse
the resentment of the enemy at Versailles.   He accomplished the task to perfection.   He began by saying that
he did not doubt the power of France — why, the figures of
the indemnity were enough to show how afraid the Germans were of their recovery ; no, what he doubted was
their military organisation, " now shattered to pieces ",
and he hastened to lay the responsibility for that on the
Empire.   Then, turning to the Left and their proposal for
the *levée en masse*, he said : " It is not possible to improvise
armies ; the Revolution itself (so often referred to) did not
improvise them ; it conducted its first war under a most
able man, whom fate had thrown into their hands, the
General Dumouriez, who commanded and made use of the
old armies of the King ; later, the Revolution had to meet
many defeats, before it could create real armies ".   The
Left did not much appreciate Dumouriez and the army of
the King.

The policy of war *à l'outrance* meant the complete
destruction of the country.   If France wished to be " a
serious nation deserving happier destinies ", they must face

the truth. It was not easy for nations to face the truth ;
he had seen that, when he had been arguing with Bismarck,
and here he added one quiet phrase — the only revenge
he allowed himself for the torture of the past week : " I
must say that victory is not always much more wise than
defeat ".

The scrutin took place at the tribune ; Gambetta (who
had taken no part in the debate) stood pale and with his
arms folded watching the bulletins drop into the urn.
Generals Billot, Chanzy, Loysel, and Mazure voted against
the terms ; Generals Deligny and Charrette abstained. The
ratification was carried by 546 votes to 107.[1]

After the result was declared, Grosjean handed in an
act of resignation on behalf of the deputies for Moselle,
Bas-Rhin and Haut-Rhin, swearing an oath of eternal
fidelity to France. That night M. Kuss, one of these
deputies and Maire of Strasbourg, died of a broken heart.[2]

Meanwhile Paris had been passing through anxious
hours. Tuesday was passed in preparation for the Prussian
entry on the morrow. General Vinoy barricaded with railway carriages all the bridges communicating with the left
bank of the Seine and the entrance to the Tuileries, the
furthest point to which the enemy were to penetrate. The
openings of the rue de Rivoli and the Faubourg St-Honoré
were also blocked and the National Guard assembled as a
second line of defence. The triumphal entry of the German
Emperor was fixed for Friday, March 3rd.

Favre had hoped against hope that the Assembly might

---

[1] Clemenceau, who voted against peace, reiterated in the closing conversations of his life his conviction that he had voted rightly. See Martel, *Le
Tigre*, p. 69.

[2] *Annales*, t. 1, pp. 109-25. The following dialogue occurred after the
reading of this manifesto and shows the state of the atmosphere :

DE TRÉVENEUC : Why should not the representatives of Alsace sit among
us ?

ROCHEFORT : You should have kept Alsace ; then you would have kept
their representatives too ; it is you, who have surrendered them.

DE TRÉVENEUC : What ! It is we, who have surrendered them ! We
fought for them while you were organising riots at home !

vote the Treaty straight off on Wednesday night, but at
three o'clock news arrived of the adjournment of the
debate.

The first day of the entry passed off without incident.
The streets were empty, the shops closed and black flags
hung out. Trouble nearly occurred at the Louvre ; the
General had obtained leave for his men to visit it unarmed ;
several officers went into the Museum carrying their arms,
but the German authorities intervened. The night was
comparatively calm ; groups of people stood about talking,
but they only showed their feelings by violent demonstra-
tions against those, who were accused of having shown
politeness to the enemy.

At the Ministry of Foreign Affairs, the evening was
spent in feverish expectation of the news from Bordeaux ;
at eight in the evening a telegram was received announcing
the vote of deposition against the Empire, and at eleven
arrived the welcome news that the ratification had been
carried.

Next morning Favre went to Versailles at seven o'clock,
but found everyone asleep ; nothing could be done till the
protocols arrived from Bordeaux, signed and sealed. They
were expected at nine but it was not till twelve-thirty that
Delaroche (son of the painter) entered with the documents ;
Favre fell on his neck, and by two o'clock was at Versailles
again.

Bismarck did not conceal his disappointment. " You
had till March 13th," he grumbled. " I understood from
you that the debate would be long." Favre replied with an
ironical courtesy, that must have been the first glimpse of
enjoyment he had known that year : " I wished to give you
a pleasant surprise ; your Excellency has neglected no
opportunity of telling me that you were in a hurry to
finish ". The Chancellor soon recovered his good-humour
and told an anecdote against himself ; he had ventured on
horseback as far as the Avenue de Neuilly, where he had

been recognised and insulted by name. " I began to understand that I had few friends at Paris ; I confess I had always suspected it."

So the state of war between France and Germany came to an end, and so the German Emperor did not ride into Paris.[1]

[1] Favre, *Gouv. de la défense nationale,* iii. 150-58.

CHAPTER VII

THE ASSEMBLY MOVES TO VERSAILLES

THE situation at Paris did not improve after the definite conclusion of peace. Jules Favre was in despair; he wrote to Thiers that the city was without a government;[1] that, while the disorders were daily increasing, no fresh troops had arrived; that Departments all over the country were without Préfets, or ruled by impossible ones, because neither Simon at Bordeaux nor Picard at Paris felt able to take the initiative; that the Assembly was lingering at Bordeaux, plotting to restore the monarchy instead of returning at once to the capital; finally, that unless Thiers at once moved the seat of government to Paris, he would resign and all his colleagues with him.[2] Thiers replied (March 5th):

You are cruel indeed, when you talk of immediate resignation on account of difficulties, which are neither my fault nor the fault of my colleagues nor indeed of anybody. The Assembly is composed of

---

[1] General d'Aurelle de Paladines (Commander of the Seine National Guard) was not at all impressed with the competence of the Ministers at Paris. " Often it was 11 P.M. and the members of the Council had not arrived. A word was given to public business and the rest of the time was buffoonery and jokes by Picard " (Deposition before the Committee of Inquiry into the Insurrection of March 18th — quoted Hanotaux, i. 159 n.). Picard protested against the suggestion that he had not taken things seriously. " Every day I sent word of it to the Chief of the Executive : I went to Bordeaux for twenty-four hours to explain the whole matter to him. It was after hearing what I had to say that the Admiral Pothuau and several Maires, who were deputies for Paris, returned with me to try to avert the threatened insurrection. . . . I appeal to all those, members of the Council or not, who knew the agony we went through " (Reclus, *Picard*, p. 282 n.).

[2] Favre, *Gouv. de la défense nationale*, iii. 185.

different parties, as you know — some of them impatient to an
unbearable degree. For the moment it is devoted to me ; I don't
know how long that will last ; it is deeply suspicious not of me but
of the whole situation, and I can't quit it for a moment ;[1] my very
colleagues in the Government need to be kept together because of
their different points of view. . . . I cannot come to Paris without
the Assembly, and it is difficult to get them to move.[2]

As to the condition of Paris, 30,000 troops were on their
way. " It is not my view that an offensive should be
started against the disturbers of the peace ; with a large
military force, a firm attitude and a little patience, it is
very probable that we shall settle the matter without a
battle. If we must fight, we will fight resolutely." He
ended on a more personal note : " My dear friend, don't
be so tiresome. Your vivacity troubles me and adds to my
anxieties. I go to bed at midnight ; I get up at four in the
morning ; I have not a single — no, not a single moment of
repose."[3]

The National Assembly did indeed call for a strong
hand ; it showed itself much too prone to party quarrels,
and constantly needing to be recalled to the national
emergency. Lacombe notes in his diary : " This Chamber
is excellent, but it lacks organisation ; I am afraid it will
wear itself out uselessly " (March 3rd) ; " I am not without anxiety for this Chamber ; it has no control and no
leader ; the Government proceeds by sudden steps which
weary the Chamber, and are only accepted because members are worn out."[4]

The Extreme Left, beaten on the issue of peace and war,
gave themselves up to petty controversies. Some of them
resigned ; Rochefort, Félix Pyat, Tridon and Malon refused
to sit any longer in an Assembly, " which has surrendered
two provinces, dismembered France and ruined the

---

[1] In the intimacy of his family Thiers expressed himself less classically :
" When the cat's away, the mice will play " (Claveau, p. 42).
[2] Bouniols, *Thiers au pouvoir*, pp. 23-4.   [3] *Ibid*. pp. 23, 32.
[4] Lacombe, *Journal*, i. 5, 6.

country "; Gambetta, who had given up his seat as
deputy for the ceded Departments, withdrew to semi-exile
at San Sebastian with the gloomy prophecy that the signature of peace meant a revolution at Paris.[1]

On March 4th, Clemenceau presented a petition from
the Positivist Club at Paris, asking that Corsica should
immediately cease to be part of the French Republic. The
Right did not mind insults being thrown at the Bonapartist
island, but they were furious about the Positivist Club.
Baze (Centre Droit) exclaimed, " The laws of France do
not recognise fantastic societies which take upon them
titles meant to disturb the country by abominable doctrines ".[2]　Audren de Kerdrel, another member of the
Right, had to remind the Assembly that the right of petition was inviolable.　On Monday, March 6th, Louis Blanc
moved for an enquiry into the acts of the National Defence
Government. " Among them are some that constituted a
grave abuse of power and have brought about the disastrous capitulation ". Delescluze openly moved that they
be accused of high treason.[3]

On March 8th, on the subject of Garibaldi's election as
member for Algeria, Victor Hugo infuriated the Right by
saying in his oracular style, " He came ; he fought ; he is
the only general that was not beaten ". De Jouvenel said,
" I ask the President to make the speaker withdraw so unpatriotic a remark ". Lorgeril called out, " Your hero was
like an understudy in a melodrama ; he wasn't beaten,
because he never fought . . . the Assembly refuses to hear
M. Hugo, because he does not speak the language of a
Frenchman ". The deputy for Paris replied : " Three
weeks ago you refused to hear Garibaldi ; now you refuse
to hear me ; I resign " — and, seizing a reporter's pen, he
wrote off a letter of resignation, and left the Assembly
for ever.[4]

[1] Mme Adam, *Mes angoisses et nos luttes*, p. 27.
[2] *Annales*, t. 1, pp. 152-4.　　[3] *Ibid*. pp. 166-7.　　[4] *Ibid*. pp. 209-11.

A fresh scene occurred. Lockroy from the Left reminded the House that Ducrot (the Royalist deputy and general) had said in his famous proclamation during the siege of Paris that he would return from a sortie " dead or victorious ". The Right called out, " Order ! It is an insult ". Finally Colonel Langlois intervened " to preach peace and calm with the gestures of a madman ".[1]

Amid these stormy incidents the Assembly paid little heed to matters of serious import ; it declared that all debts, postponed for seven months during the war, were payable within forty-eight hours — a vote which put the whole commerce of Paris " in a state of bankruptcy ".[2] A proposal to enquire into the rents, which had not been paid since the siege, was rejected, and the Government decree of February 15th restricting the allowance of 1 franc 50 cents a day to those of the National Guard, who could prove want of work, showed little realisation of the serious state of things in the capital.[3]

But the Assembly could not shirk any longer the question of its own relation to Paris ; now that the war was over, Bordeaux was clearly too far away for purposes of government.

The Right shrank instinctively from returning to Paris ; old memories of the Revolution, more recent impressions of the disorders during the siege and of the menacing attitude of the deputies for the capital — all these worked on their minds and they said to themselves : Can one imagine the Monarchy proclaimed at Paris ? On the same side there was what was called the " decentralising group ". Its policy was largely the result of the long

[1] Claveau, pp. 58-9.
[2] Hanotaux, i. 161.
[3] The Commission of Enquiry into the Insurrection of March 18, though very favourable to the Assembly, blame them " for not having prolonged enough the delays granted in the matter of debts by the National Defence Government ". As to the question of rents, it says that many of the working classes " would have liked the Assembly to remove the threat which was hanging over them " (Report, p. 78).

K

opposition of the Right to the centralisation of the
Empire. There had grown up a body of opinion anxious
to restore local life (crushed by the Préfets of the Empire),
and in some cases even seeking the revival of the old
provinces; it dwelt on the variety and richness of the
old provincial life, its charters and guilds and feudal
customs so opposed to the levelling uniformity of Napoleon's
official hierarchy. The influence of this group can be seen
in the important measure on the Conseils Généraux, which
was carried later in the year largely under their inspiration.
At the present moment it felt that the dominance and
prestige of Paris strangled and discouraged the initiative
of the provinces, and prevented France from having its
lesser luminaries, its Florence, its Venice, its Naples.[1]
Might it not be a valuable object-lesson if the Government
chose some other centre than the capital ?

Thiers also traced the action in this matter of a vaguer
group—the survivors of the Ollivier Ministry of January 2nd,
1870 (the so-called Liberal Empire), representatives of the
last constitutional Government in France. They regarded
themselves as free from responsibility for the faults of the
past régime and had rallied to the Right Centre. " They
are profoundly disappointed to find they are no longer
possible as Ministers. Daru [2] is at their head ; Brame [3]
comes next, very active and mischievous ; Buffet,[4] to
whom we offered the opportunity of re-entering office and
who refused, is annoyed and has also joined the rebels.
They have secured some Bonapartist remnants and intrigue
as much as they can ; Daru and Buffet, in sheep's clothing,

---

[1] Cp. André Siegfried's *Tableau des partis en France*, p. 193. " A curious
fact little recognised by foreigners is the political decadence of Paris . . . it
seems to have lost its influence since 1871, when the more serious Republicanism of the provinces, becoming conscious of itself, resented such Parisian acts
of caprice as the Commune and Boulangism ".

[2] Minister of Foreign Affairs in the Ollivier Ministry.

[3] Member of the party which supported the Ollivier Ministry.

[4] Minister of Finance under Ollivier. Thiers, it will be remembered, had
offered him the same post.

have entered the Commission (on the transference of the Assembly) and keep on harassing us, turning to their account the prejudices of Royalist deputies." [1] Some of the older Legitimists proposed Bourges as the seat of Government. In 1829 M. Rubichon had suggested it because " it is the dullest place in France ; there the King can found a new State without being distracted. . . . If the provinces were to send us Catos for deputies, Paris would make Catilines of them." [2] Others suggested Orleans or Fontainebleau. Even a reasonable Conservative like Lacombe preferred the places more distant from Paris. " At Versailles we shall be placed between the discontent of the capital and of the provinces ; if Paris does not send us mobs, it will send us petitions." [3]

Thiers at first favoured Fontainebleau, and on March 5th he wrote to Joly, the architect, suggesting it. Joly answered, " Impossible ". Thiers refused to give way and demanded to see plans. " Nothing ", he said, " would be easier than to turn the gallery of Henri II or the gallery de Diane into a *salle des séances* ; go home and think it over." Next morning, Joly reported that the first gallery was not wide enough, and the second not long enough. " Well," retorted Thiers, " you will build a temporary hall, then." The architect suggested Versailles ; a few hours later Thiers was wavering. " Since you want Versailles so much, go there, and be off at once." [4]

Picard, who had been at Bordeaux for the day,[5]

---

[1] Bouniols, *Thiers au pouvoir*, p. 43. It would be fairer to describe all this not so much as a Bonapartist plot as a mark of the resentment of the Right that they had so few representatives in the Ministry.   [2] Bosq, p. 62.

[3] *Journal*, i. p. 5. Jules Simon writes (*Gouv. de M. Thiers*, i, 93) : " Fontainebleau would have been a piece of folly ; Bourges would have been an act of treason ; Versailles was an expedient ".   [4] Bosq, p. 64.

[5] Jules Favre bitterly repented letting Picard go to Bordeaux for a few hours. " The very night of his departure, we were nearly swept away ; the tocsin sounded all night ; I was the only member of the Government present, and I had no official authority over the Préfet de Police or the Generals. I begged Thiers to let Picard return, which he did " (*Gouv. de la défense nationale*, iii. 185).

travelled with him ; he was a strong opponent of Fontainebleau. " At this rate ", he said, " we shall never get to Paris at all." As the train left the platform, Thiers' secretary bawled after them, " Go to Fontainebleau too ".[1]

On March 5th Thiers wrote to Favre :

The Assembly hates the idea of taking the place of the Prussians at Versailles, and it has heard that the Palace is infected ; [2] also it regards the place as too near Paris ; I think we shall find it easier to have them at Fontainebleau. I have sent Joly to you, and I ask you to send him to Fontainebleau after a rapid inspection of Versailles. . . . As for me, I regard Paris as the ultimate stage.[3]

On March 8th the Commission of the Assembly (by ten votes to four) had decided in favour of Fontainebleau ; [4] meanwhile Thiers had changed his mind. He says [5] that military reasons weighed with him. If Paris should rise, and the Assembly were far away from the capital, troops would have to be sent there to guard them and thus would weaken the army sent to suppress the rising ; whereas Versailles "dominated Paris completely by Mont Valérien".

On March 7th he wrote to Favre : [6]

The Assembly is in a state of extreme excitement ; I am going off to make a decisive effort on behalf of Versailles and I shall succeed. . . . M. Joly must put us in a hall lit by daylight, not by lamps. He must not put us where the Prussian wounded have been. We might use the Orangerie or perhaps the Gallerie de Batailles.

On his visit of inspection, Joly hesitated between the Chapel and the Theatre. Picard favoured the first, as the Salle d'Opera had no windows, but the architect pointed out that the Right would regard it as sacrilege to touch the Chapel, and decided in favour of the Theatre, which he would light by means of a glass roof.[7]

---

[1] Bosq, p. 65.

[2] It will be remembered that the Palace at Versailles had been used by the Prussians as a hospital.

[3] Bouniols, *Thiers au pouvoir*, p. 24.

[4] Lacombe, *Journal*, i. 6.   [5] *Notes et souvenirs*, p. 121.

[6] Bouniols, p. 40.   [7] Bosq, p. 65.

On March 10th, at an afternoon sitting, the Assembly debated the subject. The Government proposal only spoke of transferring the Assembly " to a place nearer Paris " ; the Commission definitely proposed Fontaine-bleau.

Louis Blanc opened the discussion with a fine defence of Paris as the only possible seat of government. " Is it possible ", he asked the Right, " that Paris frightens you? " " Yes ", answered a deputy, but his voice was soon drowned in cries of " No " from the rest of his party. To those who were afraid of Paris, the speaker replied by reading a quotation from Machiavelli : " When it is necessary to govern a city, where the temper of the people is alarming, one of the best and surest methods is to go and live there ". The spectacle of the virgin-minded idealist, the champion of pure republican principles, the enemy of " opportunism ", quoting from *The Prince*, was not without its savour.

The Government were believed to be in favour of Paris ; were they not proposing Versailles as a concession to a party in the Assembly, and did not that party really wish to transfer the capital away from Paris for good and all ? (A member of the Right answered " Yes ".) " I implore you, fellow-citizens, do not lay your hands upon the unity of the nation—(' Oh, oh ')—do not place under a cloud of suspicion that city which the Count de Chambord himself called recently ' his good town of Paris, the city of his ancestors '." The consequences of such an error were terrible to contemplate ; perhaps it would mean " that from the ashes of a fearful war, which is only just finished, there may arise a civil war more fearful still ".

Alfred Giraud replied for the Right ; he said, " We have many of us a mandate from our constituents — not an imperative mandate (we would not have accepted that) but an imperious mandate—(laughter. DUCUING : An ' Imperial ' mandate !)—to see that the Assembly does not deliberate under the threat of the Prussians or of revolution in the streets." The suspicions of France were directed not against Paris but against that turbulent minority "which lays down the law to Paris and therefore to France". The national representatives ought to be somewhere far enough to be safe from riots in the streets. " Quimper-Corentin ! " the Left called out jeeringly ; " Carpentras ! Sedan ! " At Versailles (he concluded) the danger would be the same as at Paris ; on the whole, they had better stay at Bordeaux for the present. Silva, a deputy for Haute-Savoie, speaking modestly as one who had only recently become a French citizen, made a distinct impression by his speech in favour of Paris. The Marquis de Belcastel, speaking from the Extreme Right, exclaimed : " The life of a great people is not chained to the stones of one select city ; it need not drink the waters of one sacred stream. Far from us be such idolatry ! " Millière accused the Right of Federalism (very much as his ancestors of the Mountain had accused the Gironde), and de Fresneau, a Legitimist, protested against the accusation that his party wished " to take the crown away from Paris ".

At this point Thiers rose and made one of his greatest and cleverest orations ; Claveau calls it " his Austerlitz ".[1] He was in a delicate position ; the Left wanted to go to Paris ; the Right, on the whole, to Fontainebleau ; he had to recommend Versailles as a middle course, concealing the real (*i.e.* the military) reasons, from the natural fear of alarming the Assembly and of provoking Paris.

It is necessary to listen to him for a moment as he speaks (if one is to catch anything of the parliamentary atmosphere of the time), to hear his flute-like voice, to watch his eyes gleaming behind his spectacles as he keeps them fixed upon the Assembly, sensitive to the slightest movement among his auditors, now venturing forward, now retreating a moment, caressing, soothing, explaining, throwing in here a word to please the Right, there a phrase

[1] *Souv. pol.* p. 53.

for the Left, never saying what he means till he has tentatively tested its effect, in appearance the most conciliatory of flatterers, in effect guiding the Assembly just where he wishes it to go.

He began (very wisely) far from any irritating controversy, with a bare statement of practical necessities ; he gave a frank and intimate account of his stewardship, in that deferential and conversational form that Assemblies love. The Government and the Assembly had acted with all possible speed so as not to waste the time of the country (" Time is today one of the greatest of our resources ") ; he had formed a Ministry in two days ; three days later he had met Bismarck ; peace had been made in five days — a peace lamentable indeed but which had at least saved Paris from Prussian occupation. Now the task was to reorganise the country, to work out the details of the German evacuation, to secure the services of the Bank of France, to maintain order in Paris (" There are men who would not shrink . . . from starting a civil war. They are few, I know ; I do not wish to confuse them with the honourable and sincere men for whom the Republic is the ideal Government "), to recreate the Administration, the magistrature, the Army, and finally " to concern ourselves with Europe, still agitated by the great and terrible scene it has witnessed ". Such was their task ; " we are devoting all our strength to it — sometimes more than our strength, and we are weary to death ".

All this great task could not be done " by means of a correspondence between two parts of the Government, one at Paris and one at Bordeaux. The Minister for Foreign Affairs had to be at Paris — half an hour's journey from the German Chancellor ; the Minister of Finance had to be at Paris, in touch with the Bank ; the Minister of the Interior had to be in Paris, to deal with the perils which menaced the public order. The entry of the Prussians into the capital had provoked great emotion, as was shown by the action of the National Guard in removing their cannon to Montmartre. Here there were signs of restlessness from the Right. Thiers hastened to add that the people of Paris had no culpable intentions ; they only wished to remove the batteries from the supposed danger of the Prussians being tempted to seize them. " If public order is seriously troubled, count upon our devotion in restoring it with the utmost energy." (*Great applause.*)

The Government, then, must be at Paris, but could they leave the Assembly behind them ? " One of my principal duties is not to quit you for an instant . . . to receive the inspiration of your wishes, not to impose our inspirations on you ; we have never made any such claim."

The Assembly then must move nearer Paris. Here he paused to pay a tribute to her heroic resistance during the siege. " It is not true that Paris has always been the author of civil war in France ; it is more true to say that it has been the theatre rather than the author." Then, while the Paris deputies were applauding this reassuring formula, the orator gently slid to the other side. " Paris has committed faults ; one must speak the truth to the great ones of the earth, peoples, nations, and kings. . . . Paris has committed faults and it has paid for them dearly, gentlemen, by losing your confidence." (*Sensation.*)

Paris was not yet calm enough for the Assembly ; " that is why we propose Versailles and insist on our proposal ". This conclusion was received (the official report tells us) with " numerous marks of assent " ; and here the Chief of the Executive might have sat down, but he had not yet begun what was in his eyes the more important half of his speech. Behind the practical question of danger or safety, convenience or inconvenience, he discerned a far deeper clash of political sentiments, Royalist and Republican ; he wished before he sat down to warn the Assembly against such rivalries, which would, he believed, ruin the country, and would certainly make his own position impossible.

To return to Paris would be to settle a question (he went on) which he did not wish settled. " I have been asked why. I will tell you, for the whole policy of the Government is involved in the answer. The Assembly is sovereign ; never has any Government had such a sovereignty (*Movement on the Left*) ; never has a country been so freely consulted ; never has a country answered more sincerely than at the last elections. And yet spontaneously, by an act of wisdom that is to your honour . . . you have said to yourselves, ' We will not exercise our constituent powers '."

This time it was the Right, who gave signs of alarm. What ! they were not a constituent Assembly, not free to restore the Monarchy, if and when they wished ! Thiers at once turned back to make his point again. " Let me complete my thought. You have not renounced your power ; you would not have the right to do so. . . . I only say that you are reserving it. . . . At present you have resolved that, instead of drawing up a Constitution, you will limit yourselves to the more urgent task of reorganising the country." The Right were still restless ; Thiers begged for a moment's patience. " In order to perform the pressing duties of the moment, it is necessary not to do the slightest thing that may disunite you."

This time he had found the right formula, and there was loud and general applause.

There were two great parties (he continued), Monarchist and Republican. Each was subdivided ; the Royalists were not agreed among themselves ; the Republicans also differed. " Some believe in the Republic, even when it is not in their hands ; others only admit that a form of government is republican, when it is in their hands." (*Laughter.*)

As for himself, his duty was to be loyal to all the parties which divided France and the Assembly. " I swear before my country, and (if I thought myself important enough to appeal to history) I would add that I swear before history, not to deceive any one of you, not to prepare any solution of constitutional questions behind your backs, which would be on my part a kind of treachery." [1]

Thiers then turned back to the Republicans; he reminded them that the title " Republic " had been accepted by many as a basis of unity. " The reorganisation, if it succeeds, will be done under the form of a Republic and to its profit." This laid a great responsibility on them; the Republic was in their hands; it would be the reward of their wisdom. Every time they appeared, however unconsciously, as the accomplices of disorder, they would be aiming at the Republic the greatest blow it could receive.

The orator descended from the tribune amid a tumult of applause and congratulations. " The Moderate Left ", he says, " were enchanted and expressed to me their great satisfaction. We have a majority of our own on which we can count." [2] On a division, Paris received 154 votes against 427, and Versailles 461 votes against 104. [3] It is impossible not to admire Thiers' eloquence and skill, but in the light of after events it may be doubted if on the main question he was right. It is true, that, when the time came for the move, the Commune had already broken out, and that therefore the Assembly would have had to go to Versailles in any case, but it is difficult to deny that the vote on March 10th was the last straw which irritated the Paris mob beyond endurance. Even moderate citizens felt vaguely (and the Extremists said openly) that the decision of the Assembly was a conspiracy to decapitalise Paris and restore the monarchy in a palace so full of the memories of the Kings of France. The danger at Paris might well

---

[1] This famous passage (afterwards the object of such controversy) is known to history (responsive to Thiers' modest appeal, as he perhaps suspected) by the name of the " Pact of Bordeaux ".

[2] Bouniols, *Thiers au pouvoir*, p. 44 ; in the same letter (to Jules Favre) he refers to his speech as an " improvisation, for I had not time to prepare it ".

[3] For the whole debate see *Annales*, t. 1, pp. 270-92.

have been too great for the Assembly to have stayed there, but it would have been far better if the abandonment of Paris had been forced on them by the facts and not proclaimed beforehand as a wounding suspicion. After their President had expressed their gratitude to the city of Bordeaux for its hospitality, the National Assembly fixed March 20th for their meeting at Versailles; when they gathered again, they found Paris in revolution and the Government in flight.

CHAPTER VIII

THE COMMUNE

THIS book is not a history of France; it is the political study of an Assembly. This chapter, therefore, and the two following will not contain any full analysis of the Commune — a subject which would of itself deserve a separate treatise. Rather they describe the Commune as seen by the Government and the Parliament.

It has always been felt that the Commune is somewhat of an enigma. The report of the Parliamentary Commission, which enquired into it, is full of tragic astonishment that, after the horrors of a foreign war, there should succeed — and that in a city which was supposed to be the capital of the civilised world — the horrors of " a social war such as terrified the ancient world ". The deputies, who signed the report, seem to be constantly asking themselves " Can this be Paris ? " Latinists, they look back to Rome for a parallel and quote from Sallust's *Catiline*; Christians, they seek an answer in the godlessness of the modern Babylon ; Royalists, they bitterly accuse the Empire of having corrupted its population.[1] This bewilderment, partly due to the long separation between Paris and the rest of France during the Siege, explains much by its very despair of explanation ; the capital had got out of touch with the provinces for the first time in French history.

The modern historian is puzzled, because he is not sure whether to regard the Commune as a riot on a large scale,

---

[1] Enquête sur 18 mars, pp. 1, 108. (*Annales de l'assemblée nationale*, t. 9): the Depositions are from the same volume.

or a revolution on a small one. Is it just the climax of an abnormal strain, physical and moral, caused by the Siege, the Armistice and the entry of the Prussians — an aftermath of war, to be diagnosed as *fièvre obsidionale* ? Or is it, an attempt at a real revolution with a programme of international socialism, inspired by the political ideal of local autonomy (France as a federation of communes) and the social ideal of the dictatorship of the proletariat — a kind of dress-rehearsal of the Soviet régime ? [1]

The difficulty is probably inherent in the nature of Paris ; since 1789 she had been the undisputed ruler of France ; [2] every street disturbance aimed at being a political movement. As a bitter Royalist said, she had sent out revolutions by telegraph ; in 1871, she was suffering from a sense of inferiority, driven to surrender (as it seemed) by the folly of the incompetents who directed her destinies, forced to submit to a humiliating peace and the ignominy of the enemy's troops in her midst, while an assembly of bourgeois, who deliberately refused to venture inside her walls, were trying to impose reactionary ideas on the country.

So she tried to assert her leadership in the approved manner — a rising after the model of 1830 and 1848, but this time it did not come off. The provinces, even those most hostile to Royalism, made no response to the old gestures ; their idea of democracy was no longer that of the Convention and the Terror.

Cut off from the provinces, Paris was forced to concentrate her protest within her four walls ; she had to

---

[1] The Russian Revolution and the Commune were both made possible by war and after-war conditions, but whereas Bolshevism broke out in a country weary of war, the Commune was the work of a population humiliated by the Peace.

[2] The Report of the Commission is eloquent evidence of the provincial resentment on this point — cf. p. 76 : " Paris has become the rendezvous of all who are seeking to make their fortunes, a kind of California at home. . . . In France we emigrate to Paris. We have not got those wide currents, that in neighbouring countries lead energetic pioneers far over the seas every year."

content herself with the cry " Hands off Paris ", and the programme of the leaders (that of a revolution bottled up into a local riot) had to restrict itself to a demand for municipal autonomy. Not able to speak for France, the capital repudiated France.

As early as March 3rd, the Central Committee of the National Guard considered a resolution that " in the case of the Assembly transferring the capital from Paris, the Department of the Seine should constitute itself an independent republic ".[1]

But, it might be objected, surely it is not fair to speak of the " programme " of Paris or the " policy " of Paris ; surely the movement was the act of a turbulent minority, tyrannising over the real city ; surely it had no programme, only a passion for destruction, and no leaders but an ever-changing group of ferocious nonentities. It is just at this point that the remarkable and abnormal condition of the capital (quite unlike anything in 1830 or 1848) made itself felt.

The Commune had a social side (complicated by the special siege conditions), and a political side — republicanism (complicated by the demand for local autonomy due to the quarrel with the Assembly), all influenced to a certain extent by elements of " International Socialism " ; it is in this tangle of deliberate intention and temporary disorganisation that the special character of the Commune is to be sought.

The Commission of the National Assembly in the second part of their report, entitled " Recherche des causes ", devotes several sections to the gradual demoralisation of Paris under Napoleon III. Some of their remarks are a critique of industrialism (the country-gentleman's suspicion of a big city) ; thus, it places as the first direct cause " the accumulation of masses of men in our large towns ", the existence of a class of workmen without home or family, the incessant work, all the year round, of those brought in to

[1] Simon, *Gouv. de M. Thiers*, i. 175.

carry through the vast reconstruction of the capital (there was no pause in the winter when they should have returned to their homes; " have we not seen building going on by electric light ? ") and the separation of rich and poor (" The working classes, driven out to the suburbs have lived far from any contact with the rich dwellers in the centre "). All this is put down to the account of the Second Empire. " It thought it would be able to bribe the labouring classes and dazzle Europe. . . . It refused to see the abyss which yawned beneath its feet." [1] In particular, it drew attention to the " licence allowed to the clubs and the Press during the closing years of the régime " — a policy which the Republican enemies of Napoleon (equally angry whether the unfortunate Emperor gave or withheld liberties) accounted for by his desire to give the country (on the drunk Helot principle) a specimen of what public life would be like without the firm hand of the Government.

Much of this is clearly due to the political prejudices of the Commission; great cities have managed to exist in peace, where classes lived apart, even where work was done by electric light, and where clubs and newspapers have been given a free hand. We can retain two facts as of importance; first, that by 1871 Paris had become a modern town; and secondly, that before the fall of the Empire, a spirit of revolt and opposition was abroad. To come to more recent events, it is necessary to recreate in our imaginations the long strain of the siege, the bombardment, the hunger, the suspension of business, which the Assembly had tried to close prematurely by reviving the normal régime of debts — above all, the anticlimax with which it ended. One cannot key up a whole population (especially if it be French), to a state of heroism, and then ask them to go back to the ordinary round of life as though nothing had happened. The inhabitants of Paris were

---

[1] Enquête sur 18 mars, pp. 75-6.

perfectly prepared to die in the last ditch ; what they were
not prepared for was to hear that an Armistice had been
signed, Alsace and Lorraine surrendered, and that the
Prussians were about to enter,[1] without any consciousness
of having been beaten in fair fight and without any realisation ("strung up" as they were "to a state of exaltation
by false rumours and impossible hopes kept up to the last
moment " [2]) that the state of supplies made a capitulation
inevitable.

Another dangerous symptom was the rotten state of
the National Guard. After September 4th arms had been
distributed indiscriminately, and after the Armistice no
attempt had been made to disarm them — a fault for which
Jules Favre was soon, at the tribune, to " ask pardon from
God and man ". The members of the Guard had been
" used to living without doing anything, fed and clothed
at the expense of the State . . . when food became dear,
they consumed more alcohol than bread . . . the committees of Vigilance, Superintendence, Armament and
Clothing, created in each *arrondissement*, led to the
General Federation of the National Guards and set up a
power which became a rival to the regular Government ".[3]

Moderate citizens began to leave the capital.[4] At the
same time there was an influx of troops in the process of
being demobilised ; they poured in from every railway
station and the town was full of men in uniform, who had
lost their way and strayed into the middle of a revolution.[5]

---

[1] " The entry of the Prussians was one of the principal causes of the insurrection. I do not say that, without it, the rising would not have taken place ;
I do say that the entry had an extraordinary effect in provoking it " (Thiers
before the Commission, p. 360).

[2] Enquête, p. 77.   [3] *Ibid.*

[4] Antoine Claveau says that, early in March, there was an emigration of
inhabitants from the capital to Bordeaux, who said " Paris does not feel good "
(" Ça ne sent pas bon à Paris ") (*Souvenirs*, p. 62).

[5] " We saw Garibaldians arriving in Paris in red shirts with peacocks'
plumes on the back of their heads. It was certainly like a masquerade, but it
meant that the army of the revolt was being formed " (Déposition de Choppin,
p. 455).

Lastly, on the military side, the Commune was left in possession of superb fortifications and a large accumulation of material from the Siege.[1]

To all this must be added the breakdown of central government; the committees of vigilance, largely recruited from "Internationalist" clubs, the dictatorial powers assumed by the Maires, the meetings of Maires and adjoints during the Siege to discuss problems of defence on their own — all helped to undermine the authority of the Hôtel-de-Ville. Paris neither respected nor feared its Government; it regarded the Ministers in the capital as traitors, and the Ministers at Bordeaux as strangers. When on March 18th the drums sounded to assemble the National Guard, Jules Simon called on several friends, who were officers, and found them at home in their civilian clothes. "Don't you hear the drum?" he asked. "I am not deaf." "And you refuse to come out?" "To fight? and for whom? Oh, I know, you are honest people; you are devoting yourselves to founding the Republic, but you are deceived and that twice over — by the Assembly who appointed you, and are only waiting for the moment to drop the mask and turn you out, and again, because you do not understand that the people of Paris, seeing you in the service of the Right, regard you as traitors."[2]

The Commune was not a revolution provoked by a great idea or directed by a dominating personality; rather it was a state of unrest and discontent, which attracted to itself all the floating plans of revolt and all the wandering agents of disorder. They came like vultures scenting the prey; Blanquists with their old traditions of anarchy; Jacobins, the Extreme Left of the party which had proclaimed the Government in September, and since, the bitterest detractors of it, twice suppressed by force during the

---

[1] "They (the Commune) had at their disposal immense resources such as no rebellion has ever possessed — 400,000 rifles, 3000 guns and the great fortifications of Paris" (Déposition de Thiers, p. 369).

[2] Simon, *Soir de ma journée*, pp. 182-3.

L

Siege — such men as Delescluze, Félix Pyat, Tridon, Malon, who during their short stay at Bordeaux had covered the order-paper with demands for the impeachment of the Government of National Defence ; Socialists (whether of the old French variety, dating from Saint-Simon, or the newer German collectivist type) ; members of the " Internationale ", which in 1870 claimed to have 70,000 to 80,000 members in Paris and took a large part in organising the Central Committee of the Guard.

But all these competing persons and policies (though they swelled the numbers) were really a weakness. The leadership was always changing hands, passing from the moderates to the extremists ; these varied ideas formed a vague programme, only given coherence by that effective slogan — the " Commune ". The name strictly described a form of political organisation in which the unit was a local, autonomous group ; these were to be federated into a nation and, by a curious irony of history, it was now the Mountain, not the Gironde, who proclaimed the federal principle. The theory was Syndicalist in its hatred of the State ; it would have agreed with Sorel in calling the State " a bourgeois prejudice ". Side by side with this political ideal, the name called up memories of the fierce proletarian rule of the Terror and perhaps (more distantly) ideas of property held " in common ". As Hanotaux says, " Their object was to make a Switzerland of France but a socialised Switzerland ".[1]

On his arrival at Paris, after the adjournment of the Bordeaux Assembly, Thiers found the situation becoming every moment more critical. On March 10th a Council of War had condemned Flourens, Blanqui, and Levrard to death (in their absence), and Vallès to six months' imprisonment for complicity in the rising of October 31st last year. On the same day the Council of Ministers suppressed six newspapers " for preaching assassination ". This

[1] Hanotaux, i. 169.

attack on the liberty of the Press (as it was represented by the Central Committee of the National Guard) exasperated the mob. The Prefect of the Police reported : " This decree is causing serious agitation. Even in the peaceable parts of the town many groups are discussing it in the streets ; a proclamation in red is being posted up, addressed to the Army and advocating disobedience and insurrection. The soldiers are reading it eagerly ; the affair may become serious." [1]

At the same meeting of the Council (March 10th) it was resolved " to settle, once and for all, the affair of the batteries at Montmartre and Belleville ".[2] The National Guard had taken charge of them to spare the Prussians the temptation of laying hands on them, and three or four attempts had been made by the Government to obtain their restoration by parleying. Once, success seemed so near that horses and wagons were sent to the Place Royale, but next morning the violent party prevailed and they were sent home again. The general opinion of all the supporters of the Government was that the guns must be got back at all costs, or else their prestige would suffer seriously. The business world were specially loud in their complaints ; they said to Thiers : " You will never succeed in any financial operations, if you do not put these scoundrels in their place and get back the cannon ".[3]

On the evening of March 17th another meeting of the Council was held to consider the matter. General Vinoy and Aurelle des Paladines were present ; it was proposed to remove the cannon from Montmartre that very evening ; it was urged that the Central Committee had been, more than once, on the point of consenting to their surrender ; were they likely to resist when force was used ? If they did resist, the National Guard could be called out. General Aurelle objected. " When we do call it out, we only get

---

[1] Simon, *Gouv. de M. Thiers*, i. 219-22.   [2] Favre, iii. 208.
[3] Thiers (Déposition, p. 362).

the worst battalions, who refuse to obey." It was answered that it was because they did not yet believe in the reality of the danger; at the first shot fired, they would respond.

General Vinoy objected that the Government troops in Paris only amounted to 25,000 or 30,000 men of very doubtful quality; was it prudent to oppose them to the 300,000 of the National Guard, indifferent or hostile? Would it not be better to wait till they had been able to form new regiments out of the returning prisoners? To this Thiers replied that the prisoners from Germany were an unknown quantity; they might be physically and morally unfit; if they were beaten by the rebels or fraternised with them, the very existence of the Army would be imperilled. Again, immediate action was necessary, for the Assembly was meeting on the 20th and they would insist on severe measures against disorder. Vinoy shrugged his shoulders. "Well it is possible we may succeed; issue your orders and I will obey. I am a soldier." The resolution to act at once was carried. Thiers says: "I felt that we were taking a great risk; but, after all, it was impossible to do nothing." [1]

It was obvious that, if anything was to be done, it would have to be done in the early morning, before Paris was yet awake. The troops left their barracks at 3 A.M., and by five o'clock General Susbielle (assisted by Generals Paturel and Lecomte) had seized Montmartre, while General Faron had occupied Chaumont.

Jules Ferry, the Maire of Paris, was at the Hôtel-de-Ville; the Government assembled at the Ministry of Foreign Affairs. The news of the successful operation was received with joy, and congratulations were exchanged.

As the morning drew on, alarming rumours began to circulate. At 10.30 the Prefect of the Police wired: "Very bad news from Montmartre; troops refuse to act;

[1] Thiers, Déposition, p. 362; and Simon, *Gouv. de M. Thiers*, i. 227-30.

the heights, guns and prisoners retaken by the insurgents ".[1]

The troops had soon found the occupation of the positions to be the least part of their task. There were not enough horses (the cavalry had been decimated during the Siege) ; such wagons as there were could not be taken up the steep slopes and tortuous roads of Montmartre. There were 170 cannon and the work of transport demanded a long time ; [2] time was just what the Government could not afford. The troops began by doing their best ; 70 pieces were carried down by hand. Meanwhile the quarter was aroused ; the tocsin was rung ; Bergeret arrived with the 128th Battalion of the National Guard. A crowd including women and children pushed their way among the soldiers, who were guarding the cannon not yet removed, crying, " Long live the Army ! You are our brothers. We do not wish to fight you." The troops offered no resistance, let themselves be disarmed (even sold their rifles for a few pence) and scattered. At nine o'clock General Lecomte was arrested and dragged off by the crowd. General Clement Thomas (who had resigned the command of the Guard on March 3rd) was recognised walking in the streets in uniform, and was hurried before a revolutionary court-martial on the charge of having fired on the people in the June days of 1848. Both Generals, after every kind of insult and outrage, were shot that same afternoon in the garden of a little house, rue des Rosiers.[3]

Meanwhile the Government had been pressed back to

---

[1] Hanotaux, i. 182-3.

[2] Thiers (Déposition, p. 363) says : " I could, if I liked, accuse this man or that ; I shall not do it ; I shall not specify what was the fault committed ". Jules Simon declares that no one was to blame and that the difficulties were inherent in the case. One cannot help feeling that, if the difficulties could not have been avoided, they might at least have been foreseen. It looks as though Thiers rushed into action somewhat precipitately, from fear lest the Royalists of the Assembly, now on the point of meeting at Versailles, should accuse him of doing nothing. This is certainly one of the cases where attempt is only justified by success.

[3] Hanotaux, i. 182, 186.

their second line of defence. At seven o'clock the National
Guard were called out; drummers accompanied by soldiers
paraded the streets. Everywhere the appeal failed; only
5000 or 6000 men responded. At eleven o'clock the
Minister of the Interior and the Commandant of the
National Guard issued an urgent proclamation, which was
equally ineffective. It was clear that, so far from being
able to attack the insurgents, the Government were themselves in imminent danger of attack. The insurgents,
victorious at Belleville and Montmartre, were spreading
over the rest of the city; the streets were full of revolted
Guards, arm in arm with mutinous soldiers of the Regular
Army, shouting threats of sedition and disarming passers-by.

Thiers, too restless to stay where he was, left the Quai
d'Orsay and ventured as far as the bridge de la Concorde;
he had scarcely returned when there was a noise of trumpets
and drums outside the Ministry of Foreign Affairs; everyone rushed to the windows. Five battalions of insurgents
had crossed the bridge and marched round the building
with hostile cries; fortunately they did not realise that
they had the entire Council at their mercy, for the 250
soldiers on guard were quite incapable of serious defence.[1]

It was now two o'clock in the afternoon, and Thiers
proposed that they should retire to Versailles, together with
the troops under General Vinoy's command. He reminded
them of the position, in which the Government had been
in 1848 : " On the 24th of February the King, Louis-
Philippe, asked me what was to be done ; — I told him that
it was necessary to abandon Paris, and then to return with
the Marshal Bugeaud and 50,000 men to recapture it. If
he had taken my advice, he would have saved his dynasty.
Again, Marshal Windischgraez put down the revolution at
Vienna in the same year by leaving the town, and then re-
capturing it." [2]

[1] Bosq, p. 68.
[2] Thiers, Déposition, iii. 363, and Jules Favre, iii. 216.

Jules Simon, Jules Favre, and Ernest Picard were opposed to this plan. To surrender the capital with its monuments, its munitions, and its great resources to the *émeute* seemed to them an act of despair ; it would be better to concentrate on some strategic point, which could be defended (such as the Hôtel-de-Ville), and from thence to call up the National Guard, which could not long remain inert.

Thiers replied that it was taking too great a risk to expose the Regular Army to the dangers of contact with the insurgents. Above all, the Assembly must be defended. " It is I who persuaded them to come to Versailles. . . . I should never forgive myself, if I have led them into a trap. . . . I am heart-broken but resolute. . . . The Assembly is our last hope. . . . It will be at Versailles the day after tomorrow ; it is to Versailles we must go." [1]

As the discussion became prolonged, he took upon himself to settle the matter on his own responsibility. " Our duty is to retire ", and, in reply to murmurs, " We must think of France, not ourselves." [2] At half-past three he got into his carriage and, accompanied by three Ministers, left Paris by the Point de Jour Gate, which was guarded by cavalry. The Minister for War, Jules Simon, Jules Favre, and Ernest Picard, still unpersuaded, would only promise to meet him at Versailles " if the situation did not change ".[3]

Jules Ferry, indomitable as ever, though his authority as Maire of Paris extended no further than the Hôtel-de-Ville, was not disposed to surrender it without a struggle. He had with him the 110th regiment under the orders of General Deroja, and had laid in siege provisions for ten days ; the Lobau barracks, which commanded the gardens, were occupied by 89 soldiers with 4000 cartridges. At 2.30 P.M. an officer of the gendarmerie arrived, saying, " I

---

[1] Favre, iii. 216.   [2] Simon, *Gouv. de M. Thiers*, i. 242.
[3] Favre, *Gouv. de la défense nationale*, iii. 217.

have orders to evacuate the barracks ; I can't understand why ". Ferry wired to the Prefecture of Police, " I am opposed to the execution of the order ; you clearly have not weighed the consequences ". At 4.30 General Vinoy replied, " I have given no orders for the evacuation ; I am rather disposed to increase the garrisons ". Jules Favre and Picard were both still opposed to evacuation, and it seems to have been the Minister for War, Le Flô, who insisted upon the complete execution of Thiers' plan of withdrawal. About seven o'clock the Hôtel-de-Ville received definite orders to retire. Ferry made a last appeal to Picard, who replied, " Suspend the evacuation ; I am going to discuss the matter with the General ". At ten o'clock General Vinoy confirmed his previous order and the building was abandoned. Jules Ferry was the last to leave, carrying his papers ; the insurgents were already firing from the barricades.[1]

Meanwhile the Maires and deputies of Paris were attempting the work of mediation. At a meeting, held at the Mairie of the second *arrondissement*, it was resolved that Dorian ought to be appointed Maire of Paris, Edmond Adam Préfet de Police, Colonel Langlois Commandant of the National Guard, and General Billot Commandant of Paris. A Commission was appointed to wait on the Government, consisting of Tirard, Vautrain, Vacherot, Bonvalet, Méline, Tolain, Hérisson, Millière and Peyrat. At eight o'clock they saw Favre, who asked them if it was true that the two Generals had been shot. " Alas," they answered, " it is only too certain." " That is enough for me," answered the Minister. " I can do nothing till the cowardly assassination has been punished." " But," they objected, " that means civil war." " What, then, do you call what is happening now ? " he replied. " Is it not the most hateful of civil wars ? "[2] The deputation was received more calmly by Picard, who promised that the

---

[1] Favre, iii. 217-20.   [2] *Ibid.* pp. 225-6.

Government would consider their proposals. The Minister for the Interior had himself only just escaped capture. While he had been at his Ministry (Place Beauvau) a man had rushed in showing every sign of extreme terror. " They have murdered the Generals and they are coming to kill you ! " Picard immediately inspected his defences, which consisted of twenty-five men. The officer in command said, "We shall resist, but there are not many of us ". At the same moment a battalion of National Guards arrived. Picard sent for the officer at their head, took his name and address, and in a severe tone added, " Tell your friends that we shall not allow you to enter ". The bluff succeeded, and the battalion marched on.[1]

The Maire and deputies, after interviewing the Government, returned to their place of meeting, when a messenger arrived in hot haste to say that the Hôtel-de-Ville was evacuated ; he was followed by Ferry himself. A deputation was sent to occupy the building, but they found the Central Committee already in possession. A few minutes later the house where they were meeting was itself surrounded by the Committee's troops ; they were allowed to disperse unharmed (after their names had been taken) and retired to another Mairie. Ferry himself, by an extraordinary piece of good fortune, was able to escape unnoticed by a side door.[2]

At ten in the evening, the Ministers met at the Interior, but, the situation becoming more dangerous every moment, they agreed to assemble in dead secrecy at the house of Calmon, the Under-Secretary for the Interior. Simon and Pothuau arrived rather late and, as they were ringing the bell, a man in a blouse " seemed to start up from the ground ", and said, " Do not go up ; the house will be surrounded in a few moments ! "

---

[1] Déposition (p. 401). There is something humorous about the effect on the officer of having his name taken. "He seemed much frightened", said Picard with a smile.   [2] Simon, *Gouv. de M. Thiers*, i. 243-5.

At the meeting it was resolved to propose Dorian as
Maire of Paris, and submit to the Assembly, as soon as it
met, a Bill for municipal elections. Langlois was sent for
and accepted the post of Commandant of the National
Guard ; he went to the Hôtel-de-Ville, where the Central
Committee asked him, " By whom have you been appointed ? "   " By the Government ; by M. Thiers."   " We
do not recognise his authority ; the Guard will elect its
own chief." Langlois at once sent in his resignation.[1]

It was now near midnight. Simon, Dufaure and
Pothuau repaired to the Military School, which was
General Vinoy's headquarters. It was a bitter March
night and the soldiers, gathered round their roaring fires,
seemed restless and gloomy. They drew closer together as
the Ministers approached, as though to avoid contact ;
some of them murmured that they " ought to be taken to
Montmartre as hostages ".

At last the formal order arrived for the withdrawal to
Versailles. Simon and Pothuau got into the same carriage ;
Picard and Favre were to spend the night in Paris. The
journey to Versailles lasted till four in the morning ; the
snow lay thick on the ground ; the sky was grey with
clouds. It seemed " like a retreat from Moscow " : the
soldiers marched slowly in a sulky disorder ; the officers
had to appear deaf to the oaths and complaints of their
men. Again and again they had to stop, while General
Vinoy galloped back to drive on the laggards who turned
back or sat down by the roadside. He had to beat them
with the flat of his sword : on every side murmurs were
heard, " He will get himself killed ". Inside the carriage
the Ministers were silent from fatigue and depression ;
only from time to time Admiral Pothuau said, " It was a
good thing we left Paris ; otherwise we should have had
no Army at all ! " [2]

---

[1] Simon, *Gouv. de M. Thiers*, i. 246-8.
[2] Simon, *Soir de ma journée*, pp. 185, 384.

The weather probably saved the party from attack, and they reached Versailles in safety. Simon went straight to the Prefecture, where he found Thiers up and shaving himself. The Chief of the Executive ran up to him, and almost kissed him ; he was radiant with joy. " Good ; now we can get on " ; then (changing his voice) : " It will be a long business ". " Very long ", said Simon, who did not share the morning cheerfulness of the President. " You do not wish to bombard Paris or starve it or take it by assault ; how then are you going to capture it ? " Thiers professed to laugh at his gloom. " You will say next that our troops will join the Commune ! " " I will not answer for them," said Simon, remembering his journey through the snow.[1]

Next morning Favre and Picard repaired to the Ministry of the Interior, hoping against hope that the National Guard would rally at last ; as there were no signs of any change of feeling, Picard drew up an order delegating the provisional administration of the city to the Maires, and the two Ministers left Paris by the 7.30 train. As they went to the station they " looked constantly behind them, for they knew that, if they had been arrested, they would have shared the fate of Generals Lecomte and Thomas ".[2]

Thiers' plan for the total evacuation of Paris was probably a wise one, but it came near to being carried out with a literalness that would have been disastrous. When he left Paris, his first thought had been to protect Versailles, and he had asked General Vinoy if there were any troops, who could be absolutely trusted. The General replied, " Only the Daudel Brigade ". " Very well, send it to

---

[1] *Ibid.* pp. 186-7. Jules Richard (a reporter of the *Figaro*) brought the news of the assassination of the Generals to the Prefecture. Thiers appeared, " a wrinkled dwarf, his face like that of an aged fairy, his white hair standing up in a crest, and his little hooked nose between spectacles ". He refused at first to believe it ; then he went on to justify the evacuation of Paris ; he could not allow the only Army left him by the Treaty of Peace at Paris, to be compromised. Dreyfus, *Thiers contre la guerre, etc.*, pp. 305-7.

[2] Déposition de Picard, p. 401.

Versailles." The Brigade at the moment occupied the all-important position of Mont Valérien, which was left, on their departure, with 25 soldiers and a few rifles. Fortunately the Lieutenant-Colonel, Lockner, realised how vital the post was and, when some insurgents approached, gave them ten minutes in which to disperse before he fired.

On March 19th General Vinoy wrote to Thiers urging that it should be reoccupied. In the evening a meeting of 150 deputies of the Right sent three of their number to point out the importance of the position ; Admiral Jaurèguiberry, Martin des Pallières, and Buffet saw Thiers, who replied that the weak morale of the Army made it impossible to occupy any forts ; as to Mont Valérien its military importance had been exaggerated. As they left at midnight, Pallières said, " You will be sorry for this all your life ".[1] At one o'clock General Vinoy sent another note. Thiers was in bed, and his wife read it to him ; he was at length persuaded, and on the morning of the 20th General Noël was sent with the 119th Regiment to occupy it. " I breathed again ", said Thiers to Simon. It is clear that he was on the verge of making a grave blunder.[2]

---

[1] D'Arcay, *Notes inédites sur Thiers*, pp. 181-4.
[2] Simon, *Soir de ma journée*, p. 187 ; Hanotaux, i. 184-5.

CHAPTER IX

THE ASSEMBLY AND THE COMMUNE

MEANWHILE, the deputies were arriving for the opening of
the National Assembly ; the Minister of the Interior had
wired to all station-masters to warn members to go straight
to Versailles and not to pass through Paris, but most of
them arrived in complete ignorance and, had the insurrection been better organised at the moment, many parliamentary representatives might have been captured at the
station ; as it was, only a few were stopped, including
General Chanzy, who, after a few days' imprisonment, was
released with the complicity of a member of the Central
Committee.[1]

" Versailles ", said Thiers in his evidence before the
Commission,[2] " has always been a holiday resort ; no one
expected to see an army arrive there, and nothing was
ready." The troops camped out in the Avenues, on the
Place d'Armes and on the heights of Satory. It was still
snowing, and groups of soldiers were huddled sulkily round
their fires ; they had stopped saluting their officers and
took no notice when Generals passed by. When indignant
members of the Right demanded why Paris had been
" abandoned ", supporters of the Government pointed
silently to the troops.[3]

On the heels of the refugees from Paris came the civil
administration. All the employees of the various ministries

---

[1] De Marcère, *L'Assemblée nationale*, i. 83.
[2] Enquête, p. 364.
[3] Simon, *Soir de ma journée*, p. 188.

163

had been summoned to Versailles with the exception of doctors in the hospitals, headmasters in the lycées, conservators of museums and libraries, and the heads of the Bank.[1] The Luxembourg palace was not evacuated till March 23rd, and Rampont, the director of the postal service, stayed till the 30th ;[2] the Governor of the Bank, M. Rolland, joined Thiers, but M. de Ploeuc, the sous-gouverneur, stayed behind. One of the more moderate members of the Commune, M. de Breslay, installed himself there and protected it from pillage ; it lent 20,000,000 francs to the Commune with the consent of the Versailles Government, as a ransom for its security.[3]

The Palace at Versailles was made ready for the various Ministries ; the State apartments and galleries were divided up by screens. The Minister of Justice presided in a boudoir ; Jules Simon had his office in the wing facing the Orangerie ; amid the splendours of the ancient monarchy, the " fonctionnaires " encamped like a picnic party. The floors were covered with mattresses ; the Ministers' cabinets consisted of a desk and two chairs.[4] The Œil de Bœuf, which served as antechamber to the Ministry of Interior, was as crowded with courtiers as ever it had been at a royal levée. Weiss said, as he passed through, to a waiting group of journalists: " They have just heard of the murder of the Préfet of Saint-Étienne and there are already three or four people inside, who are disputing for the honour of being assassinated ".[5]

In the midst of all this influx of visitors the newly arrived deputies found it hard to get food and shelter ; some were lodged in the Palace itself ; others were boarded out in private rooms requisitioned by Rameau, the Maire. The Vicomte de Meaux, arriving at the house assigned to

[1] Simon, *Gouv. de M. Thiers*, i. 255.
[2] Hanotaux, i. 187.
[3] See evidence of de Ploeuc (Enquête, p. 786).
[4] Simon, *Soir de ma journée*, p. 386.
[5] Bosq, p. 76. See the plan of the Palace of Versailles.

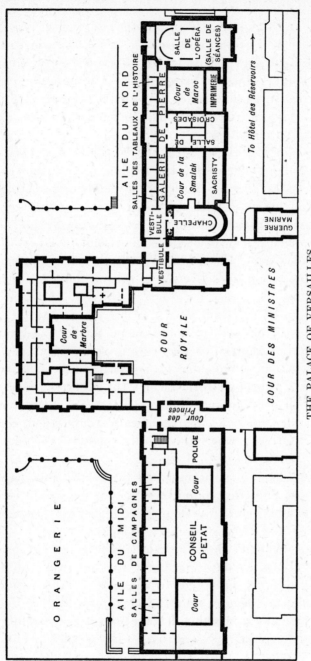

THE PALACE OF VERSAILLES

him, found them all asleep, but they said cheerily, " Certainly we will get up and settle you in ; we did it often
enough for the Prussians ". To obtain a meal was harder
still ; hungry queues besieged the restaurants ; at the
Hôtel des Réservoirs (most favoured by deputies) a meal
took two hours, and guests had to fetch their own dishes
from the kitchen.[1]

On March 20th, at 2.15, the National Assembly met
in the Salle d'Opéra. On the reading of the *procès-verbal*
of the last sitting at Bordeaux, a member, correcting the
record of his vote, said, " I voted for the transference to
Paris ; I desire to maintain my vote now more than ever ".
There was a stir of excitement, and some members of the
Left called out " Hear, hear " ; the President put an end
to the agitation by delivering in solemn tones his opening
allocution.

" Gentlemen," said Grévy, " it seemed that the misfortunes of the country could go no further ; a criminal
insurrection, that no pretext or grievance can excuse, has
added to our troubles. . . . You will know how to be
worthy of your high duties, which the situation imposes on
you, with courage and dignity. Let the country remain
calm and confident ; let them rally round their elected
representatives ; where the right is, there will the might be
also."

The phrase most appreciated by his audience was the
one about " rallying round their elected representatives " ;
the Assembly felt it was their sovereignty, which was being
attacked and their sovereignty which must be defended.
This was evident, when Jules de Lasteyrie (an old deputy,
who wore a shade over his eyes, but was far from
lacking vigour) proposed to appoint a Commission of
fifteen to co-operate with the Government. " I do not
come to make a speech ; I come to ask the Assembly to
act and to act as representative of the people." This was

[1] De Meaux, pp. 44, 45.

carried by acclamation, and the Assembly retired into its bureaux to consider his proposal, as well as a Bill presented by the Minister of the Interior to declare the Department of Seine-et-Oise in a state of siege.[1]

The Right came to Versailles in a mood of mingled anger and alarm, anger that Paris had dared to revolt against their authority and alarm lest the Government should prove unwilling or unable to display sufficient firmness. Towards Thiers their feeling was one of suppressed exasperation. They had deliberated together a few hours, after their arrival, at the Hôtel des Réservoirs and sent to demand the reoccupation of Mont Valérien ; they clamoured for instant action against Paris ; they criticised the presence of " the men of September " in the Ministry ; it was even said that there was talk of replacing Thiers by the Prince de Joinville as President of the Republic.[2] Even Lacombe, who was a personal friend and supporter of the Government, writes in his diary : " Thiers persists in keeping Le Flô as Minister for War, an excellent man, but believed by everybody to be unequal to his task. All this is sad, for Thiers' great services may most unjustly be forgotten as a result of the last few days " (March 21st). " Our apparent and unexplained inactivity irritates everybody. . . . Like all heads of Governments, Thiers pays little attention to any suggestions and attributes them to exaggeration or passion. . . . But to turn him out would be to assume a terrible responsibility."[3] So the Right were prepared to submit, half grumbling at Thiers' condescension to Republicans, half hoping that the Commune

---

[1] *Annales*, t. 2, pp. 1-3.

[2] Simon, *Gouv. de M. Thiers*, i. 293. For Republican gossip on the subject see Mme Adam (*Mes angoisses*, p. 78) : " Dr. Maure told me that de Reims said to him at Bordeaux that, if trouble arose, Aumale and Joinville would be the first to demand the honour of restoring order " ; and p. 100 : " It is said that Estancelin begged Aumale to put himself at the head of the Army to reduce Paris, but he answered : ' I do not wish to recommence my military career . . . by drawing my sword on the boulevards ' ".

[3] *Journal*, i. 7.

M

might cure him of his leanings towards the Left.[1]

The attitude of the bulk of the Republican party is well expressed by Jules Simon (from his point of view), when he says : " All members of the Assembly were full of consternation and anger, but, while the Right were hoping for revenge, the Republicans were hoping for conciliation ; the assassination of the two generals added enormously to the difficulties of the situation. On March 19th the *Journal Officiel* of the Central Committee had declared that ' these men had been executed according to the laws of war '."[2]

On Sunday, March 19th, the Central Committee of the National Guard had issued a proclamation declaring " the state of siege " at an end and announcing fresh municipal elections for March 22nd. At two in the afternoon the Maires and deputies for Paris met in the Mairie of the third *arrondissement*, and sent a delegation to the Hôtel-de-Ville ; there a long and heated discussion took place, which lasted till four o'clock on Monday morning. Clemenceau spoke first, and denied the right of Paris to rise against France ; a member of the Central Committee retorted, " We do not intend to submit any longer to rural plebiscites ; the revolution has been made ; are you for us or against us ? " Millière warned them, " If you unfurl the red flag, the Government will hurl France on Paris ".

Louis Blanc cried, " You are insurgents against the Assembly ; we cannot appear as your auxiliaries " ; Arnold (a member of the Committee) replied, " You are face

---

[1] Hector Pessard (*Mes petits papiers*, ii. 31) has a brilliant little sketch of the first contact between members of the majority of the Assembly and the Paris journalists : " We had a very low opinion of these country-gentlemen, who had become legislators after having been churchwardens for so long— they were at once timid and suspicious, penetrated with a sense of their own importance, loaded with relics and yet trying hard not to appear ' provincial ', not daring to confess their prejudices and yet suffering acutely, when the Parisians ragged them. But they soon perceived that we were the true dispensers of fame, and then they became quite human ; we learned to judge them more favourably."

[2] *Gouv. de M. Thiers*, i. 257.

to face with a force which spreads through France ; you
are unloosing civil war ".[1]

An agreement was finally arrived at. The Committee
was to hand over the Hôtel-de-Ville to the Maires ; it was
to retain control of the National Guard and was to retire to
the Place Vendôme ; the. deputies for Paris undertook to
urge the Assembly to accept remedial legislation ; Clemenceau and Lockroy were to propose a bill providing for
municipal elections " as soon as possible " ; Lockroy was
to bring forward a measure allowing the Guard to elect its
officers ; Millière was to propose that the moratorium for
debts should be prolonged for three months.

At nine o'clock the same evening, the representatives of
the Maires presented themselves at the Hôtel-de-Ville, but
the Committee refused to surrender it ;[2] in spite of this
breach of agreement the Paris deputies resolved to present
their proposals to the Assembly. They did so at five o'clock
on the 20th ; on the whole, they were well received, and
those referring to the moratorium and the elections were
referred to the bureaux " avec urgence " ; unfortunately
unpleasant incidents were always liable to break out
between the majority and the deputies for Paris ; the Right
could not dismiss from their minds the idea that all Parisians
were accomplices in crime, and they mistrusted Clemenceau
as being vaguely responsible for the murder of the Generals
(shot in the *arrondissement* of which he was Maire) ; de
Marcère relates how [3] a Committee, investigating the
question of Paris elections, called in Clemenceau and Tirard,
and were trying to dissipate misunderstandings in a spirit
of good-humour. One of the Committee made some observation on the attitude of the inhabitants of Paris ;
immediately " Tirard got up and delivered a furious har-
angue with many gesticulations, shouting louder and louder,
till in the end he became almost ill and stuttered out the

[1] Hanotaux, i. 188-9 ; Favre, *op. cit.* p. 251.   [2] Favre, *op. cit.* p. 252.
[3] *Annales de l'assemblée nationale,* i. 93.

declaration that the representatives of Paris regarded themselves as insulted and would retire. Clemenceau remained cold and haughty without saying a word, with an appearance of frigid hostility ; he took Tirard by the arm and they left the room. We were stupefied. . . . I was sent after them to bring them back, but I could not persuade them to return."

The deputies for the capital were indeed in a difficult position between the mutual misunderstandings of Versailles and the Hôtel-de-Ville ; they felt that they were the representatives of the orderly moderate population, who had no sympathy with the Commune. No doubt, as members for Paris, they could take no other line, but the orderly and moderate section of the population let down their deputies, just as they had let down Thiers on March 18th, and the small group working for conciliation in Parliament were in the exasperating situation of being considered fools, when they were not being considered traitors.

On March 20th, Clemenceau, in proposing his Bill for municipal elections, had the imprudence to say, " The Government have deserted Paris ; their post was where the danger was " (*violent protests*) ; and again : " There is no authority in Paris ". Thiers called out, " The authority is here," and Grévy protested from the presidential chair.

Ernest Picard, while not opposing the consideration of the project, doubted whether under present conditions free elections could be held in the city.

Tirard, amid renewed interruptions, said : " For two days the Government have deserted Paris " ; " after having attempted a *coup de force*, which did not come off ", added Clemenceau. The whole Ministerial bench protested : Thiers — " It is not true " ; Jules Simon — " This is the language of insurrection " ; Jules Favre — " Paris drove us out " ; Dufaure — " They seized the Ministries and chased us out ".

Tirard declared he was accusing nobody, when he said Paris was deserted, but it was a fact ; let them set up a freely elected municipal council, round which the friends of order might rally ; as to the accusation of wishing to compromise with insurrection, he replied that the walls of Paris were covered with placards announcing an election by order of the Central Committee. " As for me, I shall oppose such an election." " And I too," added Clemenceau.

The reporter of the Commission, on the proposal for the state of siege, then moved its adoption. Louis Blanc, who had much difficulty in obtaining a hearing, protested against laws of repression " in the name of Paris, now in agony ". " Talk to us of the agony of General Clement Thomas ", called out a member of the Right.

Just as the Assembly were about to adjourn, a young deputy for the Aisne, called Turquet, still covered with dust, mounted the tribune and told the story of his own arrest together with that of General Chanzy at the Paris station. He did it with great dramatic effect. Once the Assembly showed an inclination to laugh when he told them how the crowd had called out to him, " Death to the little Prussian ! " " I am blond," he explained, " and I had unfortunately a little cap on my head, which a friend of mine gave me, who had captured it from a Bavarian officer." But soon all lighter feelings were lost in a general murmur of indignation. A deputy called out, " All Europe should hear the story " ; Turquet told how he had escaped. " And General Chanzy ? " they called out. " The General is still in the Santé prison."

In the excitement, that followed, someone proposed a deputation to deliver the captive. " All, all ! " they shouted. Ernest Picard offered to accompany it ; the matter was referred to a committee but, when the time came to report, discretion had proved itself (and in this case very rightly) to be the better part of valour.[1]

[1] *Annales*, t. 2, pp. 4-16 ; Claveau, pp. 78-84.

Next day the Committee of fifteen proposed to the Assembly a proclamation to the people and the Army :

CITIZENS AND SOLDIERS,

The greatest crime, that can be committed in a nation that wishes to be free, an open revolt against the national sovereignty, is aggravating all the sufferings of our country by a new disaster. . . . The first and most elementary of your rights is at stake ; it is your duty to uphold it. Your representatives are unanimous in demanding your energetic assistance. All of us without difference of opinion implore you to rally round the Assembly, your creation, your image, your hope, and your only refuge.

Peyrat demanded that they should add the words " Long live France ! Long live the Republic ! " but, as the proclamation had been already voted, he was refused a hearing ; Millière desired to say a few words " in the interests of conciliation ", but the President had already put the order of the day to the vote. Thiers then rose and asked the Assembly to give Millière a hearing ; " we can only meet the present crisis by calm, union and respect for other people's opinions " — " And firmness " called out a member of the Right. Millière, when he did speak, contented himself with saying that the proclamation " contained some unfortunate words ".[1]

In a somewhat confused debate on the general situation, Langlois and Brisson proposed that a resolution should be carried on the spot " that the city of Paris should have a free municipal government ". Thiers replied : " Paris shall be represented in an elective system of local government for the whole country ; only, we demand time to organise such a system ". He protested that he saw little chance of conciliation with the Central Committee : " If you, M. Lockroy and M. Clemenceau, are not to be considered Republicans, who in the world can deserve that title ? Yet have they listened to you ? Have they listened to Admiral Saisset ? What can they suspect him of ?

[1] *Annales*, t. 2, pp. 20-23.

He can only be suspected of being a hero." He then proceeded to a vigorous defence of his withdrawal from Paris in the familiar anecdotal style he wielded so well ; he concluded by saying that Paris must not expect a predominant position in any new law, which might be carried : "If Paris allows itself to be dominated by a handful of wretches, . . . I say that it has given us the right to prefer France to its capital" (*loud and prolonged applause*).

Clemenceau then rose and said : "The President of the Council has just explained to us how the Government was led to drive the country into the present situation". An explosion of anger interrupted him ; he made it worse by saying that the Government were primarily responsible for what had happened.

Jules Favre called out : "That is an act of accusation drawn up before murderers ! That is what your words mean." Clemenceau tried to explain his words away — "I did not quite mean to say that ; your interruptions made me go further than I intended". Jules Favre, his face ablaze with indignation, now mounted the tribune and delivered a violent attack on the Paris insurgents, going far beyond the measured words of his chief. He read out the courageous protest of thirty-five Paris newspapers against the illegal elections ; he denounced the murder of the Generals, "disarmed in presence of cannibals who had sworn their deaths" ; he implored the National Guard to redeem their honour. "Whatever happens, the sovereignty of the people shall triumph ; no, France has not sunk so low as to bow her head before a factious and blood-stained minority."

The Assembly was in a fever of excitement. Admiral Saisset stood up and shouted, "Let us appeal to the provinces and march on Paris!" Clemenceau declared that, in view of the "provocative speech" of the Minister for Foreign Affairs, they would withdraw their measures of

conciliation; Langlois, trying in vain to make himself
heard amid the universal uproar, shouted out, "Gentlemen, the house is on fire and you indulge in private conversations!"

Thiers intervened again to restore calm. "We are not
declaring war against Paris; we are ready to open our
arms to it, if it will open its arms to us."

Finally a motion was passed declaring that the Assembly
"resolved to reconstitute the municipal administration, as
soon as possible, both in Paris and the Departments on the
basis of elective councils".[1]

The situation in Paris showed few signs of improvement;
the declaration of the thirty-five journalists (which Jules
Favre had eulogised in his speech) had been to the effect
that the convocation of electors was an act of national
sovereignty and, as such sovereignty belonged to the
Assembly, the act of the Central Committee fixing the
elections ought to be considered null and void. The Committee replied that the declaration was an act of treason
against the sovereignty of the people of Paris, and, "while
they would not touch the liberty of the Press", they warned
writers that cases of calumny and outrage would be
immediately punished.

On Wednesday, the 22nd, there was a manifestation in
favour of conciliation; a procession of 600 persons (mostly
of the bourgeois class), carrying a large tricolour flag,
marched to the Place Vendôme shouting "Vive la paix!"
The square was full of National Guards, who pointed their
rifles at them and summoned them to disperse. Suddenly
a shot was heard; the order was given to fire, and the
unarmed crowd fled in every direction, leaving 13 killed
and 8 wounded.[2] The next day the Central Committee
ordered the occupation of all the Mairies. The Maires
themselves determined to make one last effort in the cause
of peace; they issued a proclamation, associating them-

---

[1] *Annales*, t. 2, pp. 23-47.   [2] Simon, *Gouv. de M. Thiers*, i. 277-82.

selves with Admiral Saisset, the new Commandant of the
National Guard,[1] and betook themselves in a body to
Versailles.

They arrived about six o'clock in the evening. Arnaud
de l'Ariège, himself a Maire and a deputy, mounted the
tribune of the Assembly ; he belonged to that extremely
small section of fervent Catholics, who were ardent republicans, but he was much respected by his colleagues ; he
asked the Assembly, as a special exception, and in view of
the gravity of the circumstances, to allow the Maires to
take their seats with the deputies. The Right murmured,
their memories full of disorderly sittings of the Convention ; the impeccable Buffet (of whom, when he was President, it was said, " It is not that he applies the rules ; he
is the rules ") called out, " We are falling into disorder " ;
the President pointed out that those Maires, who were
deputies, could take their seats ; the others might sit in
the tribunes — he offered his own for the purpose ; Baze,
one of the *questeurs*, then explained that he had already
reserved two tribunes for them.

When the Maires entered, vested in their scarves of
office, they found that they were overlooking and almost
touching the upper benches of the Left, crowded with their
supporters ; the Paris deputies stood up shouting " Vive la
République ! " ; the Maires replied " Vive la République !
Vive la France ! Vive l'Assemblée Nationale ! "[2] The

---

[1] Saisset had been appointed to that post by Thiers on March 19th ; he
had been immensely popular during the siege, in which his son had been
killed ; he had been elected deputy for the Seine by 154,367 votes, and during
the early stages of the present disturbances, he had been recognised and
cheered by the crowd.

[2] Antoine Claveau (p. 94) and Jules Simon (*Gouv. de M. Thiers*, i. 285),
both eye-witnesses, assert that the Maires entered shouting " Vive la République ! " This is probably what happened (Jules Simon remarks : " The
extreme Republicans are sometimes rather theatrical, but we must give
them the benefit of the doubt, as the official report asserts that the members
of the Left began it (" Les membres de la gauche se lèvent en criant ' Vive
la République ! ' MM. les Maires saluent l'Assemblee et répondent ".
Annales, t. 2, p. 75). M. Hanotaux (i. 190) says " A cry of Vive la République !
burst from among them (the Maires) " ; de Marcère says : " Their appearance

Right were on their feet in a moment and surrounding the presidential chair with their protests. " We cannot tolerate that," they shouted. " Suspend the sitting. Do the Government say nothing ? " Grévy, imperturbable as ever, replied, " The Assembly have already decided to retire to their bureaux ; the sitting is suspended ". The adjournment was no doubt correct, and Grévy explained (when the House reassembled) that it had nothing to do with the presence of the Maires, but the effect was unfortunate. Whatever motive the President had for suspending the sitting, it was obvious enough why the Right demanded it. However, when the Assembly met again at ten o'clock, feelings had calmed down and the " proposition des Maires " [1] was referred to the bureaux " avec urgence ".

The Maires returned to Paris with mixed feelings ; they had experienced the jealous hostility of the majority, but, after all, their proposals had been taken into consideration without a division. They were still more encouraged, when, on the 24th, Admiral Saisset published a proclamation which began, " I hasten to inform you that (in agreement with the deputies of the Seine and the Maires of Paris) we have obtained from the Government of the National Assembly the complete recognition of your municipal franchises, the election of all the officers of the National Guard, a prolongation of the moratorium, and a proposal of relief for rents ".[2]

The words of the proclamation were more generous

(in the tribunes) provoked violent protests from the Right, on the Left a manifestation that was, to say the least of it, inopportune, and among the Centre movements of impatience and disapproval, as of a dramatic effect in bad taste " (*Assemblée nationale*, i. 93).

[1] It contained 5 clauses : (*a*) that the Assembly should remain in permanent communication with the Maires ; (*b*) that the Maires should be authorised to take, on their own responsibility, the measures necessitated by the public danger ; (*c*) that the election of the Chief of the National Guard should be fixed for March 28th ; (*d*) that municipal elections should be fixed for April 3rd ; (*e*) that the condition for eligibility should be reduced to six months' residence. (*Annales*, t. 2, p. 77).

[2] Simon, *Gouv. de M. Thiers*, i. 288.

than wise ; it put Thiers in a difficult position. He had refused to associate himself with the action of the Maires, because it might have seemed to involve direct negotiations with the insurgents, which he knew the Right would never stand ; he had told the Maires that he was prepared to support liberal measures dealing with the subjects they had raised, but he never committed himself (for instance) to the election of a chief of the National Guard. Besides, how could he promise legislation, which did not depend on him but on the Assembly ? How could Saisset " have obtained from the Government" concessions, that could only be sanctioned by a majority, which was far from blindly devoted ?

The Right were furious, when the terms of the proclamation reached Versailles. A hurried meeting of Royalists was called and it is said that a proposal was made to entrust the Government to the Prince de Joinville.[1]

Meanwhile at Paris the proclamation seemed to have produced the desired effect. The Central Committee sent " General Brunel " with one of his colleagues and a detachment of soldiers and artillery to the Mairie of the first *arrondissement* in order to negotiate ; the discussion was carried on all the afternoon. It chiefly turned on the date of the elections ; finally it was agreed to fix March 30th for the municipal elections, and April 2nd for the choice of a chief of the National Guard. Brunel appeared on the steps of the Mairie, and declared that peace was concluded ; the National Guard replied by acclamations, and in a few hours all Paris was rejoicing.[2]

---

[1] Simon, *Gouv. de M. Thiers*, i. p. 293. Tirard says in his evidence (Enquête, p. 658) : " M. Jules Simon, who was at the foot of the tribune, said to me : ' I am very anxious : there is a rumour that some member of the majority intends to propose that the command of the Army be given to Joinville ' ". It is presumably to some such intrigue that Raoul Duval refers when long afterwards, attacking the Orleanists, he said : " The Comte de Paris refused to support the resistance to the Commune by his name and presence " (de Goncourts, t. 5, pp. 206-7).

[2] Simon, *Gouv. de M. Thiers*, i. 291-2.

The Assembly had been discussing the proposal for prolonging the moratorium; after it had been carried, Tirard rose and demanded an evening sitting, in order that the report of the " proposition des Maires " might be considered. Conciliation was in the air, and it was decided to meet again at ten o'clock. At ten there were no signs of the Commission and the Assembly became anxious; at a quarter to eleven the President read a letter from de Peyramont, who presided over the Commission, which said that at 9.30 Thiers had sent for them " to communicate important information ", and that therefore they could not report that evening. At this the Paris deputies lost all control of themselves. Clemenceau rushed to the tribune; Tirard shouted like a madman. The Commission now took their seats; Peyramont told the House that, after listening to the President of the Council, they had come to the conclusion that a debate would be too dangerous : " An imprudent word might cause torrents of blood to flow ". Arnaud begged the Assembly not to adjourn, in order that the deputies for Paris might have a few moments to consult together. Thiers now mounted the tribune and appealed for calm : " Silence at the present moment is necessary for the sake of the country ; if you are an assembly of statesmen, I implore you not to ask for information, which it would be dangerous to give ". Clemenceau called out, " Gentlemen, you will bear the responsibility for what will happen ", and the House adjourned.[1]

The important communication, which Thiers made to the Commission, was that the Central Committee had repudiated the terms accepted by Brunel. " What guarantee have we ", they asked, " that the conditions offered by Saisset will be observed ? Let us begin by electing the Commune, and so remain masters of the situation ", and they issued a proclamation fixing the elections for March 26th. The first impression among the Maires was that

[1] *Annales*, t. 2, p. 111 ; Claveau, pp. 95-6.

further negotiations were impossible ; they had always maintained that the date of the election was a question of sovereignty ; to accept the programme of the Committee would be to authorise insurrection. They separated on the night of the 24th, after resolving that the " elections proposed by the Central Committee will be insincere, irregular, and uncontrolled ".

The next day two members of the Central Committee (Ranvier and Arnold) appeared before the meeting of Maires, and solemnly promised that the Hôtel-de-Ville should be surrendered to them, if they would only consent to elections the next day. The discussion was long and confused. At length it was decided, for the sake of peace and to allow the friends of order to cast their votes, that the Maires would agree, to the proposed elections. The decision was not unanimous ; 7 Maires signed the decree of convocation, 32 adjoints and 6 deputies (Lockroy, Floquet, Tolain, Clemenceau, Schoelcher, and Greppo).[1] Arnaud de l'Ariège, who was at Versailles, refused to accept it and, at the sitting of the Assembly, withdrew his proposals for a settlement in a few depressed words. Louis Blanc then moved that the Maires in authorising the elections had acted the part of good citizens. It was referred to the commission of initiative.[2]

The last hope of conciliation dawned on Sunday, March 26th, the day of the elections, but it was soon obscured by the heaviest clouds.

The party of order abstained at the polls. The total number of electors was 481,970 ; 257,773 (54 per cent) did not vote at all ; 16 candidates opposed to the Revolution were elected (their total poll being 89,731 votes), but they immediately resigned. The Central Committee also did badly ; only 13 of its members were elected, and it could count on 17 " Internationale " members ; the rest of the

[1] Simon, *Gouv. de M. Thiers*, i. 293-6 ; Favre, pp. 262-5.
[2] *Annales*, t. 2, pp. 131-2.

Commune consisted of 32 Jacobins (the party of violence headed by Delescluze and Félix Pyat) and 10 Socialists (men of theory such as Vermorel, Tridon "a kind of millionaire with a mission ", Arthur Arnould, and Lefrancais).[1]

The timidity of the friends of order is perhaps explained, if not excused, by the unexpected action of Admiral Saisset, who, passing suddenly from an excess of confidence to the opposite pole, after only holding his post at the head of the National Guard for a day or two, had dismissed his troops and sent them home. The Council of Ministers could not believe their ears when the news reached them ; apart from the wisdom or folly of the proceeding, he had no right to dissolve a body of troops, which he had been sent to command — not to destroy. He defended himself by saying that the situation was impossible, and that he could not expose his men to the formidable troops of the Revolution.[2]

On March 27th the Assembly met to consider Louis Blanc's motion approving the action of the Maires in associating themselves with the elections : the Commission had proposed that it should not be taken into consideration. Thiers, in appealing for abstinence from the pleasure of making speeches in so critical a moment, took the opportunity of answering the calumny, that was being broadcast in Paris, that the Assembly were meditating a restoration of the monarchy. "They are enemies of public order, who say we are preparing to overthrow the Republic ; I give them the lie direct ; they lie in the face of France. . . . I appeal to all parties. Do you know which of you will win the victory ? The party which is wisest."

Then he renewed the Pact of Bordeaux : " I have said before ; I repeat it before the Assembly, before the country, and before History [3] — for History has never had

[1] Simon, *Gouv. de M. Thiers*, i. 314 ; Hanotaux, i. 191, 197.
[2] Favre, iii. 266-8.
[3] Notice the curious and conscious contrast with the doubtful " appeal to History " in the Bordeaux speech.

her eyes more widely open or more attentive upon any events than it has upon the tremendous happenings of the present moment — I affirm that no party shall be betrayed by us, that there shall be no unfair solution prepared at the expense of any party ".

The Paris deputies were so crushed by the result of the elections that not a word was said in favour of Louis Blanc's motion. But the Right were also sufficiently impressed by the seriousness of the situation to preserve an attitude of moderation, and a motion to declare Sunday's elections null and void was referred to the commission of initiative " sans urgence ".[1]

With this debate, the discussion between Paris and Versailles comes to an end ; henceforward it was for the cannon to speak and the events pass out of the region of political to that of military history.

The Extreme Left sank into silence ; Delescluze and Millière resigned from the Assembly and took their seats in the new Commune ; both perished six weeks later on the barricades. Lockroy also resigned to join the Commune, but though arrested was released after a short time. Clemenceau gave up his seat and retired for the moment from the political struggle ;[2] some of his colleagues, such as Langlois, Tirard, Tolain, and Brisson, remained, taking little part in the debates except for occasional skirmishes with the Right.[3] Thus Mme Adam writes : " At Versailles

---

[1] *Annales*, t. 2, pp. 145-9.

[2] Langlois in his evidence (Enquête, p. 817) : " There are deputies who have resigned, when they would have done better to stay in the Assembly— Clemenceau, Lockroy, and others." DARU : " They have caught the infection ". " Yes."

[3] Let us collect a few; they help to give atmosphere. On March 28th the Comte de la Rochethulon showed the Assembly a paper that had been fixed to the door of his Paris house inscribed " Bon à fusiller " ; he then read a quotation from the *Journal Officiel* of the Commune : " It is said that the Duc d'Aumale is at Versailles. If it is true, it means that, from Bordeaux to Versailles, the Duke has not met a citizen. . . . Society has only one duty towards princes— that is, death." He added : " I beg my honourable colleagues on the Left, now masters of Paris, to be kind enough to tell their colleagues that I consider myself in a state of legitimate defence towards them ". On this, the Paris

the Republican Left is reduced to impotence ; they have only one aim — not to risk embarrassing Thiers. . . . On April 17th (at Quinet's house) Adam spoke in favour of a supreme effort for pacification ; Peyrat and others opposed it, because every proposal had its drawbacks. ' True,' said Adam, ' but silence and abstention, when duty prescribes action, also have their drawbacks, if only that of being humiliated and ashamed at one's inaction.' . . . The hesitations of the Left irritate Republicans in the provinces ; Quinet repeats too often his prediction that ' the mask of peace ' (with Germany) ' will conceal eternal war in every form ' . . . Louis Blanc, who is the oracle of the group, is too pontifical ; he imitates Quinet and only utters phrases." [1]

deputies rushed to the tribune ; Tirard called out, " For the last eight days we have been risking our lives, and this is the way we are insulted at the tribune ". The Count, quite composed, said that he meant his message for those members of the Left, who had joined the Commune. A moment later, when Fresneau was asking a question about the influence of the Internationale, in the present troubles, Floquet (another deputy for Paris) called out, " These people are mad ". Summoned to explain, he declared that the insult hurled at himself and his colleagues by the Comte de la Rochethulon could only be explained by supposing he had really lost his head. This naturally failed to satisfy the President of the Assembly and he was called to order. *Annales*, t. 2, pp. 151-3.

On May 6th Tolain called attention to the placards on the walls of Paris relating how four National Guards, who had laid down their arms without resisting, had been shot, and demanded an official denial from the Government ; the Royalists shouted, " No ! the previous question ! A statement by the Commune does not deserve the honour of being denied ! " When the Minister for War rose to answer, the majority refused to let him speak. " Do not answer ! Everyone knows our brave officers are not assassins." The Minister began, " In demanding the contradiction of this hateful calumny, the *honourable* M. Tolain . . ." Here the Right renewed their interruptions ; the Left took this as an insult to the honourability of their colleague, and rose to their feet ; Colonel Langlois suddenly tore himself from the grasp of his friends and rushed with clenched fists at the benches of the Right ; the sitting had to be suspended. *Annales*, t. 2, pp. 845-6.

[1] *Mes angoisses*, pp. 86, 107, 110.

CHAPTER X

THIERS AND THE COMMUNE

AFTER the failure of all attempts at negotiation, Thiers now stepped forward to lead the battle against revolution. He says himself, " We passed a fortnight at Versailles doing nothing ; they were the worst days of my life ".[1] The Right were constantly clamouring for immediate action ; even in the Council of Ministers [2] voices were raised for a counter-attack on Paris. It was urged that the withdrawal to Versailles was only defensible on the ground that the Government could not defend every part of the capital with untrustworthy and scattered troops, but now they had been concentrated in a place of safety ; now therefore was the time for taking the offensive. It would be easy to seize some fortified position, round which the National Guards, who were on the side of order, could rally ; they might occupy the Gare St-Lazare and the quarters round it, where the inhabitants had no sympathy with the Commune. Nothing could be more dangerous than to hesitate ; it meant abandoning the city to the tender mercies of revolutionaries, giving time to the other large cities of France to imitate their example — even perhaps to force the Prussian Army to an ignominious intervention for the purpose of restoring order. Every moment of inaction was an encouragement to the insurgents ; they were already saying that Versailles was panic-stricken and that the Government troops would surrender at the first shot. If they persisted in doing nothing, might

[1] Déposition, p. 364.   [2] Favre, p. 240.

they not even be driven out of Versailles by the more enterprising forces of the Commune ?

To all this Thiers replied by one argument (to his mind an unanswerable one) : " The Army is not fit for battle ; we must have time to restore its morale and to increase its numbers by persuading Prussia to speed up the return of our prisoners from Germany ; it is no good relying on volunteers ; you will not get any.[1] It is too great a risk to take the offensive till we are more certain of success." [2]

As to the possibility of being attacked, he fully admitted it ; [3] he had himself drawn up a plan of retreat. Meanwhile he gave strict orders that the troops on Satory were to be kept in the strictest quarantine from all propaganda ; whoever tried to approach them was to be shot.

It was of the last importance for the success of his policy to gain time, and it was probably for this reason that he encouraged the negotiations with the Maires, which he must have regarded as hopeless from the first.[4]

But he should not be imagined as passing the worst fortnight of his life in grim despair. He was true to his

[1] The Assembly voted a Bill for the formation of a corps of Volunteers ; the measure produced a violent contest (between the Left, who wanted them placed under the Minister for the Interior, and the Right, who favoured the Minister for War) but no recruits ; the country was too much exhausted (Thiers, Enquête, p. 365).

[2] " We shall take all the time necessary for the military education of our young soldiers. Before we begin to work our tool must be solid " (Malo, *Thiers*, p. 503). "Take Paris by surprise ! " he said. " That is easy to say. It is a gigantic undertaking to capture the fortifications of Paris " (Dreyfus, *Thiers contre la guerre*, etc., p. 327).

[3] " If we had been attacked by 70,000 to 80,000 men . . . I would not have answered for the solidity of our army " (Déposition, p. 365). At a Council of War held on March 28th he said, " Gentlemen, we shall be attacked tonight ". The Generals pointed out that a night attack was wholly impossible, and would certainly, even with trained troops, lead to disaster for those rash enough to attempt it ; however, he insisted on a promise that our troops should be kept on the alert : the night passed without any alarm (Du Barail, *Souvenirs*, iii. 261).

[4] It is said that some of the Maires, who accepted the elections dictated by the Central Committee, did so because they understood that Thiers wished to gain time. Favre, p. 263.

maxim, " Take everything seriously but nothing tragically " ; he loved the sense of power, and he had a passion
for military strategy (especially in anything that concerned
artillery) which made people call him half playfully " a
Napoleon in mufti ".

As to the actual details of warfare he was probably less
of an expert than he thought ; he nearly made a serious
mistake about Mont Valérien, but his Generals, though
sometimes rather amused, never took liberties.   General
du Barail says :

> He was proud of his marvellous faculty for assimilation ; he
> would not have talked to the keeper of a potato stall without trying
> to explain to him how potatoes should be roasted ; he delighted in
> revealing the secrets of the art of war to the generals grouped round
> him. He passed his time lying on maps ; he called councils of war,
> at which we were never allowed to utter a word, while he explained
> the situation, and criticised manœuvres with inexhaustible energy.[1]

In any case strategy was not what was wanted to recapture Paris, but common sense, firm administration and a
capacity for bringing order out of chaos. All this Thiers
had to perfection. It glows through the words, in which
he described his activities before the Commission of
Inquiry :

> There is a way of issuing orders, that I have often employed and
> always found successful — that is, not to trust to correspondence,
> but to give orders directly and *viva voce*. Every morning I called
> together all the *chefs de service* : I decided what was to be done ;
> everyone had his task assigned. We needed heavy artillery ; we
> were told where it was to be had, and we decided on the difficult
> question of transport. . . . I never gave an order without being
> sure of its execution. And I followed it step by step till it was carried
> out.[2]

The first task was to restore the morale of the troops.
Thiers raised their allowance of rations, saw that they were
well clothed, and that their officers lived with them in

---

[1] *Souvenirs*, iii. 260.   [2] Déposition, p. 365.

camp ; and himself constantly visited them to look after their welfare. In a few days they regained discipline and looked like an army once more. But it was also necessary to raise their number to over 120,000. Troops were summoned from the provinces.[1] Bismarck consented to the return of some 60,000 prisoners ; as the railways were full of returning German troops, they were sent to Hanoverian ports, and French ships landed them at Brest and Cherbourg ; but half of them, when they were arrived, were due for demobilisation, and had to be sent home. This is one of the little touches which show what a state the French Army was in. However, within six weeks the Army at Versailles reached 130,000 men, and a numerous collection of artillery was brought together with a thousand rounds for each gun. All the Army Generals flocked to Versailles to offer their services. The troops returning from Germany were organised at Cherbourg, Cambrai and Dijon, under Generals Ducrot and Clinchant ; Generals de Cissey, de Ladmirault, and Douay were put in commands of Army Corps at Versailles, and du Barail at the head of the Cavalry. General Vinoy was put over the Army of Reserve. The chief command was offered to Marshal MacMahon, famous for the taking of the Malakoff in the Crimean War ; he feared, however, that the part he had played in the defeat of Sedan would give rise to criticism of his appointment. " You have been defeated ! " cried Thiers : " unfortunately everybody has been defeated ; as for criticisms, it is for me to answer them." [2]

On April 3rd the first battle took place ; the Commune made a double assault on Courbevoie and Meudon. It was

---

[1] Antoine Claveau (p. 133) says : " I saw some regiments, whom Thiers had summoned from the provinces ; they did not look at all martial. . . . One felt that they were being corrupted by mutineers, and one could tell how bad discipline was from the way they marched. . . . Two N.C.O.'s were tried and shot on the spot. . . . In a fortnight these troops had regained all the qualities of the French soldier."

[2] Thiers, *Notes et souvenirs*, pp. 125-31.

no longer likely that they would break through, but the question everybody asked themselves anxiously at Versailles was, " How will the troops behave ? Have our men been turned into reliable material, or are they still half on the side of the revolution ? " As Thiers said, " At all costs it was necessary for the Army to commit itself ".[1]

The Palace of Versailles was full of rumours and alarms ; at half-past two a feverish sitting of the Assembly began ; Turquet rose to call attention to the salaries of teachers ; the deputies interrupted him at his first words. One said sarcastically, " This is a well-chosen moment to discuss such details ". Jules Simon in his reply said " that there were at the moment more interesting questions ". An adjournment was called for ; others demanded a communication of Government. The Minister of the Interior intervened ; he was cheered to the echo, when he said, " The Army has done its duty " ; beyond that he would only say, " We learn that a movement of retreat seems to be on the increase among the columns of insurgents in the direction of Paris ". This was not what the Assembly wanted ; " a kind of flight ", suggested the more accommodating Jules Simon. " I am only quoting from the dispatch ", answered Picard. " I do not wish to add anything."

Journault, deputy for Seine-et-Oise, followed with a cheering account of a victory at Meudon. Brame then rose and, referring to the fighting at Courbevoie, suggested that the Assembly should go in a body to congratulate the returning troops ; some members called out " Hear, hear ", but to the majority there appeared to be limits to the exultation permissible on hearing that a French army had obeyed their officers. On the proposal of Arago, the Assembly voted itself " en permanence ", and quietly discussed a Bill for the holding of elections at the *chef-lieu* of a canton.

[1] Déposition (Enquête, p. 365).

At five o'clock Jules Simon intervened to assure the House of a complete victory ; amid general relief the permanence was abandoned, and members adjourned till nine, when Thiers himself appeared at the tribune. He was so tired and hoarse that members had to crowd round to hear him. He spoke very shortly : " The facts are so satisfactory — if anything can be called satisfactory in a civil war — that the brevity of my narrative cannot diminish its importance ; " [1] he finished by saying, " I hope that the poor people who have been misled by wicked men will finish by imploring the mercy of the established Government, which will not fail them, if they lay down their arms ". (Here certain stalwarts on the Right murmured.) " Gentlemen, there can be no indulgence for crime, only for ignorance." [2]

The Assembly, as if to show its calmness of mind, proceeded to discuss a municipal law creating liberal institutions all over France, including Paris.[3] This lasted till April 14th ; after that they discussed a measure on the payment of rent and a Bill on Press offences, together with various petitions.

Meanwhile the Siege progressed. In Paris the vigorous Cluseret was " Delegate for War ", and conscription was enforced ; this was highly unpopular and led to so many desertions that it was forbidden to leave the city.[4]

On April 26th Thiers felt strong enough to take the offensive, and on May 9th won his first important success — the capture of Fort d'Issy. The day was kept as a festival

---

[1] On the side of the Commune Flourens and Duval were both killed ; at Courbevoie an incident occurred which decided the attitude of the Government troops (if they had any need for it). A doctor named Pasquier advanced unarmed towards the insurgents and said some words in favour of peace ; he was shot down, and the Versailles troops full of indignation rushed forward to avenge him. Hanotaux, i. 196 ; Simon, *Gouv. de M. Thiers*, i. 325-6.

[2] *Annales*, t. 2, pp. 217-29.

[3] For the discussion on this law (including a short-lived crisis — the first of so many — between Thiers and the Assembly) see pp. 461-2.

[4] Simon, *Gouv. de M. Thiers*, i. 352.

at Versailles ; the victors marched back singing, their cannon covered with lilies and laurels. The weather was exquisite, with spring in the air, and crowds came out to receive them, bareheaded and clapping their hands ; the windows were full of waving handkerchiefs ; Léon de Maleville, one of the Vice-presidents of the Assembly, made a speech of congratulation in the Place d'Armes, to which they replied by shouts of "Vive l'Assemblée! Vive la France!"[1]

Thiers replied to all those who came to him asking for favourable conditions of peace : "Do you speak in the name of the Commune ? If so, I cannot speak to you." When they answered that they came as private citizens, asking for an assurance that the leaders of the insurrection should be spared and that the Army should not enter Paris, he answered : "I have no engagements to make. . . . The guilty, whoever they are, will have to submit to the law . . . as for the Army, it is at home everywhere in France ; it will plant the tricolour in the capital where the red flag has flown."[2]

The serious problem of negotiation lay in the provinces ; the great Republican centres of the South were hesitating whether or not to follow the example of Paris ; Lyons had been for three days (March 22nd-25th) in the hands of revolutionary *fédérés*. At Saint-Étienne the Préfet M. de l'Espée was murdered ; at Marseilles the Commune was proclaimed and lasted thirteen days.

The Maires of Lyons, Marseilles, Grenoble, Toulon, Bordeaux, Nantes, and other southern cities came in deputation to Thiers ; they were quite outspoken in their

---

[1] Claveau, pp. 144-5.

[2] *Notes et souvenirs*, p. 135. Hector Pessard (*Mes petits papiers*, ii. 45) says : "At the Ministry of the Interior they passed their time opening letters in which correspondents, as imprudent as they were unscrupulous, offered their services and promised for a reasonable sum to bring Paris back to submission. A cynical but practical soldier wrote to Picard, ' Give me a hundred francs and I will kill my captain '."

demands. Paris had declared that the Republic was in danger : if he would assure them that the Republic was safe, they would answer for the towns they represented ; if not, they could give no assurances that the revolution would not spread over the south.

What did Thiers answer ? He says himself : " I told them that doubtless there were in the Assembly men, who favoured the restoration of the Monarchy, but there was no plan to overthrow the existing constitution and, if there were, I would take no part in carrying it out ".[1]

If that is all which he said, no one could find fault with it ; the Pact of Bordeaux guaranteed complete neutrality between Royalists and Republicans, and Thiers was pledged to resist any attempt at the moment to restore the Comte de Chambord, whether by force or by a vote of the Assembly. But it is difficult to believe that the Republicans of the South would have been contented with a declaration of neutrality, which they had all heard before, and it is hard not to suppose that Thiers promised to support the Republic by every means in his power ;[2] it is believed (though there is no direct evidence) that he entered into a secret compact with Henon, the Maire of Lyons — Thiers promised the Republic and the Maire promised support against Paris. At any rate it is a certain fact that the

[1] *Notes et souvenirs*, p. 136.

[2] Thiers afterwards maintained that he was only personally pledged not to vote for the Monarchy by the declaration to the southern delegates. Everything turns on the careful distinction between two periods contemplated by the Pact of Bordeaux : (1) a period of reconstruction during which Thiers had promised to be neutral, and (2) a period of constituent action when Thiers, like everybody else, regained freedom of action. The ambiguities underlying the Pact were (a) that no one knew exactly when the first period ended and the second began, and (b) even during the first period, " neutrality " was a difficult idea ; the actual form of government was republican, and, just in so far as the period of reconstruction was successful, the cause of the Republic gained. As Thiers said later, " Could I be expected to govern badly so as not to help the republican ideal ? " The fact of the matter is that the pact was a political reality, just as long as the dangers of France were evident enough to silence party ambitions, and not a moment longer.

radicals and freemasons of the South repudiated the Commune.[1]

On April 27th Thiers, in course of a speech on the general situation, took the opportunity of reminding the Assembly that " there exists no conspiracy here against the form of government, which you found in existence and which you are keeping in existence without committing yourselves as to the future. You have all sacrificed your personal opinions, I do not say for ever, but for the moment." Audren de Kerdrel answered for the Right. " No, gentlemen, you will not conspire against any Government but neither will you conspire against the will of the country. . . . It is because we are in such a terrible situation that we have made this great sacrifice for the good of France — the sacrifice of keeping back the expression of our real convictions." Here the Left interrupted : " What are your real convictions ? Let us hear them." " It would be disastrous ", Kerdrel went on, " to let it be supposed that we are in any doubt as to the institutions which this country needs." At this point Langlois, standing at the foot of the tribune, called out excitedly : " Yes, now is the time to speak out what we think. You shall see what we stand for ; we have been sent here to defend the sovereignty of the people — that is the Republic." He was sent back to his seat, and the President hastened to put an end to a debate which threatened to be so alarming.[2]

So far there had been no conflict between Thiers and the majority, but rumours of his interview with the southern delegates began to fly about, and on May 11th Mortimer Ternaux questioned the Government as to a statement

[1] Halévy, *Fin des notables*, p. 34. He adds that the Freemason hierarchy showed their hostility to the Commune in various ways ; they repudiated the demand of the Paris Lodges for a truce, and, in after years, they rejected the demand for an amnesty as being " political " and outside their functions (p. 36, note).

[2] *Annales*, t. 2, pp. 734-40.

professing to bear the signature of the Maire of Bordeaux, in which it was asserted that Thiers had promised, if the Commune surrendered, to let all the leaders escape except those concerned in the murder of the Generals. Ternaux was an old member of the Right Centre ; he had protested against the *coup d'état* of 1851 ; he was an old friend of Thiers, and a fellow historian of the French Revolution, having written a book on the Terror.

He was received with persistent interruptions from the Left and from the bench of Ministers ; Dufaure called out, " You are playing a sinister part " ; Jules Simon said, " You may be doing great harm to France ".

When he sat down, Thiers came to the tribune in a perfect tempest of passion ; his grey hair stood on end ; he could hardly speak for fury. He asked pardon for his emotion ; it was too much, after all his services to the country, to have to deal with such frivolous obstruction. Ternaux, sustained by the Right, protested against the phrase. Thiers shouted back at them : " I am right ; I repeat it ; I am right. . . . I cannot govern under such conditions." The Right were surprised at the outburst. " Who is attacking you ? " they asked. " My resignation is ready ", he continued, and he ended with an insulting phrase, which the Right never forgave, " There are persons here, who are in too much of a hurry. Wait a little while, and we shall be in Paris ; then there will be no more danger, and you will find the task of governing equal to your capacity and your courage." The Right protested ; poor Ternaux, hoarse and desperate, declared he had never dreamed of attacking the chief of the Executive. Thiers was implacable. " I regard myself as attacked and insulted. . . . I demand an explanation of your outrageous conduct." Ternaux bowed his head ; he said he could only regret that Thiers had broken for no reason a friendship of thirty years ; he fell ill in the December of that year, and died, it was said, of a broken heart. A vote of confidence in the Government was carried, only nine members of the Extreme Right voting against it.[1]

Thiers's bursts of temper are classical ; eye-witnesses are never agreed as to whether they were spontaneous or calculated. In this particular case it seemed out of all proportion to the circumstances. The Right had not breathed a word of criticism ; Ternaux quite sincerely believed he was helping the Government by giving them the chance of repudiating calumnies. " One does not take up a great stone to crush a fly " is Hector Pessard's comment on the incident.[2] No doubt, like many very competent people, Thiers hated being criticised ; deputies, new to public life, who had only seen the Chief of the Executive at Bordeaux, courteous, deferential and conciliatory, must have been astonished at the outburst of May 11th. But at Bordeaux Thiers was a candidate for office ; at Versailles, he knew himself indispensable. No doubt he knew that deputies were criticising him in every corner under their breath ; he had resented the committee " of supervision " as he called it — the body they had set up to work with him ; even in the calm retrospect of his *Memoirs* he says bitterly : " They would perhaps have prevented me from taking Paris, if I had allowed myself to be guided by them ".[3]

His own account of the Ternaux incident is as follows : " He questioned me, as if I had betrayed the cause of order, while I was wearing myself out in efforts to defend it ; indignant at so much ingratitude, I answered his questions harshly ".[4]

But it is hard to suppose that he had so little control

[1] *Annales*, t. 2, pp. 912-18 ; Claveau, pp. 127-31.
[2] *Mes petits papiers*, ii. 74.
[3] *Notes et souvenirs*, p. 126.
[4] *Ibid.* p. 136. It is difficult to be impressed by the pathetic picture we get, in Jules Simon and elsewhere, of poor Thiers wearing himself out to save France, while wicked deputies were always trying to obstruct his work ; it is safe to say that few sovereign assemblies have ever committed such dictatorial powers to one man — and that a man they secretly mistrusted.

over himself as to insult the majority so grievously and for
so little ; some have thought that it was all bluff intended
to divert the attention of the Chamber from the embarrassing subject of his commitments to the southern republicans.
Hector Pessard, who knew him well, believes that it
was really directed over the heads of the Right to the
Comte de Chambord, whose manifesto had appeared on
May 8th,[1] in which he said, "What I demand is to
preside over the destinies of France as head of the Royal
House ".

Au fond, Thiers hated the Legitimists ; as far as he
believed in Monarchy at all, it was in the Monarchy of
July " without priests or nobles ". " If only the Dukes
would leave us alone ", he used to say. On this occasion
he thought it safe (for whatever reason) to let himself go
and to defy their King and their Dukes — he, the little
bourgeois, who knew they could not do without him. " In
a week ", he had said, " the danger will be over." But he
knew it was not so ; he knew that, even after the recapture
of Paris, problems would remain that he alone could solve.
" Wait a little while ! " he had shouted to the Royalists.
They waited two years for their revenge.

On May 16th, as though to reassure Thiers that peace
reigned between them for the moment, a member of the
Right took the lead in moving for the restoration, at the
public expense, of Thiers' house, demolished by order of
the insurgents.[2] The same day seventeen members of the
Left proposed that the Republic should be immediately

---

[1] *Mes petits papiers,* ii. 74. See pp. 317-20 of this work.

[2] " It was decided to send the linen [from Thiers' house] to the ambulance,
the books and objects of art to the museum, and libraries ; the furniture was
to be sold by auction. The ' Vengeur ' proposed to leave one stone with the
inscription, ' Here was the house of the man, who burned Paris ' " (Malo,
Thiers, pp. 508-9). On May 16th Thiers wrote to Duvergier : " My house is
destroyed. I have neither hearth nor home, and the house where I have entertained you all for forty years, is utterly broken down. My collections are
scattered. Add several calumnies and you have the reward which the service
of one's country brings " (Dreyfus, *Thiers contre la guerre,* etc., p. 338).

proclaimed the definite form of government ; the Assembly refused to vote " urgence ".[1]

On May 22nd Thiers was able to announce the glad news that the troops had entered Paris. Henri de Blowitz, a journalist making his reputation as correspondent to *The Times*, relates that he was watching the bombardment, when a young American lady near him called out, " Look, someone is waving a white flag from the battlements ! " At the same time there was a general move forward of troops. De Blowitz hailed a cab, and drove to the Versailles Prefecture at top speed ; he found Thiers taking a walk in the courtyard, and called out, " M. le Président, the troops are entering Paris ! " Thiers gave a start and, for the moment, could not believe such unexpected piece of good fortune ; then he suddenly recovered himself and said quietly, " When did this happen ? " " At four o'clock." " Good ", said the President of the Council, who could never admit that anything happened anywhere without his knowing all about it. " General Douay was punctual to about ten minutes." [2]

As a matter of fact, the signal from the walls had been given by Ducatel, a private citizen, who, seeing that the

---

[1] *Annales*, t. 3, pp. 30-31. On May 18th the Treaty of Frankfort was ratified by 438 votes to 98 (see pp. 442-4).

[2] *Memoirs of Blowitz*, p. 35. The reference is to General Douay, who had already spent a fruitless night waiting for a supposed agent to open the gates (Thiers, *Memoirs*, p. 138). De Blowitz himself says nothing about Thiers' pretence that he had expected it, and it has the marks of one of those good anecdotes, which begin " It would be just like him to say " and end " He *said* ". But it is a delicious trait of character, and comes from Hector Pessard (*Mes petits papiers*, ii. 62), who was a great friend of Thiers and very well informed as to the *entourage* of the Prefecture. On the death of de Blowitz (1903), the following lines appeared in *Punch* :

" Sweet Peace descends on Ministers like rain,
    And diplomats see half their thraldom o'er,
Since Court can keep their secrets once again,
    Europe is free : de Blowitz is no more."

If these chapters were a complete history of the Commune, we should have had to mention Edward Bower (a master at Harrow), who was present at Paris during the Commune. He wrote a paper remarkably favourable to the Commune (*A Memoir of Mr. Bower*, pp. 336-56).

fire from the Montretout battery had demolished the Point de Jour gate and that it was deserted, had communicated with the attacking troops. Thiers and MacMahon entered the city together, and took up their quarters at the Trocadero. Thiers then returned to Versailles, where the Assembly voted by acclamation that " the armies of land and sea [1] and the Chief of the Executive of the French Republic had deserved well of their country ". In the enthusiasm of victory, resentments of the past were forgotten ; Thiers thanked the Assembly " for the greatest honour he had ever received " ; deputies crowded round to shake his hand, and Jules Simon kissed him on the cheeks.[2]

But, though the victory was now certain, there remained to be faced one of the most terrible weeks in French history. Apart from the horror of the hand-to-hand fighting at the barricades, the defenders of Paris stained their last moments by two great crimes — the burning of the monuments and the massacre of the hostages.

On Wednesday, May 24th, Versailles awoke to find the streets covered with charred pieces of paper and full of fire brigades being rushed up to put out the conflagrations in the capital. As early as May 16th, Vallès had written in his newspaper the only memorable phrase the Commune produced : " Not a soldier shall enter Paris. If M. Thiers is a chemist, he will understand what we mean." The library of the Louvre was soaked in petrol and set on fire ; the Tuileries Palace, the Hôtel-de-Ville, and the Gare de Lyon were reduced to ashes. Each evening, deputies and officials gathered on the terraces of the Versailles Palace, watching the bursts of light on the horizon and listening to the noise of distant detonations. People said to one another, " That is not far from me ; perhaps that is my house burning ".[3]

---

[1] To include the Marines.   [2] Claveau, p. 153.

[3] Simon, *Gouv. de M. Thiers*, i. 445. Claveau, p. 157. We find a touching echo of the general emotion in the MS. *procès-verbal* of the sitting of the Commission de decentralisation for May 24th, which ends " The Commission, on

On May 24th Thiers recounted the terrible events in Paris amid cries of indignation and grief. The Assembly were in a bad humour ; they suspected him of a disposition to over-clemency. He declared that punishment would be " implacable but according to the law, under the law, and by the law ". " If the laws are not sufficient ", called out a deputy, " we must make new ones." Thiers said he would leave the right of pardon to the Assembly ; a member replied, " It is a right of the sovereign and belongs to us already ". He became restless and said : " I expected a little repose ; I am in despair ; the difficulties are greater than ever. If you would relieve me from the burden, I should be grateful." " No one is suggesting it ", they cried, but the enthusiasm of Monday night had evaporated.[1]

The next day, during a statement by Ernest Picard, a voice called out " And the hostages ? " The Archbishop of Paris, Mgr. Darboy, M. Deguerry (the curé of the Madeleine), President Bonjean, Gustave Chaudey, and a great number of priests, Jesuits and Dominicans, had been seized by the Commune as hostages ; the Archbishop had written to Thiers saying that he understood that his captors were ready to exchange him for Blanqui, and imploring the Government to consent. The Council of Ministers and the Commission of fifteen appointed by the Assembly both considered the letter with deep emotion and both resolved to reject it. Thiers replied (though the letter never reached the Archbishop) : " To accept the offer would be to consecrate and extend the abominable system of hostages and allow the men, who have Paris in their hands, to multiply arrests, in order to compel the Government to consent to fresh exchanges ".[2]

hearing the lamentable news of the burning of the Paris monuments, at once suspended the sitting " (Archives of the Chamber of Deputies).

[1] *Annales*, t. 3, pp. 116-19.

[2] Simon, *Gouv. de M. Thiers*, i. 456. Claveau, p. 156.

Thiers trusted either that the gaolers would not dare to execute the prisoners, or else that the troops would arrive in time to save them. But the threat was carried out; Chaudey was murdered on May 21st, the Archbishop and his fellow-prisoners on the next day.

On May 28th Marshal MacMahon issued the following proclamation :

INHABITANTS OF PARIS,

The Army of France has come to save you ; Paris is delivered. At four o'clock our soldiers captured the last positions held by the insurgents. Today the struggle is over ; order, work, and security begin again.[1]

We, who have seen the revolutionary aftermath of the Great War, can look on the Paris Revolution not with less horror but with less bewilderment than contemporaries. The Franco-Prussian War, if not precisely the first war on the modern scale, gave the first example of the defeat of a nation on a modern scale ; and we know what social troubles and disturbances result. But we can also learn to admire the courage and resourcefulness of France, almost at her last gasp, yet reasserting her right to live.

[1] Simon, *Gouv. de M. Thiers*, i. 469.

PART II

THE NATIONAL ASSEMBLY—PARTIES
AND PERSONALITIES

(MAY–SEPTEMBER)

CHAPTER I

THE PALACE AND THE ASSEMBLY

FEW cities have had such strange vicissitudes as Versailles, such alternations of light and shade ; it was once the very centre of fashion and splendour, setting the tone to Europe and spreading faint copies of its court and ceremonial to many an emulous dukedom in Germany and Italy, the city of the Roi-Soleil and all ablaze with his glory. After a short and sharp experience in the revolutionary furnace, it sank to the condition of a museum under the July Monarchy, and of a pleasure resort under the Second Empire. It woke up again in 1871 to find itself the residence of a Prussian King, the scene of peace negotiation and of the proclamation of the German Empire. During the Commune it became an armed camp, and then, for a short but brilliant period, the political and social rival of the capital ; then, as the growing fortunes of the Republic summoned Parliament back to Paris, Versailles sank again into her dream of the past ; her parks and gardens were haunted once more by the ghosts of Marie Antoinette and her court, disturbed now and then by the bustle of a presidential election or the signature of a new treaty.

In May 1871 the city was very much alive ; the roll of drums, the crowds of deputies, journalists, ladies of fashion, kept the ghosts far away. In the great court of the Palace, Louis XIV on his bronze horse looked down " with haughty surprise " on white tents and bivouac fires ; in the Rue des Réservoirs, one could " fancy oneself in the foyer of the Théâtre-Français on a first night " ; all Parisian society was there. Officers told stories of their escapes from German prisons or from the Commune; Edmond About, the dramatist, walked arm in arm with Gustave Doré, the painter. In one group Renan held forth upon the siege of Jerusalem, and preached the necessity of a concrete symbol of authority: "Once the Holy Oil, brought by an angel and poured upon the brows of our kings, stood for such a principle — an absurd symbol, I grant you, but useful, perhaps necessary; the people always obey an authority better, when its principle passes their understanding". In another group, General Trochu defended certain members of the National Defence Government: "I saw Jules Favre perform the noblest action I have ever seen. Not a word against Jules Ferry; he is full of courage and resource." Twelve o'clock strikes, and there is a rush for seats at the hard-worked Hôtel des Réservoirs, while a battery of artillery gallops off to the front and passes the ambulances returning with the wounded.[1]

From time to time, the long files of prisoners from Paris passed through the streets — pale and in rags, but still hurling defiance at the furious spectators, who tried to throw themselves upon the hated Communards. One day the Bishop of Orleans met them, as he was going to his house in the Rue Satory. "Look!" he exclaimed, "it is an army of atheists; but the guilty are those, who have led them astray; it is the infidel writers who have pushed them on."[2]

During the critical month of May ecclesiastical ceremonies played no small part in the social life of Versailles. The Cathedral of St. Louis was crowded on Ascension Day, May 18th, when collections were made for the orphans

---

[1] Pessard, *Mes petits papiers*, Series 2, pp. 11-15.

[2] Bishop Dupanloup declared in his Pastoral, "Ah, you would not recognise the Divinity! Well, the power of Satan himself has appeared to you." He wrote privately to Thiers: "Do not strive merely to be clever and to get France out of her scrape, but make her once more religious, and therefore great" (Lagrange, *Vie de Dupanloup*, ii. 402).

of the war ; Mme Thiers and Mme la Maréchale de MacMahon took the offerings — a curious alliance in view of future events.   On May 28th the public prayers (ordered by the Assembly) to " beseech God to pacify our civil discords ", were held before a large concourse.   The Papal Nuncio, Mgr. Chigi, and two Vicars-Apostolic were present ; Thiers was in his seat, surrounded by Ministers and deputies, and to them the Bishop of Versailles addressed himself in an eloquent sermon.   " By the act that you are accomplishing ", he said, " you are declaring that there is a higher light, which you need to settle the terrible problems before you. . . . You have done a great act, and one that is profoundly instructive for the people." [1]

From the day that MacMahon's proclamation announced that the Commune was vanquished, Versailles gradually lost the look of a military camp, though it still remained a garrison town, where bugles sounded and officers galloped all day long.   In the evening it became a quiet place ; a few deputies only were able to afford hotel prices — at the Réservoirs, the Petit Vatel, the Chasse, the Plessis ; Thiers was forced by a suspicious majority to sleep every night at the Palace of the Presidency — " Palace of penitence ", he called it, for he would much rather have been in Paris.

The great moment was that of the arrival of the parliamentary trains,[2] at 11 A.M., the " Committee " train

---

[1] Dreyfus, *La République de M. Thiers*, p. 10.   On Wednesday, June 7th, a Requiem was sung at Notre-Dame for Mgr. Darboy and the other ecclesiastics, who had perished in the massacre of the hostages.   Several persons in the crowd caused alarm by their behaviour.   John Lemoinne said in the *Débats* : " Many of them had come to see what they themselves had done " (Dreyfus, p. 13).   Thiers' absence was much remarked.   " A sort of murmur rose from the crowd : ' He won't come.— Who ? — The Executive.— No.— It is impossible. — Why shouldn't he come ? — He is afraid perhaps. — You don't mean it. — One never knows ' " (Gyp, *La Joyeuse Enfance de la 3ᵉ République*, p. 61).

[2] The details that follow as to the Palace and parliamentary life are mostly taken from Paul Bosq, *Assemblée nationale*, pp. 79-107 ; Murray, *Round about France*, pp. 21-9 ; and a pamphlet called *La Marmite aux lois*.

bringing the members of various committees, who did their
work in the mornings, and at 2 P.M. the "Grande
vitesse" for the general mass of deputies. The St-Lazare
station at Paris was the scene of great bustle and animation; under the Empire it had been deserted and un-
fashionable. The Court and Ministers went to St-Cloud by
road, and it was said that on the platform you only saw
cotton-spinners from Rouen, farmers from Brittany, and
excursionists from England doing the cheap route. But
1871 reversed the fortunes of the line. At this station the
German officers from the Versailles garrison alighted in
mufti to see the sights of Paris; from this station, the
society of the capital rushed back, after their three months'
exile, to see whether the Commune had left their houses
standing, and from this station they flowed back again to
watch the political drama at Versailles. The start of the
two trains was very different; at ten, busy members of
committees got into their carriages with sheaves of papers
under their arms, turning round to throw a last question
at their escort of experts — lawyers, engineers, scientists,
from whom they had been drawing information for their
reports. But the departure of the one o'clock train was a
public event; in times of great political excitement there
was an extra supply of police — not without reason, for
it was on this platform that the Bonapartists mobbed
Gambetta in 1874. More innocent onlookers thronged to
get a glimpse of famous deputies. One day, a Bonapartist
deputy nudged a Radical and said, pointing to a loafer
with a pipe in his mouth and his cap on his ear, "One
of your constituents, I think". "He is more likely to
be one of yours", retorted the Radical. They settled
the dispute by asking him point-blank; he slowly removed the pipe from his mouth: "Je suis légitimisse",
he said.

The train was announced, and deputies hurried to the
carriages, torn between a desire to look important and

anxiety to secure an apartment for themselves. Meanwhile the Parisian journalists packed their own carriages, merry as schoolboys (their duty was not so much to take down speeches as to give to the public sketches of deputies by means of words or pictures) ; if eight Republicans or Royalists secured a carriage, their dignity soon wore off and they laughed and exchanged *bons mots*, but, if a journalist slipped in among them, they became silent and solemn.

The hour in the train, coming or going, was a unique feature of the French parliamentary life of the period, and may partly account for the restless agitation, that marked the National Assembly ; members obviously arrive more excited, when they have had a railway journey together than when each alights separately from his own car. It was in a first-class carriage that Cyprien Girerd found the famous document, which was supposed to prove the illegal practices of the Bonapartist party ; in the last year of the Assembly a crowd of Right Centre deputies surrounded the Duc de Pasquier in his compartment, urging him to take office in the Buffet Government. One of the Bonapartist plans for a *coup d'état* was to block the St-Cloud tunnel between Paris and Versailles, and catch the parliamentary train in a trap.[1]

At the Versailles station there was another crowd to greet them ; the deputies, who did not wish to walk, had to take tumble-down cabs, or choose one of the buses that always broke down on the way. One day Arago shouted, from a bus crowded with Republicans, to the Royalist general Changarnier, " Quick, general ! there is one place left " ; then seeing him hesitate : " Are you afraid, by any chance ? " " Not afraid but horrified ", murmured the General, hastening away. A good-natured and curious crowd accompanied the deputies to the Place d'Armes, sometimes right up to the door of the Palace.

[1] Du Barail, *Souvenirs*, iii. 322.

The monarchical splendours of the classical building [1]
did not perhaps delight the Royalists as much as might
have been expected. The French Monarchy had become
Romantic. Victor Hugo and Lamartine had chanted over
the cradle of the Comte de Chambord ; when the Comte
visited Paris, he did not spare a moment for the classical
Louvre ; it was *de mode* among the Legitimists to prefer
St. Louis to Louis XIV ; Versailles spoke to many of the
humiliation of their order. The Roi Soleil horrified the
dévots by his Gallicanism. But if he was hardly an orthodox Catholic, what of Louis XV ? Was he a Christian at
all ? An earnest deputy (of the Right) once asked the
House, amid loud laughter, " When our honourable President comes here to take his seat, when he passes through
the ranks of representatives, who salute him respectfully,
while the drums roll outside, do you know what is the last
statue he passes ? it is the statue of la Pompadour *en
négligé galant* ".[2] Even the Orleanist, de Broglie, in his great
speech against the Republic, appealed not to the palace,
in which he was speaking, but to *all* the royal palaces of
France.[3] The buildings might find their critics, but the

[1] Saint-Simon, who extended his hatred from the builder to the building,
wrote : " Looked at from the court, the narrowness of the place is suffocating,
and the huge wings run off on every side without any centre. Seen from the
garden, the beauty of the ensemble is delightful, but it looks like a palace
that has been burned and still lacks its top floors and its roof. . . . One
could go on for ever enumerating the monstrous faults of this palace, so vast
and built at so vast an expense " (*Cour de Louis XIV*, p. 387, Nelson edition).

[2] Speech of Jean Brunet (8/9/71). An eccentric Royalist deputy, named
de Gavardie, complained of the statues of Nymphs, which decorated the
gardens, " evidently Republican, since they are sansculotte ". After vainly
proposing that they should be properly dressed, he moved that a committee
of bishops should be appointed to inspect them (Bosq, p. 136).

[3] *Séance du 23/7/74.* " But if men should hold their peace, the stones themselves would cry out the benefits and memories of Monarchy. . . . They would
meet you in every shape, the inscriptions of our monuments, the vaults of
our palaces would recall them to the memory of all." On the other hand,
Martial Delpit, a Royalist deputy, writes in his journal : " The work of the
great King pursues me in this Versailles, where everything is so great, and we
are so small. I never appreciated Versailles so much before — this symbolical
symmetry, this complete harmony. . . . I went out (in an icy wind) to visit

terraces and the gardens — what legislature in the world
had more lovely surroundings ?   Standing on the three
pink steps of marble ("les trois marches roses" of de
Musset's poem),[1] one could see marvellous sunsets above
the trees ; on the Terrace, the cool air soothed the ardour of
political discussions, and Ministers and deputies moved
about carrying cups of coffee to the gay throngs of fashionable ladies.   In the long avenues, when debates were dull,
colleagues strolled arm in arm.   Here, in the garden, was
Thiers' favourite ride, till he became nervous at having to
pass under a bridge.   "Someone might hide", he said,
"in an angle of the masonry, and put out his arm as the
carriage passes and kill his man easily."[2]   Here, in the
moonlight of the summer of 1874, Falloux and de Broglie
walked up and down, planning together how the King
was to return in the autumn.   Here, in the garden of the
Petit Trianon, Gambetta and his beloved Léonie gave and
took the pledges of a marriage, which was never to be.

From two to three in the afternoon, the crowds of
deputies cross the Royal Court of the Palace, between the

les trois marches roses.   If I had been a poet, I should have evoked all the
different kinds of greatness from the greatest century of our history" (quoted
in Loménie, *Restauration manquée*, p. 95).

[1] De Musset's well-known poem was written in February 1849 :

> "Mais, souvient-il, mon ami
> De ces marches de marbre rose,
> En allant à la pièce d'eau
> Du côté de l'Orangerie
> A gauche, en sortant du château ?
> C'était par là, je le parie,
> Que venait le roi sans pareil
> Le soir, au coucher de soleil,
> Voir dans la forêt en silence,
> Le jour s'enfuir et se cacher
> (Si toutefois en Sa présence
> Le soleil osait se coucher). . . .
> Dites-nous, marches gracieuses,
> Les rois, les princes, les prélats
> Et les marquis à grand fracas
> Et les belles ambitieuses,
> Dont vous avez compté les pas."

[2] Malo, *Thiers*, p. 524.

" Ailes des Ministres " (the Wings, used to accommodate
the King's Ministers) on the right and left ; they pass by
the empty Chapel — once considered as a possible meeting-
place for the Assembly — and, shivering slightly at the
cold air, enter the Gallery of Tombs ; this stone hall, full
of statues reclining on their deathbeds or kneeling in
their armour, was the most animated spot in the Palace ;
it was the lobby of the House, and here at the beginning,
or during suspensions of the sittings, party groups formed
and re-formed, party manœuvres were settled and party
questions were discussed.[1] Sometimes the Gallery resounded from end to end with angry recriminations, as in
1871 when the " question of the Princes " was on the tapis,
or in 1875, when the tumultuous debate on the choice of
the 75 senators disturbed the last hours of the Assembly.
The Gallery was supposed to be jealously guarded from the
intrusion of journalists, and many were the tricks those
adventurous gentlemen played to evade the vigilance of
Baze, the stern Questeur of the Assembly ; sometimes
they slipped in, on the arm of a deputy ; at other times
they boldly crossed the hall to buy a cigar and lingered on
the way back — not always profitably, as when one of
them badgered the Duc de Broglie for information. " Sir ",
said the Duc, " can you keep a secret ? " " Certainly ",
answered the eager reporter. " Well," was the retort, " so
can I."

It was not only the journalists, who disliked Baze ;
living on his reputation as one of the Questeurs, who, in
1851, had tried to protect the Legislative Assembly against
a *coup d'état* by proposing a military guard, and had been
imprisoned in consequence, he carried his iron will everywhere ; he stopped free wines at the bar ; he reduced the
quality of food at the restaurant, and malicious tongues
said that he used the profits to send perfumes and tooth-

---

[1] The leaders of the Right used to gather round the tomb of Marie de
Medici.

brushes to his wife. Innumerable stories were told of him : how he had been heard scolding the fishes in the canal ; how, when the King of Bavaria was shown over the kitchens, he told one of his suite to tip Baze five louis ; how the journalists took their revenge by sending him a letter with an illegible signature, followed by the very legible words, " influential constituent ", and how three times the Gallery of Tombs resounded with the voice of the usher calling out in vain, " Where is the gentleman who wishes to see M. Baze ? "

At the end of the Palace's North Wing, there was a small vestibule in front of heavy red curtains, which covered the entrance to the Salle des Séances ; we lift them and are at once in the midst of the eighteenth century.

It had been Louis XV's Salle d'Opéra ; the red and gold colouring dated from the restoration by Louis-Philippe, but the plump Cupids, the flutes and violins carved on the pillars, the mirrors in the galleries, the glass chandeliers and lustres, tinkling with crowns and grapes of crystal, all recalled the light-hearted elegance of the older court, and seemed a setting for " Dresden-china pastorals among biscuit-like rocks and Grand Opera trees, in the shade of which Flora and Amaryllis might pirouette to the tune of an old minuet ".[1]   The ceiling — painted by Durameau and representing Apollo preparing wreaths for the great — had been replaced by a glass roof, which lightened the dark chamber but made it look like a railway station.

The Royal Theatre — begun by the architect Gabriel in 1753 and completed by Leroy in 1770 [2] — had seen some interesting (and one historic) scenes. It was opened at the celebrations of the marriage of the Dauphin and Marie-Antoinette, when Racine's *Athalie* and Voltaire's *Tancrède*

---

[1] Camille Pelletan, *Théâtre de Versailles*, p. 7.

[2] Saint-Simon says of the building in Louis XIV's time : " In spite of the many rooms, piled one on another, there is no hall for plays or for banquets or for dancing " (*Cour de Louis XIV*, p. 387, Nelson Edition).

were performed ; it was used for the reception of the
Emperor Joseph II. Here on the 1st of October, 1789, was
given the famous banquet to the Régiment de Flandre,
which sealed the fate of the monarchy ; Carlyle thus
describes it : " The Queen enters there, issuing from her
state-rooms, like the moon from clouds, the fairest, unhappy Queen of hearts . . . she descends amid splendour
and acclaim, walks queen-like round the tables . . . and
now, the band striking up, ' O Richard, O mon roi, l'univers
t'abandonne ', could man do other than rise to height of
pity, of loyal valour ? " [1]

During the Revolution it was occupied by the Popular
Society of Versailles ; on August 10th, 1837, when Louis-
Philippe turned the Palace into a National Museum,
Molière's *Misanthrope* was performed here, and on July
25th, 1855, Napoleon III gave an official fête here to Queen
Victoria.[2]

The architect, who had been commissioned to turn an
Opera-House into a legislative Hall, had covered over the
seats with a ballroom floor up to the height of the " pre-
miers loges " ; unlike most French assemblies, the Versailles
Parliament sat on the level and was thus obliged to dispense
with the familiar rows of ascending seats and the geo-
graphical distinctions of Mountain and Plain. The Extreme
Left was placed where the curtain fell ; here sat Littré of
dictionary fame, " the Rationalist saint " as he was called,
first to arrive and last to leave. He spent the day correcting his proofs, and was heard to complain that, as he had
to catch the morning train from Paris, " the middle part of
the day is entirely lost to me ". Bent over his work, like
a monkey, spectacled and with a blue velvet skull-cap, he
took no part in the debates and hardly lifted up his eyes
to where, at the opposite end of the curtain, on the " bench
of churchwardens " — as the Extreme Right was nick-

---

[1] *French Revolution*, Bk. VII. c. 2.
[2] The Senate sat here from 1875 to 1879.

named — sat the Bishop of Orleans, who had retired from the Academy rather than sit side by side with the Positivist Littré.

The pit was divided up by an open passage in the shape of a gridiron (thus : ⊢⌐) ; on the Right, amid a sea of bald heads, could be distinguished the white hair of the Papal Baron, de Chaurand ; on the Left Gambetta sprawled on his bench, surrounded by a crowd of supporters, whose requests he succeeded in answering, all at once, without missing a word of the debate and while throwing in, now and then, an effective interruption in his deep bass voice.

A deputy complained that " the Hall was meant for 450 members at most, while the 750 deputies and 30 employés filled it to overflowing . . . the noise round the tribune generally prevented not only the speaker's voice but even that of the President from reaching half the members ".[1] Lack of ventilation in a room, meant for night performances, was another cause of complaint. In the middle of the fierce constitutional debate of January 1875 voices were raised demanding more air — " On étouffe ici ".

Opposite the tribune, at the other end of the theatre behind a magnificent chandelier and under a recessed apse, was the Press Gallery — 50 seats for the Paris reporters and " annexes " for foreign reporters and those from the Departments. As may well be imagined, the tone of the Parisian journalists did not err on the side of respect for the majority of the Assembly. Extreme Republicanism was the vogue. Germain Casse, a friend of Gambetta, amused himself by calling the President of the Assembly a fat-head, and Camille Pelletan sat on the edge of the balustrade, his clothes untidy and his hair uncombed, sketching the bitter portraits of the Right, which he published later under the title of *Le Théâtre de Versailles*.

[1] Jean Brunet (*Séance du 8/9/71*).

Just underneath was the Ambassadors' Gallery ; here one day the Papal Legate, Mgr. Chigi, was listening to a debate on the Temporal Power, when he heard a great deal of noise above and looked up ; Pelletan caught sight of him and called out, " Hullo, here is a hostage " — a not very polished reference to the Commune.

Far different was the tone of the Visitors' Gallery ; a visit to Versailles was *de rigueur* in the world of fashion. One could meet them taking tea in the *pâtisseries*, dining in the Hôtel de Réservoirs, and buying up china in the antiquity shops. At the Assembly the great ladies of high society sat in their boxes, tittering when their husbands mounted the tribune, disappointed when they did not speak, shuddering when the wicked Republicans addressed the House. Defiant in the midst, never missing a sitting, surrounded by a court of Republican deputies, sat the wise Mme Adam, Gambetta's political Egeria ; when Gambetta's cavernous voice rolled through the Hall, the Royalist ladies shivered. " He roars ", they said one to the other. " Yes," retorted Mme Adam, drawing herself up, " he is a lion." [1] The rest of the general public were packed like herrings in the roof, where behind the grilled apertures — " ox-eyes ", as they are picturesquely called in French — they could hear, but see nothing.

The stage was surmounted by a gilt fleur-de-lys upheld by two angels ; below it was the tribune, reached on each side by steps and with two lamps on it, which were one day knocked over by an impetuous gesture of the gigantic Pouyer-Quertier.

All round were the huissiers [2] dressed in black, swords at their side and chains round their necks, moving about as

---

[1] Winifred Stephen, *Mme Adam*, p. 176.

[2] On the only occasion I visited the Chamber of Deputies, I was much struck by the paternal manner, in which the huissiers dealt with the Communist deputies, who were carrying a huge banner inscribed " Amnistie ". An unexpected sidelight on their duties as officials was revealed by the remark of one of them, " After the debate on the Amnesty we had to pick up the collar-studs, with which the floor of the Chamber was strewn ! "

debates grew warm with their soothing " Silence, gentlemen, if you please ". Near them stood the officials of the
Chamber in blue trousers and red waistcoats, presided over
by Bescherelles, a great character in his black uniform,
embroidered with gold palms, and his monocle. Even
Ministers approached him respectfully ; as was fitting, he
was a good Tory, and on the day when Thiers fell, recalling
memories of many an invasion of Parliament by the crowd,
he murmured, " This is the first revolution I have ever
seen carried out by honest men ".

Over this Assembly, in his chair of ivory and bronze,
presided Grévy, most correct of Republicans, most imperturbable of presidents.[1] He was perhaps surprised to
find himself at the head of a Royalist Assembly after having
fought in person during the street riots of 1830. But in his
mature years he was an enemy of revolutions ; he had
protested against the breaking up of the Corps Législatif
in September, and against Gambetta's refusal to convene
an Assembly ; it was he who had moved the famous
amendment to the 1848 Constitution — " The Assembly
delegates its powers to a citizen who receives the title of
President of the Council of Ministers ". When this was rejected as a result of Lamartine's great speech, after which
Louis Napoleon was elected President and destroyed the
Assembly, many an enemy of the Empire said pensively
to himself, " Ah, if only the Grévy amendment had
passed ! "

It was said of him that he had a real authority as
President, when he was not asleep, and there were times
when his attention wandered from the debate below (as on
the celebrated occasion which led to his resignation), but
it was never safe to assume that he was asleep. Jules
Simon describes him at meetings of the party under the

---

[1] " His round hat and long coat . . . seemed to say to the majority, ' I
am only the servant of the people ' — like Roland in his slippers before Louis
XVI " (Bosq, *Assemblée nationale*, p. 20).

Second Empire " looking as if he were slumbering in his armchair, sunk in immovable calm but following all that was said with his malicious eyes, stroking his bald head and his large whiskers, occasionally dropping a word that was listened to with respect, in a tired voice, with a serious, deliberate slowness that marked a balanced mind ".[1] His enemies said he was incurably lazy, and that he kept out of active politics from fear of responsibility ; that under an appearance of deep sagacity and virtue he concealed an amorous disposition, love of public-houses, and an insatiable avarice. A few days before he was elected President of the Republic to succeed MacMahon, a well-known journalist said of him, " He drinks, he has love-affairs, and is correct ; he is just the President to suit France ".[2]

Physically he was certainly not lazy, for he walked every day from his Paris house to the St-Lazare station ; he was an excellent billiard-player[3] and an adept at chess, where it was noted that he played a defensive game. It was rather caution than indolence, which kept him from playing a more active part. His mind was not very much open to new ideas ; his chief political conviction was scrupulous adherence to the letter of the law. In his one great speech — against the prorogation of the powers of Marshal MacMahon, delivered with slow, deliberate gestures and concentrated irony,[4] he attacked the proposal as unconstitutional ; in 1875 he refused to vote for the Republic, because he did not believe the Assembly had constituent powers. His character, wary and reserved, was as antipathetic as possible to Gambetta's flamboyant exuberance ; when Gambetta refused to convoke the National Assembly, Grévy said to him, " You are destined

---

[1] Simon, *Soir de ma journée*, p. 327.

[2] A. Vandam, *My Paris Notebook*, p. 338.

[3] One day a journalist asked an innkeeper in Grévy's district what he thought of the then President of the Republic. " What a billiard player ! " he exclaimed, " the best stroke in Franche-Comté " (*Portraits de Kel-Kun*, p. 7).

[4] Lacombe says of the speech that " it fell like a weight " (*Journal*, i. 241).

to die in the skin of a rebel ".[1] After Gambetta's Grenoble speech, Grévy said, " He floats on top, because he is completely empty ".[2] Years after, when Gambetta was President of the Council and Grévy President of the Republic, a lively discussion was dividing the Council of Ministers on the reform of the magistracy ; Grévy seemed asleep ; suddenly he said, " M. Gambetta, will you allow me an observation ? " All the Ministers leaned forward respectfully : " Do you know what I should do in your place ? " he went on in his slow drawl. Gambetta bowed interrogatively. " Well, in your place I should do nothing at all." [3]

As President of the Assembly he was so afraid of his personal feelings that, when Gambetta spoke, he either left the debate in charge of a Vice-President, or allowed the orator liberties he would never have conceded to another.[4]

He broke with the parliamentary tradition of presidential jokes, set by Dupin in the Assemblies of the Second Republic ; he was majestic and severe. " Looking at his shrewd solid face," a journalist wrote, " I used to see suddenly, plodding before my eyes through a restful country scene, the great white oxen, who all day long turn up the heavy soil in Doubs or Haute-Saône." [5]

It was said of him that he rang the presidential bell sharply with never more than three notes, and then leaned forward to assure his thrifty mind that he had not damaged the furniture.[6] But he was a good President, calm, impartial and with an imposing air, which kept both sides of the Chamber in order. One would not have supposed that in duller moments of the debate his eyes wandered to the ladies' gallery, but so it was ; this austere lawyer had been

[1] Grenville Murray, *Men of the Third Republic*, p. 55.   [2] Bosq, p. 146.
[3] Pessard, *Mes petits papiers*, i. 111.
[4] Murray, *Men of the Third Republic*, p. 56.
[5] L. Hubert, *Figures parlementaires*, quoted p. 130.
[6] Vandam, *My Paris Note-Book*, p. 250.

P

a friend and associate of Alfred de Musset, and it was said that his success with women was not less marked, because in his slow, deliberate way he studied the moves of the game, as though he were sitting at the chess-board.[1]

[1] *My Paris Note-Book,* pp. 328, 336.

CHAPTER II

THE ROYALIST PARTY AND THE QUESTION OF THE PRINCES

AFTER the defeat of the Commune, the National Assembly begins to occupy the foreground. From its first meeting in February till the end of May, the unceasing whirl of events had called for action rather than deliberation ; the settlement of the terms of Peace and the struggle with the Commune had thrown Thiers and the Executive into prominence, but the Royalist majority had no intention of being kept any longer in the shade, and it is the object of this and the following chapters to make a closer acquaintance with the personnel of the Assembly and the formation of parties.

The period from May to September (when the Assembly separated for their holidays) contains three notable political events, each of which shows a different section of the Assembly beginning to function. First, in June, the question of the position of the Orleanist Princes and the publication of the Chambord manifesto gives an opportunity of studying the parties of the Right. Secondly, the Republican successes at the July elections mark the beginning of party organisation on the Left. Thirdly, the " proposition Rivet ", which defined and regularised Thiers' powers, naturally leads to a consideration of Thiers' political action, and especially of his relation to the Left Centre, the nearest approach to a Ministerial party, which the abnormal state of French politics allowed.

(a) THE CÔTÉ DROIT FROM 1789 TO 1848

When in 1789 the States-General became the National Assembly, the Estates of the Noblesse and the Clergy took their seats on the right of the President's chair. They came for the most part slowly and reluctantly, partly under pressure from the Crown, partly as the result of internal discord. It was not many days since — at the opening ceremony — the Nobles had walked in procession, conspicuous in their cloth of gold, with their silk cloaks and lace waistcoats, wearing their plumed hats *à la* Henri Quatre ; the clergy in cassocks and cloaks, the Bishops in violet soutanes and rochets, while the Third Estate followed in sober black coats.[1]

Now the Right had ceased to be two separate Orders and had become merely a political opposition, generally outvoted, hooted from the gallery, " sheep before their butchers ", as one of their number described them. But such sentimental considerations must not blind us to the fact of their complete political incapacity. Mirabeau judged them with his usual sense of reality when he wrote : " The Right are no good for anything ; the stupid and senseless way they behave during the debates makes it impossible to take them seriously ".[2] No doubt the abolition of the Orders and the organisation of democratic suffrage under the new Constitution left them without any *raison d'être* and put them in the position, fatal in an elected assembly, of members without constituents. Still they had before them a task which might have called forth the highest qualities of statesmanship — the cause of social order to defend, a Church to protect against spoliation, and the great problem to solve of royalty and its place in the new world. Not one of them tried to face that question of monarchy in a democracy which gave Mirabeau, when it

---

[1] *Memoirs of the Marquis de Ferrières*, p. 14.

[2] Ferrières, p. 381. " La manière gauche et insensée " recalls Rivarol's epigram, " Le côté droit etait si gauche et le côté gauche si peu droit ".

was too late, the chance of showing his political genius.

They had effective orators — Cazalès, d'Espremesnil, the Abbé Maury. But Maury cared for nothing except his Cardinal's hat, and Cazalès left France the moment that his hopes for the new democracy were disappointed.[1]

Most of their faults may be put down to inexperience of public life. The Left were also new to parliamentary life, but many of them were lawyers and business men, who learned their trade quickly. The Right learned nothing; they remained to the end country gentlemen, who had never seen the inside of a Government office, and *abbés de salon*, whose wit and gallantry made them as unfit for the tribune as for the pulpit. Every evening, when the candles in the hall of Assembly were lit, they hurried off to their suppers, trusting to some ill-defined agreement that no constitutional business would be discussed in the evenings. They returned one morning to find that all hereditary titles had been abolished in their absence.

Party leaders and party discipline they had none; unlike the English aristocracy, their only idea of corporate obedience was in war; at the Assembly each man thought he had done his duty, if he had interrupted Mirabeau with some such witty rejoinder as " Vous êtes un bavard, voilà tout ", or if he had contemptuously condescended to fight a duel with a bourgeois, who could not be expected to know what honour was. Brilliant eccentrics like Montlosier, devoted to music and magnetism, setting off one day to geologise on Mount Valérien,[2] sat side by side with M. de Laqueville, who only had two maxims in his head, " We cannot compromise when honour is at stake " and " No yielding to rebels "[3] — the corpulent Mirabeau, brother of

---

[1] " Maury had no ideas at all about the future of France; Cazalès' ideas were false" (*Memoirs of Montlosier*, p. 245; chapters 10 and 11 of that work contain a brilliant and pitiless analysis of the Right by one of its members).

[2] " If the convulsions of nations ", he says, " have their importance, the convulsions of the globe are still more impressive " (p. 274).

[3] Montlosier, p. 255.

the orator, shouting joyously to a meeting of aged clergy and bishops, while the mob were breaking the windows of the club, " Gentlemen, fall into line, fall into line ". Gay, brave, undisciplined, extravagant in character and action, they found themselves unable to live in their own country, and they wearied out the patience of Europe by their fantastic behaviour as *émigrés* ; those, who remained, died like gentlemen in the Terror, but they had not a glimmer of concerted policy beyond futile conspiracies to get the King out of Paris.

It is true they received no support from the Government. Louis XVI and his Ministers were terrified of being compromised, if a nobleman were seen inside the Palace. But the Right were as incompetent in the defence of their own order as in the defence of the monarchy ; after throwing away their privileges in a burst of imprudent emotion on the night of August 4th, they ruined the proposal of an Upper Chamber, which would have preserved some of their political functions, from jealous suspicions that only some of them would be selected.

Above all, the Right shared that fatal error of aristocracies in a revolution : they half welcomed its excesses on the ground that the worse it became, the sooner it would end — " I cannot help remarking ", says de Ferrières, " on the lack of political wisdom in the behaviour of the nobles and bishops ; as their only wish was to dissolve and discredit the Assembly, far from opposing its worst decrees, they showed an indifference beyond belief ; they left the Chamber, when the President put the question, urging their party to follow them, or, if they stayed, they told their supporters to take no part in the debate. . . . Firmly believing that the new order of things could not last, they hastened on their own ruin in the impatient hope of pushing the revolution to its doom. . . . They showed an insulting want of respect for the Assembly, and the people in the galleries ; they paid no attention to the speeches, laughing

and talking at the top of their voices."[1] Such conduct
was natural in a privileged caste, whose only notion of
public life had been loyalty to the King and contempt for
the common people.[2]

It was not till the Restoration of 1815 that this mob of
courtiers became a Royalist party. Between 1789 and
1815 events had happened, of which even the most stupid
could hardly fail to read the lesson ; for it was one of
Napoleon's qualities that he made pupils even in the ranks
of his bitterest enemies.

On July 3rd, 1790, Mirabeau wrote to Louis XVI in a
letter full of political sagacity :

Part of the policy of the National Assembly — and the most
important part — is clearly favourable to the monarchy. Is it of
no importance that we are without Parlements, without *pays d'état*,
without privileged corporations, without clergy and noblesse ? The
idea of forming only one class of citizens would have delighted
Richelieu . . . several reigns of absolute government would not
have done so much for the royal authority as this one year of
revolution.[3]

Under Henri IV and Louis XIV the French monarchy
had won its popularity by satisfying the longing of the
people for unity, central government, and national leadership. The scandals of the Regency and of Louis XV had
shaken the prestige of the Crown, and Louis XVI was not
the man to recover it. It was left to Napoleon to realise
Mirabeau's ideal. Napoleon taught the lesson that so far
from Order and the Revolution being incompatible things,
it was only possible to establish a vigorous Government by
accepting its leading principles — the " career open to

---

[1] Ferrières, p. 309.

[2] In de La Gorce, *Histoire religieuse de la révolution*, i. 217-22, there is an
interesting discussion of the qualifications of the Right to take part in the
debate on the Civil Constitution of the clergy. He concludes that, though
they had sincere and able speakers among them, they were " lacking in faith " ;
by 1815, after the sufferings and trials of the aristocracy and clergy, they had
again attained to faith in their principles.

[3] *Correspondance*, ii. 75.

talents ", fair taxation, and undisturbed possession of the sold property of the Church ; henceforward only the most fantastic *émigrés* could suppose that the old France might be restored.

The monarchy was also obliged to accept from Napoleon the centralised administrative system, which under all changes of political régimes has remained down to the present day the chief feature of public life in France. Napoleon had satisfied two great demands of the Revolution — Equality and Fraternity ; he had done nothing at all for liberty. His continual wars had made the country a vast barracks, and it was this, even more than his final defeat, which had alienated from him the rising generation.[1] It was here that the restored monarchy had its chance of popularity and stability ; accepting the " conquests of the revolution ", it offered peace and parliamentary government — a monarchy, liberal, constitutional, and centralised, not for war or despotism but for the direction of national life under the new conditions of a transformed France, something between the nonchalant, ill-organised despotism of the eighteenth-century monarchy and the merciless concentration of the Empire.[2] This is

---

[1] Take, for example, two reminiscences, the first of a Republican, the second of a Royalist. Odilon Barrot (*Mémoires*, t. 1, p. 7) says : " I remember the feeling of indignation, with which I saw for the first time, child though I was, our soldiers marked with the letter N. ' Why,' I said bitterly to a friend, ' not long ago I saw a flock of sheep, that were marked like that with the initial of their owner.' " Berryer, in his great speech on the revision of the Constitution (July 16th, 1851), said : " At twenty years of age I was still an Imperialist. Oh, the glory of the Empire ! I left college with the sound of the cannon of Jena in my ears ; what head would not have been turned at such a moment ? But I saw, I studied ; I began to understand . . . I felt the despotism and it spoiled the glory for me."

[2] The restored monarchy regarded the Empire, not the Republic, as its chief enemy. The Regicides were only exiled ; Ney was shot. The bitterness of the opposition to the Restoration was due to the coalition of Bonapartists and Republicans. Both in 1830 and 1848, the Republicans had Bonapartists in their ranks ; they did not talk much about the Empire, but they demanded a strong foreign policy and the defence of oppressed nationalities — Poland, for instance. It was at St. Helena that Napoleon discovered he had been the champion of oppressed nationalities ; it may have

not the place to ask why the Restoration ended in a collapse. We are more concerned with a division in the Royalist ranks which proved to be of permanent importance.

This division might be expressed in conventional terms as the conflict between the Liberals and the Ultras, or the Moderate and the Extreme Right; more generally, the conflict between the "politicians" and the "country gentlemen".

The term "country gentlemen" by no means implies stupidity or obstinacy; their leader was Chateaubriand, who, if not a great thinker, was a brilliant writer. His complaint was that the Ministers of Louis XVIII, pursuing a policy of so-called liberalism, were really perpetuating the administration of the Empire; that they were more anxious to conciliate opponents of the monarchy than to win the support of its friends. "It is well known", he said, "that the maxim of the Ministerialists is Alliance with the Jacobins as a last resort; alliance with the Royalists never. To this Royalists must answer Alliance with honest people of all opinions."[1] "Honest people" meant ordinary voters — mostly from the country —, who were too sensible and straightforward to be taken in by the subversive sophisms of politicians — always the dream of conservative statesmen. They had no objection to liberal institutions; Chateaubriand himself had a certain weakness for democratic suffrage, which was shared by many Legitimists; after all, the peasants, who went to Mass every Sunday, were more likely to vote straight than middle-class financiers.[2] Their objection was rather to

been true of Italy, hardly of Germany or Spain. But the opponents of the Vienna settlement all appealed to the Emperor's memory, and Napoleon III was brought up in this creed. It was not till the *coup d'état* of 1851 that Bonapartists and Republicans took different roads.

[1] De Loménie, *La Carrière politique de Chateaubriand*, i. 215.

[2] Balzac's bitter hatred of the Orleanist régime was mostly based on his view that Guizot, by his maxim "Enrichissez-vous", had replaced marquises by bankers in the social world.

the administration and personnel of the early Restoration. The Empire had been "abolished but not replaced", and the Government offices were full of ex-agents of the Empire; [1] all they asked was that the monarchy should rely upon its real supporters. Served by such men, monarchy could bring forth its real social and political fruit; it could create a landed aristocracy with the right of primogeniture; it could encourage in the provinces guilds and aggregations of interests. In a speech, made during the year 1818, Chateaubriand said, " The new monarchy has as yet hardly any of its proper elements, except the King; the aristocratic part is a mere fiction ".[2]

Chateaubriand was of course something of a free-lance; most of his party failed to grasp his large ideas, but it was in these circles that there grew up a feeling for the " Romantic Monarchy ". The noblesse of 1789 had cared very little for the person of Louis XVI, whom many of them despised; the new nobility were devoted to their King, whom they surrounded if not always with the halo of divine right, at least with all the associations of history and tradition. The old aristocracy had been Voltairian, sceptical, contemptuous of the Church; but since Louis XVI died for his faith, it was the mode to regard Altar and Throne as inseparable. The new nobility experienced something of the feeling of the Cavalier for his King. After the dry dogmatisms and the equally dry negations of the eighteenth century, after the cold and correct efficiency of Napoleon, France felt a need for emotion, and it was this need that Chateaubriand satisfied — rather self-consciously perhaps. The new monarchy, surrounded by its faithful nobles, blessed by the Church of God,

---

[1] " When the new deputies ventured into the Government offices, they could not get over their surprise to find almost unchanged the personnel of the Empire and even of the Republic " (de La Gorce, *Louis XVIII*, p. 51).

[2] Loménie, *op. cit.* i. 264.

appealing not to the middle-classes alone but to the humblest of its subjects as their father and protector, advised by Parliament but free, in the name of the nation, to resist imprudent counsellors, found for the artist and poet its outward (though, alas ! only its outward) expression in the Anointing of Charles X at Rheims.

The " Chambre Introuvable " of 1816 is an admirable example of the " country gentleman " type ; it differed from the Right of 1789 in being prepared to learn — slowly at first, but in the end with relish — the lessons of constitutional government, so that while the deputies were — in the famous phrase — " more royalist than the King ", in their anxiety to serve his interests even against his wishes, they were more parliamentary than the old parliamentarians. In many ways they recall the Extreme Right of 1871–5 : they have the same hatred of the Empire, as represented by the fiery La Bourdonnaye, who cried, " We need fire, executions, tortures ! ", the same zeal for religion, as seen in the mystical discourses of de Bonald, whom they admired without understanding, the same nuance of liberalism which led them to extend the suffrage beyond the limits prescribed by the Government, the same curious blend of loyalty and independence towards the sovereign,[1] ready to go to remarkable lengths in protesting against his refusal to take their advice, but at once closing their ranks, if anyone else ventured to criticise anything he did.

If, for the country gentlemen, the Constitution was an addition to the glory of the Crown and the sign of its bounty, for the " politicians " the King was there chiefly to work the Constitution. The Orleanists — and most of them came from the " politicians " — had little feeling for the Crown as such ; they removed the aristocracy from the

---

[1] At the Séance Royale of 1816, a deputy of the Right rose and said, " I demand the right to be heard from my lord the King " ; he had to be called to order by the Duc de Richelieu (de La Gorce, *Louis XVIII*, p. 53 ; in the text I have compressed the historian's brilliant account of the Chambre Introuvable).

steps of the throne and put the middle-class in its place ; they frowned on the Jesuits, and polished up the old weapons of Gallicanism to keep the Church in its place ; " Sans noblesse et sans prêtres " was their motto.

In their eyes the chief function of the King was to be the hereditary President of " the best of republics " ; [1] his model was to be that of an English sovereign, whose title was to be that of William III, and his rule (as time went on) something like that of Queen Victoria.

It is easy to smile at the bourgeois Louis-Philippe, holding an umbrella in place of a sceptre, shaking everybody's hand instead of giving his own to be kissed, protected by the fat members of the National Guard in place of the flashing " régiment du Roi ". It is, none the less, an interesting experiment to watch — this " Victorian period " of France.

Queen Victoria and Louis-Philippe had only to see each other to fall in love. Each adored family life ; each had a good deal of personal influence, more or less hidden under the conventions of constitutional government ; each had a Protestant Minister who loved peace — Guizot and Aberdeen — and Queen Victoria's indignation, when Dean Hook preached before her on the text " Hear the Church ", is not unlike Louis-Philippe's complaint that it was really not decent under a monarchy, and in his presence, to sing the verse in the Magnificat — " He hath put down the mighty from their seat ". But the real conditions of the sovereigns, the statesmen, and the peoples were quite different in the two countries.

Queen Victoria's accession to the throne had been tranquil and unchallenged ; Louis-Philippe stood between the elder branch of the Bourbons, whose feelings he had

---

[1] See, for example, in Barrot's *Mémoires* (i. 128), the argument, by which the author persuaded Lafayette to give his consent to the July Monarchy : " Hereditary monarchy depends upon public opinion, not every five or ten years, like the President of a Republic, but every day and every moment of the day ".

outraged beyond the hope of pardon, and the Republicans, whose game he had spoiled by accepting the crown ; this gave him a feeling of insecurity and made him terrified at every movement towards the right or left,[1] always anxious to leave things as they were at home, and abroad to maintain a policy of caution, which called out Lamartine's famous criticism, " La France s'ennuie ".

This fear of political danger — personally he was highly courageous — was not combined with a readiness to stand on one side ; in forwarding the policy of doing nothing, he was never himself still for an instant. Queen Victoria's influence was, for the most part, hidden, cautious, indirect. Louis-Philippe was far the abler of the two ; his own views were very often wise and upright, but he could never keep himself in the background ; he regarded himself as personally concerned in everything that occurred ; his Ministers were there to defend *him* ; deputies who voted against *him* were asked to the Palace and lectured (" être chambré " the French called it) ; he said to three members of the Left, who came to remonstrate with him, " I don't know what you mean by talking about the ' policy of my Ministers ' ; I would have you know, gentlemen, that there is only one policy, and that is my own ".[2] His ideal would have been to be his own Prime Minister and to defend his measures at the tribune ; by the irony of fate it was his old enemy, Thiers, to whom this combination of functions finally fell.

The statesmen, who supported the July Monarchy, were among the most brilliant and honest that France has known ; it was not their fault if they were in a false position. The English Constitution had the advantage of being venerable in its prestige, and at the same time elastic

---

[1] Barrot says (i. 218) : " I found the King pacing up and down his study in the greatest agitation. . . . " You don't know what has happened ", he said ; " they are driving me out into the unknown ; yes, my Ministers are proposing to lower the electoral qualification to 200 francs."

[2] Barrot, i. 271.

in its provisions. The French Charter of 1830 was new, artificial, patched up to meet a crisis ; yet the Doctrinaire party talked as though this rough-and-ready compromise represented some final and esoteric theory of government. The *juste milieu*, the balance of classes and interests were *a priori* desirable, whether people desired them or not. It was one of them who said, "I disdain a fact"; and even Guizot, the wisest of them, resigned office and left the dynasty to its fate rather than admit the smallest modification in the qualification of voters. They might honestly believe this the path of political safety, but it seemed unnecessary that it should be spoken of as the only path of political righteousness.

The electorate, also, were hardly ready for the delicate adjustments of the *juste milieu*. The Orleanist party and policy were quite new. It had to meet three ancient parties. It had to set itself against the prestige of Legitimacy, the legend of Bonapartism, the popularity of the Republicans. It was a difficult task for the French bourgeois, and it is not very surprising that he ended by losing his head.

The French bourgeois combines in a curious way complete self-satisfaction with a great fear of being laughed at ; he felt himself derisively watched by the old nobility ; in the end, he seemed to himself rather ridiculous, sallying out in his National Guard uniform to defend against an *émeute* a man, who had been put on the throne by an *émeute*.

There is a kind of bourgeois fatalism, which considers a revolution as a chronic malady which cannot be prevented ; in presence of democratic socialism, waiting for its chance with eager patience, with its chiefs, orators, newspapers, subscriptions, plans, places of meeting . . . what do we find in the conservative camp ? neither unity nor agreement nor leadership . . . an émeute will always find men of goodwill to support it ; a patrol never.[1]

---

[1] *Memoires du Marquis de Boissy*, t. 1, pp. 110, 111 (from the Preface by Paul Breton).

It is possible to hold that the Orleanist experiment ought to have succeeded ; it is not possible to think that the political condition of France had more than a superficial resemblance to that, which made the Victorian period in England a political success.

(b) THE ROYALIST PARTIES FROM 1848 TO 1871

> Good was it in that dawn to be alive,
> But to be young was very heaven.

So in two famous lines Wordsworth hailed the first French Revolution ; less sonorous and with a still quicker growth to sad maturity, they would apply to the Second — " the social and democratic Revolution " of 1848. This time, it was not only man's political freedom that was to be for ever assured, but his whole position in society. The great industrial problem — how new and flexible it then seemed ! — was to be solved at a stroke, and, as the Peers of the July Monarchy hurriedly quitted their seats in the Luxembourg Palace, their places were taken by working-men in their blouses, under the presidency of Louis Blanc — the first Socialist Convention, but it was a Socialism premature and Utopian, *sans son livre et sans ses cadres.* Karl Marx had not yet written his book on Capital, and the trades-unions had not yet been organised.

I once heard a distinguished and friendly French critic of English life declare that in some ways his own people seemed to him the oldest in the world ; in comparison, the English seemed like children with their naïve belief in the good intentions of politicians, and in the possibility of universal peace and brotherhood. But (if it be a disease to believe in politicians) the French too have had their attacks, and 1848 was a serious case.

It was the Revolution of the Romantics ; '89 had been classical in its admiration for Greece and Rome ; '48 was tinged with the vague Christianity of the Romanticists.[1] Reason was the presiding deity of the First Republic ; the name of God was constantly on the lips of the Second [2] — and Victor Hugo was His prophet.[3] After singing the praises of the Christian Monarchy, he became the poet of the people whose voice is God's — and was not the prince of poets, Lamartine, at the Foreign Office ? [4]

The first act of the Provisional Government had been to abolish the death-penalty for political offences ; admirers of the Girondins rather than of the Mountain, they hastened to repudiate the guillotine and the Terror. Then came the great adventure of Universal Suffrage, tried for the first time in France, by which, without transition of any kind, the electorate was increased from 200,000 voters to 9,000,000. It was a radiant Easter Sunday after Mass when they voted, and Lamartine's lyrical description was not wholly undeserved :

At sunrise the people . . . formed into columns . . . under the direction of the mayors, curates, instructors, justices of the peace, . . . and proceeded by villages and hamlets to the principal places of voting. . . . In the towns, it was the same. . . . Citizens were seen . . . to carry their written suffrages to the ballot and, pausing sometimes to modify them under the influence of a new idea or of a sudden feeling of repentance, deposit them in the urn and go home with satisfaction depicted on their countenances, as from a pious ceremonial.[5]

To the modern student of democracy this may read like a piece of satire, but it was 1848 and the dawn of a new age ; so men thought, and children too. Juliette Lambert (afterwards, as Mme Adam, to be the Queen of

---

[1] Faguet has defined Romanticism as Christianity without the doctrine of Original Sin.

[2] And the presiding genius of the Third Republic was Positivism.

[3] It was during the Constituent Assembly, after the exile of Ledru-Rollin, leader of the Extreme Left, that Victor Hugo (as Ollivier says) " leaped into his vacant place ".

[4] Thiers, who did not relish the intrusion of poets into politics, said of him : " When he shuts his eyes, he sees statues ".

[5] Lamartine, *French Revolution* (Bohn translation), p. 474.

the Third Republic) was at school in 1848 ; the lessons
were badly prepared, and the Revolution was pleaded as an
excuse. The mistress waxed sarcastic : " I fail to see how
the Republic can be any concern of yours ". Juliette's
voice was heard : " But, Mademoiselle, it interests us
passionately ".[1]

Even the Legitimists joined in the universal enthusiasm.
After all, Universal Suffrage had overthrown the hated
bourgeois monarchy ; during the revolutionary tumult
which swept away the Chamber of Deputies, a Legitimist
member, de Genoude, had cried, " We can do nothing
without the consent of the country ; in 1830 you refused to
appeal to the people, and you see what is happening ".[2]
The Marquis de la Rochejaquelein openly defended an
" appeal to the people ", and the Legitimist *Gazette de
France* made itself the organ of this demand, containing
such statements as " Tell the people you are neither for
Divine Right nor for any absolute right ; that for you
monarchy is a delegation from the country ", and " Outside Universal Suffrage there is no safety for France ".[3]
Many a staid Royalist in 1870 blushed to remember his
escapades of twenty years before. Beulé, the Minister of
the Interior in '73, who hoped to see the King restored,
while he was in office, had played truant as a schoolboy,
and been seen on the barricades in a fantastic dress ;
Chesnelong, the ambassador, who in '73 believed he had
persuaded the King to accept the Crown, had said to a
democratic candidate in '48 : " Citizen, will you promise
never to support a monarchical restoration ? "

The enthusiasm of the Royalists for the Republic was
short-lived but sincere ; it would not be just to apply to
Legitimists the charming reply of the ingenuous Republican,

[1] Stephens, *Mme Adam*, p. 25.
[2] Falloux, *Memoirs*, i. 268.
[3] Quoted by a Bonapartist deputy, Prax-Paris, in a speech on November
18th, 1873, when trying to persuade the Legitimists to vote for a " referendum ".

Q

who had become a Senator under the Second Empire. Asked why, in 1849, he had called on the Right to shout " Vive la République ! ", he answered, " Oh, that is simple enough ; at the moment we were living under a Republic ".

Even more remarkable was the manner in which the Church rallied to the new régime. For the moment, the younger Catholics were somewhat tired of monarchy ; the Restoration had not realised their hopes ; the Catholic revival under Chateaubriand had been more literary than orthodox, and a caustic critic made the celebrated remark, " I should be glad to know the name of Chateaubriand's confessor ". How superficial it was could be seen by the violent and credulous hatred of the Jesuits, which contributed so largely to the downfall of Charles X.[1] The 1830 revolution was marked by the most violent anti-clericalism. Priests dared not wear their cassocks in the streets, and the palace of the Archbishop of Paris was sacked by the mob. The July monarchy showed itself very timid in ecclesiastical matters, kept the clergy under the heel of their bishops, and refused the promised permission for free Catholic schools. A fervent and talented generation of Catholic leaders was growing up, which was tired of official religion ; some of them looked to the Republic for protection against the monarchy, others to the Pope for help against the dull Gallicanism of the Established Church. They had their orator in Montalembert, the famous author of *The Monks of the West*, their statesman in Falloux, their preacher in Lacordaire, who had been condemned by the courts for opening a free school, and now took his seat in the Constituent Assembly of 1848 to prove the sincerity of the sermon, in which he had cried (under the arches of Notre-Dame), in answer to the Republicans, " Are

---

[1] It is remarkable that even Charles X, extreme as he was supposed to be in Church matters, was a Gallican; Henri V, if he had ascended the throne, would have been the first ultramontane King of France.

they Frenchmen ? So am I. Patriots and liberals ? So am I." The Abbé Lammenais, who began as their leader, passed from belief in the omnipotent Pope to belief in the omnipotent people.

This party welcomed the Revolution as an emancipation. In many parts of the country priests might be seen blessing the planting of "trees of liberty". The *Univers* published an article in which it said, "Royalty has no more partisans today. . . . It was the theology of Gallicanism [1] alone which consecrated the Divine Right of Kings. . . . Catholic Theology has proclaimed the Divine Right of peoples. . . . If the French Republic will give the Church at last that liberty, which everywhere the crowned heads refuse, or seek to wrest from her, there will be no better or more sincere republicans than French Catholics." [2] What was more surprising, the French Bishops showed no great objection to the change ; this was partly because the voters — especially in the country — as yet unorganised and inexperienced, were remarkably amenable to Church influence. There were Departments in the West where the list of successful candidates was drawn up by the Bishop himself ; the Bishop of Chalons wrote to the *Univers* that Liberty, Equality and Fraternity were the Gospel in its simplest form ; another Bishop said in his Pastoral that Universal Suffrage was the realisation of St. Paul's social ideal : "there is no difference among you between commoner and noble, bond and free ".[3]

All eyes were turned towards the Legitimist Pretender ; what position would he take in this new world ?

The Comte de Chambord was now twenty-eight years

---

[1] *Gallicanism* may be defined (in the abstract) as the French Church, ecclesiastically free from the Pope's claims, and politically under the control of the Crown ; *Ultramontanism* as the French Church, politically free from State control and ecclesiastically subject to the Vatican.

[2] Falloux, *Memoirs*, i. 276-7.

[3] Quoted in Émile Ollivier's *L'Église et l'état au concile du Vatican*, i. 358-9.

old ; he had been born on September 29th, 1820, seven months after the murder of his father, the Duc de Berri, younger son of Charles X. It was the heyday of mystical Romanticism. The posthumous birth of the Duc de Bordeaux — for such was his title — was hailed as super-natural, and he was called "the child of miracle"; the castle of Chambord was bought for him by public sub-scription ; Chateaubriand brought water from the Jordan for his baptism ; Victor Hugo acclaimed him as "the glorious child, the angel promised to the earth by the martyr who has left us for the skies "; and Lamartine did not shrink from recalling memories of the Epiphany — "like those Kings from the East, an instinct, which my soul does not understand, makes me adore a child ".[1] Before the boy was ten years old, the worth of such adulation was exposed ; on August 2nd, at the palace of Rambouillet, Charles abdicated in his grandson's favour, while in the midst of the Paris Revolution Louis-Philippe was pro-claimed Lieutenant-General of the realm.

The act of abdication passed over the King's eldest son, the Duc d'Angoulême, and appointed the Duchesse de Berri as Regent for her son. Damas, tutor to the Duc de Bor-deaux, came to tell the child that he had become Henri V. He was playing with his sister ; on hearing the news he burst into tears. "What! dear papa, who is so good, cannot make France happy ; they wish to make *me* King. How stupid ! "[2] The Body Guard — still faithful to the elder line of Bourbons — assembled in the Palace ; the swords flashed ; the White flag dipped and, as the child passed along the lines, he heard — for the first and the last time — the cry of " Vive le Roi ! "

But Louis-Philippe would not be content with the title of Regent, and the sad, slow journey to exile began ; the little Duc de Bordeaux, whether he was chasing after

[1] Reclus, *L'Avènement de la 3e Republique*, pp. 194-5.
[2] De Luz, *Henri V*, p. 23.

butterflies or being carried in his tutor's arms dressed "in his bright-blue frock, turn-over collar and white trousers", softened all hearts; [1] at Carentan a hostile crowd had assembled, but when, from the windows of the first carriage, the Duke and his sister put out their heads, bowing right and left and blowing kisses, the women wept, and the men muttered, "How pretty they are, the poor innocents!" [2] The exiled monarch took refuge in Holyrood, but the Scotch winter proved too much for them, and they moved to Austria, where the Emperor — with much reluctance — lent them the castle of Hradschin at Prague.

In 1832 the young Prince's mother, the high-spirited but wayward Caroline of Sicily, landed in France and tried to rally adherents. She was betrayed to Thiers and imprisoned at Blaye, where she was found to be with child, upon which she informed the scandalised and incredulous Legitimists that she had been married to an Italian Count; after the first movement of horror, [3] a bitter conflict broke out in the entourage of Charles X; one party held that, in spite of her fall, she still remained Regent and that therefore her son should be brought up as future King of France. The other party held that Charles' eldest son, Angoulême, had not really consented to the abdication of his father, and that he was therefore Louis XIX, but had delegated his powers to Charles X, who therefore remained King. This complicated theory was patronised by the all-

[1] Lucas-Dubreton, *Charles X*, pp. 219-26.

[2] Barrot, *Mémoires*, p. 169.

[3] The judgment of de Blacas — censor of etiquette at the Hradschin palace — is delicious in its terse finality. "A fault might have been pardoned; a marriage cuts the Duchesse de Berri off from the Royal family" (Lucas-Dubreton, *Charles X*, p. 240) — Thiers' conduct in exposing the Duchess's state remained one of the permanent grievances of the Legitimists against the Orleanists. The Marquis de Castellane relates an instance as late as 1871. "I said to the Marquise de Juigné, my mother-in-law, that I had been to write my name in the visitors' book of the Orleans Princes. . . . I received a roll of bread full in my face; she apologised: 'I could not help it; those people who tried to bring shame on the Duchesse de Berri — their own niece'" (*Men and Things of My Time*, p. 124).

powerful de Blacas. When Chateaubriand in his rôle as knight-errant presented himself at Hradschin to intercede for the Duchesse de Berri, a ridiculous scene took place; the poet threw himself on his knees before the young Prince, exclaiming, " You are my King ; I come to take my orders from you, and from you alone will I receive them ". The child turned pale and ran away, leaving the disconcerted Peer on his knees.[1]

Embittered controversies about a crown, which neither party can give or take, have something infinitely wearisome and absurd in their very nature, and the subject would have been hardly worthy of mention but for its effect on the young prince's education, and the question how far he was to be trained for the throne. Charles X, lethargic and unenterprising, would never take the trouble to make up his mind whether he was still King or not ; to the solemn appeals of his followers he answered, " I cannot say ; you must be content with the principle of Legitimacy ". It did not seem to him of much importance how the Duc de Bordeaux was brought up ; in his view all that a King needed was to know enough Latin to follow the Mass, and to be able to ride a horse correctly.

As the doubt subsisted, it was agreed that " the Prince's head must not be turned ".[2] In 1833, when he came of age, the Austrian Government was persuaded to refuse passports to French Royalists, who were eager to cross the frontier with their loyal addresses ; when, on the feast of the Epiphany, the " cake of the Kings " was divided up and the Prince " got the bean ", his family were anxious as to the effect on his mind, and, when the Legitimists sent him a present of sword and spurs, they were seriously alarmed ; after all, was he not the son of the headstrong Caroline, whose portrait he was not allowed to have in his

---

[1] Lucas-Dubreton, *Charles X*, pp. 241-2.
[2] For these details on the youth of the Duc de Bordeaux see Lucas-Dubreton, *Charles X*, ch. ix.

room ? Who could tell what wild strain he might not have inherited ? Signs were not wanting to disquiet. The boy was haughty and passionate ; in the streets of Prague he insisted that everybody should make room for him ; he seized his mathematical tutor, who was of European eminence, by the collar and drove him from the room. He adopted special oaths to imitate Henri IV ; he refused to learn carpentering, because it was not " a trade for a King " ; his teachers reported that he was " impatient, at times, of study and work . . . proud, intractable and obstinate, but always of an elevated and cultivated mind ".

Repression was the order of the day ; for punishment he was forced on his knees for a long time, then made to put on a shirt shaped like a sack and sent to bed to be talked to by his confessor. The effect of all this was to check impetuosity, but to weaken initiative. In 1839 Falloux met him with his tutor, the Duc de Lévis, and made the comment : " His chief fear was to leave the Prince to himself ; he would have been excellent in charge of a rash Pretender ; his methods were dangerous in dealing with a Prince so naturally self-controlled as the Comte de Chambord ".[1] The old hastiness of temper could only be traced in a determined obstinacy and a keen sense of personal dignity ; it was replaced by a deliberateness, which sometimes verged on scrupulousness.

He had been much influenced by his aunt, the Duchesse d'Angoulême, daughter of Louis XVI ; she had been in prison with her aunt, Mme Royale, and knew by heart, the last will of her father. " If my son is unfortunate enough to be King " were the opening words ; they made a deep impression on the young Henri. Bishop Frayssinous, his tutor, tried to efface it by suggesting St. Louis's words to his son as more appropriate, " If God gives you the honour of being King " (" fait la grâce d'être roi "),

[1] Falloux, i. 204.

but to the Prince the crown was always a burden rather than an object of ambition.[1]

The presiding spirit in this education was de Blacas, the favourite, whom Louis XVIII had sent away in disgrace. Tall, impassive, in his impeccable clothes and light wig, he stood for a cold and courtly correctness; his enemies called him "the undertaker at the funeral of the French Monarchy". The Jesuit fathers, Deplace and Druilhet, were originally among the Prince's tutors, but the outcry was so great that they had to be sent away.[2] De Blacas revenged himself by dismissing General d'Hautpol, whose influence he thought too liberal, and the Duchesse de Gontaut, guilty of having spoken in favour of the Charte and of having hinted in a letter that a reconciliation with the Orleans was desirable.

So the Duc de Bordeaux was left entirely in the hands of those, whose influence led Chateaubriand to call the Palace "the Museum of Prague". On the whole, it is remarkable how largely the Count de Chambord escaped the evil effects of such an education; this was partly due to the increasing independence of his character; his conversation — often brilliant enough — was followed by periods of reserve, when he used to say half seriously that the wily Louis XI was his favourite French king.

He had a most attractive manner, courteous and considerate; his regular features and clear blue eyes predisposed visitors in his favour. Falloux met him, when he was fourteen and was fascinated by him. "You come from Prague", the boy greeted him; "you must be hungry; you shall lunch with me; otherwise I should

---

[1] De Roux, *Origines de la 3e République*, p. 160.

[2] Charles X wrote : "If, compelled by reasons due to the evils of the time, I have had to withdraw from M. Deplace the charge of my grandson, I feel none the less that I must express the merited regrets which his departure inspires in me, and recognise the good service he has rendered to his pupil". Henri added in his testimonial, "They would never have left, if my wishes had been of any force" (De Luz, *Henri V*, p. 60).

lose half of your visit, and I do not wish to lose any of it."
And, after the meal, he put a lily-of-the-valley in his guest's
buttonhole, saying, " I decorate you with my order " —
green and white were then the Royalist colours.[1] But deep
down in his character was a mistrust of Royalist France,
due perhaps in part to the isolation in which de Blacas had
kept him.[2]

When he grew older, the Royalists came to see him
incessantly — at one time of his life his chief occupation
was interviewing members of Parliament and receiving
deputations — and they returned charmed and impressed.
But, *au fond*, he had a profound suspicion of statesmen.
Louis XVIII had loved to talk to them ; Louis-Philippe
rejoiced to intrigue with them and against them. The
Comte de Chambord was never at his ease with the Royalist
parliamentary party ; he had not forgiven them for
deserting Charles X ; his very simple and upright nature
shrank from the compromises, of which political life is
made up. In a sense he regarded them as a kind of aristocracy coming between him and his people.[3] If he seemed

[1] Falloux, i. 74-5.

[2] In this sense de Flahaut's mot is just. A lady, who had met the Comte
de Chambord at a picture gallery in Rome, said to de Flahaut, " To think that
so charming a prince should have enemies ! " " Ah, Madame," he replied,
" if it were only a question of his enemies ! " (Falloux, i. 201). During this
visit to Rome (1839) we have a glimpse of him in the Duc de Broglie's Memoirs :
" We [his father and himself] had stopped by chance opposite the tomb of
the Stuarts, scupltured by Canova near the entrance of St. Peter's. We saw
a small group approach, in the centre of which was a fair young man with a
fine face and strongly marked Bourbon features. It was the Prince ; it was
Henri V, come to gaze on the tomb of James III. We moved away, at once,
much touched by the meeting. How surprised I should have been, if I had
been told that, thirty-four years later almost day for day, I should offer the
crown to the Comte de Chambord and he would refuse to take it from my
hands ! " (*Revue des Deux Mondes*, 15/1/25, p. 333).

[3] If the Comte ever demeaned himself so far as to read Mirabeau, he would
have agreed with the following words in the famous speech on the Veto :
" There will always result from the choice of representatives of the people
a kind of actual aristocracy . . . equally hostile (in certain cases) to the
monarch and the people ". In a pamphlet, issued under the inspiration of
the Comte de Chambord, he concedes — though reluctantly — the annual
vote of the Budget by Parliament, afterwards withdrawn in 1887 by the Comte

sometimes to prefer the company of the faithful comrades of his exile, it was not because he thought them wiser, but because they offered him less advice. Nothing perhaps is so important to remember, as an explanation of his subsequent behaviour. Father Marcel, the Capucin, who saw him often, when the Comte was at Versailles in 1873 playing his last card, records his impression in the revealing words, " He mistrusted all these people ".[1]

Most important of all the influences on his character was Religion, and it came less from his surroundings than from himself. He was the first of the Bourbons to show this type of piety ; Henri IV weighed Paris and the Mass in the same scales; Louis XIV was a statesman before he was a Churchman ; Louis XVI, if genuinely religious, showed it more conspicuously in prison than on the throne ; Louis XVIII was an amiable sceptic of the eighteenth-century kind ; Charles X devoted his later years to a real if retarded piety — for all of them religion was important as a support to the throne ; for the Comte de Chambord, religion was the reason why kings existed.

Debarred by his lameness from active exertions and so thrown back upon himself, ardent in temperament yet contemplative and disciplined, he had a nature apt for mysticism ; true to the best mystic type, he combined a sweetness and unassuming gentleness of personal demeanour with a flash of authority in his blue eyes, when his God-given right was questioned. He would pardon a thousand enemies, but he would not even appear to surrender a

---

de Paris ; he trusts the deputies " to think twice before they disorganise everything by refusing supplies. If the Assemblies of France do not deserve the honour of such a trust, then France does not deserve the honour of a free constitution " (de Roux, p. 165). See in de Luz, pp. 280-84, various formulae — from supporters of the Comte rather than the Comte himself —expressing his views on the relation of Parliament to the Executive : " We must give up parliamentary government to keep the reality of *constitutional* government " ; " He wishes that monarchy shall be really a power, not a doll moved by the strings pulled by parliamentary leaders " ; " something between the ancient Monarchy and the English form of Parliamentary Government ".

[1] Hanotaux, ii. 304.

single principle. The contrast of the active and mystical temperament was clearly shown by the bewilderment of Bishop Dupanloup at the idea that a scruple of honour about the flag should hold back the Comte, when his troops demanded he should lead them to battle. " What a psychological enigma ! " the Bishop exclaimed.[1] He would have been less puzzled, if his studies had included the psychology of the mystics.

It was said that the Comte de Chambord was under the control of clerical influences : it is true that he was more likely to listen to a bishop than to a deputy. But here too he went his own way, alone with God.[2] For him the Restoration was no triumph of personal authority or political combinations ; it would be, in the literal sense of the word, a miracle. " If France is to be saved," he said, " God must reign there as master, and then I can reign there as King." [3] While anxious counsellors waited on his word, while delegates from the Assembly wept and trembled in his antechamber, while his representatives in France strove to explain and tone down his latest manifesto, the Comte was on his knees in chapel, expecting the sign from heaven.

The effect of this was to produce the appearance of quiet fatalism in his conduct. " I expect little from the wisdom of men," he said, " and much from the justice of God." But mysticism must not be confused with dreaminess ; the mark of the mystic in him was not that he did not know what he wanted, but that he would never be content with what he thought second best.

On June 3rd, 1844, he formally announced to the

---

[1] Falloux, ii. 479.

[2] In 1877 he wrote : " No one can doubt that I am disposed to leave to the Church the liberty, which belongs to her and is necessary for her spiritual government. But the clergy cannot be too careful not to interfere in matters that belong to the temporal authority" (Bernanos, *Grande Peur des bien pensants*, p. 112). When Leo XIII tried to rally the Comte to the Republic, the old Prince, now near his death, replied, " I thought that the Church forbade suicide " (*ibid*. p. 154).

[3] Reclus, *L'Avènement de la 3e République*, p. 197.

Powers his position as claimant to the throne ; he protested against " the change introduced into the legitimate succession in France " ; he declared he would never renounce the rights he held " by birth, according to the ancient laws of France " ; but he added, " I do not wish to exercise them, until in my own conviction Providence shall call me to be truly useful to France ".[1]

From that moment till his death, he upheld that claim unswervingly and with spotless honour. There are few positions more trying to human dignity and intelligence than that of Pretender to a crown. There is the perpetual contrast between the magnitude of his claims and the straitened conditions of his actual existence, always verging on tragedy or comedy. To maintain a show of ceremony, of which the substance is only a dream ; to assume the dignity of a King and accept the genuflexions of a small band of devotees, who address the monarch as the source of all favours and yet know in their hearts that they are giving everything and receiving nothing ; to divide one's attention fairly between those, whose very fidelity has made them exiles from their country, and those who, with no such claim on their Prince's gratitude, are yet living among his future subjects, and therefore far better able to judge the state of opinion at home ; to issue manifestoes, which combine the dignity of royal proclamations with the persuasiveness of electoral addresses — and all this under the eyes of a foreign Court, where the reality of monarchy throws into relief the mockery of a King without subjects, and where the forms of diplomatic courtesy thinly disguise the contempt felt for a dynasty, that could not keep its throne ; to declare and believe oneself indispensable to the national well-being, and yet see the nation cheerfully dispensing with one's services ; to feel the heart-throb and the words clamour for utterance at every crisis in one's country's fate, and yet to have every public statement

---

[1] Hanotaux, ii. 122, *note*.

treated as an act of personal aggression; to be thought indifferent if one is silent and, if eloquent, ambitious — all this requires either the talent of a consummate actor or the simple directness of an honest man.

All this was still harder in the case of the Comte de Chambord, who had never ruled, for whom Monarchy was a vocation romantically distorted by distance and hope long deferred, not modified by any first-hand experience of men or things in France, and who had to decide, far from home, bewildering problems of Restoration policy, when every concession seems a bargain for the Crown — as though one were saying, " I am your King by Divine right, but I will surrender this or that, if you will only be kind enough to have me back ". The burden of a long exile either stiffens or loosens the convictions. Either the Pretender becomes ready to come back on any terms, or the conscience becomes steeled against concessions and regards it as a point of honour to seem a Don Quixote rather than a Bolingbroke.[1] Jules Simon, in his amusing sketches *Nos hommes d'état*,[2] tells the story of a poor madman, who thought he was the claimant to the throne, and " appeared every day on the pier at Havre, bowing most politely to the right and left, saying to himself, ' Things are going well ; it will be next month ' ". Whatever it might cost, the Comte de Chambord was resolved to have nothing in common with that lunatic.

He solved the moral problem by an integrity and loftiness of spirit,[3] which did not need a crown or a throne

[1] See Shakespeare's picture (in *Richard II*) of the Pretender courting the crowd : " With humble and familiar courtesy " (Act I, sc. 4).

[2] P. 104.

[3] Vassili, in his highly imaginative chapter on the Comte (*France behind the Veil*, pp. 112-22), pays him a just tribute : " He was one of the characters who reconcile one with humanity " ; Louis Veuillot spoke of his " striking personal uprightness, his moderation, his long and silent consideration of our needs, the seriousness of his character, the courage with which he has despised the pursuit of a political career, less precious in his eyes than the peace of his conscience and the honour of his name " (Bellesort, *Les Intellectuels et l'avène-ment de la 3ᵉ République*, pp. 55-6).

to be royal, and which deeply impressed all who met him. The claim on his intelligence was harder for him to meet.

In November 1846 he married Marie Thérèse Béatrix Gaetano of the Ducal house of Modena — "a family of the Middle Ages", so Thiers spoke of them; "they have political ideas of the most reactionary kind and their religion is *outrée*".[1] Her family was the only reigning family, that had never recognised the Orleans dynasty, and she did not conceal her animosity against them.[2] Though the Comte lived on terms of the greatest intimacy with her, it does not seem that he let her talk politics. Three years older than her husband, she was not beautiful and one side of her face was disfigured. She accepted his desire for the Restoration, but secretly she feared Paris, its pleasures and its dangers alike. She knew she was not attractive, and was ashamed she had no children; her imagination was full of murders and assassinations. "If my husband were to reascend the throne," she used to say, "the best thing for everybody would be that I should be killed."[3] Simple and natural in her talk, with her fine hair and white teeth, dignified in her black dress and plain white collar, she stitched away at her tapestry, and grew old and deaf in an isolation she gladly accepted; a friendly visitor in 1873 found her, "in spite of all her attempts at being amiable, unable to talk about anything but pilgrimages".

---

[1] De Marcère, *Assemblée nationale*, ii. 40.

[2] She used to say, "That Clementine (Duchess of Saxe-Coburg) makes me dine opposite a picture of Louis-Philippe in his red trousers; does she suppose I like it?" (Hanotaux, ii. 259). "The hatred of the younger branch is a second nature to her, a monstrous twist of mind that makes her add unconsciously at the end of the Lord's Prayer, 'and from all the Orleans family. Amen'" (De Luz, p. 130).

[3] Hanotaux, ii. 259. Mme de la Ferronays reports that the Countess said to her, "'The more one is a Royalist, the more one should desire my death, because I have no children'. I replied by the banal consolation, 'Madame will have children when she lives at the Tuileries'. She seized my hands with a movement I shall never forget, and gazing fixedly at me she said, 'My dear, do you believe what you say or do you say it only to please me?'" (De Luz, p. 128).

They lived in the castle of Frohsdorff in Austria, be-queathed to them by the Duchess of Angoulême; some-thing of that fateful and melancholy personality (she had shared Louis XVI's captivity) seemed to brood over the house. Lackeys in the blue livery of the House of France moved solemnly through the hushed rooms beneath the pictures of Henri IV on his horse, and Marie Antoinette in the days of her radiance. The long evenings passed slowly; " one could not get rid of the feeling that they were all waiting for something ".[1]

But to return to the Second Republic. The enthusiasm of the Right for democratic institutions had not survived the " June days ", when the Socialist Revolution had to be fought in the streets; all the Conservative parties united — in the famous " Réunion de la rue de Poitiers " — to defend the cause of order, and obtained a majority in the Legis-lative Assembly of 1849. Together they voted the laws, authorising " free " Catholic schools, the expedition to Rome to save the Pope from Garibaldi, and the law of May 31st limiting Universal Suffrage. But party interests and party divisions soon made themselves felt; Louis Napoleon, the French President, whom the Right had hoped it would be so easy to use as their tool, was busy forming a party of his own. The Orleanists were indignant at the refusal of the Legitimists — on two separate occasions — to recall their Princes from exile. The motion was opposed by Berryer, the Legitimist leader. " Revolutions ", he said, " may disinherit the future; they cannot annihilate the past; a Bourbon can only return to France as King." [2] At the critical moment, when Napoleon asked the Assembly

---

[1] Vassili, p. 114; de Sugny, a devoted Royalist, says of a visit in 1873 : " We felt leagues and leagues from France; this cloister-like castle in the depths of Austria had a sad and frozen look. . . . We were among people, who had spent their lives in dreaming and who regretted being woken up " (*Fusion monarchique*, p. 302).

[2] *Fusion monarchique*, p. 30. After the second rejection (in March 1851), the Duc de Nemours, one of the Orleanist Princes, wrote, " We cannot work in alliance with the Legitimists " (*op. cit.* p. 35).

to revise the Constitution in order to allow his re-election as President, the Right were divided.[1]

The Comte de Chambord constantly appeared on the Rhine, at Ems, Wiesbaden, and Cologne, to keep in touch with his supporters. He did not really feel free to act till the death of Louis-Philippe in 1850 ; then — after having a Requiem sung for his soul and sending a letter of condolence to the widowed Queen — he assumed the direction of his party in the famous circular of Wiesbaden.

The first question he had to decide was : Should he appeal to arms ? Among his counsellors, the Duc de Cars advocated an insurrection ; he was a little man " outwardly calm and inwardly ardent to temerity . . ., who never appeared in society and mistrusted the salons as much as the tribune ".[2] Though the Comte de Chambord still retained him in his councils, it was clear that he meditated no immediate action ; in 1848 he had said to a French Republican that he would embark on no enterprise against established authority, and did not wish to take any initiative, having no personal ambition.[3]

Another question was that of the " Appeal to the People ", which had been advocated by La Rochejaquelein and de Genoude. The Circular repudiated this position in no uncertain terms : " Mgr. the Comte de Chambord has formally and absolutely condemned the system of an appeal to the people, as implying the negation of the great national principle of hereditary monarchy ". Rochejaquelein immediately protested against what he called the " senseless action ", which excommunicated him from the party. But the bulk of the Royalists had never gone so far as the Appeal group ; what exasperated them in the Circular was the absence of all reference to the wish of the people, or to *rapprochement* with the Orleanists, and above all, the appointment of a directing Committee of five, three

[1] See pp. 266-7.   [2] Falloux, i. 222.   [3] Hanotaux, i. 146.

of whom had no connection with Parliament at all.[1] "An act of gross stupidity"; "our Waterloo" — so the Liberal Royalists described it. Guizot said, "A few more circulars of this kind will render the most excellent Messages fruitless".[2]

All the misunderstanding between the Comte and his followers lurks in that first difference. The Prince was in a sense liberal in his views; he was known to be in favour of granting large powers to Local Councils; he was credited with advanced views on Labour problems; at Venice, where he sat with Falloux in a gallery of the Doge's Palace, watching a reception of the Austrian Emperor in St. Mark's Square, and talking politics with him, he "seemed quite in favour of Universal Suffrage".[3] After a great speech, in which Berryer traced out the programme of a Monarchy at once traditional and modern, the Comte replied in a glowing pronouncement, known as the Circular of Venice — "The day when France shall be convinced that the traditional and age-long principle of hereditary Monarchy is the surest guarantee of the stability of her Government and the development of her liberties, she will find in me a devoted son, eager to rally round him all the capacities, all the talents, all the glories of France, all the men who by their past services have deserved the gratitude of the

[1] The Duc de Lévis, the Marquis de Pastoret, the Duc de Cars, General Saint-Priest (an obscure deputy) and Berryer.

[2] *Fusion monarchique*, p. 15. General du Barail (*Souvenirs*, iii. 419) says that "La Rochejaquelein, the Marquis de Pastoret and the Duc de Valmy interviewed the Prince at Ems in 1849; they promised him that France would elect a Chamber that would place him on the throne. 'What!' he replied, 'you wish that I should submit my hereditary right to the vote of an Assembly!'. Recognising in that answer the blood of Henri IV, they offered to bring him back at the head of the Army. 'What!' he replied, 'you wish that I, the King, should enter France, bathed in the blood of my subjects!' The three visitors bowed their heads, and retired in silence; all three were included in the Emperor's first promotion of senators." De Luz (p. 150) has shown that the story is inaccurate, but it may have a certain symbolic value.

[3] Falloux, ii. 33. The Comte lived in the Cavalli Palace on the Grand Canal; his mother was at the Vedramini Palace. After the cession of Venice to Italy, he expressed his displeasure by selling his house.

country ".[1] But the liberties he was ready to bestow on others he claimed for himself ; he was not willing to be the figure-head in any parliamentary constitution ; the liberties he believed in were only safe, if protected by his own universally recognised authority ; if the Parliamentary Royalists accepted that, and worked with him, he was eager to share the task, but, if they tried to tie him down to be the mouthpiece of their policy, they must find some-one else to play the part ; it was not worth while being the heir of a hundred monarchs and appointed by the Voice of God, only to say ditto to a Council of Ministers. Let that be clearly understood. Yet up to the last, Henri could never persuade himself that it *was* clearly understood.

The *coup d'état* of 1851 had a remarkable result (so close observers remarked) in stiffening the Comte's views on authority, perhaps because he observed how willingly France had accepted strong government.

During the Second Empire, two problems presented themselves as of special importance for the Royalist party and its chief.

The first was that of Abstention. The Prince immediately issued instructions that no Legitimist was to take the oath to the Empire, or to recognise it by sitting on any elective body ; a large group of Royalists — especially in the West and South — at once obeyed and retired to their châteaux, giving themselves up to works of charity or to the management of their estates. For them the King's word was law,[2] whether he were on the throne or in exile. These afterwards formed the Extreme Right of the National Assembly, where they bore the mark of this twenty years' exclusion from public life.

The liberal and parliamentary group protested, and

---

[1] *Fusion monarchique*, p. 29.

[2] The Duchess of X, hearing an Orleanist say the Comte de Chambord had made a mistake, answered, " Sir, the King cannot make a mistake ". " Good," was the reply, " then you will recognise the infallibility of the Comte de Paris when he is on the throne." " Oh, that is different."

" tasted a joy not without its savour, that of remaining firmly Royalist while completely in disgrace with the King ".[1]

Berryer was the orator of this group; Falloux its statesman. At the Constituent Assembly of '48, an observer describes his " high pale brow, his soft mild eye . . . regular features and pointed beard elongating the oval face, like that of a Crusader kneeling in monumental marble ".[2] Famous in Catholic circles as the Minister who carried the Bill allowing them to open their schools, he was admirable in the art of managing men. Ollivier, who did not like him, and quotes maliciously his nickname " Fallax ", yet admits that he came nearest to his idea of what a statesman should be; he adds, " He thought himself irresistible; when he heard that someone had spoken evil of him, he said, ' Ask him to lunch '; under all these flowers, he was as hard as a rock ".[3]

In pure Legitimist circles there is a legend that Falloux detested the Comte de Chambord, " seeing in him not only a man, who did not appreciate him, but also a King, who meant to be his master ".[4] This is much exaggerated; but it is true there was little cordiality between them. Falloux came to believe and to say (sadly but firmly) that the Comte was impossible, while the Prince saw in Falloux the very incarnation of the dreaded Prime Minister of his sleepless nights, who would say to him suavely but unmercifully, " Your Majesty reigns; you do not govern ".

Falloux protested to the end against the policy of abstention; he pointed out in a letter to a friend (1852) that the Royalists had recognised the Second Republic;

---

[1] Falloux, *Souvenirs*, quoted *Fusion monarchique*, p. 112.

[2] Corkran, *Constituent Assembly*, p. 313; Grant Duff notes in his diary for December 29th, 1859 : " Today M. de Falloux came to call on us . . . my wife, who had never seen him before, said . . . that he looked just like a gentleman of the Ligue, come out of his grave " (p. 51).

[3] *Empire libéral*, ii. 173.   [4] Loth, *L'Échec*, p. 117 (quotation).

yet what régime could be more of a denial of all their principles ? How could the Revolution, Bonapartism, and Socialism be combated by private virtues and without public action ? " What you call preserving the French aristocracy, I call destroying it." [1] In 1861 he made the same point in a letter to the Comte himself [2] against the refusal to allow Legitimists to take political action in common with the Catholics of other parties ; nor did he mince his words :

We protest against a command imposed without discussion, and subordinating a majority to a minority. . . . Whenever the King has been lost in the party leader, France has shrunk from the Monarchy. . . . Your servants may be divided into two classes ; those, who borrow from you, and those, who bring you something worth having. . . . I know what heroic self-control it needs for a King not to say to himself, " The friends, who follow me most promptly, are the most devoted ". No, Monseigneur, they are not the most devoted, they are the most isolated, that is all.

The Comte was inflexible ; he said he was far from thinking himself infallible, but it was his duty to form a clear idea of the questions submitted to him. If others preferred opinions he regarded as highly dangerous, " I leave them the full responsibility for their conduct ; I shall certainly not give them any advice ". He observed the same attitude to Falloux's friends ; he rebuked Resseguier, who had taken his seat in the General Council of the Basses-Pyrénées, and that in terms like those used by a schoolmaster to an erring pupil : " I am compelled to receive you badly, and I refuse you my portrait ; you must say everywhere that you have been badly received. . . . I am seriously annoyed with your friend M. Falloux . . . those, who act with you, make the mistake of giving to the [Imperial] Government an honourability — the word is bad but it expresses what I mean —, which ought to be refused it. . . . I cannot approve of dis-

[1] Falloux, ii. 211-15. [2] Ibid. pp. 345-63.

obedience to orders, which I have given after long reflection."[1] Charles Lacombe, one of Falloux's young supporters, was also rebuked by the Comte for criticising Abstention, and replied quite in his leader's style : " It is the vice of the present régime to substitute orders for discussion ; the school, that at present predominates in the party, concerns itself with questions of persons, sends orders, and is ready to condemn all, who disagree, as disobedient. . . . Let the young Royalists, who are so devoted to you. work freely in your service."[2]

The second — and by far the more important — question, with which the Prince was faced, was that of his relation to his cousins, the Orleans Princes and their supporters.

By a curious coincidence, the Comte de Paris, the heir to the July Monarchy, was also grandson to the last reigning king, and his father had also died in his childhood by a violent death — not in this case by assassination, but as the result of a terrible carriage accident.[3]

But his parents were very different from the Duc and Duchesse de Berri. His father, the Duc d'Orléans, said in his will, " My son must, before all things, be a man of his time and nation — a Catholic and a servant, jealous and passionate, of France and of the Revolution ".[4] The Comte de Chambord was brought up by men ; the Comte de Paris had a mother of vigorous and original character — " the adorable Hélène ", as Thiers used to call her. During the '48 Revolution she went to the Chamber of

---

[1] Falloux, ii. 322-7.   [2] Lacombe, i. 256-64.

[3] His body, as he lay dying, was found in the road by some workmen, who said, " What a pity ! such a fine young fellow ! " ; when they heard he was the Duc d'Orléans, they carried him into a small shop. Here the Royal family assembled to watch the long death struggle (de Flers, *Le Comte de Paris*, p. 15). The Queen of the Belgians, Louis-Philippe's daughter, wrote to Queen Victoria : " My father and mother are both grown old in looks and their hairs are turned quite white. The first day my poor father could do nothing but sob, and it was really heart-breaking to see him " (*Letters of Queen Victoria*, i. 414). If any Legitimist wanted to see the usurper " paid out ", he had his desire that day.   [4] Hanotaux, ii. 127, *note*.

Deputies to claim the Regency on behalf of her son; her mourning veil was half drawn from her pale face; her blue eyes searched the Assembly for friends; her cheeks flushed at the welcoming applause. She held the Comte de Paris by the right hand; on the other side was the little Duc de Chartres; they were dressed in black with white, open collars falling back on their shoulders, and seemed " to have stepped down from Vandyke's portraits of the children of Charles I ".[1]

The Republicans shouted her down, and she fled to Lille, where she determined to appeal to the General of the garrison. The young Comte de Paris — ten years old, just the age of Chambord, when he too trod the path of exile — cried, " I am sure the soldiers will welcome me as one of their own children ", but their suite hurried them away.[2] They resided at the castle of Eisenach, which belonged to Hélène's uncle, the Grand Duke of Saxe-Weimar. The Duchess brought up her children to love France before all; they used to make little raids together across the Alsace border, and carry back the soil of their native land in trowels.[3] During the Crimean War, while the ladies made clothes for the wounded round the tea-table, the Comte pored over the map of Sebastopol, and knew the forts as well as if he had been there.[4]

He was to see real fighting in the American Civil War, in which the two brothers fought for the North on the staff of General McClellan; during the retreat from Chicka-

---

[1] Lamartine, *Revolution of 1848*, p. 101.

[2] De Flers, p. 44: "The Comte de Paris, on seeing the carriage which was to carry him away into exile, obstinately refused to get into it, and, when he found himself shut into it against his will and placed on his feet near his mother, he stamped violently and struck the floor of the carriage, saying that he did not wish to leave Paris; that his father had told him to stay there all his life, whatever might happen, and that there was nothing to fear, as he saw walking freely in the streets all those good National Guards, whose uniform his grandfather loved so much to wear, and who would be able to defend him, if the rebels and the men in blouses tried to attack him again" (*Souvenirs du Comte de Pontecoulant*, iv. 389).

[3] De Flers, p. 52.　　　　　[4] *Fusion monarchique*, p. 131.

hominy, the Comte, " easily recognised by his head-dress *à la* Henri IV ", made superhuman efforts to stem the rout.[1]

But, though a brave fighter, Paris was of a more studious and reflective turn of mind than his livelier brother. He wrote his first book at the age of twenty-two — *Damascus and Lebanon*, a record of travels to the East ; it was followed by *A History of the American Civil War*. His great interest, however, sedulously encouraged by his democratic mother, was the condition of the working classes ; he constantly visited Lancashire ; he attended a Christmas feast for the poor at Blackburn Town Hall ; in '63 he wrote a study of the cotton famine, *Xmas week in Manchester* and in '69 *Trades-Unions in England,* in which he defended freedom of association and profit-sharing.[2] Jules Simon went with him to Manchester, and was struck by his sound economic judgment ; " he had deep sympathy for the working classes, but he was free from all sentimentality ; he had no conventional prejudices, but he had no use for Utopias ".[3] At Rochdale factory the workmen were always offering him beer, "which he took with good grace ". A Legitimist would have said that beer was not the only thing his family had taken from the mob with good grace.

During the Empire, it was fashionable for Republicans to coquet with Orleanists, and Gambetta visited the Comte's Twickenham residence in 1865 with his friend Clement Laurier. Over their cigars the conversation became very free. " Your young republicans ", said the Comte, " are very foolish to frighten the bourgeois by memories of the French Revolution ; the times have changed. France is

---

[1] De Flers, p. 80. They were forced to leave America owing to the strained relations between France and the North over the Mexican expedition.

[2] De Goncourt notes in his diary for June 2nd, 1873 (Extracts, in the Nelson edition, p. 204): " I cannot get over my disgust, when I read on the fourth page of a newspaper among the advertisements — ' The second edition has just appeared of *The Situation of the English Working Classes*, a work in which M. le Comte de Paris has shown himself a thinker and a citizen ' . . . Pretenders who make themselves Socialist writers ! Pouah ! "

[3] Simon, *Soir de ma journée*, pp. 95-7.

no more threatened by a European coalition. There is no more any question of throwing down the head of Louis XVI as a desperate challenge to Europe " ; Gambetta burst into a long laugh. " In your family ", he said, " that would not worry you much." Imagination reels to think how the Comte de Chambord would have treated any light allusion to Égalité's vote for the death of Louis XVI ; the Comte de Paris, like a good host, professed not to have caught the remark.[1]

But the two young Princes were not the only representatives of the Orleanist House — far from it ; behind them were grouped " the uncles ", many and brilliant — Nemours, Montpensier, Joinville, Aumale, Ponthièvre, Alençon. Thiers loved to make malicious references to the two princes in the Tower and Uncle Richard, but the Orleans were a united and affectionate family. The education of the sons of Louis-Philippe was famous ; they attended the Collège Henri IV, and won prizes without any favouritism ; special orders were given that their breakfasts were only to cost half a franc per head, and their dinners two. Talleyrand said of them, " As young men, they are remarkable ; as Princes they are unique ".

The eldest of the royal brothers, the Duc de Nemours, was " of striking likeness to his great ancestor Henri IV, as Rubens portrayed the Béarnais ".[2] But the two most distinguished were the Prince de Joinville and the Duc d'Aumale.

Joinville was thirty, when the Second Republic was proclaimed ; he had distinguished himself in the Navy. It was he, who had brought back Napoleon's ashes from St. Helena in 1840, and had declared, on hearing that the English fleet would attack, " We will fight to the death ". He was no doubt a gallant sailor, but somewhat overfond of Platonic challenges to England ; in 1844 his pamphlet *Notes sur les forces navales de France* roused violent indigna-

---

[1] Pessard, *Mes petits papiers*, i. 129.   [2] Bodley, *France*, p. 550.

tion in England, and caused copious underlinings in Queen Victoria's letters. " And this *all* after our having been on such intimate terms with him and having *sailed* with him ! If he comes here, what *shall* we do ? Receive with open arms one, who has talked of ravaging our coasts and burning our towns ? You know how we like him, and that therefore it must be very annoying to us to see him get himself into such a scrape." [1]

Aumale, four years younger, was the most accomplished of the family ; he had won a great military reputation in Algeria. At the capture of La Smala he said to a Colonel, who complained that there was no way of retreat, " I belong to a race which is not used to retreating ". A captain murmured, " Enough follies have been committed today ". " Captain ", replied the Duke, " if anyone has been guilty of folly today, it is I, myself ; I am in command and I intend to be obeyed." [2] In '48 he was Governor-General, but he resigned at once, and sailed off to join his exiled family in England. Joinville was with him and, as they sighted Brest, the Admiral, who was escorting them, said, " Well, shall we land ? " They bent their heads in silence.[3] Like all the Orleans Princes, he had a remarkable diversity of tastes ; want of concentration was perhaps their principal weakness. Thiers — very unfairly — called them " slackers, smokers and idlers " ; [4] Napoleon III said of them, " They do not exert themselves, yet they get on ". The Comte de Chambord had only one interest in life ; if he asked you to step into the next room, you knew he was King. But the Princes were able to play many parts. If the time came, they were ready to rule. Meanwhile the Comte de Paris had his Political Economy ; Aumale could

---

[1] Queen Victoria to King Leopold (*Letters*, ii. 11). There is a reference in *Vanity Fair* (ch. xxii) : " Brighton is now only a hundred minutes off (from London) . . . and may approach who knows how much nearer, unless Joinville comes and untimely bombards it ".

[2] Du Barrail, *Souvenirs*, i. 205.   [3] E. Daudet, *Duc d'Aumale*, p. 92.
[4] De Marcère, *L'Assemblée nationale*, i. 293.

play the grand seigneur in his castle at Chantilly ; he and
Joinville could act the part of deputies at the National
Assembly, and a stupefied Bonapartist watched them
" waiting in the queue at the ticket office, putting the
change in their pockets, or shaking hands in the House
with neighbouring members, getting up to let members
pass, leaning forward to listen to conversations in front
or behind. One would never have guessed they were
Princes." [1]

For the moment they were in exile, and it lasted from
'48 to '71. They did not in the least regard exile as a
tribute to their position ; they did not hug it as a recognition that they were not as other men. The Comte de Paris
referred to " what is ironically called our privileged
state " ; frankly they wished to get back to France, almost
at any price.

Aumale bought Orleans House at Twickenham, and
filled it with art treasures — Italian, Spanish, Flemish, and
French ; in his study hung the ivory-handled sword of
the great Condé.[2] The Duke, who had great literary gifts
and became a member of the Academy, was working at a
History of the House of Condé, which the French Government would not allow to be sold in France. In '61 he
wrote his famous letter on the History of France to the
Prince Jerome Bonaparte, ending with the famous apostrophe :

You, who treat with an arrogance born of good luck and with an
injustice due to unmerited success, those ancient races, who have
long reigned over a generous nation . . . you, who enjoy the
accumulated fruit of so many labours, so much wisdom, so much
glory, and who put it every day in peril, be assured that, if you do not
leave these evil ways, it will not be to the Bourbons or the Orleans
— to whom at least no one has dared to address such a reproach —

---

[1] Loudun, *Journal de Fidus*, March 1st, 1872.
[2] In 1830 the last of the Condés, the Duc de Bourbon, was found hanging
from his bedroom window ; he left his castle of Chantilly to Aumale.

it will be to you and your family that will be applied those words of your uncle to the Directoire, " What have you made of France ? "

The publisher of this pamphlet was sentenced to a fine of 5000 francs and six months' imprisonment.

All the Orleans Princes had, almost to excess, the political prudence of Louis-Philippe ; Aumale had also inherited much of his wit and freedom of judgment. After the Orsini outrage, someone said how well the Emperor had behaved — " Like my father ", said the Duc, " every time they tried to assassinate him, but afterwards not a week passed without his committing some great fault." [1] Gambetta said to him, " I don't suppose you like Universal Suffrage ". " Like it ! " he answered, " what do you mean by that ? It is a question of time and occasion, not a question of principle." [2] He was the democrat of the family, " as proud to be the son of the soldier of 1793, as to be descended from St. Louis or Henri IV ".[3]

De Goncourt in one of his vivid portraits describes him (after 1870) " as the type of old cavalry colonel — the slim elegance, the furrowed face, the grey little beard, the baldness, the voice broken with giving commands ; his colour is slightly orange, his eye is grey like a bird's. When he is concentrating, his forehead wrinkles in the shape of a lampstand." [4] Yet, for all his military appearance, it is a question whether he was not at his happiest among his books and pictures at Chantilly.[5]

---

[1] De Goncourts, t. 5, p. 101.   [2] Bosq, p. 152.
[3] *Fusion monarchique*, p. 54.   [4] De Goncourts, t. 5, p. 167.
[5] Disraeli, who knew him well, wrote : " I do not know his equal ; such natural ability, such extreme accomplishments and so truly princely a mind and bearing. Between the Comte de Paris and the Comte de Chambord he has been sat upon in life and has had no opportunity " (*Life of Beaconsfield*, v. 297). Bodley (*France*, p. 551) writes : " It is vain to regret that the heir of Louis-Philippe was not the gallant and gifted Prince [Aumale] ; yet one may picture the destiny of France, had the fortunes and honour of the Orleans family been in the hands of one, who combined all the qualities, which touch the sympathies of the conflicting elements of the nation. The man of culture would have appealed to the literary and artistic instinct, widespread among

The contrast is striking between the Comte de Chambord, on the one side, childless, lame, and isolated, with little knowledge of the world outside a cold, stately palace in southern Austria, and, on the other hand, the prolific Orleans family, brilliant and diversified, travellers, writers, soldiers in two continents. Yet it is a mistake to confuse mobility with audacity, or to suppose that a military career necessarily encourages initiative. Though the Comte de Chambord had never seen a battle, no general ever disposed his troops with more authority or lost a fight with more gallantry. The Orleans were men of the world ; they had all the qualities of the average man. Such gifts may be sought after, when it is a question of setting up a new monarchy (as witness the success of the Coburg family in supplying " kings on demand "), but, when a fallen dynasty has to be restored, there is generally needed more appeal to the imagination. Weiss, the *enfant terrible* of the Royalist party, says, with much truth :

The Orleans Princes are a family of brilliant second lieutenants, and their head, the Comte de Paris, is a learned professor of political economy, in fact a John Stuart Mill . . . they are not at the head

the French people. The heir of the Revolution of July would have rallied the solid middle class. The descendant of Henri of Navarre would have conciliated the Royalists. But the quality to have touched the hearts and imaginations of the people was that of the soldier, the dashing horseman of Horace Vernet's paintings, the grave warrior who directed the trial of Bazaine, confounding the excuses of the faithless Marshal with a phrase that rang out like a trumpet-call to duty and patriotism — ' Il restait la France ' " (1873 — Bazaine had pleaded as an excuse for having surrendered Metz that, after the fall of the Empire, " nothing was left "). In a curious report on the politics of the French Army in 1876 for Gambetta's use (quoted in Gheusi's *La Vie et la mort singulières de Gambetta*, pp. 182-5), the author — supposed to have been the General Gallifet — says: "The Duc d'Aumale continues to rally round him the Generals and the *chefs de corps*, who have no definite political opinions. . . . In spite of his letter of August 9th, 1870, to the Minister of War, he never cared to take part in the last campaign, for what could have prevented him from going to serve as a volunteer like his brother, the Prince de Joinville, and his nephew, the Duc de Chartres ? . . . In the National Assembly, he never entered frankly on his rôle, contenting himself with representing every kind of echo and hope. He is a fine fellow without any striking points, ambitious without daring, a prince without pride."

of a great national party. Their noble qualities cannot be prized too highly, but I fear that in an hour of need . . . they would not give France a Gustavus Vasa nor a Conradin nor even a Charles Edward ; they would be excellent as private citizens, and I should admire their patriotism, abnegation and honesty without any reserve, if I believed that the honesty and patriotism of a descendant of Henri IV and St. Louis are enough, when they only equal in kind and degree the honesty and patriotism of the ordinary man.[1]

The idea of a Fusion [2] between the two monarchical parties seems to have begun during the Legislative Assembly of the Second Republic, in which Legitimists and Orleanists sat and voted side by side. Salvandy [3] went to see Louis-Philippe, who was favourable but alive to the difficulties. He said : " My sons ought to be always ready to reunite. . . . My grandson can only be legitimate King by the abdication or death of the Duc de Bordeaux." But the realist old monarch had little faith in the Comte de Chambord or his supporters ; he thought them political pedants. " What are abstract principles worth in politics ? ' Legitimacy ', ' Sovereignty of the people ' are only words. . . . I do not think that Fusion will ever come off, because the other side will do nothing to make it possible." He added : " My rôle in the world is over. The matter can only concern my sons, and they cannot act till all my family are agreed." [4]

Louis-Philippe died on August 26th, 1850. The Comte de Chambord had a Requiem celebrated at Wiesbaden in

---

[1] Weiss, *Notes et impressions*, p. 331 ; Bodley (*France*, p. 553) says of the Comte de Paris : " He has none of the qualities so essential for a crowned ruler of France after a century of revolution, but his domestic virtues, his hereditary Teutonic temperament, his interest in social questions, and his love of rural pursuits, would have made him an admirable King of England ".

[2] A counsellor of the Comte de Chambord wrote : " His Highness blames the word ' Fusion ' as indicating a fusion of political doctrines ; it should be replaced by the word ' Reconciliation ' " (Hanotaux, ii. 139).

[3] An ex-Minister of the July Monarchy, who was *persona grata* with the Legitimists for having refused to support the famous motion which pronounced a *flétrissure* on the deputies, who had been to pay their homage to the Comte de Chambord at Belgrave Square.　　　[4] *Fusion monarchique*, p. 8.

the presence of a thousand Legitimists, and after this sign
of goodwill, waited for his cousins.

The history of the debates on the Fusion from 1850 to
1870 is like the history of the clouds at sunset — nuances
of light and darkness, ambiguities which hover between
day and night, words and actions, which lose their outline
as we gaze upon them and melt into their opposites.[1]

Thiers once said that the Comte de Chambord " hated
his cousins, really hated them ".[2] No one, who had once
recognised the Prince's Christian magnanimity, would
suppose that he harboured such feelings. There were
always endless difficulties about their meeting, but, when
they did meet, they generally parted in mutual esteem and
affection. Only, the Comte de Chambord's likes and dis-
likes never interfered with his calm political judgment.
The Orleans Princes might be admirable young men ;
they might be quite guiltless of any responsibility for the
usurpation of Louis-Philippe, but by their position they
symbolised a great act of national apostasy from the pure
principle of Legitimacy. A lady of his Court asked how
she should behave, if she met the Princes in society : he
replied, " Until they have returned to their duty, you will
not know them ".[3]

For that act of rebellion an act of reparation was
necessary. This is what he described as " resuming their
places in the Royal family " ; he would make the Confiteor
as gentle as possible ; he would try to spare them any
painful repudiation of their father or their ideas ; but
the act must be unconditional ; that would be the proof
of its sincerity. The Comte, who had refused to offer
conditions in order to gain a throne, would certainly not
offer them to unite his own family ; he held out the vague
hope of complete understanding — on the Flag and all

---

[1] References, when not otherwise marked, are to the classical account of
these negotiations in Desjoyeaux's *Fusion monarchique* (chs. i. and ii.).

[2] De Marcère, *Assemblée nationale*, ii. 39.   [3] Hanotaux, ii. 126.

other questions —, when once they had returned to the fold. It was the same vicious circle which was, later, to make impossible all agreement between the Comte and the National Assembly, the one saying " No concessions, till I return ", the other " No return, till you concede ".

Louis-Philippe had said that nothing could be done till all his people were agreed ; in the Orleans family everything was settled by family councils, and their attitude varied as different members took the lead ; an envoy of the Princes, to whom a representative of Chambord complained about the difficulties of an arrangement, replied : " Is it not obvious that the action of one man is easier to secure than the co-operation of five or six people ? "

The Duc de Nemours was the strongest supporter of the Fusion ; he had affectionate memories of the Court of Charles X, and he regarded Legitimacy almost as if it were the Ark of the Covenant, on which his own family had laid sacrilegious hands.

Joinville had a less mystic sense of kingship ; he said of the July Monarchy, " Born of an *émeute*, it was overturned by an *émeute*". He therefore supported Fusion, but without any repudiation of 1830 ; he remembered that even the most venerable monarchies had always been founded by someone. " My father had the qualities of the founder of a dynasty. Aumale perhaps could have done it, but what could the young Comte de Paris do ? "

Aumale was himself too much of a Liberal to believe that Fusion was either possible or desirable.[1] In 1851 he wrote, " The Legitimists do not want Fusion ; what they want is submission ", and in a letter to Thiers he was ready to discuss " alliances with the Left ". However, he was not by character inclined to take the lead, and he " accepted " Fusion as the wish of his father and of

---

[1] A few days before his death, he said, speaking of the suspension of Louis XVI by the Legislative Assembly : " It was just ; he had forgotten his Coronation Oath ; he had called in the foreigner ; it was just " (Loth, *L'Échec*, p. 175, *note*).

the wisest counsellors of his party.

Queen Marie Amelie, the widow of Louis-Philippe, had a strong leaning towards Fusion. " I wish for union ", she said with great energy to Guizot. But her enthusiasm waned. She found the Legitimists expected her, after having been Queen of France, to become Duchess of Orleans ; " they wish us to pass under the Caudine forks ".

The most active opponent of the Fusion was the Duchess Hélène. In 1849 she told the Duchess of Dino that it would disgust her supporters in France ; she felt that she could not dispose of the future of her children while they were yet under age ; " Paris [the Comte] cannot become the servant of the Comte de Chambord ". She went for a walk with Thiers, one windy day at Claire-mont, and exclaimed vehemently : " This is all intrigue ; if circumstances alter, I will go on to Strasburg bridge, when the moment comes, and call on you and other friends. Then I will consult with you and act as you advise. But at present it is all intrigues of *émigrés*." [1]

As far as all this exchange of views can be dignified with the name of negotiations, it falls into three stages :

(1) *The Venice Circular* (January 22nd, 1851).—In this document, the Comte de Chambord inserted the significant phrase, " I venture to hope that with the aid of all good citizens *and all the members of my family*, I shall not be wanting in . . . the perseverance necessary to accomplish the work of national regeneration ". Two months later, this opening for agreement was closed by the refusal of the Legitimists to vote for the repeal of the laws of exile. The Comte de Chambord held strongly that it was part of the dignity of members of the Royal Family to remain in exile, and, on the Legitimist benches, much alarm was felt at the

---

[1] De Marcère, *Assemblée nationale*, ii. 38, and Pessard, *Mes petits papiers*, ii. 68. In her will, dated January 1st, 1855, she says : " Her sons should ever bear in mind the political principles, which have made the glory of their house, which their grandfather faithfully observed on the throne, and which their father, as his will bears witness, ardently adopted " (Bodley, *France*, p. 550).

rumour that Joinville was to stand for the Presidency of the Republic. It was known that Louis-Philippe had said on his deathbed, " As for you, Joinville, remember that if they offer you the Presidency, you are to accept it ". The Princes were furious. " The Comte de Chambord ", wrote Aumale, "threw a few shovelfuls of earth on the ditch, that yawns between us ; the Legitimists hastened to open it up again."

(2) *The Jarnac Embassy* (1852). — This time the *démarche* came from the Princes ; all the family, except the resolute Duchess of Orleans, concurred. The Comte de Jarnac was sent to Frohsdorf with a letter of submission to be presented to the Comte de Chambord, provided agreement could be arrived at on three points : the constitutional monarchy, the Tricolour Flag, and the " recognition of the historical fact " of Louis-Philippe's reign. It was clear that the whole matter was beginning to hinge more and more on the question of the Flag. It could not really be expected that the Princes should acknowledge their father to have been a usurper any more than that the Comte de Chambord should admit that his grandfather had violated the Charter ; as Guizot said, " Great acts of political reconciliation are not concluded in the confessional ". If Chambord would accept the Tricolour, the Orleans would regard the fact as a sufficient tribute to their dynasty.

It did not appear that the Comte de Chambord would be inflexible on the point. It was said that one of the reasons which prevented him from going to the Austrian Court was that he would have to go in full uniform, and he did not choose to wear the white cockade. But, if he was not inflexible, he was mysterious ; he sent a message to the envoy of the Princes that " there is no sacrifice he would not be prepared to make to France and in France ; he could not admit any intermediary between France and himself ". In a personal interview, the Count told de

S

Jarnac that he would be happy to see the Princes, if they returned " unconditionally ". After this, there was no more to be said ; de Jarnac regretted he could not deliver his letter of submission, and the Duchess of Orleans wrote triumphantly, " Let us keep ' ourselves intact for the future ".

(3) *The De Nemours Interview* (1853). — In November, de Nemours visited Frohsdorf. The Comte de Chambord met him with the words, " I know you come to tell me in the name of your brothers and yourself, that I can count on you ". " I come ", replied the Duke, " to bring you the expression of our feelings. Many bonds unite us already ; in the past, the memory of our common ancestors ; in the present, our common misfortunes, and I can add, the conformity of our opinions in the future." The Comte nodded assent, and they parted friends. The social barrier seemed about to fall down ; the Comte visited Louis-Philippe's widow, and had a rather embarrassed conversation with her about her private concerns. He seemed himself to feel that de Nemours' visit implied some form of political engagement, and, four years later, in a private letter to Berryer, he referred to " engagements made and promises given unconditionally ". The Princes were alarmed ; Joinville (supported by Thiers) demanded a firm repudiation. De Nemours took the other side and the dispute was referred to Victor de Broglie ; on his advice [1] de Nemours sent the letter of January 15th, 1857, which brought the matter to an abrupt conclusion by the statement of the three fundamental points of difference — the Tricolour Flag, the re-establishment of constitutional government, and " the cooperation of the national will in the Restoration ". Only the first had been discussed and no agreement had been reached. The Comte replied with

---

[1] In a testamentary note, dated 1877, left by Nemours to Alençon, his brother, he says : " Condemned by the result of the arbitration, I signed out of loyalty to my brothers, a letter which was contrary to my opinions " (de Luz, p. 221).

his favourite formula : " We cannot dispose of the destinies of the country far from France and without her consent ".

This time Fusion seemed to have been done for. The next year, the Princes passed through Brussels without calling on the Comte and — according to Thiers [1] —the Comte de Paris, who had just come of age, wrote to a friend that he adhered to his mother's opinion and desired to keep away from Fusion.

However, as Chambord had not gone beyond oracular generalities, as the letter of 1857 did not represent the views of the whole Orleans family, and as the Comte de Paris had not officially given his opinion, the door was still ajar.

What was the effect of all this on the Orleanist party ? Of course, in a sense, there was no organised party after 1848 ; the bourgeois, who had supported the July Monarchy, seemed to have found expression for their conservative instincts, first in a strong Republic and then in the Empire. The Duc d'Aumale, in a pamphlet on the parties under the Second Empire, uses the following significant words :

I prefer the title " constitutional party " ; those who use the name " Orleanist " look too much as though they were confining it to the personal friends of the Princes. . . . This continually embarrasses them, for it puts their personal opinions too much to the fore at the expense of the great principle they represent. . . . The Princes have a great number of personal friends, but they have never demanded from their followers the kind of loyalty, that pretenders demand from them ; for them there is no King of France outside France ; they have never preached abstention. . . . You may be sure that in the heart of every French Liberal, who does not believe in the Divine Right of the Republic, there is a hidden Orleanist. [2]

These last words give the key to the hesitation of the Princes ; their party had its Right wing and its Left. The

---

[1] Letter of 6/2/57, quoted Bosq, *Assemblée nationale*, p. 247, *n.* 1.
[2] *Écrits politiques*, pp. 168-70.

Right wing saw in them the representatives of Monarchy and, as the only chance seemed to be for a united monarchy, they were ardent Fusionists. The Left wing saw in them the representatives of the " principles of 1789 ", which would be compromised by any connection with the unpopular elder branch ; they therefore remained Separatists, not in the sense of expecting or desiring another 1830, or a throne to be won at the expense of the Bourbons, but in the sense of waiting on destiny. The Comte de Chambord was not immortal and he had no children ; at his death the Liberal Monarchy would descend upon the Comte de Paris, the next heir, without any serious rival ; or, if Monarchy was impossible, might not a Republic find a place for democratic princes — as Regents, Lieutenant-Generals, perpetual Presidents, like the Dutch Stadtholders, or what not ? It is natural enough that the Princes, freed from an immediate decision by the difficult behaviour of the Comte de Chambord, should have wavered between the Right and Left, hoping to make the best of both worlds. Unfortunately, when they did make up their minds, it was too late, and they lost both ; France would not have them as Kings, nor the Republic as citizens.

The Orleanist Left — under the various names of Regentists, Pure Orleanists or Separatists — rallied round the Duchess of Orleans. In France it was represented by Jules de Lasteyrie and De Mornay ; " Why ", they asked, " should we throw in our lot with an unpopular Monarchy ? " Thiers hovered on the edge of this group ; he wrote to the Duc de Chartres (July 5th, 1870) : ". . . Your claims on the future are based solely on your ability to give us liberty ".[1]

It was this group, that refused to support the Revision of the Constitution asked for by Louis Napoleon. The Duchess of Orleans would listen to nothing, that might postpone the restoration of her son. " She was one of the

[1] Bouniols, p. 4.

noblest and bravest creatures I have ever known ", says
de Broglie ; " she only had one weakness, common enough
in her sex, that she could never make her reason control
her passion, and supposed that all, who would not sacrifice
to her fancies, were either traitors or cowards." [1] He adds
that he can only account for Thiers' opposition to revision
by supposing that he hoped to be elected President himself
in 1853, if the law, which disqualified Louis Napoleon,
was maintained. Thiers summed up his views in a letter
to the Duchess (February 1851) : [2]

> The Empire comes nearer every moment. It can only be prevented
> by one candidature — that of Joinville (for the Presidency in 1852).
> His candidature will condemn him to be a loyal President of the
> Republic ; if after four years, he is obliged to retire, he will have
> added four years to the eighteen which France owes to the Orleans
> family (*i.e.* " eighteen years of good monarchy — 1830 to 1848 —
> and four years of good republican rule "). . . . We must recall him
> to France ; for that we need 360 votes. All the difficulty lies there.
> If the Fusion is made and is known, we win the Right and lose all
> the Left. I do not say that all idea of Fusion should be condemned
> for that, but I say we must be careful to know what we are doing.
> The Orleans family represent all that is good in the French Revolu-
> tion.

Thiers persuaded some of the Extreme Right to vote
against the Revision on the ground that the Comte de
Chambord's chance was precarious ; the Fusionists and
Bonapartists voted for Revision ; the Republicans and
Thiers' group against. With the death of the Duchess of
Orleans, the Orleanist Left tended to break up, and from
1871 to 1875 most of them passed over to the Republic,
under Thiers' guidance. The *élite* of the party had
accepted Fusion, which seemed the right policy, but they
lost as well as gained by it. Men like Renan and Taine,
who hated the Republic, hated one thing still more —

---

[1] *Revue des Deux Mondes*, 1/6/25, p. 607.
[2] Halévy, *Le Courier de M. Thiers*, pp. 275-7.

clericalism. They would have welcomed an Orleanist
dynasty, but they feared an alliance with the elder branch.
Taine felt no confidence in the " clerical and Austrian
upbringing of the Comte de Chambord ".[1]

The Legitimists also had their natural suspicions of the
Orleanist Left as allies ; had not de Tocqueville, one of
their prophets, said, " For us Liberals Legitimacy will never
be more than a means " ? Had not Daru and Buffet —
both Orleanists — been Ministers under the Liberal Empire,
and resigned their posts not out of loyalty to monarchy
but because they thought the Referendum of 1870 endangered parliamentary government ? Did not Prévost
Paradol, the most brilliant of Orleanist journalists, say in
his book, *La Nouvelle France*, the Bible of French Liberals :
" We must consider calmly and without prejudice the case,
in which the State, failing to find a suitable sovereign,
accepts the Republican form of government. It is true
that we shall regard the political machine as lacking one of
its important springs . . ., but the Republic, all the same,
is a form of government . . . which is most acceptable
and most worthy of the loyal support and sincere respect
of all good citizens " ? [2]

The Legitimists observed that the Orleanists always
had their pockets full of alternative constitutions in case
monarchy was impossible, combinations which they produced with the utmost complacency, when monarchy *did*
prove impossible, paving the way for the Republican Constitution of 1875.

The Orleanist Right — ardent for Fusion — formed the
most brilliant and the most interesting of the Opposition
groups under the Second Empire ; veterans of the July
Monarchy, like Guizot and Molé, mingled with the future
leaders of the Right Centre in the National Assembly, the

---

[1] Bellesort, *Les Intellectuels et l'avènement de la 3ᵉ République*, p. 220.
[2] P. 152. Gambetta scribbled in the margin of his copy : " Bonne
conclusion ".

three Dukes, de Broglie, the statesman, Audiffret-Pasquier, the orator, Decazes, the diplomatist. Their turn of mind is perhaps best represented by the Duc de Broglie ;[1] characteristic of the group was his subtlety of reasoning, his somewhat abstract way of regarding problems, his passion for history and religion (he was the author of the famous study on *The Church and Empire from the days of Constantine*), his delicate literary style — fitter perhaps for the lecture-room than the tribune — his curious mixture of unyielding conviction and scrupulous caution, that made him (as a devoted admirer called him) a consummate leader of retreats.[2]

What were the ideas in the minds of Royalists under the Second Empire ?

The policy of an Opposition is moulded by the Government it opposes ; under the First Republic, Royalism had stood for order against anarchy ; under the Second Republic, for Property against Socialism. The Second Empire claimed to be the ideal mixture of liberty and authority ; on the side of authority, it stood for centralised administration and the negation of parliamentary government ; on the side of liberty, it stood for universal suffrage, unmutilated and entire.

As against the Empire, then, Royalism stood for two Liberal principles — decentralisation and full parliamentary government : and one conservative principle — the reform, or " organisation ", of Universal Suffrage.

As for decentralisation and Parliament, it is not perhaps fanciful to say that the Orleanists cared more for

---

[1] See pp. 470-9 for a fuller study.

[2] The Duke's father in his *Views on the Government of France*, had expressed constitutional opinions not so very different from those of Paradol : " A Republic, which approaches to constitutional monarchy, or a constitutional monarchy, which approaches a republic, and only differs from it by reason of the nature and permanence of the Executives — these are the only alternatives left to lovers of liberty " (quoted de Roux, p. 38). These two books — of de Broglie senior and Paradol — had a great influence on the Constitution of 1875.

parliamentary institutions, while the Legitimists preferred liberties at a greater distance from the Crown, local and municipal in character.[1] This policy of decentralisation had been adopted under the Empire by Royalists and Republicans at the Congress of Nancy ; among the Legitimists there were some, who carried it as far as Regionalism, and dreamed of reviving the Provincial Estates of the ancient monarchy.[2] More moderate minds were content with restoring to municipal and General Councils some of the powers, which, from de Tocqueville to Taine, all the great thinkers of France had claimed for them.

The question of reorganising the vote — " finding a counterpoise to the brutality of number " was the approved phrase — had been constantly kept before the Royalist party by Falloux, who declared he would rather have a Republic with a sensible suffrage than a monarchy with votes for everybody. As far back as the days of the Second Republic, the Fusionist Committee had proposed as an electoral body " delegates of the municipal councils, and of professional corporations, the presidents of tribunals of commerce, etc." [3] The National Assembly of 1871 buzzed with such schemes — indirect suffrage, representation of interests, " adjonction des plus imposés " ; [4] they failed,

---

[1] Modern French Royalists have dropped the epithet " Parliamentaire " from their description of Kingship, and, *en revanche*, have stressed very vigorously the epithet " décentralisatrice ". See Charles Maurras, *Enquête sur la monarchie, passim.*

[2] Louis Veuillot wished each province to have its own magistrates, budget, militia and university, " only subject to the control of the General Assembly on points that concern the unity of the nation " (Bellesort, *Les Intellectuels*, p. 56).

[3] *Fusion monarchique*, p. 47. See de Luz, p. 277. Amédée de Margerie writes : " The Comte de Chambord desires — if I understand him rightly — a universal suffrage, from which ' the nomad element ' (voters who have not resided long in the constituency) should be removed, and interests be represented as well as numbers " ; he approves of de Franclieu's pamphlet advocating the representation of professional interests (Agriculture, Property, Industry, Commerce, Manufactures, Science).

[4] *I.e.* the presence at meetings of the municipal council of voters, who paid the most taxes, to settle the local budget.

because nothing is harder than to persuade an Assembly to disfranchise the electors, who have chosen it. Also, the electoral triumphs of February 1871 had reconciled many Royalists to Universal Suffrage ; they called themselves " liberal conservatives ", sincere lovers of freedom, though more and more embarrassed as the free institutions, so Royalist in 1871, gradually swung to the side of the Republic.

On the question of education the Comte de Chambord wrote (January 30th, 1865) : " Above all, let us preserve the labouring classes from the tyrannical and hateful yoke of compulsory education, which would complete the ruin of paternal authority and destroy the last traces of respect in the family and in the State ".[1] On industrial questions he wrote (April 20th, 1865) : " We must oppose association to individualism, to unlimited competition the weight of common defence, to industrial privilege the voluntary and regulated establishment of free corporations. We must give to the workers the right to combine. . . . It is natural that in these associations there should be formed . . . Syndicates, Delegations, Representations — whatever name they may bear —, who can enter into relations with employers, or Syndicates of employers to settle peaceably conditions of work and especially questions of wages." [2] Many Legitimist writers, such as de Luz and Beau de Loménie, believe that the Comte's progressive ideas on social questions helped to alienate rich Orleanist indus- trialists like the Duc de Pasquier.

There was another question — not the less serious, because it was not formally before the two Royalist parties — the religious question. As Royalists, neither Legitimists nor Orleanists interfered with the Vatican Council of 1870, but as Catholics many of them took part in the violent infallibility controversy and the jealousies and resentments of that period still lingered, even though

[1] De Luz, p. 290.   [2] Ibid. pp. 294-5.

for Frenchmen the proclamation of infallibility was so
soon followed by the earthquake of invasion and defeat.
The Comte de Chambord, though brought up under
Gallican influences, had become an ardent convert to
Ultramontanism ; he was heard to say : " It is less the
vices of Louis XV than the Four propositions of Louis XIV
that I am expiating today ".[1] It was significant that,
many years after, he declared his deepest feelings had
been understood by one, who was not even a Royalist —
though he rallied to the throne —, the mystical Ultramontane journalist, Louis Veuillot,[2] and the one councillor,
who seems to have influenced him, was Mgr. Pie, Bishop
of Poitiers, one of the champions of Papal claims at the
Council.[3] It added to the Comte de Chambord's mistrust
of the Assembly that its ablest members had belonged
to the Liberal party during the Council — de Broglie, de
Meaux and, above all, Dupanloup, Bishop of Orleans, who
declared that, while they personally accepted infallibility,
it was not the right moment (*non opportunum erat*) to make
it a dogma. In one of his few personal criticisms, the
Comte said : " Dupanloup has been telling me that it is
not the right moment to declare in favour of the White
Flag — for him it is never *opportunum* ".[4] It is true that
the Bishop had accepted the decision of the Council with
almost over-zealous alacrity, but the adhesion of opponents
after the victory is rarely received with enthusiasm by
those, who have borne the burden and heat of the day ; it is
said that the Papal Legate at Paris would have preferred
the Republicans to a Government counselled by Dupanloup.

---

[1] Loth, p. 459. The Propositions enunciated Gallicanism.

[2] It was he who said : " Si le Comte de Chambord accepte le drapeau
tricolor, il sera peut-être mon Roi ; il ne sera jamais mon homme ".

[3] Ollivier (*Empire libéral*, xiii. 127) describes him as " tall and majestic
in appearance ; his writings show the vigour and elegance of a robust theo-
logian . . . in the pulpit, his sermons never rise above the level of a well-
informed and lively conversation . . . without weakening in his Legitimist
and ultramontane convictions he usually shows a grace and charm of manner,
except in rare moments of passion ". [4] Loth, p. 158.

The Legitimists were apt, during the National Assembly, to suspect the Orleanists of lukewarmness in the cause of the Temporal Power, while the Orleanists were continually embarrassed by the attitude of Legitimist bishops, whose "charges" and pastoral letters irritated King Victor Emmanuel, and Bismarck, then engaged on his struggle with the Church; the Republican opposition made the most of the situation, to confirm their war-cry "A Restoration means War".

During the Second Empire, the Catholics had begun by rallying to the régime. The priests, led by Veuillot, proclaimed Louis Napoleon the new Constantine and the modern Charlemagne; the Emperor retorted by showers of favours; Préfets were ordered to enforce the observance of Sunday; the Army took part in religious processions; provincial Councils were again allowed to meet; the Emperor suggested to the Pope that (in return for a revision of the Organic articles of the Concordat — hated by the Church — and a modification of the marriage clauses in the Code Civil to bring them into accordance with Canon Law) Pius IX should crown him at Paris. But the Pope was afraid of Austria; besides, he could not forget that in his youth Louis Napoleon had been a Carbonari, and had taken arms for Italian independence.

Falloux was disgusted with the Catholic adulation of the Empire. He declared: "The Bishops are elevating the beauty of the Empress to the rank of an imperial institution"; he said to Veuillot: "I know Louis Napoleon better than you; never expect from him a sincerely Catholic policy; he retains his youthful ideas of the Papacy". In 1859 the Empire swung from the Right to the Left; when the soldiers marched through Paris on their way to fight for Italian independence, they were cheered in the popular quarters of St-Antoine. But Catholics began to desert and return to the Royalist ranks. Veuillot said: "Louis Napoleon is, after all, only a Louis-Philippe brought up to date ".[1]

Through most of the nineteenth century, almost as much in the political as in the ecclesiastical world, — Dupanloup had been one of the leading figures in the Church of France. This section may fitly be concluded with a picture of this most distinguished representative of Liberal and Catholic Royalism in the National Assembly.

Born in 1802 of peasant stock from Savoy, he soon became known as a Paris priest ; " there are few churches in the capital I do not know ", he said in one of his speeches. In 1827 he was confessor to the then young Comte de Chambord, then still Duc de Bordeaux ; when they met in 1871, the Comte recalled those distant days and added with a smile, " What I had to say then cannot have been very interesting ".[2]   He also taught the Orleans Princes their catechism ; during the war of 1870 he met the Prince de Joinville, serving incognito, and recognised him by his blue eyes, saying, " Monseigneur, you will get killed ".[3]

He had heard Talleyrand's last confession (" he must have listened to some jolly things " was the universal comment) ; in 1835 he was made Curate of la Madeleine ; in 1837 he became head of the seminary of S. Nicolas de Chardonnet, where he aided the young Renan to quit a vocation, from which he was in revolt ; in 1841 he was Lecturer at the Paris Theological Faculty, and caused a violent tumult by reading a letter of Voltaire's in which he declared his intention of denying the authorship of a comedy. Dupanloup's comment was : " These men are not a sect of philosophers ; they are liars ".[4]

Under the Second Republic, he was a member of the famous commission, that prepared Falloux's law on Secondary Education ; Falloux has described how Thiers used to leave the head of the table, when Dupanloup was speaking,

---

[1] Article on Cavour (Paléologue) (*Revue des Deux Mondes*, November 11th, 1925, pp. 153-177).   [2] De Meaux, p. 123.
[3] *Fusion monarchique*, p. 153.   [4] E. Faguet, *Mgr. Dupanloup*, p. 28.

and stand opposite to him, wrapped in admiration.[1] They always remained friends, even in the violent controversies of the National Assembly. " We must never break with Thiers ", he said to Falloux; " his good qualities are greater than his faults." [2] He accepted the bishopric of Orleans in 1849, after persistent refusals, through the persuasions of the Cardinal Archbishop of Cambrai. He wrote to Falloux : " Satius est Dei causa servitutem subire, quam, crucis fuga, perfrui libertate ".[3] In 1854 he became a member of the French Academy, from which he was to resign, in 1873, rather than sit side by side with the Positivist Littré. At the Vatican Council he led the opposition to Pius IX ; it was under his roof that de Broglie drew up his manifesto against infallibility for the *Correspondant*; he was even accused of having asked the French Government to interfere by evacuating Papal territory, which would certainly have brought the Council to an abrupt end, but there is no real evidence of this.[4] When Orleans was captured by the Germans, he interfered to save the town from levies, and, during the second occupation, he was imprisoned in his Palace; when the Germans illuminated his windows, at the news of the capitulation of Paris, the indignant Bishop had the lights extinguished at once.[5] When told that he was chosen as a candidate for the National Assembly, he cried, " At my age ! With all my other work and my broken health ! . . . Well, if necessary, I will give my life for them." [6]

For all his sixty-eight years, he was one of the most active deputies at Versailles ; in the Chamber he never seemed able to sit still for a moment on his bench ; he went backwards and forwards, then started up again to suggest an argument to a speaker, or give a word of command to his friends, or a piece of advice to a Minister.[7]

---

[1] Falloux, i. 425.   [2] *Ibid.* ii. 507.   [3] *Ibid.* i. 496.
[4] See the discussion of the evidence in Faguet's *Mgr. Dupanloup*, p. 99.
[5] Lagrange, *Vie de Dupanloup*, ii. 398.   [6] *Ibid.* p. 398.
[7] Bosq, *Assemblée nationale*, p. 266.

He was up at four o'clock in the mornings ; he had hosts
of hard-worked secretaries, and at night Vicars-General
hurried from his villa to Versailles and back again, bringing
proofs of his speeches or carrying back his corrections.[1]

He might aim at being a statesman-Bishop, but he had
no taste for worldly delights ; he hated luxury and receptions. When he was working, the door was locked and the
bell plugged up ; he went to bed at nine, and his friends
had the greatest difficulty in forcing upon him an important
visit to the Comte de Chambord, because it involved
travelling all night ;[2] he worked with his windows open at
all seasons, and he loved walking in the woods, however
cold the day. He was a striking figure, whether pacing
along the avenues of Versailles in his much-worn cloak, or
standing at the tribune in his violet cassock. His purple
cheeks, in which the blood seemed always coursing, his
eagle nose, his dark piercing eyes, his prominent chin, all
spoke of the fighter, softened by the crown of grey hair.
A fighter he was to his finger-tips ; but also he was incom-
parably the best educator of his day, not in the sense of
drawing up programmes or promulgating theories, but, in
Renan's phrase, he was " an awakener of the mind " ; as
a Bishop (so Renan shrewdly observes) he was more popular
with the laity than with his clergy, whom he worked to
death. In the rest of his famous portrait[3] Renan says :
" His conception of the world was very aristocratic, but he
admitted three aristocracies — the *noblesse*, the clergy and
literature ". No man cared less for science, or speculation ;
he loved the classics as " a gentleman's education " ; at the
Orleans seminary he was fond of presiding at performances
of Sophocles in Greek, and one of his great speeches in the
Assembly was a defence of the humanities ; like all great
teachers, he loved children ; he used to say, " My hair has
grown grey in their service ", and his methods of teaching

---

[1] Bosq, *Assemblée nationale*, p. 87.   [2] Falloux, ii. 470, 477.
[3] Quoted Faguet, pp. 13-18.

the Catechism are still in use. Like most Frenchmen, he adored his mother ; he taught Renan never to finish a letter to his mother without the word " respect ".

Combined with all this gentleness, he had the heart of a soldier. Ollivier is too hard on him when he says : " His heart was tender and aflame with charity, and yet when roused he never hesitated to attack his neighbour un-justly " ; [1] Falloux is more just when he says : " He had all the vehemence of conviction, and all the delicacy of charity ".[2] His warm heart loved souls, and hated systems, which he thought harmful to them. He could cry in full Assembly, " You pretend that Religion is threatening you ; how can it threaten you, when you possess none ? " ; in the debate on Rome he cried, " No, the King of Italy shall not make his bed there "; he was the Church Militant incarnate. He was a real liberal, nobly and sincerely a lover of freedom, a true representative of the great Catholic movement of '48, yet unlike it in supporting monarchy and opposing Papal infallibility ; Hanotaux says of him, " He missed in succession the rôles of Bossuet and Richelieu ".[3]

His position in the National Assembly was striking and curious. No English elective assembly has ever included princes or bishops ; a more decorous setting is reserved for coronets and mitres ; even among French Catholics there is a division of opinion as to the advantages of episcopal deputies.

He made it a rule never to interfere in purely political discussions (though it is said he had much influence behind the scenes) ; he reserved his rolling periods for such subjects as the Papacy, Army Chaplains, and, above all, Education. Even so, it was difficult for him to restrain himself ; the pulpit is very different from the tribune, and the devout silence of a deferential congregation from the tumult of a political assembly. Interruptions excited him ; he had to

[1] *L'Église et l'état au concile*, i. 443. [2] Falloux, i. 424.
[3] Hanotaux, i. 243.

bite his lips to keep back invective and repartee. In his speech on the Superior Council of Education he cried, " We, Bishops, may be useful to you, even when we fall under your shots ", and he made the gesture of shooting.[1] The Left were furious, but, though they loved to provoke him, they respected his sincerity and ardour. The Republican Tolain called out, " A Bishop does not frighten me " ; Félix Pyat said, " We must forgive him ; he is a Bishop " ; and those two interruptions perhaps best sum up their attitude.

On the whole, his greatness of soul and heat of conviction were among the most enduring supports of the sorely tried Catholic majority. That such a man should have been without influence on the counsels of the Comte de Chambord is a sign of the difficulties which Royalist deputies were called upon to face.

Fusion, so far a pious aspiration, had now to be translated into terms of political reality ; would the nearer possibility of a Restoration, only feasible if the two Royalist parties stood shoulder to shoulder, bring them more closely together ? or would the actual confrontation of real problems only serve to bring out the latent differences ?

(c) THE QUESTION OF THE PRINCES

It was the weakness of the Orleans family that they never appeared in public without an escort of personal questions — repeal of the laws of exile, right to sit as deputies, reintegration into the Army, restoration of property ; all this was as different as possible from the dignified aloofness of the Comte de Chambord, who only asked for one thing, to be recognised as King. With

---

[1] Faguet, p. 115. In another debate he was quoting a " disgraceful piece of materialism " ; the Left reminded him that it was written by Napoleon's doctor. " He may have been Napoleon's doctor," retorted the Bishop, " he would not have been mine " (*Séance du 18/6/75*).

the exiled Princes it seemed a secondary question whether they should ever again have the crown in their family; their first desire was to get back to France at all costs, and resume their rights as French citizens.

This difference of attitude was clearly shown at the outbreak of the War of 1870; many Legitimists considered this as a heaven-sent opportunity for their King, and never opened their newspapers without hoping to see that the Comte de Chambord was with the Army. On August 18th the Comte had left Frohsdorf, and was at Yverdon on the Swiss frontier; he left a sealed letter for his wife which contained the words, " I am under no illusions; I know that I shall probably meet death where I am going ".[1] His plan was to put himself at the head of a body of volunteers on the right of the French Army in retreat.[2] He characteristically concealed the whole transaction from the Marquis de La Ferté — his agent in France —, who reached Geneva on September 15th, and appealed to him to land in Brittany, and exhort the country to drive out the foreigner. He added :

You will have the Orleans Princes at your side; you will re-constitute the House of Bourbon on the best and most solid basis. If you are to die, I may be allowed to say that it will be a glorious end; I do not suppose you will succeed in driving out the Prussians; they are too strong, but, some day, there will be peace and on that day, Monseigneur, you will have fought for the deliverance of France and will be carried on their bucklers; that is how you will regain your throne; that is the true way of ascending it for a descendant of Henri IV.

The Comte " did not believe the plan possible ".[3] In a letter of October 1st to the King of Prussia, he says : " I had to yield before the most pressing representations, when I was going to the frontier ";[4] nothing more is known. It is probable that he saw the impossibility of

---

[1] De Roux, p. 171.
[2] De Luz, p. 310.
[3] *Bureau du roi*, p. 157 (cp. Lacombe, i. 234).
[4] De Roux, p. 171.

T

collecting a Royalist Brigade, when so many Legitimists were serving with the regular Army ; Bismarck said : "He will never be King of France, because he cannot swim across the Seine with a sword in his mouth ".[1] But it would be a complete mistake to regard the Comte as a coward ; perhaps his delicate conscience regarded the Restoration as too serious a matter to be snatched from the nation in some moment of martial enthusiasm. He confined his intervention to such acts of sympathy as putting the château Chambord at the disposal of the Red Cross ; meanwhile his Manifestoes made it clear that he did not regard it as necessary to cross the frontier in order to speak as King. In September he wrote : " At all costs the honour and territory of France must be kept intact " ; in November, he proposed as a " talisman capable of chasing away the invader, a national government having right as its basis and honour as its principle " ; in January 1871 he protested against the bombardment of " the city of Clovis and Charlemagne, St. Louis and Henri IV ".[2]

The Orleans Princes were held back by no scruples ; for them the war was like the sound of a trumpet to the war-horse, or the first glimpse of home to an exile. The Comte de Paris, after having applied in vain to both the Imperial Government and the Government of National Defence for leave to join the Army, made a desperate appeal to be allowed to take part in the defence of Paris ; he offered to serve under an assumed name and to return to exile after the last shot was fired. " You must know what I suffer ", he wrote to the General Chabaud-Latour (January 17th, 1871), " in being condemned to remain an inactive spectator of the heroic struggle of my countrymen. I must say that such a possibility had never entered my mind. . . . It seemed to me . . . that no one could forbid an Orleans to take his place on the fortifications of Paris, the work of

[1] Loth, p. 127. [2] Loth, p. 124.

my grandfather, the soldier of Jemapes." It had been objected that " their names might serve in the capital as a pretext for civil war " ; on the contrary, the only result (he pleaded) would be to rally round the Republic those Liberals, " who might have been frightened by the sound of the word ' Republic ', and would be reconciled to this form of government by our adhesion to it ".[1]

As soon as the Empire had fallen, his uncles Aumale and Joinville crossed to Paris with the Comte de Paris's younger brother, the Duc de Chartres. Aumale immediately sent for Bocher and d'Haussonville, two of the most eminent Orleanists, and asked them to inform the National Government of their arrival. " You see," he said, " we have rallied to the cannon ; we have come simply as Frenchmen and as soldiers. The most obscure and dangerous post will suit us best." The Government professed themselves much moved at their offer, but they were unanimous in asking them to go away. Jules Favre said : " We should run the risk of seeing a large part of the National Guard, who are devoted to them, attempting to escort them to the Hôtel-de-Ville ". General Trochu said : " The most fatal thing that could happen would be to divide our forces in the presence of the enemy ". Reluctantly the Princes left the city.[2]

Their next attempt was more romantic. Joinville and Chartres landed at Havre, and succeeded in reaching Tours, the seat of the Delegation Government. Chartres slipped into the Army under the name of Robert le Fort. Joinville, after having been refused by the Government, planned to enter Paris as a gardener, with a check handkerchief and red umbrella, but he finally presented himself at the defence of Orleans, where the soldiers admired his courage in the trenches. " You don't mind the shells, then ? " they enquired. " I am deaf," he replied. " I can't be as afraid

[1] De Flers, *The Comte de Paris*, pp. 114-16.
[2] D'Haussonville, *Journal*, pp. 122-8.

of them as other people." [1] On December 30th he was discovered and expelled. "The Prince ", wrote Gambetta, " has committed a most serious fault in secretly entering France and joining the Army, where, if his presence were known, it might become an element of disorder." [2] When Aumale wrote to Gambetta expressing astonishment that they asked for everybody's help except that of the Princes, the Dictator of Tours replied that, " after Joinville's campaign ", he could not give them a military command.[3] Such an attitude was intelligible in men, to whom the Fourth of September was more memorable for the proclamation of the Republic than for the fall of the Empire.

But one is surprised to find it in so detached an observer as Thiers ; he flew into a temper, whenever the Princes were mentioned. " They are a thousand times in the wrong," he said to d'Haussonville ; [4] " their friends are advising them very badly. It is a crime to compromise all the efforts I am making by personal preoccupations. It means throwing us straight into civil war. I shall tell everybody what I think. Ah ! the Princes are always like that. I snap my fingers at the Bonapartists ; they are dishonest ; one cannot say or think too much evil of them. But the Orleans ! if they are pursuing selfish ends at such a moment, I shall treat them in the same way as I treat the Bonapartists." Old d'Haussonville, a loyal and gallant servant of the Orleans family, not at all frightened by Thiers' tantrums, protested. " Put yourself in their places ; think of the patience, with which they have borne the sorrows of exile for twenty-three years ; they are more

---

[1] One night, when he was staying with l'Abbé Denis, curé of St-Hilaire Mesmin, he said, " Poor France ! what will happen to her ? " " Ah ! " replied the priest, " the 1830 revolution began all this. Louis-Philippe occupied a throne which did not belong to him " ; and (the Prince remaining silent) he went on : " France will only find rest and stability, when she returns to the principle our fathers abandoned eighty years ago ". " M. l'abbé," Joinville replied, " I have always thought that " (*Fusion monarchique*, p. 153).

[2] *Ibid.* p. 154.   [3] *Ibid.* p. 157.

[4] D'Haussonville, p. 20.

sincere than you think ; you only knew Louis-Philippe, when he was old and a bit sceptical. Think what he was at twenty in the days of Jemapes and Fleurus ; all these Princes are Frenchmen to their finger-tips. If I were one of them, I would not be convinced by your reasons : I would come to France." [1] But Thiers persisted in his prejudices. "It is Joinville, who has planned this coup ; he is capable of any trick. Ah ! I know them all well, except the young ones ; the Comte de Paris would make a very good constitutional monarch, I should think, but he has written some absurd letters to democrats. They are all on the beg for thrones. Except the old King, whom I liked, and the Duc de Nemours, I have much to complain of their conduct — I except the young ones." [2]

Meanwhile important negotiations were going on in the South of France. The Royalist Laurentie, almost eighty years old, had been living at Bordeaux during the siege of Paris, bringing out a provincial edition of the Legitimist paper, the *Union* ; he had been a violent Ultra during the Restoration, had attacked Villèle for being too moderate, and had sat in Polignac's office at the time of the Ordonnances. In his old age he had calmed down. "Who knows ", he wrote, " if God does not will that I, worthless as I am, after having made war so long against these poor princes of the Revolution, should now have some part in their return to dignity and duty ? " The Duc de Decazes, a personal friend of the Orleans Princes, was living at his château, La Grave, and informal conversations took place between him and Laurentie. They were not without storms. Decazes, who had perhaps never forgiven the Ultras for their attack on his father (Louis XVIII's favourite), talked tentatively about abdication or the adoption of the Comte de Paris by the Comte de Chambord. [3]

After the February elections, Thiers had forbidden the Princes to approach Bordeaux, and Thiers had quarrelled

---

[1] *Ibid.* pp. 113-117.   [2] *Ibid.* p. 139.   [3] De Roux, pp. 176-8.

with de Broglie about their motives in a railway carriage. Thiers had far too sound a judgment to suppose that they had either the ambition or the power to be serious rivals to himself or to the security of the Republic ; they were far more dangerous haloed with the prestige of misfortune and the romance of exile. The very way to disarm persons of their easy-going temperament was to throw them back into the security and comfort of a social life they had missed for so long.[1] The true explanation of his attitude is probably to be found in Rémusat's phrase to the Princes, " You embarrass him, as you always have " ; he could exercise his wit on the Comte de Chambord without scruple, but he felt that he had an obligation to the children of his old master, which made him uneasy.

For the moment, his policy was clear ; by refusing to support the abrogation of the laws of exile and the validation of their election, he would force them to negotiate with the Legitimists for their votes ; if the negotiations broke down, he would be free from their presence ; if they succeeded, the Legitimists could be trusted to exact terms that would extinguish Orleanism as an independent force.

Thus a most serious problem was forced upon the Orleanists, and without much time for reflection — that of their relations with the Legitimists, without whose votes their Princes probably could not return from exile. The Bishop of Orleans wrote to Joinville urging him to support the Fusion ; skilfully adapting his own classical enthusiasm to the nautical profession of the Prince, he quoted Horace, " ' O navis, referent in mare te novi fluctus ; fortiter occupa portum '. A ship beaten by the storm needs not merely a roadstead but a harbour. Give us the spectacle of the House of Bourbon respecting the principle it represents, and

---

[1] See the opinion of the Legitimist La Ferté : " I said that they could not be at the same time Princes and citizens ; by being elected deputies they could only lose their prestige ; nowhere was it more necessary than in France to keep up one's position " (*Bureau du roi*, p. 188).

not violating it by personal rivalries ; show Europe and the world the noblest royal family under the sun reunited at last, and drawing strength from its union for the prosperity and honour of France." [1] Aumale sent back a declaration, in which the House of Orleans pledged itself not to oppose a restoration of the legitimate monarchy. [2]

But it was evident, from a visit of General Ducrot to Aumale, that the Legitimists would demand more than this. Ducrot was a distinguished soldier ; he had been lieutenant-colonel under Aumale in Africa. In 1869 he wrote from Strasburg describing the German preparations ; [3] at Froeschvillers he resisted a whole German army with one division. At Sedan, after MacMahon was wounded, he was in command for a few moments, and had the good sense to order a retreat on Mezières, which would have saved the army ; at the Siege of Paris he acted with great courage and energy. [4] In politics he was a strong Legitimist. Thiers said of him that " he had a pint of blood too much " ; he attacked Garibaldi in the Assembly ; he said that Picard and the Republicans in the Government were " incredibly feeble ". When at Bordeaux Thiers said there was not a general who would act at Paris, unless the Assembly were near by to support him, Ducrot answered, " I should not hesitate ; I would prefer not to have the Assembly on my shoulders ". When the Prussian

---

[1] *Fusion monarchique*, p. 181. Even more august ecclesiastical influence was brought to bear in favour of the Fusion. Pope Pius IX wrote directly to the Comtes de Chambord and Paris begging them, in the interests of France and the Church, to come to an agreement, which should facilitate the Restoration. He received from both the most filial assurances, and he said to de Rossi, " I think I have united the princes of the House of France ; the Monarchy will be restored " (Loth, p. 78). [2] Hanotaux, i. 152.

[3] He wrote to General du Barail : " War is certain and imminent ; we are not ready, but we shall muddle through " (Du Barail, iii. 135).

[4] He was never allowed to forget the promise, which he made before his sortie that " he would return dead or victorious ". Adam, the Republican, once tried to provoke him to a duel by saying to his face " neither dead nor victorious " (Mme Adam, *Mes angoisses*, p. 147). General Le Flô defended him warmly : " Is it his fault that he is not dead ? he did his best, like Ney at Waterloo " (Claveau, p. 58).

General Manteuffel arrived unexpectedly just before a dinner that Thiers was giving to some deputies, Ducrot declined to sit down at table with him, and left the Prefecture.[1]

The General arrived at Biarritz on March 12th ; he did not come in any official capacity, but he had consulted one or two Orleanist friends before coming. He told the Princes that the partisans of the Fusion were alarmed at the development of revolutionary ideas and at Thiers' intrigues for power ; a united royal family was necessary, and it was for them to take the first step by making their submission to the Comte de Chambord ; after that, there would be no difficulty in obtaining a majority for the abrogation of the laws of exile and the validation of their elections. This was going too fast for the Princes ; they replied that, according to the information they had received, the recall of the Comte de Chambord would be the signal for civil war ; considering the attitude of Thiers, it would be better to wait till the Royalists in the Assembly had come to some arrangement with him ; meanwhile they could enter the Assembly and discuss the whole matter with their fellow-deputies. Ducrot thought he saw signs of a reluctance to accept the Fusion, and added very frankly : " Either the Monarchy will attach itself once more to the chain broken in 1830, or it will cease to exist ; personally I should not hesitate to vote against abrogation and validation, if you appeared at the Assembly without having given previously pledges of submission to your King ". Aumale fired up — " My dear general, you will do as you please, and we shall do the same " ; and on this note the first interview ended.

That evening Aumale sent again for Ducrot, and said : " Old friends cannot separate like that ; I think we can come to an agreement by a slight modification of your

[1] Thiers, *Souvenirs*, p. 192 ; Chalvet-Nastroc, *Les Projets de restauration et le général Ducrot*, p. 33.

programme. The abrogation of the laws of exile must come first ; it is the opening of the breach ; if Thiers cannot prevent us from entering, he will be forced to surrender. But, if we were to begin with a visit to Geneva (where the Comte de Chambord then was), he could use it to attack us and remain master of the situation ; abrogation first, then validation, and then the Geneva visit." The General once more defended his own opinion, but respectfully deferred to the decision of the Princes.[1]

On March 17th the Princes moved to the old episcopal palace of Dreux, and it was here that they received a more official deputation ; three Legitimist deputies of the Moderate Right came to plead the cause of Fusion — de Meaux, de Cumont, and de Maillé. The Vicomte de Meaux, deputy for the Loire, was an accomplished type of the Liberal Catholic ; he was son-in-law of Montalembert and a member of the " Falloux group ". Smiling and amiable, he was a busy member of the Assembly, and secretary of many commissions ; his polished style and literary graces made his speeches acceptable and are conspicuous in his *Souvenirs politiques*, one of the most attractive records of this period.

Cumont also belonged to the Falloux group [2]; he was older than de Meaux, rather a haughty-looking aristocrat with monocle and dry sarcastic voice — like a nobleman of the old régime ; but, under his hard manner, he had virtues unknown to the contemporaries of Talleyrand ; for, after writing some memoirs full of malicious portraits of his colleagues in the Assembly, he felt scruples of conscience, and burned them all.[3]

Count Armand de Maillé was of a line famous in chivalry ; he had distinguished himself in the war at the

[1] *Fusion monarchique*, pp. 177-81.

[2] Castellane in his *Men and Things of my time* (p. 46) calls him Falloux's aide-de-camp; at the February elections, Falloux stood aside to give him a seat.

[3] Lacombe, *Journal*, ii. 325 (Appendix article, by Lamy).

head of the Anjou battalion, and was a devoted Royalist, but he knew how to speak to his King, when it seemed necessary, the language of the firmest independence.

At the interview, Aumale did most of the talking — brilliant but rather heartless, de Meaux thought him ; he began by declaring that they would offer no opposition of any kind to the restoration of Henri V. " But ", he went on

it is not us, whom you have got to rally to your side. The House of Orleans has no party, strictly speaking — except perhaps a few sons of my father's Ministers — but they correspond to a certain state of feeling, certain prejudices, if you like, in the French people — to their taste for a Monarchy " without priests and nobles ". For this reason in 1830 we had the greater part of the country with us ; this sentiment may have taken other directions since, but it is not extinct ; if we were to recognise at this moment the rights of the elder branch, you would have gained a few more Legitimists, but that would be no guarantee of success ; what you have got to do is to rally to your side and to your Prince that portion of French society, which we represent.

The tendency of this answer was clear ; the Orleanists were prepared to acknowledge the Comte de Chambord, if they obtained guarantees that he was " up to date " in his views on Monarchy ; the Legitimists offered what assurances they could ; they sincerely declared themselves " lovers of liberty, free from every thought of reaction " ; they added that — as far as they knew — the Comte de Chambord had no intention of asking France to give up her flag or her constitutional liberties. De Joinville, who was deaf, stood a little on one side, but, at one point, he intervened with more spontaneous feeling than his brother. " In a word, gentlemen, if we held the crown of France in our hands, we would place it on the head of the Comte de Chambord and not of the Comte de Paris ; do you not agree, Aumale ? " The Duke assented with a gesture ; but they added, " we do not hold the crown of France in our hands ".

No formal agreement was drawn up, but it was settled that the question of a visit to the Comte de Chambord should be decided by a joint meeting of the deputies of both parties. As they left the Palace, they compared impressions ; they were agreed that the Princes did not wish to take any initiative, that they did not intend to support or oppose the Restoration, and that their only positive desire was — to remain in France.[1]

Scarcely had the three deputies returned to Bordeaux than the Commune broke out. Some doubts were felt about the safety of the Princes ; the Paris newspapers openly spoke of murder. The Préfet of the Loire was assassinated, and, on March 31st they received a telegram from London to the effect that certain suspicious individuals had set out for Dreux. Thiers took advantage of these rumours to make another attempt at getting them out of France ; Leblond — the procureur-général at Paris — in forwarding the London telegram, added, " It is most regrettable that the Princes should persist in remaining in France, in defiance of the law ". The Princes, after a few days spent in hiding with a friendly deputy at Marcouville, Léon Vingtain, were preparing to leave France when the Duc d'Audiffret-Pasquier, informed of the situation by Bocher, persuaded them to stay at his château de Sassy. He told Thiers, next time they met, that the Princes were his guests and he hoped no one would venture to lay a finger on them.

The Duc de Pasquier is one of the most interesting figures of the Right Centre. His father, Audiffret, was an able financier and Receiver-General from 1839 to 1856 ; his uncle, Pasquier, was the well-known Chancellor of the Chamber of Peers under the July Monarchy. His nephew used to relate, as an example of how people respect a Government, which sees justice done, that in 1848, when the Chancellor left his carriage at Tours, the mob wished to burn it,

---

[1] *Fusion monarchique*, pp. 182-4.

but, when they found out the name of the owner, they showed every mark of respect, saying, " He is the man who judged Teste ".[1] The Chancellor adopted his nephew, and left him the beautiful castle of Sassy in the Department of Orne.

The Duke, though he was a faithful Orleanist, felt that the " plaque of the Holy Spirit ", which his uncle had worn, ought to be returned to the descendant of Charles X, and placed it in the Comte de Chambord's hands at Venice.[2] In 1840 he was a member of the Conseil d'État, but he left public affairs under the Empire, devoting himself to the administration of his mines at Anzin ; in the Right Centre he belonged to the group called " the three Dukes " (including de Broglie and Decazes), and in some ways he seemed the most gifted ; he was generous and courageous by nature, a charming talker, endowed almost beyond any deputy with the difficult art of rousing to enthusiasm a meeting of colleagues in a committee-room ; and, at the tribune of the Chamber, capable of producing one of the great oratorical sensations of the Assembly — the attack on the Army Contracts of the Empire. His appearance was not distinguished ; he was small, nervous, and alert, his eyes grey and restless, his face long, the nose thin and prominent — " the nose of the doctrinaire " ; but he had the commanding manner of the aristocrat, one of the last survivors of the old legal families with their honest independence and hatred of all that was underhand ; [3] he had, far more than the Duc de Broglie, that openness, without which an aristocrat can hardly succeed in a French Assembly ; he was not only a personal friend of the Orleans family, but he represented, far better than his brother Dukes, the intense Orleanist hatred of the

---

[1] One of the corrupt politicians of the epoch (Lacombe, ii. 17).

[2] *Fusion monarchique*, p. 116.

[3] Du Barail, who met him at dinner without knowing who he was, says : " He had free manners, and was a little dominating. . . . I took him for a *procureur* accustomed to treat everybody as criminals " (*Souvenirs*, iii. 382).

Empire.[1] Yet, with all these gifts, he never succeeded in playing a leading part; he had a hot temper and an impatience of control, that made him sometimes a difficult colleague; he was not personally the least vindictive; he used to say, "I have no hatred for mankind; I like discussion, and accept it without bitterness";[2] and, again, "Hatred slips through my fingers".[3] But he could not resist the instant retort; Claveau justly says, "There was never a man less inclined to turn the other cheek".[4] He was also exceedingly versatile, and the older politicians, while they liked hearing him talk at the party groups, shook their heads over his want of solidity. "He is like a brilliant firework, breaking out in a hundred different places."[5] Like many impetuous people, he was not too sure of himself; a little more experience of public life, which he missed under the Empire, would have steadied him. A great admirer of the Restoration period, he was always going to write a Life of the Duc de Richelieu, but he never did; he performed yeoman service first to the cause of the Fusion, and then to that of the Republic, but he was never admitted into Ministries of the Right or Left. Deschanel well describes him as "a tribune of the aristocracy, impatient of control, all nerves and quicksilver".[6] Lacombe, who knew him well and liked him, notes the general impression in his Diary: "His nature is generous and changeable, never so ready to calm down as when he has lost his temper; unreliable as a leader, powerful as a helper".[7] "He has a generous and impulsive nature; I understand his impatience and disgust, but in politics it is a duty to restrain one's feelings."[8]

---

[1] The feud between Bonapartists and Orleanists always seemed more bitter than between Bonapartists and Legitimists, partly because the Orleanists were rival vendors of a "popular monarchy", and partly because the Emperor had confiscated the property of the Princes.

[2] E. Daudet, *La Vérité sur la restauration*, p. 64.

[3] *Portraits de Kel-Kun*, p. 29. [4] Claveau, p. 105.

[5] E. King, *French Statesmen*, p. 200. [6] *Gambetta*, p. 218.

[7] *Journal*, ii. 45. [8] *Ibid.* ii. 60.

At the moment, he was full of generous ardour to protect the Princes against Thiers' persistent ill-will. They arrived in the middle of April ; they were known as " the comtes de Vineuil ", and the children called them uncle. Every day they rode in the park, and in the evening Orleanist councils were held in the famous library of the castle. Pasquier was cautious about any very close union with the Legitimists. " Do not compromise yourself," he said to Aumale ; " wait for events ; the Comte de Chambord will prove impossible, and then naturally France will have to choose between a radical republic and a republic with a Prince at the head." [1] It was a tempting prospect ; Louis-Philippe had told Joinville to accept the Presidency of a Republic, if it were offered him ; the promise to Chambord, that they would not be rivals for the crown, hardly applied to offices less than royal. But, for the present, the Princes refused to commit themselves. Aumale professed Fusionist sentiment : " I am always regarded as a man of 1830, but I would give much for 1830 never to have happened ". When pressed for an immediate decision, they answered that their only desire was to enter the Assembly, and to claim their rights as ordinary citizens ; the other questions must be settled by the Comte de Paris himself ; they promised " not to bring to bear upon him any influence unfavourable to conciliation ". [2]

The Comte de Paris — now thirty years old — was care-

---

[1] Loth, p. 73.

[2] On January 31st the Comte de Montalivet — a close adviser of the Princes — sent Thiers a letter from Georges Picot, his son-in-law, in which he said : " At present we must use the republican form of government in order to reform the country, corrupted by the Empire " ; he added himself : " One of the friends of the Princes said to me the other day, ' When one considers what the rôle of monarchy would be in face of the foreign occupation, one feels that, if the Republic did not exist, it would have to be invented ' " *Courier de Thiers*, p. 426). On February 13th Montalivet wrote to Thiers : "I am writing today to Joinville hoping that he will leave it entirely to you to save France " (*ibid.* p. 428). This proves no hideous Orleanist plot, only that certain Orleanists still hesitated to throw in their lot for the moment with the Legitimists.

fully watching events from London ; he was assisted by
the advice of that distinguished friend of his family, the
Duc de Broglie, not yet leader of the Conservatives in the
Assembly, but ambassador to the Court of Queen Victoria.[1]
The attitude of the Comte himself was that the question
of return from exile ought not to be confused with questions
about the Monarchy ; it ought to be settled on its own
merits. The larger constitutional questions had been
wisely postponed by the Assembly ; could not the Princes
themselves claim a Pact of Bordeaux ? On February 18th
he wrote to the Comte de La Palice : " I have no hostility
towards the Legitimists, but . . . I ought not to take part
in any negotiations, which might seem to have for their
object to dispose of France without her consent ".[2] On
February 26th he wrote to d'Haussonville : " As for me, I
am a claimant — to the rights of a French citizen . . . as
to the form of government, who could be in a hurry to
assume such a task ? "[3] " My plan will be to make
myself really acquainted with a country I have learned to
love from afar."[4] In a declaration to be shown to members
of the Right, he says the same thing : " What is done in
France and by the representatives of France, will be well
done. Whatever should be attempted apart from them,
would be premature and barren. I have no thought of
personal ambition. . . . If a political agreement is made,
all the stipulations ought to bear on the Constitution ;
questions of persons cannot be the object of any conditions."[5]

The Duc de Broglie strongly urged the same policy ;
it was necessary for the Princes to preserve their independence, in order that they might treat on equal terms

---

[1] The Comte de Paris wrote : " It is a great joy for me to feel in sympathy
with the representative of France here ; to understand what I feel, one must
have lived for long years with the Flahauts and Persignys "—the ambassadors
of the Empire (*Fusion monarchique*, p. 177).

[2] *Ibid.* p. 172.   [3] *Ibid.* p. 174.   [4] *Ibid.* p. 187.

[5] Hanotaux, i. 152.

with the Comte de Chambord. If the Legitimists compelled them to pledge themselves to an immediate " visit ",
they would appear " as if dragged behind the Royalist
party, not placed at their head ".[1] It was resolved — as a
last attempt to escape the meshes of the Legitimist net — to
appeal once more to Thiers, and the old Comte d'Haussonville was sent to interview him at the Versailles Prefecture.

He offered on behalf of the Princes that they would
resign their seats, and opened the interview (May 17th-
18th) with refreshing frankness. " It is useless for me to
speak, unless you will grant me two things — one is that
I have much affection for you, and the other is that I am
not quite a fool. I am deaf, it is true, but not blind ; even
with my deaf ear, please believe that I can distinguish
what sounds false in what is said to me, and I have eyes
to detect anything underhand in conduct. It is very
convenient for me to look as though I believed everything,
but, though I am good-natured, I am not anxious to be a
dupe." Thiers replied by a long exposition of his political
views ; he spoke calmly except when he mentioned the
Princes. " Our only chances are two — a moderate
republic or a constitutional monarchy ; you know which I
prefer personally . . . but a sensible man must consider
the opinion of the country. At the present moment, the
Republicans are, I do not say the most numerous, but
the most decided and energetic party ; they are more and
more in control of the towns. We must therefore move
towards the Republic, at least temporarily. Will it last ?
I can't say ; I am doubtful myself. But that is not a
reason for declining to try it loyally. . . . We must make
it last out — one year, two years, who knows ? — for the
time we need to reorganise." He professed himself sceptical
about the Fusion. The Comte de Chambord was " a child
or a fool, gently but unshakeably obstinate " ; Aumale
was " ambitious ". He appealed to the Pact of Bordeaux ;

---

[1] *Fusion monarchique*, p. 180.

" I must render back intact and uninjured the deposit I have received ; I cannot enter into any arrangement for the advantage of anyone . . . you wish to raise the question of the Princes, in the Chamber, do you ? Very well ; I shall leave it to the Chamber, but I shall point out to them that there are three rival dynasties, and to grant such an advantage to one of them is upsetting the balance to their exclusive advantage. . . . If the Princes were living quietly in some obscure place, I should ignore their presence in France. That is all I can say." The Comte d'Haussonville went home, and said to his son with tears in his eyes, " There is nothing to be done with M. Thiers ; you must make your terms with the Right ".[1]

The Princes wished for their independence, but they wished still more for the end of their exile ; they immediately resumed negotiations with the Legitimists. On May 27th Aumale issued a second declaration, in which, while stating that the question of the Restoration was for the moment " reserved ground ", he added, " However we can affirm that in the House of Orleans, there are neither claimants to the throne nor rivals for it ".[2]

The Comte de Chambord was rather perplexed at the decision, thus thrown upon him ; he was not inclined to bargain. De Blacas wrote on his behalf to La Ferté, his agent in France : " To take a high tone with the Orleans Princes is not only in complete accordance with the dignity of Monseigneur, but is also politically sound ". He criticised the over-eagerness of certain Fusionists : " Really, there must be times when they think that the restoration of Monseigneur is only desirable to make sure the rights of the Comte de Paris ! " [3]

If the Comte de Chambord would offer no conditions from the Orleanists, he was far from happy as to the

---

[1] Hanotaux, i. 248 ; Denis, *Histoire contemporaine*, pp. 68, 69 ; *Fusion monarchique*, p. 188.

[2] Denis, *op. cit.* p. 67.   [3] *Bureau du roi* (Noailles), pp. 196, 197.

U

condition they offered — the famous " Visit ". " Certainly ", de Blacas wrote, " a visit from the Comte de Paris to Monseigneur would have a great effect, and by removing all uncertainty would perhaps determine the attitude of many people, who cannot at present make up their minds. But you may be sure that great inconvenience would probably result from it. One cannot suppose that they should meet without saying anything to one another, and yet are you not convinced that, if they do talk, points of disagreement will at once arise ? [1] If we have occasion to go to England, a short visit in that country *en passant*, which would only leave time for politeness and effusions, would perhaps be well timed. But a prolonged visit, a life together, for several days would be too dangerous to risk."

What, then, was to become of the Abrogation of the laws of exile, for which the Visit was to be an equivalent ? The question was most " embarrassing " ; " the best plan perhaps would be to combat the idea . . . of the admission of the Princes to the Assembly by the consideration of the inconvenience, that might result for themselves ; if they had been admitted at Bordeaux (as they demanded), would they not have found themselves, as Princes of France, face to face with the Paris insurrection ? The Duc d'Aumale felt this so keenly that he refused the power they wished to confer upon him.[2] Might there not still occur situations as critical and compromising ? "

However, the Comte de Chambord was unable to maintain his opposition, in view of the fact that the repeal of the exile laws would probably have been carried, in any case, by Legitimist votes ; he finally consented upon a promise that the Comte de Paris would visit him immediately after the vote of repeal.[3]

The matter was referred to a Committee consisting of

[1] Especially, of course, about the question of the Flag.
[2] See p. 167.
[3] *Bureau du roi*, p. 201.

six Legitimists and six Orleanists, known in parliamentary slang as the Twelve Apostles. The six Legitimists included the three visitors to Dreux — Maillé, de Meaux, and Cumont ; there were three other deputies — the Viscount de Gontaut-Biron, the Comte de Resseguier, and Charles de Lacombe.

Gontaut-Biron was destined to be Ambassador to Berlin and was a great success in that delicate post — " a skilful and very amiable diplomat of ancient family ", so Bismarck summed him up.[1]

Resseguier was an ardent Catholic ; he had collaborated for *Lives of the Saints,* and was an organiser of Peter's pence ; like Cumont, he wrote some acid memoirs, and burned them for fear of giving pain to others.[2]

Lacombe is one of the most charming figures in the National Assembly. Now thirty-nine years of age, he had been brought up in the very bosom of the Liberal Catholic school ; educated by Père Gratry at the College Stanislas (of whom he says, " He knew at once how to check and spur on the young "), he began his career as a writer under Dupanloup. Montalembert introduced him to Falloux, saying, " Take care not to become more friends with him than with me ". He was presented to the Comte de Chambord in Italy (1852), and wrote, " His claim and misfortunes filled me with enthusiasm ". Berryer said to him in 1867, " Be the introducer of my memory to your generation ", and he devoted himself to writing the life of the great Royalist orator.[3] In 1861 he wrote a favourable review of the eighteenth volume of Thiers' *Consulate and Empire* ; as a result, they became fast friends even through

[1] Hanotaux, i. 376.

[2] His well-known lines on Thiers give a taste of his lost memoirs :
> " Ah qu'il eût mieux servi son honneur et la France,
> Qu'il eût été meilleur citoyen et plus grand,
> Si, plus ambitieux, il eût de préférence
> Choisi le premier rôle au lieu du premier rang "
> (*Fusion monarchique,* p. 188).

[3] *Journal* : Notice biographique, pp. viii, xx, xxi.

all the bitterness of the National Assembly, and the Right always sent Lacombe to Thiers as their most persuasive ambassador ; his political Diary — a most valuable document for the inner life of the Assembly — shows him a tireless exponent of moderation, loved and trusted by all parties, and only hampered by an invincible nervousness, that made him unable to approach the tribune without days of terror and prayer ; he was Falloux's political correspondent, and in their letters Lacombe, though the younger man, is full of caution, and checks the exuberance of the older Royalist. " The majority ", he says, " show a want of experience and an instinct for what is extreme " ; again : " I came to the Assembly as a champion of order and liberty, not as a Legitimist. . . . I attend Fusionist meetings, because, if the Republic becomes impossible, France ought not to be left without resources, but, even if a complete agreement were arrived at, I do not agree that we are bound to accept the consequences without further consideration ".[1]

" You desire a change of government. Such an adventure ought not to be tried without being sure of the means of success ; can you rely on the Assembly or on the cities ? "[2]

Of the six Orleanist deputies, the President of the Committee was a distinguished professor and journalist, St-Marc Girardin. He had met Hegel at Berlin, and had succeeded Guizot at the Sorbonne as Professor of History ; he also wrote for the *Journal des Débats*. He was an ingenious speaker, but less successful as Vice-President of the tumultuous Assembly. De Meaux says of him : " He was too upright in character, and too enlightened in intelligence not to be conciliatory ".[3]

De Corcelles, in whose house the Committee met, was also a Liberal Catholic. A devoted supporter of Pius IX,

---

[1] Letter of 26/4/71, *Journal*, i. 10-13.   [2] Letter of 20/5/71, *ibid*. i. 22.
[3] *Souvenirs*, p. 135.

he had been sent to Rome as ambassador by Louis Napoleon, and returned to his post in 1873 for three years ; he had great influence in the Assembly, where he was regarded almost as an ancestor ; he was rather isolated from parties and stood apart from lobby intrigues ; " his attitude was reserved without being haughty ".[1] He had voted for the Republic in 1848, and was still prepared to accept one, if Thiers governed it on right lines ; he cared more for the Church than for systems of government.

Jules de Lasteyrie, the grandson of Lafayette, naturally inherited an instinct for the July Monarchy ; at the moment, he was an ardent Fusionist, going so far as to say that " he considered himself a Legitimist ".[2] In reality he belonged to the Orleanist Left, which, more and more disgusted at the concessions of the Princes to the Comte de Chambord, ended by supporting Thiers and the Republic, and by sharing what Lasteyrie called " the fine unity of ideas and of minds at once brave and balanced ", which he found in the Left Centre party.[3]

The Comte de Mérode, brother to an Archbishop and uncle to de Meaux, was not a very active member of the Assembly, but was an ardent Fusionist ; he had a shrewd mother-wit, which often summed up situations picturesquely. " The Comte de Chambord ", he once said, " is like a Bishop in partibus, who will not enter his diocese, till all the people have made their Easter communion ; his letting his friends vote for a Senate is like a Bishop allowing the faithful to eat eggs in Lent." [4]

---

[1] De Marcère, *Assemblée nationale*, i, 168.   [2] *Fusion monarchique*, p. 192.
[3] Mme Adam, *Mes angoisses*, p. 143.
[4] Lacombe, i. 177. De Broglie calls him " the most charming mind I have ever met ; he is at once gay and serious, just and amusing, full of good sense and originality. . . . In public assemblies, though he never spoke nor aspired to an active rôle, he always exercised a real influence by his art of summing up characters and situations in a lively and amusing way ; his *bons mots*, never unkind but always funny, were repeated from bench to bench and had more effect than many speeches " (*Revue des Deux Mondes* (1/6/25), p. 597).

The General Chabaud La Tour had been aide-de-camp to the Duc d'Orléans and in the '48 revolution had put himself at the disposal of the Duchesse ; he was tall, with a great air of distinction and a strong voice. A gallant soldier and a first-rate engineer, he defeated Thiers himself in the Assembly on the question of the Paris fortifications ; later, as Minister of the Interior, he was to show how faithful he remained to the political ideals of the July Monarchy.

The sixth Orleanist was naturally Pasquier, as representing his guests. At first his party had been inclined to insist that the Visit should be paid in France. Pasquier even quoted the remark of the Maréchal de Biron to Henri IV, " There is no King of France outside France ". However they did not insist and, when the representatives of the Comte de Chambord demanded that the Comte de Paris should visit him at Frohsdorf and at the same time express " the wish that France should restore the Monarchy ", the Princes consented. On these terms the Legitimists were authorised to vote for the abrogation of the law of exile.[1]

The scene now shifts to the Assembly. The political situation at the end of May was full of stress and strain ; the Commune had just been put down, and the Right, convinced that it would provoke in the country a great reaction towards Conservative principles, had secured for the beginning of July the fixing of the by-elections — so numerous (as a result of options and resignations) as to

---

[1] *Fusion monarchique*, pp. 192-3. During the discussion, Bocher and the Duc de Decazes (Orleanist deputies) had a long conversation with La Ferté, the Comte de Chambord's representative. They were inclined to put forward difficulties ; if they promised the Visit, they would lose 50 votes. " Well," the Marquis replied, " at any rate you gain 200." They objected, again, that it was a long journey to Frohsdorf. La Ferté, who knew of the Comte's projected journey to France, assured them that only a few hours' journey would be needed. Later on, Aumale told five Legitimists that not only the Comte de Paris, but all the Princes would visit the Comte after the vote (*Bureau du roi*, pp. 202-4).

constitute a miniature General Election. Thiers, on the other hand, was equally confident that an appeal to the country would result in a vote of confidence in himself.[1] The two parties eyed one another narrowly, like adversaries who long to come to blows but for the moment cannot do without each other. Lacombe wrote anxiously to Falloux :

> The Right and Thiers are like two people who, *au fond*, ought to agree, but have ceased to see one another and only know each other through the gossip of their entourages. . . . I have often told Thiers that he ought to have intermediaries between himself and the Chamber, whose duty would be to prevent misunderstandings. I always say to members of the Right that, instead of indulging in suspicions and sallies against Thiers, they ought to surround him with counsel and advice.[2]

Two questions were a special source of irritation. In the first place, the Right objected to the presence of the three " September " Ministers — Simon, Favre and Picard ; in the second place, they were annoyed at the proposals, which were constantly circulating among Thiers' followers,

---

[1] Thiers' general sentiments may be gathered from the following extracts from his letters. On May 10th, writing to de Broglie, he still professes himself satisfied with the Assembly (" It is getting wiser every day "), but this is introduced by the rather equivocal reflection, " As things are going well on the field of battle [Paris], they are naturally going well in the Assembly ". The Bonapartists are not to be feared, unless the restoration of the Bourbons is proposed : " If the country is placed between the choice of a restoration and the Socialist despotism of the Empire, it might well incline to the latter. If not driven to such a choice, it will rally to a moderate Government, that will give peace at home and abroad " (Bouniols, p. 64). On the 16th, writing to an old Republican, Duvergier, he is annoyed at old Orleanist friends, who are rallying to the Right Centre and the Fusion : " Most of my friends are behaving very badly, because they have not been given offices or embassies or Marshal's batons. Nothing can give an idea of the conduct of the Darus, the Lasteyries, etc. The Legitimists and Orleanists wish me to give the Republic over to them ; I am convinced that for the moment nothing is possible but the Republic." To another Republican he writes the same day : " I am hardly alive today at all ; I work 20 hours out of the 24, and a handful of nuisances — disappointed of office — attack me, as if they belonged to the Commune ; the Legitimists, who have joined the Orleanists but are not *united* to them, would like me to give the Republic over to them . . . if we try to overturn the Republic, we shall have another terrible civil war on our hands " (*ibid.* pp. 66-9).

[2] *Journal*, i. 23.

in favour of regularising and extending his powers by a new law.

On the question of the Princes, Thiers did not find in the Left Centre the support he had expected in resisting the return of the royal exiles. Some of them like himself were old friends of the Orleans family, and felt that to oppose would be invidious ; others believed that respect for Universal Suffrage forbade a Republican from voting against the decision of the constituencies, which had returned Aumale and Joinville.[1] Others urged that it was a matchless opportunity for a bargain — abrogation of the laws of exile in exchange for an extension of his own powers.[2]

When Thiers heard that the Legitimists were to support the Princes, he decided to give way ; he promised the Right to remove one or two of his more obnoxious Ministers, and to support Abrogation, on condition that the Princes consented not to take their seats, and to prevent any other member of the family from standing at elections. It was agreed that a solemn covenant should be drawn up — with all the formalities of a duel — in a small hunting-lodge at St-Germain, to which Aumale and Joinville were to repair, furnished with full powers to answer for their nephew and brothers. Batbie and Pasquier were to be witnesses ; Thiers was to be accompanied by Casimir-Périer (son of the famous Minister of Louis-Philippe) and the Duc de Broglie, who had come from London to take part in these proceedings.[3]

On May 31st some members of the Right interviewed Thiers, and found him ready to accept the arrival of the Princes. " I will settle the question in half an hour ", he said gaily. He seemed quite definitely to have moved

---

[1] Even Louis Blanc, on the Extreme Left, voted for the repeal of the laws of exile ; Edmond Adam, the shrewd Republican deputy for Paris, said to him angrily, " Have you learned nothing in your exile ? " " I have not forgotten my principles," he replied (Mme Adam, *Mes angoisses*, p. 151).

[2] Pessard, ii. 84.   [3] *Fusion monarchique*, p. 196.

towards the Right. At the meeting of the Council, that evening, he said suddenly :

Well, gentlemen, we must give up the idea of prolonging my powers. After all, the Assembly could always turn me out if they pleased ; besides [turning to the representative of the Right in the Cabinet], my friend Larcy will be pleased if we give up the idea. Ah, you don't speak ! Aren't you pleased ? I wager it is not enough ; your friends wish to go much further ; they do not think they are sufficiently represented in the government.

The " September " Ministers intervened ; Favre and Simon said they were ready to retire, if their places were given to Republicans ; Picard said he would rather be driven out than resign. Thiers watched them slily " like a cat watching mice ".[1]

Ten days later everything seemed suddenly changed. In the morning of Friday, June 2nd, de Broglie and Casimir-Perier called on Thiers, to settle the final arrangements for the agreement with the Princes. As they entered the Prefecture, they were asked to wait a few moments in the ante-room ; the door of the study opened, and a group of deputies of the Left and Left Centre — Rivet, Arago, Lefranc, Feray — came out from Thiers' presence. The two groups eyed one another with surprise and suspicion. When the two representatives of the Princes were admitted, Thiers informed them in an embarrassed speech that, though personally he had no need of further guarantees, yet the Left, whose support was necessary, demanded more. On being asked to explain himself, he lowered his voice, and added that in return for supporting the Abrogation, they wished to see his own powers extended for three years. The two deputies in reply expressed their astonishment ; they had come to put the finishing touches to a settled agreement ; they were perfectly incompetent to discuss new conditions, and they left the house, passing in silence

[1] Lacombe, i. 30.

and with an ironical bow their colleagues of the Left, who had been waiting for them in the ante-room.[1]

That afternoon (Friday, June 2nd) the matter was brought before the Assembly. To the general surprise, it was first introduced by an ultra-Radical, the eccentric deputy for Paris — Jean Brunet;[2] he argued that the punishment of exile should be abolished altogether, and urged that the population of Paris, after experiencing the spectacle of so many arrests as a result of the Commune, should be reassured by the spectacle of the abrogation of all laws of proscription.[3] Neither the general principle invoked, nor the particular people for whom sympathy was asked, interested the Right, and they turned to the motion — proposed by an obscure Legitimist, de Vaulchier and backed by many signatures from the Right and Right Centre — which declared the abrogation of " the laws of April 10th, 1832 and May 26th, 1848, concerning the princes of the House of Bourbon ".

Henri Brisson from the Left asked what was meant by " the House of Bourbon " ; did it include the elder and the younger branch ? Baragnon, a leading Fusionist, replied : " The authors of the proposal might have used a more general expression — ' The House of France ' ". These words produced the most intense excitement ; the Right yelled themselves hoarse with applause ;[4] Brisson called out amid the cheers of the Left : " Then the Fusion is accomplished ; we warn the country ". Thiers walked up

---

[1] I have adopted the Duc de Broglie's own account (quoted *Fusion monarchique*, p. 197) because (unlike Lacombe, i. 31) he was an eyewitness. Hector Pessard says he himself was present (*Mes petits papiers*, ii. 85), but his love of the ludicrous always makes one suspect exaggeration. The Duc's account is also amusing in a sardonic kind of way ; the discerning reader will not fail to guess why the Duc was none too popular in the Assembly.

[2] His complete lack of humour is shown by the preamble to his motion —" In view of the necessity of re-establishing peace and *fusion* in France . . ."

[3] *Annales*, t. 3, p. 214.

[4] *Annales*, t. 3, p. 215 ; the *Temps* said the Right were as " happy as grown-up children " (Halévy, *Fin des notables*, p. 21).

and down the lobbies, his hair standing up with excite-
ment ; meeting two Fusionists — Decazes and the young
Marquis de Castellane—he accused them of wishing to snatch
away his authority from him. Deputies of the Right and
Left crowded round him, exchanging violent accusations.
Thiers shouted to Bocher : " You are mad ; you want civil
war ; the Orleans Princes want to play the part of Louis
Bonaparte in 1849 ". " With this difference," replied
Bocher, " that one was a scoundrel, and the others are
honourable men." " Certainly ", answered Thiers, calm-
ing down, " they are honourable ; as for saying Prince
Louis was a scoundrel, I do not deny it, but it is rather
strong language." The same evening, at a crowded reception in the Prefecture, he again addressed Castellane :
" How am I expected to govern with Aumale at Chantilly,
Henri V at Chambord, and Prince Jerome Napoleon at
Prangins ? The Orleans Princes are unpatriotic ; I served
their father ; if he had listened to me, he would not have
lost his crown ; today the Princes are on the way to ruin
themselves and ruin France." [1]

An agitated meeting of Fusionists was held at the
house of de Corcelles ; Pasquier and Decazes violently
attacked Thiers, and it was at first resolved to declare
open war upon him at the Assembly. But on reflection
it was decided to send Lacombe to remonstrate with
him.[2]

Lacombe found him at the early hour of half-past seven
on Saturday morning sitting at a table surrounded with
documents. He pointed to them, saying, " I am making
myself *au courant* with all the affairs of State, but I demand
not to be harassed. As for the Princes they are deceiving
you Legitimists ; I have seen letters from the Comte
de Paris saying it is impossible to come to an agreement
with the Comte de Chambord." Lacombe shrugged his
shoulders. " That is not the question," he replied ; " the

[1] Pessard, ii. 89-91.   [2] Lacombe, i. 33.

question is whether you are going to keep your word. The Princes have agreed to all your conditions and now you demand a new clause — the prorogation of your powers." " Oh, you exaggerate its importance ; I did not suggest it ; it came from the Left. Besides, three years of power ! With my character, if they worry me, I shall resign in a week." He got more and more excited, with his eye on the coming elections. " The Assembly is becoming more unpopular every day ; the country will not hesitate, when it has to choose between them and myself." Lacombe made a fine reply : " It is only too true that France has always preferred being governed by one man to being governed by an assembly, but it is not for you, an old master in the parliamentary world, to exploit that feeling ". Thiers cooled down ; he said he was tired, and wished to be left alone, but he followed his visitor to the next room, saying, " You Legitimists are only a minority ; you would not have a hundred seats, if there was a General Election ". Lacombe replied that he did not speak on behalf of the Legitimists, but of the great Conservative majority, which included such men as the Duc de Broglie. " Oh, the Duc de Broglie ! " interrupted Thiers ; " he is an intriguer." At this moment Calmon, the Under-Secretary for the Interior, entered and Thiers concluded : " Well, the proposal for the prolongation of my powers will be made to-night ; I shall myself demand *urgence*, and if you reject it, I shall resign ".[1]

Lacombe left in the utmost consternation, but the situation was less alarming than it seemed. On hearing that, at a meeting of the Left Centre, 27 votes were cast against the prolongation of his powers, Thiers saw he could not insist on the point ; [2] he determined, however, to make

[1] Lacombe, i. pp. 34-7.
[2] Pessard, ii. 91. Three of Thiers' Ministers — Lambrecht, Pouyer-Quertier and Larcy — threatened to resign, if the proposal for the prorogation of powers was made.

one last effort before the Commission of the Assembly, to which the motion to recall the Princes had been referred ; he proposed that all claimants to the throne should be excluded from all public offices for two years, and that, " if one of the Princes or their partisans (even without the knowledge of the Princes) inspire the Chief of the Executive with anxiety and suspicion, he shall have full and entire liberty to make them change their places of residence or conduct them back to the frontier ". He spoke for an hour with vigour and energy. " I have saved France," he said, " and you wish to provoke civil war ; how do you expect me to raise a loan of two milliards in the midst of the sterile agitations of parties ? " Decazes, white with rage, exclaimed : " You are comparing the House of France to the Bonapartes ! It is a gratuitous insult. The second clause of your proposals puts the Princes in the position of ex-convicts under the surveillance of the police." An altercation followed between Pasquier and Thiers on the question how far the Princes were bound by their promise to him ; " I am speaking politely to you," said the Duc, " try to do the same to me ".[1]

On Monday, June 5th, tempers had cooled down. Thiers explained that the exclusion from public office only referred to their seats in the Chamber ; he was ready to accept guarantees on the old conditions. On Tuesday he was still hesitating,[2] but the fear of a crisis induced him to drop the obnoxious Clause Two, and accept the conditions, which Pasquier announced to the Commission on Thursday

---

[1] Pessard, ii. 94 ; but de Broglie says (*Revue des Deux Mondes* (15/3/29), p. 371) that his nephew d'Haussonville, who was a member of the Commission, told him that same evening that, after Thiers had read his proposal, " glacial silence followed, and all those who were present began to blush for shame. Thiers put back the paper in his pocket without anyone thinking it worth while to answer him."

[2] In his speech of June 8th Thiers said : " The day before yesterday I was still in doubt . . . but I said to myself that I had not the right to bring upon France the inevitable trouble, which would result from a change of the persons responsible for government " (*Annales*, t. 3, p. 293).

morning on behalf of the Princes — " Abrogation of the
laws of exile ; validation of elections ; promise not to sit
and not to allow any member of their family to stand again
as a candidate ".[1]

The debate in the Assembly opened at two o'clock.
Thiers was in his place unusually early ; he was somewhat
nervous about his speech ; he said to his Minister, Lambrecht : " I have to walk on eggs and I am seventy-
four ; I have no longer got the necessary agility ".[2] The
tribunes were full of spectators ; crowds of Parisians,
especially ladies, had arrived by the " parliamentary
trains " ; lovers of excitement hoped for " scenes ". It
was known, of course, that the Right and Left Centres
were agreed, but it was hoped that in regions of the Left
there was still enough indignation smouldering to create
an incident. On the contrary, the debate opened on a note
of calm not far removed from dulness. This was largely
because the two questions of Abrogation and Validation
were introduced separately, and the reporters of the
Bureaux solemnly discussed the question, to the lay mind
quite meaningless, whether people, who were forbidden by
law to set foot in France, could be elected deputies.

The Report of the Commission on Abrogation was read
by Batbie (Right Centre), deputy for Gers ; he was chiefly
remarkable for his corpulency ; " he had two legs which
seemed to walk with regret, and a voluminous stomach " ; [3]
he had been lecturer on " Droit Administratif " at Paris,
but his appearance of ponderous law-learning concealed a
mind full of subtlety and charm. He was the wittiest of
talkers, and his fat face easily wrinkled into a smile ; in
the Assembly he was nicknamed " the subtle elephant ",
or " an animal who has swallowed a code ", or " the wittiest
of mastodons ". Later on, Thiers was to suffer dearly for
underrating his intelligence. At the moment, however,

---

[1] Pessard, ii. 94-7.   [2] De Marcère, *Assemblée nationale*, i. 154.
[3] *Portraits de Kel-Kun*, p. 89.

things were too delicate for fireworks, and he contented himself with the usual arguments ; he laid special stress on the election itself. " We, who hold our powers from Universal Suffrage, have no right to cross-examine the electors as to the reasons of their choice." He disclaimed emphatically all political intentions. " What we propose is to adjourn all constitutional questions, and perform an act of justice." Barthélemy-St-Hilaire, the philosopher-secretary of Thiers (he had translated Aristotle), reported in favour of Joinville's election ; he could not resist a dig at the ultra-democratic principles of the Conservative Batbie, who accepted the decision of three constituencies as the verdict of the sovereign people : " If it is right to feel respect for Universal Suffrage, that respect should not become a superstition ". Barascud, a member of the Right, reported in favour of Aumale's election ; then a member of the Left read a declaration on behalf of nineteen deputies representing departments still occupied by the Germans, in which they demanded the adjournment of the question as likely to " create alarm and division and hinder the re-establishment of French credit ". Leblond, the procureur-général, who had tried to turn the Princes out of France, suggested in his soft, dreary voice that the majority " carried away by generous sentiments, were going to weaken the powers of the Head of the State " ; the Right protested, and Batbie, declaring that any such motive would have been unpatriotic, called on Thiers to speak for himself.[1]

The President of the Council now mounted the tribune, and delivered one of his most celebrated speeches ; it did not please the Right as much as they had expected ; de Broglie bitterly comments, " He began by enumerating all the reasons against the measure, and ended by supporting it ".[2] He had promised to vote for the Princes, but not to speak for them, and he allowed himself the sweet revenge

---

[1] *Annales*, t. 3, pp. 284-91. [2] *Fusion monarchique*, p. 197.

of saying more discreetly before the Assembly what he had said so intemperately in front of Fusionist deputies. That part of the speech may seem unbalanced and wanting in foresight; the perils he evoked so solemnly were non-existent. But Thiers was much less eager to prove the peril of recalling the Princes than to explain to the Right — and to the country already preparing for the elections — the dangers of turning him out of office; here he had a remarkable success. He spoke for two hours, and never were his peculiar gifts more visible. He made use of an engaging frankness, seeming to admit every member of the Assembly into the inner counsels of his mind, and yet there was hardly a statement that was not subtly qualified; he caressed both sides of the House, but he committed himself to neither. His exposition was so clear that a child could have understood it, and yet the language was so carefully chosen that there were few statements to which he could have been pinned down. He spoke as a historian — judging his own time as if it had been the Consulate or the Empire — and he spoke gently and with such charm that he was never interrupted. Yet his claim to judge all parties so serenely, implied, as it was meant to imply, an appeal to the electors to place him, by their confidence, above and apart from all parties. Claveau, a shrewd observer who heard the speech from the secretaries' table, writes: " It is really incredible how many precautions, reserves and nuances he put into the countless circumvolutions, of his speech; it recalled the picture of an immense cobweb; all the parliamentary flies were caught in it ".[1]

He began upon the pathetic note; if he had been able to listen only to " deep and ancient memories and affections ", he would not have hesitated a moment, but he had " great and painful duties to perform "; he had at first been opposed to the measure, which he now supported. These words reassured the Right, who settled down in their

[1] Claveau, p. 166.

places, prepared to listen in silence to the story of doubts, which they now knew were ended. He did not suppose for a moment that there was any intention of enfeebling his authority, but it had been said that the measure had no political bearing. " We must not close our eyes to the facts ; the country will regard it as a great political action." The Right began to get restless, and he hastened to the calmer waters of contemporary history.

He spoke of the great victory they had won over the Commune, and the impression it had made abroad : " Europe has congratulated me, and I have accepted their congratulations on behalf of my country ". But there still remained agitation in France ; the anarchical passions had been reduced " to powerlessness, not to calm ". Two remedies were necessary ; first, not to give any cause for further excitement, and secondly, to give work, " the most powerful diversion we can offer to passions, whether good or evil ". " What is necessary for the leaders of industry to regain courage and initiative ? I answer, gentlemen, for all to hear — Confidence."

He then turned to the financial problems of the evacuation. Here Thiers spoke in moving terms of the humiliation of foreign troops in the country. " Ah ! if you only knew the details ! Not to be able to order a movement of soldiers without asking for the consent of a foreigner ! To fear at every moment that some young Frenchman, proud and imprudent, inspired by the most generous of feelings, should provoke a collision ! " [1] He spoke of the difficulty of collecting money : " There is no more productive duty than that on tobacco ; today it produces nothing ". In a few days would come their appeal to the credit, that is to the confidence of Europe ; they trusted the resources of France. " Only one thing is in doubt — the preservation

---

[1] Referring to this period, at a later date, Thiers used to say, " One shot from a gun and our loan was ruined " (Dreyfus, *La République de M. Thiers*, p. 30).

X

of order at home." For this reason he had hesitated to
support the measure before them ; at last he had accepted
it with the " guarantees loyally offered ".

He was aware that to many people the measure
appeared simply as an act of reparation to the Bourbons,
and he added : " I am not afraid to mention the name here,
for to do so would be to shrink from mentioning the name
of France ". While the enthusiastic applause of the Right
was dying away, he gently reminded them that much could
be said in favour of exiling claimants to the throne ; he
said : " They are laws not of proscription but of precaution, based on the principle that two Governments
cannot exist together on the same soil ". He related how
he had said to Louis Napoleon in 1849 : " These imprudent
republicans, who have recalled you, do not know what they
are doing ; you will be their master but you will never be
mine ".

He then brought back their minds to the circumstances
and conditions of the Bordeaux Pact. He began by saying
some words in favour of the National Defence Government
— an action not without courage, when he was being pressed
to remove his September Ministers and the Assembly itself
was on the eve of voting a hostile enquiry into their actions :
" The Fourth of September delivered you from the Empire,
and at the time you were most grateful for the service ".
But he drew a distinction between republicans ; Paris
could not help resisting ; she was a fort that could not
surrender without orders. It was those outside Paris (the
Delegation of Tours), who were responsible for the imprudence of prolonging the War ; and he described their
conduct — in a famous allusion to Gambetta — as " a
policy of raging madmen that put France in the gravest
peril ".

Having thus inserted a wedge between the Moderate
and the Extreme Lefts, he continued : " At Bordeaux,
gentlemen, you wished to take the Republic out of the

hands of bad republicans ; you did not wish to overthrow the Republic ". He himself had accepted the Government on these conditions, and he sought every moment to be faithful to them. As to his own convictions, he had struggled for forty years to secure for France constitutional government, as it existed in England. " At Washington the people are free in a great and noble fashion, but at London they are perhaps freer still ", because the sovereign recognised that " Monarchy is a republic with a hereditary President ". The French Princes had not recognised this (that sentence was meant for the Comte de Chambord) ; in any case, the questions, " which divide us, can be postponed " ; the urgent " task of reorganisation unites us ".

He had been accused of governing " in a republican sense " ; well, of course he could not help governing as well as he could, even at the risk of strengthening the Republican form of government ; but he declared that in no instance (and he gave as an example the appointment of officers) had he asked to what party a man belonged. The mention of the Army was the occasion of an eloquent passage about the common soldier, whom Thiers declared he loved " as a man loves his own child ". Praise of the Army was always welcome to the Assembly, and amid the warmth of sympathy produced by his words, Thiers felt strong enough to recount his interview during the Commune with the delegates from the cities — the very information he had angrily refused to Mortimer Ternaux a month before. According to his own account, the assurances he had given on behalf of the Republic came to little more than a reminder that the Assembly had reserved its constituent rights ; he threw out two formulae destined to great notoriety in the political world — " We must make a loyal experiment of the Republic " and " The Republic has never succeeded in the hands of republicans " — ancestor of the later and more famous phrase, " The Republic without the Republicans ".

Returning more closely to the measure before the House, he declared that not only was it dangerous for a Republic to admit the Princes, but that their own dignity was not served by becoming deputies. "God has made them princes, and princes they ought to remain." However, as they insisted on returning to France, he had reluctantly consented. "But I said to myself that I could only excuse myself by warning my country. That is what I am doing now." He concluded with an appeal to their confidence : "I remain in office, convinced that I am fulfilling a great duty, asking you to trust me still, if you think I deserve it, and saying to you once again : No, I will not deceive any party ".[1]

The enthusiasm provoked by this speech took away most of the effect from some rather isolated protests from the Left, and on a division the abrogation of the laws of exile was carried by 472 votes to 97 ; on the validation of the elections the majority dropped slightly (the votes were 443 to 111).

The Princes had won ; after twenty-three years the gates of France were again open to them. Whether they had not paid a heavy price in the alienation of Thiers and the close alliance with the Legitimists, might be a question, but it was not a question they bothered their heads about much in the high spirits of the moment.

The Comte de Paris had been detained at Twickenham by the birth of a daughter. On June 12th he wrote to d'Haussonville to thank him for his services : "Without thinking of the past or worrying about the future, I am full of joy at this great act which makes me a Frenchman like my countrymen ".[2] On the same day he rushed off in a hansom through the pouring rain to the French Embassy ; he longed to put his foot on what was technically French soil, and to express his gratitude to the Government. He was received by Gavard, the " conseiller de l'ambas-

[1] *Annales*, t. 3, 291-300.   [2] *Fusion monarchique*, p. 205.

sade ", who persuaded him to write a dispatch to the French Government, thanking them for allowing him to return. Gavard forwarded it as from " His Royal Highness Monseigneur the Comte de Paris ", for which Favre gently scolded him.[1]

On Friday, June 9th, Bocher, the faithful friend of the Princes and the administrator of their property, threw open his salon to the Princes for a reception of deputies of the Right and the Right Centre ; even members of the Extreme Right were present. Decazes, seeing the fiery Legitimist Dahirel, nudged his neighbour to draw attention to his arrival.[2] The Fusionists formed an animated group ; they talked of sending delegates to the Comte de Chambord to ask him respectfully to return to France. Lucien Brun, leader of the Ultras, played the part of a graceful skeleton at the feast ; " gay and smiling but with long face and disdainful lips ", he expressed a polite doubt whether the Comte de Chambord would let his movements be regulated by parliamentary votes.[3]

On the following Monday, June 12th, Thiers gave a reception to meet the German Commandant from Rouen. At ten o'clock the Princes, who had warned the President of their intention, entered the salon ; the ladies at once rose ; the gentlemen grouped themselves round the door — there was a moment of acute embarrassment. Thiers at once introduced such of the Ministers as were present ; when Favre shook hands, he looked " like a criminal undergoing sentence " ; even Thiers seemed less himself than usual. But the courtesy of Aumale soon broke the ice. Mme Thiers begged him to be seated ; he declined

[1] *Ibid.* pp. 203, 206. De Broglie was in France by the bedside of his son, who was wounded at the attack on Fort Issy and whose life was despaired of ; he had received the Last Sacraments, and the Duc was unable to be present at the debate of June 8th, but when his nephew, the young d'Haussonville, returned in the evening, his first question, after he had spoken of his son, was " What happened in the Assembly ? " His son recovered, and had a long career in the Army.

[2] *Fusion monarchique*, p. 204.   [3] Pessard, ii. 107.

with a smile, saying, "I do not forget that I am in the presence of the Chief of the Executive of the French Republic ".[1] The Legitimists grumbled, saying that the Duke was always dragging his family to the Left.

The Republicans, too, were not pleased, and Thiers — his eyes still on the elections — hastened to reassure them. The *Gaulois* having announced that the Princes had "dined at the Presidency", the *Journal Officiel* of June 14th gave a formal denial: The Princes had simply arrived at the reception, where no one expected them;[2] their presence showed that while remembering the past, they understood and accepted the present.[3]

On Saturday, July 1st, the day before the elections, Thiers had no more fear that his domestic arrangements would be used to mislead voters, and he gave a brilliant dinner to the Princes. There were twenty-nine guests; the Duchess de Chartres and the Comte de Paris (who had just arrived from Paris) sat on the President's right; the Comtesse d'Haussonville and Joinville on his left. Chartres and Aumale were present, four Ministers, the two Vice-Presidents of the Assembly, the Legitimist Duc de Bisaccia and his wife, the Legitimist Marquis de Castellane and his wife. Never again was such a dinner to be possible in Republican France. In the evening the salon was full of deputies; the Princes stood in the middle, and Thiers

---

[1] Pessard, ii. 115, and Martial Delpit, *Journal*, p. 190 (quoted Denis, p. 76).

[2] This is slightly disingenuous; Thiers had certainly been warned before, but from the rather embarrassed manner of their reception, it looks as though he had not informed his guests.

[3] *Journal Officiel*: "The master of the house remembered that he had been the Minister of their father and that today he was Head of the Executive of the Republic, and the presence of the Princes at the reception showed that, while they recall the past, they understand and accept the present. There is nothing in this, that does not conform to the policy inaugurated by the liberal vote of the Assembly. Republicans can, without feeling any embarrassment, proclaim their deference to Princes, who bear a glorious name nobly, and M. Thiers can honourably receive in his house members of a family, whose policy has always been to respect most sincerely the wishes of the country " (Loménie, *Restauration manquée*, p. 110).

made the introductions. The deputies of the Right were in the highest spirits — " We are all sovereigns here ", they chuckled, referring to the vote of the Assembly recognising its own constituent powers. De Meaux, describing the scene enthusiastically to Falloux the next day, said, " It was the Monarchy holding a reception under the Republic ".

The conversation turned on the Fusion ; the Princes declared they were going to Bruges to make their submission to the head of the family ; Thiers seemed enchanted. One of the guests having said, " The only person we miss at your dinner is the Comte de Chambord ", he replied, " He will be welcome ; I do not despair of having that honour ".[1] The Comte de Chambord arrived at Paris the next morning, when perhaps the festal lights were hardly extinguished at the Prefecture, but he was in no mood to attend Republican receptions.

(d) THE CHAMBORD MANIFESTO

The first public utterance of the Comte de Chambord, since the meeting of the National Assembly, had been a letter, dated May 8th (during the Commune), addressed to General de Carayon-Latour, Legitimist deputy for the Gironde ; it ran as follows :

MY DEAR FRIEND,

Like you I am watching the cruel vicissitudes of this hateful civil war, following so closely on the disasters of an invasion, and my heart is torn with grief ; I need not tell you how much I agree with the sad reflections these events suggest to you, and how well I understand your anguish. When the first shell of the invaders burst over Paris, I remembered nothing but the grandeur of the city where I was born, and I uttered a cry which was heard all over Europe ; that was all I could do, and, now as then, I can do nothing but mourn over the horrors of this fratricidal war. But be confident ;

---

[1] Dreyfus, *La République de M. Thiers*, p. 84 ; Falloux, ii. 471.

the difficulties of this tragic undertaking are not too great for the heroism of our Army.

You tell me that you live among men of all parties, who are anxious to know my will, my desires, my hopes. Make them acquainted with my most intimate thoughts and with all the feelings of my heart. Tell them that I have never deceived them, that I never will deceive them, and that I ask them, in the name of our most dear and sacred interests, in the name of civilisation, in the name of the world, that witnesses our misfortunes, to forget our dissensions, our prejudices, and our resentments. Warn them against the calumnies, that are being circulated to make people believe that, discouraged by the excess of our misfortunes and despairing of the future of my country, I have renounced the joy of saving it.[1]

It will be saved on the day when it ceases to confuse liberty with licence, when it no more looks for safety to these governments of adventurers, who after some years of false security precipitate their country into terrible disasters. Above the political agitations there is a France which suffers, which does not wish to perish, for, when God exposes a nation to such trials, it means that He still has great designs for it.

Let us recognise that the true cause of our disasters is our desertion of principle ; a Christian nation cannot with impunity tear out pages from its long history, nor break the chain of its traditions, nor write at the head of its history a denial of the rights of God, nor banish all mention of religion from its laws and its public teaching ; under such conditions it will never do more than pass from one form of disorder to another ;[2] it will swing perpetually from Caesarism to anarchy — two forms of pagan decadence equally shameful ; it will not escape the punishment of peoples, who are unfaithful to their vocation.

The country understood all this, when it chose for its representatives men like you, who know the needs of their time, and yet are fully aware of the principles necessary for every society, that wishes to preserve its honour and its freedom ; it is for these reasons, my dear friend, that in spite of prejudices, that still remain, all that is good in France longs for the monarchy ; the glare of burning Paris shows them the true way ; they feel that they need order, justice, and integrity, and that they can only find them in the Monarchy and its traditions.

---

[1] A reference to rumours of abdication.

[2] " Elle ne fera jamais qu'une halte dans le désordre."

Attack with all your force the errors and prejudices, that enter too easily into the most generous minds. It is said that I claim unlimited powers ; would to God that such a power had not been so rashly granted to those, who in the days of crisis offered themselves as saviours of the country ! We should not then have to lament today over the misfortunes of France ; [1] what I claim — as you know — is to work for the regeneration of the country, to give free play to all its legitimate aspirations, to preside over its destinies at the head of the Royal Family, while at the same time submitting confidently the acts of the Government to the real control of freely chosen representatives.

It is said that the Monarchy of tradition is incompatible with the equality of all before the law ; answer that I am not ignorant to such an extent of the lessons of history and the conditions of the life of nations. How should I tolerate unfair privileges for others, who ask for no privilege for myself except that of devoting all the moments of my life to the happiness and safety of France and to suffer always, before I share the victory with her ?

It is said that the freedom of the Papacy is dear to me and that I am determined to obtain effective safeguards for it. [2] It is true ; the liberty of the Church is the first condition of peace and order throughout the world ; to be the protector of the Holy See was always one of our titles to honour and the most undisputed cause of our greatness among the nations ; only during the greatest disasters has France abandoned this glorious rôle.

I shall be recalled — be sure of it — not only because I represent a right, but because I represent order and reform, because I have the authority needed to put right what is wrong and to govern according to law and justice, in order to repair the evils of the past and, at the long last, to prepare a future for France. It will be remembered that I have the ancient sword of France in my hands, and in my breast the heart of a King and father, who belongs to no party. I am not a party, and I do not wish to return to reign for the benefit of a party ; I have no wrongs to avenge, no enemies to

[1] The Count's style is always too grand and elusive to condescend to proper names ; the reference is probably to the Second Empire — less probably to the National Defence Government.

[2] One of the effects of the French defeat was the withdrawal of French troops from Rome, which was occupied by Victor Emmanuel ; Pius IX became " the prisoner of the Vatican " and Catholics throughout the world — especially in France — were very anxious as to whether the Italian Government would allow the Pope freedom of communication with the faithful.

remove, no fortune to recover except that of France ; [1] I am able
to choose from every quarter servants, who will loyally take their
part in the great work ; all I bring back with me is religion, concord
and peace ; the only dictatorship I wish to exercise is that of mercy.
For in my hands, and in my hands only, mercy is also justice. It is
for these reasons, my dear friend, that I do not despair of my country,
and do not shrink before the immensity of the task ; it is for France
to speak and for God to act " (" La parole est à la France et l'heure
à Dieu ").

HENRI [2]

This letter is given in full, because, unlike many manifestoes and public documents, the Comte de Chambord's
declarations do express his most intimate thoughts ; the
whole of his character is there already in this early letter to
Latour, as it is in the more famous Salzburg letter, in which
for the last time he forfeited his chances of a crown. It is
all there — the generous and chivalrous style, too lofty to
demean itself to details of persons or parties, the conception of a Restoration as an act of national repentance, that
no more admitted of negotiation or bargaining than a
penitent's confession to a priest, the direct appeal to " all
that is good in France " over the head of Parliament,[3] the
almost perverse frankness — ever the joy of his opponents,
that seemed to single out for reference the very points,
which prudence would have passed over ; thus the allusion
to the independence of the Papacy was taken as justifying
the fear of a Royalist intervention in Italy, and did incalcul-
able harm at the July elections. In the debate on the
Princes, M. Ducarré said it seemed " like a page from the
famous collection *Gesta Dei per Francos* " ; [4] three trusted
leaders of the Royalist party did not hesitate to say to the
Comte's face : " Your manifesto produced a profound im-

---

[1] It is hardly possible to suppose an allusion here to the demand of the
Orleans Princes for the restoration of their property, confiscated by the Empire,
but the phrase is not very happy.   [2] Lacombe, i. 264-7.

[3] Lacombe says (i. 21): " The very fact of having written the letter
without consulting a single member of the Chamber shows a deplorable
prejudice ".   [4] *Annales*, t. 3, p. 300.

pression by its truly royal tone — even opponents have
spoken of their admiration. But the feeling did not last
long ; we cannot conceal from your Royal Highness that
it has been interpreted, commented upon, and exploited so
as to have exercised undoubtedly the worst possible effect
on the elections." [1]

The Comte de Chambord passed the months of May and
June in a state of anxiety and impatience ; [2] he was at
Bruges (he had gone there to be nearer France), and he
passed long hours in church, plunged in solitary prayer
and meditation. The subject of all this restlessness was
characteristic. He was not troubled by the thought that
negotiations for his return might break down in France ;
what troubled him was the feeling that things were going
too smoothly. He was particularly annoyed by the visit
of the three deputies to the Princes at Dreux ; he suspected
them of having said that he was willing to give up the
White Flag. He rebuked La Ferté, his representative at
Versailles, for having thanked the deputies for the visit ; [3]
he sent de Blacas to Versailles to discourage Legitimists
from negotiating with Orleanists. His deep mistrust of
politicians made him prefer to see his cousin personally ;
he disclaimed any idea of seeing Aumale, whom he had
never liked. " The Comte de Paris is my heir, if I have no
children ; I want to come to an understanding with him,
but I have no terms to accept." He refused to see several
deputies, who were pressing for an interview ; he did not
wish his views to reach Europe " par ricochet ", as the result
of a talk. He must declare himself publicly ; he must not
leave his cousins to nurse impossible illusions. De Monti,
who was with him at the time, says : " We had great

---

[1] *Fusion monarchique*, p. 214.

[2] His only public utterance in June was another letter to Carayon Latour
(June 6th) congratulating MacMahon on the repression of the Commune: "I
knew what was to be expected of the illustrious Marshal and the brave Generals
under his orders " (Loth, p. 226).

[3] Lacombe, i. 52.

difficulty in persuading him not to do something violent ; he is as fiery as gunpowder ; he gets it from his father and mother. He is not always easy to deal with ; he could not stand the idea that he had been committed without his consent and that his cousins believed in an agreement which did not exist." [1]

One can follow the perplexities of the Count's supporters, day by day, in the correspondence between Blacas (resident at the King's Court) and the Marquis de La Ferté Mun, who from 1850 to 1870 belonged to the Royalist Committee at Paris, and after 1871 was the official representative of the Comte de Chambord " *auprès de la majorité royaliste de l'Assemblée Nationale* ".[2] The Marquis belonged to a family of proved Legitimist fidelity ; his father and uncle were among the fourteen Royalists (out of the 200 that had promised), who assembled in 1814 on the Place Louis XV to proclaim Louis XVIII.[3] He himself had resigned the Army rather than serve the July Monarchy, though he came of a military race, and had himself the appearance and courage of a soldier.[4] However, he had married the daughter of Molé, ex-Minister of Louis-Philippe, and this made him suspect to the Ultras.[5]

On February 27th, Blacas wrote to La Ferté, " not officially but as a friend ", to warn him of the " extremely difficult position ", in which he would find himself placed as the Comte de Chambord's representative in France : [6]

Ernest [a pseudonym for the Count] has decided not to accept

---

[1] Lacombe, i. 52.

[2] This correspondence is published by the Marquis de Noailles in *Le Bureau du roi*.

[3] *Bureau du roi*, pp. 214-215.

[4] " In the June days of 1848 a young French *mobile*, hardly sixteen years old, dashed at a barricade to snatch the Red Flag, and fell backwards struck by a bullet. Seeing M. de la Ferté dash forward to take his place, he cried, ' Ah, you have all the luck, big National Guard ; it is you, who will tear the flag down.' ' No, my child, it will not be me ', he answered, and, taking him in his arms, placed the flag in his hands, and leaped down again " (Falloux, ii. 476).   [5] Loménie, p. 124.   [6] *Bureau du roi*, pp. 176-8.

the Tricolour ; he no longer regards it as a reserved question but as a settled question. . . . This decision must not yet be divulged, and, considering the difficulty of its being carried out, it should not be divulged till the latest possible moment. Therefore for you it still remains a reserved question. . . . You can cautiously prepare public opinion for it by saying, for example, that the moment seems ill-chosen for adopting a flag, which has cruelly cancelled its ancient glories in the minds of men, and which at present decorates the arsenals at Berlin ; emphasise with all your power the following consideration — that the first thing to be done is to recognise the principle [of monarchy] without any conditions ; say you are sure Monseigneur will not accept any. If the Chamber were to decide purely and simply to declare the traditional and hereditary Monarchy re-established in France in the House of France, everything and everybody will find themselves back in the same position as at the end of July 1830 ; there will be no more need for Fusion negotiations and conditions ; Fusion will be implied in the facts. . . . It will be enough for Monseigneur to make one step towards the French frontier for the whole country to be covered with white flags. . . . The invariable reply [to questions about Fusion] is that Monseigneur is always ready to take the hand offered to him, and to forget all the past ; he only demands pure and simple recognition of his claim, which puts everyone back into their proper places. But no conditions about the Flag or about anything else.

The Marquis was heart-broken at this letter and his reply (on March 3rd) [1] is full of despair. The day before, he had been present at the debate on the Treaty of Peace, and he had thought there was no further kind of sorrow left him to endure ; the news of the Comte de Chambord's determination showed him this was not so, " for today I can no longer retain any hope of seeing the return of that noble family, which could alone still have saved my poor country ". He could have understood the question being " reserved " ; but " to see it settled, when it is impossible for anyone, who has breathed the atmosphere of France, not to realise that even among the most devoted Legitimists everyone feels in his inmost heart the obstacles, that cannot

[1] *Bureau du roi*, pp. 180-7 (from Bordeaux).

be surmounted, erected by indestructible prejudices — all this drives me to despair ". The country was longing for security and repose ; hence the general movement towards monarchy. " But it would be the gravest of errors to regard the movement as purely Legitimist. It is above all a Conservative movement in a crushed nation, whose wounds still bleed and which longs for a remedy. France would never pardon the party, which should disunite the friends of order, who are making such efforts today to save the country together." They had made great sacrifices ; they had compelled Larcy (Thiers' Minister of Public Works) to accept Jules Simon as Minister of Public Instruction : Thiers himself was exceedingly flattered by the sincere support of the majority in the Assembly ; " honest republicans capable of conversion " were being carried in the same direction. All this would be ruined by the disunion of the Conservative party ; " the peasants would vote for the Empire ; there can be no doubt of that . . . it would be the end of the Legitimist party ". He felt as much as anybody the sacrifices involved in a surrender of the White Flag, but " can one hesitate when it is a question of saving France, and France can only be saved at this price ? "

He went on to recall the Comte's own words to the Duc de Nemours : [1] " We cannot dispose of the destinies of the country, far from France and without her consent ". Did not that mean that it was to be settled " in France and together with France " ? " I cast myself at the feet of Monseigneur and beseech him to reflect that this new attitude will seem in conflict with that declaration."

It had been objected that the Tricolour was the flag of Revolution ; that was no longer true. It had put down the '48 Revolution at Rome ; it had stopped the massacre of Christians in Syria ; the Commune had repudiated it in favour of the Red Flag ; the War of 1870 had

[1] See p. 265.

purified it by " the blood of all that heroic band of nobles
— the Bouillés, the Luynes, the Charettes ", who had
poured it out for France. He concluded with a last appeal :
" France is lost, if the King does not return, and I am sure
the King cannot re-enter France with the White Flag. . . .
I would give everything in the world for Monseigneur to
be able to inform himself by consulting the men here,
whose judgment is to be trusted. . . . Adieu, my dear
friend ; may God assist us ; I shall never despair of His
mercy."

On April 2nd, de Blacas announced that the Comte
was setting out for Bruges ; [1] he was convinced that
the time had not yet come for a public appearance, but
he wished to be near France and also within reach of
England, in case of a rising in Brittany. There was a
rumour of a Bonapartist revolt after the reoccupation of
Paris by the Versailles troops ; in that case the Breton
Legitimists would have marched on the capital with the
Comte at their head : " in the present state of things,
Monseigneur believes that interviews with politicians or
more or less authorised members of the Chamber, laden
with conditions, programmes, etc., would be more harmful
than useful ; [2] ignorance of Monseigneur's whereabouts
would make such *démarches* more difficult ".

The Marquis was meanwhile placed in the most inextricable of false positions ; for example, after the
negotiations with the Orleanists, which ended in the repeal
of the laws of Exile, the Comte de Maillé (Fusionist) paid
him a visit. He had received a memorandum from one
of his colleagues, Gabriel de Saint-Victor, deputy for the
Rhône Department, who had himself been attached to
the " court " of the Comte de Chambord, in which the
latter assured him that he had heard from the Comte's

[1] *Bureau du roi*, p. 193.
[2] He adds, " I include among the awkwardnesses to be avoided (if it can
be done honourably) the visit of M. Decazes " — always the *bête noire* of the
Legitimists (*ibid.* p. 195).

own lips that he would accept the Tricolour.[1]   But another Legitimist deputy, the Marquis de Partz, expressed himself as more than sceptical about this astonishing production, adding, " I believe he is far from having consented to sacrifice his Flag ".[2]   La Ferté, in reporting the incident, says :

You will understand how false my position was knowing Monseigneur's feelings and yet under orders not to allow them to be guessed. I answered : " My dear friend, I do not know if you are acquainted with the instructions we have received since 1856. . . . Monseigneur has always replied by the words ' It is a reserved question '."   Maillé read the instructions and then exclaimed, " Ah ! I was sure of it ; Monseigneur feels that it is a sacrifice he must make, when the time comes ".[3]

Maillé went off full of joy to inform the Right Centre, and in the middle of June, Dampierre (a Legitimist) wrote to the Comte de Chambord assuming that an understanding had been arrived at. The Comte was stupefied[4] and replied : " I have learned with infinite regret, and not without displeasure, that several Legitimist deputies have entered into engagements, which would result in a serious surrender of principle ".[5]   In his own diary he noted : " Certain of my friends have engaged themselves, almost in my name, on the Flag question without any authority from me. So I was obliged to publish the Chambord manifesto." [6]

On May 21st the Marquis, after attending a service at Versailles, where (he says) " all servants of the Monarchy receive a deep impression of the presence of the Great King ",[7] sent off a desperate appeal to the Comte. He did

---

[1] Quoted de Roux, p. 185.

[2] On June 27th *Le Figaro* said : " We feel able to say (without fear of contradiction) that the august representative of the monarchical principle in France . . . will accept the flag of France ; this is a declaration of immense importance " (Loménie, p. 113).

[3] *Bureau du roi*, pp. 204-5.　　　　　[4] De Roux, p. 185.

[5] *Fusion monarchique*, p. 209.　　　　[6] De Roux, p. 187.

[7] *Bureau du roi*, p. 206.

not mince his words : " Not only does Monseigneur run the risk of being accused of having contributed in the present and in the future to the ruin of his country, by preventing a return to Monarchy and by sacrificing the hereditary principle, which he represents, to a personal repugnance, but also of being charged without fail by his own party with having led them into error by reticences, of which the great majority of Royalists have never had any idea, and which in their eyes would completely justify the behaviour of the Orleans Princes ".[1] He pointed out again that the Comte's decision, if adhered to, would be the end of the Legitimist party, and concluded : " God and Monseigneur will pardon me, I hope, this cry wrung from my despair. But the memory of Henri IV and the sacrifices he made for his country seem still to authorise me to count on some other ending to our hopes, some other reward for our patriotism and our fidelity, than what lies in store for us as a result of Monseigneur's actual decision. I ask Monseigneur to accept the respectful homage of one, who will be to his last breath the most faithful and devoted of his subjects, but who certainly at the moment is among the most unhappy."

On May 24th the Comte sent in his own hand the following characteristic reply : [2]

I have received your letter, my dear La Ferté, and I recognised in it your devoted heart and your excellent intentions. But your observations have made no difference to my decisions, which have been long and maturely considered, and now are settled beyond the possibility of change. The question of the Flag is not for me merely a question of an easily understood repugnance ; it is a question of principle. With the symbol of the Revolution it would be impossible for me to do any good, or set right any evil ; why is there so strong a desire that I should accept colours, which have waved over so many crimes and which have always represented the overthrow of the Legitimate Monarchy ? If all this means nothing,

---

[1] That is (I suppose) in resisting complete Fusion.
[2] *Bureau du roi*, p. 208.

Y

there is no reason to attach any importance to one colour rather than another, and therefore I can keep my own. But if, on the other hand, it stands for a complete order of ideas (and that is what I believe), I ought not, and I will not consent to abandon the Flag of my fathers, which for me means respect for religion, protection for whatever is just, whatever is good, whatever stands for the right, united to what the needs of our time demand, while the Tricolour symbolises the Revolution under all its aspects and — what is more — is now filling the arsenals of the foreigner, who has defeated us.[1]

I have shown by what I have constantly written — and particularly by my last letter [2] — that I understand the needs of my time, and that I am ready to devote myself wholeheartedly to the greatness and the reconstruction of France. If my country, weary of so many changes and so many fruitless experiments, desires at last to have done with them, let her take me with my principle and its symbol. I belong to her with all my soul, with all my heart, and with all the intelligence God has given me. But if she wishes to remain in the rut of revolutions, I can be of no use to her, for I will never be King of the Revolution or of any semi-Revolution. In that case I shall wait till, taught better by events, France understands at last where the port lies after the storm. But we shall not be driven to this hard extremity. Courage, then, my dear La Ferté ; the sadness of a friend like you deeply distresses me. All the same, you will understand that, sure of being on the side of the truth, I can only obey the orders of my conscience ; I embrace you cordially and count upon you more than ever,

HENRI

Soon after the receipt of this letter the Marquis went to see the Comte at Bruges.[3] He was received with all possible affection, and they sat together on the same sofa to discuss the dispositions of the Royalist party. " Monseigneur," began the Marquis, " there are many among your friends who must be humoured." " They are the most worthless," retorted the Comte. " Oh no, Monseigneur, but they need

---

[1] The idea that one abandons a flag, because it has been defeated, is one of the odd gaps in the Comte de Chambord's generosity of outlook, due perhaps to his solitary existence.

[2] To General Carayon-Latour.   [3] *Bureau du roi*, p. 213.

gentle treatment." "Pooh," repeated the Comte, "they are the most worthless." "No, Monseigneur." This second contradiction provoked one of the Comte's rare outbursts of passion, of so violent a nature that the Marquis said to him: "Monseigneur, I shall never speak of this scene, and it is not for my sake that I shall keep silence about it". The Comte made no answer, and the Marquis resumed his argument; he declared that every one of the "old and faithful nobility" would join him in his protest against the White Flag. "Oh", answered the Comte, struggling with his impatience, "the Legitimists!" La Ferté, hurt by the scorn in his voice, replied: "A Legitimist is before all the most faithful of patriots; we have always cried 'God and the King', because we have always identified our King and our country. The day you separate them, Monseigneur, will make us unhappy indeed, but we shall never abandon our country."

The Comte replied that he did not wish to separate himself from France, but the Tricolour was the symbol of the Revolution. The Marquis answered that, on the contrary, the Tricolour had just defeated the Red Flag, which was the real symbol of the Revolution. He went on to urge that there was no historical ground for this insistence on the White Flag, since the old Army had flags of all colours, and concluded: "Like a doctor you must take your patient as you find him, and give him the medicine he needs, and then perhaps you will cure him. But if you expect to cure him simply by appearing at his bedside, you will not succeed." "I should feel myself unable to do any good", returned the Comte, "unless I came back completely myself" (" tout entier ").

La Ferté tried another line of attack. "Monseigneur, I do not know a better Christian than you; consult the Holy Father." The Comte thought for a moment, then replied: "No — in matters of dogma the Pope is infallible, not in political matters."

The Marquis began, " Well, then——" but checked himself in time,[1] and continued : " Well, Monseigneur, I have an infallible means for you to recover your flag ". The Comte looked astonished. " What do you mean ? " The Marquis meant that he was to accept the Tricolour, and after five or six years, when France had recovered her strength, he should chase the Germans from Alsace-Lorraine and then demand the White Flag in exchange. The Comte remained unconvinced, and the interview ended, " with much kindness on his part, but more coldly than usual ". La Ferté then related the conversation to Blacas and Monti, who were waiting in an adjoining room. Blacas' comment was, " You are a gallant fellow ".

On June 29th [2] La Ferté returned to the charge ; he asked Blacas to lay before the Comte the instructions, issued from Frohsdorf on November 25th, 1856, which said that he was " free from all engagements and far removed from all prejudices " on the Flag question ; this had been taken to mean that he would choose the right time and moment for a decision, and that he would consult the wishes of the country — " today Monseigneur abandons all precedents, and has resolved to announce his own decision to France ". On June 30th, after the great military review at Longchamps,[3] he wrote that " the effect of Thiers' speech on the Loan and against the Income Tax, the prodigious success of the Loan and the attitude of the public at the Review, where there was enthusiastic applause for Thiers and MacMahon and none at all for the Assembly, all showed that the moment was more than ill-chosen for the proposed manifesto ; the people had seen the national flags carried by thousands and applauded in the streets — and now they were to be asked to abandon them ! "

On June 30th he made a last appeal : " Has Mon-

---

[1] I am not clear what La Ferté was going to say ; possibly " Why, then, do you support the Pope's temporal power ? "

[2] *Bureau du roi*, p. 223.   [3] *Ibid.* p. 226.

seigneur considered that by making the Flag a question of honour, he thereby compels France and the Army and the Princes to make it also a question of honour ? " [1] As the month of June drew to an end, it was evident that some decision would have to be arrived at. Joinville went to Paris, under the name of " Colonel Lutteroth ", to arrange details of the Visit on behalf of the Orleanists ; the Marquis de la Ferté said to him : " M. le Comte de Chambord is no longer in Belgium ; he is in France. I shall at once transmit your request [for an interview] and I hope to be able to give you a reply tomorrow or the day after." [2]

On the night of July 1st, the Comte took the train for Paris. A certain brusque impetuousness is, at first sight, an unexpected trait in his cautious character, but is not uncommon in people, who live secluded and independent lives. They are so used to remaining inactive, when all the world expects them to move, that they sometimes enjoy movement, when all the world expects inaction. It is perhaps a certain compensation for seeming stiff on great matters to allow oneself freedom in smaller ones. Certainly the events of the next few days were fantastic enough for the Arabian Nights. It is to be hoped that the Comte de Chambord, who was something of a Romantic, appreciated that aspect, for, if so, it was the only amusement he ever got out of his political adventures.

He took a passport in the name of Mercoeur, and he travelled all night ; as the morning sun rose over the country he had not seen for forty years, he noted in his diary : " Chantilly ; beautiful woods ".[3] He arrived at Paris at 5 A.M. on Sunday, July 2nd, the day of the elections. He was attended by the Count de Monti and de Vanssay ; as the carriage which had been ordered was not there, they took a cab like a party of tourists. His first desire was a very human one — to see the great city, so changed since his childhood : he went first to Notre-Dame-

[1] *Bureau du roi*, p. 227.   [2] *Ibid.* p. 229.   [3] De Roux, p. 188.

des-Victoires, where he heard Mass, then to the Sainte
Chapelle in memory of St. Louis, and to the Pont-Neuf in
memory of Henri IV.   After that, they visited the Tuileries,
now a heap of ruins.   There remained only the Pavillon de
Marsan, where he was born ;   he could see the windows, in
front of which he used to play at soldiers ; [1] his eyes were
wet with tears [2] and the cabman said to him, " Don't cry
so much, bourgeois ;   it was worse during the Siege when
they ate my horses ".[3]   After *déjeuner* at a restaurant in
the Rue de Marivaux, he went to the Avenue de Villars to
the house of Baron de Nanteuil.   La Ferté went to visit
him, and asked whether he had read the letter, in which he
reminded him of the Instructions of 1856.   " Yes."   " Well,
Monseigneur ? "   " It makes absolutely no change in my
resolve.   For me it is a question of honour."   " I am afraid,
Monseigneur, that you will make yourself impossible and,
when France needs a King, she will turn to the Comte de
Paris."   " He will never be legitimate King, for I shall never
abdicate."   " Monseigneur, you will do worse :   you will
say ' No ' to France, and she will certainly take it as an
abdication."   La Ferté then asked whether the Comte had
any more to say to him : " No," was the answer, " later on,
I shall send you the reply for the Comte de Paris."   " I
shall have the honour to send it," replied the Marquis,
" but it will be the last service I shall be able to do for
Monseigneur."   The Comte stopped in his walk up and
down the room, saying, "Ah, I regret those words ".   The
Marquis bowed, and took his leave of his master ; they
never met again.[4]   In the afternoon, the Comte set off for
his chateau at Chambord ;   from the station of Blois

[1] *Bureau du roi*, p. 229.

[2] Thiers ungenerous comment (in conversation) was as follows : " He wept
over the ruins left by the Commune ; if you think a blubberer can govern a
nation, you are wrong : if I had wept at the gates of Paris, I should never
have got inside " (de Marcère, *Assemblée nationale*, ii. 40).

[3] Halévy, *Fin des notables*, p. 25 ; Loth, p. 131 ; *Bureau du roi*, p. 229.

[4] *Bureau du roi*, pp. 230-32.

(where he stayed the night at the Hôtel de l'Angleterre) he sent the following answer to the Comte de Paris :

M. le Comte de Chambord was glad to hear the expression by the Comte de Paris of his desire to visit him. M. le Comte de Chambord is in France. Therefore the moment, indicated by him before, has now come to explain himself on certain reserved questions ; he hopes that nothing in his language will be an obstacle to that union of the House of Bourbon, which has always been his dearest wish. Nevertheless loyalty demands that the Prince, his cousin, should be informed that M. le Comte de Chambord thinks it necessary to ask M. le Comte de Paris to put off his visit till the day not far off, when he shall have explained his whole mind to France. He would have wished to receive his cousin's visit at Chambord, but at present he thinks it better not to prolong his stay in France : on leaving Chambord he will return to Bruges, where he will be from July 8th to the 16th.[1]

It would be hard to say whether the Comte de Paris and his friends were more perplexed by the cold correctness of the note, which read like the reply to an invitation to dinner, or by the phrase " reserved questions " : the Comte de Paris asked Pasquier what the words meant ; the Duke replied that he had never heard of them.[2]

They were soon to know : La Ferté, directly after his painful interview with the Comte de Chambord, went to the house of the Bishop of Orleans. He did not find him at home, but Falloux was staying there as his guest, and La Ferté told him with tears in his eyes that the Comte was about to issue a manifesto in favour of the White Flag. The effect was like that of a bombshell at a wedding-party. Since the dinner of the Princes with Thiers, the Royalists had been living in an atmosphere of almost religious ecstasy. Falloux, who had come up for an

---

[1] Falloux, ii. 473.

[2] *Fusion monarchique*, p. 211. In communicating the letters to the Legitimists, Pasquier said : " We have made engagements to you and, if they are not accepted, it is not our fault. We shall not allow you to copy the note ; a document when copied is always published and for our part we are anxious not to cause any bitterness " (Loménie, p. 125).

Academy election, had spent the Sunday listening to rapturous accounts of the famous dinner to the Royalist deputies, and rejoicing with the Bishop of Orleans over the near prospect of a Restoration.[1]

When the first movement of horrified incredulity was over, a largely attended meeting of Royalists was held on Monday in one of the bureaux of the Assembly, and it was unanimously resolved to send a deputation to Chambord to represent that " to sign such a manifesto would be equivalent to signing an act of abdication ". The Comte de Maillé consented to go (he was not perhaps a very tactful choice, as he had been a member of the suspect deputation to Dreux), and Gontaut-Biron, one of the " twelve Apostles " ; they were joined by La Rochefoucauld, Duc de Bisaccia. In appearance he resembled his famous ancestor, the author of the *Maximes*, and in elegance of manner, but he had no pretensions to cleverness or eloquence ; he was somewhat pompous (it was said he always walked as though preceded by a master of ceremonies), but he had the good sense of a country gentleman. His wife, the Princess de Ligne, was a famous Parisian hostess ; his son-in-law, the Duc de Luynes, had been killed in the war.

Many of the deputies expressed the opinion that Dupanloup should go also, and Falloux went to the Assembly, where he met him in the Galerie des Tombeaux — the Versailles lobby. The Bishop refused ; he hated travelling at night. At his Versailles house, the door was shut at nine every evening and the bell prevented from functioning. Falloux put his back against one of the monuments, and talked till he had won his point. He said, " Side by side with the noblesse, the clergy of France should be represented ; as the attachment of the *Tiers état* to the Tricolour is undisputed the King will see that the whole nation demands it ".[2]

[1] Falloux, ii. 472.   [2] *Ibid.* ii. 477 ; De Meaux, p. 117.

The four deputies left that evening, accompanied by
Laurentie, director of the Legitimist organ, the *Union*, and
the young Cazenove de Pradine — deputy for Lot-et-
Garonne — the darling of the Assembly ; he had been
seriously wounded at the battle of Ligny, where he had
fought with the greatest courage ; his charming face and
seductive manner won all hearts and his colleagues called
him Eliacin ; but he had also all the intemperance of youth,
and an impatient Royalist said of him, as he mounted the
tribune to make some imprudent motion, " He is only good
at getting himself killed ".[1]

The Castle of Chambord is near the city of Blois ; it
had been given to the Maréchal de Saxe as a mark of public
esteem after the victory of Fontenoy, and the illustrious
General had died there, surrounded by actresses and
comedians. When in 1821 it had been given to Henri in
the burst of loyal enthusiasm that hailed his " miraculous
birth ", Paul-Louis Courier, the famous Radical pam-
phleteer, wrote sarcastically : " Chambord is full of the
young Prince's ancestors, and for that reason I regret he
should live there . . . here Louis, the model of Kings,
lived with Montespan and La Vallière, and all the wives
and daughters, whom it was his good pleasure to take
away from their husbands and relations . . . by this door
the mistress entered in the evening and the confessor in
the morning ".[2] Victor Hugo described it as being " lovely
as a fairy palace, and stately as a King's dwelling " ;
the ancient castle had now to witness the unaccustomed
scene of a King refusing to reign, and courtiers telling the
truth.

The Comte had arrived on the night of Monday, July
3rd, and stayed for three days, going for long walks in the

[1] De Meaux, p. 208.
[2] Pamphlet of 1821 ; Courier was condemned to two months' imprisonment and 100 francs fine, rather perhaps for irreverence to the aristocracy
(who, he said, had won their advancement " by means of women ") than for
an attack on the Crown.

park and receiving many visitors — curés, sisters, peasants.
On Tuesday, Cazenove de Pradines saw him, and it is said
he fell at the King's feet to implore him to make
concessions — in vain ; [1] the official deputation was introduced on Wednesday, July 5th. The Comte's attendants
crowded into the passages, full of agitation. " Spare no
pains to succeed," they cried to the deputies, " or all is
lost."

The Comte himself remained completely · calm ; he
invited the three delegates from the Right to be seated,
and assured them that they might speak openly without
offending him. De Maillé spoke first.[2] He gave a short
sketch of the negotiations with the Orleanists from the
beginning of the Assembly, referring to the Dreux interview, which he said had obtained the honour of Monseigneur's approbation (as a matter of fact the approbation
had been given by La Ferté and repudiated by the Comte) ;
coming to the question of the Flag, he repeated the Comte's
own declaration of 1856 — that he would not take a
decision upon it " far from France and apart from France ";
he interpreted it as meaning that he would follow the
opinion of the country. " Now it is beyond question that
the country desires the Tricolour unanimously." " Not
perhaps so unanimously as you think ", replied the Comte.
" The Tricolour ", continued de Maillé, " is the symbol of
the modern régime ; it is for the people the sign of freedom
from the old pre-Revolution abuses. If Monseigneur gives
it up, he must give up the crown of France." The Comte
replied : " I cannot return to France without my principle
and my flag ; I am sure that with the Tricolour I should
no longer be myself, and that I could not give to France the
services she expects from me as the representative of order
and liberty ". De Maillé replied boldly, " The White Flag

[1] De Roux, p. 188.
[2] De Maillé drew up the *procès-verbal* of the interview (see *Fusion
monarchique*, p. 212).

does not belong to you exclusively : it is the flag of France, not of your family.[1] There is not a Legitimist who will follow you in the way you propose." If we had not the report signed and accredited by witnesses, it would be hard to believe the Comte's reply : "That proves", he said, speaking to men, who had grown grey in the service of monarchy, "that revolutionary ideas have taken root more firmly than I thought". The deputies now passed to the most passionate supplications. "Have pity on this great Legitimist party, which for forty years has given up careers, honours, fortunes for you." "If the manifesto appears, the party will disappear." "Yes," replied the Comte, "if you desert me." La Rochefoucauld fell on his knees begging him not to reject the flag, under which his son-in-law had died at Coulmiers.[2] De Maillé cried : "Have pity on our children, on us, on France". The Comte remained inflexible : "I have reflected much on this subject ; for me it is a question of honour and political integrity. I can say no more ; let us part ; we shall always be friends."

The deputies sadly took their leave : Dupanloup was then introduced. The interview was not an easy one ; the Comte did not particularly like the Bishop, whom he looked upon as a kind of Modernist (to ante-date the phrase) because of his opposition to Papal Infallibility. He opened the conversation with a good-humoured refer- ence to the last time he had met the Bishop — as con- fessor in his childhood, but he would not speak any more about politics, as he had exhausted the subject with the three deputies. The Bishop urged that the failure of

---

[1] Hector Pessard (ii. 111) adds here — I do not know from what source — "It was *our* ancestors that made the White Flag glorious for the glory of your ancestors. We, their descendants, have perhaps the right to believe that our honour is not committed to the exclusive maintenance of this flag, and we may be allowed to believe, Sire, that the honour of your faithful servants is not less sensitive than your Majesty's."

[2] *Fusion monarchique*, p. 217.

a Restoration would give the Church up to her worst
enemies ; the Comte agreed, but did not see how his
manifesto would hasten such a calamity. The Bishop
urged him to come to Versailles, or else to summon deputies
of all parties to Chambord ; he replied : " It would be
useless ; I have made up my mind ".[1]

After the Bishop, Laurentie was introduced. " From
you, my friend," said the Comte, " I am ready to hear
anything, for I am sure of your feelings and your intentions." " Well, Monseigneur, why raise the question of
the White Flag ? " " It is not I who raise it ; I have
been compromised by those, who have no authority to act
in my name ; I must make known my resolution to France."
He then showed Laurentie a copy of the manifesto and
made some alterations, by his advice.[2]

The Castle emptied ; the visitors returned to Versailles.
Laurentie wrote to a friend : " In twenty-four hours we
have lost the fruit of twenty years prudence ". Dupanloup,
as he was jerked about in the uncomfortable carriage, which
took them back to Blois, kept on exclaiming, " What an
amazing psychological problem ! What moral blind-
ness ! "[3]

The Comte left Blois by the night train with the
manifesto in his pocket. He slept soundly during the whole
journey, but Vanssay, his attendant, could not settle down
and, when they reached Paris, asked him anxiously
whether the manifesto was to be altered. " No," answered
the Comte, " send it to the *Union* to be printed as it is ;
it is my last word." He did not stop at Paris, but went
straight back to Bruges, leaving behind him the capital he
was only to see once again in his life.[4]

The manifesto appeared in the evening papers of
Thursday, July 6th. It ran as follows :

---

[1] Lagrange, *Vie de Dupanloup*, ii. 404.   [2] Loth, p. 159.
[3] Falloux, ii. 478-9.   [4] Loth, p. 160.

PEOPLE OF FRANCE,

I am among you ; you have opened the doors of France to me, and I could not refuse the happiness of seeing my country again, but I do not wish by staying any longer to furnish new pretexts for excitement at a time when there is so much restlessness.

Therefore I am leaving this château of Chambord, which you gave me, from which I took the name I have been proud to bear for forty years along the paths of exile. As I leave France, it is in my heart to tell you that I am not separated from you ; France knows I belong to her. I cannot forget that the right of the King is part of the nation's inheritance, nor can I refuse those duties towards the nation, which it imposes upon me.

These duties I shall carry out, on my word as an honest man and a King. With the help of God we will found together, and when you will, a government in conformity with the real needs of the nation, widely based on administrative decentralisation and local liberties.

As a guarantee of the public liberties, to which all Christian peoples have a right, we shall grant Universal Suffrage, honestly practised, and the control of two Chambers. We shall resume the national movement of the end of the last century,[1] restoring to it its true character.

A minority in revolt against the wishes of France made it the occasion of a period of demoralisation by falsehood, and of disorganisation by violence ; their criminal conspiracy imposed a revolution on a nation, that only asked for reforms and, since, has driven it to the edge of an abyss, in which it would a few months ago have perished but for the heroic efforts of our army.

It is the working-classes, the labourers in the country and the towns, whose welfare has been the constant object of my most anxious thought and my most welcome studies, and who have suffered the most from this social disorder. But France, cruelly disillusioned by unprecedented disasters, will understand that it is impossible to return to the truth by exchanging one error for another, that we cannot evade eternal necessities by temporary expedients.

France will recall me and I shall come to her with all that I have — my devotion to her service, my principle, and my flag.

On the question of the Flag mention has been made of conditions

---

[1] Apparently the Royal programme of 1789.

to which I cannot submit. People of France, I am ready to do everything to help my country to rise from her downfall and resume her position in the world ; the only sacrifice I cannot make to her is that of my honour.

I belong to my time with all my heart : I pay sincere homage to all its greatness and, whatever has been the flag under which our soldiers have marched, I have admired their heroism and thanked God for all, which their courage added to the treasure of our national glory.

There must be no misunderstanding or reserve between you and me. No, it is not true what ignorance and credulity have spoken of — class privileges, absolutism, and intolerance, and I know not what else — tithes and feudal rights — phantoms which the most daring calumny is trying to evoke before you. But I will not, for that, let the standard of Henri IV, François I, and Jeanne d'Arc be snatched from my hands.

With that flag the national unity was effected ; with that flag your ancestors, led by mine, conquered Alsace and Lorraine, whose faithfulness to us is still a consolation in our disaster ; it has conquered the barbarians in their land of Africa, which witnessed the first war-like actions of a Prince of my family. It will conquer the modern barbarians, by whom the world is menaced. I shall entrust it without fear to the courage of our army. They know it has never followed any path but that of honour. I received it as a sacred legacy from the old King, my grandfather, when he died in exile ; it has always for me been bound up with the thought of my distant country. It floated over my cradle ; I wish that it may overshadow my tomb. In the glorious folds of this unspotted standard I shall bring you order and freedom. People of France, Henri V cannot abandon the White Flag of Henri IV.[1]

The French people, to whom the Comte appealed, had so completely lost the memory of the White Flag that the manifesto seemed like a lesson from a history book — with the history somewhat imaginative. In a matter so exclusively French, we can only quote the conclusions of the careful appendix to M. Desjoyeaux's *Fusion monarchique* : [2]

The Ancien Régime had no national flag. There were French arms such as the white cross on a red ground of the Picardy regi-

[1] Lacombe, i. 279-81.   [2] Pp. 438-61.

ment, and the blue banner with a white cross; the dynasty also had its emblem — the blue banner with golden lilies carried by twenty-four of our kings and which passed from the Capetian Kings to the Valois, from the Valois to the Bourbons.[1] . . . Since 1789 [2] there is a single French emblem — the Tricolour; the White Flag, in the sense given it by the controversies of 1870–73, dates from the Restoration.[3] . . . It was abandoned by Louis-Philippe in favour of the Tricolour, and for forty years, under Monarchy, Republic and Empire, the flag of France has been the red, white, and blue.

At Versailles the depression and despondency among the Royalists were universal. " Never ", says Falloux, " have I seen such complete unanimity in despair." [4] Vitet, a distinguished Orleanist, sat in Dupanloup's house, his head in his hands, murmuring, " Oh, the blood of Charles X ".[5] Lacombe notes in his diary : " The Manifesto is full of fine feeling, but it is no good hiding the fact that it is a farewell to France ".[6] Another Royalist deputy wrote in his journal : " No doubt it is very fine to drape oneself in one's dignity and make one's father's flag a winding-sheet, but France, poor France, who will help her ? " [7]

On Thursday, July 6th, a large meeting of Royalist deputies was held in the house of Resseguier, opposite the Palace of Versailles; many deputies talked of resigning their seats and retiring from the Assembly; others pro-

---

[1] " The white plume, to which Henri IV bade his followers rally, was not a flag but a feather which he wore as leader of the Huguenot party " (*Fusion monarchique*, p. 448).

[2] " La Fayette in 1789 gave the cockade of three colours to the Paris National Guard : white was worn as a cockade by all the army in 1786 ; red and blue were the colours of Paris " (*ibid.* p. 451).

[3] " The Provisional Government of 1814 hesitated before adopting the white cockade, and were finally influenced by the action of Marshal Jourdan, who made the troops at Rouen adopt it " (*ibid.* p. 458) ; cp. Halévy, *République des ducs*, p. 57 : " The White Flag had been the flag of the King and his family, never the flag of the Army . . . the royal regiments marched under a mixture of colours, in which it is easy to recognise the Tricolour, . . . in 1815 the White Flag was only an insolent invention of *émigrés* ".

[4] Falloux, ii. 477.　　　　[5] *Ibid.* p. 482.　　　　[6] Lacombe, i. 43.

[7] Martial Delpit (quoted Denis, p. 90).

posed that a protest should be sent to the newspapers.
This was accepted, and it was resolved to convene a larger
meeting that evening in the rooms of La Rochefoucauld at
the Hôtel des Réservoirs ; about eighty members were
present and Falloux was invited to take part. Count
Benoist d'Azy, Vice-President of the Assembly, took the
chair, and Larcy, Minister in Thiers' Cabinet, proposed a
form of protest. There was hardly any dissent. Du Temple,
an eccentric member from Brittany, a fervent mystic, a
virulent opponent of Thiers, an implacable enemy of the
Orleanists, who, he declared, had " consecrated the right
of insurrection by the July colours ", defended the Comte
de Chambord. " Here ", he cried, " is an unhappy King
without money, power or soldiers, who returns after forty
years of exile, and his supposed followers repudiate the first
word he utters ! I do not belong to your party ", and he
walked out. He was followed by Fresneau — a gentleman
in a long coat, who looked like a professor at a seminary,
but had already distinguished himself in the Assembly by
screaming out to the Paris deputies that they were
" covered with blood " — and La Monneraye, another
Breton deputy. The rest of the meeting unanimously
accepted the following declaration :

The personal inspirations of M. le Comte de Chambord concern
himself alone. However they may be judged, it cannot be denied
that they have a quality of sincerity, pushed to the point of self-
sacrifice *which inspire respect* ; [1] after, as before, this grave document, those, who support the principle of hereditary and representative monarchy, because they see in it a pledge of security for
the country, remain devoted to the cause of France and her liberties ;
full of deference for her will, they do not give up the flag she has
chosen, made glorious by the courage of her soldiers, and become,
in opposition to the blood-red banner of anarchy, the flag of social
order. [2]

---

[1] These words were added by Falloux to emphasise the reference to a
possible abdication contained in the word " sacrifice ".

[2] Falloux, ii. 484-5. Loth, p. 168.

A copy of the Chambord manifesto had been sent to the Comte de Paris ; he replied in a letter, marked confidential, so as not to aggravate the situation :

The Comte de Paris is very grateful to the Comte de Chambord for having informed him of his decision ; he acknowledges the perfect loyalty of his behaviour ; he thinks that the visit, which he is still disposed to pay, would under the present circumstances run the risk of bringing about explanations which it seems to him preferable to avoid. This is the motive which has caused him to postpone it.[1]

The Fusionist campaign now came to an end, and its leaders turned their attention to securing conservative guarantees within the existing form of government.

There remained for the Comte de Chambord an act of discipline to be carried out ; generous towards his enemies and courteous to all, he yet had for his servants the most inflexible standard of obedience. His friendship was only to be had at this price ; the poor Marquis de la Ferté was now to experience this.[2]

Writing from Bruges in a letter dictated to Blacas, the Comte reminded the Marquis of his words, " It is the last service I shall do for you ", and went on to criticise his conduct :

Your position at Versailles imposed upon you the duty of supporting Monseigneur in a matter which he regarded as concerning his honour ; instead of that it has come to his ears from several quarters that — contrary perhaps to your intentions — you let it be understood that the manifesto was contrary to Monseigneur's previous engagements, and even allowed the opinion to be expressed in your presence without protest that the act was equivalent to an abdication.[3] Monseigneur concludes therefore, to his great regret

---

[1] *Fusion monarchique*, p. 223 ; Hanotaux, ii. 121. In handing the answer back to La Ferté, Joinville said : " We have all seen the grief of the Legitimist party ; we all understand it, the Prince most of all ; we share it and we respect it (his voice shook with emotion) " (*Bureau du roi*, p. 236).

[2] *Ibid.* p. 238. It is perhaps fair to add that La Ferté's remonstrances seem to have been more candid than tactful.

[3] The reference, I suppose, is to his interview with Falloux and Dupanloup.

Z

and mortification, that you separated yourself from him at Versailles too violently for him to be able to keep you in the functions, which he has hitherto entrusted to you.

De Blacas, writing in his own person, added, " We saw, quite as much as you, how difficult was the question of whether the right moment was chosen for the manifesto ; the result has not completely justified your fears ".[1] But La Ferté was not reassured. " The manifesto ", he replied, " having its origin in regions that are idealistic but impracticable for the France of today, has won respect and admiration, while people have been stupefied by its language of another age. . . . I have seen the impression produced on General Changarnier, on General Ducrot, on Marshal MacMahon ; all his staff talk in the same tone." [2] In a farewell letter of the same date to the Comte himself [3] he refused to discuss the charges brought against him : " My conscience tells me I have fulfilled my duty to the last with courage and at the cost of great distress, as a gentleman, whose feelings may have been hurt, but who can never forget the kindnesses, with which his King has honoured him for so long ".

On the Left, writers adopted their classical tactic of praising the Comte de Chambord for his disinterestedness and sense of realities. Victor Hugo wrote :

> C'est bien ; l'homme est viril et fort qui se décide
> A changer sa fin triste en un fier suicide,
> Et qui, se sentant grand surtout comme fantôme,
> Ne vend pas son drapeau même au prix d'un royaume.

On the other side there was a certain movement of admiration and sympathy in the Church and the Army. The Comte notes in his diary of July 14th : " The effect, of which so many weak minds were afraid, is better than was expected ".[4]

The one gleam of consolation in the despair of the

---

[1] *Bureau du roi*, pp. 241-3. [2] *Ibid.* pp. 244-6 (July 22nd).
[3] *Ibid.* pp. 246-7. [4] De Roux, pp. 191, 192.

Royalists had been, as Falloux had noted, its unanimity ;
even this small comfort was not to last long. All sections
of Royalists supplicated the Comte de Chambord to preserve the national flag and almost all concurred in the protest of July 6th ; the sudden and unexpected shock of the
obstacle put almost all the deputies instinctively on the
defensive, but as the shock wore off, differences began to
assert themselves. The Extreme Right began to repent of
having seemed to oppose the royal will. Their watchword
was " Cover the King at all costs ; do not desert him in
public ". Such an attitude was chivalrous enough ; unfortunately, if the King was blameless, someone else must
have been to blame. Old memories and resentments began
to revive ; it was remembered that the Orleanists, only
half forgiven, had played a prominent part in what had
occurred, and that Falloux, the old opponent of royal
commands, had helped to draw up the protest of the
deputies. A legend began to circulate that the Orleanists
had plotted to force the Comte's abdication. Falloux was
shown two letters from an ardent Royalist at Nantes :
the first, immediately after the Chambord manifesto, said,
" All is ended " ; the second, a few days later, said, " I
have been made to understand my mistake ; M. le Comte
de Chambord was disgracefully deceived ; I recognise that
he was in a state of legitimate defence ".[1] It was said that
the Comte de Chambord meant to reserve the whole
question of the Flag until he was restored ; he hoped that
the universal enthusiasm accompanying his return would
make it possible to restore the White Flag, but the unscrupulous schemes of the Orleanists drove the Comte to
a premature disclosure of his unpopular intentions. It is
probable enough that some such scheme was in the Comte
de Chambord's mind,[2] but it could only be justified by a

[1] Falloux, ii. 488.
[2] The Comte certainly hoped that the restoration of the White Flag
would be easier amid the triumphant scenes of his entry to Paris ; it was
expected there would be a snowstorm of white emblems to welcome him —

complete neglect of the representatives of the nation, who were surely bound to inform themselves as to the King's intentions, before they restored him. Laurentie and Poujoulat, the editors of the *Union*, and de Saint-Chéron, author of the Royalist *Correspondance*,[1] rallied to the personal policy of the Pretender.[2] More serious still was the split which ensued in the ranks of the parliamentary Legitimists. Hitherto they had all met together at the Hôtel des Réservoirs ; now, about eighty deputies of the Extreme Right broke off to form a group called the Chevaux-Légers ("light horsemen "), not, as might have been thought from their independent cavalry tactics, but

the " window plebiscite ", as it was called with reference to the scenes of 1814. This is what made the situation in 1871 and 1873 so paradoxical : the Comte de Chambord, so idealistic in his fidelity to his flag, was worldly wise enough to see that it could not be made a condition of his return. This led to every kind of ambiguity ; the Comte, first of all, wished to keep his intentions secret ; at last in 1873 he promised or seemed to promise that there should be no change before his return. The deputies thought this meant he would give way ; he really meant to reserve the question, because he believed France would accept the White Flag, when they once saw him on the throne. But his hatred of the very shadow of deception made him tear his plans to pieces, and twice he declared himself prematurely ; his lofty idealism always triumphed over his best-laid plans.

[1] *I.e.* information sent by the Paris Royalists to the provincial papers.

[2] The following extracts give some idea of the tone of the Press. *Bien Public* (Thierist) : " It is the affirmation clear and unambiguous of the royalty of divine right. It is too late ; France has forgotten it." *Temps* (Centre) : " A flag is a symbol . . . the White Flag is a reversal not only of the French Revolution and its consequences, but to a certain extent of modern thought itself ". *Gazette* (Orleanist) : " The question has always seemed to our friends one reserved for the nation ". *Univers* (Ultramontane) : " Henri wishes to keep his flag ; he has certainly the right to it, and it is his duty. The Protestant traders from Holland trampled on the Cross in order to trade with Japan ; a man, who aspires to wear the crown of France and still keeps the glory of it on his brow, cannot begin by an act of apostasy " (de Luz, pp. 359-61). *Le Français* (Orleanist) : " A great party faithful for long through all vicissitudes, forced to choose between its Prince and its country, decides for its country not without regret but without hesitation ". *La Revue des Deux Mondes* (Orleanist) : " The manifesto of July 5th is a naïve abdication, all the more characteristic for being absolutely unconscious ". *Journal des Débats* : " This is the language of another world and another time, the language of the Encyclical, the Syllabus. It is the theocratic language of the Papacy applied to the Monarchy, as complete, as absolute, as dogmatic in the case of the State as in the case of the Church " (Loménie, pp. 140-42).

from the name of the street where they met.

The Moderate Legitimists (nuance Falloux) formed the Réunion Colbert. Their meetings were presided over by Audren de Kerdrel, one of the wisest and most disinterested of their number, deputy for Île-et-Vilaine : he had been a leading member of the Conservative party in the Assembly of '48 ; " blond as a cherub, with curly hair, supple as a waltzer, he was cursed with one of those pretty faces which prevented his audience from taking him seriously ".[1] He had been elected to the Corps Législatif, but had resigned rather than vote the Empire. Now he was thin and shrivelled, like a Don Quixote ; he had a string of Christian names like a hidalgo — Vincent-Paul-Marie-Casimir ; he was nicknamed the Impulsive, and he could never sit still on his bench for a moment. This, and his habit of always appealing to the " loyalty " of his colleagues, made the reporters call him " the loyal puppet on strings ".[2] But his chivalry and honour were real and impressive.

The Extreme Right may be divided without offence into the mystics and the courtiers — the one with their eyes fixed on Heaven, the other looking to the Court of their exiled King. One of the most perfect types of the mystic was Belcastel, Marquis and " Chevalier of the Order of Pius IX " ; his hollow face with the deep-set eyes of the dreamer, and his lyrical style of oratory often excited the Assembly to laughter. For him Paris was " the hell of Dante ". " In the country ", he used to say, " we have kept the faith of our fathers in God." He voted against Thiers' title, refusing to " accept the Republican label even for a day ". Once only, four years later, when it was clear all hope of a Restoration was at an end, did he speak burning words of remonstrance, which moved the Assembly to its depths.

[1] Guyho, *Hommes de 1852*, pp. 33, 105.
[2] Bosq, p. 180 ; Claveau, p. 55.

Another of the same class was the Marquis de Franclieu, " the queerest, maddest, most reasonable, obstinate, honest, violent, adorable of old men ", a Republican called him.[1] He was a Legitimist *à l'outrance* ; for forty years in his ancestral château he had hated the Orleanists. In 1875 someone said to him : " If the Comte de Chambord dies without male issue, the Orleanists would become Legitimists ". " Never," he cried. " Legitimacy will die with him." [2] He combined with this a real liberalism in matters of the Press and decentralisation, which made people speak of him as a " white radical ".

To the same political family belonged the old Breton deputy Dahirel, " type of the old Royalist in his short Breton waistcoat, smoking his little wooden pipe ",[3] an ex-magistrate who had resigned in 1830, and the Viscount de Lorgeril, famous as an interrupter ; he was the " lyre of the party, an Aeolian harp ever ready to sound under the soothing influence of a breeze from Frohsdorff ".[4] On the strength of his collection of poems, called *The Spark*, he was supposed to have told Victor Hugo to his face that his style was not French.[5] He called Thiers " a sinister old man ", and he was full of eccentric ideas of reform. He refused subsidies for the Opera as immoral ; he thought the pay of Ambassadors too large, as under a republic France had no chance of getting allies. He once proposed a stamp on picture postcards, and on being asked ironically if he would put it on the face of the portrait, he replied to his interrupter (not without effect), " There are certain faces which a stamp would suit ".[6]

Side by side with these picturesque country gentlemen

[1] Pelletan, *Théâtre de Versailles*, p. 102.   [2] Denis, p. 643.
[3] De Marcère, ii. 131.   [4] *Portraits de Kel-Kun*, p. 188.
[5] As a matter of fact, he protested against Victor Hugo's praise of Garibaldi as the only General on the French side who had not been conquered, saying, " L'Assemblée refuse la parole à M. Victor Hugo parce q'il ne parle pas français " (*i.e.* as a Frenchman) (Séance du 8/3/71, *Annales*, t. 1, p. 209).
[6] Bosq, pp. 137-8.

were the politicians of the Ultras ; the most competent
was Lucien Brun, deputy for Aix, who had made his reputation as a speaker at the Lyons bar. He was born on the
slopes of the Jura, and his tall figure, large body, and
swarthy complexion (brown like his name), recalled the
type of vigorous mountaineers. His shaven face gave him
the look of a Jesuit ; his thick eyebrows and disdainful
smile showed the fighter. He was a direct and energetic
speaker and a good tactician, who never allowed his cool
judgment to be swept away by Fusionist eloquence : he
knew his Comte de Chambord too well.

The Baron de la Rochette, sad-faced with grey
whiskers, under his cold and courteous irony,[1] was violent
in his affections and aversions. In 1873, after the collapse
of the Restoration, he said, " I am at the end of everything " ; [2] he died in 1876 broken-hearted by the disputes
and acrimony, which marked the disappearance of the
Royalist majority.

The Baron de la Bouillerie was the only member of the
Extreme Right, who was ever a Minister. Obedience to the
Comte de Chambord was part of his religion ; it was permitted to remonstrate before the royal decision ; after,
there was no course but blind submission. A colleague in
the 1873 Government speaks of his " charming ease of
manner ; he only wanted a blue ribbon to look like an
eighteenth-century statesman ".[3]

It is not probable that the Chevaux-Légers wanted the
White Flag or had much hopes of a Restoration. But they
were resolved that, if France could not have Monarchy, at
least she should have no rival form of established Government, if they could help it—and this resolve was not least
among the obstacles, which beset the ill-starred Royalist
party in the National Assembly.

[1] Hanotaux, iii. 397.   [2] Denis, p. 409.   [3] Du Barail, iii. 380.

CHAPTER III

(a) THE VETERANS

EARLY in July, Thiers half ironically congratulated the Duc de Broglie on the virtual abdication of the Comte de Chambord, which seemed to leave the road open for the Orleans Princes; the Duc replied: " The suicide of the Comte de Chambord does not console me for the resurrection of Gambetta ".[1] Before describing this success of the Republican party at the elections and the re-election of their leader, a word should be said about the Republican party, its past fortunes and its actual condition.

Political inexperience was the fault of most of the leaders of the French Revolution. They had to improvise parliamentary government in a few years, and in the midst of ever-growing confusion and anarchy. With imperturbable vanity they rejected all examples from foreign nations, and accepted as an axiom that all the past history of France must be reversed.

Because Government had been tyrannical, it must now be jealously checked. The formula of all revolutions has well been described as follows: " Whenever reforms are demanded and the Government is not trusted, there will be a revolution ". The Constituent Assembly treated the Executive as a public enemy, harassing and impeding Ministers in every possible way, and deliberately forbidding its members to take office; this jealousy, which had begun

---

[1] Quoted *Fusion monarchique*, p. 220.

as a prejudice, became a passion, when the Government were suspected of treachery during the war, and the Republic arose not as a theory (there was no Republican party before the Tenth of August) but as a military necessity.

The first French Republic was sustained by that passionate desire for national unity, which was one of the sustaining causes of the Revolution. France was to be " one and indivisible " ; all distinctions of classes and provinces were to be merged in that patriotic ardour, which showed itself in resistance to the invader. Of that unity Paris was the heart and soul, and the Girondists fell, because they seemed to represent the provinces against the capital. This national self-consciousness expressed itself in the desire for the Rhine frontier, which (as Sorel has shown) was a more real motive in the advance of the French armies than Republican propaganda. This lack of theory is shown by the fact that the Convention governed without a Constitution ; the visionary Jacobin Constitution was laid on the shelf by tacit consent.

For the moment, the war crisis called out all that was best in France, and little attention was paid to the Reign of Terror at home. But you cannot permanently govern any nation in such a manner ; Robespierre's policy of annihilating every sect but his own was bound to fail. At the Thermidorian reaction an attempt should have been made to put an end to the government of a clique, and call the people into the national councils. But the Thermidorians were themselves for the most part a fraction of the Terrorist clique, opposed to the guillotine, because their names were next on the list. They inaugurated the new Constitution by violent interference with the freedom of election, and the Directoire was a long struggle, in which at last the quarrels of the governing class allowed the people to enter on the scene with their champion Bonaparte.

The Constitution of 1795 was the first attempt to establish a normal form of Republican government. It has certainly left behind neither mourners nor imitators. Its defects were due not so much to too much theory as to a rather childish attempt to construct constitutional checks — the division of power among five Directors, and the provision that they should be chosen by one Council from a list presented by the other — a precaution easily nullified by the Lower Council, which sent to the Upper a list consisting of the five candidates they wanted plus a number of nonentities. However, the Constitution contained the interesting innovations of a Second Chamber, and a partial renovation of deputies. With a tolerably efficient government and some moral support from public opinion, it might have worked passably.[1]

Curiously enough the most fantastic of Republics was that, under which Napoleon was First Consul. It was drawn up by Sieyès and, with its elaborate mechanism of a Tribunat, which debated and did not vote, and a Corps Législatif, which voted laws but did not debate them, almost justified Burke's sarcastic delineation of his mind.[2] The working of the Constitution, however, fully bore out the terse definition of the crowd, who first heard it read, " C'est Bonaparte ". As the continuation and consummation of the Revolution the rule of Bonaparte rallied almost all Republicans, and it was not till 1815 that there was an independent party of that name. Napoleon on his return from Elba attempted to gain their support by the " Acte Additionnel ", which proposed " to surround the rights of the citizens with safeguards, to give to the representative system all its extension and to confer prestige and power on the bodies intermediate between the people and the Throne ". Under the Second Restoration and the July Monarchy, the Republican and Bonapartist parties worked

[1] For a favourable picture of parliamentary life under the Directoire see Gaston Dodu, *Le Parlementarisme et les parlementaires*, Pt. IV., ch. i.

[2] I refer to the passage in the "Letter to a Noble Lord " beginning "Abbé Sieyès has whole nests of pigeon-holes full of constitutions ready-made, ticketed, sorted, and numbered ".

hand in hand, as it was the fashion to regard Napoleon as the great revolutionary and champion of liberalism in Europe. The more serious risings under the July Monarchy were accompanied by cries in favour of that Poland, about which Napoleon spoke so much, and for which he did so little.

In 1848 Bonapartists and Republicans triumphed together. The Second Republic attempted, at the beginning, to copy the gestures and attitude of the First ; its " Mountain " deputies sat on their upper benches, and defied the President according to the best precedents of the Convention, but the chief instruments of the Terror were blunted by Lamartine, that very romantic successor of the Girondins, who abolished the death penalty for political offences, and reassured the Governments of Europe as to his peaceful intentions. The people were obsessed by social and industrial questions, and Bonapartism easily adapted itself to such new interests : a popular autocrat is always the dream of Socialists. Louis Napoleon set the example — so fashionable in pretenders to the Crown — of an intense interest in the working classes. The split between Republicans and Bonapartists ruined the 1848 Constitution. Certainly the device of an elected President over against an elected Assembly was a dangerous one, though with a Parliamentary President, like Thiers or Cavaignac, it might have worked. But Louis Napoleon was no figurehead ; he was a man with a mission and a programme of his own, and a profound faith in both. His name seduced at once the peasants, terrified at the prospect of a revolutionary attack on property, and many of the workers in towns, who sympathised with the author of " the extinction of poverty ". The schism between Republicans and Bonapartists was complete. After the *coup d'état* it was against the Republicans, that the main severities of the President were directed, and not a single member of the party was elected to the first Corps Législatif of the new régime.

A small group of the veterans from the Mountain of 1849 sat upon the Extreme Left of the National Assembly of 1871. They were more respected than followed by the younger Republicans, who called them " Les Vieux ". " They proclaimed a certain number of principles, and the object of their whole lives was to remain unshakeably faithful to them. Their ideal was consistency ; they cared for nothing else. They refused to admit that the course of time or any events or unforeseen catastrophes could change an iota of their views. . . . You could see it even in their dress. Most of them adhered to the fashions of their youth ; they cut their hair and shaved in the same way." [1] Gambetta's friend, Mme Adam, says : " More and more they play the part of great Elysian shades, astonished at terrestrial arrangements ; for them ' Republic ' is a solemn ritual word ".[2]

If a group of such independent characters could have recognised a leader, it would have been Louis Blanc : they did actually begin by assembling at his house, but, unwilling to admit even a shadow of party discipline,[3] they ended by meeting at each other's rooms in turn.

Louis Blanc is a strange example of the literary man in politics. Under the July Monarchy he had written *The Organisation of Labour, History of Ten Years* and the first part of *The French Revolution*. In the '48 revolution he was the representative of advanced socialism, and became president of the Commission on Labour. He was the idol of the crowd and the bugbear of the Conservative majority of the Constituent Assembly,[4] who prosecuted him for complicity in the June riots and forced him to take refuge in England. In fact, " il ne méritait ni cet excès d'honneur

---

[1] Lockroy, *Au hasard de la vie*, pp. 244-5.

[2] *Mes angoisses*, p. 267.

[3] In 1875, when Gambetta ordered the party to vote for the Constitution, Blanc protested against the new and strange idea of party discipline.

[4] " A serpent could hardly have excited more fear and aversion " (Corkran, *Constituent Assembly*, p. 36).

ni cette indignité ". He was not a man of action. When
the mob broke into the Chamber and carried him on their
shoulders, he kept on pitifully exclaiming, " Your place is
not here ! " [1] His character was full of the contradictions
of a writer on politics, who has no idea of statesmanship.
He was so small that a stool had to be placed for him at the
tribune : yet there was resolution in his olive complexion,
his strong chin, and dark eyes. His voice was soft and
unctuous ; he " kept his words in his mouth for a moment,
as if they were delicious sweets " ; [2] " all the grasshoppers
of the South sang in his utterance " ; [3] yet there was sometimes a tone of bitterness, the regret of the popular hero
whose name was now forgotten. " He had the mildest of
characters ", said one of his colleagues, " but he nourished
terrible resentments : one felt the Corsican in him. He
passed his life in daring strokes, and he was the most prudent
person in the world. I never met a man so full of contradictions." [4] It was not only in reference to his stature that
Heine called him " a curious mixture of a Lilliputian and a
Spartan ".[5]

The June days of 1848 and the Commune of 1871 had
cured him of his Socialist dreams, but he remained an
impenitent Radical, hostile to Second Chambers and it
was said he was in favour of abolishing the offices of President and Préfet alike. He swore by Rousseau like all

[1] Simon, *Soir de ma journée*, p. 193.
[2] De Goncourts, *Journal* (Nelson edition), p. 130.
[3] Bosq, p. 211.   [4] Lockroy, p. 243.
[5] Grant Duff, who met him in London in 1853, says : " He looked as the
first Napoleon might have done if seen through the wrong end of an opera-
glass " (*Notes from a Diary*, p. 10). For an Irishman's recollections of him see
Justin McCarthy's *Reminiscences*, i. 118-24 : " He had deep, dark, lustrous
eyes, which gave infinite variety to every word he spoke. He had a graceful
presence, if we make allowance for his want of stature — and small delicate
hands. His voice was strong, clear, sweet and thrilling. . . . He gave a series
of lectures in London public halls. . . . I remember the close of one lecture
(on the wits and satirists before the French Revolution) : he suddenly made a
deliberate pause for a moment and, looking fixedly around his audience, finished
with the slowly-spoken and emphatic words, ' Then for a time laughing went
out of fashion '."

dogmatists ; he said to Victor Hugo, when the two democrats were discussing the eternal subject of the comparative
merits of their two apostles, " Rousseau was the friend of
the humble, while Voltaire was the friend of the great ".
Victor Hugo retorted : " Rousseau turned Robespierre and
St-Just, who called themselves friends of Nature, into wild
beasts and sectaries like you : I detest Rousseau because
he was a bad father ".[1] Louis Blanc's chief remaining
influence was as an orator ; with all his short-comings, his
sincerity and literary power made him effective at the
tribune, and his speeches on the return to Paris and on
Universal Suffrage are still worth reading.

Then there was Edgar Quinet, the "grey-haired
cherub". He was one of the many historians of the Revolution, and a friend of Michelet, though the friendship was
rather shaken by the fact that Quinet did not mention his
predecessor in his book. He was all gentleness and
candour ; he protested against the stupid ferocity of the
Terror.[2] The revenge he dreamed of for those, who had
exiled him, was the establishment of a generous and
indulgent Republic. Even when driven by his conscience
to interrupt in the debate, " he would rise in his enormous
overcoat, that reached down to his heels, show his great
bald head, look round, and sit down without a word ".[3]
His old-fashioned integrity found little to attract it in the
noisy opportunism of the younger Gambettists. He often
said, " What drives me to despair is that every day France
loses a little more of her divinity ". His colleague, Edmond
Adam, who often walked with him in the Versailles Park,
when the sun was setting and debates were dull, said,
" Quinet sees the unseen and makes us see it ".[4]

Victor Schoelcher, another exile, who had been on the

---

[1] Mme Adam, *Mes angoisses*, p. 293.
[2] Pessard, i. 134. [3] Bosq, p. 140.
[4] Mme Adam, *Mes angoisses*, p. 91. Michelet is said to have called him —
in a public lecture at the Collège de France — " the soul of a hero in the body of
a saint " (Grant Duff, *Notes*, p. 55).

barricades during the *coup d'état*, had played a leading part in the abolition of slavery, and was an opponent of the death penalty. He still dressed in the old fashion, " the large trousers, the long coat folded like a skirt, the black stick with the silver handle".[1] He glided along like a ghost, and he was never known to laugh ; but he had still energy enough to say to a Bonapartist, *en pleine séance*, " I declare that you have uttered an infamous lie ".[2]

Alphonse Peyrat represented a more militant type of Republican : he had not been a member of the 1848 Assembly, but he had written Marrast's speeches for him, and he had no sympathy with the half-measures of Quinet which " emasculated the Revolution of all that was most powerful in it. Ferocity was necessary then and may be so again." [3] He was a resolute opponent of the Church, and indeed his chief claim to remembrance lies in the peroration of the great speech delivered by Gambetta six years later, when he quoted as having been said " by my friend Peyrat " the famous war-cry, " Clericalism is the enemy ". What he had really written was " Catholicism is the enemy ".[4]

Félix Pyat, another member of the '48 Mountain, had become involved in the Commune, and retired to England. During the two Republics and the Empire he had incurred sentences amounting to 212,000 francs, 29 years' deportation, 5 months' prison, 5 years' surveillance, and 10 years' " interdiction of civil rights ". In 1848 he had written the well-known play *Le Chiffonnier de Paris*, in which a ragpicker strikes a crown in the streets with his stick, and " with a proud gesture " throws it into the gutter.

In June 1871 neither of the leaders of the 1848 Extreme Left was in the National Assembly. Ledru Rollin, " the

---

[1] Lockroy, p. 245.   [2] Séance du 1 août 1874.
[3] Winifred Stephens, *Madam Adam*, pp. 100-101.
[4] In the " Opinion Nationale" under the Empire (de Marcère, *Histoire*, i. 209).

father of Universal Suffrage ", was not elected till 1874.
Victor Hugo had resigned. He had found himself ill-
prepared by his rôle of prophet of Patmos in the Channel
Islands for the noise and rudeness of an unsympathetic
Assembly.[1] He gave up politics and resumed his rightful
throne as Grand Cham of French literature. If he hardly
resembled Doctor Johnson in his morals, there was a
certain similarity in conversational gruffness and tenderness to children. Both had also a robust patriotism. When
Moltke, as a great admirer of his work, sent to him in
Switzerland asking permission to call on him, Hugo replied
gently and quietly, " No, sir, never ".[2]

(b) THE REPUBLICANS UNDER THE EMPIRE

It was one of the disadvantages of the dictatorial
Government of the Second Empire that it could never
find place for a normal Opposition. Under a constitutional
régime opposition is so safe and so familiar that no one
takes it too seriously. When it raises its tone too shrilly,
people remember that, after all, it is a case of the Outs
attacking the Ins. Under the early Second Empire
criticism was certainly not easy : to a Government, which
identified itself with the nation as a whole, opposition
seemed akin to treason, and the men, who accepted such
risks, either became martyrs or tribunes.

The first six years was the era of martyrs — Republican
opposition took the form of abstention. Some were already
in exile : those, who remained, resolved that they would
never take the oath, in order to serve the Empire as deputies
or officials. Jules Simon has left an account of the *diners
des morts* at which, every month, a small group of Republicans met under the chairmanship of General Cavai-

---

[1] For his unfortunate début, see pp. 126-7. Malicious journalists said they
had seen a proof of one of his speeches, to which he had added with his own
hand the words " Explosion d'enthusiasme " (Bosq, p. 88).

[2] Lockroy, p. 292.

gnac, Louis Napoleon's unsuccessful rival at the Presidential election.[1] Here it was the fashion to treat the new régime with contempt rather than hatred. " It cannot last ", they said ; " it is only a third scuffle like Boulogne and Strasbourg." The exiles, with their luggage still unstrapped, dreamed of returning in a few days to sit on the High Court of Justice, which should condemn the usurper. At the first Paris elections some voices were raised for sending deputies to sit in the Legislature, but the majority decided to " leave the Empire in its isolation " : a Republican candidate came forward, refused the oath and retired. By 1857 it was clear that the Empire was going to last, and the younger Republicans were impatient at the abstention imposed on them by their elders. " You have had your turn," they said ; " when will ours come round ? " But in stricter circles it was still *de mode* to be shocked at the election of the five famous Republican deputies. Even at the 1863 elections Jules Simon, though convinced of the futility of abstention, felt such repugnance to taking the oath that he had to be pushed into a carriage by his friends, and dragged to the Hôtel-de-Ville, " like a criminal to the scaffold ". He signed himself " Jules Simon, rentier ", " so as not to compromise the Institut ".[2]

The second period was that of the orators. In 1857 the Five took their seats — Jules Favre, Ernest Picard, Émile Ollivier, Henon, and Darimon. The Empire, utterly disdainful of the art of eloquence (Louis Napoleon had begun by abolishing the tribune and making members speak from their seats unreported), had failed to realise the importance of the orator. In constitutional States speeches count for something, but not for much ; under a despotic régime, when there is no freedom of speech or of the Press, the voice of the parliamentary orator, who cannot be suppressed by the magistrate or silenced by the gendarme, becomes the very embodiment of the public

[1] *Soir de ma journée*, p. 43.   [2] *Ibid.* p. 61.

2 A

conscience : " It seemed as if the whole life of the nation had taken refuge in their breasts ".[1]

At the elections of 1864 the Opposition was swelled by Royalist recruits — old Orleanists like Thiers, and Legitimists like Berryer. They formed a quasi-alliance with the Republicans ; they deliberated together for common action. " Ah ", said the Conservatives, " if all Republicans were like you ! " " They are like us ", answered the Left.[2] Orleanists and Republicans seemed on the best of terms. Laurier and Gambetta visited the Comte de Paris at Twickenham, and Jules Simon accompanied him on his tour to Lancashire. There were moments of embarrassment in this new *rapprochement*. The Duc de Chartres presented himself before a French Republican Congress at Zurich. Everything went so well that a friend of the Duke suggested they should all lunch together ; a severe democrat answered suspiciously, " It will be a light lunch, won't it ? " " Evidently ", adds the Duc de Broglie, who tells the story, " the danger of contact with Princes seemed to him to increase with the solemnity of the meal and the quantity of the food." [3]

In 1869 starts the third period — that of resistance. It is true there were no armed risings, but Paris had become once more the centre of violent opposition. A younger generation was pushing its way forward. Never was more incendiary language held at public meetings ; the police were constantly called in to intervene ; observers, who recalled that period to their memory, saw already the Commune in germ.

The Imperial system was cracking in all directions ; the Emperor's will power was failing with his health. The confusion and ineffectiveness of his foreign policy was revealed by the shameful termination of the Mexican expedition, and the permission given Prussia to crush

[1] *Soir de ma journée*, p. 67.   [2] Simon, *4 septembre*, p. 257.
[3] *Revue des Deux Mondes* (1/11/25), p. 142.

Austria at Sadowa caused universal restlessness. Louis-Napoleon had succeeded by his personal charm in detaching one of the Five — Émile Ollivier — , and entrusting him with the task of transforming the Empire into a constitutional Monarchy. But, in spite of the plebiscite which gave a majority to the new Liberal Empire, the position of the dynasty was evidently in peril. Nothing could show this more clearly than the fact that, after the first defeats of 1870, the Empress Regent assured her husband that it was not safe for him to return to Paris.

But from 1869 a study of the Republican party necessarily resolves itself into a study of Gambetta.

(c) GAMBETTA — (TO THE JULY ELECTIONS)

During the years from 1864 to 1869, at almost every sitting of the Corps Législatif, there might have been seen seated at a corner by the window overlooking the President's garden a young spectator almost as regular in his visits as the deputies themselves. The officials of the Chamber crowded round to make way for him ; they never asked for his ticket ; they escorted him to his place, and took care to turn out any tactless visitor, who might have innocently occupied it. He knew them all by their names ; he had a shake of the hand and a joke for each of them. His loud and hearty laugh dominated the conversations around him ; as soon as he had taken his seat, he began to tell stories full of flavour and malice with irresistible verve. When the debate began, he leaned forward, his arms crossed, his back rounded, his beard tangled, contemptuous of the empty adornments of toilette. In the lobby he could imitate a speech to perfection. All his hearers laughed and applauded him ; they were never tired of hearing him talk. His good-humour equalled theirs : if anyone interrupted him with a *bon mot*, he doubled himself up with laughter ; he congratulated the author ; he repeated and developed

the idea. As he left the House to describe the events of the
day in the Café de Madrid, the same phrase was on every
lip, " Gambetta should be a deputy ".[1]

He was born at Cahors (Gascony) in 1838, and his
father, Joseph, was a grocer from Genoa. Long after, in
the Assembly, a Bonapartist deputy flung at Léon the
supreme insult from a Corsican, " You are a scoundrel
and, what is worse, a Genoese ".[2] Cahors is a little town
built above the red and green waters of the Loth, which is
spanned by three bridges, one of them turreted and very
old : the narrow valleys all around, with their dark grass
and rough yellow soil, are scented with orange-blossom
and verbena. Under the Cathedral stood the grocery of
the Gambettas, the doors decorated with designs of sugar-
loaves, and on the sign-board the words " Genoese bazaar " :
the father, Joseph Gambetta, felt so strongly that Italy
was his native land that for a time he refused to let his
illustrious son be buried in the Panthéon rather than in
the once-Italian Nice. Gambetta himself wrote of Italy :
" I breathe more freely there than elsewhere, and I feel
myself completely at home ".[3]

It is always interesting to trace the mingling of French
and Italian blood. Both nations have inherited the Latin
genius, but in spite of sentimental affinities they never
seem to get on well together. From the day when Charles
led his French army into Florence, and petulantly exclaimed in the course of protracted negotiations, " We shall
sound our trumpets ", provoking Capponi's famous retort,
" And we shall ring our bells ", down to the " monstrous
ingratitude " of 1870, when Italy did not stir a finger to
help the Emperor Napoleon, who had fought for her
liberties, they have been incapable of understanding each

---

[1] Simon, *Soir de ma journée*, pp. 73-6 ; Pessard, i. 69.

[2] Fidus, *Journal* (i. 266). It will be remembered that Genoa had
attempted to annex Corsica.

[3] Marzials, *Gambetta*, pp. 14, 15 ; Laur, *Heart of Gambetta*, p. 266 ;
Deschanel, *Life of Gambetta*, p. 7.

other. The Italian idea of politics has always been that
of cold and polished cunning, sometimes hidden under
diplomatic affabilities, sometimes openly moving to its end,
realist, business-like, bent on results. The French statesman is far more effusive, more sentimental, more concerned
with general ideas and far-reaching ideals.

But a mingling of the strains has produced great characters — Napoleon for example, who united to the directness and realism of the Italian, the large ideas and logical
lucidity of the French. Gambetta was no Napoleon : a
certain diffusion of energy and incoherence of thought in
his mind contrasts with the purposeful concentration of
Bonaparte. But, all the same, beneath a certain ease and
openness of manner, there was an inner complexity ; at
first sight one would have thought him a perfect type of the
southern Gascon, as known in literature and romance —
exuberant, full of high spirits, inexhaustibly fluent, ambitious, audacious, impulsive, *bon camarade*. But underneath
all this there was the cool calculation and the positive aims
of the descendant of the Genoese traders, who fought
Venice for the mastery of the seas — the qualities of the
parliamentary strategist, the political opportunist, the
leader of men. The two strains in his character are well
marked in a phrase he loved to use, " To govern France you
need violent words and moderate actions ".[1]

The following picture of his boyhood comes from
Madame Adam : [2]

He was always making speeches everywhere. One day in the
country he went into a church, mounted the pulpit and preached.
" Suppose the curé came in ? " " He would listen to me." As a
child he was always jumping on people's shoulders ; he knocked
everything down, as he passed along. He had exuberant animal
spirits. When he was about fourteen, he turned out the lights
and, by the flame of the burning punch, he fascinated his audience

[1] Cf. Hubert, *Figures parlementaires*, p. 207 : " Under the riotous scarlet
of his speech there lay hid a prudent and well-balanced mind ".

[2] *Mes angoisses*, p. 262.

with his improvisations. He made speeches to his sister in Greek and Latin; the little child sometimes showed her admiration by saying, "I am frightened". . . . . His father said, "If he loves the Army so much, it is because of one of our Corsican friends, whom we knew in the garrison at Cahors. When Léon came to Paris, he found this friend a captain in the imperial guard. Till the fourth of September, he always went to dinner at the officers' mess."

He·lost his right eye, while watching an apprentice at a cutlery; a steel drill broke, and wounded him.[1]

His mother devoted herself to the future greatness of her son: she loved to tell how a soothsayer had told her before his birth that her son would govern France.[2] She used to say to him, "Your country is your vocation; you must know everything, so begin about it at once".[3] It was she who persuaded his father to send him to study law at Paris.

It is usual to describe his life in the Quartier Latin as one of glorified Bohemianism, composed of endless cigars and interminable conversations in cafés. Guizot dismissed him in the portentous phrase, "I have heard that the young man frequents wineshops".[4] Rouher spoke of him as a "Bohemian, who could be bought for five hundred francs a month".[5] His Southern accent was voted impossible, his gestures vulgar (he spat during his speeches), his dress was untidy, and a friend said to him, "There is one gulf you will never fill up — that, which divides your waistcoat from your trousers". Even Republicans described him as "one of the riff-raff of the party", or "a commercial traveller", or a "provincial grocer".[6] He dominated his fellow students by his frank and exuberant personality. "He was full of the joy of life and the joy of speech. A loquacious Roman, grafted upon a Gallic stock, he deafened and stunned even himself with the clangour of his own words, made the very windows tremble with the claps of

[1] Gheusi, *Vie et mort de Gambetta*, p. 29.
[2] W. Stephens, *Madam Adam*, p. 180.   [3] Laur, p 47.
[4] King, *French Political Leaders*, p. 97.   [5] Pessard, i. 278.
[6] W. Stephens, *Madam Adam*, pp. 110-11.

his thunderous eloquence, and then would generally finish up with an outburst of noisy laughter. He was already hailed as a ruler by the general throng of his companions." [1] " In the Conférence des Avocats ", he writes to his family, " I was cheered and almost carried aloft in triumph. So many mouths congratulated me all at once, so many hands were held out to mine that I was wild with delight." [2] Jules Simon describes his visits : " He sat down in a chair near the fireplace and smoked half a dozen cigars. His conversation was, it is true, rather like a monologue, but it sparkled with verve. He waved his arms, shook his hair over his face and threw it back with a rapid gesture of his hand. His sonorous voice had at times an accent like thunder. We had to blow out the candles to persuade him to go." [3]

In a well-known passage, written after Gambetta's death, Weiss has pointed out that this life was in itself a real political education :

Before Gambetta the Republicans lived in secret societies, or in a little circle of initiates, separate from common life, less desirous of spreading their doctrines than of guarding their idol from profanation. . . . But Gambetta learned his trade from the accidents of everyday life in the Paris of 1861 to 1868, so wide, so picturesque, so varied, where there was a lesson everywhere for anyone who could learn, where in an hour's conversation at the café Veron or the café Voltaire there was displayed more political genius than ever came to birth during five or ten years in a Minister's study ; where it was possible to secure a finer taste for literature at a meeting of artists than in the Academy ; where at a gambling-house one might meet a clever Turk, who, though he might let himself be cheated by charming women, could explain to you with the utmost thoroughness the political game of cards at Cairo or Constantinople ; where one might jostle at a Concert Musard a man, who might seem the victim of a fixed idea, but who will be two or three years later the victor at Sadowa and the master of Germany. [4]

---

[1] A. Daudet (quoted Marzials, p. 18).   [2] Deschanel, p. 11.
[3] *Soir de ma journée*, p. 323.   [4] Weiss, *Combat constitutionnel*, pp. 310-11.

It was by means of this quality of learning from men rather than from books that he strove hard to deliver the Republicans from their three chief faults — narrowness, pedantry and love of violence, all due to a certain seclusion from the main currents of national life. He had the statesman's power of assimilation, of picking up information from the right sources. It has been said of a famous Prime Minister in our own day, " No one is more ignorant of a matter when he starts, and no one learns more quickly as he goes along ". This was also true of Gambetta and it brought the same inconveniences ; they were both too liable to be influenced by their immediate milieu. " What is his opinion ? " it was asked. " The opinion of the last person he has spoken to."

But it would be a mistake to suppose that all Gambetta's studies were in the café or the restaurant. Like many students, he read more diligently than he would have cared to own. But he read with a practical object — politics. He knew little history, and his friends used to tremble, when he put historical examples into his speeches. His love of strong government and hatred of muddled rhetoric already showed themselves. He preferred Danton and Mirabeau to Rousseau and Robespierre. He had not a trace of philosophy.[1] He admired Proudhon, a writer of vigorous epigrams rather than a maker of systems. His marginal notes on Prévost Paradol's *France Nouvelle* show shrewdness rather than profundity. He was attracted by Auguste Comte, and did much towards making Positivism the religion of the Left in place of Victor Hugo's Deism.

But he loved literature for itself, or rather perhaps for its sound. He used to recite passages from *Les Misérables* in the café : one evening, when the company were quoting Rabelais, he repeated two pages by heart without hesitating

---

[1] " Unfortunately he had no general culture, which made him look at big questions with blinkers on " (a remark of Clemenceau, quoted in General Mordacq's *Ministère Clemenceau*, iii. 166).

for a word.[1] Nor was Zola right in calling him a " Philistine of the Philistines " ; he could not bear music, but he was a lover of pictures. In a letter from Brussels he describes Millet's " Angelus " enthusiastically and treats a Reynolds " Mother and Child " as " the gem of the collection ".[2] Above all, he adored Nature. He cried to his friend Spuller, as they were watching a sunset over the sea, " Do you understand ? Do you see ? Are you able to feel ? "[3]

Naturally he loved the orators best — Bossuet, Vergniaud, Demosthenes ; " Oh, how I am longing to speak ! " he wrote to his father. " My tongue is on fire."[4] When his father wrote in alarm at some of his advanced ideas, he answered : " As for the great idea of God, I am too rational both in politics and ethics to give it up. Besides, as you very justly said, it is one of the most valuable resources of eloquence."[5] One has heard of the God of the poets and the God of the philosophers and the God of the saints : I have never met a more naïve profession of faith in the God of the public speaker.

In 1860 he wrote to his father : " Why should I hide it from you ? I am devoured by ambition."[6] Without calling his sincerity in question it could hardly be doubted to which side the ambitious son of a grocer would attach himself.[7] The Empire was on its last legs ; the concession of the Liberal régime under Ollivier seemed to the hot Parisian youth the first admission of defeat.

On November 14th, 1868, Gambetta leaped into the oratorical fame, which he coveted so earnestly. He spoke in defence of the editors, who were prosecuted by the Government for having opened a subscription to erect a memorial

---

[1] Freycinet, p. 162.   [2] Marzials, p. 209.
[3] Mme Adam, *Nos amitiés*, p. 79. Spuller called him " the most melodious of Virgilian pipes ".
[4] Deschanel, p. 8.   [5] *Ibid.* p. 15.   [6] *Ibid.* p. 8.
[7] Halévy, *Fin des notables* (p. 111) puts it well : " Gambetta did not detest the Empire ; he did not know how to detest anyone. His real nature was made up of amiable scepticism. But the Empire had no need for the eloquence of young men."

to Baudin, the Republican deputy, who had died heroically at the barricades resisting the *coup d'état* of 1851. In his speech for the defence Gambetta took the Catilinarians as his model, shouting down magistrate and prosecutor with his voice of thunder, and appearing as though he wished to break through the walls of the court and penetrate into the very presence of the Emperor.

" Listen [he cried in his peroration], for seventeen years you have been absolute masters, ruling France at your discretion. . . . We do not ask what use you have made of her treasures, her blood, her honour, and her glory. . . . But there is one thing, which is the best evidence against you, for it bears witness to your own remorse — I mean the fact that you have never dared to say, ' We will celebrate the Second of December : we will place it among the public festivals of France as a national anniversary ' — and yet all the régimes, that have followed one another in this country, have honoured the day of their birth. They have fêted the Fourteenth of July, the Tenth of August, the July days of 1830, the Twentieth of February : there are only two anniversaries — the Eighteenth of Brumaire and the Second of December — , which have never had a place among such festivals, because you know that, if you wished to do so, the conscience of the world would repudiate them. Very well, then, *we* claim this anniversary which you would not keep. *We* take it for ourselves. We will keep it always and for ever. Every year it will be the anniversary of our dead, till that day when the country, become its own master again, shall impose upon you the great public expiation in the name of liberty, equality, and fraternity." (To the Avocat Impérial) : " Ah, you shrug your shoulders ". — THE AVOCAT IMPÉRIAL : " But this is no longer a speech for the defence ". GAMBETTA : " Be assured that I am not afraid either of your contempt or your threats ".[1]

He lost his case, but he won his reputation. The court echoed with applause. From that moment he stepped forward into the front rank of the Opposition — and he deserved his success. Ollivier has perhaps the right to retort that, after all, the Fourteenth of July and the Tenth

---

[1] Reinach, *Discours de Gambetta*, pp. 13-14.

of August were also anniversaries of acts of violence;[1] but none the less the passage remains a classic of French eloquence. It would be a mistake, however, to suppose that this austere Republican passed the evening of his triumph by the graves of the December martyrs ; he spent it in a café repeating the speech amid the enthusiastic applause of the company, striking the table and exclaiming, " I told them some home-truths ".[2]

In 1869 he was elected to the Corps Législatif for Paris and Marseilles ; in the capital he had to take an oath to accept the Radical provisions of the Belleville programme, including the separation of Church and State, and the suppression of standing armies. He must have had his tongue in his cheek, for he was never a Radical in the strict sense of the word ; he had far too strong a sense of authority and the necessity of shelving awkward questions (" il faut sérier les questions ") ; he was the founder of Opportunism, and the stern Radicals fought him to the death. When in later life he became the champion of the Army and of a tolerant policy to the Church, he put aside the pledges of his youth with a smile. When people asked him how he was going to " cut off his [political] tail ", he answered, " Never ! I shall put it into a dress-shirt, and introduce it into good society ".[3]

Years after, Belleville had its revenge, when Gambetta

---

[1] *Empire libéral*, t. xi. p. 97.

[2] One cannot represent in English the full flavour of the French " *Je leur ai dit leurs quatre vérités* " (de La Gorce, *Second Empire*, v. p. 19).

[3] Pessard, i. 275. Laurier once reproached Gambetta with having been too faithful to the Belleville programme : " You have fine qualities, but you have not enough ingratitude. You will never have the courage to cut off your tail." " I shall not cut it off : I shall drop it off so quietly that no one will notice it." " But my violent patriot, you promised to suppress the War Budget, the Navy and standing armies." " I will multiply them by three." " You will make education compulsory and turn out the Jesuit teachers ? " " I shall do all that, when I am in power or have influence with those in power." " You will suppress the Budget of Cults ? " " I shall make Paul Bert [a notorious anti-clerical] Minister of Cults to frighten the Church, and tell him to make the concessions necessary to any Government " (Mme Adam, *Mes angoisses*, p. 336).

flung at the mob, which refused to hear him, the famous apostrophe, "Drunken helots". At Marseilles he secured the moderate liberal vote, and the Préfet even suspected the Superior of the Jesuits of having voted for him. Thus in Parliament he represented at once the Radicals and the Moderates ; he chose Marseilles as his constituency.[1]

In the Corps Législatif he continued the rôle of Danton ; his hollow voice resounded through the Chamber, and the milder members of the Left pulled him back by his coat-tails. The ladies in the gallery sat entranced, as if they were watching a melodrama ; the bourgeois muttered, "He has no *tenue* whatever ; he is not *sérieux*". He shouted to Ollivier, "We accept your liberal empire as a bridge to the Republic, that is all ".[2] In his speech against the plebiscite he definitely asserted his preference for the Swiss and American type of Republic as against the English form of democracy.

In the same speech he cried to the Imperialists : "You have committed five fundamental violations of Universal Suffrage. You have established the hereditary principle as a dogma ; you have established two Chambers ; you have declared the Head of the Executive irresponsible ; you have declared your Constitution to be unchangeable ; you have deprived the people of their constituent powers."[3] Two, if not three, of these violations were committed by Gambetta himself, when he accepted the Republic of 1875.

But there were signs already that he was more than a wordy agitator. In 1863 he had asserted his independence by supporting the candidature of the brilliant Prévost Paradol against the wishes of his party. This was not only an act of generosity towards an Orleanist, but it showed a striking difference between Gambetta and the average Republican, who looked on Prussia as "Protestant and

[1] De Roux, p. 11.
[2] E. King, *French Political Leaders*, p. 80 ; Murray, *Men of the Third Republic*, p. 40. [3] Reinach, *Speeches*, p. 39.

liberal " and rejoiced that the Emperor let her crush the " Ultramontane and despotic Austria ". Gambetta had far more sympathy with the Orleanist view, so strikingly expounded by Thiers, that Sadowa was really a French defeat. In 1869 he wrote to his father of " the hatred he had vowed to the victors of Sadowa ". So, when war was declared in 1870, though he condemned the manner of the rupture, he voted for the Army credits (10 Republicans voted against and 7 abstained), and said, after the debate, to a Bonapartist deputy : " It will be all the better for your Emperor, if he can wash away the Second of December in the waters of the Rhine ".[1]

On the Fourth of September, when the mob invaded the Corps Législatif, it was Gambetta's voice that alone was able to dominate the tumult. It was he, who proposed the deposition of Louis Napoleon ; it was he, who suggested that they should go to the Hôtel-de-Ville to proclaim the Republic. " For twenty-four hours ", he says in his evidence before the Commission of the National Assembly (September 7th, 1871), " I made the very greatest efforts to induce the Corps Législatif to proclaim the deposition of the dynasty and the constitution of parliamentary government. This solution failed, because we had to do with men who were timid and hesitating. Then spontaneously the people of Paris began to move." [2]

In the Government of National Defence, Gambetta became Minister of the Interior : on October 7th, after Paris had been invested, he left in a balloon, with the German bullets whistling round him, to organise the Delegation at Tours. " I shall come back with an army ", he said as he left the capital.

He did not come back with an army, but for three months he was the very incarnation of French patriotism. His conduct of the war has been very diversely judged ; he has been called the dictator of incapacity, and Thiers

[1] Deschanel, p. 49.   [2] Marzials, p. 73.

referred to his policy as that of a "raging madman". On the other hand, the German Emperor, quoting Schiller's verse, "Can I bring armies out of the earth by stamping my foot?", said, "I know somebody who can do that — Gambetta"; and General von der Goltz said he had performed the work of a giant.[1] Such a matter must be left to the judgment of military experts.[2] One might accept Clemenceau's verdict: "He conducted the war neither well nor badly, rather perhaps badly than well, but he certainly *did* conduct it as well as he could".[3] He had the gift of inspiring leadership and, on the whole, he rallied all parties to the flag, though there are points, on which it is difficult to acquit him of party spirit, such as the dissolution of the Conseils Généraux, because of their Royalist tendencies, the expulsion of the Orleans Princes from the Army, and the attempt to disqualify the Bonapartists from standing at the February elections.

At the opening of the Assembly he regarded the violent attacks upon himself with contempt "Don't worry," he used to say, "time will carry all this away." But he was troubled by the misunderstanding between Paris and the Assembly. "If this goes on, a bloody conflict is inevitable and no one knows what may result." He thought of going to Paris to calm their suspicions. "We dissuaded him. Five months of absence had put him out of touch. Besides, his health was seriously upset. His face was red, he coughed and was feverish. We begged him

---

[1] Hubert, *Figures parlementaires*, p. 205.

[2] See Deschanel for a favourable summary (pp. 118-33).

[3] Martet, *Clemenceau*, p. 280. Cf. the judgment of Foch (in 1904): "In history the glory of Gambetta will be this — he understood that the centre of the power of a State is not its capital, but the nation itself. . . . Unfortunately it is difficult to escape entirely from the ideas of one's time. . . . He could not escape entirely from the opinion, that links the fate of the nation with that of its capital. To these armies, which he had so magnificently created, he gives as their first objective the deliverance of Paris . . . an offensive beyond their strength" (quoted Dreyfus, *M. Thiers contre l'Empire*, etc., p. 242).

to seek a warmer climate." [1] He resigned his seat and retired to Spain, to San Sebastian.

He set out for his Spanish holiday in a mood of great depression: " I am broken down ", he wrote to a friend, " by all the troubles that have befallen us. Faced with the odious cession to the enemy, which the Assembly has just sanctioned, I can only retire : I shall wait for republican France to find herself again." [2] Yet for himself and his party nothing could have been more fortunate than these months of forced retirement, for it enabled him to avoid all connection with the Commune. In France the Republican party was grievously weakened and divided by the pronouncement of its leaders for and against the Paris insurrection. It required a leader, who had never made a public reference to the matter.

Many people wondered at the time how Gambetta regarded the Commune ; a person in authority said to Freycinet (the close personal friend of the " Dictator of Tours ") : " Gambetta is playing a very ambiguous part in Spain. He has been seen in Madrid in spite of his supposed illness. The Commune has ramifications abroad." [3] In later life political opponents shouted across the floor of the House, " Do you repudiate the Commune ? " He always refused to answer,[4] only too happy that Providence

[1] Freycinet, p. 265. " Thiers sent a message to Gambetta by Antonin Proust that he counted on his patriotism to withdraw for a time " (Malo, p. 494).

[2] Deschanel, p. 141.

[3] Freycinet, pp. 270, 271. This suspicion was perhaps founded upon the fact that he was in touch with some Spanish Republicans : he met the great orator, Castelar, and said of him, " These Spaniards are born for (literally ' in ') the tribune ".

[4] Thus on the ninth of January 1873, during a speech by Dupanloup, Bigot (Centre Droit), deputy for Mayenne, suddenly called across the Chamber, " M. Gambetta, do you repudiate the Commune ? " Gambetta answered, " I reply to M. Bigot that he has no right to question me . . . probably his old profession of purveyor to the parquet has confused his head ". (In 1868 Bigot had been Avocat Général at Angers.) Grévy, with his usual partiality as President, wherever Gambetta was concerned, mildly rebuked Bigot and called Gambetta to order.

had kept him far away from that great source of division
between Republicans. But such records as we possess do
not suggest any great mystery in his attitude. He was
embittered against all parties. He naturally had little
sympathy with the monarchical Assembly he had left.
" What criminals not to have foreseen the conflict ! " [1]
Yet he adds : " The insurrection will be conquered and it
is necessary it should be. . . . I believe that the movement will be defeated." [2] True, he added : " Later we
will give them an amnesty ". But his sympathies were
mostly with the future Republic : " It runs the greatest
risks. . . . We shall have to spend our lives preparing a
new generation capable of founding it." [3]

But with returning health his natural optimism revived.
One who knew him well said that he never looked backwards, but always forwards — a fact that added to the
gaiety, if not to the consistency of his career. The announcement of the July elections made him prick up his ears like
a war-horse. But he hesitated to return to a Parliament,
which he knew to be personally hostile to himself : " My
own feelings are against being a member of an Assembly,
which I regard myself as finished with ".[4] Had not Thiers
publicly called him " a raging madman " ? Would it not
be better to wait for a later and less aristocratic Assembly ?
Two letters probably decided him. One was from Spuller,
a close friend and political adviser : " The proper rôle for
you is that of a Republican O'Connell. It is you, who must
undertake the arduous task of reconciling these two French
parties, who are fighting one another. . . . The more
violently you have been treated, the easier it will be for
you to moderate. Come back to the Chamber. When
once you are there, no one will ever dare to say, without
fear of contradiction and criticism, that your policy of

[1] Freycinet, p. 269.
[2] Letter to Spuller (Hanotaux, i. 177, and Freycinet, p. 268).
[3] *Ibid.* [4] Letter of June 6th, 1871 (Deschanel, p. 144).

honour and courage was not the only course worthy of the Republic and of France." [1] The other letter was from the Chamber itself. Edmond Adam, Republican deputy for Paris, whose brilliant wife was to exercise such an influence over Gambetta himself, wrote in terms of gentle reproof : " We are annoyed with you, dear friend, for having avoided all responsibility in the struggle between the Commune and Versailles. Take care not to become an exile out of touch with our ideas like our dear friends, the proscripts of 1851. Your duty is to be among us to defend your friends." [2]

Courage was a quality, in which Gambetta was never lacking, and the suggestion that he was skulking in his tent, when there was danger to be faced, sent him hurrying over the Pyrenees as an electoral candidate. On June 26th he addressed a meeting of Republican delegates at his old stronghold, Bordeaux. [3]

Election speeches (unless they are delivered by such masters of style as Burke or Disraeli) have rarely any of the salt, which preserves, and it is probable enough that the reader, who turns to the text of the Bordeaux oration, may see in it nothing more than a string of democratic platitudes. But the student of politics knows that there are other tests than literary for judging the importance of a speech. It must be related to the circumstances of the moment. From this point of view Gambetta's words were a turning-point in his own career and in the fortunes of his party.

To us, who are familiar with the long duration of the Third Republic in France, sometimes inglorious, often agitated, but on the whole outwardly respectable and completely free from daring experiments in social matters, the terror which the word " republic " evoked in many minds during the year 1871 may seem hard to understand. Yet we must remember that up till then French republics

---

[1] Deschanel, p. 144.   [2] Mme Adam, *Mes angoisses*, p. 155.
[3] Reinach, *Speeches*, p. 61.

2 B

had been short-lived and tempestuous. " Three times ",
cried an Orleanist of very moderate views, " the republic
has been tried in this country and three times it has perished
in blood and imbecility." The First Republic recalled the
Terror ; the Second the June insurrection ; the Third
(only a month ago), the Commune. The " imbecility "
seemed even more marked. In the First Republic the
corrupt and incompetent Directoire ; in the Second the
fanatics of the clubs ; [1] in the Third the amateur strategists
and administrators of the Gambettist régime.[2] In the eyes
of many timid bourgeois the Republic meant taking public
affairs out of the hands of the *classes dirigeantes* and delivering them over to fanatics ready for any violence, their
brains full of empty Utopias, and occasionally pausing in
their denunciations of one another to join in a general
anathema on everybody, who had not swallowed every
clause of the Republican Credo from his cradle.[3] It was
this fear of Socialist theory and violence which drove the
peasants to seek protection for their property from Louis
Napoleon in 1851, and might still (in 1871), now that
Napoleon was fallen, drive them into the arms of the Comte
de Chambord.

Gambetta knew all this, and knew moreover that to
many people he was the very incarnation of wild republicanism. In his first speech, therefore, after his return from
Spain, he sounded the note of practical statesmanship and
large-minded moderation. Never did any sucking dove
roar more gently. It did not cost him anything to be
moderate. It was his real nature. He was far too great an

[1] See for two classical satires on the clubs of 1848 — *Jérome Paturot*,
ch. xi., " Les Clubs au vinaigre et au camphor ", and ch. xx., " Malvina au
club des femmes ", and Flaubert's still more delicious sketch in *Éducation
sentimentale*, pp. 408-18.

[2] Not the least amusing piece of reading (I am told) in the archives of the
Chamber of Deputies is the report of the Commission, that revised the " grades "
of Gambetta's Army.

[3] In the 1848 Revolution the Républicains de la Veille (*i.e.* who had been
Republicans before the Revolution) claimed to form a kind of aristocracy.

admirer of order and discipline to feel any great admiration for wasteful revolutions. A young Republican may use violent language about an expiring Empire, but no Republican, unless he is a fool, rebels against a Republic. He was far too easy-going, too large in his human sympathies, to be a party fanatic, and he was anxious to show that he had too firm a grip upon realities to encourage wild theories or speculative solutions. First of all, he wished to prove that the Republican party was not a party of violence or disorder. He appealed to the delegates to show "patience and wisdom in their political action, to offer to France the spectacle of a party disciplined, firm in its principles, hard-working, vigilant and resolved on every effort, which may convince France of its capacity to govern. . . . The heroic days of our party, its age of chivalry, are passed, now that many of our hopes are fulfilled. . . . Now it is our duty to be as calm, as patient, as methodical, as skilful as we were enthusiastic and vehement" in the last days of the Empire.

He did not let these generalities blossom in the void. He took two steps of *rapprochement* — the first towards the President of the Republic. Thiers had said : "The future will belong to the party which is wisest". Gambetta accepted the challenge : "We accept the formula. We must become 'the wisest'. That will not be difficult for us for the excellent reason that the policy of our party is the only one that is truly wise and fruitful in results." He did not mention Thiers by name, but he said : "The present form of government commands the respect of all : whoever threatens it is a rebel". But, while he offered support to Thiers, he did not offer alliance. "I know a passion stronger than that of exercising power : it is that of controlling a loyal Government firmly, justly, sensibly." To a friend, who congratulated Gambetta on the good effect made by his speech in presidential circles, he answered : "Thiers knows he has nothing to fear from me. Did I

not make room for him at Bordeaux, when I might have
stayed ? Though he was too old to fight, he went all over
Europe to look for allies, when Jules Favre refused to cross
the Channel for them." [1] Next, with the true eye of the
strategist, he turned to the peasants — the vast majority of
the French electorate. The Republicans had up till then
been mostly a town party and had thought it rather good
form to sneer at the stupid dwellers in cottages, and call
the National Assembly " a pack of rustics ". Gambetta
sternly rebuked such language : " We should wish that
there was a ' rural Chamber ' in the deep and true sense of
the words, for such a Chamber would be composed not of
ignorant squires but of free and enlightened peasants ".
It was true there was a gulf between the town and country
voters, but it was due to ignorance. " The peasant,
devoted to work on his land, does not perceive the world
beyond except through legends and rumours. He is at the
mercy of clever tricksters. He is told, again and again, that
it was Napoleon, who gave him his land. He confuses
Napoleon with the Revolution : he is not far from the belief
of Mme de Staël that Napoleon was ' Robespierre on
horseback '. Well, we must pull him off his horse. We
must prove to the peasant that it is to democracy, to the
Revolution that he owed not only his land but his rights." [2]

Secondly, Gambetta wished to show that the Republican

---

[1] Mme Adam, *Mes angoisses*, pp. 165-7.

[2] The most important political event from 1871 to 1875 was the conversion
of the peasants to Republicanism. In 1871 they still regretted the Empire.
" Parish roads, crossing the cantons in all directions and reducing the difficulties of agricultural transport, railways covering the country and overcoming
distances, treaties of commerce opening up new markets, the postal rate at
twenty centimes, and the telegraph had (under the Empire) multiplied the
value of the soil tenfold. On the roofs tiles and slates replaced the thatch :
on the sideboards white bread in place of the old buckwheat. . . . Armed with
the vote, the peasants had felt their moral as well as their material condition
improved. The Préfet was particularly anxious to please them ; the authorities
spoke to them more politely ; the gentlemen no longer said to them, ' Hé,
l'ami ' [Hi, friend] . . . the French peasant is very sensitive to such nuances
of language " (Weiss, *Combat constitutionnel*, p. 104).

party had abandoned the visions of social Utopias, and would henceforward concentrate on a few urgent practical problems. " The more we specialise, the more we centralise our efforts on a given point, the more readily we shall raise up devoted supporters in the ranks of universal suffrage. . . . Our party needs a programme that is clear, precise and opposed to all chimeras." What was the policy upon which they were to concentrate ? The education of all, and conscription. " I shall see with patience the postponement of important questions, that can wait, that are side-issues, dependent on the realisation of these first and capital necessities." This was the first declaration of the famous policy of opportunism ; " Take questions in their right order " (" Il faut sérier les questions ") was the later formula.

The education of all — in body and mind : this double preoccupation made Mme Adam call Gambetta's ideal " the Athenian Republic ". " It was the inferiority of our national education which led to our defeat. . . . We have only one task — to instruct the people. . . . I demand that Science should leave its books, its libraries, its academies, its institutes, and descend into the streets and the humblest schools." Here he added a tribute to Positivism : " One of the greatest thinkers of our time, Auguste Comte, said that education should begin with the exact sciences ". No doubt the phrase implied a tacit criticism of religious education, and anticipated the demand for an instruction, which should be " free, compulsory, and secular ". But the speech contained no actual attack on Clericalism.

The second part of the educational programme — compulsory military service — roused no such controversies, and was soon to be realised by the National Assembly itself. " Side by side with the teacher we must place everywhere the gymnastic and military instructor. It must be well understood that in France, when a citizen is born, he is born a soldier, and that, whoever shirks the double duty of civil and military instruction, must be deprived relentlessly of his rights as a citizen and an elector."

Thirdly, Gambetta's aim was to show that the Republican party had thrown off its narrow exclusiveness and had become national. Doubtless there were some severe words as to the policy of the Royalists. "Does France wish again to abdicate and to be overturned into the dynastic rut ? . . . Today one hears on all sides of plots and intrigues in favour of this dynasty or that : the only question is which pretender shall claim the ruins of our menaced country : all that must end. We must resolutely dismiss these scandalous examples of covetousness and think only of France. . . . We are not rich enough to afford a monarchy." He warned the peasants that the Royalist deputies had introduced a motion to restore the right of the eldest son to inherit.[1] But there were no violent attacks upon the majority of the Assembly ; to them he said : " You wish to govern the Republic. . . . Well, we only ask of you to do one thing first — to recognise it. Once you have recognised it, we shall be perfectly ready to admit your taking office. For we wish to show the country the spectacle of Republicans by birth, who remain in opposition, face to face with converted Royalists, who shall be compelled by the unity of the Republican party and the legitimacy of the Republic to accomplish the reforms we demand."

Gambetta adopted the same tone at Paris, where he secured over 60,000 votes. On July 2nd he declared in an electoral placard : " Gambetta is not on any special list of candidates. To add his name to your voting papers

---

[1] This refers to a proposal of Mortimer-Ternaux, Brun and Baragnon, "taken into consideration " by the Assembly on June 23rd. Baragnon denied that he wished to revive the *droit d'aînesse* : " We are only proposing to modify clause 832 of the Code Civil ; at present it provides that every part of the inheritance must be formed of the same quantity of real estate, personal property and other kinds of wealth. We alter it in such a way that each part may, if necessary, be formed of only one kind of wealth " (*Annales*, t. 3, p. 569).

means founding the Republic by conciliation : it means creating the true balance of power (by giving the Republic two chiefs, one for the Whig section, the other for the Tories, Gambetta and Thiers), which will finally shut the door on the Royalist conspirators." [1]

How were these advances received in Government circles ? Hector Pessard says that Thiers was at once " delighted and anxious. He did not expect and perhaps did not even hope to find so much wisdom in one who, he vaguely foresaw, might be a rival and a successor." [2] Edmond Adam said to Gambetta : " Your speech is masterly. Its wisdom and balance have stupefied your enemies. Thiers said to St-Hilaire that he was much struck by its wisdom." [3] The *Bien Public*, in an article inspired by Thiers himself, mingled praise and blame : " One may hate this man : one may fear and oppose him. One cannot feel indifferent towards him. He has been someone, who counts, and so he will always be : he has been associated with the very life of France : he is a force, perhaps at this moment a danger. If he had been better advised, he might perhaps have been a hope for the future. Let us beware that he does not become a scourge." [4]

After his election, the tone became more cordial : " We suspect in him an immense ambition, a complete abandonment in the sphere of practice of the principles he has defended in theory, a determined resolution to grasp power at all costs. We wish to know for certain." [5] Thiers' friends were less satisfied. Leon Say, the new Préfet of the Seine, wrote in the *Journal des Débats* : " Must not a nation be very weak or very blind to entrust power again to a man, whose rule, though so short, was so full of the gravest faults and has been called the dictatorship of incapacity and official falsehood ? " [6]

[1] Halévy, *Fin des notables*, p. 116.   [2] Pessard, ii. 138.
[3] Mme Adam, *Mes angoisses*, p. 166.   [4] Pessard, ii. 138.
[5] Halévy, p. 117.   [6] Quoted Denis, p. 46.

Meanwhile France was being called upon to elect 118 deputies. The date had been chosen by Pasquier, partly in order to bring forward the question of the Princes' elections (Joinville had been elected in two Departments and therefore would have to be replaced in one), partly because he hoped that so soon after the suppression of the Commune there would be a violent reaction against demagogues and democrats. It was true that very few of the seats were held by the Right, for the vacancies were due to one of two causes — the resignation of a large number of deputies (all from the Left) after the vote in favour of Peace, and the multiple elections of February (Thiers had to be replaced in 26 Departments, Trochu in 9); but these candidates had been elected as persons in the public eye, rather than as party representatives, and their constituencies might now feel free to vote as they wished. The alarm of the Republicans might seem to justify the hopes of the Right : the Left were ill-organised and they were apprehensive that the bourgeois would vote conservative from fear of the Communards, and that the lower classes would sullenly abstain in despair.[1]

Thiers did not share this alarm. If, in one sense, the Republic might have seemed compromised by the Commune, in another sense it was the Republic that had vanquished the insurrection. "France is Thierist", he said, "and Audiffret is a bungler. Universal Suffrage will declare for me. We shall have Republican elections, very moderate and cautious."[2] At the same time he decided not to interfere openly on one side or the other — not that he held the belief of many, caused by the scandalous official candidatures of the Empire, that Government should remain neutral,[3] but because "the Government had no interest in

---

[1] Pessard, ii. 127.   [2] Dreyfus, *La République de M. Thiers*, pp. 70-71.

[3] In England we are so used to Government candidates that it seems a surprising thing that in France the Government is commonly expected to express no electoral preferences. It shows what enormous influence Administration is suspected of wielding.

interference, its popularity in the country being still unimpaired ".[1]

What he would not do himself, however, he could do through others. The majority of the Assembly considered that they had struck a good blow for their cause in persuading Thiers to dismiss Ernest Picard (one of the " men of September ") from the Ministry of the Interior on the eve of the elections, and to replace him by Lambrecht, a somewhat vague adherent of the Right. But Ministers of Thiers were expected to forget all other loyalties, and de Broglie sadly comments, " In place of a compromising ally Thiers put in a docile servant ".[2]

Meanwhile at the Interior Thiers worked through Calmon, the *chef de service*, an ex-official of the July Monarchy, now devoted to his new master and ready to instruct the Préfets, who had been carefully selected by Picard. Thiers even wrote to Auguste Mame, a well-known Catholic editor at Tours, in favour of Calmon's candidature : " I do not wish in the least to renew the scandal of official candidatures, which consisted in subordinating the interests of the administration to electoral interests, but a Government should be allowed to have its friends and to agree with them on the choice of good representatives, provided that only lawful means are used and never threats or bribes. . . . I know that you are independent, and I ask you to resist a kind of conspiracy against my friend M. Calmon, who wishes to be a candidate for your Department, and who by his merit and position, and large property in Touraine has a very real claim to stand in your constituency." [3]

In some Departments the Royalist candidates claimed Thiers' name for themselves, and accused the Republicans of being rebels against his authority. In the Département du Nord the Monarchists asserted that the Chief of the State was on their side. Thiers made no sign, but, when

---

[1] *Notes et souvenirs*, p. 171.   [2] Quoted Dreyfus, *op. cit.* p. 76.
[3] Bouniols, *op. cit.* p. 76 : Calmon was not elected till 1873.

Testelin, one of the Republican candidates in the same Department, was accused of having been ready to negotiate with the Commune, Thiers' secretary, Barthélemy-St-Hilaire, wrote : " It is your enemies and the enemies of M. Thiers who spread such disgraceful stories. You may remind them of the affection and esteem, which M. Thiers showed you when you came to see him." [1] The Right were indignant,[2] and, if Testelin had not obtained an overwhelming majority, would have tried to unseat him.

But the need for intervention or pressure was very slight. The chief difficulty in the way of Left candidates was the want of efficient organisation. The February elections had been quite free from electoral committees (hence, said many critics, the excellent results) ; little had been done to improve matters in July. Gambetta had not yet had time to create local groups with that *coup d'œil*, which made his brain " a small atlas of France ".

In Paris the famous journalist, Émile Girardin, grouped moderate opinion by calling together a committee representing 19 newspapers, mostly Legitimist and Orleanist, who had united during the siege in criticising the Government of National Defence, and which took the name of " *Union parisienne de la Presse* ". They put forward a list of moderate Conservatives, and paid a marked tribute to

[1] Dreyfus, *op. cit.* p. 73.

[2] For another example see Simon (*Soir de ma journée*, pp. 204-5) : " M. Rémusat and I were going from a meeting of the Council to the Assembly, when we met Vitet, Saint-Marc-Girardin and other members of the Right . . . they were much excited and received us with violent reproaches because of St-Hilaire's letter to Boysset " (President of the Saône-et-Loire General Council : the Republic was mentioned as the " only Government under which France could find safety "). " We waited for them in the outer room, while they went in to see Thiers. We heard the noise of a stormy discussion. After a quarter of an hour we saw Thiers come out. He was full of energy. He had received them, as a man who was devoting himself to saving France and who would not any longer put up with the distraction of their silly disputes. He had said to them, ' I await you at the tribune ; I summon you there to have an explanation with me before France and before history '."

the Government by including General de Cissey, the new Minister for War. Meanwhile the Republicans were hopelessly divided : 22 Radical deputies published a manifesto, which was immediately answered by 122 members of the Moderate Left. The number of electoral lists became so great that it was even suggested that Thiers should be asked to nominate the candidates himself.

Thiers had a Central Committee presided over by a friend, Charles Renouard, and at the last moment it rallied to the " *Union de la Presse* ", which carried most of its candidates, with the paradoxical result that, in place of the violently Radical representatives of February (two of whom had actually perished in the Commune), Paris returned, under the patronage of Royalist newspapers, a list of Moderates, most of whom became supporters of Thiers' Government.[1]

Five Radicals were returned — Gambetta ; Claude Corbon, who had been Vice-President of the Constituent Assembly of 1848 ; Scheurer-Kestner, an Alsatian chemist and friend of Gambetta ; Pierre Brelay, who in 1848 had been Commandant of the artillery in the Paris National Guard ; and Laurent-Pichat, a friend of Victor Hugo and himself a poet. On the Moderate list, Mgr. Freppel was beaten. A Bishop — even if an Alsatian — was too much for the Paris electorate. On the contrary, they elected Pressensé (Moderate Left) minister of one of the Protestant chapels in Paris, whose virulence won for him in the Assembly the ironical nickname of the " gentle pastor ". Of the same list were : Alfred André, a banker, a strong Thierist, and Denormandie, an *avoué* of Paris, a clear and witty speaker,

[1]

	February	July
Extreme Left . . .	19	5
Left	2	2
Left Centre	1	12
Right Centre and Right . .	..	3

(See Pessard, ii. 128-33 ; Dreyfus, *op. cit.* pp. 82-4.)

more of a Conservative than a Republican ; [1] Wolowski, a Pole who had become a naturalised Frenchman, and Professor of Political Economy at the Institut (Left Centre); [2] Pernolet, a Catholic Republican (Left Centre), who had been Maire of the thirteenth arrondissement during the siege, and whose mellifluous eloquence in the Assembly on one occasion filled 17 columns of the report ; Louvet (Left Centre), another Paris Maire, director of a lace-making industry ; Drouin (Left Centre), a rich Paris chemist, president of the tribunal of commerce ; Dietz-Monin (Left Centre), an Alsatian industrialist ; Paul Morin (Left Centre), head of aluminium works ; Ploeuc (Right), one of the governors of the Bank of France, who had maintained the institution during the Commune ; Krantz (Left Centre), an engineer who was to be one of the first reporters on the Channel Tunnel ; Lefebvre (Right), " an expert in finance, with light curly hair, who spoke like the angel Gabriel, and became a charming embodiment of Christian charity by attaching his name to the best projects of social beneficence " ; [3] Sébert, President of the Chamber of Notaires (Left Centre), who had refused to submit to the Commune ; and Ferdinand Moreau (Left Centre), a stockbroker. De Cissey, the Minister for War, was also returned. The list testifies on the whole to a rally of professional and business men to Thiers.

The other deputy on the list was destined to be of more parliamentary importance : Édouard Laboulaye (Left Centre) had been Professor of Comparative Legislation ; he became famous by his book, *Prince Caniche*, a satire on Bonapartist administration. He stood as an Opposition candidate at the 1866 elections. After his defeat he was

---

[1] Both André and Denormandie belonged to the group of " Conservateurs républicains ", which hovered between the Right and the Left Centres, supported Thiers till his fall, and then were not far from accepting Royalist overtures.

[2] As the list began with André and ended with Wolowski, it was jocosely called the Alphabetical List.   [3] Du Barail, iii. 441.

presented by the Strasbourg students with a silver ink-
stand : in 1869 he rallied to the Liberal Empire (on the
principle that " the best Constitution is the one you have,
provided you make use of it "), and his lectures were
interrupted by cries of " Give back the ink-stand ! " [1] But
his most important influence was as a lover and champion
of American ideas.[2] His book, *Paris in America*, was much
read ; he helped to create an admiration for Washington,
Franklin and Lincoln. Though himself a Catholic, he was
a fervent admirer of the Unitarian, Channing : though he
had never been across the Atlantic himself, his rooms were
full of presents from America, and in his library at Glatigny
(a pleasant suburb of Versailles) he had an antique volume
containing the constitutions of the original States of the
Union. His large contributions to the legislative work of
the National Assembly are interesting, as based upon a
clever and persistent appeal to Anglo-Saxon ideals of
liberty.

The Comte de Chambord's letter on the Pope's temporal
power had a pernicious influence upon the fortunes of his
party. As if this were not enough, a certain number of
Bishops addressed petitions to the Assembly " inviting the
Government to concert measures with other nations to
restore to the Pope the conditions necessary for the free
government of the Catholic Church ".[3] The Republicans
replied that this was equivalent to war with Italy, and
De Meaux, looking back at the July elections, says sadly
that " the principal authors of the Royalist defeats were
Thiers and the Bishops ".[4]

The Right retorted by accusing the Republicans of
being communards, but the peasants were not frightened :
reassured by Gambetta's Bordeaux speech, they eagerly

---

[1] In 1873, when a Commission of which Laboulaye was the reporter,
delayed its report, Baragnon enquired whether it was still " in M. Laboulaye's
inkstand ".

[2] Gambetta called him " an American from Seine-et-Oise ".

[3] Dreyfus, *op. cit.* p. 78.   [4] De Meaux, p. 57.

welcomed the denunciations of the Ancien Régime, with which the Left stuffed their rural addresses, such as the following : " The peasants alone paid taxes ; the nobles and priests, who possessed two-thirds of the land, paid nothing towards the public expenses ".[1] The country voter showed no gratitude to the majority of the National Assembly for having allowed him to vote in his own commune, instead of having to walk to the chief town of the canton. The Republicans swept the constituencies : La Vendee, the very type of Catholic peasantry, returned a candidate of the Left. General Faidherbe (Left Centre), " the brilliant conqueror of the Moors . . . kind under a dry manner . . . rigid as a Puritan ",[2] obtained 103,438 votes in one Department and 151,470 in another : [3] the Gironde Department, which in February had returned a list including Decazes and General Carayon-Latour, now voted a list headed by Fourcand, the democratic Maire of Bordeaux.

The Bonapartists made an attempt to re-enter political life. Prince Jerome Napoleon, leader of the democratic section of the party, said in a public letter to Jules Favre that " the only source from which a Government can draw legality and strength in France is an appeal to the people ",[4] i.e. the plebiscite. But their hour was not yet : their leaders, Rouher, Ernest Dréolle, and Baron Jérôme David were all defeated. A few isolated supporters of the Empire were elected — Jean André, an obscure notary in Charente chosen to replace the Bonapartist deputy, Peconnet ; and Soubeyran, who had served in the Finance Ministry of the Empire but always boasted of having voted against the

---

[1] Dreyfus, *op. cit.* p. 79. [2] Freycinet, p. 219.

[3] He resigned in August rather than recognise the constituent powers of the Assembly.

[4] Hanotaux, i. 254. Pasquier, speaking on June 27th, expressed an ironical hope that Prince Jerome would be elected to the Assembly : " He must wish to tell us where and on what battlefield he has served his country : he will tell us what has happened to France while he was smoking his cigarette in his palace at Caserte or on the terraces of Prangins ".

war. A more important person came in for Vienne —
Pierre Magne, who under Napoleon III had been Minister
of Finance and Public Works. But his personal loyalty
to the Emperor did not prevent him from sitting in the
Orleanist Right Centre, and afterwards becoming their
Chancellor of the Exchequer.

The result of the elections did not add to the reputation
of the Duc de Pasquier for political sagacity.[1] It was
not the last time he was to stake the fortunes of his party
upon a hazard and lose. De Broglie says philosophically :
" The February elections had swung further to the Right
than was justified by the Royalist reaction. A swing-back
in the opposite direction was inevitable." [2] Martial Delpit,
from the Legitimist ranks, was less resigned : " The great
danger ", he wrote in his diary, " is that an honest republic
is one of the most difficult things to realise : it at once
tends to become Jacobin or Socialist ".[3]

(d) GAMBETTA AT THE NATIONAL ASSEMBLY
(JULY TO SEPTEMBER)

The July elections had been a great victory for the
Republic, but the question remained — What kind of

[1] Here are the results : complete accuracy is difficult as some of the
deputies, who were replaced, had not declared their affiliations :—

	February	July
Extreme Left . .	36	42
Left	20	38
Left Centre . .	11	24
Thiers . . .	26*	..
Trochu . .	9	..
Bonapartists . .	1	1†
Right Centre . .	5	9
Right . . .	10	3
Extreme Right . .	0	1
	118	118

* In all but three of these Departments he was replaced by members from the Left.
† Counting Magne and Soubeyran as Right.

[2] Quoted Dreyfus, *op. cit.* p. 91.   [3] Denis, *Histoire contemporaine*, ii. p. 47.

Republic ? And, as Gambetta again took his seat on the benches of the National Assembly, he had a difficult problem before him. Was he to accept the leadership of Thiers (in whom the country had expressed its confidence) at the cost of his own convictions, for, if Thiers was a Republican (and it was as yet by no means clear), he was certainly the most conservative of all possible Republicans ? Or was he to lead a violent Radical opposition, thus alienating the Moderate Left and repudiating his own counsel of moderation at Bordeaux ? He determined to do neither, but to adhere to a programme of " independent support ". There was to be no open breach with Thiers, but there was to be no surrender to his influence. Gambetta resolved to unite all Republicans from the moderate to the extreme Left as a disciplined, compact and independent wing of Thiers' supporters. Such a feat could not be carried out by means of the tempestuous eloquence, which so far had been the chief manifestation of his character. It needed patience, moderation and skill. He revealed these new qualities in the years from 1871 to 1875 — perhaps the brightest period of his chequered and uneven career.[1]

It is possible to see Gambetta's problem in the concrete by considering the case of Edmond Adam, Republican deputy for the Seine. During the Commune, most of the deputies of the Left, terrified at being regarded as accomplices, " ate out of Thiers' hand." Adam, though he protested against such docility, himself felt the impulse to enlist under Thiers in the Left Centre. " If we had not been resolved to be loyal to Gambetta," writes his wife, " Adam, disgusted at the Commune and disturbed by the revolutionary logic of the Radicals, . . . would have joined

---

[1] De Meaux, an irreconcilable but not an ungenerous opponent, after denying that he was a great statesman or a great orator, adds : " His rôle was that of a party leader. One should have seen him sometimes bringing his troops to their feet and rousing the storm by a word uttered from his place or from the tribune, and sometimes, by a wave of his big hand, imposing silence and repressing untimely excitement " (*Souvenirs*, pp. 244-5).

the Left Centre [but] they detest 'the madman of Bordeaux'.[1] *Au fond* Adam is much nearer [to the Left Centre] than to the Socialism of Louis Blanc or the Positivism of Littré or the Jacobinism of Peyrat, but as deputy for Paris he is classed as a Radical and he is a good party man."[2] Adam himself said to Gambetta, soon after his return : "We will make agreements with the Left Centre easy for you. . . . We cannot be led by Louis Blanc. Without you we shall end by going over to Thiers."[3]

But the relation of Gambetta to Adam and his wife is important enough to require more detailed treatment.

Edmond Adam had been Conseiller d'État in 1851, but had resigned after the Second of December. During the last years of the Empire he had founded a new paper with Peyrat, *L'Avenir National*. He had been Préfet of Police under the National Defence Government, but had resigned after the *émeute* of October 31st. Tall, energetic, with commanding gestures, he was faithful to his cause and his friends. When Rochefort was implicated in the Commune, Adam wrote a letter calling him "my friend", and was cold-shouldered in the Assembly. He interceded also for Ranc as "the combatant of Tours and Bordeaux". He spoke his mind roundly to Grévy for his unfairness as President to Gambetta. But he was no fanatic : he always endeavoured to keep up good relations between Thiers and Gambetta, and he had the courage to abuse his own party for their narrowness and pedantry :

You must destroy the idea that you are Hottentots. Only the other day General Changarnier said to me : "You yourself and two or three of your colleagues of the Union Républicaine, and half a dozen of the Left Centre, are the only men of the world you have got". Don't laugh, Gambetta. Be sure of this — that one does not get far in Paris, unless one belongs to a presentable set. You can keep up an opposition in cafés, but to govern you must have good

---

[1] *Mes angoisses*, pp. 143-4.   [2] *Ibid.* p. 87.   [3] *Ibid.* p. 166.

society on your side. Your sons (alas! too many of you are bachelors) must be *gens bien élevés*.[1]

It was the task of his wife to realise this ideal, to educate the Republican party, and to begin by polishing its leader. Juliette Lambert was born in the little Picard town of Verberie. Her father was a doctor of the traditional Voltairean type, though very un-Voltairean in his love of social equality. "If you must worship something", he used to say, "worship the sun." "Christ came to save what He called men's souls : we come to save society" (*la personne sociale*). "I rejoice to see you talking to a workman, as if he were your brother."[2] His daughter sometimes laughed at him, and she was soon removed from his influence, but it was easy to see that she inherited his fiery democratic idealism. She first appeared in Paris *chez* the Comtesse d'Agoult, an important social figure in the late fifties, the mother of Mme Émile Ollivier, and the friend of Liszt. It was here she met Edmond Adam, and after her marriage with him she opened an opposition salon under the Empire.

She first met Gambetta at this salon : it was not without many hesitations. One of her friends described him as belonging to the riff-raff of the party. Another said : "You cannot imagine the vitality of the fellow : if only he were better put on, I would introduce him to you. But it is impossible. Nevertheless he is a man of letters." Even Adam himself was more than doubtful. "His accent is impossible. He is insolent in discussion. Moreover, I do not wish you to hear the way he talks of the Republicans of 1848. He is worth knowing, but he is a Bohemian, vulgar, brutal . . . a typical man of the masses, a Danton, only more crafty." Hetzel, the publisher, who knew Gambetta through his brilliant fellow-provincial Alphonse Daudet, was consulted. He also pronounced him impossible :

---

[1] Mme Adam, *Nos amitiés politiques*, p. 117.
[2] Winifred Stephens, *Mme Adam*, p. 17.

" You should hear Alphonse describe his family, blatant windbags of Provençals.   He himself is a kind of political commercial traveller, provincial to the marrow of his bones, a one-eyed grocer with his shirt and cravat and trousers all tumbling down." [1]

Nevertheless it was decided to ask him for one of the Friday dinner-parties.   He said to his boon companions at the Café Procopé :   " I shall accept.   It will be curious to see what kind of a woman Adam's bourgeois wife is." [2] On the eventful evening,[3] the salon was full : the Marquis de Lasteyrie (an Orleanist friend of Thiers, grandson of Lafayette) was there to make his report to Thiers, who was " greatly interested in the young monster ".   All the guests were in evening dress.   Gambetta arrived in a nondescript kind of coat and a waistcoat, buttoned up to the throat, with a flannel shirt showing through.   He tried to excuse himself :   " If only I had known . . ."   " You would not have come ", replied Mme Adam with a smile ;   " that is not nice of you."   Lasteyrie whispered to his hostess in despair, " If only he had come in a workman's blouse, I might have passed him ".   " The only way to rehabilitate him ", she replied, " is to give him the place of honour." " You are right ", answered the Marquis, " otherwise the servants might neglect him.   Besides we shall see whether he appreciates the grand manner."   He did appreciate it, for, as Mme Adam took her embarrassed guest by the arm and placed him at her right hand at the table, he leant forward and whispered, " Madame, I shall never forget the lesson you have taught me ".

For seven years their friendship was deep and strong. She made him a man of the world, taught him manners, and sent him to a new tailor.   When he returned to the National Assembly in 1871, he still wore his white drill trousers and

---

[1] *Ibid.* pp. 110-11.
[2] Vassili, *France from behind the Veil*, p. 193.
[3] Probably in 1866 or 1867.

panama hat. But he steadily improved, and many years later she saw him at the Opera faultlessly attired, with light gloves, and a gardenia in his button-hole, and felt a creator's pride.[1]

During the war her sympathy and loyalty increased. A fervent patriot, she looked on him as the embodiment of La Revanche : when he came to Versailles in 1871, she constantly received him at her house, went to the gallery of the Assembly to applaud his speeches, kept up a constant correspondence with him, and even became intimate with those " blatant windbags ", his relations. " We must serve him ", she exclaimed, " who has never despaired of his country." [2]

On his side, Gambetta felt towards her an unbounded reverence and gratitude. " She had been very beautiful, and was still extremely handsome : above all she was full of graciousness, tact and goodwill." [3] It is natural to ask whether there was anything romantic in their relationship, and it is refreshing to be able to answer (in a matter so nebulous) with a direct negative. Vassili [4] represents Gambetta as saying : " I would never have dared to allow my thoughts to rest on that idea. . . . I would not have had the courage to make her unhappy. . . . That woman would never suffer more from anything than from the loss of her illusions, and she sees in me the man she has created, and not the man that I really am." On her side, she was devoted to her husband and, after his death in 1875, to his memory. In 1877, when Gambetta was fighting for his political life against the last attempt of a Conservative Government to destroy him, a woman of the Quartier Latin, who had been his mistress at Paris and Bordeaux, threatened to sell to the Bonapartists a photograph of

---

[1] Winifred Stephens, *Mme Adam*, p. 112.
[2] *Ibid.* p. 178.   [3] *Ibid.* p. 173.
[4] *Op. cit.* p. 201. I have already warned the reader that Vassili's conversations with eminent persons must be taken with a grain of salt, but, in this case, the sentiments he attributes to Gambetta seem natural and just.

herself, upon which, in the middle of the War, he had written, "To my little queen, whom I love more than France". She wished to be revenged upon a rival who had displaced her in Gambetta's affections. Mme Adam sent for the jealous woman, and said : "Are you going to give this up to the cruel enemy of him whose life you have shared ? " " I am avenging myself." " You once loved M. Gambetta ? " " With all the passion and devotion I have." " Well, Madame, respect this feeling of yours, which has exalted you, and do not let yourself be ruled by the lowest instincts of hate." " It is this woman who has taken my place, whom I wish to wound through him." " How much do you want ? " " They are worth 30,000 francs to M. Rouher (the Bonapartist leader), but I will take 6000." " Come, then, with the papers and the photograph, and say to yourself that you are doing a good action." The papers were brought and burned. A month later she said to Gambetta, " This woman was worthy to be loved, but not so much as our . . ." There she paused, and he replied with a laugh, " Thank you, my sister, for your absolution ".[1] It is a fine example of devoted loyalty, but there is not a word that could have passed between lovers.

This is of importance, because it limited the influence of Mme Adam. Gambetta was exceedingly susceptible to feminine influence. He needed it to bring out the best in him, and in this sense her friendship was a constant inspiration. But he needed to have his heart touched, if he was to be permanently influenced. She has been called his political Egeria, but that name rightly belongs to another. She did him inestimable service in keeping the party together, helping moderate counsels to prevail, and maintaining contact with Thiers. " She moved about, the only lady at the receptions, from some old dry doctrinaire of

[1] See the touching description in Mme Adam's *Après l'abandon de la revanche*, pp. 56-65.

the Left Centre to some fiery Republican from the
South." [1] She was in truth " the Queen of the Third
Republic ".

But she did not impress her views upon Gambetta as
much as might have been supposed. It was partly that he
had hardly any formed doctrines. [2] True to his opportunist
doctrine, he did not consider questions, till they arose, and
the only problem, that mattered at the moment, was to
prevent disputes among his followers, and lead them to the
definite proclamation of the Republic. But it was already
possible to see divergencies of opinion between the two
friends. Mme Adam was a passionate Nationalist devoted
to the union of the whole country against Germany. She
said to Gambetta : " If I believed that Bismarck supported
the Republic and that therefore it did not stand for Revenge . . ." " What then ? " " I should not serve the
Republic." " I thought you were a Republican before
everything." " No, I am French before everything, then
a lover of liberty, and then a Republican." " And always
and everywhere on your own " (hors des rangs). [3] She hated
the petty intrigues of Freemasonry against the Church.
" Are you going to fight Clericalism ", she asked, " by
means of Freemasonry ? It will be anti-Liberal : it will
make the Republic detested." [4]

When the Republic had triumphed, and Gambetta

---

[1] Winifred Stephens, *Mme Adam*, p. 173.

[2] One remembers Clemenceau's verdict (*Martet*, p. 280) : " He had profoundly generous impulses. His philosophy was beautiful and noble. . . . I
liked Gambetta and respected him. He didn't know very well where he was
going, but he went with ardour." " He had a fine soul, [but] he had the terrible
fault of never being able to carry anything through right to the end " (Mordacq,
Ministère Clemenceau, t. iii. p. 166). Bodley believes that in his later days
Gambetta lost all belief in the parliamentary republic. " In my belief, the
Liberals, who detested autocracy on principle, . . . were quite right to mistrust him : I hasten to add that he was equally justified in giving them cause
for mistrust. The regret expressed in these pages at his career cut short would
be meaningless, if the only promise he had given were that of a parliamentary
statesman " (*France*, pp. 600-601).

[3] *Nos amitiés*, p. 16.   [4] *Ibid.* p. 262.

began to play with the idea of an agreement with Germany, based on a joint hostility to the Church, Mme Adam broke off relations with him. She lived to welcome the Russian alliance, which she had foreseen; she lived through the Great War, devoting herself to the soldiers, who christened a gun in her honour. She returned to the bosom of the Church: " I remembered how for centuries France had been superbly patriotic, how for centuries the association between God and the King, God and *la patrie*, had been perhaps more essential than I had ever believed ".[1] One of her last books by its title — *The Time of Revenge for Bismarck's Insolence* — linked victory with old memories of the defeat.

But to return to 1871 — Gambetta was already passing under the influence of another woman, who was to be the romance of his life, and to have a real influence on his politics. In 1869 he was speaking at the Corps Législatif, when his eye fell on a tall woman with a severe type of Roman beauty, gazing at him long and fixedly from the gallery. She was always present, when he spoke, and one day he sent a letter to her by an usher. She opened it, tore it up, and disappeared.[2] They did not meet again till August 1871, when he again sent her a note at the Assembly. " At last I see you once more : is it really you ? " This time she slipped the letter into her bodice, and disappeared.[3] They met again at the house of a wounded friend, and he told her of his love. " No," she answered, " you cannot love me. I am unworthy of your great destiny. I will not hear of your love, till I have told you the story of my sad life." They agreed to meet early in the morning (it was now the autumn of 1871) " by the side of the Petit Trianon at Versailles where two branches of the Grand Canal make a sort of cross ".[4] There she told him about herself : she was the second daughter of Colonel François-Émile Léon,

[1] Winifred Stephens, *Mme Adam*, p. 206.   [2] Laur, *Heart of Gambetta*, pp. 4-5.
   [3] *Ibid.* p. 10.   [4] *Ibid.* pp. 16, 17.

who had served under the Duc d'Orléans, and, in consequence of some story discreditable to his honour, committed
suicide in 1860. Her own name was Léonie : her two sisters
had been seduced, and she had gone as governess to
Mocquard, chef du cabinet under the Empire, and there
she had been seduced by his son. " You cannot love me ! "
she cried. " Gambetta can have nothing in common with
a dishonoured, ruined girl." Gambetta replied in a burst
of confident affection. " My mind ", he said, " has very
many dear friends : my heart has not even one. The public
love in a rough way, but its affections cannot satisfy my
longings for a really trustworthy friend. My heart is lonely
as yours is. Why not join our two hearts together and make
a paradise of our two solitary lives ? "   But she was implacable : she could never be " the guardian of his home ",
but she wished to be " the guardian of his political honour
and of his affectionate heart, only too easily influenced ".[1]
She was a devout Catholic, and refused to accept civil
marriage. After consultation with her director, she be-
trothed herself " by present vows " (equivalent under
unavoidable circumstances to holy matrimony), and they
exchanged rings. Gambetta said, " Be my wife in secret,
dear adorable one ".[2]

Gambetta himself called her his Egeria, and he wrote to
her : " I can never decide whether my heart or my head is
the more delighted ".[3] Up to 1875 her influence upon him
was mostly on the side of moderation. " Be more and more
persuasive ", she urged. " Offend no one. Try to inaugur-
ate a policy of results." [4] " Let the country feel that the
old political parties might possibly adapt themselves to a
new form of government." She warned him against declaring in favour of separation of Church and State, or
encouraging conflict between the schools and the Church.

---

[1] " Without me ", she added, " it will always be at the mercy of vulgar
adventures or treacherous ambitions " (Laur, pp. 25-7).
[2] *Ibid.* pp. 52, 57.   [3] *Ibid.* p. 80.   [4] *Ibid.* p. 37.

" The clergy are so powerful : would you set them against us ? " " Let us discriminate ", he answered. " I have gone over to the free thinkers : I consider that nothing can surpass human science, and yet I cannot help feeling awed and touched, when I think of these men who are spoken of so disdainfully, and who form the lower clergy. I cannot help liking the humble curé." " Bravo," she replied.[1] At this time we only get one hint of her later pro-German influence. One day Gambetta arrived, his blood boiling at some insult of Bismarck, and she said quietly : " Tell me about your mother ".[2] It is not till after 1875 that her true rôle began. But it would not be possible to picture Gambetta's career at the Assembly without remembering these stolen meetings in the Versailles Park.

We must now turn from women to politics — in spite of Talleyrand's *mot* (when Thiers complained that he *would* talk about women), " Women *are* politics ". We must consider the parties, which Gambetta had to guide in the Assembly.

The Left of the Assembly consisted of three rather undefined groups. (*a*) The " Union Républicaine " (about 86 deputies) : this was Gambetta's party. It had begun under the Empire and consisted of younger men, who had

[1] *Ibid.* 39-41.

[2] *Ibid.* p. 46. On February 23rd, 1878, Gambetta wrote to her that the idea of a personal interview with Bismarck was " the result of your inspiration, and of the clearness of your intelligence ". The limits of this book do not allow me to spare more than a passing reference to the painful theory that she was a German spy. Léon Daudet, in his *Drame des Jardins*, represents her as being first in the Secret Service of the Empire, before joining that of Germany, and that, when Gambetta found it out, he killed himself by snatching the pistol she was pointing at herself. The only evidence for this is that she brought up a young man, whom she called her nephew, that he was educated in Germany, that he was an employé in a factory and paid for by Henckel, a German industrialist in close relations with Gambetta. Gheusi (Gambetta's cousin) holds that perhaps she was sent to find out his political plans, but in that case she really became fascinated by him (*Vie singulière de Gambetta*, p. 247). For a rather hostile summing up ending, however, with a not-proven, see de Roux, pp. 298-301. My own feeling is that her strict Catholic views, which seem to have been sincere, make it most unlikely that she was a spy of Bismarck.

been disgusted by the unpractical idealism of the Mountain.
The Radical party (as they were called) prided themselves
on being implacable realists. Alphonse Peyrat said that
" the men of '48 failed to understand that a Government
should prefer its existence to its principles ". They laughed
at the scruples of the older men about taking the oath of
allegiance to the Empire. Rochefort said : " I never break
my promises : I have sworn to break my oath and I shall
keep my word to break it ".[1] Most of these men had rallied
to Gambetta's opportunism. Twice they deliberated on a
recourse to violence, when a Conservative victory seemed
likely, but on the whole, they were agreed that " the
heroic age of the party was past ". René Goblet, a lawyer
from Amiens, was one of Gambetta's devoted followers :
he had the head of a cherub, and the small round figure of
an *abbé galant*, but he spoke with vigour and sincerity.
When he distinguished himself, his leader used to say,
" The little fellow has shot up a whole peg in my estima-
tion ".[2] Edmond Lepère was another of his lieutenants
with " a talent for speaking and a good heart . . . superior
to most of the party " (says a critic from the Left Centre),[3]
and always ready to warn his leader against dangerous
ideas. Turquet (who became Under Secretary for the Fine
Arts and married Miss Montgomery, an English art
connoisseur) " reddened with pleasure when Gambetta
pinched his ear with Napoleonic familiarity ".[4] Jules
Cazot, newly elected deputy for Gard, had been Gambetta's
Secretary-General during the war, and " was much respected for his firmness of principle, and profound erudi-
tion ".[5] Alphonse Gent, one of Gambetta's fiery Préfets,
who is said to have proposed to him to " raise the South ",
had been returned for Vaucluse.

Clément Laurier, Gambetta's most intimate friend, had

---

[1] De Roux, p. 9.　　　　[2] Mme Adam, *Nos amitiés*, p. 269.
[3] De Marcère, *Histoire de la république*, ii. 197-8.　　　　[4] Bosq, p. 92.
[5] Freycinet, p. 167.

also been returned at the July elections. Together they had visited the Comte de Paris at Twickenham with the words " Monseigneur, you see two Republicans " : together they had appeared on the Belleville platforms during Gambetta's ultra-Radical phase. During the war, he had used his considerable financial ability to negotiate a loan for 250,000,000 fr. in London ; he had sent a message to the Préfets : " War to the bitter end, to the last stage of exhaustion ". But he had never been happy in the midst of popular agitation : under an audacious manner, bristling with sceptical epigrams, he concealed the instincts of a Conservative. During the disorders of the closing years of the Empire his devotion to Gambetta alone kept him by his side. " I cannot get used to this kind of life ", he used to say ; " you will see : if these people become masters, they will end by burning Paris." [1] The Commune seemed to him the fulfilment of his worst fears, and at the National Assembly he ended by going over to the Right Centre. They retained their affection for one another. Freycinet describes how he dined at the Palais Royal with the two parted friends : " We hardly touched on the sad subject : Laurier spoke of the horrors of the Commune and the necessity of carrying out the restoration of national life : Gambetta listened sadly without comment ".[2]

On one side of Gambetta's group lay (b) the Extreme Left, consisting of about ten intransigent members, mostly from the Assembly of 1848.[3] Among the newer recruits was Alfred Naquet, a doctor and chemist of Jewish extraction, physically deformed and " with the crooked nose of Punch ".[4] He was a fervent apostle of Divorce, and, under the Empire, was condemned to prison for his book *Religion, Property, and the Family.* His interventions were almost as embarrassing to the Left as irritating to the Right. He proposed a complete amnesty for the

[1] Pessard, i. 274. [2] Freycinet, p. 165.
[3] See above, pp. 354-8. [4] Claveau, p. 229.

Communards. He asserted in full Assembly that " morality, merit and demerit are but accidents of the constitution, and there is no more demerit in being evil-minded
than in being one-eyed or hump-backed", and he quoted
a famous phrase from Taine's *Introduction to English
Literature* : " Vice and Virtue are products, just as
vitriol and sugar are products ". It was a shrewd blow,
for Taine was now posing as the Conservative champion :
he wrote a somewhat embarrassed letter to the *Journal
des Débats* : " To say that virtue and vice are products,
just as vitriol and sugar are products, is not to say that
they are chemical products. . . . However well one knows
the composition of vitriol, one does not pour it into
one's tea. The evil man deserves blame, disdain and
punishment. . . . A hump-back is not admitted into the
Army, and confirmed evil-doers should be excluded from
society." [1] In later life, Naquet became guide, philosopher
and friend to the abortive Boulangist movement.

On the same benches of the Extreme Left sat also
Charles Boysset, an avocat who had written for Proudhon's
Peuple : the Moderates called him " un vieux routier de
1848 ". He proposed the suppression of the Budget of
Cults and declared solemnly, " The dogma of Universal
Suffrage is intangible " ; [2] and Francisque Ordinaire, who
had fought under Gambetta, and afterwards distinguished
himself by calling a Commission of the Assembly " a Commission of assassins ".

On the other side of Gambetta's group was (c) " La
Gauche Républicaine ", the Moderate Left (about 100
deputies). It had originated with the majority of the
National Defence Government, who had voted for peace, and

---

[1] Taine, *Life and Letters*, iii. 71, 99-101. Everything turns of course upon
the precise meaning of merit and demerit : Naquet would not have denied that
the evil-doer ought to be punished. But he would have said that he no more
" deserved " blame than vitriol does. It is difficult to resist the impression
that, when he coined the phrase, the historian held the same opinion.

[2] Mme Adam, *Nos amitiés*, p. 228.

had forced Gambetta to give way at Bordeaux.   There still remained smouldering resentments, but the leaders of the Moderate Left were for the moment without much influence on the party : of the " four Jules ", who formed its back-bone, Grévy was President of the Assembly, Favre and Simon were members of the Government, and were re-garded with the suspicion that deputies in France always feel towards colleagues, who have become Ministers, while Ferry was too unpopular with his fellow-members to have much influence.[1]

The main bulk of the Moderate Left consisted of Re-publicans, who had been respectable local representatives of their principles, most of them members of the bourgeoisie. Some had historic names : Hippolyte Carnot, who had been Minister of the Interior in 1848, was son of the Organ-iser of Victory ; Sadi, his son, engineer and deputy for Côte d'Or, was to be President of the Republic in later years.   Oscar Count de Lafayette (another great Republican name) had been an artillery officer in Italy.   Pascal Duprat, a Professor of History, " with his long hair flowing down to his collar ", had been an 1848 man.   Two other members of the party had been members of the National Defence Govern-ment — Arago and Dorian ; the first was easy-going, without resentment, and always eager for reconciliation ; the second was a silent, hard-headed industrialist.   Duclerc, President of the Gauche Républicaine, was a very moderate demo-crat[2] and a great friend of Gambetta.   On the whole a group easily dominated by the " Dictator of Bordeaux ", but his team needed careful handling, and Gambetta showed

[1] When Ferry made a successful speech in the Assembly, Gambetta said to his friends that it "stuck like a bone in their throats ".   "Not at all ", answered Adam, " and the proof is that, if we were not determined to be just, nothing would induce us to praise him " (*Nos amitiés*, p. 257).

[2] " As to Equality ", he said in conversation, " I think the time has come to reverse the machine backwards :   otherwise with Universal Suffrage it means the systematic destruction of every kind of superiority " (*Nos amitiés*, p. 253).   Later, he tried to arrange a private meeting between Gambetta and Marshal MacMahon.

to the full his capacity for lobby intrigues and for managing men. His *mot d'ordre* was to lay aside differences and to concentrate upon securing a definite Republic. Some months after his return, Mme Adam wrote :

> Gradually influence is being transferred to our party : Louis Blanc and the Extreme Left are more and more playing the parts of great Elysian shades. . . . The young men, who follow Gambetta, want to become useful and practical. They desire a Government appropriate to our democratic conditions without dogmatism. . . . A serious element of support for the Radical Gambettists is that of the leaders of commerce and industry at Paris, who during the Siege learned to hate the phrase-making of Favre and Trochu, and to respect Gambetta. These men want a Republic that should organise social conditions, but at first be content with little more than applying progressive reforms after methodical study.[1]

In order to prepare his group for the responsibilities of office, he started in November (1871) the journal entitled *La République Française*. It had its headquarters at the Chaussé d'Antin, the street in which Mirabeau died. His friends took over the various branches of the work — for example, Freycinet wrote on Public Works, and Paul Bert on Education : Gambetta regarded himself less as a journalist than as a Prime Minister directing his " shadow Cabinet ". Most evenings he would sit there till midnight smoking incessantly, revising the front page, describing the sitting of the Assembly — " an indescribable centre of force ".[2] The title " République Radicale " had been suggested, but rejected as likely to alarm the Moderates. The tone of the paper was often uncertain and inconsistent : " On the first page it would preach moderation : on the third it would give notoriety to some victims of the Commune ".[3] But it was not so much to settle points of policy that Gambetta used the organisation of the paper :

---

[1] In other words they discovered to their great relief that Gambetta had not a glimmering of sympathy with Socialism (*Mes angoisses*, p. 267).
[2] Deschanel, pp. 152-3.   [3] Pessard, ii. 257.

he wished to teach practical administration to men, who often had no experience of it at all. The office resembled a G.H.Q. It had its bureaux, its dossiers, its cards, its clerks, its provincial correspondents — all the apparatus of a Government Department.

If Gambetta did his best to discourage differences in open debate, he could hardly suppress them in private conversations ; and in the diaries of Mme Adam we can trace the beginning of divergencies, which were to break out later in the party.

We are so used to a state of political life, in which the main questions are social or diplomatic, the advanced parties taking an international position on both, that it is rather hard to throw our minds back to the Assembly of 1871, where the main question was one of political power and constitutional organisation, and where the Left was militarist and nationalist on foreign questions, and con-servative on social questions with no very great differences on either from their opponents on the Right. There have been few Parliaments, in which there was so much agree-ment, even on general political principles ; hence " les fureurs Versailloises ". Men quarrel more violently over means than ends. In 1904 d'Haussonville wrote : " We [the Right] were as liberal as our opponents on the Left. . . . We had no systematic spirit of reaction against the French Revolution. We considered its social work and the greater part of its political work as definite and final. If we worked for a Restoration, it was because we saw in Monarchy the most certain means of assuring the necessary liberties in France and consecrating the legitimate consequences of the Revolution." [1]

In the Corps Législatif of the Empire, the Republican Opposition had posed as anti-militarist. Jules Simon had cried in 1867 : " If we cannot have an army without the military spirit, then I demand an army that shall not be

[1] Loth, L'Échec, p. 415.

an army ". Such outbursts no more prove him a Pacifist than the opposition of the Tories to William III's standing armies prove them to be Quakers. The Left criticised the declaration of war against Prussia, but after Sedan they adopted the war and made it their own. Gambetta and the Extreme Left had voted for its continuance : the Moderate Left had voted for peace : the new members elected in July had voted neither way. But all were agreed that the Army must be reorganised on the basis of Conscription, and that then France must wait her opportunity for revenge. Few of them would have agreed with Renan at the famous dinner-party on September 6th, 1870. Renan had been developing his favourite thesis of the superiority of the German people. Berthelot had said : " It is all up with us, and nothing is left save to bring up a generation to avenge us ". " No, no," cried Renan who had got up all red in the face, " not revenge ! Let France perish, let our country perish : there is something higher than our country — there is Duty, Reason." " No, no," they all shouted at him, " there is nothing higher than one's country ! " " No ! " yelled Saint-Victor, still louder and quite angry, " do not let us be aesthetes : don't let us go in for Byzantine philosophy." Renan " got up and walked round the table somewhat unsteadily, waving his short arms in the air, quoting Scriptural passages very loudly, and saying that they contain everything ".[1] Gambetta at this time still retained his bellicose patriotism : he even suspected Thiers of being too cautious. On September 4th, 1874, he wrote to Mme Adam : " The memory of this sad and tragic anniversary always puts my mind into mourning ".[2] Like so many Frenchmen he adored the Army. A spectator describes how in the Assembly generals and officers pressed round him like courtiers.

There were many military deputies on the Left of the Assembly — Billot, who had been Chief of Staff to Bour-

---

[1] De Goncourts (Nelson edition), pp. 102-3. [2] De Roux, p. 63.

baki, and " who could not make a speech without an entirely unnecessary profession of Republican faith " ; [1] General Chareton, who had " picked up his Republican ideas at the Polytechnic school " ; [2] Colonel Langlois, who had been wounded at Bezenval, gesticulating amid the stormiest scenes of the Assembly (Mme Adam says, " he made one forget his best qualities by his continual bawling ") ; [3] General Pellissier, who defended Garibaldi at the tribune ; Tamisier, an artillery officer, who had been a representative in 1848, and Commandant of the Seine National Guard in 1870 ; Denfert-Rochereau, defender of Belfort, and president of the Union Républicaine, who " in an incoherent speech defended voluntary obedience in the Army ".[4]

If the Left were not Pacifist, neither were they Socialist. Even the leaders of the Commune were not all Socialists : Delescluze always objected to " theories, which are utterly opposed to the national spirit ", and put on a frock-coat and tall hat to be killed in at the barricades. The Blanquists wished for the gradual abolition of property, but not till Universal Suffrage had been " educated ". Marxism had not yet become the Gospel of the working-classes. In the Assembly there were a few old-fashioned theorists — Godin demanded State assignats ; Esquiros had published a *Gospel for the People* in 1840 ; Greppo had supported Proudhon's famous aphorism, " Property is theft ", but " he only wished for peaceful reforms by common agreement ".[5] The most interesting of these deputies was Tolain, who was himself a worker in bronze, and could be seen every morning doing his own shopping, smoking his pipe and " pressing a lobster tenderly to his heart ".[6] The Assembly asked him to explain what he meant by Socialism, and courteously gave him a whole sitting : his definition was " uniform conditions of work

[1] Claveau, p. 341. [2] Du Barail, iii. 398. [3] *Mes angoisses*, p. 271.
[4] Claveau, p. 345. [5] *Soir de ma journée*, p. 19. [6] Bosq, p. 134.

for everyone " ; he was listened to with polite incredulity. Even in his own party he found more sympathy than support ; Adam said to him : " There is one thing which cannot be changed, and which is against the realisation of your ideas, and that is a man's own character ".[1]

Gambetta himself was not at all interested in social theories ; as he said later in a famous phrase, " There is no social problem, only social problems ". He was, above all, anxious to gain for the Republic the confidence of business men and peasants. Few things were more marked in the future than the disappointment of the working-classes with Opportunism.[2]

What of religious questions — at all times one of the great resources of the Left ? [3] In the Assembly Paul Bert represented the pure anticlerical spirit : he was a doctor, who had made important studies in fermentation. During the war he was Gambetta's Préfet at Lille. He loved to describe clericalism as worse than the phylloxera, which was ravaging the vines of the South, and to attack Catholic schools. Many of Gambetta's friends protested. Lepère declared that " for Bert Science had only been a stage : he now dreamed of having all the education of France in his hands ". Spuller, who was a Deist, also opposed his influence.[4] Mme Adam begged Gambetta not to " force us to swallow these scientific-political theories ". Gambetta

---

[1] *Mes angoisses*, p. 270.

[2] Zévaès, speaking of the year 1885, says : " The working classes were discontented. The Republic, which they had been the first to support, was for them synonmyous with social progress and emancipation. But what reforms had been accomplished ? The laws protecting the workman were in so elementary a state that in practice they could be considered as non-existent. The average day's work was 11-12 hours in workshops and factories, in which there were no regulations as to safety or health. The average salary was for workmen 5-6 francs at Paris, 3 fr. 50 c. in the provinces : for women 2-3 fr. at Paris, 1 fr. 64-2 fr. 15 c. in the provinces. The miner was paid on an average 3 fr. 79 c. a day of 10 hours, and there were no precautions against accidents " (*Au temps du Boulangisme*, pp. 14-15).

[3] A journalist wrote : " Apart from anticlericalism, the Republic (*i.e.* the party) suffers from want of raw material". (Halévy, *La Fin des notables*, p. 127.)

[4] *Nos amitiés*, p. 129.

himself was somewhat impatient of these disputes : he allowed himself in some of his public speeches to use violent language about religious education. On the other hand Leonie kept him in some sort of touch with Catholic circles, and he never brought forward any educational scheme.[1] He was convinced that it was no part of the duty of Opposition at the moment to propose constructive legislation.

As to religious convictions, while on the Right Catholicism was almost *de rigueur*, the aspect of the Left was multi-coloured. There were some practising Catholics, notably Arnaud de l'Ariège, " with a head like a Crusader ", who tried to reconcile the Pope and democracy in his book *The Revolution and the Church.* He wrote : " Were it not for the servile and tyrannical complicity of the priests, all other kinds of despotism would be impossible ". He wrote pamphlets urging the Pope to abandon Rome, and quarrelled with his Republican wife because he insisted on their son receiving his first communion.[2] There was his father-in-law, Victor Guichard, " the last of the Gallicans ", " tall, bent and white-headed ", " un vieux Voltaire, ennemi de la prêtraille ".[3] There was Étienne Lamy, who had been a student with the Dominicans at Sorrèze, an earnest and laborious deputy, who worked at a report on the Navy for four years before he published it.[4]

Then there were Protestants, like Leroyer, a Lyons avocat, who was destined to cause a parliamentary crisis by a word of two syllables, Pressensé, the pastor-deputy for Paris, Henri Martin, who wrote a history of France in fifteen volumes and ordered that he should be buried in a Protestant cemetery, and Eugène Pelletan, who spoke in so deep a voice that Thiers said to him, " In a fountain the

---

[1] Jules Simon introduced a Bill for compulsory education, but it was altered by a Committee of the Right and then dropped (see de Roux, p. 345).

[2] De Roux, p. 25.   [3] Claveau, p. 311.   [4] Bosq, p. 133.

tap is as important as the water supply : take care of your tap ".[1]

The old Republicans of the Hugo school had been Deists, always coupling God and Freedom. The young generation were scientific Positivists. Clemenceau wrote in a thesis of 1865 : " We shall never know anything about first causes for the very simple reason that there are none ".[2] Gambetta and Ferry learned their Positivism from Littré who, though he never spoke, was a remarkable influence in the Assembly. He had been a pupil of Comte, and had written on Medicine, but his great work was the famous *Dictionary of the French Language.* Mme Adam, who met him under the Second Empire, " worshipped his character but disliked his extreme views ; he seemed to her to take the mystery out of life ".[3] He said of her — shrewdly and truly : " We shall see this pagan turn Christian ".[4]

Many of the younger members of the Left were also becoming Freemasons : Gambetta had been initiated during the 1869 elections at Marseilles ; Jules Simon, Arago, Ferry and Littré were all admitted within the next few years. At that time, although the rites still made

---

[1] *Bosq,* p. 97. Under the Empire the Jeromists (the democratic section of the Bonapartists, who rallied round the Emperor's cousin) were politically, if not denominationally, Protestant. One of their journalists wrote : " The mission of Prussia is to make Europe Protestant, just as the mission of Italy is to destroy the Papacy " (de Roux, p. 26). Renan, who belonged to the same circle, said : " Catholicism stultifies the individual : education by Jesuits or lay brethren arrests and restricts all power to achieve, while Protestantism develops it " (de Goncourts' *Journal* (Nelson edition), p. 100).

[2] De Roux, *Origines de la 3e République,* p. 22.

[3] Winifred Stephens, *Mme Adam,* pp. 68-9.

[4] Six months before his death, there arose in his soul " a deep persistent sorrow for his past sins ". He withdrew from his Positivist friends, and sent for the Abbé Huvelin and talked long with him about it. He said : " What I feel is not what you call contrition, it is just simply heart-break ". He had not time to arrive at explicit Christianity, for he worked according to his slow and minute methods. He already believed in the existence of the invisible world and the survival of the soul. On the day of his death, he was baptized at his own desire and in his daughter's presence. He was buried with the usual Catholic rites (Statement by von Hügel quoted in the Introduction to Huvelin : *Some Spiritual Guides of the 17th Century,* pp. xv-xix).

mention of God and a future existence, members were allowed to believe what they liked : in 1877 the Grand Orient suppressed all mention of the Great Architect of the Universe, and the English Lodges seceded.[1]

A passage in Mme Adam's diary [2] brings out the religious condition of the Left : " We liked Arnaud de l'Ariège, only we put in a caution against his clericalism. Among us, only Spuller was a Deist, and Arnaud the only Christian. He (Arnaud) smiled at our negations : Spuller attacked them, half laughing, half serious, 'regretting more and more, the better he knew us, his small hopes of meeting us again in another world ' ; Peyrat, Paul Bert and Gambetta were always at him, and I joined them, to the chagrin of Adam, who is himself a Deist, and hopes (like Spuller) ' to meet me in the hereafter '." [3]

When Gambetta took his seat at Versailles, a *petit frisson* ran along the galleries, and the deputies pointed him out one to another. At the Republican Bordeaux he had seemed quite in his element : at the elegant Versailles he seemed like a monster let loose.[4] It is true he looked wild enough with his characteristic gesture of throwing his head back like a lion. His personal appearance is familiar from photographs ; the general impression he produced may perhaps be suggested by combining various appreciations — first that of a personal friend : " His face was strikingly sympathetic . . . his voice warm and sweet, and his pale face was lit up by the wonderful smile that won all hearts ".[5] Next that of an American lady who had married a French

---

[1] De Roux, p. 29.   [2] *Mes angoisses*, p. 209.

[3] The following passage from the debate of January 9th, 1873, on Higher Education illustrates the same point. Dupanloup, who had the habit of addressing his opponents as though he were taking a Mission service, said to the Left : " Yes, you have this faith within yourselves, whoever you are ; when you violate it, when you deny God, when you make yourselves the independent masters of your consciences and your lives, there is left only disorder and confusion in life and conduct (*Loud applause on various benches. Interruption from some benches on the Left.*). Gentlemen, you may contradict me on all these points (*Several members of the Left* : ' No, no.' ' We agree.')."

[4] Pessard, ii. 134.   [5] Freycinet, p. 113.

statesman : " His appearance was against him : he was dark and heavy-looking with an enormous head. He was not a ladies' man, though he had some devoted women friends ".[1] To a political journalist he recalled Danton : " The brave lips, the large open hands, the one eye always fixed, the sculptural vigour of neck and arm " [2] A social satirist thought he had " the fat and oily face of a money-changer " [3] A bitter political enemy describes him as a " subtle adventurer with a gilded tongue, cunning as a Greek, loved by women, expert in cruel acts of malice . . . one eye shining, while the other is cold, an evil-smelling cigar in his mouth, his coat stained and his nails dirty, more jovial than perverse, without traditions or ancestors ".[4]

Whatever doubts were felt about his face or clothes, no one could long doubt his immense power of attraction. He started with the feeling of the House dead against him : before he had returned to Versailles, the very mention of his name had been the signal for a storm. On June 13th (on a debate upon a proposed Commission to enquire into the acts of the Tours delegation), Lepère called him " the man who carried from Paris to the provinces the very soul of France . . . the Carnot of the national honour ". The Right retorted : " All Gambetta's secretaries were in the Commune ". " He has ruined France." " You are defending a régime of tyranny and terror." [5] When he came to the Assembly, it was the fashion to regard him as a complete outsider, " rolling on his bench, as though he were at a public-house, fat, red, laughing, and careless ".[6] There was almost a crisis, when Thiers shook hands with him. Yet before the end of the Assembly he was seen walking about,

---

[1] Mme Waddington, *My first Years as a Frenchwoman*, p. 22.
[2] Kel-Kun (*Nouveaux Portraits*, p. 15).
[3] De Goncourts (t. 5, p. 93), 10/9/73.
[4] Bernanos, *Grande Peur des bien pensants*, p. 109.
[5] *Annales*, t. 3, pp. 361-2. A speaker was actually interrupted by the majority for speaking of the " honourable M. Gambetta ".
[6] Fidus, *Journal*, 1/3/72.

arm in arm with Legitimist Marquises. He won over opponents by his *bonhomie* and ease of manner. De Castellane (an elegant of the Right, who had called Gambetta " a talented lawyer who had ended up by being a tenth-rate dictator ")[1] narrates how the " dictator of Tours, who had a liking for me, sat down on my bench in a sprightly mood, and taking a teetotum from his pocket, marked on each side Republic and Monarchy, turned it round, and when it stopped ten times at the word ' Republic ', walked away splitting with laughter ".[2]

But he had a hard time at first — especially at the tribune. Continual and contemptuous interruptions broke the thread of his discourses. The secretaries' table was just under the tribune, and Bethmont leant forward to encourage the orator : Gambetta replied with a glance at the Right of the Assembly, " I should like to see that bench of Irishmen fly into the air ".[3] After the debate, de Meaux expressed his surprise and disappointment to Laurier, who replied : " What do you expect ? There is a degree of hostility, which no orator, however great, can overcome. Besides, when one has been treated like a god for six months, it is not pleasant to have to change." [4] The time was to come, when he would dominate the clamour of the majority, and a still stranger time when, at one of the most confused and exasperating moments which marked the last year of the Assembly, Ministers trembled on their benches below him.

It has been said that what the National Assembly lacked most was men of action. Many of its leaders had worked out a theory of politics to its last refinements : they had discussed and demonstrated to the applause of salons and lecture-rooms. They had hardly ever addressed a crowd, and they were startled by this irruption of a man

---

[1] " Twentieth-rate " in the original, but in English we do not seem to go beyond ten (*Annales*, t. 3, p. 392).
[2] Castellane, *Men and Things of my Time*, p. 125.
[3] De Meaux, pp. 243-4.   [4] *Ibid.*

of the people, who had no use for their airs and graces, and little respect for their speculation. They might sneer at him, and call him a drunkard, but they could not deny that here was somebody who knew how to play the game of politics in a democracy.

He would mount the tribune and address the House in his deep voice,[1] his two fists grasping the marble, with his head thrown back, and sweeping gestures. The style of his speeches was not always precise or correct, the constant repetition of words, the accumulation of synonyms, the successive refinements of a phrase, which was always growing and never-ending, " vast showers of great abstract nouns — all carried off by rapidity of movement ".[2] He was at his best before some vast audience in the sun-swept Midi : it took him some time to find a style, which would suit the Assembly, but he achieved it. If he did not learn subtlety or elegance, he did something to catch the tone of the most gentlemanly of all French Parliaments.[3]

---

[1] " He relied greatly on the sonorous quality of his voice, from which he obtained striking effects " (Martet, *Clemenceau* (English translation), p. 280).

[2] Faguet, *Propos littéraires* (2), p. 341.

[3] Which did not prevent its being a stormy Parliament. Members were allowed much licence in personal attack, provided they made handsome explanations at the debate on the *procès-verbal* the next morning. Ludovic Halévy records (in February 1881) that Gambetta " spoke with real enthusiasm of the reactionary Assembly of 1871. He spoke of it as an artist might speak : it was a pleasure to make speeches before such a Chamber ; the instrument responded. The National Assembly was full of intelligent and cultivated persons belonging to all parties. It is better to have to do with intelligent enemies than with stupid friends. It was the orator speaking : he recalled his past battles. It was a pleasure to convince and subdue an Assembly that resisted him. It was like mounting a difficult horse, that was strong and generous. The actual Chamber [of 1881], though it was under his thumb, seemed to him empty and stupid " (*Vie de Gambetta*, Gheusi, pp. 254-5). Camille Barère, his secretary, says of his speaking : " I asked him once whether he felt nervous. ' Yes ', he answered, ' when I catch the Speaker's eye [*demande la parole*]. Then I feel a shudder from my head to my feet. It is a bad moment, but, as soon as I am at the tribune, I feel myself at once in full possession of my resources.' He began heavily like a great bird who has difficulty in spreading his wings. Then suddenly he was on the wing and soared to the heights of eloquence. As far as I know, he never prepared his speeches " (*ibid.* p. 314).

His first intervention at Versailles was on July 22nd, during a debate on the independence of the Papacy, and (without his intending it) it was sensational enough.

Several Bishops during the July elections had signed petitions asking the Government to take diplomatic steps with the object of defending the spiritual freedom of Pius IX, menaced by the entry of Victor Emmanuel into Rome. At Mme Adam's salon all was fury and indignation. " It is an intolerable insult ! " cried Gambetta. " These people are out of their mind ", said Challemel-Lacour ; " when we could not keep Alsace and Lorraine, we are to make war to get back the Pope's States for him." Spuller added, " It will throw Italy into the arms of Germany ". Gambetta then said, " I will make my entry on this question ".[1]

Thiers shared their views on the imprudence of the petitions. " These people are absurd ", he said ; " they have no feelings as Frenchmen. They are like the monks of the Ligue." But he himself was an old defender of the temporal power of the Papacy. " St. Peter has touched my heart ", he would say with a smile. " I am the only person in Europe who defends the clergy " ; and he would recall how in 1850 he had tried to place in their hands the teaching of all the children in France.[2] Pajot, a municipal councillor of Lille and a member of the Extreme Right, was the first reporter in favour of the petitions : he quoted several passages from Thiers, such as the maxim that " when the Pope descends from his throne, he will be no longer free ". He reminded the House how, during the war, Pius IX had intervened in favour of France, " while the Kingdom of Italy, which has cost us so much money, so much blood and such cruel defeats, has so far repaid us by treachery and desertion ". No one wished for war, but " between an armed struggle, which is not permitted us, and an inert resignation, there must be some other solution possible ". Tarteron, a Toulon avocat, spoke in favour of

[1] *Mes angoisses*, p. 182.   [2] Pessard, ii. 139-140.

the other petitions : he was remarkably sane and moderate when left to himself, but " he could not refuse to follow his friends on the Extreme Right ".[1] He ended with a motion that the petitions be referred to the Minister of Foreign Affairs. Thiers now intervened in a dexterous speech. He repudiated none of his past opinions ; he had never been in favour of Italian unity, " not only because one should not voluntarily create at one's doors a new great power, but also because I was certain that the unity of Italy would favour the unity of Germany, both by example and by material help. Again, it was impossible to create the unity of Italy without destroying the temporal power of the Holy See. In my opinion no Government should commit the fault of offending the religious consciences of its people." However, regrets were now too late : a united Italy existed, and had already friends at all the Courts of Europe — in Russia because of the Pope's sympathy with Poland, in England, " not at all displeased to see a new fleet in the Mediterranean, which might become a rival to us ", in Austria resolved, as they could not recover Italy, to live on good terms with her — and yet the petitioners demanded of him that France, alone of the Powers, should arouse the suspicions of this new power, which might play an important part in the future. He appealed to the majority to put themselves in his place. What would they do ? Patriotism and prudence alike demanded a policy of peace. He had treated the Pope with every respect and had offered him a refuge in France, if he felt inclined to leave Rome. He was ready to join with the other Catholic Powers in demanding the spiritual independence of the Papacy, so important to a nation like France, which by its Concordat made the assent of the Pope necessary for the appointment of its Bishops : that was all he could promise.

When the long applause that followed Thiers' speech

[1] Lacombe, ii. 85.

had subsided, the Bishop of Orleans made his first appearance at the tribune. He began by expressing his gratitude for Thiers' sympathetic reference to the Papacy,[1] but the combative Bishop was never happy, unless he was attacking something or somebody. His red cheek glowed, his long hair strayed about his cheeks, as in envenomed phrases he hurled his scorn at Italy and her King : " Ungrateful Italy waited so courageously for the hour of our disasters, and seized the moment to throw itself bravely on its prey ". He spoke sarcastically of the " gentlemanly King." He cried : " It is impossible that eighteen centuries of greatness and benefit should end by making the successor of St. Peter into the private Chaplain of Victor Emmanuel. . . . Neither the great Emperors, Constantine or Theodosius . . . nor the proudest conquerors, Attila or Genseric, have stayed in Rome. They pillaged it and fled, and this poor Victor Emmanuel . . . has hardly dared to be seen there. He arrived in the morning and went away the same evening. He felt he could not make his bed there." It was an eloquent speech, and roused the Catholic majority to enthusiasm : the Bishop took the opportunity to make some general exhortations. He rebuked the people, who said the Bishops wanted war. He rebuked the people who, at the last elections, had spread reports that the Catholics wished to revive " dîmes, corvées et billets de confession ", adding in one of his flaming phrases : " Let me tell you there is not much difference between those who calumniate priests and those who massacre hostages ". He rebuked those, who thought the problem of the Papacy was " a foreign question ". No question was more relevant to the work of the Assembly than the restoration of Religion. " Without God there is no liberty, no morality, no equality, no society."

[1] He was not really satisfied. M. Delpit, who visited him next day, writes : " The Bishop was sad and troubled as to Thiers' intentions . . . he regarded him as shrunk both physically and morally. He thought his speech of yesterday very feeble " (quoted Denis, p. 40).

Thiers intervened again to remind the Assembly that he could promise nothing, which was against the political security of his country. When Belcastel (Extreme Right) ascended the tribune, the members of the Right, afraid that the extreme Catholics would compromise their cause, forced him to come down without opening his lips.[1]

It looked as if the debate were finished, and that the Right and the Left would be forced, for very different reasons, to leave the matter in Thiers' hands. Marcel Barthe, a member of the Left Centre, proposed an order of the day which, without referring the petitions to the Minister of Foreign Affairs, simply said : " The National Assembly, confident in the patriotism and prudence of the Chief of the Executive of the Republic, passes to the order of the day ".

Thiers, without " advising or demanding anything ", suggested that the proposed motion " corresponds to your feelings and the reality of things ". It was at this point that, amid general excitement and cries of " Écoutez ! " Gambetta intervened. In a strong and calm voice he spoke a few words to the effect that he and his friends accepted the order of the day, which Thiers wished for. If he had proposed that the Vatican should be burned down, he could not have caused a greater sensation. A deputy of the Right said to a friend in the gallery : " It is as clear as day : Gambetta and Thiers have a secret agreement. Is not the decoration of General Faidherbe as Grand Officer of the Legion of Honour (after he had dedicated his book on the war to Gambetta) a striking proof of the agreement ? " The tumult in the Assembly was continuous. Keller, ex-deputy for Alsace Lorraine, now member for Belfort, declared that the moment Gambetta accepted an order of the day it must become unacceptable to the Right. Thiers replied firmly that to abandon a

[1] The Baron Chaurand called out : " In the name of the Holy Father, come down from the tribune, M. de Belcastel ! "

motion, simply because it was accepted by another party, was " to use the language of Discord itself, for, if Discord had a voice, it would use just such words ". As to Gambetta's support, " I do not seek for an agreement with anyone, but, when it happens, I do not run away from it ".

The confusion was redoubled by the fact that amid the excitement it was difficult to distinguish the different motions that were made. Finally Gambetta pointed out that the motion accepted by Thiers contained no reference to the Minister of Foreign Affairs. Dupanloup retorted that, in that case, they would insist on the words being put in. Thiers, forced to give way by the excitement of the majority, said : " I accept the reference to the Minister as interpreted by the words ' patriotism and prudence ' ". Gambetta refused to accept the reference. He was so violently interrupted that he cried : " Your interruptions remain anonymous. If you would be good enough to make interruptions individually, your names will be in the Official Report tomorrow, and you will find a reply — my own personal reply if necessary " (" *Order !* " *from the Right* : DE JUIGNÉ : " *It is a challenge to the Assembly !* ").

Finally, the motion of Barthe was lost by 394 votes to 257, and a form of words, combining reference to the Minister with confidence in Thiers, was carried by 431 to 82.[1] Though Thiers had ended by giving way to them, the Right were full of suspicions, and whispered darkly that Thiers had chosen Gambetta as " his Dauphin ". But to understand more fully the relations between Thiers and the Right it is necessary to take a comprehensive survey of his policy and administration from June to September.

---

[1] *Annales*, t. 4, pp. 243-63 ; Claveau, pp. 189-191 ; Pessard, ii. 141-7 ; *Mes angoisses*, pp. 183-5.

CHAPTER IV

THIERS, THE GOVERNMENT AND THE ASSEMBLY

(a) THIERS AND HIS MINISTERS

THE temporary Constitution, which the National Assembly had patched up at Bordeaux, was a strange affair. On paper it looked ultra-parliamentary, for the head of the State was appointed by the Assembly and could at any moment be dismissed by them. But Constitutions are made by persons, and not persons by Constitutions. Under the next President, MacMahon, who regarded himself as a kind of irresponsible constitutional monarch, and left to Ministers a free hand in Parliament, never appearing or taking part in its debates, the Assembly was able to exercise its sovereignty. But Thiers was not going to let himself be trapped into a position like that which he had tried to impose on Louis-Philippe —" Le roi règne et ne gouverne pas " ; he was the last person in the world to become a figure-head. His love of power and his passion for administration were far too strong for that. With slight exceptions he governed the country himself. He appointed Ministers, who were docile and obedient : [1] he was ready to sacrifice one or two of them, when the Royalist demands became too emphatic to be resisted, but their replacement made little difference to general policy. The Assembly had no real way of influencing the Government except by dismissing Thiers, and that they did not dare to do ; for

---

[1] " Gambetta openly mocks at Thiers' Republic and his inferior Ministers " (Mme Adam, *Mes angoisses*, p. 234). Jules Favre said to Ferry : " His Cabinet, composed of the very cream of eloquence, has to be rationed as regards speeches " (Malo, p. 554).

he represented the compromise agreed upon at Bordeaux, and the majority had not at the moment either a successor or an alternative policy available. Thiers was able to control them by one of the most seductive gifts of eloquence, that ever held a deliberative assembly captive. But still more effective than his lucid exposition was the threat of resignation : he had only to fold up his papers and leave the tribune with a frown to convert a hostile audience into a crowd of trembling suppliants.

The Constitution, which the Assembly found so embarrassing, seemed to Thiers almost perfection.[1] It gave him work as full and as varied as perhaps fell to the lot of any modern statesman.

He rose every morning at four o'clock, and paid a visit to his stables. He was not a strikingly competent equestrian, but an assiduous care for his horses tickled his semimilitary pretensions of being a " Napoleon in mufti ". At five o'clock he returned to his study, where his Secretary-General was waiting for him : this was the distinguished savant, Jules Barthélemy-Saint-Hilaire. Tall and ascetic-looking, with the stoop of the scholar, he had first of all (in 1840) devoted himself to Cousin, when he was Minister of Education, and now had become henchman to Thiers, working twenty hours a day, without a penny of remuneration. Thiers said of him, " He keeps me straight : I never knew an idea of mine, that was not the better for having passed through his head ". St-Hilaire was simple and austere in his tastes. " They tell me ", he said of Rochefort, " that he is too fond of gambling, suppers and women. All that is waste of time : a sojourn in New Caledonia will do him good." Though not a Christian, he

---

[1] It is true, that in a moment of petulance, he wrote to Guizot that he would have preferred the Constitution of 1848 with its President elected by the people and independent of the Assembly (Bouniols, p. 98). But he would have missed the right of appearing at the tribune and charming a suspicious audience. A dumb Thiers is unthinkable. He used to say, " A King has his Constitution : a General his victories : I have only my voice " (Bosq, p. 116).

accepted the Cartesian proof of God's existence, and the
Stoic morality ; though he had spent his life translating
Aristotle, he preferred Plato.[1] He was a sincere Republican,
and is said to have influenced Thiers in that direction. He
held " that for the last hundred years France had been
governed in defiance of common sense ".

Every morning, after he had left Thiers' study, he
used to interview the journalists in his own room from
seven to ten : a shirt hung over the principal chair, and a
portmanteau stood in the corner. He used to draw attention to it with a smile : " It is packed, messieurs : they
can turn us out of office, whenever they like ". " His first
word to all reporters ", says one of them, " was, ' I don't
know anything ', and that was his last word too." [2]

At six o'clock, when Thiers had finished going through
his mail, private audiences began. It was at this time the
President saw the directors of the financial departments, the
chiefs of the administrative services, and Generals. " He
liked to know the business of his Ministers a little before
they did — an arrangement not always appreciated by
them." [3] He also interviewed police agents and informers,
for he never lost his taste for the political underworld.
While such people were waiting in the ante-room, St-
Hilaire would discreetly draw the journalists apart into
another room. Thiers said with a laugh, " It is by using
such rascals that one helps honest men ".[4]

At 11 A.M. the Council of Ministers met (every day but
Sunday), and sat for two hours. After *déjeuner* (at which
he usually had places for twenty guests) he received visitors
again, and, till his presence was required at the Assembly,
the staircases of the Prefecture were thronged with deputies,
ambassadors and maires. He was often kept at the Palace
by meetings of the Assembly and Committees till seven

---

[1] Acton, *Letters to Mary Gladstone*, p. 39.
[2] Bosq, pp. 121-6 ; de Marcère, *Assemblée nationale*, i. 29.
[3] Simon, *Gouv. de M. Thiers*, ii. p. 241.   [4] *Ibid.*

o'clock : then followed dinner and the evening receptions.
Thiers himself was severely dieted : his meal consisted of
soup, roast veal and sweetmeats with two glasses of Bordeaux ; he liked coffee, but it was bad for his nerves, and
Mme Thiers sternly warded it off. He was also fond of
eels, another forbidden luxury, which is said to have been
smuggled secretly into his study by his lifelong friend and
fellow historian, Mignet, now seventy-five years old to his
seventy-four.

As soon as he had finished his own meal, he skipped
round the table, asking if the food was good, talking politics
to a deputy, or painting to an artist, or strategy to a general.
If he received a telegram, he opened it saying, " The business of France before everything else ". After dinner he
sat in an armchair and took a doze ; Mme Thiers would
put her finger to her lips, and the guests would tiptoe into
the next room, till the evening reception began.[1]

The crowds that flocked to these parties were not
attracted by the quality of the refreshments : in fact many
of them on leaving were observed to slip into the cafés
of the Avenue de Paris.[2] They came to hear the best
conversation in France. Thiers was generally in the
highest spirits. Jules Simon says that he could not have
got through the business without his " native gaiety ".
Mme Thiers was sleepy and bourgeoise ; Mlle Dosne, the
sister-in-law, was more alert,[3] but it was the incomparable
master of the house that men came to hear — his anecdotes,
his explanations of everything under the sun, his sparkling

---

[1] Bosq, pp. 117-18.

[2] After a dinner given by Thiers to celebrate a rather precarious arrangement between Thiers and the Right, a deputy said to de Meaux, " Our new
majority and the menu are of about equal value " (de Meaux, p. 90).

[3] Waddington's American wife says : " I believe Mme Thiers and Mlle
Dosne were very intelligent, but I cannot truthfully say that they had any
charm of manner. They never looked pleased to see anybody, and they had
comfortable naps in the armchairs after dinner " (*First Years*, p. 30). Mme
Thiers' " fashions in dress were considered as a protest against the corruptions
of the Empire " (Malo, p. 525).

indiscretions, his endless jokes, though members of the
Right sometimes thought the latter in somewhat doubtful
taste.[1]

When Thiers retired to bed, he had one thorn to his
pillow : he wanted to live at Paris. Now and then he paid
a flying visit to the Élysée, but the Assembly was always
restless during his absence. When he attended a reception
at the capital, a carriage waited at the door to bring him
back to Versailles before midnight. Even at Versailles he
would have liked rooms at the Palace, but deputies objected to his being too near quite as much as to his being
too far off, and so he returned mournfully to the Palace
of the Présidence — " Palais de pénitence " as he ruefully
called it. He sometimes enjoyed a malicious revenge at
the expense of the Right. One evening, at an official dinner,
a Royalist General noticed a fine lily sweeping to the right
and the left. Was it meant (someone asked) as an emblem
of the dissensions between Orleanists and Legitimists ?
" What ! " Thiers answered with a smile, " an interpellation about a flower ! You must ask my gardener : he is
a clever fellow, but rather mischievous." [2]

Thiers had included in his original Ministry three " men
of September ". The Right had grumbled, but consoled
themselves with the reflection that at least some of those,
whom they regarded as responsible for the disastrous
Peace, would be associated with its signature. But, now
the Treaty was signed, schemes were laid for getting them
out of office one after the other — " eating the artichoke,
leaf by leaf " as it was jocularly called.

The first victim was Ernest Picard : personally he was
popular for his wit and high spirits, but on the eve of important elections a Minister of the Interior becomes an
important person, and hitherto his choice of Préfets had

---

[1] Larcy said : " Thiers has adopted a Voltairean tone not natural to him.
At meetings of the Council he allows himself irreligious pleasantries and dirty
stories which I never heard from him before " (Falloux, ii. 509).

[2] Dreyfus, *La République de M. Thiers*, p. 68.

been (in de Broglie's words) " detestable ", that is, democratic. On May 30th, General Ducrot violently attacked
him for the appointment of a Préfet for Nievre, whose name
had figured on the electoral lists of February side by side
with two Communards. A Royalist called out, " The best
way to restore order is for the men of September to retire ".
Picard gave as good as he got : where (he asked) were his
critics on the 4th of September ? They were everywhere in
flight, disclaiming all responsibility and leaving the burden
of national defence on the shoulders of those they were now
denouncing.[1]

But in the end, at a private interview with Casimir-
Perier and de Broglie, who appealed to him to work more
cordially with the majority, Thiers promised them a new
Minister of the Interior : [2] an excuse was found in a violent
dispute with Dufaure, the Minister of Justice, whom Picard
accused of not restraining the Press from abusive attacks
upon him.[3] Picard himself was not reluctant to go, as he
objected to the " transportation *en masse* " of the Communards.[4] He resigned on May 31st, and Thiers at once
nominated him Governor of the Bank, " not as a favour but
as an act of justice and good administration ".[5] Picard,
however, refused, and accepted the post of Ambassador
at Brussels. Lambrecht, the Minister of Agriculture and
Commerce, took his place. He was a Legitimist, but his
nomination gave little satisfaction to the Right, who said
that Thiers regarded him as an oracle, because he always
echoed the opinions of the Chief of the Executive. His
place was filled by Victor Lefranc, a popular member of
the Left Centre, who inaugurated his new career by saying,
" Everyone knows that I know nothing about Agriculture
or Commerce ".[6] During the debate on the Princes, he had
accused Thiers of being an Orleanist, but as Minister he

[1] *Annales*, t. 3, pp. 182-90.
[2] *Memoirs of de Broglie (Revue*, 15/3/29), p. 378.
[3] Thiers, *Notes et souvenirs*, p. 152.   [4] Reclus, *Ernest Picard*, p. 303.
[5] *Ibid.* p. 311.   [6] Bosq, p. 49.

often displeased the Gambettists, who called him a tool of the Right.[1] The next " leaf " was the Minister for Foreign Affairs, Jules Favre. This time the resignation was due to matters of a private nature. An *avocat* named Laluyé, a former friend turned enemy, had been arrested during the Commune. He accused Favre of having put him in prison because of certain compromising facts in his possession, and he published documents, which proved that the Minister, while living with a married woman, had made a false statement in order to legitimate his children. Favre with great imprudence determined to prosecute him, and took as an opportunity of resignation the resolution of the Assembly, which had referred to him the Petition of the Bishops. Thiers wrote him a letter of regret : " I began, and hoped to finish with you the cruel task, which the country has imposed upon me for six months : I shall never cease to love a colleague, who has assisted me by his patriotic courage during the painful negotiations of Versailles ".[2] Favre was acquitted on the charge of wrongful arrest, but during the trial he admitted the truth of the charges against his private conduct. " I lost my head," he declared, " and, when the child was baptized, his father and mother were described as married ".[3] His political career was at an end, though he sometimes returned to speak at the tribune in an Assembly, where many members refused to speak to him.[4]

---

[1] He was always welcome at Mme Adam's, but he was often ragged there. On one occasion they drew up a list of his inconsistent votes. He replied in his inimitable accents, " The Centre is sheltered from all pressure from Right or Left, and is therefore independent " (*Nos amitiés*, p. 233).

[2] Bouniols, pp. 92-3.

[3] See *Empire libéral*, x. 511-13. Ollivier adds that Napoleon III, though he knew the facts, refused to allow his police to take action.

[4] He bore his destiny with a calm courage. " It is a real advantage ", he said, " to abate somewhat of the good opinion, which one is tempted to entertain of oneself. I should desire nothing, did I not occasionally fall to thinking that the unrelenting animosity, which does me honour, deprives me of the power to be useful " (de Coubertin, *Evolution of France*, p. 13). In spite of his fiery eloquence, his nature was sweet and yielding.

Thiers' choice of a successor for the Ministry of Foreign Affairs caused some surprise.   Charles de Rémusat was not a member of the Assembly, and did not become one during his term of office.[1] He was living in his Château de Lafitte, near the Pyrenees, when his son Paul (deputy for La Haute Garonne and Thiers' secretary during his European journey) fetched him to replace Jules Favre. He had been a typical member of the Orleanist aristocracy ; Minister of the Interior in 1840, he had proposed the return of Napoleon's ashes. He had studied philosophy and written on Abelard ; he had also specialised in English History (the fashion had been set by Guizot), and had published studies on Canning, Wesley and Bacon ; his *England in the Eighteenth Century* (1852) contains one of the few French lives of Burke. Thiers had the highest opinion of his " prodigious culture often subtle to profundity, his gentle and amiable mockery ",[2] and above all his ministerial docility.[3] Jules Simon says with gentle irony : " Thiers used to say, ' What a style Rémusat has ! It is important to have a real writer at the head of the Foreign Office ', which did not prevent him from covering his ministerial minutes with corrections." [4] Other people regarded him as an elegant sceptic " asking questions, but never answering them ".[5]

The replacement of a man of September by an Orleanist might have seemed a success for the Right, but they sus-

---

[1] The attempt to get him elected for Paris in 1873 was one of the immediate causes of Thiers' downfall.

[2] Thiers, *Notes et souvenirs*, p. 176.

[3] Mme Adam says that " though very independent, he has a remarkable faculty of assimilation " (*Nos amitiés*, p. 257).   When he was dying, in 1875, he said to Thiers : " At our age the parting cannot be for long ".   Thiers left the room brusquely, murmuring, " Poor Rémusat is wanting in tact " (Falloux, ii. 205).

[4] *Soir de ma journée*, p. 201.

[5] Joseph d'Arcay in *Notes on Thiers*, p. 219.   In 1872 he said to Lacombe : " You are lucky if you know what France will be like in four years.   I do not see so far ; I should wish to know what it will be like in four months " (*Journal*, i. 102).

pected he was only too ready to follow Thiers in any political evolution.[1] De Broglie says, "Rémusat has courted democracy, like a great nobleman who is blasé and, tired of the salon, goes off to win popularity in the servants' hall ".[2]

The third of the men of September in the Government was Jules Simon, the Minister of Education.

The University don has always played a larger part in Continental politics than with us. There were about twenty in the Assembly of 1871, and the generation after the Dreyfus case has been called " the Republic of Professors ". This is partly due to the French respect for polished oratory. The professor is generally an expert in extempore speaking ; he is less inclined than his English confrère to lean gracefully over his notes. At exciting moments of French history the lecture-rooms have been political storm-centres. It may also be due to the fact that in France Education has been so constantly the field for political and religious controversy. From the top to the bottom of the educational ladder there has been the never-ending contest for the soul of the child — University against Bishop, and village *instituteur* against *curé*.

The class of political professors was very favourably represented by Jules Simon. He hardly prepared his speeches, except for a card with three or four headings which he rarely consulted. He, too, had delivered his political lecture. A few days after the *coup d'état* he appeared at the desk and began : " Gentlemen, I am here Professor of Moral Philosophy. It is my duty to teach you, and to set you an example. The right has been publicly violated by the man, whose business it was to defend it ; tomorrow

---

[1] Before he was appointed Minister, he wrote to Simon : " I am as opposed to the Assembly as I am in sympathy with the Government " (*Gouv. de M. Thiers*, p. 247).

[2] *Revue des Deux Mondes*, 15/3/29. The Duke was so bitter that people suspected him of wishing the Foreign Office for himself. He says himself, " I knew Thiers too well to suppose that we could work in the same Council ".

France is called upon to say, by her vote, whether she approves of this violation of right or condemns it. If there should only be one voting-paper in the urns for condemnation, I claim it in advance : it will be mine." Then, when the tumult of applause had somewhat died down, he added : " I accept your cheers as a promise. If you ever allow yourselves to give way to shameful acts of weakness, remember this scene, and say to yourselves that you have broken your word." [1] Also he represented the anticlerical tradition ; he was a fervent Deist ; his republicanism dated from the days, when it was advanced to believe in God and not in Christianity. At the National Assembly he did not feel on easy terms with the Positivism of Gambetta and his group : later still in the history of the Third Republic he joined forces with the Catholic Right in opposing Secularism, and delivered one of his greatest speeches in the Senate against the proposal " to banish the Name of God from the schools ".

When he was thirteen, his Breton family was ruined financially : he was left with six francs in his pocket, and walked to Vannes, where he taught himself, and gave lessons at thirty sous an hour. He was the best of Victor Cousin's pupils at the Sorbonne, and became Professor of Philosophy at Caen in 1836, and afterwards at Versailles. After the famous lecture on the *coup d'état* he was suspended, and during the Empire interested himself in industrial problems, writing on " The Working Woman ". He accompanied the Comte de Paris on his trip to inspect conditions at Manchester, and (after a long struggle with his conscience) took the oath of allegiance to the Empire, which enabled him to join the Opposition in the Corps Législatif.

His appearance suggested a gentle sadness, as of a Marcus Aurelius brooding without bitterness over the sorrows of the world. He used to walk slowly to the

[1] *Soir de ma journée*, p. 14.

tribune, as though absorbed in some melancholy reverie ;
he climbed the steps with bent head and bowed shoulders.
His tired voice seemed as if it would never carry. Yet,
once there, he drew himself erect ; his voice filled the
Chamber ; he walked up and down, decorating his phrases
with the nervous gestures of his *loquacissimae manus* ; he
was insinuating, clever, unctuous, captivating, always
watching every corner of the Assembly, pricking up his
ears at every sound. He was fond of ingratiating caresses.
Dupanloup, who could not abide him, said, " He will be a
Cardinal before me " ; and in fact there was something in
him of the bland Italian Cardinals, who tried to win back
Luther by their charm, and arrest the Reformation by a
formula. When, as President of the Council in 1877, he
defended counsels of moderation against Gambetta's
war-cry, " Clericalism is the enemy ", his speech was so full
of sugared periods and balanced concessions, it swayed so
gently from Right to Left that deputies, who heard it, must
have felt almost sea-sick.

But he could strike other notes as well. In his attack
on Marshal MacMahon in 1873, " though the most temperate
of orators, he managed to produce all the effects of a
speaker of vehement eloquence. There was no violence of
language, yet, when it was over, every member of the
Right felt as if he had been beaten." [1] His physical
appearance also witnessed to a mixture of qualities ; his
nose stood for Jewish cleverness ; his large brow and
temples for philosophic depth ; his blue eye looked gentle ;
his lips smiled enigmatically, like " a threat disguised by
charm ".[2] Both his gentleness and his subtlety were mis-
leading. His gentleness concealed a will of iron, as was
shown in his contest with Gambetta at Bordeaux in 1871 ;
his subtlety concealed a simple and straightforward nature.
Someone called him " an honest Talleyrand ". When it

[1] King, *French Political Leaders*, p. 101.
[2] Kel-Kun, *Nouveaux Portraits*, p. 1.

was said to him that he could turn Thiers round his little finger, he replied, " I could do what I liked with him, if only I could persuade him that I am unscrupulous ".[1]

His political ideals were simple and a little academic — Free Trade, Free (and compulsory) Education, a free Press and a free Church (abolition of the Concordat) ; but he was patient and ready to wait. His life had not been passed like that of Hegel amid the distant sounds of the Jena cannon, but in the tumult of *coups d'état* and street riots ; his work on Stoicism had been burned by the Communards.

In happier times he might have been a great Minister, brave, honest and broad-minded : he was perhaps a little too honest and a little too subtle for the bitter politics of his day. His real place was neither in the Government nor the lobbies, but at the tribune of the Assembly. As Thiers' Minister of Education he alone of the men of September remained in office, till very near the end of the Presidency. This was partly due to Thiers' respect and affection for him, which was so strong that he was nicknamed " the beloved disciple ". One day, when Simon left a meeting of the Council to answer an interpellation at the Assembly, Thiers followed him down the stairs, saying, " Defend yourself well so as not to leave us ", and sent a note after him, " Defend yourself well, not so as to satisfy yourself or to relieve your own feelings, but so as to make sure not to leave us ".[2]

He also kept office by an ingenious manipulation of his three offices — Education, Cults and Fine Arts.[3] In Church affairs he generally accepted the episcopal candidates of Chigi, the narrow-minded Papal Nuncio, saying in his suave voice, " Is the man sound doctrinally ? " — secretly not at all sorry to widen the breach between Catholicism and modern thought. Meanwhile, as Minister of Education, he leaned towards Anticlericalism, favouring

---

[1] De Goncourts, t. 5, p. 78.   [2] Simon, *Gouv. de M. Thiers*, p. 244.
[3] " The True, the Good and the Beautiful ", as Batbie called them.

it in his appointments, and instilling it into the *Journal des Instituteurs*.[1]

The Bishop of Orleans was not deceived ; it was difficult to say which he disliked more — the concessions to Anti-clericalism or the concessions to Ultramontanism. He was tireless in his attacks. He wrote to Thiers : " If you separate from him, we can come to an agreement. If not, it is war." Simon bore no malice, and proposed Dupanloup as Archbishop of Paris : he refused, saying, " At my age and with my broken health it would be madness ".[2] Thiers answered, regretting the difficulties in the way of a choice, " that all enlightened Catholics would have ardently desired. But everything is difficult in the times, in which we live, and it is one long torture to be in power in the middle of parties, which are always at each other's throats."[3] Mgr. Guibert, the Archbishop of Tours, was appointed, and held the see till his death in 1886.

Jules Simon was an enthusiastic believer in the three-fold Republican formula — Education Free, Compulsory and Lay. In the last months of 1871 he introduced a Bill making education obligatory : the state of the Treasury did not allow of making it free of charge, and the only step towards *laïcité* was the withdrawal of the right, by which a Congregationist had only to present his " letter of obedience " to be accepted as a teacher. Thiers, who had more or less promised not to accept compulsory education, put his name to the Bill " after making a face ".[4] He knew

[1] Mme Adam says : " Going backwards and forwards to Versailles, we often meet in the train deputies of the Right, who sing the praises of Simon; never was a Minister so kind to his opponents : he refuses them nothing. We laugh up our sleeves ; actually he is laicising France as fast as he can ; he gives secret but enormous appointments to the anticlericals " (*Mes angoisses*, p. 298).

[2] Lagrange, *Vie de Dupanloup*, ii. 405.

[3] Bouniols, p. 83.

[4] *Soir de ma journée*, p. 218. He wrote to Dupanloup (9/11/71) : " There is no need for alarm. . . . Free Education is rejected, because the Budget does not allow it. Obligation does not imply the exclusion of any school " (Halévy, *Courier de M. Thiers*, p. 460). On July 2nd, Pius IX wrote to his " dilettissimo

the majority would not accept it.   A Commission, presided over by Dupanloup, rejected compulsion as " incompatible with liberty of conscience ", and amended the Bill so as to place public schools under a commission, in which the parents had a majority.   The National Assembly did not find time to discuss the subject.[1]

In educational administration Simon's chief task was to recreate the school.   Most of the teachers had enlisted in the war ; there was not a single pupil left in the Teachers' Training College, and the schools had been used as barracks and hospitals.   The personnel was singularly lax in discipline.   A professor boxed the ears of his rector in public ; another wrote in an article, " I am asked if I am for Paris or Versailles ; they are both of them assassins.   However, if I must choose, I should prefer Versailles." [2]

As Minister of Fine Arts he persuaded Thiers to sanction the Artists' School at Rome, and to decorate the famous actor, Régnier.[3]

The third ministerial change was not political in character.   General Le Flô, the War Minister, was an Orleanist. He had been through the African wars, and in 1848 was one of the famous *questeurs* of the Legislative Assembly, who were dragged from their beds by the police of the *coup d'état* (he fought the whole way from his bedroom to the front door) ; he had been Minister of War on September 4th, and had been retained by Thiers, but " though he would have commanded a division to perfection, as an administrator he was less useful ",[4] and in May 1871 he was sent as ambassador to St. Petersburg, where his military

figlio Adolphe Thiers " : " Vi prego di far tutto, che da voi puo dispendere, per rimettere sempre piu in onore la Nª Santa Religione, e specialmente per dare alla istruzione il carattere eminente Catholico.   Sara questo una dei mezzi potenti per formare opposizione al commune, alla internazionale, e le tutte istituzioni distruzzitrici della societa " (*ibid.* p. 460).

[1] See de Roux, pp. 345-6, and de Meaux, pp. 78-80.
[2] *Soir de ma journée*, p. 216.
[3] Simon presented him to his pupils, saying, " He is not only your master but ours also " (*ibid.* p. 219).   [4] Thiers, *Notes et souvenirs*, p. 152.

straightforwardness made him acceptable to the Czar. He was succeeded at the War Ministry by General de Cissey, also an Orleanist and an old African campaigner. His appointment was well received, as, without being brilliant, he was open-minded and saw that important changes in the Army were due. However, Thiers was far too ardent a military expert to allow his Minister to be more than a chief clerk, and sometimes compelled him to do things he disliked, as when he forced him to strike off the Army List the name of Jerome Napoleon, under whom de Cissey had acted as Chief of Staff.[1]

The Minister of the Marine and the Colonies, Admiral Pothuau, had no pronounced political views. Gratitude for promotion inclined him to Orleanism. Like most French sailors, he was more liberal than the soldiers, and at the same time a fervent Catholic. He followed Thiers in the ranks of the Left Centre.

Larcy, the Minister for Public Works, was the most " to the Right " of the Government. He was the son of a Sous-préfet of the Restoration, and had resigned from the magistrature as a protest against 1830. He continued in Thiers' Government till 1872, but he was not much use as a link with the Right. His gentle temperament involved him in a continual case of conscience ; he was torn between attachment to Thiers and to his Royalist friends, just as in a later Government he was to be torn between his parliamentary allies and his loyalty to the Comte de Chambord.

The Minister of Finance, Pouyer-Quertier, was also a Legitimist, though not so pronounced a partisan as he afterwards became. He was one of the picturesque, and even legendary, figures of the Assembly. Radiant with health and good-humour, he was described as a mixture of a Norman and a Yankee ; he had 1800 workmen spinning for him at Rouen, and was a convinced Protectionist.

[1] Du Barail, iii. 291, 398.

Gigantic in stature,[1] vigorous in action, he took the tribune by storm and he argued by blows of the fist. It is said that, when he accepted office, he carried off the whole of the Exchequer in his hat : since then, he had helped Thiers in raising the Loan, and he was more than useful as a negotiator with Bismarck, who admired his powers of drinking. After a long night's bout, he woke up fresh next morning and knocked at Bismarck's door to propose a cup of tea.[2] He secured for France the important iron mines of Villerupt by saying : " If you were the conquered party, I would not force you to become French, but you force me to become German ". " What do you mean ? " said the Chancellor, " who talks of taking away Normandy from you ? " " It is simple enough, Prince : I am one of the owners of the Villerupt forges. So you see that from that point of view you are making me a German." " Well, well : don't cry. I'll let you keep Villerupt, but don't ask for anything else, or I'll take it back." [3]

Thiers reigned as a benevolent despot over his Council : the only thing he feared was the mordant tongue of his Minister of Justice. Jules Dufaure had been an *avocat* at Bordeaux. He had been Minister of the Interior under the Second Republic, and of Public Works under Louis-Philippe. It was said of him that his ideas were Left Centre, and his sympathies Right Centre. He was a Catholic and went to Mass at five o'clock in the mornings. His austerity made people call him a Jansenist : " his only reading was the Mass-book and Tacitus ".[4]

---

[1] " His shoulders were made for responsibility " (Hanotaux, i. 96). " One day I saw him at the station catching a train : he took the employee by the shoulders and pushed him out of the way " (*Kel-kun*, vol. iii.).

[2] Claveau, p. 314. The Marquis de Gabriac, French Chargé d'Affaires at Berlin, says : " The two guests did one another mutual honour, and I am obliged to admit that in the new passage of arms repeated from the Homeric heroes, in which each of them sought to dominate his adversary, Prince Bismarck and Pouyer-Quertier miraculously preserved their positions " (Hanotaux, i. 342).   [3] Lawton, *The Third French Republic*, p. 47.

[4] De Goncourts, t. 5, p. 296.

He used to roll towards the tribune, looking like a peasant. His cravat was always coming loose, and the gallery watched with endless amusement his attempts to hitch his trousers and waistcoat together. He always looked bad-tempered, and his wretched voice wandered all over the place, but his speeches generally effected their object. He introduced the style of the *avocat* into the Chamber ; Lacombe says of him : " He enters on a theme as if he were hewing out a path, pushing ahead, striking heavy blows and never looking to the right or the left to see if there might not be other ways to take ".[1] His style was precise and vigorous, his dialectic close and clear, and he was a master of the phrase that stings ; at a famous crisis, when Target had spoken for five minutes and decided the issue not by his argument but by the votes he commanded, Dufaure referred to the hon. member's " *weighty* speech ".

He had rather limited interests, and Thiers said, " He will never make a good President of the Council ; he does not know which way the Danube flows ". However, he held that office twice without conspicuous failure. On the whole he was respected for a roughness that (as in the case of Doctor Johnson) expressed an honest independence and concealed a brusque kindness in action.[2]

(b) THE TREATY OF FRANKFORT AND AFTER

It will be remembered that at the time of the Franco-Prussian War Russia had repudiated that article of the 1856 Treaty, which referred to the neutrality of the Black Sea. A Conference was held in London, and France was invited to take part, but Bismarck, by delaying the passports, had prevented Jules Favre from attending ; he was afraid that the matters in dispute between France and Germany might be brought before the assembled Powers. Even when the preliminaries of peace had been signed at

---

[1] Lacombe, ii. 19.   [2] Bosq, pp. 230-5. Freycinet, p. 384.

Versailles, Jules Favre still entertained hopes of an appeal to the London Conference. He bombarded the Duc de Broglie (now ambassador to England) with " slushy and wordy rhetoric " (so the ambassador described it) ; he appealed to Spain, Austria, Russia, and even to Turkey for support, only receiving in reply the assurance that, if Lord Granville, the President of the Conference, would take the first step, they would follow his lead.

De Broglie turned a deaf ear to his instructions ; he was convinced that such a step, possible before the signature of the Preliminaries, would now be fatal : Bismarck would have regarded it as a breach of France's plighted word, and would probably have given the order for his troops to enter Paris. " The treaty ", he said to Lord Granville, " is detestable, but it is not we, who will violate it. Our only duty is to carry it out. It is you — it is Europe, who will not be able for long to support the master you have accepted." He told his Foreign Minister that he would not intervene without direct orders from Thiers himself, and on March 13th, when the Conference resumed its sittings, he only inserted one topical phrase in his opening address. After praising the method of Conference, he expressed " his regret that in recent years this rule has so often not been applied ". Even this was too much for the German ambassador, and the other Powers had some difficulty in persuading him to sign the protocol. Thiers approved of his ambassador's caution :

Our excellent Jules Favre has not enough experience and is too much troubled to see clearly what should be done. It would have been absurd to attempt anything at this moment. As the neutral Powers (great or small) do not wish, or are not able to take any serious action, we should have looked like cry-babies shrieking, because they have to have their teeth out. Worse might have followed. We should have cast doubts upon the execution of the Treaty and the Prussians would have slowed up the evacuation of our territory — even if they had not done more.[1]

[1] *De Broglie* (*Revue*, 1/3/29), pp. 147-50.

The definite negotiations for a Treaty were therefore left to the two Powers concerned, and were begun at Brussels on March 24th. France was represented by the Baron Baude, her ambassador in Belgium, and de Goulard, a deputy of the Right Centre and a personal friend of Thiers ; Germany by the Count von Arnim, Minister of Prussia to the Holy See, and Baron von Balan, the ambassador at Brussels.

Meanwhile the Commune had broken out at Paris, and the crisis made negotiations exceptionally difficult. Bismarck seemed torn between two apprehensions — one that the Versailles Government, strengthened by the accession of the prisoners, whom Germany had allowed to return, would vanquish Paris, and then become powerful enough to repudiate the Peace Preliminaries ;[1] and the other that the Commune might be victorious and repudiate the debts of France.[2] He pretended to lean for a moment towards a Bonapartist Restoration. " The party of the Empire is probably the one, with which we could most reasonably flatter ourselves as to the prospect of establishing tolerable relations between France and Germany." [3]

His policy therefore was to make the conditions more severe ; he demanded that the five milliards indemnity should be paid in coin ; that the railways in ceded territories should be handed over to Germany ; that the commercial treaty between France and Germany (dating from 1862) should be renewed ; and that an indemnity should be allowed to Germans expelled from France. The French, on the other hand, offered to pay one milliard of the indemnity in specie and the rest in bonds ; they

[1] In his speech to the Reichstag (24/4/71) he said : " I cannot resist the impression that the French Government would seem to cherish the hope of obtaining, later on, when it has recovered its strength, other conditions than at present " (Hanotaux, i. 277 n.).

[2] In the same speech he said : " If the French Government does not succeed in suppressing the insurrection, what collections of troops will be able to be formed in France and under whose orders ? " (Hanotaux, i. 277).

[3] Hanotaux, i. 279.

demanded that French territory should be evacuated by July 1st, and that Germany should take over the National Debt in Alsace-Lorraine.

The French were severely handicapped by the Commune. Bismarck was always threatening to put it down himself, which Thiers rightly regarded as the last drop in the cup of national dishonour, and Favre was obliged to ask for the speedy repatriation of prisoners to form an army against the insurgents. Thus (as Sorel says) " every advantage obtained for the benefit of social order was paid for by a retreat upon the field of diplomacy ".[1]

The Brussels discussions dragged on without result. On March 30th, General von Fabrice, who was acting at Rouen as German provisional plenipotentiary, publicly declared that these delays would lead to a state of war. On April 26th Favre wrote in despair : " I can only explain it by a fixed intention of breaking off entirely ". On May 3rd, General Fabrice wrote to Thiers that " the French proposals at Brussels were contrary both to the spirit and the letter of the Preliminaries ". If the negotiations did not come to a satisfactory conclusion, they would occupy Paris and compel the French armies to retire behind the Loire. Thiers at once decided that speed was of the first importance. On May 4th, the Brussels Conference was brought to an end, and on the 5th Favre and Pouyer-Quertier were sent to Frankfort to open direct negotiations with the Chancellor ;[2] they were given full powers to negotiate with the duty of referring to Versailles before

---

[1] Quoted Hanotaux, i. 285. Bismarck wrote to General Fabrice on April 18th : " If the Versailles Government has seriously the intention of ending the insurrection, and arriving at a definite Peace with us, it should treat the Parisians more firmly " (Dreyfus, *M. Thiers contre l'Empire*, etc., p. 331).

[2] Hanotaux, i. 281-8. They had some risks to run on the way ; as the train passed near the walls of Paris, a " well-dressed " man approached them, and said : " You are the citoyen Favre, and you are going to Pantin. We will see to you all right." At the Pantin station there was a raging crowd, held back by the troops : Favre had refused a German escort " (Favre, *Gouv. de la défense nationale*, iii. p. 351).

concluding. They at once called on Bismarck at the Swan Hotel ; the Chancellor seemed restless and annoyed. He kept studying the features of Pouyer-Quertier, whom he had not met before. He complained that " the gravity of events in France is such that we should have the right to consider the Treaty of February 26th as non-existent. We do not suspect the good faith of the French Government, but we fear that they are not strong enough to overcome the difficulties, that threaten them. We let them raise the Army to 100,000 combatants : we sent them back over 80,000 prisoners. Yet they seem more exigeant than ever. They seek to prolong the siege of Paris to eternity. They have not yet restored all the captured ships. Your plenipotentiaries at Brussels systematically adjourn all discussion." Favre replied : " I offer to put an end to all these delays by concluding a definite treaty on the spot ". Bismarck was visibly relieved. " If we agree on the war conditions," he said, " I think we shall easily settle all the other questions." But, with his love of the melodramatic, he still persisted in appearing next day at the hotel in full uniform and reading an ultimatum. " The Paris insurrection ", it said, " has compromised the future, on which we were counting ". Unless France granted them terms which placed the interests of Germany beyond the effects of disturbance, German troops would enter the capital to restore order.[1]

Bismarck added that the ultimatum was happily not needed, " thanks to the sincerity of the French explanations ", and negotiations were opened. They lasted three days : the Treaty of Frankfort was signed on May 10th. Bismarck adopted his usual tactic of severity of language, designed to make every concession appear as a gracious condescension. He gave Favre a rap over the knuckles, apropos of the London Conference, without mentioning it directly. He complained of a dispatch sent to the French

---

[1] Favre, *ibid.* p. 352.

ambassador at St. Petersburg : " I place upon record your
persistent attempts at European interference ".

A warm discussion took place on the evacuation of
territory.   Favre declared occupation useless.   " You are
masters of Alsace-Lorraine, and you have us by the throat :
you are reducing our people to despair."   " You forget ",
Bismarck replied, " that the occupation bears still more
heavily on us.   Our Army is the nation.   We demand the
right to decide when our troops are to be withdrawn, not
in order to keep them uselessly in France, but in order that
we may not be compelled to send them back later."   In
the end, the provisions of the Peace Preliminaries were
aggravated.   The evacuation of the Departments of Oise,
Seine-et-Oise and Seine-et-Marne was to take place not
after the payment of the first half-milliard of the indemnity,
but " after order had been re-established ", or after the
payment of the third half-milliard ;   thirty days after the
recovery of Paris, 500 millions were to be paid ;   a milliard
before the end of 1871 ;   another half-milliard before May
1st, 1872 ;   the other three milliards before March 2nd,
1874.   The indemnity was to be in coin, not notes, and the
evacuation was to take place step by step, as the payments
were made.   France and Germany were to adopt a system
of reciprocal commercial dealings on the footing of the
most favoured nation.   Pouyer-Quertier, an ardent Protectionist, fought hard for liberty of tariffs.   Bismarck
answered that he would rather " begin the war of cannon-
balls again than expose himself to a war of tariffs ".

On the question of territory, the French Finance
Minister secured Villerupt.[1]   He had learned the lesson
(which Favre never learned, and Thiers did not always
remember) that Bismarck liked a man who stood up to
him, and talked over matters in a business-like *insouciant*
manner :   the Chancellor abhorred emotion and despised
dialectic.   Belfort had been saved for France at the

[1] See p. 435.

Versailles Preliminaries. The French now asked for a strip
of territory round it to make the place defensible ; the
Germans were agreeable, on condition that a slip of
country (10 kilometres) on the Luxembourg frontier was
conceded to them in exchange. It abounded in iron, and
the Emperor wished to possess the graves of so many of his
troops. The matter was left to the choice of the National
Assembly.[1]

On May 13th the Treaty was formally laid before the
Assembly, and a Commission appointed to consider it.
Thiers was summoned before it. His dictatorial tone
showed how three months of power had changed him. The
Treaty was his work, and he did not like to hear it criticised.
One of the members suggested that France would have got
better terms, if they had asked for support from England.
Thiers angrily charged him with letting out diplomatic
secrets and falsifying them.[2] Another member declared
that the Treaty sacrificed French commerce. Thiers
answered hotly : " Do those, who blame the Treaty, want
war ? If so, let them have the courage to say so. It is
easy to grumble." [3] But the most vehement dispute took
place on the question of Belfort. Thiers, who looked upon
himself as the saviour of Belfort, regarded any sacrifice
as worth while, which made the place defensible. A Commission of officers reported that it was more important to
keep the Luxembourg frontier than to round off Belfort.
Thiers was furious, and tried to persuade them of their
error. Two Generals came over to his side, but two others
remained unconvinced.

On May 18th both parties appealed to the Assembly ;
de Meaux, as reporter, pointed out that the increased
severity of the Treaty was due to the insurrection still
raging at Paris. " Nine months ago it was the Empire that
brought the foreign armies into France ; today it is the

---

[1] See the whole account in Favre, pp. 352 *sq.*
[2] De Meaux, p. 53.   [3] Favre, *ibid.*

Commune which keeps them still outside Paris." Admiral Fourichon urged that the Treaty should be voted in silence and without debate. General Chanzy, who had commanded the Army of the provinces, argued that as the Treaty aggravated the previous terms, negotiations should be resumed. " Is it impossible that we should come to an understanding with Germany without recourse to arms ? " He strongly opposed the proposal to surrender the rich minerals of the Luxembourg frontier, in order to secure a useless increase of the Belfort area. Peltereau-Villeneuve, a member of the Right Centre, protested against the " cruelty of disappointing the communes on the Luxembourg frontier, who had rejoiced in being saved for France, and now were to be told that they were to become Germans after all ". Depeyre excited the anger of the Left by declaring that the final disaster of the war " had been the work of the republican dictatorship ", and provoked a warm reply from Lefranc. Thiers, in his speech, had two objects. First of all, he wished to point out the futility and danger of further negotiations. In the course of his argument he turned to Chanzy and addressed to him the famous phrase : " The hon. General has said, ' It is the diplomatists who sign treaties '. Permit me in my turn to say ' It is the soldiers who make them '." Chanzy retorted proudly from his place : " Then you should have let the soldiers do it " : he had a right to say so, for he had voted against the Peace Preliminaries.

In the second part of his speech Thiers had to defend the strategic value of his pet scheme for accepting the increase of the Belfort territory. An eye-witness describes his triumph with gentle irony. " He treated those, who were of a different opinion, as men ignorant of history and geography. . . . He began a lecture on strategy for the benefit of the weaker members of the Assembly. . . . We thought at one moment that he was going to favour us with the plan and programme of the next campaign against

Prussia." [1] The clause in favour of the Luxembourg exchange was voted according to Thiers' wishes by 433 votes to 98 ; the Treaty, as a whole, was carried unanimously.[2]

The German occupation cost dear — more than a million francs per day. The troops had to be lodged as well as fed. Special barracks had to be erected, and it was not without difficulty that the foreigners were prevented from using Catholic churches for Protestant services. In occupied territory hunting had to be forbidden from fear of arming the inhabitants, and it needed special negotiations to allow the keepers of forests and custom-house officers to carry rifles. Attacks on Germans had to be tried, when demanded by the Army of Occupation, and much trouble was caused by the acquittal of two accused persons by the jury in the Departments of Seine-et-Marne and the Seine.

This difficult situation was much eased by the German Chief Commander, the Baron von Manteuffel, a chivalrous enemy much in sympathy with France. He showed tact towards the conquered, and real courage towards the military party in Prussia. It was he, who unmasked the hostile schemes of von Arnim (afterwards German Ambassador at Paris), and got him dismissed. He had his headquarters first at Compiègne, afterwards at Nancy. France was represented there by the Comte de Saint-Vallier, ex-Ambassador in Württemberg, who proved a tower of strength.

Twenty Departments still remained in occupation. Of these, the forts of Paris, Seine, Seine-et-Oise, Seine-et-Marne and Oise were liberated after the end of the Commune, and before the end of 1871, also those of Eure, Seine-Inférieure, Somme, Aisne, Aube, Côte-d'Or, Haute Saône, Doubs and Jura. In September Bismarck offered the immediate evacuation of six new Departments, if the fourth

---

[1] M. Delpit, p. 157 (quoted Hanotaux, i. 300).
[2] *Annales*, t. 3, pp. 62-84.

half-milliard was paid, and certain advantages were given to manufactured goods coming from Alsace-Lorraine. The Assembly, after a special night-sitting, authorised Thiers to accept the proposal by 533 votes to 31.[1]

The indemnity had been fixed at 5,000,000,000 fr. It was reduced to 4,675,000,000 by the concession of the railways in Alsace-Lorraine. According to the Treaty, half a milliard had to be paid a month after the recovery of Paris, and another milliard in 1871. The first half-milliard was paid in July (125,000,000 in bills of the Bank of France, and the rest drawn on German and English Banks); Bismarck refused to acknowledge payment till it had all been counted, which delayed the evacuation considerably.[2]

To raise the money, Thiers rejected the idea of a patriotic subscription or of a special war tax, and appealed for a loan. In one day (June 27th) it was covered two and a half times — a spectacular demonstration of the excellence of French credit.[3]

On June 20th, Thiers presented his Budget: he explained that the Public Debt (*i.e.* war loan and indemnity) had increased by 8,000,000,000 fr. : the interest on this was 356,000,000. 200,000,000 was added as a Sinking Fund.

Of this, 556,000,000 had to be raised by taxation.[4] He proposed to double the fees on registration and stamps, and to increase (*a*) the duties on sugar, wine, coffee and alcohol by 30-50 per cent ; (*b*) the tobacco duties by 20 per cent ; (*c*) the postal service by 20 per cent. These resources reached about 350,000,000 fr. : 200,000,000 was

[1] Malo, p. 543.

[2] Reclus, *L'Avènement de la 3e République*, p. 122.

[3] The interest was 5 per cent : 2,500,000,000 came from Paris ; 1,250,000,000 from the provinces ; more than 1,000,000,000 from abroad. The next day the Assembly received the Minister of Finance with three cheers. *The Times* said that the result was " miraculous " (Dreyfus, *La République de M. Thiers*, pp. 61-2).

[4] In his preliminary sketch, Thiers had not included the indemnity for the invaded Departments, the maintenance of the Army of Occupation, and the new military reorganisation. It was found that 750,000,000 of fresh annual receipts was needed (Hanotaux, i. 347).

still needed. Thiers rejected the income tax, "for the valuation of which we have only the declaration of the tax-payer himself, too insecure a foundation to build upon, or else an inquisition into private fortunes by Treasury officials, an odious and arbitrary method ".[1] Land could not be "loaded with fresh burdens". He therefore proposed to revive the tax on raw materials, abandoned by the Empire in its Free Trade mood. "We had only one thing to fear," he says; "the resistance of the great manufacturers, a resistance which I had resolved to combat with all my power." [2] But these struggles belong to the next session of the Assembly.

(c) GENERAL ADMINISTRATION

(1) *Ecclesiastical.* — As a rule, Thiers kept himself from interference in religious questions. Once, however, it seems that he forgot his caution, and, as the incident throws some light on the situation, it is worth a moment's notice.

At Paris the Commune had been defeated and paralysed, but the state of affairs at Lyons, "the second capital of France ", still gave cause for anxiety. During the war the Red Flag had flown from the Mairie, and during the Commune repression had been difficult and dangerous. At the July elections, the city had chosen deputies of highly democratic opinions, and the new municipal council soon showed its Radical tendencies.[3] It began by forbidding religious Orders to teach in the schools (an action contrary to the law of 1850) ; then it forbade the traditional Catholic festivities of the Assumption and substituted for them, on Sunday August 13th, a *fête des écoles*. The children were

---

[1] Thiers, *Notes et souvenirs*, pp. 159-62. He declared to the Left, who defended the Income Tax : "It would be a tax of discord. . . . I will never flatter the popular passions and I would rather leave the Government than consent" (Dreyfus, *La République de M. Thiers*, p. 64).

[2] Thiers, *op. cit.* p. 162.

[3] For this incident see Halévy, *Fin des notables*, pp. 55-8.

led into the public gardens, and, after a feast costing 26,000
fr., addresses were given in the finest anticlerical strain.
Barodet, the *adjoint*, who was to be elected at Paris two
years later in circumstances of great political excitement,
spoke of " morality based on science ".   Another speaker
said : " If we have removed religious instruction from our
programme, it is only because we see in it a usurpation
of the State on the domain of the individual ".[1]   It was
even asserted in some papers that " children, parents and
National Guards were led past barrels of wine given away
free, and that, when the fête ended at six in the evening,
children, parents and lady teachers had to be removed in
carriages ".   The *Salut Public* spoke of " this deplorable
orgy ".[2]   On August 21st the matter was brought before
the National Assembly by Monnet and Chaurand, members
of the Right.   Jules Simon denied all responsibility ; he
had himself written to the Rector of the Academy (the
highest local educational authority) expressing astonishment at " a great fête at such a moment, and at such
enormous expense in the present condition of our finances ".
The Rector replied that he was opposed to the whole thing,
and the Minister concluded : " It was the authority of the
Préfet, that approved and authorised it ".[3]   As to the decree
of the municipal council excluding religious instruction,
" we shall take the steps necessary to stop " such illegality.

The Préfet at Lyons was Valentin, one of the Préfets
of the National Defence, and hateful to the Conservatives.
He was under the control of the Minister of the Interior ;
so Lambrecht was sent for.   He was ill, but he left his bed
to tell the Assembly that the fête was " mischievous in its
object and blamable in its execution ".   No one could
suppose that so timid a Minister was responsible, and the
Assembly began to suspect Thiers, who was known to grant
interviews to Préfets without deigning to consult the
Minister responsible.   Chaurand declared : " We have now

---

[1] *Annales*, t. 5, p. 37.   [2] *Ibid.* p. 38.   [3] *Ibid.* p. 34.

evidence that the Sous-préfets correspond directly with
other authorities at Versailles without transmitting their
dispatches to the Minister of the Interior ". "Then let us
have an inquiry ", called out a deputy ; but the majority
shrank from a direct challenge to Thiers. De Broglie,
who happened to be present, declared that what was necessary was an act of confidence in the Government,[1] and an
order of the day was carried accordingly.

(2) *Personnel.* — Although it does not figure much in
parliamentary debates, the appointment of Préfets always
plays an important part in French life.[2] Under Thiers
none of the Préfets of the Empire were employed, though
this exclusion did not extend to Sous-préfets. At first most
of the Préfets of the National Defence were maintained, till
April, when changes began.

Of the 89 Préfets, about ten were kept where they were :
others changed their Departments, but a quarter of the
personnel were still "men of September ". Ten new
Préfets were Legitimists, including the Marquis de
Nadaillac, a celebrated anthropologist, at Pau, and Lavedan,
one of Dupanloup's friends, at Poitiers ; [3] de Guerle, an
Orleanist who had corrected the proofs of Aumale's *Letters
on the History of France,* was sent to La Rochelle. Thiers
professed to give to every Department, after consultation
with the deputies, the Préfet, who represented its nuance
of opinion, but the Royalists complained they were
neglected.[4]

---

[1] He said : " In times of difficulty and trouble, such as these in which we
live, the Government may sometimes lack the force necessary for putting the
law into execution : it is for you to give them that force. *(Loud applause)* "
(*Annales,* t. 5, p. 44).

[2] It used to be said in French rural districts that the greatest grumblers
against the Government were the first to approach, hat in hand, saying,
" Bonjour, M. le Préfet ".   [3] De Roux, pp. 134-6.

[4] Hendlé at Lille seems to have been the first Jewish Préfet of the Third
Republic : when the people of Lille prepared a hostile demonstration against
the Royalists (returning from Antwerp, where they had presented a White
Flag to the Comte de Chambord), he stopped their train outside the town and
sent them home in a bus (Halévy, *Fin des notables,* p. 97).

When it was decided to dismiss Jules Ferry and appoint a Préfet for the Department of the Seine and Paris, the Right hoped the post would be given to Augustin Cochin, a famous Catholic member of the 1849 Commission on Education, and popular at Paris for his many charities. But Thiers professed to be afraid that he was too clerical for the capital, and kept Cochin close to him at Versailles, as Préfet of Seine-et-Oise. His salon soon outshone the rest : he and his wife devoted themselves to repairing the ravages wrought by the civil and foreign wars, and to caring for the prisoners of the Commune confined in the neighbourhood.[1] The Prefecture at Paris was given to Léon Say, Left Centre, Protestant and Anglophile, who controlled the important *Journal des Débats*.

(3) *Military.* — Thiers greatly loved military affairs, partly because they provide an ideal opportunity for an administrator, and partly because he was very conscious of himself as the historian of Napoleon, but mostly because he sincerely loved his country.

The 29th of June was probably the proudest day of his life : it had been decided that the recent success of the Loan and the reawakening of French industry justified a great military review — so dear to the French heart. The date had first been fixed for Sunday June 18th, on the great hippodrome at Longchamps. Thiers was on tenterhooks : " every moment he was opening windows, consulting barometers and weather reports ".[2] It was put off to June 25th, and then to June 29th, because the ground was soaked. The papers began to whisper that the Government were afraid of Communard outrages, and that they did not dare to confront the people of Paris with General

---

[1] Falloux, ii. 527. He died in March 1872, writing a pathetic and unfinished letter to Thiers : " Your powerful mind will end by seeing in Jesus Christ the true God come on earth. . . . The Republic has been killed by its children . . . by Robespierre and Marat, then by all the makers of phrases, plots, debts and stupidities, who have three times mounted the popular chariot."

[2] Pessard, ii. 151.

Gallifet, noted for his severity during the insurrection.

June 29th dawned bright and radiant : 120,000 men took part in the review, " their bearing confident, and proud from having forced the walls of Paris, that had defied the Prussians ".[1] The infantry were massed in the centre ; the cavalry (15,000 in number) and artillery were placed in front and on the wings. Marshal MacMahon galloped down the front of the troops and the march-past began.

As they went by, the Army, that had defeated Russia and Austria under the Empire, that had fought so valiantly and so tragically against Prussia, that had saved Paris from the Commune, all hearts were stirred. Thiers in the central pavilion, surrounded by deputies and diplomats, the President of the Assembly on his right, his favourite, Jules Simon, on his left, " bit his lips, rubbed his hands together, let his spectacles fall from his moist eyes, hardly able to control himself, shifting his feet, marking time to the trumpets, and, now and then, drawing himself erect with incomparable majesty ". When, at the end, the Marshal came round to salute him, Thiers took his hand and stood sobbing, unable to speak.[2]

The crowds acclaimed the soldier and the statesman, and went home, quiet and serious, without the usual comic songs. Thiers gave a dinner to the heads of the Army, and, after that, a reception to deputies of all colours. But even from such a day of patriotic triumph politics were not quite absent. Royalists complained that Mme Thiers *would* talk to the Extreme Left, and that her husband, when listening to the crowd, had been heard to remark, " Notice how they shout ' Vive la République ' ".[3]

It was necessary to keep the Army intact, to present a bold face to Prussia, to cow the revolutionaries, and to furnish a basis for the new military reorganisation. The supreme command was retained in the hands of MacMahon.[4]

[1] Thiers, *Notes et souvenirs*, p. 149.   [2] Pessard, ii. 152.
    Ibid. p. 153.   [4] Thiers, *op. cit.* pp. 151-2.

Meanwhile Thiers laboured to create 150 regiments of infantry (3000 men in the field, 1000 in the depot of each regiment), and a force of artillery with one gun for every thousand men.[1] He was ably assisted by the Army Commission of an Assembly, which contained so many distinguished generals, and which was to devote most of the year 1872 to the great problem of Conscription.

The only military emergency outside France was in Algeria, where the decree of the National Defence Government, giving the Jews equal rights, had caused an Arab insurrection.[2] After the death of the ring-leader, the Government appointed a Civil Governor, Vice-Admiral de Gueydon, on March 29th.[3] He at once demanded troops. On April 30th, Martial Delpit (deputy of the Right) received a letter from him, in which he said that, " if there is longer delay, there will not remain to France one colonist or one square inch of ground in Africa ".[4] But it was not till June 16th that Thiers was able to write : " Now that we have chased the formidable insurrection from Paris, I can send you troops — three brigades, each of 5000 men ".[5]

(4) *After the Commune.* — Thiers has been severely criticised — especially by Clemenceau — for the cruel repression of the Commune. He has been taken as the typical bourgeois, who sheds blood like water, because he is frightened. It is not easy to assess responsibilities in this matter. No one denies that the behaviour of the troops of the Government was (in many cases) ferocious. Paul Bourget, who was an infant at the time, " saw wounded people having their skulls broken by the butts of rifles " ; a doctor, who opposed the massacre of the wounded, was dragged to the wall and shot. At the Prison de la Roquette

---

[1] Hanotaux, i. 233-4.

[2] See in Daudet's *Lettres de mon moulin* (pp. 247-69) the essay called " A Milianah " for the way in which the Arabs looked down upon the Jews : the decree was modified on October 7th, 1871, but not abolished.

[3] Denis, p. 13.   [4] *Ibid.* p. 14.   [5] Bouniols, p. 75.

a *chef de bataillon* stood at the door, as the prisoners were led in, saying " Left " or " Right " at his fancy : those led to the left were shot. Captain Guercin had Millière shot on the steps of the Panthéon, saying, " I have read articles by you, which disgusted me. You detest Society : very well, it is going to drive you out." It is said in an official report that 17,000 people were shot down in the streets after surrender.[1]

Vassili records a conversation,[2] in which Thiers defends

the order which I had given to Gallifet to show no mercy. . . . In order to oblige the Prussians to recognise that we were strong enough to rule France . . . we had to drive out of the minds of all our opponents the idea that we had not got power enough on our side. . . . This severity had the result that out of the moral ruins left by the Empire . . . rose a government which won for itself the esteem of Europe. I may deplore it, but I cannot regret it : one cannot be sentimental in politics.

De Meaux says that, while " Gallifet distinguished himself by pitiless severity ", the other Generals, Ladmirault and MacMahon, " disapproved of the execution of prisoners, who had surrendered ", but could not succeed in preventing it everywhere. This suggests that the extent of the reprisals depended more on the character of the General than on instructions from Thiers.[3]

Hanotaux says that after the massacre of the hostages, " on both sides the word of command was to be ' No quarter '. The soldiers, black with smoke, were the blind

[1] Bernanos, *La Grande Peur des bien-pensants*, pp. 75-8. Millière's widow prosecuted Guercin for murder : the civil court at Versailles declared itself incompetent.

[2] *France from Behind the Veil*, pp. 106-8. The conversation is placed at St-Germain, a few weeks before Thiers' death, and " was written down in my diary, when I got home ". I should doubt the authenticity of it : Thiers himself says, " I gave the strictest orders that the anger of our soldiers should be restrained " (Dreyfus, *M. Thiers contre l'Empire*, etc., p. 345).

[3] Quoted Dreyfus, *La République de M. Thiers*, p. 66. After May 29th Thiers ordered General Borel to cease fire : " After the battle is over, it is a monstrous irregularity ". He complains that the magistrates have " no heart and no political sense ". He tried to save Crémieux and Rossel, and he saved Lullier, " a dangerous madman but with qualities " (Malo, p. 515).

instruments of public vengeance, sometimes also of private grudges. They no longer knew what they were doing. Their chiefs did not always take account of the formal orders, which had been given by MacMahon forbidding useless violence." [1] It is evident that street fighting is not only the most ferocious form of warfare, but also that in which control from above is least effective.

In the trial of the 35,800 prisoners [2] Thiers had little part. They came before Councils of War, subject to the final decision by himself as advised by a Commission of Pardon set up by the Assembly.[3] Beyond insisting that every case should be tried by law, he did not interfere. He understood the fury of the moment. "It was impossible", he says, "to grant an amnesty : that would have been against all human conscience, since beyond doubt those responsible for the massacre of the hostages were among the number of prisoners." [4] But, though he stood for the most part on one side, he did not share the political passions of the Assembly. "If he had not had to count with the Assembly, he would have been merciful to those who survived the civil war." He used to say to deputies of the Right, "There are many abnormal cases [de malades] among these scoundrels ".[5] Occasionally he did intervene. He sent for Bergeret, who had set fire to the Tuilleries, and said : "Well, old rascal [grand gamin], they have forgotten to shoot you, have they ? I will arrange the matter with St. Hilaire, who is the kindest of men." [6] Bergeret was sent abroad with a false passport. He also saved Rochefort in spite of the opposition of his Ministers.

[1] Hanotaux, i. 219, 221.

[2] Up to 1875 the arrests reached 43,501. In 1873 the total number of condemnations reached 13,450 (Zévaès, *Histoire de la 3ᵉ République*, p. 81).

[3] On June 17th, 1871, out of 9600 persons summarily condemned the Commission recommended 1891 to mercy (Hanotaux, i. 227).

[4] *Notes et souvenirs*, p. 154.

[5] Pessard, ii. 53. He added : "They have killed poor wretches, who revolted without knowing why. Their chiefs left them and took to their heels " (Malo, p. 516).   [6] Malo, p. 516.

Favre and Cissey told him that opinion was unanimous against him. Thiers replied : " He was mixed up in the destruction of my house ; if I let him be shot, I shall incur all the odium of personal revenge ".[1] He was sent to New Caledonia, from which he escaped before long.

(5) *Foreign Affairs.* — If a foreign policy means the power to influence the affairs of other countries, France had no foreign policy in 1871. Apart from her special relations with Germany, her representatives abroad could only do nothing with dignity, and keep one eye open for possible friends.

Thiers adopted the policy of using aristocratic families for diplomatic work, partly because they " had the tradition ", partly perhaps because it weakened the Royalist party in France. " They have no title to these appointments ", said an angry Republican, " except their titles." [2]

The Viscount de Noailles was sent to St. Petersburg, but was soon replaced by General Le Flô, who from " being an overtired Minister of War became an incomparable ambassador ".[3] The Czar, like most autocrats, was fond of frankness — in foreigners —, and appreciated his military straight-forwardness. Russia " was beginning ", says Thiers, " to find cause for disquiet in the developing powers of her neighbours, neither did she forget her old jealousy of England, kindled afresh every day by events in Central Asia. She therefore looked upon France as a useful and probable ally in the future." [4]

Thiers' optimism was perhaps somewhat premature, but he preached it to Le Flô with dignity and patience. He

[1] On 10/1/72 Rochefort wrote to Mme Adam : " You tell me that Thiers saved my life. I agree, and it is impossible for me to forget it " (Malo, p. 516).

[2] Thus, in the case of his most successful appointment (at the beginning of 1872) of the Comte de Gontaut-Biron (Legitimist deputy for the Basses Pyrenees) at Berlin, Thiers writes : " A nobleman, who is of the old Sèvres pattern, and not of the new, has much influence with the King of Prussia, who is at heart a Legitimist " (Hanotaux, i. 376).

[3] De Roux, p. 134.   [4] *Notes et souvenirs*, p. 167.

must not be present at the fêtes given to the Prussian officers. " Bismarck has covered Gortshakoff with caresses. . . . Your only dignified attitude is to be quiet, and appear to notice nothing. Protest gently to the Czar without bitterness, like a calm person, who is not to be deceived, because he is not inclined to illusions. Be philosophical and patient without being a dupe." [1] And again : " France needs to be more reserved than ever, or people will say we are knocking at all doors, and they are all shut. . . . After two or three years of good government, France will be as strong and as much considered as ever. . . . Show your-self convinced that an alliance between France and Russia would procure for Europe a new equilibrium . . . helpful for all the states threatened by Prussia. . . . If the door opens, you must enter, but you must not do anything com-promising to get it open." [2] " Persist in your reserve with all the good grace possible : an alliance, which is possible but not certain, is like a woman who must not be rushed." [3]

The ambassador at Vienna was the Marquis de Banne-ville, diplomatist by career. Austria was divided in feeling : there was still soreness against Prussia as a result of Sadowa, but the Hungarians reproached France with her friendly attitude to Russia, and the Austrian-Germans " naturally through pride of kinship ranged themselves with our conquerors. Besides the ruling Minister in Austria, Count Andrassy, was favourable to Prussia." [4] Thiers, as an old friend of Austria, wrote to his ambassador : " In my opinion, France and Austria are (in the present state of the world) *necessary* allies : they must not say so, nor, above all, write it down, for that would excite alarm by suggesting immediate plans, but they must practice an alliance with-out professing it : I have defended this policy for twenty-five years. [5]

[1] Bouniols, pp. 117-21 (letter of 4/9/71).   [2] *Ibid.* pp. 122-9.
[3] *Ibid.* p. 140.   [4] Thiers, *Notes et souvenirs*, pp. 167-8.
[5] Bouniols, p. 106.

Two ambassadors were necessary in Italy. To the Vatican Thiers sent Count Bernard d'Harcourt, a diplomatist by career, and a fervent Catholic. He was instructed[1] to assure Cardinal Antonelli and the Pope that " I have taken and shall always take great trouble to avoid any measure and any nomination, that may increase the difficulties of the Holy Father ".[2] The position at the Quirinal was more embarrassing. In 1870 Victor Emmanuel had desired to rush to the help of his old ally, and had only been restrained by his Ministers, who pointed out that to support France meant to lose Rome. Thiers sent to him Fournier, who, though he was a Catholic and a member of the Right Centre, was also a convinced supporter of Italian unity, and even gave a dinner in honour of Renan, when he visited Rome. The two ambassadors were always at loggerheads.[3] Thiers wrote to his representative at the Quirinal : " The King knows that I would not have brought about the unity of Italy nor that of Germany, but it is quite another thing to undo what has been done. . . . What I ask of him is to make the Pope's life supportable. If he does not treat him properly, the Pope will end by leaving Rome, and I know of no greater peril for the unity of Italy." [4]

In England, the Liberal party under Gladstone was more interested in Social Reform than in Foreign Affairs : the Court was pro-German, and the Liberals were on the whole prejudiced against the Second Empire.[5] De Broglie had therefore plenty of leisure at the London Embassy.

---

[1] Bouniols, p. 96 (letter of 11/8/71).

[2] The French Government still kept the frigate *L'Orénoque* at Civita Vecchia in case the Pope wished to leave Rome : Thiers offered him a château at Pau.

[3] De Roux, p. 134.   [4] Bouniols, pp. 178-80 (letter of 6/4/72).

[5] Thomas Carlyle, whose influence can hardly be imagined today, wrote to *The Times* (November 11th, 1870) a letter which ended : " That noble, patient, deep, pious and solid Germany should be at length welded into a Nation, and become Queen of the Continent, instead of a vapouring, vainglorious, gesticulating, quarrelsome, restless and over-sensitive France seems to me the hopefullest public fact that has occurred in my time " (*Critical Essays*, vii. 251).

In 1872 he protested against the reception of Napoleon III
and the Empress at Buckingham Palace on the occasion of
the National Thanksgiving for the recovery of the Prince
of Wales. " He laid stress on the few opportunities which
he had, as ambassador, of seeing the Queen, of which he
made no complaint, but it made any attention to the ex-
Emperor on public occasions more marked." Granville,
the Foreign Secretary, replied that " the admission of the
Emperor and Empress had no political significance ".[1]
Most of the ambassador's time was taken up by the question
of the Treaty of Commerce (the famous Free Trade pact
signed between Cobden and Louis-Napoleon), which after
ten years was now on the point of expiring. Thiers, a
vehement Protectionist, desired to let it drop, or at least to
modify it, so as to allow his proposed duty on raw materials.

Bouillé (Legitimist deputy for Nièvre) was ambassador
at Madrid : the Marquis de Vogüé,[2] a grey-haired Legitimist, friend of Berryer and a member of the Academy
of Inscriptions, was sent to Constantinople, where he
caused some excitement by taking a seat in presence of the
Sultan without being asked.

A few minor posts went to Republicans. Arago was
sent to Switzerland ; Ernest Picard, after resigning the
Ministry of the Interior, went to the Brussels embassy ;
and Jules Ferry was appointed ambassador at Athens,
" because of his Greek style of beauty ", said a malicious
colleague on the Left.[3]

(d) THIERS AND THE RIGHT : FALLOUX AND DE BROGLIE

Thiers' political ideal was a situation so complicated
that it needed a clever man to unravel it, so elastic that the
last word remained with the most eloquent, so difficult that

---

[1] Granville to Lyons, ambassador at Paris, 1/3/72 (Newton, *Lord Lyons*,
p. 297).

[2] Deputy for Cher : he was father of the political novelist, who wrote
Les Morts qui parlent.

[3] Said by Boysset (Mme Adam, *Mes angoisses*, p. 288).

all eyes were turned to the experienced veteran, so urgent
that the safety of France hung in the balance, so many-
sided that only a man of universal competence could deal
with it, so dangerous that a slip would mean disaster, so
disputed that no party could get the upper hand, and all
must submit to an umpire. Such a situation he found in
1871. Too much peace, and the parties would find out
that he was not indispensable : too much war, and he
would perish in a party conflict. Never did an acute mind
relish the razor-edge more deliciously.

His long experience had left him rather a Gallio in the
matter of constitutions : he found it hard to believe that
people really held " principles " on such a matter. He
agreed with Pope's dictum :

> For forms of government let fools contest :
> Whate'er is best administered is best.

For the Divine Right of Kings he had the contempt of a
Minister, long tried by Louis-Philippe ; [1] he thought " the
Dukes " snobs, and the Comte de Chambord — worst of
faults — a Romantic.

Towards the Orleans family his attitude was complex ;
he had real feeling, not for the dynasty, but for the exiled
family. Yet he persistently treated the Princes as grown-
up children with the patronage of one, who had known their
father. As to the Fusion, he was convinced (as the result
of trustworthy reports from Vienna) that the thing would
not work ; he regarded Orleanism as impossible without
the Legitimists, and intolerable with them.

As to the Republic, he had said contradictory things,
at one time that a republic " always ended in blood and
folly " : at another time that " all Europe was on the
march towards republicanism ". For the Republican party
he had little sympathy. He had no use whatever for the

---

[1] He characteristically dismissed monarchy as an extra obstacle for an
overworked Minister.

Radical programme — Compulsory Education, Anticlericalism and a Single Chamber. He looked on Universal
Suffrage as " a serious difficulty, for which perhaps in time
we shall find a remedy ".[1] He treated Gambetta with his
demand for *guerre à l'outrance* as a *fou furieux*. He formu-
lated his feeling in two famous phrases : " The Conservative
Republic " and " The Republic without the Republicans "
(*i.e.* the Republic governed by himself). When finally he
did declare for them, he tried to leave the impress of his
personality on a proposed Constitution full of checks and
guarantees.

Except on the one point of monarchy, Thiers would
have seemed Conservative enough to please the majority
of the National Assembly ; yet curiously enough it was
not so.

Thiers was a liberal but never a democrat. Even his
Liberalism has been limited to liberty of the tribune and
liberty of the Press, so that Lamy [2] can speak of his
" scepticism tempered by two superstitions ". His one
passion was efficient government, and he believed with all
his heart in the administrative hierarchy left by Napoleon,
" which Europe envies us ". He was utterly opposed to
any idea of Decentralisation. He said (in the 1849 Commission on Education) : " In England everything is
municipal : with us Staff work is always necessary. Do
you suppose that our magnificent and unrivalled Jardin des
Plantes could now be comparable to the institutions created
by private enterprise in England, unless it had been founded
by royal authority under Louis XIII and protected by
every succeeding Government ? In France the State
has to do everything : it has to rear horses ; it alone
can undertake the manufacture of Gobelin tapestries or
of Sèvres china." [3] Thiers combined with this adminis-

---

[1] Bouniols, p. 273.

[2] In a brilliant study of the difference between Thiers and the Assembly
in an appendix to Lacombe's *Journal* (ii. 302-3).

[3] *Procès-verbaux* of the Commission (published by H. de Lacombe), p. 191.

trative severity an easy *camaraderie* with people, who were
abhorrent to the Right. " Did you join the Commune ? "
he said half jestingly to some Parisian. " No ? You were
wrong : *il faut être de tout.*"

The Conservative majority held precisely opposite
views. They disliked Centralisation : they were champions
of local liberties, but they disliked still more his easy-going
tolerance. He believed in " material order " : as long as
the streets were quiet, all was well. They believed in moral
order.

More than any Government since the French revolution, the
Assembly believed in the power of ideas. . . . Deeply Christian,
they owed to their religious faith their certainty of judgment on
moral questions, the stability of the family, the functions of property,
the limits of personal freedom, the duties of public authority. . . .
[For them] the essential element in Order was to refuse to admit or
tolerate an equality between different doctrines. They thought that
the principal duty of Government was to maintain the beliefs, which
were in conformity with Christian civilisation, the historical genius
of the race, and to fight the opposite beliefs.[1]

Lamy's analysis of the different kinds of Conservatism,
held by Thiers and by the majority of the Assembly, is
subtle and instructive. It may perhaps be simplified by
saying that Thiers was an old man full of political experience, and who prided himself on knowing how to govern.
On the other side were a crowd of deputies, mostly new to
political life. Many of them had spent the last twenty
years in their châteaux, where their public duties were
confined to presiding over agricultural societies ; they were
then thrown into political life full of good intentions and
with a more or less clean slate, on which to write their reforms, and to satisfy that itch for legislation, which marks
every deputy that is worth his salt.[2]

---

[1] Lacombe, ii. 302-3 (by Lamy).
[2] See in the Annexes to the *Annales* of the Assembly the long lists of projects by private members, especially on electoral reform.

Thiers was always exasperating the Assembly with his seventy-four years, and they were always irritating him with their up-to-date ideas.[1] In August, Ernoul said : " Deputies work in commissions, study a scheme, and prepare it carefully. Then Thiers comes along, finds it all wrong, alters everything, wants to do it again, criticises everything, and treats the deputies as if they were little boys." [2]

If one thing irritated Thiers more than the rest, it was the pretence of the Royalist majority to be liberal : was he not himself a Grand Old Liberal ? Had he not in a famous speech under the Empire defined the " necessary liberties " ? They were constitutional and parliamentary liberties, but this new-fangled liberty in administration, this desire to give powers of local government to Conseils-Généraux and Departmental Commissions — all this meant the kind of muddle, which his orderly mind abhorred.

During the Commune, the Assembly were discussing a provisional Bill on the subject of municipal elections : in face of the preposterous claims made by the Paris rebels on behalf of local autonomy, it might have been supposed that the current would set towards reaction. But the majority were anxious to show by a gesture of serenity that their

---

[1] A Conservative party out of power for twenty years, and after a restricted régime like that of the Empire, comes back bubbling over with ideas. Halévy sums it up well (*Fin des notables*, p. 49) : " They were men of education and culture, a real *élite* such as one only finds in a Parliament elected by surprise. They had no kind of parliamentary experience : they had no tried chiefs. The Duc d'Aumale might have known how to lead them. But the patriotic prince and soldier of the House of Orleans desired above all to recover his rank in the Army, and Thiers had got him to promise not to sit in the Assembly, to which he had been returned by the electors of Oise. Albert de Broglie showed promise of the qualities belonging to a leader, and Thiers (perhaps on purpose) had asked him to take the French embassy at London. So Thiers remained alone, dominating the inexperienced crowd, that spoke confusedly by the voices of the Dupanloups, the de Meaux, the Ernouls, the Wallons, the Lucien Bruns — as also of the Belcastels, and Franclieu, Knight of the Papal tiara and the fleur-de-lys."

[2] Journal de Fidus, 6/8/71.

liberal principles were still untroubled.[1] Clause 9 provided that (for the present) only the Maires of the communes, whose population fell below 6000, should be elected by their municipal councils : the rest were to be nominated by the Government. On April 8th, Antonin Lefèvre-Pontalis (Right) moved to extend the right of election to all councils. " The election of Maires ", he said, " was for us a programme of opposition under the Empire : it is right, therefore, that today it should become a programme of Government." Ernest Picard, who was then Minister of the Interior, asked for the postponement of so large a question, but the amendment was carried by 279 votes to 269.

The sitting was at once suspended, and Thiers was sent for : he apologised for his absence.

> Busy about your closest interests. . . . I could not believe for an instant that a doubt was possible on the question before you. . . . What ! you ask us to maintain order, and at the same time you take away from us the means for maintaining it ! . . . I appreciate the intelligence of our great cities : I do them all possible justice, but you cannot be unaware that the demagogic party is powerful there by very reason of its audacity. . . . I care too much for the interest of my country and the accomplishment of the overwhelming task you have laid upon me to hesitate in making it perfectly clear that, if the clause you voted were not amended, I could not keep on my shoulders the burden of power.

The Assembly had to eat humble pie, and, as a result of numerous abstentions, a compromise was carried by which the Government obtained " provisionally " the right to appoint Maires in all communes, where the population exceeded 20,000.[2]

---

[1] Under the Empire the Royalist and Liberal Oppositions had drawn up at Nancy, in 1863, a programme of which the object was " to emancipate the Departments ". Halévy has shown (*Fin des notables*, p. 49) that the idea of local liberties was a favourite doctrine of the liberal aristocrats down from the time of the Fronde.

[2] *Annales*, t. 2, pp. 340-47 ; cf. Thiers' letter to General Bourbaki, Commandant of the 6ᵉ Corps d'Armée (2/9/71) : " I cannot allow the municipal council [of Lyon] to act like the government of a federal state, ordering, commanding, convoking the National Guard, as though it were an army

On June 27th the debate began upon a much larger and more important measure, introduced by the De-centralisation Commission " on the organisation and attributions of the General Councils of the Departments ", whereby it was proposed to check the powers of the Préfets by associating with them a Departmental Commission, elected by the Council. Thiers did not intervene in the Assembly debates, but he spoke his mind before the Commission.[1]

I do not disguise at all our differences of opinion. They are such that, if we were in a normal situation and I were the King's Minister, and if I could see one party ready to replace the other in the Government, I should hand in my resignation. I have always been a resolute supporter of the French system of administration. There is not another in Europe as good as ours. In each of our revolutions everything would have collapsed in disorder without it. . . . There is not a clause in your Bill that is not fated to be given the lie by the facts. . . . The Préfet is reduced to a subordinate rôle. . . . The Bill makes him a kind of clerk charged with drawing up reports for the General Council and carrying out its decisions. You have set up a Departmental Commission : I disapprove entirely of the institution. . . . The only Préfet I understand is one, who has a real responsibility and the zeal and devotion, which result from that. . . . But to place at his side a body to prevent him from acting is to put him in an impossible position, especially when we have to deal with a character as quarrelsome as the French.[2] You are

belonging to them. This is the way the Commune of Paris acted, and I will not allow any revival of it. Unfortunately the gentlemen of the Right, who call themselves Decentralisers, have involuntarily helped to spread the idea of the ' independent commune ' " (Bouniols, pp. 112-13). Faguet says : " For Thiers, centralisation had the charm of a poem. . . . Every kind of independ-ence, communal, Departmental, Provincial, was for him a secession " (*ibid.*).

[1] What follows is from the *procès-verbaux* of the Commission on Decentral-isation, which I was kindly allowed to examine at the Archives of the Chamber of Deputies. (See Appendix.)

[2] So Thiers said to Falloux : " Your friends are seeking a false popularity . . . look at their law on Decentralisation. It is absurd. My friends force me not to go to the Assembly. I would make a fine scene there : I would smash their law to pieces. What is this invention of a Departmental Commission ? It is a stick between the Préfet's legs to trip him up " (Thiers' actual phrase is much more vigorous). " Administration would be impossible in such condi-tions " (Falloux, *Memoirs*, ii. 499).

giving all the administration of the communes to this Commission. . . . The Commission will not do all this work : you will not find men to do it. Business will suffer. If that is what you want, I will never consent to it. At my age I will never consent to lend my name to the dislocation of our administrative system.

These incidents happened not only when the Right were trying to reform the Government in a democratic direction [1] but also when they were trying to stimulate the administration against demagogy. That too Thiers regarded as outside their province. On August 24th the Vicomte de Meaux spoke in favour of the immediate dissolution of the National Guard on the ground that it was in contradiction with the military institutions intended for the future [2] and could only be an element of disorder in the country. The feeling of the Assembly was with him : even Jules de Lasteyrie said, " Though I am the grandson of the National Guard,[3] I shall vote for their dissolution ". But unfortunately, in rejecting the argument that the Government were sufficiently armed, de Meaux gave instances of their weakness, concluding with the assassination of the Préfet at St-Étienne by the National Guard, which had not yet been dissolved. Amid the excitement provoked by these words, he felt he had gone too far. He added : " Do I wish to attack the Government ? " Thiers interrupted him furiously : " Accuse them. It is more honest." De Meaux hurriedly finished, and Thiers rushed

[1] Another example concerns the freedom of the Press. On April 12th it was decided (on the report of de Broglie) that Press cases should be sent to a jury. On July 3rd a Bill was introduced for the *cautionnement* of newspapers (*i.e.* paying deposits). It received Government support, and was carried. But the Marquis of Castellane (from the Extreme Right) opposed it in the name of liberty. Thiers remarked to Falloux : " I am very glad his mother is no longer here, for I should not have wished to distress her ". His mother, a niece of Talleyrand, had just left the room (Falloux, *Memoirs*, ii. 500).

[2] Universal Conscription had already received the support of the Army Commission. Thiers had spoken strongly against it : he was in favour of professional armies. He would therefore specially resent the argument that the National Guards must be dissolved to prepare the way for Conscription.

[3] Denis, p. 30. Lafayette was his grandfather.

to the tribune, where he played the comedy of provoking the Right to interrupt him, and, when he did not succeed, pretending he had been interrupted and lashing himself into a fury :

" It is not just to say that all the National Guards of France are culpable and dangerous." (" *Hear ! hear !* " *from the Left.*)

From the Right : " We did not say that : we protest."

THIERS : " I ask that you will be good enough not to interrupt me." (*Murmurs from the Right.*) " I declare that the material order of France is not in danger." (*Assent from the Left. Renewed murmurs from the Right.*) " I declare it." (*Renewed murmurs.*) " It is not those, who interrupt me, who have to answer for it : it is I, who answer for it on my honour. . . . What ! you have, between Paris and Versailles, this Army which forced the gates of Paris, which still consists of 120,000 men, and, protected by such a force, you are not feeling safe ! "

DUC DE BISACCIA : " We protest against such an accusation."

Voice from the Right : " There are no people here, who are afraid."

THIERS : " If I were a weak man, I would flatter you. Instead of that, when I think you are mistaken, I regard it as my duty to tell you so." (*Noise.*) " If, when the Government, that you have set up, believes that you are mistaken, you do not wish even to listen, there is only one thing to do." (*Exclamations.*) " Gentlemen, after the numerous interruptions I have had to put up with, I am perhaps justified in saying that I have difficulty in obtaining a hearing." (*No.*) " From the number of voices in this Assembly, which protest against my words, I believe that the confidence, which I need, is much shaken." (*No, no.*) " . . . I have only one word to add. I know the resolution demanded from me by this scene. I have no more to say to the Assembly." [1]

With these words Thiers left the House, which was seething with excitement and confusion. Finally General Ducrot persuaded him and the Assembly to accept the following amendment : " The National Guards shall be dissolved in all the communes of France, as far as circum-

---

[1] *Annales*, t. 5, pp. 117-28. De Meaux says that Thiers drew up his resignation, but a friend snatched the paper from him, and tore it up (*Souvenirs*, p. 67).

stances and the progress of military reorganisation permit. This operation shall be carried out by the Government on its own responsibility, and as soon as possible." [1]

Outside the Assembly, Thiers' attitude to the Right is best illustrated first by his relations with Falloux, and secondly by his growing antagonism towards the Duc de Broglie, still ambassador at London.

By his refusal to enter Parliament, Falloux had placed himself in the irritating position of an external oracle, who was perpetually lecturing the Comte de Chambord on his duty to the Royalists, Thiers on his duty to the Assembly and the Legitimists on their duty to the Orleanists, without really having any defined responsibility to speak for anyone. His highly sensitive independence, and perhaps his weak health, forbade his being the accredited agent of anybody.

During the Commune, Falloux was all on fire for action. He blamed the Assembly for its subservience to Thiers. " Of course he will compel you to accept his ideas as far as he can, but I still remain convinced that the day, when you, in your turn, say to him, ' Choose between the majority and the minority ', he will return to you." As for the Assembly, he was convinced they must restore the Monarchy : " A Republic in France does not pacify : it destroys. . . . You, who are young in the Assembly and the Press [he was writing to Lacombe], do not abuse your modesty : do not prolong the truce too long : that is all right in peace time, but in war you should seize your arms (whatever stage of military instruction you may have

---

[1] Thiers carried out the dissolution of the National Guards in his own time (*e.g.* " The National Guard at Lyons being one of those that the Assembly wished to dissolve, we must obey the recent law " (letter to Bourbaki — Bouniols, p. 113). He said to Falloux : " It is necessary that a National Guard should have committed a fault for me to dissolve them. I cannot make enquiries whether the Battalions are what *you* call good or bad." Falloux replied : " Never has a society been more attacked and less defended " (Falloux, ii. 505). However, most of the Guards were suppressed in three months (Dreyfus, *La République de M. Thiers*, p. 120).

reached) and rush to the battlefield, instead of advancing step by step." [1]

In reply [2] Lacombe tactfully suggested that, if Falloux were in the Chamber " in the midst of the difficulties of the conflict ", he would calm " these outbursts of holy impatience ". An open conflict with Thiers would mean a crisis not merely in the Ministry but in the Government. " Have you the means of success ? In the Assembly, where, the last few months, the Right has rather lost than gained ground, precisely because it has always been more concerned with the end to be attained than with the means for attaining it ? In the towns, where so many evil passions still exist, and where you have no army to preserve order ? " Such being the case, the best policy for the Right was to " surround Thiers, to advise him, to keep him well informed. In order to succeed, the movement to restore the King must feel it has Thiers behind it ; if one were forced to work for it *without* him, at least one must take care not to seem to be striving for it *against* him." [3]

The end of the Commune seemed to Falloux the ideal moment for a Restoration. " The *status quo* or the *provisoire* (whatever title is given it for ornament) will never be anything but an instrument for the decomposition of France, till it has become totally corrupt." [4] Feverish with an impatience, partly perhaps accounted for by his physical sufferings, he wrote to Thiers himself : " You seem to think that the pacification of the country could be attained, if you reorganised it without giving it a Constitution. . . . You cannot have believed that our dear wounded France, once restored to health, could remain on her feet without conviction, without compass, republican

[1] Letter of April 28th (Lacombe, i. 13-17).
[2] Letter of May 20th (Lacombe, i. 21-4).
[3] An admirable piece of psychology (where the young man saw further than the old one) ; the leaders of the Right were always ready to make reasonable concessions to Thiers : but they never knew how to appeal to his *amour-propre*.   [4] Letter to Lacombe, May 22nd (i. 25).

or monarchist, under the Bonapartes or the Bourbons, as chance or the caprice of the crowd may bring it about. You cannot have resolved in your great heart and mind that statesmen should abdicate from the most important decisions that affect their country." Did he believe that the Royalist cause could gain by further waiting ? " That will not be gaining time but failing to recognise the precious moment, which Christianity calls a gift from Providence and the world calls an opportunity." " People say, ' The towns are Republican,[1] the peasants Bonapartist and the army hesitates between the two '. My answer is : You are shutting yourselves up in a vicious circle. The states- men wait for the country to give the signal, and the country waits for the signal from its statesmen." [2]

Falloux received no answer to this letter, and his sus- picions became darker. He now accused Thiers not merely negatively — of hindering Monarchy, but positively — of encouraging disorder. He spoke of his refusing to dissolve the National Guard, allowing the municipal councils to break the law,[3] continually insulting the majority of the Assembly : " His faults may deserve indulgence, for they go with rare qualities and eminent services, but they must not cause us to be complaisant to them, or else the result will be to draw down upon all the territory of France a hateful and bloodthirsty state of anarchy, which will be our last convulsion before our mutilation and final subjection

---

[1] Falloux is recalling Lacombe's letter of May 20th.

[2] Falloux, ii. 454-63. I think this last judgment is true : the best authori- ties seem to agree that, though the party divisions were sharp, the majority of the country, exhausted by the double disaster of the war and the Commune, would have accepted any solution.

[3] Taine writes (7/9/71) : " In my opinion another cause for anxiety is the composition of many of the municipal councils, not only at Lyons but in the little towns, like Lodère. They are composed of ' reds ', stupid and declama- tory, who have inherited the style, the violence and the folly of the ancient Jacobins " (Vie, iii. 171). M. Delpit writes (Journal, p. 141) : " Here we are in a state of alarm, almost of consternation, at the result of the municipal elec- tions (April 30th). It is said that Thiers and Picard are rubbing their hands and saying that it is a good lesson for the Assembly " (quoted Denis, p. 20).

beneath the combined yoke of the Bonapartes and Prussia ".[1] The Chambord manifesto destroyed his hopes of a Restoration, but strengthened and inflamed his demand that Thiers should maintain order. During a visit to Paris, he went to see Thiers personally.[2]

" It is useless ", Falloux said, " to worry about a final solution, if the *provisoire* continues as it is now, for in a few months there will be no more society for any of us : we are hasting towards an abyss, in which all solutions and ambitions will be swallowed up together." Thiers shrugged his shoulders ; he pointed out that all danger from the Internationale was over. " You may be reassured : I have my eye on everything." " You mean your functionaries : that is an eye which never sees far." Thiers began to lose his composure : " Then you come here to tell me that I do not know how to govern ? " He began to march up and down the room exclaiming, " I know what your friends want — my place. Very well, let them take it. . . . Now there is no more danger, everyone can succeed me, and your friends are able to rise to that kind of courage." Falloux sprang up and advanced towards Thiers, saying, " M. Thiers, you have already said that at the tribune ; [3] I thought you were ashamed of having said it. I warn you that I will not let you say it again before me." The conversation had become so warm that the ladies left the room.

As usual, when his anger was met with firmness, Thiers calmed down and explained that he had not meant to attack the military and political courage of the Right ; he then settled down to a calmer style of reasoning. With

[1] Which shows that the generally well-balanced Falloux had, for the moment, lost his head (letter of June 6th, Lacombe, i. 38-40).

[2] This visit seems to have been about the middle of July. The Duchesse de Galliera (daughter of the old Sardinian ambassador) and the Marquise of Castellane had called at the Presidence on their way to the gallery of the Assembly, and Falloux was invited to meet them (Falloux, ii. 494-507).

[3] At the *séance* of May 11th (see p. 192).

great skill, he pointed out that the Assembly were at one moment enfeebling the administration (by defending decentralisation and freedom of the Press), and at the same time accusing the administration of not being energetic enough. The discussion then turned on the National Guard, after which Falloux left the house exclaiming, " What a noble page in history you refuse yourself ! " Thiers followed him out, worn with excitement, and murmuring, " You exaggerate, you exaggerate ".

On his return Falloux confessed the scene to Dupanloup, who said, " You and I must never break with Thiers ; he must find us at his pillow, as friends up to the last hour ". Thiers himself sent a message to say that he felt no resentment. Falloux dined there the next day, and Mme Thiers said, " It is a good thing to get my husband used to contradiction ".[1]

All the same, a long personal and political friendship was ended. Thiers' comment was, " Falloux has become a fanatic ". Falloux felt that Thiers " was on his decline, morally and politically ". Lacombe, the distressed friend of both, wrote to Thiers : " Allow me to say that if you enfeeble the Assembly . . . it is your own strength, that you will diminish ; "[2] and to Falloux : " I hope still that the reconstitution of the majority, so as to force their will on Thiers, may be the benefit resulting from this melancholy situation ".[3]

Thiers' relationship to Falloux concerned his own past : his attitude to Duc Albert de Broglie vitally affected the future of both.

It is one of the boasts of the French Republicans that, under their form of government, class distinctions do not exist. Such a claim may or may not be justified by the facts ;[4] in any case the Republic of 1871 was as yet too

---

[1] Falloux, ii. 510.   [2] Letter of 15/8/71 (Lacombe, i. 48).

[3] Letter of same date (*ibid.* p. 50).

[4] See for a discussion of the whole question Bodley's *France*, Bk. i. ch. iii. (" Equality ").

precarious and too unsettled for such a result to have been achieved.   The Duc de Broglie can best be understood as a typical aristocrat, just as Thiers was the *petit bourgeois in excelsis*, and Gambetta the son of a grocer.

The de Broglies [1] came from Italy. It is said that in 1644 a Piedmontese captain entered the service of France, and did much work for Mazarin in the days of the Fronde. He is described as " brave and supple " ; the second epithet was constantly stressed by their enemies, as indicating some Machiavellian strain in the race.   St-Simon paints the de Broglie of his day as " full of artifices, intrigues and contrivances ".[2]

Duc Albert's father Victor was one of the leaders of that section of the nobility, which rallied to the house of Orleans, and he played an important part under the July Monarchy as a member of the group of Doctrinaires, rigid in principle, aiming by every device of study and experience at making themselves experts in politics, but perhaps too aloof from the man in the street, and too contemptuous of the opinion of others.[3]   The position of a Liberal aristocrat was none too easy in France ; as Whig Nobles the de Broglies would have shone in the House of Lords, but across the Channel such compromises were less easy.   De Broglie says that, when his father returned after the Revolution to the family château, " the survivors, who recalled the old Marshal de Broglie [4] . . . in his proud military costume . . . some-

[1] Pronounced " de Breuil ".

[2] Hanotaux, ii. 35, and *French Political Leaders*, ch. x.   The connection of the name with the Italian word Broglio or Imbroglio was not forgotten in the political controversies of 1873–7.

[3] Victor de Broglie was once turned out of office for saying disdainfully in answer to repeated parliamentary interrogations : " Is it clear now ? "

[4] He was *Victor-François*, commandant of the Camp at Paris : he left for Germany with the emigration, and served with the English and Russian troops against France, dying in 1804 : his son, *Victor-Claude*, fought for the United States, and, having imbibed an enthusiasm for liberty, was cut off by his indignant family.   However, he refused to accept the decree of suspension against Louis XVI, and was guillotined on June 27th, 1794.   His son, *Achille-Victor* (died 1870), was the father of Albert.

times presiding over the Estates of the nobles of the district, sometimes solemnly taking his place on the bench at church to be censed by the *curé*, sometimes galloping over the plains followed by an army of squires and outriders [1] . . . could not recover from their surprise as they met the new Duke, alone and on foot, a stick in his hand, and dressed severely, with nothing to recall the orders of chivalry ".[2]

In the case of Albert, his position was complicated by the fact that he was not only a Liberal aristocrat, but also a liberal Catholic. His mother, Albertine, daughter of the famous Mme de Staël,[3] was a Swiss Protestant, full of piety and charm : the only service held at Broglie was family prayers and the reading of a chapter from the Gospels. The old Duke Victor was a Catholic after the style of Rousseau's Vicaire Savoyard. "There is no middle course ", he said to a brother-in-law, " you must either be a philosophical Christian like me,[4] one who is sorry to be able to go no further, or else, like your sister, you must be a Christian out and out. . . ." " Jesus Christ was merely a philosopher like Socrates or Confucius, although He was superior to both of them." [5]

In accordance with an arrangement, usual at the time, the sons of mixed marriages were brought up as Catholics, and the daughters as Protestants. As will have been gathered, the old Duke was not a very inspiring or orthodox teacher of Catholicism ; he rarely went to Mass, and he

[1] Victor in his *Memoirs* (p. 2) describes him as " clad in a hunting-dress, braided all over, surrounded by the nobility of the neighbourhood, all wearing similar dresses, the gift of the Marshal, for whose pleasure the forest at Broglie used to re-echo the cry of a hundred hounds and the gallop of fifty horses ".

[2] *Revue des Deux Mondes* (15/12/24) (De Broglie, *Souvenirs*), p. 776.

[3] Said to have been Mme de Staël's daughter by Benjamin Constant. One day in the Assembly, Gambetta, watching the Duke's nervous hands, said to a neighbour, " The hands of Constant ".

[4] He had himself written a *Traité sur l'existence de l'âme*. He tells us of his childhood : " I still see from here the spot near the bathroom, where, I know not why, I was struck by the idea that I was *myself*, and could not be any other but myself. The ideas of identity, personality and necessity, suggested themselves to me under their rigidly metaphysical forms " (*Memoirs*, i. 16).

[5] Victor's *Memoirs*, ii. 20.

gave his son Bossuet's *Exposition de la doctrine catholique* " to show him that the differences between Protestantism and Catholicism were not so important as Protestants made out ".   When Victor became a Minister of the Crown, he gave up taking Albert to Mass, and his mother conducted him to a specially orthodox Protestant chapel, where he had to " listen to a sermon of an hour and a half, austere and monotonous in form, without any other food for the feelings and the imagination than the singing of psalms in bad French verse " : the result was that he " dreaded his Sunday holiday almost as much as his week-day lessons ".[1]

With such a training, he had to find out his religion for himself.   He was always a fervent son of the Church, but he attached himself early to the Liberal Catholic school. " Closely united to one another, too closely perhaps, too much separated from the multitude by the grave charm and intimacy of their union . . . they comforted themselves by that very union." [2]   A follower of those who fought the despotic State in 1840, and the despotic Papacy in 1870 — Falloux, Dupanloup, Montalembert — he wrote liberal articles for the *Correspondant*; he drew up (for Dupanloup) the manifesto against Papal Infallibility.   It is clear that such theological views definitely weakened his position as leader of the Right.   In 1874, when his Government suspended the *Univers* — the newspaper of Louis Veuillot, that fierce Ultramontane said : "*Au fond*, we believe that there has been more Liberal Catholic bitterness than diplomatic insistence " ; [3] and it is said that Cardinal Chigi, the Papal Legate at Paris, secretly preferred the Republic to de Broglie.

Born of such rigidly upright parents, a Doctrinaire and a Calvinist, brought up under the religious severity of his

---

[1] *Revue des Deux Mondes* (1/1/25), pp. 63-4.
[2] Halévy, *Fin des notables*, p. 153.
[3] De Meaux, p. 204. Veuillot's Papal propaganda was alleged to have alarmed Germany.

mother and the political austerity of his father, it was to
be expected that Albert would be high-minded and disinterested : the danger was that he might have about him
a touch of the prig. As a boy, his terror was that he
would have to board with other boys. On his first arrival
at Paris he confesses that he was " rather solitary, a stranger
to my generation " : his only diversion (and that a passionate one) was to prepare speeches, and fight for majorities
at political debating societies. He adds : " I have been
reproached with a strictness of behaviour and manners,
which was often taken as haughtiness. . . . A little more
life in the world and society would perhaps have made me
more flexible." [1] A diplomatic career (at Madrid, Rome
and London) taught him cleverness and resource rather
than that particular instinct that marks the real statesman.
However much one may admire him, it is hard not to feel
that the Duke was rather inhuman.[2] His tutor, Le Père
Doudan, — a priest of much subtlety and brilliance —
wrote to him, when he was twenty-four : " May God preserve you from pride, from vanity, from insolence, from
scorn of your fellow men, from being wedded eternally to
your own opinions, from a mocking and dictatorial attitude ;
in short, from all the vices that intellectual superiority
brings in its train, and especially from the worst vice
of all, the vice of flattering yourself that you do not make
others too conscious of your superiority ! In a word,
my son, I wish you what you can never attain." [3] De
Meaux, who was a devoted follower, says (more mildly) :
" He was more at his ease dealing with ideas than with
men ".[4] This aristocratic morgue, which would have

---

[1] *Revue des Deux Mondes* (15/1/25), pp. 334-5.

[2] After reading a novel by Octave Feuillet, he gravely asked whether one
of the heroes in it was still alive and, on being answered, said : " Why waste
one's time in writing about things that have never existed ? Life is too short "
(Vassili, p. 158). This is carrying the historical temperament very far !

[3] Quoted in Deschanel's *Gambetta*, p. 167 (letter of 22/7/45).

[4] De Meaux, p. 144.

seemed distinguished in England,[1] appeared unsociable in
France. " He had never been frivolous, and had but
seldom shown himself amiable. He had no indulgence for
others, perhaps because he never had any for himself." [2]
His contempt for meanness struggled with a desire to be
loyal to his supporters. " It is the ' Spiritual Combat ' in
action ", an observer remarked. Even his magnanimity
seemed charged with disdain : " It is so tiring to hate ", he
used to say.[3] A certain shyness and a very strict moral
sense concealed a not unkind heart. The American wife of
a French deputy tells the story of how " a deputy once
asked the Duc de Decazes for something . . . he was kind
and courteous, but did not do what the man wanted. He
then went to the Duc de Broglie, who was busy, received
him very curtly, cut short his explanations, and was in
fact extremely disagreeable, but actually did the thing that
was wanted. The man loved Decazes and hated de
Broglie." [4]

His upbringing and temperament had a strong influence
on his political views : the cultured *via media*, which he
affected, does not flourish in democracies — especially in
French democracies. It really needs the atmosphere of
our House of Lords : failing that, de Broglie asked himself,

---

[1] In some respects the Doctrinaires rather modelled themselves on English
statesmen : they also had what M. Faguet has called — in the case of Guizot —
a " taste for unpopularity ". The Duke spoke of his father as having " a
contempt for the arts of winning popularity with the masses " (quoted
Deschanel, *Gambetta*, p. 166).   [2] Vassili, p. 157.   [3] De Meaux, p. 145.
[4] Mme Waddington, *First Years*, p. 64. Marshal MacMahon, when he was
President of the Republic, said to the Duke : " You can't be Minister of the
Interior : you would annoy all the deputies, who had business with you " (de
Meaux, p. 149). The following story (even if apocryphal) is too amusing
to omit : " A Parisian notary, Senart, deputy for Seine-et-Oise, used to
come to the Assembly in a black suit and white shirt. One day de Broglie,
then President of the Council, comes to the Assembly in the driving rain. In
the vestibule of the Palace he sees a distinguised-looking fellow, who bows as
he passes. Without paying much attention, the Duke says, ' Mon garçon,
take my umbrella to the cloak-room and, as it is dripping, take care of the
floor '." It is said that Senart's was the vote that carried the Republic in
1875 (Zévaès, *Histoire de la 3ᵉ République*, p. 128).

" Could not the cultured and refined tone of the National
Assembly be preserved, after its separation, in some kind
of Senate or Second Chamber ? " He played with the idea
of creating an aristocracy in a country, where, since 1789,
monarchies and republics flourish, but aristocracy never
seems to take root.

He wrote to Thiers on May 16th, 1871 : " I have made
you my confession of faith, or rather of scepticism. I do
not believe either in the Republic nor in Legitimacy.
Whoever brings me these magical formulae for curing our
evils, seems to me always either a charlatan or a fool.
But I believe in the good sense and united action of honest
men whether under a Prince or a Republic." [1] His ideal
was a Senate representing all the best talent in the country,
and presided over by a Prince of the blood, Aumale for
example. Thiers laughingly called it a *République princière*:
the Legitimists murmured that the Orleanists were not
really Monarchists, but Oligarchs.[2]

A contrast with Gambetta brings out the Duke's own
character. The social difference between the two rings in
the words used by de Broglie in 1877 : " He, who bears the
name of Marshal MacMahon, cannot become the ally and
hireling of the hon. M. Gambetta ".[3] Gambetta, always a
generous opponent, though he called his rival " Machiavelli
of the lobbies ", and " Orator without a voice ", yet, when
the Extreme Right deserted him in 1874, exclaimed,
" They are fools : they have only one man, and they throw
him over ".[4]

In the political drama the two were foils to one another.
When the Duke came into power, Edmond Adam said to

---

[1] Halévy, *Courier de M. Thiers*, p. 430.

[2] " One of the ideas of the Right Centre corresponded to an old dream of
all the Frondes and Ligues. Always, when the nobles have tried to dominate
the State, they have taken princes of the blood as their chiefs" (de Roux,
p. 141). He points out that Duke Victor in his *Views on the Government of
France* desired an Upper Chamber including the great proprietors and all
descendants of the great families of Peers (*ibid.* pp. 38-9).

[3] Hanotaux, iv. 45.   [4] Bosq, p. 229.

Gambetta : " He is a great orator, who has never influenced a single vote, and whose speeches must be read to be admired. He is by nature loyal, and he has to behave like a Machiavelli. All his good qualities (and he has many) are faults. His reserve makes people think him contemptuous. He needs a Chamber of Peers under a monarchy — and a different voice. Look at him ! He has not the attitude of a man who leads his troops to victory." [1]

Gambetta was a born leader, superbly at his ease with men, pinching his favourites by the ear, *bon vivant*, full of *camaraderie*, encouraging his party by his presence, and checking them by a gesture. The Duke was shy, haughty in manner and preferred to buttonhole deputies in corners. Gambetta was an orator, full of vigour and *entraînement*, sweeping impetuously to his point with his lion-like profile and tempestuous hair, dominating the tumult, drawing on the enthusiasm of the moment, turning interruptions to account, an " opportunist " in speech as well as policy. The Duke's face was colourless below its ample forehead : only the dark eyes were active. His nervous laugh, his spasmodic gestures and twitches of the shoulder, showed that he was not at his ease. His voice was poor and weak (" he speaks as others gargle ").[2] His style was polished to perfection, the arguments solid, the language beautiful : every word carried. They had " a strange elegance and perfection ",[3] but they seemed nearer to an article in a review than to the action, which Demosthenes regarded as the soul of oratory.

Gambetta was hampered by no metaphysics or general views. The Duke was by temperament reflective, large rather than clear in his views, made cautious by an over-subtle psychology — as a student, historian of nations and

---

[1] Mme Adam, *Nos amitiés*, p. 465.

[2] Bosq, p. 227. After a failure at the tribune a friend said to him, " It is only the voice you lack ". " Ah," he replied sadly, " is not that everything for the orator ? " (de Meaux, pp. 145-6).

[3] Lano, *Après l'empire*, p. 199.

Empires,[1] as a Christian always interrogating his own conscience. His hesitations came from the same source as his haughtiness — his alert and sensitive conscience. He seemed to his opponents to lack openness. What he lacked was hopefulness — less serious as a moral, more serious perhaps as a political defect. He had Gladstone's profound belief in God without Gladstone's exuberant power of persuading himself that God was on his side.

Yet with all these defects he had a power and effectiveness quite outside Gambetta's range. One felt the stern sense of duty, the forceful personality, the scholarly distinction, the rich, well-balanced mind. His courage was passive rather than active. He was a Cato, the worthy champion of lost causes rather than a Caesar of the *victrix causa*. His greatest speech was the defence of a policy he knew to have been overwhelmingly defeated;[2] his next greatest was a protest against a republic he knew to be inevitable.[3] He advocated with skill and dignity the 1873 compromise with Thiers on Ministerial responsibility, though he had next to no confidence in it ; he defended the constituent powers of an Assembly of whose mandate he was not wholly convinced.[4] In 1877, though he conscientiously appealed to the electorate, he felt that a *coup d'état* would have given better results.[5] Perhaps it was as well that he failed, for failure and suffering called out the real courage of his character. After his death, his valet said, "He waited for his end as if he were waiting for his

---

[1] A Royalist said to the bunglers of Seize Mai 1877 (de Broglie and others) : "Write history, gentlemen : do not concern yourselves with making it " (Maurras, *Enquête*, p. 318). [2] In the Senate after the 1877 elections.

[3] 1874, against the Casimir-Périer motion.

[4] " I have seen his noble mind struggling against the thought so disconcerting for him that, after three years, the Assembly had perhaps ceased to be the exact expression of the country's will " (Daudet, *Chronique*, p. 200).

[5] " On seeing the crowd in the Champs-Élysées at their ease, elegant, walking in the sunshine from the Arc de Triomphe to the Obelisk, de Broglie said to me : " These people are more ready for a *coup d'état* than for the effort we are going to ask from them " (de Meaux, p. 315).

coach ".[1] His highest efforts were a satire on the successful
and an epitaph on those who had been beaten. It was a
great tribute to him that, in the last desperate battle for
the Conservative cause, the Marshal sent for him : it was
profoundly characteristic that the messenger found him
reading Tacitus.[2]

Thiers and the old duke Victor de Broglie had been
friends and colleagues under the July Monarchy.[3] But in
the son's account of their relations can be felt the slight
nuance of an aristocrat speaking about a bourgeois : " Born
of a family of little reputation, and himself exposed to many
insinuations, some mere calumnies, the rest exaggerations,
Thiers found in my father a benevolent judge, whose
austere morality gave the younger statesman a standing in
the eyes of the public. . . . But my father often used to
say to me, ' There is nothing to be done with him today :
he is in a bad mood : you can see it by his face '." [4]

Albert never felt much attraction to Thiers : with his
own deeply philosophic and distinguished mind he regarded
him as the incarnation of the commonplace. He seemed
" a little man from the South, in a hurry ".[5] They were
both historians, and each wrote of an Empire, but how
different the Duke's reflective investigation of the influence
of Christianity upon the Roman Empire,[6] and the superficial animation and lucidity of Thiers' picture of Bonaparte !
De Broglie has himself finely analysed the incompatibility
of temperament :

Thiers' conversation, which ravished his audience, always left
me cold and unresponsive. He had two faculties, rare in them-

---

[1] Daudet, *Chronique*, p. 233.   [2] Hanotaux, iii. 615.

[3] " Saint-Marc Girardin tells me that the Duc de Broglie has not any
authority over Thiers, but has a certain influence from the memory of his
father " (Lacombe, i. 27).

[4] " Il a sa mauvause figure " (*Revue des Deux Mondes* (1/1/25), pp. 67-8).

[5] Halévy, *Fin des notables*, p. 155.

[6] De Broglie's *History of the Church and the Empire* is still referred to with
admiration (*e.g.* by Duchesne) : Thiers' *History of the Consulate and the
Empire* is hardly read in France.

selves, which perfectly explain his ascendancy in debate. He knew
at once how to give an elegant and distinguished form to commonplace ideas, and how to bring the most difficult ideas down to the
understanding of the lowest intelligences by the clearness of his
explanations. . . . Neither of these methods appealed to me : the
commonplace ideas wearied me . . . and, as to the others, I was
vain enough to believe that I could grasp them without other
people taking the trouble to bring them down to my level.[1]

One of the Duke's first pamphlets was written to support
Thiers' celebrated work on Property. The author was not
flattered. " You don't know these doctrinaires," Thiers
said to a friend, " they never talk of other people's works
except to put one of their own productions in their place." [2]

The moment Thiers came to power, he sent the Duke to
the London Embassy. If he wished to keep a rival away
from the Assembly, the purpose was hardly fulfilled. De
Broglie visited Versailles in March and May, and he was
constantly seen moving about the groups of deputies. A
journalist remarked, " He is not slavishly bound down to
any ideas of residence ". He defended himself against the
charge of having intrigued against his Government. Indeed, at this time he still hoped that Thiers might lead
a Conservative majority.[3] But suspicions began to grow.
Thiers said of him, " Il a des calculs " and " On ne peut
vivre avec lui : il a un mauvais caractère ". " Take away
the epithet ", de Broglie said to a friend, " and you have
the truth." Another time Thiers said : " France is content
for the present and does not worry about the future."
" True," was the Duke's acid comment, " we all know
that France is seventy-four years old, and has no children."[4]

Officially, the correspondence still continued courteous

---

[1] *Revue des Deux Mondes* (15/1/25), p. 348.　　[2] *Ibid.* (15/5/25), p. 413.

[3] " In my opinion Thiers ought to have installed the Conservative party
in power . . . and to have allowed the attempt at a Restoration to go on (if
he did not wish to take part in it himself). . . . If (as was only too likely) it
had failed, he could have asked the Royalist party to constitute a form of
government, at the head of which he would naturally have been placed "
(*Revue des Deux Mondes* (15/3/29), pp. 376-7).

[4] *Revue des Deux Mondes* (15/3/29), p. 388.

— in spite of a violent protest of the Ambassador against the fact that one of the leading Communards had reached London in disguise with a passport signed by St-Hilaire.[1] Thiers wrote to tell him how his son had been wounded at the capture of Fort Issy, and praised his courage and devotion : [2] later on, he referred to the effect of the Chambord manifesto in producing " a little more patience among the various parties".[3] Later in the month his tone slightly changes : " I despair of ever coming to an agreement with you about Home policy. I only care for one thing — the peace of my country. . . . France is a charming mistress, but very uncertain : one would feel the reproach of loving her too much if she were not one's country." [4]

Such was the position at the end of the first session of the Assembly at Versailles — the Right disappointed at the failure of the Restoration movement, suspicious of Thiers, but forced to work with him, *faute de mieux* ; Thiers himself for the very same reasons inclined to evade a decision, to rely upon his new title of President [5] and the popularity revealed at the July elections.

Falloux had been over-excited, when he said that the country was moving to the abyss, but he had a real reason for impatience. Every week made Thiers more at home in his quasi-Republican régime, and the country more used to it. The possibility of a successor seemed very remote : the Orleanists wanted the Duc d'Aumale or the Prince de Joinville, and the Legitimists would accept neither. Thiers chuckled to himself — " They have no one ".

(e) THE LEFT CENTRE AND THE PROPOSITION RIVET

" France is Left Centre." — ROYER-COLLARD.
" The Left Centre is most convenient : I never worry about it and it always follows me." — THIERS.

[1] *Ibid.* p. 381. This probably refers to Bergeret (see p. 453).
[2] Letter of 10/5/71 (Bouniols, p. 62).   [3] *Ibid.* p. 82 (letter of 11/7/71).
[4] *Ibid.* p. 90 (letter of 20/7/71).   [5] See the next section of this chapter.

" A French Centrist is a man, who has never been able
to make his mind up." — GRENVILLE MURRAY, *Round
about Paris.*

The Left Centre of the Republican party [1] was naturally
marked out as Thiers' *point-d'appui*, but the relation was
not always easy. They had to play the part of a Ministerial
party without having a majority, and with a Government,
in which colleagues of the Right were always disputing
their influence.

It was not till the fall of the President in 1873 that the
Left Centre really became a Thierist party. Till then it
was not very clearly distinguished from the Right Centre.[2]
French parties lack the sharp separation of our own parliamentary forces. The two Centres sat very close together,
and a slight shifting of seats is almost imperceptible compared to our " crossing the floor of the House ". Movements from the Left to Right Centre and back were constant. A group of nine members, called the " Conservateurs
républicains ", sat on the dividing line (or fence), and
a larger group (the group Target) were responsible for
Thiers' downfall in 1873 by transferring their votes to the
Right. So, afterwards, the Royalists hoped to get a majority
of one for the monarchy by detaching votes from the Left
Centre, and in 1875 the Republic was carried — also by
one vote — largely by the efforts of two brothers-in-law,
both ex-Orleanists, who sat on each side of the invisible
line of absolute neutrality which is the exact centre of the
Chamber.[3]

[1] In reading descriptions of the members of this party we come across such
phrases as " Not more republican than necessary ". " His republicanism was
of a mauve tinge." " Not a violent republican — et nullement *de la veille* "
(the title proudly claimed by the Republicans, who had held the faith under
the July Monarchy). Many of the leaders were Free Traders, a fact which was
destined at one famous crisis to strain their relations with Thiers.

[2] Thus Feray, one of the founders of the Left Centre, voted (up till May
1873) with the Right on the question of the Princes, with the Left on the return
to Paris, and abstained on all constitutional questions.

[3] Pasquier and Casimir-Périer — their policy was called the Conjunction of
the Centres.

The Left Centre was composed of four elements —
Orleanists, who preferred a Republic to the Comte de
Chambord, but who would have preferred the Comte de
Paris to a Republic ; *Industrialists*, who wished, as far as
possible, to preserve the *status quo* ; *personal friends of
Thiers* ; and lastly, a *group of newer deputies*, anxious to
show that Republicanism had shaken off its old violence
and pedantry, and could produce tolerance, good-humour
and common sense,[1] " a little inclined from inexperience
not to measure the difference between the ideal and the
real, but honest and moderate ".[2]

The origin of the party illustrates the combination
of these four elements. The story is told by de Marcère,
deputy for the Nord, a lawyer sprung from an old Norman
family who " made his way without concessions or intrigues ",[3] by sheer sincerity. On his arrival at Versailles
he gathered a group of new members, which met at the
Hôtel-de-Ville (Salle de Justice) and, after a long debate,
whether they should call themselves " Républicains conservateurs " or " Conservateurs républicains ",[4] decided for
the former. At first he had four supporters : Gailly, who,
as Maire of Charleville, had bravely gone through the
German occupation and bombardment ;[5] Philippotaux,
Maire of Sedan, who had been seized as a hostage during
the war ; Dureault, and Félix Renaud. Their numbers soon
rose to sixty. They included deputies of distinction, such
as General Chanzy, afterwards Governor-General of Algeria,
who accepted the Republic on the understanding that it

---

[1] Laboulaye came nearest to the English idea of an M.P. His impartial
humour was not always acceptable amid the solemnity of French party
struggles.   [2] Pessard, ii. 39.

[3] Mme Adam, *Mes angoisses*, p. 87 : " Marcère, with his cold smile, was
nicknamed Robespierre by the ladies. I don't know why " (Lano, *Après
l'empire*, p. 280).   [4] De Marcère, *L'Assemblée nationale*, i. 107, 108, 133.

[5] It was he, who six years later (June 6th, 1877) in a famous scene (com-
memorated in prints and pictures) interrupted Fourtou's tribute to the National
Assembly for having liberated the territory of France, by pointing to Thiers
and calling out, " There is the liberator of our territory ".

had "nothing to do with the Republic of discontented factions and social rebels " : [1] he accused Gambetta of " turning republicanism into a sect ",[2] and then declared that, if the country turned to Radicalism, "we shall be driven into the arms of Monarchy ".[3] De Freycinet, who knew him during the war, describes him as " a real leader . . . firm without haughtiness, brave without rashness ".[4]

To the same group belonged Bardoux, a lawyer of Clermont-Ferrand, " liberal, a lover of order, who respected the rights of others, very broad-minded and *au fond* Catholic, as he showed in his last moments ",[5] " a poet and at the same time an Auvergnat, positive as a boiler and dreamy as a troubadour ".[6] His black, shaven cheeks and melancholy air gave him the look of a priest ; his long black hair, thrown back, recalled " a revolutionary student ".[7] He was a great worker [8] and his politeness bordered on unctuousness. Dufaure said of him, " He is everybody's best friend ".[9] As Minister of Justice he always promised the same post to at least four candidates.[10]

Ricard came to the Assembly from Niort with a great reputation for eloquence at the Bar. He had to learn the familiar parliamentary lesson that success at the tribune requires other qualities. His thick lips and lion-like appearance seemed vulgar.[11] He valiantly denied himself the tribune for a time, and confined himself to committee-rooms and party gatherings. " I am voluntarily dumb ", he said : his enemies called him " The Mirabeau of com-mittee rooms ".[12] He was to gain himself a place later as the great orator of the Left Centre, strong enough to stand up to Gambetta, but he was removed from the service of

[1] De Marcère, *L'Assemblée nationale*, i. 224.   [2] Pessard, ii. 284.

[3] Mme Adam, *Nos amitiés politiques*, p. 27.   [4] Freycinet, p. 212.

[5] De Marcère, *Hist.* ii. 197.   [6] Pessard, ii. 175.

[7] De Goncourts, t. 5, p. 234.

[8] " A deputy, whose laziness was proverbial, said to me, ' I am president of such and such a commission '. Seeing me smile he added, ' It's all right ; Bardoux is secretary ' " (*Kel-kun*, p. 344)   [9] Bosq, p. 97.

[10] Daudet, *Chronique*, p. 99.   [11] *Kel-kum*, p. 288.   [12] Bosq, p. 190.

the Third Republic by an early death.

Lanfrey, member for the Bouches du Rhône, was never an orator ; his gifts lay along the line of philosophy and history. His chief distinction was that he had attacked the Napoleonic legend in his *History of Napoleon* (1865–1875). " His victories were either treated as unimportant, or else attributed to his Marshals." [1] The author himself, " cold and correct, looked like a diplomat with his enigmatic smile ",[2] and he was actually sent as ambassador to Berne from 1871 to 1873.[3]

Scherer was a still more prominent literary figure, known to us as the friend of Matthew Arnold.[4] His father was Swiss, and his mother had English blood ; he himself knew England, and was married to an English wife. He had been Protestant Professor of Theology at Geneva, " that home of large instruction and lucid intelligence ".[5] There he abandoned Christianity for Hegelianism after an agonising struggle. Long afterwards someone quoted Guizot's judgment on Lammenais as an evil-doer. " Evil doer ! " he cried, " M. Guizot does not know what it costs." [6] Sadness and disillusion followed ; [7] after 1870 this Hegelian wrote : " The charm, which once drew us towards Germany, is broken for ever ".[8] He became more and more disgusted with the phrases of democracy. " Humanity as a whole inspires me neither with respect nor tenderness : I

---

[1] Claveau, p. 114.   [2] Bosq, p. 191.

[3] His *Letters of Everard* (correspondence during the Assembly) showed " his astonishing pride which spared nobody : Gambetta was an actor, Dufaure an incompetent, Thiers an old mummy, the Assembly a carnival in which servility and charlatanism joined hands " (Bosq, p. 192).

[4] Who introduced him to the British public in " A French Critic of Milton " (*Mixed Essays*, p. 237).   [5] *Ibid.* p. 253.

[6] *Les Intellectuels et l'avènement de la 3ᵉ République* (Bellesart), p. 75.

[7] Matthew Arnold notes that he has not the elasticity and cheerfulness of Sainte-Beuve (*Mixed Essays*, p. 253).

[8] In an essay on Goethe (Bellesart, p. 79) ; Matthew Arnold urbanely opines that " he is not warped by injustice and ill-will towards Germany, although the war has undoubtedly left him with a feeling of soreness " (*Mixed Essays*, p. 280).

repudiate solidarity." [1]   He wondered whether Democracy would not be for France " what the invasion of the barbarians was for the Roman Empire ".[2]   But his hatred of clericalism [3] kept him in the ranks of the Left.

While de Marcère was forming his group of " Républicains conservateurs ", a group of industrialists and important persons from the provinces was gathering round Feray, owner of a large cotton-spinning factory at Essonne.   It contained deputies like Cordier, a Protectionist, manufacturer of printed calico, and Delille, President of the General Council of Creuse.   Their policy was " the reconstruction of the country by means of liberal institutions, and under the form of republican government actually in existence, other constitutional questions being reserved ".   The words " actually in existence " were only carried after a long debate.[4]

Thiers naturally kept his eye on the two groups, and at his suggestion they were fused into one.   It was not without trouble.   " The programme cost much sweat and oil. . . . Commas had their importance and full-stops were serious matters." [5]   Fourteen members of the Group Feray seceded to the Right Centre, and three to the intermediate " Conservateurs républicains ".

The new Left Centre was naturally patronised and kept in touch with the Government by the undefined group, who were the personal friends of Thiers.   They were not all like Jean Maure, who never appeared anywhere without a letter from his beloved Thiers, and yet at the beginning of each session wrote to the President of the Assembly : " Circumstances more powerful than my will do not allow me at present to offer my resignation, and my many

---

[1] Bellesart, p. 79.

[2] Bellesart calls him the Professor of Despair (p. 80).

[3] Taine says of him : " He is always irritated : his grievance is that everyone is clerical . . . he has the Protestant and Jansenist bitterness of a Camus " (*Vie*, t. 3, p. 226).

[4] De Marcère, *L'Assemblée nationale*, i. 107.   [5] Bosq, p. 187.

infirmities forbid me to take part in the work of the Assembly ".[1]

The following *amis de Thiers* are worth a moment's notice :

Charles Bertauld had been Professor of the Code Civil at Caen, and was an effective speaker, combining the dialectic of the lawyer with a real Norman caustic humour.

The Comte Horace Choiseul-Praslin was another friend. He was ambassador in Italy from May to November 1871, and later it was he who proposed that the President had " deserved well of his country ".[2]

Léon de Maleville was a veteran of politics, full of jollity and anecdotes. He had been secretary of the Interior under the July Monarchy, and Minister of the Interior under the Second Republic. He looked on himself as Thiers' official agent ; he loved taking messages backwards and forwards from and to the parliamentary groups ; he went about enrolling a devoted bodyguard for him ;[3] he loved the intrigues of the lobbies and would sit " near a large stove " in the Salle des pas perdus, giving audiences to his clientèle.[4]

Léon Say was perhaps the most interesting of the group. He was a political economist and a convinced Free Trader. This annoyed Thiers, who called him " a great egoist ", and did not at first give him a place in the Ministry, making him instead Préfet of the Seine. He was a Protestant and a great admirer of English ways. In October 1871 he went to London to present a gold medal to the Court of Aldermen, as a commemoration of British services in revictualling Paris. It was said of him, " He always has

---

[1] Bosq, p. 103.

[2] The Comte had a sharp tongue. The Duchesse de Broglie married her son (Amédée) to Mlle Say, daughter of the sugar-refiner. At the reception the bride dropped an ice. " You have a spot of sugar on your gown ", he said maliciously. The retort was *foudroyant* : " I prefer a spot of sugar to a spot of blood " (the Duc de Praslin, his father, had murdered his wife). (Vassili, p. 160). 　　　　　[3] Mme Adam, *Mes angoisses*, p. 141.

[4] De Marcère, *Histoire de la République*, ii. 93.

a British M.P. with him ".[1] Such society, however, did not
affect him with dulness, as Frenchmen sometimes expect
from such contacts. He was square-faced and thick-built,
and so witty that he never bored the Chamber even on
finance. His favourite recreation after a hard day's work
was to go to a small theatre in the boulevards, and read a
rather lively " yellow-backed novel ".[2]

Thiers, himself an ex-Orleanist, was busy persuading
Orleanists to follow him in his evolution towards the
Republic — among them two sons of famous Ministers of
the July Monarchy.

Auguste Casimir-Périer was the son of Louis-Philippe's
Minister, who in his day had been the very embodiment of
authority and courage. The son had none of his father's
firmness. He was amiable and easy-going, a devoted friend
of England. He had pursued a diplomatic career in England
and Belgium ; he took his seat in the Assembly as member
of the Right Centre ; he had visited the Orleans Princes in
1868 and had written of the Second Republic, " France was
not ripe for institutions, which demand a long and severe
education in self-government ".[3] Gradually he came under
Thiers' influence, and declared that " his private attach-
ments [to the Princes] did not influence his political convictions ".[4] He told Lacombe that he " feared the Princes
were at the mercy of *intrigants*, and that he desired a
Conservative Republic ".[5] It was he who in 1874 brought
forward and nearly carried the famous resolution in favour
of the Republic, and in 1875 the negotiations for the Constitution were partly concluded in his house, a " massive,
square building of uncertain design " a " Left-Centre

---

[1] Goncourts, t. 5, p. 297. Other " British " members of the Left Centre
were Daniel Wilson, son of a Glasgow foundry-man, married to a daughter of
Grévy (whom he drove from the Presidency of the Republic by his corrupt
practices), and Waddington, who had been educated at Rugby and Cambridge.

[2] Mme Waddington, *My First Years*, p. 21.

[3] E. Daudet, *Vérité sur l'essai de restauration*, p. 120.

[4] Murray, *Men of the Third Republic*, p. 285.

[5] Lacombe, i. 87 (17/2/71).

Hotel " the unkind called it.[1]

Charles, Comte de Duchâtel, was also son of a well-known Minister of Louis-Philippe. Earlier in 1871 the Princes had stayed in his father's château at Lagrange.

Another personal friend of the Princes was Roger du Nord, a diplomatist who belonged to the Orleanist section of Paris society. He was " a complete gentleman with fine manners and attractive behaviour " : the meetings of deputies at his Hôtel du Cours-la-Reine had almost the air of a salon. His personal friendships placed him in the ranks of the Right Centre, but his devotion to Thiers more than balanced his Orleanism. " You know how devoted I am ", he would say, " to the Orleans family, but I am not one of those who push them forward." [2] He ended by following Thiers, after his fall, to the Left Centre.

Jules Lasteyrie was the grandson of Lafayette, and inherited his instinctive dislike of the Legitimists. He soon ceased to act with them, and followed Thiers.

The Left Centre fluctuated between 100 and 120 deputies : it was from this *milieu* that the demand originated for strengthening Thiers' constitutional position. Attempts had been made, but without success, to raise the question in June. Since then, his prestige had been much increased by the Chambord manifesto and the July elections.[3] At the beginning of August, Rivet, an obscure

---

[1] *Kel-kun*, p. 234.

[2] De Marcère, *L'Assemblée nationale*, i. 165.

[3] Thiers said to Falloux : " The founder of the Republic in France is M. le Comte de Chambord. Posterity will call him the French Washington " (Falloux, ii. 494). As to Thiers' popularity in the country it is to be noted that on June 20th the municipal council of Toulouse voted an address which, while denying the constituent power of the Assembly, called on them to prolong the powers of Thiers for two years, " so that no intrigues against him may be successful, and all threats of a *coup d'état* may be removed ". It was sent to all the communes of France, and called forth a remarkable response : 24 communes accepted it *in toto*, and many more put forward the same views. Halévy calls it " un véritable mouvement d'opinion communale " (*Fin des notables*, p. 282).

deputy of the Left Centre (an ex-Préfet of the July Monarchy), announced his intention of proposing the prolongation of Thiers' powers. He was "fat and healthy . . . an excellent fellow of the bourgeois class, a little conceited and naïve "[1] — evidently a *porte-parole*. Who was behind him ? Thiers himself always denied that he had anything to do with the matter. He told Larcy that he "did not desire it but was obliged to follow the Left ".[2] In the Assembly he declared he had demanded nothing for himself and, imagining that he caught a murmur of incredulity, he added, "I hope that nobody will wish to doubt my statement ".[3] In a sense, of course, these are the conventional disclaimers of politicians. There are other ways of getting your friends to propose what you want than "asking" for it. It is certain that he disliked the title *chef de l'Exécutif*, and it was said by his friends that the Germans would hesitate about accepting financial terms, unless they were sure of his remaining in office.[4] The Right grumbled that he wanted "the dictatorship in name and fact for three years ", and "that his ideal was that of the First Consul ".[5] Yet it may well be believed that, whatever his ambitions, he honestly hesitated. His Ministers constantly kept before him the dangers of the attempt ; the Right were sullen and not the less hostile that they were helpless ; on the Left, there were many deputies, who believed that the Assembly ought to be dissolved before long, and they did not at all relish the idea of asking it to legislate (by proroguing Thiers' powers) for a future that did not belong to it. Thiers himself, when a five-years tenure was proposed, said half jestingly : "You will take away the only hold I have over the Assembly —

[1] Claveau, p. 224.   [2] Lacombe, i. 47.
[3] Dreyfus, *La République de M. Thiers*, p. 117.
[4] The Emperor of Germany "did not conceal his liking for Thiers, speaking of him as a wizard, a siren whose song was irresistible, unless one filled one's ears with wax " (Claveau, p. 197).
[5] Delpit, p. 217 (quoted Denis, p. 102).

the threat of resignation ".[1] Finally, it is said that Rivet
settled the matter by declaring he would bring forward his
proposal anyhow, whatever the Government said.[2] Rivet
himself had been one of the signatories of the decree, which
chose Thiers as head of the Executive. " That was a
nail in the shoes of the Royalists ", he said ; " my new
proposal will be a fish-bone in their throats." He was not
far wrong : the Royalists themselves preferred the more
elegant simile of a " tile falling on their heads ".[3]

On Tuesday August 1st, the Right Centre group, led
by St-Marc Girardin, sent five of its members to confer
with five members of the Left Centre. Both parties played
the game so popular in French politics, known as *jouer au
plus fin* : de Maleville, on behalf of the Left Centre, gave
assurances that they did not wish to bring forward the
" proposition Rivet ", but were compelled " by the force of
circumstances ". One deputy was about to raise the
question ; another had a proposal on the paper to extend
Thiers' powers ; Rivet added that " Thiers knew of the
proposal and supported it ". The Right Centre were not
behindhand in finesse. Vitet, the diplomat of the group,
" made objections without being too precise " ; his duty
was " to leave the door open for a compromise at the very
moment of seeming to shut it ".[4] At a meeting of the
Right Centre on Thursday, the feeling was hostile, but " it
was thought that something might be done, if only to
humour the whims of this poor country, which thinks it can
be saved by formulae ".[5] In other words, they did not feel
strong enough to face the public opinion now so clear in
Thiers' favour, and it might be a good opportunity to

---

[1] Bosq, p. 256. Jules Simon says that Thiers said to a friend : " I desire
nothing for myself. I only accept duties. When the Constitution is made, the
attributions of the President will be clearly defined. Today I only retain my
liberty of action, because I can always offer my resignation " (*Gouv. de M.
Thiers*, ii. 259).

[2] Pessard, ii. 163.   [3] Delpit, p. 215 (quoted Denis, p. 103).
[4] Lacombe, i. 44.   [5] *Op. cit.* p. 45.

extort, in return, some new arrangement for the real responsibility of Ministers.

The motion was put forward by Rivet on August 12th. It ran as follows :

THE NATIONAL ASSEMBLY [1]

Considering that, to satisfy the wishes of the country and the most pressing interests of credit and industry, it is urgent to give to the established Government new guarantees of duration and stability :

As amended by the Commission

THE NATIONAL ASSEMBLY [2]

Considering that it has a right to use the Constituent power, which is an essential attribute of the sovereignty, with which it is invested, and that the imperious duties, which it had to assume from the very beginning, and which are still very far from being fulfilled, have been the only obstacle, till this moment, to the exercise of this power ;

Considering that, till the establishment of definite institutions in the country, it is urgent, on account of the interests of commerce and industry, that our provisional institutions should possess for the public, if not that stability which is the work of time, at least such stability as can be assured by voluntary agreement and the cessation of party strife ;

Considering that a new title, more precise in its terms, without effecting any substantial change, may result in making clearer the intention of the Assembly to continue in a spirit of sincerity the " loyal attempt ", begun at Bordeaux ;

That the extension of the powers conferred on the Head of the Executive, and henceforward limited to the duration of the Assembly, removes from these powers any element of uncertainty and instability without allowing

---

[1] *Annales*, t. 4, p. 641.   [2] *Ibid.* t. 5, pp. 201-2.

the sovereign right of the National Assembly to receive the least injury, since in any circumstances the final decision belongs to the Assembly, and since a system of new guarantees gives us an assurance of the maintenance of these parliamentary principles, which are at once the protection and the honour of France :

DECREES—

1. M. Thiers shall exercise, with the title of PRESIDENT OF THE REPUBLIC, the duties assigned to him by the decree of February 17th last.

DECREES—

1. The Head of the Executive shall take the title of PRESIDENT OF THE REPUBLIC, and shall continue to exercise, under the authority of the National Assembly (and as long as it is sitting), the powers delegated to him by the decree of February 17th, 1871.

2. His powers are prolonged for three years.

Nevertheless, if during the interval the National Assembly should decide to dissolve itself, the powers of M. Thiers, which are bound up with those of the Assembly, shall only last during the time necessary for the constitution of a new Assembly, which, in its turn, will have the duty of taking a decision on the question of the Executive.

3. The President of the Republic is charged with the duty of promulgating laws.

He superintends and assures the execution of laws.

He presents Bills to the National Assembly through his Ministers.

The representatives and ambassadors of foreign powers are accredited to him.

He has his residence at the seat of the National Assembly : he is

2. The President of the Republic promulgates laws, after they have been transmitted to him by the President of the National Assembly.

He superintends and assures the execution of laws.

He has his residence at the seat of the Assembly.

lodged at the public expense, and receives a salary voted in the Budget.

4. He presides at the Council of Ministers, the members of which he appoints and dismisses.

He appoints a Vice-President from the Council.

In case he is absent or unable to act, the Vice-President takes his place in presiding over the Council and in his other duties.

5. The diplomatic agents, the commanders of the armies on land and sea, and all the magistrates and functionaries of superior rank are appointed or dismissed in Council of Ministers.

6. All acts of the Executive must be countersigned by a Minister. The Ministers are responsible to the Assembly.

He can speak to the Assembly, whenever he thinks it necessary, after he has informed the President of the Assembly of his intention.

He appoints and dismisses Ministers, and these Ministers are responsible to the Assembly.

All the acts of the President of the Republic must be countersigned by a Minister.

3. The President of the Republic is responsible to the Assembly.

On behalf of the Right, Adnet proposed the following Bill: " The Assembly, confident in the wisdom and patriotism of M. Thiers, continues its support to him, and in the name of the grateful country confirms the powers, which were conferred upon him at Bordeaux ". In a few words he demanded " urgence " for his proposal, " evidently inspired ", he said, " by the same thought " as that of Rivet. This was met with indignant denials from the Left, who saw clearly that a few words of compliment were hardly the equivalent of the title of President conferred for three years.[1]

Thiers hastened to the tribune. He assured the House that the question had been raised " without his participation and without his desire ". The murmurs of polite assent to this improbable statement did not seem to satisfy

[1] A deputy called out, when Adnet read his motion, " Why, it is simply a vote of confidence ! " (Bosq, p. 257).

him, and he added : " I hope that no one wishes to raise
any doubts as to my statement ". He ended by demanding
that both proposals should be referred to a Commission
" with urgence ". The Assembly was in a state of violent
excitement. Groups were formed ; insults were hurled
from one bench to another. The Legitimists, who had
apparently not been informed of Adnet's motion, were
perplexed, and the Duc de Bisaccia demanded a short
suspension of the sitting. Grévy, who had been trying to
restore order for a quarter of an hour, gladly left the chair
and there was an interval of twenty-five minutes before the
debate was resumed.[1] The two proposals were then referred
to the same Commission. Belcastel then rose from the
Extreme Right, and proposed that the Assembly should
not separate, till it had proclaimed a definite form of government. The Right Centre, who preferred any state of uncertainty to the Comte de Chambord, expressed their
resentment by voting against the proposal for " urgence "
on this motion,[2] and the next day a similar motion by
Dahirel (Extreme Right) was rejected altogether.[3]

The reception of the " proposition Rivet " in the House
had alarmed the Left.[4] Their fears were justified, for the
Commission elected by the bureaux contained nine opponents of the scheme and only six supporters.[5] The dis-

[1] *Annales,* t. 4, pp. 641-3 (cf. Claveau, pp. 201-2).

[2] It was rejected by *assis et levée,* by a very small majority : the Bureau
was divided on the question by 4 votes to 2 ; Castellane (Extreme Right) rose
from his secretary's place and demanded the *scrutin* ; Paris (Right Centre)
persuaded the House not to " raise even the appearance of doubt " against a
decision of the bureau (*Annales,* t. 4, p. 644).

[3] *Annales,* t. 4, pp. 650-54. The proposal was to appoint a Commission of
fifteen to prepare a Constitution. Boyer, who as reporter had to propose the
rejection of the motion, was in a rather difficult position, as he was himself a
Legitimist. He reported that the Commission did not believe that the public
tranquillity was assured enough to justify constitution-making.

[4] " Aug. 12th — Figure attrapée des Rivistes " (Lacombe, i. 46).

[5] The Right had Benoist d'Azy, Vitet, Callet, Delacour, Bottieau, Beulé,
St-Marc Girardin, Perrot, Léonce de Lavergne. The Left claimed de Maleville,
Ricard, Moreau, Rivet, Bertauld, de Goulard (de Marcère, *L'Assemblée
nationale,* i. 169).

The Duc de Broglie was violently attacked by Thiers for having left the

cussions of the Commission took place in an atmosphere of growing excitement. "Everything was in movement : each group met in council of war ten times a day, and sent its staff officers to carry ultimatums to the Presidency and to rival groups." [1] The Right vehemently opposed the idea of setting up Thiers as a dictator ; they passed from crises of depression when they believed that a dissolution was near,[2] to bursts of excitement, when they looked about for a successor to Thiers — MacMahon, Changarnier, Aumale, even Grévy, who enjoyed a certain prestige among them as a personal enemy of Gambetta.[3] Thiers shrugged his shoulders, saying, "Everybody is marching over the precipice with a light heart " : Grévy wondered whether it would not be best to " lead the country towards a dissolution ".

However, the outlines of an agreement began to emerge. The Right Centre were not prepared to find a successor for Thiers, and the state of the country, still occupied by foreign troops and hardly yet recovered from the Commune, did not lend itself to experiments. Since the Chambord

London embassy, in order to come and vote against the Head of the State. He defends himself in his *Memoirs* (*Revue des Deux Mondes*, 15/3/29, p. 382) ; he declares that he had resolved not to be present at all, and had even put off a visit to arrange about his son's marriage till the latest possible date, in order to be absent from the discussion. To his great chagrin he arrived at the Assembly on the very day when Rivet brought forward his proposal. He resolved to use the occasion to procure an agreement between the majority and Thiers. At the meeting of his bureau he spoke in this sense, adding that he had " felt in his discharge of his ambassadorial duties how great was the prestige of Thiers' name in Europe, and that his own person supplied the place of a government for France ". He wished to be a member of the Commission, but the votes were equally divided between him and Bertauld (Left Centre), who was elected as being the elder of the two. On the other hand, it must be remembered that he was one of the signatories of Adnet's motion, which Thiers much resented (Lacombe, i. 46). Gambetta in his bureau opposed the " proposition Rivet " on the ground that the Assembly ought to be dissolved to make room for a real Constituent Assembly (Deschanel, *Gambetta*, p. 149).

[1] Pessard, ii. 163.

[2] Lacombe, i. 47 *n.* : " Aug. 15 — I met Depeyre, and Resseguier who said to me, ' We shall be forced to dissolve ' ".

[3] Lacombe, i. 55 : " Our friends are very excited. There is a question of finding someone to succeed Thiers " (cf. de Marcère, *op. cit.* i. 169).

manifesto, the Orleanists had no hope of a Restoration, and
the best they could do was to accept Thiers quietly in the
hope that Providence would remove the obstacles — or
to speak more frankly, the obstacle [1] — that stood between
them and their hopes.   Ricard, who played the part of
negotiator " with his frank, reassuring laugh ", made it
clear that all that was wanted was the title of President.
Thiers, though he protested he had not desired the title,
would now regard refusal as a definite vote of no
confidence.[2]   Might it not be possible to concede the
title in return for fresh assurances that the President
was responsible to the Assembly, and a solemn declaration that the whole arrangement was provisional, since
the majority intended before long to decree a definite
Constitution ?

This was the main purport of the report, read on behalf
of the Commission by Vitet.   He was nicknamed " the last
of the Doctrinaires ", and he had the academic tinge of
that Right Centre school.   In 1824 he was Professor at the
École Normale ;   in 1830 he was appointed Inspector of

[1] One of the Orleanist wits made facetious enquiries as to " the King's
favourite dishes, and regretted that he had not a passion for *pâté de foie gras*
and mushrooms.   Emanuel Arago, in a similar spirit of humour, swore in his
sonorous voice that he would enter the service of Henri V and himself super-
intend the royal kitchen to protect the life of a monarch so useful to Republicans " (Pessard, ii. 165).   It was a common Orleanist prayer that God would
either " open the eyes of the Comte de Chambord — or else close them ".

[2] In a letter to Guizot (August 18th), after inviting him to pay a visit to
study the political situation, Thiers adds : " I say this, assuming that the result
of this crisis will be that I become President of the Republic : otherwise I
shall become once more what *au fond* I really am, a true philosopher ".   The
letter is delightfully characteristic.   Guizot had complained that the Constitution was not " logical ".   Thiers gently reproves him for ignoring the facts
" from the depths of your peaceful and studious retreat ".   As for himself, he
would love to retire from politics, and become " a true philosopher loving only
one thing in human affairs — the spectacle of the universe ruled by God, Who
is able to be ' logical ' — a spectacle, which I shall often enjoy at the Ob-
servatoire — the only one worthy of men that have lofty thoughts in their old
age ".   He adds : " I am not an ambitious man, satisfying my sense of power :
I am a philosopher in despair, because I am condemned to rule ".   Guizot must
have smiled indulgently, as he read this in his Norman home (Bouniols, pp.
97-100).

historical monuments. Guizot wrote : " I found him the
most fitting person to carry out and popularise the restoration of the old monuments of France. He had already been
noticed for his taste for the beautiful, and for his subtlety
at once critical and sympathetic." [1] Tall, thin and austere,
he combined a severity of dress with occasional elegances
such as a " cravat of olive-green with white spots, artistic-
ally pinned to his chest ".[2] He had a slight air of disdain
which marked " the grand bourgeois ". He was a violent
opponent of the Empire to the point of saying that the fall
of Napoleon was a compensation for the loss of Alsace-
Lorraine, and he was one of the most animated actors in
the demonstration which ended in the *vote de déchéance*.
During the Siege of Paris he became an ardent Republican
and spoke of burning the city rather than surrender. But,
on his arrival at Versailles, his old Orleanist associations
got the upper hand. It was said that he never forgave
Thiers for not making him Minister of Education.

When he rose to introduce his report on August 28th,
the galleries were crowded to hear him : everyone expected
a treat in the style of the Academy, where " a reserve is
slipped into the middle of a concession and an epigram into
a compliment ".[3] Thiers and his friends were to be praised
with a *sous-entendu*, that the French appreciate beyond all
other people. His audience were not disappointed ; he
read loudly and in a serious voice, giving weight to such
phrases as the following : " No one of course can doubt
that the honourable authors of the proposal, when they
decided after a long and prudent hesitation to bring it
forward, had serious motives for what they did, and believed
they were fulfilling a duty, but I shall allow myself to say
that they would have acted more wisely and done a greater
service if they had at least adjourned their proposal.
(*Loud applause from the Right. Murmurs on the Left*)."
He went on to describe with gentle irony the motives

---

[1] *Histoire*, ii. 67.   [2] Claveau, p. 73.   [3] *Ibid*. p. 217.

mentioned in the preamble — the danger to credit and capital caused by the present uncertainty. " The proposal has not failed (contrary, no doubt, to the intention of its authors) to increase the very evil they wish to cure." They had themselves created the idea that, unless some new powers were granted to the Government, its position would be compromised, and this had forced the hand of the Commission. " Now that the public expect a solution, to adjourn the question would be difficult and would be taken as a refusal."

For this reason the majority of the Commission, who had regarded the original proposal as " useless, inopportune and even dangerous ", were prepared to see whether a compromise were not possible. First of all, did the new title " President of the Republic " imply any alteration of the Bordeaux pact ? The authors of the proposal denied that it did. The Commission had accepted it " not only because of their assurances, but from a calm appreciation of the bearing of this change, more difficult to refuse than compromising to accept ".

The reporter went on to the question of the duration of the President's powers. If the Assembly were to recognise him for three years, what would become of its sovereignty ? The Commission met the objection by " filling up a gap, which the authors of the proposal admit to have been a mistake ", and adding a clause that he always remained responsible to the Assembly.

But in that case why select three years ? How unwise to give a public " rendez-vous to the fury of parties ! " and he recalled the famous problem, " twenty years ago ", of the Prince-President's re-election, which had cast such tragic shadows before it. " It is then far better to limit the powers of M. Thiers to the duration of the Assembly, remembering that owing to his responsibility a divorce remains always possible (*Murmurs on the Left*)."

A question had arisen as to whether in Thiers' peculiar

position as President and deputy it would not be wise to restrict his communications with the Assembly to messages — as in the case of the American President ; Vitet's paragraph on this subject is a *chef-d'œuvre* of irony : " Do not believe that the least touch of such irreverence has entered into our report. When we ask that M. Thiers should have among us the privilege of approaching the tribune in a different way from the rest of us " (*i.e.* after notice given to the President) " and that a certain amount of solemnity shall precede it, we are addressing to him at once an act of homage and a request to be economical of his strength, and to reserve himself by preference for the great problems, which are illuminated by his words and are fit for his powerful mind." As to the general constituent power : " If for the present we content ourselves with holding it in reserve, it is all the more reason . . . for proclaiming openly that we possess it. So we ask you to make a declaration to that effect in the preamble of the Bill." In a peroration skilfully framed to appeal to the Royalists, Vitet spoke of the spirit of compromise necessary to save France " now as in the days of Henri IV ".[1] The Right, seeing that the " proposition Rivet " had been transformed into something acceptable, received the report with growing enthusiasm.

The Left were sulky and vexed at its language.[2] Thiers was so annoyed that he prepared his resignation.[3] Dufaure on behalf of the Government soothed his feelings by moving a new paragraph to the preamble : " Taking also into consideration the eminent services rendered to the country

---

[1] *Annales*, t. 5, pp. 198-202. For the amendments of the Commission see above, the right-hand list on pp. 492-4.

[2] De Marcère (i. 169) says that " the report was drawn up in a tone of notorious hostility, that was meant to hurt " ; someone called it " orné et perfide ".

[3] De Marcère, i. 169 ; Pessard, ii. 169. Thiers probably refers to this in his letter to Hénon : " My situation is wearisome . . . to the point of inspiring me, *as during these last days*, with an ardent desire to resign " (letter of September 1st, Bouniols, p. 109).

by M. Thiers for the last six months, and the guarantees offered by the duration of the powers he holds from the Assembly ". The President of the Assembly refused to allow further discussion, and the debate was resumed on Wednesday August 30th.

It was not so stormy or so difficult as was expected. Those members of the Right in the Commission, who had not accepted the Vitet compromise, put forward two amendments by the mouth of Lavergne. They demanded (*a*) that the words, equating the duration of Thiers' powers to that of the Assembly, should be omitted as inconsistent with the declaration that he was always responsible to it ; (*b*) that the President should only communicate with the Assembly by messages. But both these amendments were withdrawn the next day. The Commission accepted the clause recognising Thiers' services, which was carried,[1] and Dufaure in return expressed the Government's approval of the amended scheme. Most of the discussion turned on the words of the preamble recognising the Assembly's constituent powers. The Left Centre, still full of hope that the Republic would be proclaimed, accepted the words. The attack came from the Left ; Pascal Duprat, a veteran of 1848, whose grey hair swept his collar, while not proposing immediate dissolution, wished to limit their task to the Budget, the reorganisation of the Army and the reform of electoral laws, but he would go no further. They had not the right to give a Constitution to France. The February elections had been held (under the clause of the Armistice) " on the question whether the war shall be continued " ; in most constituencies the candidates had no opportunity of meeting the electors ; even where they had, no constitutional questions had been raised. Étienne Lamy, making his first appearance as a " Catholic Republican ", urged that the demand for stability, so clamorous in the

---

[1] 36 members of the Extreme Right (plus a few Bonapartists) voted against.

country, could not be satisfied by any modification of
Thiers' title. What was wanted was a Constitution, and
the present Assembly was incapable of producing one,
because " a majority cannot be formed in favour of any
government whatever ". The only remedy was an appeal
to the country. " In these days of tribulation you have
shown wisdom : show now the still greater wisdom of
knowing when to end your existence." Colonel Langlois
denied that any Assembly could be constituent : " I am a
Republican and I assert the permanent sovereignty of the
people ". From the Extreme Left, Louis Blanc declared
that a Constitution could only be set up by an Assembly,
whose mandate was undisputed : " Your mandate is not
indisputable, and the proof is that even in this Chamber it is
disputed ". Naquet appealed to the elections of July 2nd,
which "have effaced, annulled and annihilated the vote of
February 8th ".

In reply General Ducrot read the Assembly's manifesto
of March 21st, issued unanimously against the Commune,
containing the words " You have committed to us the task
of saving, organising, constituting the country ".[1] " We
hold from your free vote the great and beneficent principle
of national sovereignty." St-Marc Girardin pointed out
that the " proposition Rivet " was itself an exercise of constituent powers. " They have been kind enough to bring
before us a chapter to write ; some day we can finish the
book, but we are in no hurry." Pagès-Duport,[2] amid tremendous applause from the Right, read a passage from
the *Journal Officiel* for September 10th which said : " The
electoral colleges are convoked . . . to elect a National

---

[1] The word " constituer " may mean simply " to set on its feet ".

[2] An extreme Legitimist at the moment, he had been to visit the Comte de
Chambord during the Empire, and increased his reputation as a Royalist by
wearing an enormous fleur de lis and undergoing imprisonment at Mazas.
He was a well-known speculator, and the story ran that, being one of the first
to hear the news of the Austrian victory at Novara, he rushed to the bank,
bought shares, and made a fortune. Later his Royalist views became less
extreme.

Constituent Assembly " : [1] de Kerdrel quoted a list from the Department of Doubs, in which Ordinaire (the name of the Radical candidate) figured, and which was headed " Scrutin of February 12th, 1871. List of candidates for the Constituent Assembly." [2]

The next speaker (from the Right Centre) was Numa Baragnon. His nickname in the Assembly was " Frère Numa des Entonneurs ".[3] His fat, jovial face was decorated by " six chins so full of fat, that they seem to push the mouth up to where you would expect the eyes to be ; his black moustache and bald head, adorned by two tufts of hair, his bulbous nose, all spoke of the man, to whom politics are a game, which he enjoys playing ". He was from Nîmes and had all the *fouge du midi* ; he was described as " a boxer on the Royalist side ", " a curious mixture of the local *avocat*, the chief waiter and the public-house politician ". His vehemence, " hot and artificial ", his southern accent, his gesture as he struck the tribune with both his fists and threw back his head to shout with all his lungs, made people call him " the Gambetta of the Right ". De Marcère describes him as " eloquent, fluent . . . a bit vulgar, but alive and awake, with a touch of Gasconnade ; he was ready to thunder from the tribune at the slightest provocation, a good companion and sometimes sincere ". After the Fourth of September he wrote : " Republic and fatherland are two inseparable expressions ". His enemies said that he added, " I don't know what will come of September 4th, but I know I shall ", and that he only became

[1] Langlois retorted that the words only concerned the Department of the Seine ; the *General* Election was not held till February. The legal authors of *Les Constitutions de la France* (Duguit et Monnier) quote this decree among others as proving that " as a question of law the Assembly was constituent ". The decree of February refers to *the* National Assembly, and probably therefore to the September decree.

[2] Ordinaire replied that this was a relation of his of the same name. He had been elected in the Department of Rhône on a list headed " Candidate for the Assembly, National and not Constituent. "

[3] " The quaffers or drinkers " (a character in Rabelais).

a Royalist, after having been refused at Bordeaux as Republican candidate. Like Gambetta, he was subtle as well as noisy; his bursts of temper were well-timed to interpret the feeling of the majority. His good-humour kept the Royalist party going through difficult days [1] — on the whole, a man without many principles, but *bon camarade*, who put his money on the wrong political horse, and who risked and took his loss like a sportsman.

In the present debate he was serious and quiet; he said he felt no need to appeal to decrees or documents. The powers of the Assembly could not depend on the will of the National Defence Government. On the contrary, that Government, by overthrowing the Empire, had made it impossible for the representatives of the nation to meet " without having the right to build on the spot, where the authors of the Revolution had only left ruins ". It was not his fault that his reference to the Fourth of September provoked a violent scene. Testelin, a Republican doctor from Lille, called out, " If it had not been for the Fourth of September, you would still be licking the Emperor's boots ". The words burst like a bomb : the whole Assembly rose to its feet, calling out " Order, order ! " ; several deputies dashed with menacing gestures towards the Extreme Left, where a few members supported their colleague by cheers. Grévy put on his hat and prepared to adjourn the sitting, but the majority demanded disciplinary measures. The President sent the *huissier* to conduct Testelin to the tribune, and formally called him to order. Testelin expressed his regret and declared rather disingenuously that the words were not addressed to the Assembly. On this Grévy withdrew his censure, to the

---

[1] See Pelletan, *Théâtre de Versailles*, pp. 99-102 ; Bosq, p. 179 ; *Kel-kun*, ch. xvii. ; de Marcère, i. 311 ; Claveau, pp. 109, 232. Lacombe thought him " a delightful character, and so subtle " (i. 248) ; " a clever politician, very open, and wonderfully at his ease " (i. 159). He was " moderate by nature ; but afraid of being compromised in the eyes of the Extreme Right, if he showed it too much ".

great discontent of the Right.

The President of the Assembly somewhat regained their sympathies by the very little support he gave to Gambetta, whose protest against the constituent powers was interrupted by the most violent clamour from the Right: " You confiscated all the liberties of the country ". " You seized the power without right and ruined the country." Grévy, who hated Gambetta all his life, gently rebuked the Right and severely scolded the Left when they cried " Order ! " [1] Gambetta shook his flowing hair and defied the Assembly : the " proposition Rivet " was a mere piece of trickery. Was it possible to decree " stability by decreeing titles " ? and how was it possible for an Assembly, whose title was contested, to set up a Constitution ? He used the rather curious argument that the Constitution of 1849 had fixed the number of constituent assemblies at 900, whereas the present only had 750 deputies. He denied that, in face of public opinion, the Assembly would dare to use its constituent power, and declared (very rashly as it turned out) that he would not accept " even a republic set up by an incompetent Assembly ". After his speech [2] the constituent powers were voted by 434 votes to 225.

The debate was concluded on Thursday August 31st, when Amédée Lefèvre-Pontalis spoke for the Extreme Right. He regarded the scheme of the Commission as absolutely useless. " Do you imagine you can reassure the leaders of industry by saying : The situation is saved, because we now have a president of the Republic instead of a head of the Executive ? It is as if, at a critical moment, an industrialist were to send for the director of his factories and say : Instead of calling you director, I shall in future call you Governor, and the situation will be saved." [3] Ernest

---

[1] " Be good enough to keep silence yourselves, gentlemen. It is not your business to repress the tumult."   [2] *Annales*, t. 5, pp. 234-52.
[3] *Ibid*. t. 5, p. 259.

Picard, though he had already left the Government, spoke in favour of the scheme, and his calm, good-humoured tone put the Assembly into a good temper : " We have today a Government, which is reorganising and healing the country. We cannot, we have not the right to indulge in party divisions. If I am wrong, may I be cursed by the Left and excommunicated by the Right." [1] The debate was concluded by de Tocqueville, brother of the famous historian, so thin and old that he seemed like a ghost. He spoke from the benches of the Left Centre and declared : " The country has confidence in M. Thiers. . . . This illustrious statesman has contracted a marriage of reason with the Republic." The project as a whole was carried by 491 votes to 94. Many deputies abstained. A member of the Extreme Right, who voted for it, says : " I voted as a result of discouragement and weariness of futile resistance ".[2]

The Ministry immediately resigned as a matter of form, and were all reappointed, Dufaure with the new title of Vice-President of the Council. Even Larcy, whose Royalism was shocked by the " proposition Rivet ", consented to return to his Ministry after a letter from Thiers in which the new President promised " to remain the vigilant guardian of the conservative and liberal ideas, to protect which they had always fought together " ; [3] but he had misgivings. " Thiers' impressions are, I like to believe, sincere, but they are very changeable. . . . My hope is to form in the Council of Ministers a block to resist his caprices." [4] It needed a cleverer man than Larcy to resist Thiers in his own

---

[1] *Annales*, t. 5, p. 263. The words, though received as a joke, probably expressed some of his bitterness at the universal unpopularity of the men of September. In private, he criticised the "proposition Rivet", because the Commission, by omitting a clause in the original scheme, had left unregulated the question of the transmission of powers. " The mandate of the Assembly and that of the Head of the State end on the same day. The Government is destined to disappear, just when its functions are most necessary " (Reclus, *Picard*, p. 321).　　　[2] Vinols (quoted Denis, p. 109).

[3] Denis, p. 110.　　　[4] Lacombe, i. 56.

Council. The Right tried to persuade themselves that nothing had happened but a change of title. Such was not the impression of the country. The *Siècle* wrote : " One great fact dominates the two-days debate — the installation of a President of the Republic, and therefore the institution of a French Republic ".[1] Thiers himself, in a message of thanks to the Assembly, spoke of their having " voted him to the highest magistracy of the Republic ".[2] The same day he wrote privately to the Radical Maire of Lyons : " The Republic is proclaimed, and I am become its Head : I shall not betray the Government of which I have become the Head ".[3] He wrote to de Broglie : " I regret, my dear Duke, a difference of opinion, that I see no reason for. . . . It would perhaps have been better if it had been less open.[4] . . . As to my new title and the prolongation of my powers, I know that you have always supported them. . . . I have never cared for them." [5]

(f) Conclusion

When the penitent Thiers asked Falloux to dinner after their little " scene ", the Presidential household was much divided on the question — Are we to move to Paris ? Mlle Dosne declared that it was absurd for the Government to remain at Versailles : Mme Thiers retorted, " We shall not be in Paris a fortnight, before M. Thiers is assassinated ". Falloux judged that the President, while he believed it *de bon ton* to sigh for his beloved Paris, was

---

[1] Loth, p. 179.   [2] *Annales*, t. 5, p. 279.   [3] Bouniols, p. 108.

[4] De Broglie also refers to " a disagreement that my conscience would not let me pass over, but which no one regretted more than I did " (Halévy, *Courier*, p. 445). He wished that the proposal had been " less personal to Thiers and had given to France the guarantees of a regular Constitution (real responsible Ministers), at least for a few years. . . . Thiers and his salon were all fire and fury against me " (*Revue des Deux Mondes*, 15/3/29, p. 384).

[5] *Ibid.* (13/9/71), p. 130. The Duke wrote : " There is always an advantage in calling things by their right names. I shall certainly not cure myself of the disease of agreeing with you, and regretting it, when I cannot always do so " (Malo, September 4th, 550).

not at all anxious to go there.[1]

The matter came before the Assembly : the Baron de Ravinel, a young deputy of the Right Centre, who acted as aide-de-camp to Buffet, brought forward a Bill of two clauses. The Assembly, the Pouvoir Exécutif and the Ministers were to remain at Versailles ; the services of public administration to be moved from Paris to Versailles. A Commission of twenty members was to co-operate with the Government in giving effect to this measure.

The debate was opened on September 5th by Naquet, the Jewish doctor from the Extreme Left.[2] Addressing himself to the chief reproach brought against Paris, he declared : " I claim that Paris has only carried out the revolutions, which were approved by the public sentiment of all France ". He was interrupted by a great shout from the Right : " What about the Commune ? " In answer, he essayed an elaborate piece of Republican casuistry to show that the only just revolutions were successful insur-rections. In countries like Spain, when the riots spread from Barcelona to Cadiz, and from Cadiz to Valladolid, it caused endless trouble, whereas in centralised France it was all over in a few days. " This country is indeed for-tunate to have a capital, which carries out the revolutions herself." " All this is very cheering for us ", said a member of the Right, " if we go to Paris." Another commented, " It is a course of lectures on Comparative Revolutions ".

Ravinel, the author of the proposal, replied that, so far from being hostile to the Republic, he wished to make a loyal experiment in this form of government under re-assuring conditions — that is far from the tumults and passions of Paris. This reference to the Republic was much interrupted " by the Left, because they did not believe him, and by the Right because they did ".[3]

[1] Falloux, ii. 510, 511.   [2] Annales, t. 5, p. 386.
[3] Claveau, p. 238. The words are significant as showing the views of Buffet, always less anti-Republican than his colleagues of the Right Centre.

On September 7th, Cézanne, the reporter, spoke for the measure. He was one of the conservative members of the Left Centre, who generally voted with the Right. He declared that personally he was attached to Paris " by every fibre of his heart and intelligence ". But, even though Paris was the heart of France, " the brain can live at some distance from the heart "—an anatomical metaphor much admired by the Right. He concluded : " As for me . . . my hand on my heart, and in presence of my country, which for the first time hears my humble voice, I declare that I will not take the responsibility of leaving this Palace, where we deliberate in profound peace, to go of my own free will to face the storm. (*Loud and long-continued cheers from the Right and Centre.*) " [1]

As at Bordeaux, Louis Blanc was one of the leading champions of Paris ; perched on a stool, the diminutive deputy declared that " France in opposition to her capital would mean France in opposition to herself. If you find Paris absorbs too much of France, develop municipal liberties by your laws all over France : revive local life everywhere . . . but, in the name of Heaven, do not take from a city, whose splendour all the world envies us, one of the prerogatives, of which she is proud."

The discussion was resumed on September 8th, and the familiar arguments were tossed from one side to the other. The chief incident of the day occurred when Lucien Brun, speaking from the Extreme Right, declared that " Providence has placed you in a position——" He could get no further. The Deists of the Left shook their fists at him. " He has not the right to say we are the adversaries of Providence." " It is not Providence which has brought us to Versailles." The Protestant pastor, Pressensé, foamed at the mouth, as if he had been called an atheist. " We believe in God as much as you, and more perhaps." Arnaud, the Catholic Republican, protested against the insult to

[1] *Annales*, t. 5, p. 441.

his " party " — a party consisting of two, himself and Lamy. Brun replied : " If the word Providence shocks you, invoke the Devil if you like, but allow us to invoke God ". The tumult lasted half an hour.[1]

Dufaure, speaking in the name of the Government and of Thiers, proposed to accept the *status quo* — the President and Ministers at Versailles and the administrative services at Paris. A certain number of the Right Centre, knowing Thiers' wishes, rallied to the compromise. In particular the Target group voted with the Government, and the second clause (Transfer of Ministries from Paris) was rejected, to the indignation of the Right, by 345 votes to 305.[2]

On September 13th, Thiers sent a message to the Assembly supporting the proposal for a prorogation. " After so many efforts, we should demand today an instant of repose : the country would be too just, too sensible, too accustomed to measure the limits of human strength to reproach us." It was necessary for members to return for the sessions of the General Councils in their own Departments, and to let the country tell them *dans l'intimité du foyer* what were its thoughts and wishes. It was not surprising (he said) that members were profoundly moved by the question at issue between republic and monarchy. "We should be worth less, if we were not so moved." But the emotion was communicating itself to the country and a short interval would make for calm and serenity. The controversial questions of taxation (especially the much-discussed Government proposal of a duty on raw materials) were adjourned. The Assembly separated on September 16th.[3]

---

[1] *Annales*, t. 5, pp. 467-8.   [2] *Ibid.* t. 5, p. 486 ; Claveau, p. 250.

[3] *Ibid.* t. 5, pp. 590-92. One other point should be noted, which marks this session of the Assembly — the large number of Commissions of Enquiry, that had been appointed, and were sitting behind the scenes (on the National Defence Government, on the Bordeaux Delegation, on the War Contracts, on the Commune, etc.). As Jules Simon says, " Half the Chamber were holding an enquiry into the behaviour of the other half " (*Gouv. de M. Thiers*, ii. 7).

The Bill for the reform of local government passed with some compromises both on the political and administrative side. Thus the champions of local liberties reluctantly conceded to the Government the right of dissolving the Departmental Councils, and to the Préfet the surveillance over the village communes. But the institution of a Departmental Commission to check the Préfet went through safely, and was, from the point of view of De-centralisation, a " most important creation ".[1]

The first session of the Assembly closed during a period of tranquillity such as France had not known for over a year. Many regarded it as deceitful ; Falloux was not alone in thinking that the country was drifting towards an abyss — towards a new Commune and a second German invasion.

It was not to be so ; France was at the beginning of a quiet era, agitated no doubt (when is a French Republic not agitated ?), but free from great political convulsions. The friends of Revolution were discouraged by the defeat of the Commune ; Paris seemed to have returned to moderation and the Republicans in Parliament studiously avoided social problems. The new generation, stupefied and sobered by events, was more interested in reflection than in action. Paul Bourget says, in his famous preface to *Le Disciple*: " In our schoolrooms we were not gay. We said to ourselves that our work was to make a new France. . . . We knew that the resurrection of Germany at the beginning of the last century had been above all a spiritual achievement, and we realised that it was the spirit of France that must be cured."

In the absence of any steady current of popular opinion, the work fell upon the Parliament, and France has had few better-intentioned, more brilliant and more embarrassed Assemblies than that of 1871. The Royalist majority, clear in its devotion to monarchy, was torn by divisions, and,

[1] Barthelemy, *Gouv. de France*, p. 156. See Appendix.

at the very moment that Legitimists and Orleanists were shaking hands in the Assembly, the claimant to the throne himself publicly announced just those differences they were endeavouring to conceal. In such a state of confusion they fell into the hands of the cleverest statesman of the day. Thiers led them by his *distinguo* — first, the period of reconstructing France, on which they were all agreed, and only then the constitutional settlement, about which they differed. The majority accepted this, partly out of real patriotism and partly from an obscure feeling that, after the republic had done the dirty work, the monarchy might make its entry with clean hands.

Thiers did not agree with them : in his view it was just the dirty work, in which the country was interested — and in the one person who could do it, himself. Personally, he would far rather be President of a republic than Prime Minister of a monarchy. The country would be grateful to him for his good administration, and a new republican party under Gambetta was offering new pledges of moderation. But Thiers knew he must conceal his scepticism about a Restoration, till he was strong enough to defy the majority in the Assembly.

In the end, he showed his hand too soon : in 1873 the Assembly woke up to the facts, brushed Thiers aside and asked whether it was yet too late to restore the monarchy. There may be other opportunities of describing that last and desperate struggle.

APPENDIX

APPENDIX

THIERS AT THE COMMISSION OF DECENTRALISATION

(August 2nd, 1871 : from the Archives of the Chamber of Deputies)

M. LE PRÉSIDENT and M. le Ministre de l'Intérieur are introduced.

THIERS : I thank the Commission for having secured for me an opportunity to arrive at an agreement, by calling me to their deliberations. I have a great desire for conciliation in spite of differences of opinion, which I do not disguise at all.

These differences of opinion are such that, if we were in a normal situation and I was King's Minister, and if I could see one party ready to replace the other in the Government, I should hand in my resignation.

I have always been a resolute supporter of French administration. There is not another in Europe as good as ours. In each of our revolutions everything would have collapsed into disorder without it. I only say this in order that you may recognise how far I have to go to accept your Bill. There is not a clause in it, that is not fated to be given the lie by the facts.

Thus, the Préfet is reduced to a subordinate rôle. The Bill makes him play a part, that is not his proper part. The Préfet is not only the representative of the executive ; he is the representative of the State. The State has to be represented not only at Paris but in the provinces. The Préfet alone can discharge that duty. Now the Bill makes him a kind of clerk charged with drawing up reports for the Conseil-Général of the Department and carrying out its decisions.

You have set up a Commission ; I disapprove completely of this institution. However, I do not oppose it. I should have understood, though I could not have accepted, that the Conseil, meeting from time to time, should appoint a Commission to watch over the execution of its decisions. But I have always believed that there is only one kind of good government and one kind of real liberty.

Good government means unity of action; real liberty is the opportunity of dismissing the authority, to whom the action has been entrusted. But once you have set up an authority, you must not enfeeble it but let it act.

The Préfet ought to be placed in such a situation. He should be left to act, and the Conseil should be allowed to stop him, if it is not content. This is what the First Consul did. The only Préfet I understand is one, who has a real responsibility and the zeal and devotion which result from it, and so applies himself with all his heart to the administration entrusted to him. But to place at his side a body to prevent him from acting is to put him in an impossible position, especially when we have to deal with a character as quarrelsome as the French. Still I understand a Commission, which should be the continuation of the Conseil. I understand it as an experiment. It is just possible it might succeed, though I do not believe it, but a body of men governing with the Préfet I could never have accepted, if I had taken part in the debate. It would have been necessary, if the Commission were a Commission of surveillance, that the Préfet should be president. However, the Assembly has committed itself, and I recognise that it would be difficult now to make it change its mind.

If the powers of the Commission have been reduced to those of surveillance only, it would have been less embarrassing to have someone else and not the Préfet as president, but you have given to the Commission the administration of the entire Department.

The first danger implicit in having a Commission of direct action is that it may absorb all power into itself. Assemblies, when they last, end by becoming personified in a committee. The Commission will be the real Conseil-Général. However much trouble you take to create more interest in the administration of the Department, you will find it very difficult to secure it; the Department is not like the old province; the ancient provinces were real little nations, to which everyone felt loyalty. Now, when the Conseil meets on a Monday, no business is more pressing than to end on the Saturday. You want to increase these sessions, to have two a year. You can do so without any danger; no one will come. But four or five of the keener people will take hold of all the business of the Conseil. They will find electoral advantages in doing so; the Commission will be the ladder leading to a seat in Parliament. The Commission will be the place, where several determined men will seek to become the masters, and they will succeed. The Conseil will let them do it without interference.

You are making this law with the old Conseils in mind, not those the next elections will give you. You give a Department very large powers and you never consider that the Conseil may abuse them. You will have some Conseils where the idea of disorder will find credit ; at Chambéry and Nice you will have Conseils with Separatist ideas.

To give the verification of its own elections to the Conseil is a serious mistake ; the mistake is to consider the Conseil as sovereign. Above the Conseil-General there is always the State. If you make the Conseil decide on the elections, you put everything in the hands of the majority. If you had put the decision in the hands — I do not say of the Conseil de Préfecture (though it is the best jurisdiction but it is no longer in fashion), but with an appeal to the Conseil d'État, which has always been impartial — you would have done a sensible thing.

LENOEL : Clause 47 allows recourse to the Conseil d'État in case of violation of the law, even in the case of validation of elections.

CHRISTOPHLE : Clause 16 formally excepts the verification of powers.

THE PRESIDENT OF THE COMMISSION : The Commission had proposed recourse to the Conseil d'État but the Assembly rejected it after listening to the arguments of a Minister, M. Victor Lefranc.

THIERS : This is not one of the things I mind most. What I mind most is the public danger. The provision that the Conseil may meet at the demand of two-thirds of its members is inadmissible. No one in a State may meet except at the orders of the supreme authority. Otherwise, there is no security. Under a monarchy, the Chamber of Peers itself cannot meet except when called by the King. This applies *a fortiori* to a Conseil-Général. Under a Republic, only the sovereign Assembly can convoke itself. Beyond that, everything of the kind is dangerous. We have thoroughly defeated material disorder. I answer for it with my head ; with an army like ours, numerous and reorganised, we shall not have even an attempt at disturbance. But moral order can only be restored after a long treatment. What is there to prevent a Department with a detestable majority from assembling on its own ? The will of two-thirds will be enough, and that at the bidding of a Commission, which will represent all its power. This clause is not voted ; I implore the Commission to give it up.

The Conseil is to have two sessions a year ; that is quite enough. If extraordinary sessions are necessary, let it demand an authorisation from the State through its Préfet.

Moulin : An idea very common nowadays is to allow the Conseil to meet on its own.

L. Brun : I put in the two-thirds instead of one-half.

Thiers : I admit that the Commission has only deferred to a very general feeling. I share the feeling but not the opinion, to which the feeling has given rise in many minds. There is a recent experiment, that is decisive — I mean the dissolution of the late Conseils by a Government, which was the most unpopular we have ever had. The Delegation of Tours was not even in agreement with the Paris Government. Public opinion was violently excited, and yet not a Conseil-Général dared to meet.

Several members : Because it was against the law.

Thiers : You want to make a law, that shall be orderly ; take care you do not make one that is disorderly. It is a great mistake to say that it is Paris, that must be resisted ; Paris has not made all the revolutions. It has not even made one, that any of the big cities would not have made in its place. It is the expression of the opinion of the moment. In 1815 it brought about the Restoration, which all France wanted ; in 1830 all France made the revolution ; in 1848 there was no more resistance to it at Bordeaux or at Rouen than at Paris. It is a mistake to suppose that Governments are overthrown by caprice. They fall because they feel that opinion is hostile ; they hesitate and are troubled ; the Government of Louis-Philippe was attacked several times. It fired the cannon resolutely, as long as it felt opinion was on its side ; once only a revolution at Paris failed — the 18th of March — , because I had France behind me and I did not hesitate. If opinion had been divided, I should have hesitated myself and been beaten. Paris is only the readiest instrument in the hands of the rest of France. When you think you are giving powers to the Departments, they will not use them ; only the dangerous people will use them. Recently when we were at the gates of Paris, seventeen Departments in the South demanded to meet. What would have become of France ? Your measure is good for nothing except to create difficulties. I pass to the final clauses which allow Conseils to act together.

Moulin : Only for objects of Departmental utility.

Thiers : If that is so, why not let the common action go on between the Préfets ? You mistrust the Préfets. They are passionately devoted to the welfare of their Departments. If several Departments want a common road, the Préfets take up the matter; they come to Paris.

MOULIN : For twenty-nine years I have been a member of the Conseil-Général of Puy-de-Dôme, and I can assure you that I have never seen the Préfet display all this zeal for the welfare of the Department.

THIERS : You are making a law with the Empire in mind, and it has disappeared. The Préfets of the Empire had only one object — the elections. In ordinary times an agreement will always be possible for a real need through the Préfets.

WADDINGTON : The law has two considerable guarantees : (1) the Préfet can always be present at these meetings ; (2) to be carried out, the decisions must be approved by all the Conseils concerned.

REVERCHON proposed : " These meetings must be announced beforehand to the Préfets and shall not take place, unless the Government during a delay of . . . months has raised no objection."

THIERS : I should accept that.

There is something more. It is impossible to say that the Government cannot dissolve the Conseil without a special law. At least a fortnight is necessary to obtain a law. Almost always after a revolution laws are made with a view to the past [*i.e.* to the danger of Paris] and not to the future. Paris has just given us a reassuring exhibition. In the Conseil Municipal there is a majority in favour of order. There is no more resistance in Paris ; it is elsewhere. Put this in, that we cannot dissolve a Conseil without referring it to you at once, and I accept.

The publicity of sittings is also a bad thing. The Conseils are administrative bodies. When there is no publicity, there is every chance of their doing business for business' sake. Now, you will have to have special halls for discussion. Orderly people will not come to the sittings ; you will only have the disorderly. One cannot do business like that.

TARGET : We have had publicity for four years. It has not turned out so badly. What is more, the Corps Législatif voted it last year ; it is difficult to go back.

THIERS : Again, you have given to the Departmental Commission all the most important parts of the administration of the communes. It is true you have taken from it the ordinary communal budget, but these will no longer give rise to any difficulty ; they are decided beforehand. What is important is the extraordinary budget

— the " centimes additionnels ", the loans for new establishments. All this you have left to the Commission.

On clause 88 (declaration of public utility for public roads) : This is a misunderstanding of all the principles of equity. Nothing is more sacred than property. Nothing is more serious than expropriation for public utility. One cannot leave it to the Conseil. You are giving not the " tutelle communale ", for the word is not exact, but all the administration of the communes to the Commission. Then we must say that the offices of the Préfets no longer belong to them but to the Commission. The communes only work under the direction of the Préfets and Sous-préfets ; one Department sends to the Prefecture 8000 communal affairs a year. The Commission will not do all this work ; you will not find men to do it. The affairs will suffer. If that is what you want, I will never consent to it. At my age I will not lend my name to the dislocation of the French administrative system.

La Bassetière : If the Commission consented to reserve all questions concerning the administration of the communes till the vote of the law on the communes, if it consented to wait for the issue of the experiment of Departmental Commissions, would this concession satisfy M. le Président du Conseil ?

Thiers : If you would consent to withdraw this clause, I should be very grateful. I only ask for the withdrawal of the clauses about the administration of the communes.

La Bassetière : It is quite understood that this is a bargain ; that, if the Commission gives way on this point, it will be on condition that the rest of the law is untouched.

Thiers : Yes, it will be a bargain. I came here with ideas of conciliation. Otherwise I should have asked you to make the Préfets presidents of the Commissions, but it has been pointed out to me that the Assembly has already committed itself on this question. What is the danger at present ? It is that little by little you get possession of all the powers. The Commission of Enquiry on the events of March 18th have just sent for General Bourbaki to give evidence without consulting the Minister for War ; it is a usurpation. I shall defend the Executive ; I will lay down the powers entrusted me, untouched as I received them.

On clauses 35 and 36 : Lucet : In case of dissolution, what will happen to the administration of the Department ?

Thiers : The obligation to refer to the Assembly is a sufficient guarantee. Besides in the Assembly there will be discussions, which will have their influence on the electors. We must have a longer delay for the convocation.

On clause 44 (declaration of public utility) : CHRISTOPHLE : This declaration is surrounded with guarantees.

THIERS : In order to use it, the Conseil must have broken the law ; it will not break it.

Clause 51 (resolutions on economic questions) : THIERS : Very well, since it is voted.

Clause 71 : THIERS : We should have wished, since the Préfet is not president, that the president should always be the eldest and that the Préfet should be present *ex officio*. . . .

ERNOUL : In the course of the discussion M. le Chef du Pouvoir has said several times, " Your law is detestable ; it is a muddle ". I ask him, if we are making a bargain, not to use such language in the Assembly.

THIERS : All I can give you is my silence ; you shall have it.

CLASSIFIED LIST OF AUTHORITIES

The list only contains books, which are quoted with reference to the period February–September 1871.

Works by deputies are marked †.

When the political tendency of any work is marked, the special colour is noted in brackets, *e.g.* (Legitimist) (Left).

CONTEMPORARY AUTHORITIES

ADAM, MME JULIETTE (Left).

Mes angoisses et nos luttes (1871–3).

Nos amitiés politiques avant l'abandon de la revanche (1873–5).

Reminiscences (in semi-diary form) largely consisting of letters and conversations. A vivid picture of Gambetta and his group.

ANNALES DE L'ASSEMBLÉE NATIONALE. Debates, Reports of Commissions, etc., 1871–5.

BOSQ, PAUL. *Souvenirs de l'assemblée nationale.* Lively reminiscences of a journalist, full of anecdotes and lobby gossip.

BUSCH, DR.

Our Chancellor.

Bismarck in the Franco-German War.

The well-known record of Bismarck, which " Boswellises " his talk.

†CASTELLANE, MARQUIS OF (Right). *Men and Things of My Time* (translated by de Mattos). Unfortunately most inaccurate.

†CHESNELONG, CHARLES (Legitimist). *Les Derniers Jours de l'empire et le gouvernement de M. Thiers.* He did not become a deputy till 1872, but the first volume of his memoirs has some interesting matter, such as Thiers' description of his " Belfort interview " with Bismarck, quoted in the Additional Note to Chapter V (Part I) of this book.

CLAVEAU, ANTOINE. *Souvenirs politiques et parlementaires d'un témoin* (1871–3). He was one of the official reporters of the Assembly. The book is a lively account of debates, at which he was present — so detailed that it can almost be used as a supplement to the official reports.

CROWN-PRINCE. *Diaries of the Emperor Frederick* (translated by Frances A. Wells). Contains a few pages on the Peace Negotiations at Versailles.

†DAMPIERRE, MARQUIS DE (Right). *Cinq ans de ma vie politique.* This, I think, is privately printed. I have been unable to get a copy,

though constantly promised one. It is quoted by De Meaux and Denis *op. cit.*

†De Broglie, Duc (Right Centre). *Souvenirs.* Published in various copies of the *Revue des Deux Mondes* : it is, I think, in course of being published as a separate work. A very characteristic work with all the author's literary elegance, power of historical analysis, and slightly mordant humour.

†De Marcère (Left Centre). *L'Assemblée nationale de 1871* (2 vols.). Distinguished in style : its point of view is that of a penitent Republican. The anecdotes tantalise by their rarity.

†De Meaux, Vicomte de (Right). *Souvenirs politiques.* De Meaux (though technically a Legitimist) is a spiritual child of the Right Centre Doctrinaires with their rather literary liberalism and their high-minded detachment.

D'Haussonville, Comte. *Mon journal,* Part II. Part of this diary, by the old friend of the Orleans Princes, is quoted in Denis *op. cit.*

Dreux-Brézé, Marquis de (Legitimist). *Notes et souvenirs.* A violently anti-Orleanist collection of documents by one of the Comte de Chambord's confidential agents.

Du Barail, General. *Mes souvenirs.* In 1873 was Minister of War in the Cabinet of the Right. Vol. III. c. 12 is about the National Assembly.

†Ducrot, General (Legitimist). Extracts from Memoirs are printed in Chalvet-Nastroc, *Les Projets de la restauration et le général Ducrot.*

Falloux, Vicomte de (Legitimist). *Mémoires d'un royaliste* (2 vols.). Vol. II concludes with an account of the Assembly. The style is distinguished, and the comments on the Comte de Chambord's policy trenchant.

†Favre, Jules (Left). *Gouvernement de la défense nationale.* Vol. III, which goes down to the Treaty of Frankfort, covers part of the period. Authoritative and well documented.

Fidus, *Journal.* Under this pseudonym, Loudun, a Bonapartist, gives his impressions (naturally hostile) of the Assembly.

Freycinet, C. de (Left). *Souvenirs.* Chapters 8 and 9 cover the period. The treatment derives its value from the author's intimacy with Gambetta.

†Gambetta. *Discours* (collected by Reinach).

Goncourts. *Journal* (Vol. 5). The well-known diary by Jules and Edmond (this part is by Edmond alone). Has some vivid portraits of politicians.

Gyp. *La Joyeuse Enfance de la Troisième République.* A semi-autobiographical romance of the lightest character. Conveys some of the political and social atmosphere.

Kel-Kun.
   Portraits.

Nouveaux portraits.
> Anonymous sketches of deputies. Amusing in a rather elaborate
> way. The portraits of members of the Right are mostly satirical.

†LACOMBE, CHARLES (Legitimist). *Journal politique* (2 vols.). Indispensable to a student of the Assembly. Does for the " inner life " of the Right what Mme Adam does for the Left.

†LAMY, ÉTIENNE (Left). His *Review of Lacombe's Journal* (printed as an Appendix) is a brilliant summary of the relations between Thiers and the Right.

†LOCKROY, ÉDOUARD (Left). *Au hasard de la vie.* A few sketches of Republican deputies.

MARMITE AUX LOIS. A pamphlet (in the Bibliothèque Nationale) describing the life of the Assembly in a familiar style.

PELLETAN, CAMILLE (Left). *Théâtre de Versailles — l'Assemblée au jour le jour.* A vehemently Republican sketch of the Assembly during its two last years.

PESSARD, HECTOR (Left). *Mes petits papiers* (2 vols.). A brilliant (if rather malicious) study of the period (Vol. II refers to the Assembly) by a journalist, who was a friend of Thiers.

REPORT OF THE COMMISSION ON DECENTRALISATION. MSS. in the Archives of the Chamber of Deputies.

SIMON, JULES (Left). *Le Soir de ma journée.* Reminiscences (partly by Simon himself, partly by his son Gustave from recollections of conversations). Admirably vivid and witty. Forms a good supplement to the more formal
> *Gouvernement de M. Thiers* (2 vols.). Like all his works, full of benevolence agreeably tinged with malice.

TAINE, HIPPOLYTE. *Sa vie et correspondance.* Vol. III covers the period 1871–5. There are some political allusions. Taine was a Conservative but not a clerical, and drifts rather uneasily between the Orleanists and Thiers.

†THIERS, ADOLPHE. *Notes et souvenirs* (1870–73). (Translated by F. M. Atkinson.) Naturally contains important material, but is discreet to the point of dulness. One misses the verve of Thiers' speeches and conversation.

†VINOLS, BARON DE (Right). *Journal,* quoted by Denis *op. cit.*

WEISS, J. J.
> *Combat constitutionnel.*
> *Notes et impressions.*
> Weiss was the *enfant terrible* of the Right, who afterwards rallied to the Republic. The first work (published after our period) contains a brilliant and devastating essay on " Les Illusions monarchiques " (p. 67). The second work, consisting of letters and essays, some of which were written in 1871, show him as still a Royalist, though a very independent one.

Later French Authorities

BARTHÉLEMY, JOSEPH. *Le Gouvernement de la France.* A well-known survey of French institutions : c. 9 contains a description of local government, which refers to the decentralising policy of the National Assembly.

BELLESORT, ANDRÉ. *Les Intellectuels et l'avènement de la Troisième République.* An interesting study of such writers as Hugo, Flaubert, Veuillot, Taine and Renan.

BERNANOS, GEORGE. *La Grande Peur des bien pensants.* A life of Drumont: brilliantly and bitterly anti-Semitic. Has some virulent pictures of political leaders.

BOUNIOLS, GASTON. *Thiers au pouvoir* (1871–3). Selections from Thiers' political correspondence with some lively footnotes.

COUBERTIN, PIERRE DE. *Evolution of France under the Third Republic* (translated by Isabel Hapgood).

D'ARCAY, JOSEPH. *Notes inédits sur Thiers.* Of little value.

DAUDET, ERNEST (Orleanist).
   Duc d'Aumale.
   Trois mois d'histoire : la vérité sur l'essai de la restauration.
   The latter work is a history of the Royalist campaign in 1873 ; has some portraits of the leaders.

DE FLERS. *Le Comte de Paris* (translated by Constance Majendie).

DE LUZ, PIERRE (Legitimist). *Henri V.* An excellent study of the Comte de Chambord by a Legitimist admirer.

DENIS, SAMUEL (Orleanist). *Histoire contemporaine.* Vol. II. describes the work of the Assembly.

DE ROUX, MARQUIS. *Origines et fondation de la Troisième République.* Makes use of much recent material. Impartial and independent.

DESCHANEL, PAUL. *Gambetta.* Probably the best book on the Republican leader.

DESJOYEAUX, CLAUDE-NOËL. *La Fusion monarchique* (1848–73). A standard account of the negotiations from an Orleanist point of view.

DICTIONNAIRE PARLEMENTAIRE. A biographical dictionary of deputies.

DREYFUS, ROBERT.
   M. Thiers contre l'empire, la guerre et la commune (1869–71).
   La République de M. Thiers (1871–3).
   Excellent studies of the period and the statesman.

FAGUET, ÉMILE. *Mgr. Dupanloup.* A sympathetic study by the well-known French Liberal.
   Propos littéraires (Series 2). Contains an interesting study of Thiers as a speaker in the essay on " L'Éloquence politique ".

GHEUSI, P. B. (Left). *La Vie et la mort singulières de Gambetta.* Written by Gambetta's cousin : contains some family traditions, but nothing sensational. Rather a glorification of his relative.

HALÉVY, DANIEL. *La Fin des notables.* An excellent title. The design of the book is to study the period 1871–7 as the last effort of the aristocracy to rule. The author on the whole regards their failure as inevitable. It is continued in a second book, *La République des ducs.*

    Le Courier de M. Thiers. Contains a great deal of Thiers' correspondence, woven together with comments — " almost a biography ", as the author describes it.

HANOTAUX, GABRIEL. *La France contemporaine* (4 vols. ; translated by J. C. Tarver). Remains (though new material is accumulating) a classical study of the period by a distinguished statesman. The tone is Gambettist, but the author tries to understand the Conservative standpoint.

HUBERT, LUCIEN. *Figures parlementaires.* A study of Presidents of the Chamber and Senate, including Gambetta, Grévy and Buffet.

LAGRANGE, L'ABBÉ. *Vie de Dupanloup.*

LANO, PIERRE. *Après l'empire.* Some venomous (even libellous) portraits of Royalists.

LAUR, FRANCIS. *The Heart of Gambetta* (translated by Violet Montagu). A " sentimental " history of Gambetta's relations with Léonie. Has little political value.

LOMÉNIE, EMMANUEL BEAU DE. *La Restauration manquée.* The author declares " Toutes mes hérédités sont orléanistes ", and his grandfather, Beau, sat in the Centre of the Assembly and voted for the Republic. But the book is a strong criticism of the Orleanists.

LOTH, ARTHUR (Legitimist). *L'Échec de la restauration monarchique.* An able statement of the case against the Orleanists.

MALO, HENRI. *Thiers.* The best and most complete life of Thiers.

MARTET, JEAN. *Clemenceau* (translated by Milton Waldman). A well-known record of conversations with the Tiger. It contains some appreciations of politicians of the period (as does General Mordacq's *Le Ministère Clemenceau*, Vol. III). Clemenceau was one of the last survivors of the Assembly, though he resigned after the Commune.

MATTER. *Bismarck et son temps.*

NOAILLES, MARQUIS DE. *Le Bureau du roi.* A very important book (published 1932). The second part is taken from the papers of the Marquis de la Ferté Mun, and forms practically our only authority for the inner history of the Chambord manifesto.

RECLUS, MAURICE.

    L'Avènement de la Troisième République (Series " L'Ancienne France ").

    M. Thiers (Series " Le Roman des grandes existences ").

    E. Picard (Essai de contribution a l'histoire du parti républicain).

ZÉVAÈS (Socialist). *Histoire de la Troisième République* (1870–1926).

ZEVORT (Left). *Histoire de la Troisième République* (4 vols.).

ENGLISH AUTHORITIES

ACTON, LORD. *Correspondence.* Several letters are from France, where as a Liberal Catholic he came in touch with the Right Centre.

ALGER. *The New Paris Sketch Book.* A description of Paris by an English resident (1887). Contains some sketches of politicians.

BLOWITZ, HENRI. *My Memoirs.* He was correspondent to *The Times.* Chapter 2 describes experiences during the Commune.

BODLEY, J. E. K. *France.* The classical study of French politics by an English thinker. The author is definitely anti-Republican and slightly pro-Empire.

KING, EDWARD. *French Political Leaders.* Another (rather slight) book by an Englishman on French politicians.

LAWTON. *The Third French Republic.*

MARZIALS, FRANK. *Gambetta* (in the " Statesmen " Series).

MURRAY, GRENVILLE EUSTACE CLAIRE. *Men of the Third Republic.* Sketches of prominent politicians by an Englishman, who knew France well.

  Round about France. A rather satirical description of French politics in 1877.

STEPHENS, WINIFRED. *Madam Adam* (from Louis-Philippe until 1917). A useful sketch of her life.

VANDAM, ALBERT.

  My Paris Note Book.

  Men and Manners of the Third Republic.
    Full of slightly irritating gossip about the Second Empire and the Third Republic. The author, who poses as having inside information, is anti-Republican and rather a friend to the Empire.

VASSILI, COUNT PAUL. *France from behind the Veil.* This book is pretentious, like its title. The conversations are not reliable (for example, his talk with the Comte de Chambord in the Versailles Park (1873) : all the other evidence is to the effect that the Comte never went outside his house). It may be read with amusement and used with caution.

WADDINGTON, MADAME. *My First Years as a Frenchwoman* (1876–9). The authoress was an American. She married Waddington (deputy of the Left Centre in the Assembly) in 1874, but c. 2 contains some interesting impressions of the National Assembly — mostly of a personal nature.

INDEX OF NAMES

2 M

THE END

Printed in Great Britain by R. & R. CLARK, LIMITED, *Edinburgh*

STUDIES IN MODERN HISTORY

EDITED BY
PROFESSOR L. B. NAMIER

(All prices are net)

MACMILLAN AND CO. LTD., LONDON

STUDIES IN MODERN HISTORY

(continued)

————

DISRAELI, GLADSTONE AND THE EASTERN QUESTION: A Study in Diplomacy and Party Politics. By Prof. R. W. Seton-Watson. Illustrated. 21s.

ENGLAND UNDER GEORGE I: THE BEGINNINGS OF THE HANOVERIAN DYNASTY. By Prof. Wolfgang Michael. Translated and Adapted from the German. 21s.

ENGLAND UNDER GEORGE I: THE QUADRUPLE ALLIANCE. By Prof. Wolfgang Michael. Translated and Adapted from the German. 21s.

LETTERS FROM GEORGE III TO LORD BUTE, 1756–1766. Edited by Romney Sedgwick. 18s.

THE WHIG PARTY, 1807-1812. By Prof. Michael Roberts. 25s.

THE BEGINNING OF THE THIRD REPUBLIC IN FRANCE: A HISTORY OF THE NATIONAL ASSEMBLY (FEBRUARY—SEPTEMBER 1871). By Rev. Canon Frank Herbert Brabant, M.A.

(All prices are net)

MACMILLAN AND CO. LTD., LONDON

Date Due